*Cervantes
and the Humanist
Vision*

CERVANTES

AND THE HUMANIST

VISION: A Study of Four

Exemplary Novels

ALBAN K. FORCIONE

———

Princeton University Press
Princeton, New Jersey

For Suzanne

Noli de fructu sollicitus esse.
Ipse erumpet suo tempore,
cum Deo videbitur.
—Erasmus

CONTENTS

CONTENTS

PREFACE AND ACKNOWLEDGMENTS

THIS BOOK BEGAN in 1973, when my research for what I had intended to be a short article concerning the source and structure of Cervantes's *La Gitanilla* burgeoned in a way I had not foreseen. I found the article impossible to conclude and soon realized that, if I wished to arrive at satisfactory answers to the various questions that the short story raised, I was going to have to face squarely one of the central problems of Spanish literary history—the nature of the impact of Erasmus's thought on Spanish letters and specifically on the work of Spain's greatest writer. As I absorbed myself in the gigantic *oeuvre* of Erasmus and the rapidly expanding body of scholarship on Christian Humanism, I became increasingly convinced that Cervantes's *Exemplary Novels* are the works that reveal most decisively the presence of Erasmism in Spanish literature and that their literary qualities can be understood and appreciated properly only if they are situated in the cultural context of Christian Humanism. This book attempts to argue my convictions, and its growth from an unfinished article and a pile of research notes on the principal concerns of humanist writings—religion, morality, nature, government, marriage, education, literature, and language—will continue in a follow-up study, *Cervantes and the Mystery of Lawlessness*, a book devoted entirely to the story that I consider ideologically Cervantes's richest and formally his most complex work of short fiction, *El casamiento engañoso y el coloquio de los perros*.

As the book grew, I began to recognize that its roots reached back well beyond my frustrated efforts to deal with *La Gitanilla*. In reality it was an attempt to answer a question that had been troubling me since the spring of 1960, when I had just completed an undergraduate thesis on the theme of madness in Cervantes's and Erasmus's writings. The thesis owed a good deal of its inspiration to Americo Castro's *El pensamiento de Cervantes*, and I was, of course, delighted when, shortly before my graduation, one of my teachers arranged a luncheon with the retired master of Cervantes studies. I had never met Professor Castro, but the encounter was far different from anything I had anticipated. After politely inquiring about my work and learning of my interest in Erasmus and Cervantes and my admiration for his classic work linking the two giants of the European Renaissance, he looked at me mischievously, paused, and then remarked with the slightest trace of irritability: "There is absolutely nothing of Erasmus in Cervantes's work!" The statement allowed for no response. There seemed to be no irony to moderate its definitive tone, and the conversation immediately turned to other subjects. He had categorically disposed not only of my undergraduate paper but also of his own epoch-making study of Cervantes's fiction and European humanism. As I had not yet acquainted myself very well with the recent redirections of his thought and his determination to account for Cervantes's achievements exclusively as products of Hispanic culture, I found his uncompromising rejection of his earlier conclusions utterly baffling. The unsettling effect of this encounter continued long after the luncheon, and fifteen years later, as I found myself laboring to restore Cervantes's fiction to its rightful place within the literature of humanism and, by doing so, to "recuperate" some of Castro's finest work on the subject, I realized that my book was to some extent a response to a provocation implicit in his words.

Any book dealing with such inexhaustible fields of study as Cervantes and European humanism is bound to amass a large number of debts to the numerous scholars who continue to enrich our understanding of these areas with new information and interpretation. In footnotes to my text I have tried to give credit to those who have contributed concretely to its arguments. Among Cervantists, however, I would make special mention of Castro, everywhere a demanding guide and a generous antagonist, and Joaquín Casalduero, whose fine analysis of the *Exemplary Novels* remains the foundation on which all subsequent studies of the ideology of Cervantes's short stories must build. At the same time I would express my obligation to certain writers who have influenced my understanding of humanism and my method of literary study in a decisive, if a more general way: the late Marcel Bataillon, the late Hugo Friedrich, Northrop Frye, and Ira Wade.

I am particularly grateful to Stephen Gilman and Luis Murillo, who read the completed manuscript, offered helpful criticisms and suggestions for improvements, and generously shared with me their considerable knowledge of Cervantes and Golden Age culture. Thanks are due to others who read portions of the manuscript and were forthcoming with valuable advice, criticism, and encouragement: Robert Hollander, E. C. Riley, Ronald Surtz, and Harvey Sharrer.

My greatest debt is to my friend and colleague Suzanne Nash. Without her interest and confidence the research and writing of this book would have been a lonely and probably interminable task. She was always ready to listen, read, challenge, encourage, and provide a dialogue that brought to life even the most remote concerns of my study. Her presence was a constant reminder of the enduring values of the humanist tradition of civilized conversation.

I am grateful to the American Council of Learned Societies for a grant that enabled me to find my way about in Erasmian studies with some degree of confidence and to the Research Committee of Princeton University for generously supplying funds to cover typing expenses.

I have provided English translations for all quotations in foreign languages (except those in the footnotes). I have used a number of translations of Cervantes's works, frequently modifying them to bring out the sense of the Spanish necessary to my argument. They are: J. Ormsby's and J. M. Cohen's translations of *Don Quixote*, N. MacColl's and W. Starkie's translations of *The Exemplary Novels*, H. Oelsner's and A. B. Wellford's *Galatea*, E. Honig's *Interludes*, and L. D. Stanley's *The Wanderings of Persiles and Sigismunda*. Translations of all other works cited are my own unless otherwise indicated.

Princeton, 1981

*Cervantes
and the Humanist
Vision*

Madness and Mystery:
The Exemplarity of Cervantes's
Novelas ejemplares

IN HIS LITERARY testament, the mock-epic *Viage del Parnaso*, Cervantes describes his frustration when, on entering Apollo's dazzling garden, he finds himself excluded from the ceremonial gathering of the great poets beneath the laurels of Parnassus. Likening the indignity to the mistreatment of Ovid in his exile, he allows his "Juvenalian anger" to vent itself in the composition of some autobiographical verses. Addressing his complaint to the god of poetry, he reminds him of the authenticity of his vocation and proceeds to pass review of his considerable achievements as a writer. Cervantes prefaces his surrender to anger with an acknowledgment that the literary products of the indignation of fools are generally full of perversity. But a more interesting note of self-deprecation sounds in the middle of his list of accomplishments, in the qualification attached to his defense of his collection of short stories, *Las novelas ejemplares*:

> Yo he abierto en mis Nouelas vn camino,
> por do la lengua castellana puede
> mostrar con propiedad vn desatino.[1]

> (In my novels I have opened a way,
> Whereby the Castilian tongue can display
> An absurdity with propriety.)

---

[1] *Viage del Parnaso*, ed. R. Schevill and A. Bonilla (Madrid, 1922), p. 55.

In its reference to the "desatino con propiedad," the tercet presents the exemplarity of the tales in an odd perspective, a perspective that is all the more striking when one considers it beside the emphatically doctrinaire pronouncements of Cervantes's prologue to the tales: "I have given them the name of *Exemplary*, and if you look at it well, there is not one of them from which a profitable example could not be extracted . . . perhaps I would show you the savory and honest fruit which could be derived from them. . . . If in any way it comes to pass that the reading of these novels could tempt one who should peruse them to any evil desire or thought, rather should I cut off the hand with which I wrote them than bring them out in public."[2] The paradoxical understatement of the *Viage* is much more elusive than the closed, conventional discourse of the prologue, but its ambiguities might, in fact, tempt us to suspect disingenuousness in the latter and to read both as implying Cervantes's awareness that the exemplarity of his tales is not to be sought where expected.

If we look at the testimony of one of Cervantes's most illustrious contemporary readers, we discover a striking failure to find any notable exemplary content in the tales. Introducing his own collection of novellas, *Novelas a Marcia Leonarda*, Lope de Vega praises the formal excellence of Cervantes's tales, but adds: "I confess that they are books of great entertainment and that they could be exemplary, like some of the *Tragic Histories* of Bandello, but they should be written by men of learning or at least by great courtiers, men who are able to discover in a 'disillusionment' (*desengaño*) remarkable *sententiae* and aphorisms."[3] Apart from what it reveals about Lope's ambivalent personal feelings toward the literary successes of his great rival, the commentary is most interesting in its insistence that the excellences of Cervantes's short stories are to be found exclusively in their pleasant fictions. Quite explicitly, Lope refuses to acknowledge that the *Exemplary Novels* offer any edifying doctrine commensurate with their entertaining effects, and in making his judgment, he invokes a narrow and well-defined conception of exemplarity in short fiction. His em-

---

[2] "Heles dado nombre de *Ejemplares*, y si bien lo miras, no hay ninguna de quien no se pueda sacar algún ejemplo provechoso . . . quizá te mostrara el sabroso y honesto fruto que se podría sacar. . . . si por algún modo alcanzara que la lección de estas novelas pudiera inducir a quien las leyera a algún mal deseo o pensamiento, antes me cortara la mano con que las escribí que sacarlas en público" (*Obras completas*, ed. A. Valbuena Prat [Madrid, 1956], pp. 769-70).

[3] "Confiesso que son libros de grande entretenimiento y que podrían ser ejemplares como algunas de las Historias trágicas del Bandelo, pero habían de escribirlos hombres científicos o por lo menos grandes cortesanos, gente que halla en los desengaños notables sentencias y aforismos" (ed. F. Rico [Madrid, 1968], p. 28).

phasis on erudition, wit, courtly philosophy, and a type of discourse in which univocal doctrinal content can be clearly isolated and indeed even dissociated from its fictionalization through reductive *discursus*, aphorism, and *sententia* recalls methods of novella writing which had developed in courtly circles of Italy in the sixteenth century and were to flourish in the academic novellas of seventeenth-century Spain. As Walter Pabst has demonstrated in his comprehensive account of the historical development of the early European novella, the sixteenth century witnessed a striking transformation of the genre in its form, its social function, and its reception by its readers. The change paralleled an increasing interest throughout Europe in the vulgar tongues as the proper instrument of self-expression and communication for the new culture of court and city, and it was undoubtedly a response to the ascendance of the courtly society with its widely orchestrated ideal concerning the individual as a socially perfectible being. Castiglione himself gave the genre a type of canonization which was to be frequently repeated and which we find echoed in Lope de Vega's observations on Cervantes. If the courtier is indeed to achieve the polish required to distinguish himself within his society, he must master the arts of good speech ("bel parlare") and the strategies of competitive conversation. The proper models for wit, verbal resourcefulness, propriety, and grace in the use of Italian lie in the tales of Boccaccio, and the successful courtier would do well to study them in order to cultivate the arts of extemporaneous composition.[4] While such a con-

---

[4] *Novellentheorie und Novellendichtung: Zur Geschichte ihrer Antinomie in den romanischen Literaturen* (Heidelberg, 1967), chap. 2. Pabst traces the novella's intimate connection with courtly values and philosophy from Masuccio's incorporation in his tales (1476) of the qualities of wit prized by the dominant social class of his time through the academic implementations of Castiglione's formulas for *novella*, *facezie*, and *motti*, such as G. Parabosco's *I Diporti* (1550), to Lope de Vega's conception of the writer of novellas as the "grande cortesano," proclaiming the fashionable worldly wisdom of his own times in "desengaños notables." For the extremes to which the dissociation of fiction and erudite commentary could lead, see Pabst's discussion of G. Giraldi Cinzio's *Hecatommithi ouero Cento Novelle* (pp. 89-90). One can contrast Lope's emphasis on *"ciencia"* with G. Sermini da Siena's description of his collection of tales (*Novelle*, 1424) as a modest "basket of salad" which is not for the learned: "di questa non dia ad uomini di grande scienza, perchè non è vivanda da loro" (Pabst, *Novellentheorie*, p. 76). Castiglione's theories on the art of facetiae and novellas appear in the *Libro del Cortegiano*, 2:42-100 (see ed. E. Bonora and P. Zoccola [Milano, 1972], pp. 150-205). An indication of the popularity and topicality of Castiglione's discussion is the fact that his basic distinction between insubstantial tales dependent entirely on the oral performance of their teller for success and tales valuable for their inherent, "fixed" content, a distinction which, as Pabst points out, incorporates a *topos* deriving from Cicero's *De Oratore*, is echoed by Cervantes's Cipión in *El coloquio de los perros*. However, the interesting thing about Cervantes's discussion of the "ingenious tales"

ception of the art of the short story brought with it the elevation of a genre which had been traditionally consigned to the marginal and even subliterary spheres of man's reading experience, it undoubtedly blinded its adherents to the numerous possibilities which the form had cultivated in its historical development and excluded from serious consideration all narrative procedures and even types of tales that failed to focus on the social graces and urbane wisdom of "courtly philosophy."[5] It is surely such a blindness which Lope, the most worldly of Spain's great writers, reveals in his failure to find any exemplarity worthy of comment in Cervantes's tales. It is even possible that Cervantes's refusal to employ the traditional frame—a courtly society of teller and recipient—with its conveniences for both reader and author as a closed, determining structure which reduces the contained fictions to a univocal exemplarity and thereby fixes the reader's response to them, was for Lope a sign that the *Novelas ejemplares* belonged to a conventional type of writing aiming at the modest goal of entertaining its audience.

If Lope and, presumably, numerous readers who shared his expectations concerning the form and proper subject matter of the novella were inclined to discount the exemplarity of Cervantes's tales, we must consider the possibility that Cervantes's allusion to the "proper *desatinos*" of his fiction was in fact an admission of their modest intention of supplying permissible entertainment for a public which did not always welcome the edifying assaults on its sensibilities of traditional devotional readings or of the more austere genres of "honest entertainment." Apart from the salaciousness of some of the tales in the collection, Cervantes's willingness to use the designation "*desatino*" may be his way of acknowledging and dealing with the disdain which the short story had suffered in official circles from its very

---

which, through the "clothing of words" and their teller's gesticulations, make "something of nothing," is its transformation of the literary doctrine. Far from standing as a statement of the author's artistic program and his fundamental theory of the short story, as Ortega has suggested, the *topos* forms part of a dense system of elements in the tale pointing up the universality of illusion in human experience and specifically the deceptive potential in literature.

[5] For the "misreading" and resulting impoverishment of the *Decameron* in sixteenth-century Italy—e.g., its readers' concentration on the two days offering triumphs of verbal ingenuity, their perception of the frame primarily as an exemplification of the general aesthetic doctrine of unity, and their condemnation of its plague description for its apparent disruption of a uniform elegant tonality—see Pabst, *Novellentheorie*, pp. 74-79. Though their profound themes are rooted in sixteenth-century thought, Cervantes's tales, in their conceptual density and complex mixture of tonalities, can be seen as representing a rediscovery by the novella tradition of the broad dimensions that are visible in its founder and in all his authentic descendants.

beginnings and which persisted through the sixteenth century despite the peculiar sanction it received in the courtly society of Italy. The authors of early novella collections frequently had to recognize the embattled status of their fiction, its disruptive subject matter, its potential for debasing its readers, and the contempt that it excited in orthodox quarters. The excesses of their justifications can, in fact, be read as testimony to the validity of their opponents' claims. If the genre was generally looked upon as a vulgar form of entertainment, the designation *novella* and its cognates were themselves occasionally invoked as terms of derogation. For example, Chrétien de Troyes, Ramón Lull, and Juan Manuel suggested that one of the worst insults a knight could endure was to be regarded as a *novelero*, a teller of novellas.[6] One of Cervantes's predecessors in Spain, Juan de Timoneda, intitled his volume of tales and anecdotes "the collection of lies"—*El patrañuelo*—, suggested to his reader that his creations should be taken purely for "pasatiempo y recreo humano," and added: "my native Valencian tongue intitles such confusing imbroglios (*marañas*) *Rondalles*, and the Tuscan calls them *Novelas*."[7] And it is possible that Lope's introduction to his collection of novellas, which attributed their composition to the persuasiveness of a "woman reader," his beloved Marta de Nevares, remarking: "I never thought that it would occur to me to write novellas," is to some extent motivated by the traditional scorn with which the genre was treated in academic circles.[8]

At the same time, in referring to his absurdities as *proper*, Cervantes may well have been adopting a defensive posture, ironically acknowledging the traditional disrespect for short fiction and carefully reminding his audience that his own tales should not be judged according to conventional prejudices. His words may in fact be simply a translation into a more severe paradox of a contradiction latent in the

[6] See W. Krauss, "Novela-Novella-Roman," *Gesammelte Aufsätze zur Literatur- und Sprachwissenschaft* (Frankfurt am Main, 1949), p. 64. W. Pabst points out that the term preserved certain despective connotations of its Latin root *novus*—e.g., "surprising," "odd," "comical," "foolish," "fanciful," and "mendacious." A sixteenth-century editor of the earlier novellas wrote: "Nuova, volea dir Piacevole per semplicità, e stravaganza onde è rimaso a noi Nuovo pesce [joke]. . . . Di qui le favole, e li racconti piacevoli Novelle fur dette" (see Pabst, *Novellentheorie*, pp. 15-16, 21-22).

[7] "semejantes marañas las intitula mi lengua natural valenciana *Rondalles*, y la toscana, *Novelas*" (ed. R. Ferreres [Madrid, 1971], p. 41). E. C. Riley points out that the "word *novela*, as well as being unflatteringly interchangeable with words like *patraña*, or 'deceitful fiction,' must have conjured up for the public the names of Boccaccio and Bandello," authors associated with licentiousness (*Cervantes's Theory of the Novel* [Oxford, 1962], p. 102).

[8] "nunca pensé que el novelar entrara en mi pensamiento" (*Novelas a Marcia Leonarda*, p. 28).

phrase *"novela ejemplar"* and as such a characteristically indirect way of pointing simultaneously to the literarily revolutionary and the morally legitimate character of his literary undertaking.[9] The same intention could well have motivated the exaggerations and reiterations concerning their exemplarity in the prologue. Cervantes, as we have noted, is prepared to cut off his hand before allowing it to write a word that might provoke an evil thought in his reader. E. C. Riley is certainly right in suggesting that "the excessive insistence of Cervantes undoubtedly reflects anxiety," and that he may have been eager to dissociate himself from the notoriety enjoyed by the classical Italian *novellieri*, whose names, well known in Spain, had become "bywords for salaciousness."[10] However, there is something yet more revealing in the paradox which he voices while complaining of his mistreatment in the garden of Parnassus, and it explains in part why for Lope de Vega the true exemplarity of the tales may have passed unnoticed. It is perhaps well to recall Cervantes's self-deprecatory discussion of the literary merits of *Don Quixote* I on the eve of Don Quixote's third sally. In the midst of the various denunciations of the work—the improvisational monstrosity resembling Orbaneja's formless paintings, the masterpiece for an audience composed of the "stultorum infinitus numerus," the hodgepodge of "baskets and cabbages"—Don Quixote notes that "to say amusing things and to write humorously is the gift of great geniuses" because "the cleverest character in comedy is the clown, for he who would make people take him for a fool,

[9] An interesting testimony to the paradoxicality and possible audacity in the combination of terms for Cervantes's audience can be found in G. Argote de Molina's prefatory address to the reader in his edition of the *Libro llamado el Conde Lucanor* (Seville, 1575). He justifies the book as an "exemplario," a "libro de buenos consejos," which adopts the methods of the ancient sages, Socrates and Plato, and Jesus Christ in their utilization of *"cuentos"* and *"parabolas"* in order to convey ancient philosophy and divine wisdom. He distinguishes his *"exemplario"* sharply from the popular forms of *"nouela"* and *"fabula,"* "los quales tienen vn solo intento que es entretener con apazible, y algunas vezes dañoso gusto." To appreciate the forcefulness of Cervantes's assertion that he was doing something new and valuable, as well as the freedom and originality with which he created the exemplary novella, one must bear in mind the traditional prestige of the *exemplum* in Spain (see Pabst, *Novellentheorie*, p. 100) and the absence both of an established indigenous tradition of novella literature and of the academic-courtly circumstances which in Italy focused attention on and to some extent schematized the Italian short story. In 1590 the Spanish translator of Giraldi's tales introduced his work with the hope that his audience will see "que se estima esto tanto en los estrangeros, para que los naturales hagan lo que nunca han hecho, que es componer Novelas" (Pabst, *Novellentheorie*, p. 104).

[10] *Cervantes's Theory of the Novel*, p. 102. Riley points out that Cervantes may have intended the title of his collection to be *Novelas ejemplares de honestísimo entretenimiento*.

must not be one."[11] In its association of the "discreet madman" and the *Quixote*, the phrase casts a revealing light on the "proper absurdities" which Cervantes offers as the designation of his tales, and in both cases the paradoxes look back to the fundamental paradox animating the thought and writings of the Erasmian reformers, men inspired by their profound sense that ultimate truth lies beyond the canonized forms of culture—the deadening letter—and that it can be reached only if one transcends the logic of the letter. As Erasmus asked repeatedly, was not the most sublime source of truth veiled in the humble form of a carpenter's son in Nazareth? And did not the wisest of the ancient sages pronounce his universal truths from an oafish face and a slovenly figure laughable to all who gazed upon it until they beheld the wonders of the spirit concealed within?[12]

Cervantes's description of his tales as *"desatinos"* is, then, neither the defensive invocation of a *topos* of novella composition nor an admission that his tales are primarily aimed at furnishing pleasing entertainment. In the tradition of Erasmus's meditation on the *Sileni Alcibiadis*, it is rather an invitation to look for the truth beneath the surface, in the remote or concealed areas where Lope de Vega, a man of radically different disposition and a man whose spiritual formation was the product of very different historical circumstances, was temperamentally unprepared to look. As Cervantes insinuates in his prologue, "lofty mysteries" lie concealed within his trifles: "they hold hidden some mystery which elevates them" ("algún misterio tienen escondido que las levanta"). "He who says 'mystery' says 'pregnancy' (*preñez*), an impending truth which is hidden and recondite, and any truth which exacts a price in its communication is more highly esteemed and more pleasureable," Gracián was to say in his poetics of wit a few years later.[13] For the critic, a reader whose business it is to transcend, insofar as it is possible to do so, the historical rootedness that inevitably mediates and conditions our perception of the past, Cervantes's words offer not only an invitation to look within, but a challenge to look backward in history as well, to the humanist writings of nearly one hundred years earlier, the writings of Cervantes's

[11] "Decir gracias y escribir donaires es de grandes ingenios: la más discreta figura de la comedia es la del bobo, porque no lo ha de ser el que quiere dar a entender que es simple" (*Don Quijote de la Mancha*, ed. L. A. Murillo [Madrid, 1978], 2:64; all subsequent volume and page references to the *Quixote* in my text are to this edition).

[12] See "Sileni Alcibiadis," *The "Adages" of Erasmus*, ed. and trans. by M. Mann Phillips (Cambridge, 1964), pp. 269-72.

[13] "Quien dice misterio, dice preñez, verdad escondida y recóndita, y toda noticia que cuesta, es más estimada y gustosa" (*Agudeza y arte de ingenio*, ed. E. Correa Calderón [Madrid, 1969], 1:88).

spiritual fathers, men who understood that the loftiest teachings concerning man's religious, ethical, political, social, and domestic life could be conveyed perhaps most effectively in the disjointed discourse of a fool.

Since Américo Castro's declaration in *El pensamiento de Cervantes* (1924) that "without Erasmus, Cervantes would not have been the writer he was,"[14] the attempts to locate the spiritual and intellectual sources of Cervantes's fiction in Erasmus's writings have retreated from the forceful conclusions of Castro's epoch-making study. The reaction was in part attributable to the gradual revision in historical studies of the excessively secularized conception of the European Renaissance, rooted in Burckhardt's classical interpretation, which informs Castro's entire argument, and in part due to the closely related correction of a traditional misconception of the modernity in the critical tendencies of Erasmus's philosophy. If the crucial period in Cervantes's spiritual development was no longer to be viewed as an era of unbounded individualism, audacious free inquiry, subversive ethical naturalism, heroic hypocrisy, and exhilarating liberation from confining religious traditions, the greatest humanist of the late Renaissance could no longer be regarded as simply the iconoclastic precursor of modern rationalism, the "Voltaire of the Sixteenth Century." However, more important among Cervantists was the emphatic change of direction that marked Castro's own thinking in the twenty years that followed the publication of *El pensamiento de Cervantes*. During this period, years of cultural breakdown and exile for Castro, he devoted his inexhaustible intellectual energies to comprehending the structure of a text larger and, in its contradictions, even more complicated than the *Quixote*—that of Spain itself. As he focused his attention on the peculiar dynamics of Spanish history and looked more searchingly and exclusively for inspiration in contemporary existentialist and vitalistic philosophy in his efforts to deal with the intractable complexities of historical process, he found himself compelled to doubt the fundamental premises and methods of the intellectual history (*Geistesgeschichte*) which he had practiced so successfully, and ultimately to deny the validity of its privileged categories of historical understanding—the generalized structures of ideas and values, the *Weltanschauungen*, as well as their specific historical formulations such as Renaissance, Counter-Reformation, and Rationalism—the very categories that he had taken for granted in his previous efforts to account for Spain's position in Occidental history and for its principal cultural creations

---

[14] (Barcelona, 1972), p. 300.

such as the *Quixote*. [15] One of the results of the profound reorientation
in his thought was a thorough disdain for the lifelessness and inauthenticity of abstraction and a heightened sensitivity to its potential—
in the form of ideology, unexamined assumptions, cultural common-
places and axioms—for the suppression of human freedom, the cur-
tailment of individual growth, and the general impoverishment of
man's experience. Castro is not the first Spaniard whose intellectual
evolution is mirrored perfectly in his rereadings of Cervantes's multifaceted and ultimately elusive masterpiece. Whether as guide or
provocation, the *Quixote*, the work that revolutionized literature by
calling into question all traditional assumptions concerning literary
value, implicitly disclosing the poverty of the ideologies reflected in
them, and endowing the nontranscendent particulars of ordinary experience with poetic dignity, now offered Castro something far more
profound than the monument to Renaissance ideas and cultural tensions which he had constructed so painstakingly and persuasively in
his *El pensamiento de Cervantes*. If the vision and structural dynamics of
the work itself seemed to vindicate the value and integrity of the
individual human life in all its singularity, the very possibility of its
creation in Spain of the early seventeenth century by a man driven by
a particular sense of his own marginality and alienation pointed to the
very concrete preoccupations and tensions which account for the peculiar historical life of Spain and its uniqueness in the Occidental
world.

Castro's insight into the depths of Spanish historical life and into
Don Quixote as a creation within a particular historical scenario led
him to his most profound writings on Cervantes's art. As a result of
his effort, we understand the uniqueness, the value, and the place of
the *Quixote* in literary history as never before, and his quixotic refusal

[15] In elaborating the central category of his new historical method—the *morada
vital*—Castro glances at the lifeless abstractions, the disembodied "essences" of *Geistesgeschichte*: "No existe un Gótico, un Renacimiento, un Barroco o un Neoclásico que,
desde un espacio irreal, condicione el fluir de la historia como la luna interviene en
las mareas" (*La realidad histórica de España* [Mexico, 1954], p. 49). In Chapter Two,
"Enfoque de la historia," Castro reveals the sources and direction of his developing
philosophy of history. He acknowledges the fundamental place of Dilthey's *Lebens-
philosophie* in his conception of the dynamic process of history, and he makes it clear
how his thought is conditioned and developed in his engagement with the ideas of
such prominent spokesmen for vitalism and existentialism as Bergson, Nietzsche, and
Kierkegaard. Another disciple of Dilthey whose central conceptions concerning historical process—e.g., the "la razón vital," "la razón histórica," and "la circunstancia"—are clearly influential in Castro's intellectual development and his reconsideration of Cervantes's work is J. Ortega y Gasset.

to permit the republication of *El pensamiento de Cervantes* until shortly before his death in 1972 is a characteristic sign of the intensity and intellectual integrity which marked his own life-long quest for truth. However, as valuable as it is, *El pensamiento de Cervantes* is not the most precious victim that Castro sacrificed on the altar of the vitalism informing his new conception of historical process and value. In his general hostility to the abstracting tendency in thought and literary creation and in his particular disdain for the official set of values that stultified the consciousness of Cervantes's contemporaries and blighted their institutions, Castro came to look upon all of Cervantes's overtly exemplary writings that fail to dignify the sphere of individuality and ordinary experience as somehow lifeless, worthy of historical recuperation only as documents of the tensions alive in Cervantes's consciousness. While brilliantly illuminating the perspective of marginality from which the *Quixote* appears to have been conceived, Castro's influential essay, "The Exemplarity of Cervantes' Novellas," has had the effect of widening the historical gap separating us from the tales, the very gap that his early *El pensamiento de Cervantes*, which considered Cervantes's *oeuvre* as a unified totality and the product of a single consciousness, had undertaken to overcome. [16] With Castro's essay we

---

[16] In presenting Cervantes as an embattled pioneer of enlightenment in the repressive era of the Counter-Reformation, Castro insists on the normative and rationalistic tendencies of his art. There were "determinadas realidades, tanto físicas como morales, que para él son de existencia tan evidente como esta luz que nos alumbra. Entre esas realidades morales hay algunas cuya existencia se establece dogmáticamente, y que son en Cervantes verdaderas tesis de combate" (*El pensamiento de Cervantes*, p. 123). Thirty-five years later he writes that the *Quixote* is impenetrable to the reader who would "enfocarlo como un arsenal de ideas y doctrinas" and, in a judgment that would definitively dispose of his early "classic" of Cervantine scholarship, he proclaims: "Los resultados desprendibles y objetivables de todo aquel proceso quedaban en penumbra; los bienes o los males, los pensamientos o las creencias, la doctrina o la retórica perceptibles en el *Quijote* son cosa secundaria en él, mero combustible para que no cese el martillo de la forja vital" ("Prólogo" to *Don Quijote de la Mancha* [Mexico, 1960], pp. xx-xxi). In another influential exposition of his vitalist reading, he admits his error in having argued that "a Cervantes le interesaba en ocasiones determinar cuál fuera la realidad yacente bajo la fluctuación de las apariencias" and insists that "lo dado, las realidades inmutables y objetivadas frente al correr mismo de las vidas, no juega papel esencial en el libro máximo de España." The work presents human experience, and "el vocablo 'experiencia' no se refiere entonces a nada racional y científico" ("La palabra escrita y el 'Quijote,' " *Hacia Cervantes* [Madrid, 1967], pp. 383-84). The characters of the *Novelas ejemplares* are unfortunately born as such rationally determined essences, "tipos alimentados por un ideal trascendente a ellos y válido y grato para las gentes . . . son personajes 'sustanciales' aristotélicamente, sustancia de virtud; no se hacen a sí mismos, no poseen un *sí mismo*, van adonde 'les han dicho' que tienen que ir . . . ." ("La ejemplaridad de las novelas

find the dichotomy of the "two Cervanteses," a conception which, in one form or another (see below), has plagued a good deal of modern Cervantine criticism, resurrected in a particularly disturbing version. Castro would appear to be no longer interested in the content of the tales, reads Cervantes's emphatic assertion in the prologue—"the clamorous pretension to morality"—as a confirmation of the absolutely doctrinaire and trivial nature of the ethical vision exemplified in his fictions, finds in his willingness to create characters according to ideas—that is, the conventional technique of exemplary fiction—a renunciation of his artistic self, and devotes the major arguments of the essay to an analysis of the motives for Cervantes's silencing of his authentic voice. No longer writing from the perspective of the outsider, creating "madmen in collision with society's normal ways of thinking," subjecting all "vulgar experience" to ironic treatment, and affirming the primacy of a "profound and imperishable vital reality" over the lifeless "truth of moralization," Cervantes conceived the *Novelas ejemplares* from a vital situation firmly fixed within the cultural horizons of the official Spain, a Spain that had finally consented to make him its own after he had endured a life of frustrated ambitions, physical exile, poverty, social degradation, and spiritual alienation. Cervantes's affirmations in the prologue to the exemplary stories are the revealing statements of a new man, one "circumspect and tranquil," who "proceeds with a consciousness of being a responsible member of a community in which he is of some importance." The greatest writer of Spain determined to "moralize from above," assuming, as moralists generally do, that society would reward his concerned pronouncements with status and esteem. While acknowledging that this change of perspective, the "swing of the pendulum of Cervantes's art toward exemplarity," must be viewed as the necessary result of the complex personal, social, and historical circumstances of Cervantes's existence, Castro's analysis of the process is frequently marked by a disapproving, even disdainful tone: Cervantes wishes to "pontificate in that society in which he believed himself to be duly established."

---

cervantinas," *Semblanzas y estudios españoles: Homenaje ofrecido a Don Americo Castro por sus ex-alumnos de Princeton University* [Princeton, 1956], p. 311). In characteristic metaphors Castro emphasizes the historical perishability of all art conceived in such abstract terms. "Envejece . . . lo concluso y definido, lo objetivado sin enlace con un vivir incierto. Se agostan incluso los sistemas de pensamiento y las teorías científicas. . . ." [Works which maintain] "viva su eficaz y perenne realidad" are those "creados por el genio humano, no como entes, sino como existentes" (p. 297). This judgment rests to some extent on the questionable assumption that the historical vitality of a work of literature is dependent on its projection of the dynamic, unpredictable flow of real experience.

In his stories he chooses to offer his public "archetypes of social perfection, in order to become respectable," and, as an exemplary writer, he can feel important within the social hierarchy. He writes as an "inoffensive conformist," a "gentle moralist," proposing an ideal "valid and acceptable for the people among whom he lived and desired to live in a respectable way and not as a pariah." A severe judgment of Cervantes's inauthenticity is clearly audible throughout the explanation of his apparent determination to endorse the official convictions of his society, and, when Castro goes on to consider the way in which this development is reflected in *Las novelas ejemplares*, he does not stop short of implying that their composition was in a sense an act of self-betrayal. Two of the novellas, which are most interesting and valuable because their author's authentic voice asserts itself and appears to be in conflict with his exemplary voice, require revision if they are to be allowed in the collection. They must be "pruned and touched up." If the concealed metaphor of grooming might hint at pretentiousness or a desire to please finer company, the harsh figure of excision suggests the spiritual violence that frequently accompanies self-betrayal. The lifelessness of academic art is the ultimate result of the savage self-repression: "The rebel writer becomes, in a certain way, an academic." With the *Persiles* the process is complete: no longer can we discern, as is still the case in "some of the twelve novellas," the coexistence of the "Cervantes who lives his art 'from outside' and the Cervantes who aspires to implant himself 'within' the area of the currently reigning codes of value."[17]

Castro's basic thesis is engaging, and, whether or not his speculations concerning the motivations and tensions troubling Cervantes's consciousness are valid, his analysis of the singular features and effects of the artistic product of the author's "authentic" voice is an incisive and convincing summary of the interpretations advanced in his major essays on the *Quixote*. However, as a study of the exemplarity of Cervantes's fiction, the argument falls victim of its narrow, polemical assumptions concerning the nature of exemplary art—"exemplarity, as a goal which is utilitarian, goes beyond and deforms authentic art"—and fails to offer its reader any insight into the particulars of the rich exemplary vision that informs the short stories. Indeed, Castro's abbreviated description of the tales as conformist, abstract, and devitalized, a description that in reality amounts to defining them by negative contrast with the *Quixote*, would suggest that they belong to

[17] See "La ejemplaridad de las novelas cervantinas," pp. 297-315.

a type of conservative fiction which has flourished in every age since the invention of printing and which owes its stability and resiliency to its fulfillment of the primarily social function of confirming established values, supporting vulgar prejudices, cultivating pleasurable sentiments, and trivializing subversive preoccupations. The short stories, which enjoyed an extraordinarily rich and productive historical life and which, as recently as 1795, were celebrated by Europe's most imposing man of letters as providing the classical models, both in form and vision, for modern writers of novellas, are reduced to the status of bland and comforting entertainment, the kind of literature which H. R. Jauss, in a metaphor which no doubt would have been pleasing to Cervantes for reasons very different from those informing it in Jauss's studies of literary reception, has referred to as "culinary reading." Indeed Castro at one point in his argument refers to the "formas de vida apetecible" of Cervantes's exemplary fiction, resurrecting at once one of the age-old *topoi* of derogation that have beset the European novella from the earliest period of its history.[18] The fact is that Castro's reading of the *Novelas ejemplares* in some ways represents the culmination in the development of the central tendencies of the Romantic reading of Cervantes's works, which, while leading to a profound understanding of the *Quixote*, a full appreciation of the essential qualities of novelistic fiction, and the due recognition of the revolutionary role of Cervantes's masterpiece in the evolution of literary forms and the creation of the novel, has resulted in the loss of Cervantes's works in which the potentialities are more restricted by the cultural and literary horizons surrounding their original creation.[19] Castro himself noted in his reconsideration of the blindness in his own early reading of the *Quixote* that Cervantes's masterpiece could be re-

---

[18] See Goethe's letter to Schiller, December 17, 1795, *Goethes Briefe*, 4 vols. (Hamburg, 1962-1967), 2:210. For Jauss's discussion of the type of literature that avoids troubling the receiving consciousness with the unfamiliar experience that might provoke a change in its comfortably assumed horizons, see *Literaturgeschichte als Provokation* (Frankfurt am Main, 1970), p. 178. For the conventional unfavorable view of novellas as "food for the senses," see the sixteenth-century judgment of J. de Zurita: "algunos libros han de quedar para ocupar la gente sensual, que no sabiendo ocuparse en cosas más altas, por fuerza han de tener algunos manjares gruessos en que se entretengan" (cited by A. González de Amezúa y Mayo, *Formación y elementos de la novela cortesana* [Madrid, 1929], pp. 82-83).

[19] A very different evaluation of the results of the Romantic "misreading" of *Don Quixote* can be found in A. Close's recent *The Romantic Approach to "Don Quixote"* [Cambridge, 1978], a study which reached me after the completion of this introduction.

covered from the drastic reductions of its potentialities which generally characterized its readings in the first two centuries of its historical
existence only following the radical modification of consciousness and
the revisions in philosophical and literary orientation brought about
in the period of European Romanticism.[20] What Castro's writings do
not indicate so explicitly is that the reformation of the European literary horizon which enabled the expansion of the *Quixote* to the fullness of historical life which was potential but unrealized in it earlier
would lead to the severe attenuation of Cervantes's exemplary fiction,

[20] See "Prólogo" to *Don Quijote de la Mancha*, pp. xiii-xiv, also "La palabra escrita
y el 'Quijote,' " p. 389. A glance at the complicated historical life of the *Quixote*
would confirm the usefulness of a fundamental distinction in the current aesthetics of
reception between the immediate and potential meanings of a literary work and the
recognition that the distance between the two can vary a great deal in different types
of works and as individual works are subjected to the readings of different periods.
In fact, in its "expansion," a phenomenon all too readily dismissed by an influential
school of contemporary readers as the growth of a distinguished body of "erroneous
interpretation," the *Quixote* is the preeminent case of a literary work that, before it
can become fully meaningful, requires a profound alteration in its public, a process
which can unfold in decades or centuries and which can in some instances be effected
by the powers of its own imaginative energy. "Der Abstand zwischen der aktuellen
ersten Wahrnehmung eines Werks und seinen virtuellen Bedeutungen, oder anders
gesagt: der Widerstand, den das neue Werk der Erwartung seines ernsten Publikums
entgegensetzt, kann so gross sein, dass es eines langen Prozesses der Rezeption bedarf,
um das im ersten Horizont Unerwartete und Unverfügbare einzuholen" (Jauss, *Literaturgeschichte als Provokation*, pp. 192-93). Clearly there was much in the *Quixote*
that was both "unexpected" and "unusable" for Cervantes's contemporary readers,
and the impoverishing "improvements" of Avellaneda's reconstruction of the masterpiece, as well as Sancho Panza's indignation at the gluttony and drunkenness of the
"impostor" whose life is chronicled by the Tordesillan historian, are eloquent testimony of its "irrelevancies" for its contemporary readers (see *Don Quijote de la Mancha*,
2:488-89). See also M. M. Bakhtin's observations on the "immortal, polysemic"
novelistic images which live different lives in different epochs and his judgment of
Don Quixote as the classic example of the phenomenon of "re-accentuation" in literary
history. "The historical life of classic works is in fact the uninterrupted process of
their social and ideological re-accentuation. Thanks to the intentional potential embedded
in them, such works have proved capable of uncovering in each era and against ever
new dialogizing backgrounds ever newer aspects of meaning; their semantic content
literally continues to grow, to further create out of itself." Bakhtin notes that the
process can bring contraction as well as expansion, and his words on the dangers of
"impoverishment" could stand as a summary of the excesses of both the Romantic
interpreters of *Don Quixote* and their adversaries, the so-called "hard" readers. "Especially dangerous is any vulgarizing that oversimplifies re-accentuation (which is
cruder in all respects than that of the author and his time) and that turns a two-
voiced image into one that is flat, single-voiced—into a stilted heroic image, a Sentimental and pathos-charged one, or (at the other extreme) into a primitively comic
one" ("Discourse in the Novel," *The Dialogic Imagination*, trans. C. Emerson and
M. Holquist [Austin, 1981], pp. 410, 421-22).

which, to be sure, speaks much more directly and exclusively to its immediate audience.[21]

If the *Novelas ejemplares* are to be recuperated in the extraordinary fullness of *their* original historical existence, an effort must be made to probe their exemplarity and its historical sources more searchingly than Castro's pronouncements on their dubious authenticity would encourage. Castro is, of course, perfectly aware of the direction that such an undertaking must follow, as he, more than any other literary historian, first opened our eyes to the matrix of cultural values, spiritual preoccupations, and literary systems in which they were born. Even in the grudging tones of his late work, Castro implies that the fundamental conclusions concerning the origins of Cervantes's ideas and values in Erasmian thought, presented in his now forbidden *El pensamiento de Cervantes*, are still valid. He argues that, following the death of the austere monarch, Philip II, "there flourished in Spain a Christian neo-humanism," concerned with preparing man for the afterlife but at the same time determined "not to forget the flesh and blood individual of this world." And it was precisely in this neo-

[21] Ironically Castro is the twentieth-century reader who has done most both to sustain the life of Cervantes's exemplary fiction and to complete the historical process of its loss, and one should not underestimate the severity of the rift separating the rationalism of his original conception of Cervantes as the most distinguished early spokesman for a minority tradition in Spain espousing enlightenment, rationalism, cosmopolitanism, and Europeanism from the vitalism informing his subsequent attachment as a critic to novelistic values and qualities, a philosophical vision intimately connected with them, and a belief in the causal relationship between their discovery and cultivation and the peculiar tensions of Spanish history. The recent study of Castro's writings on Cervantes by A. Close (*The Romantic Approach to "Don Quixote,"* chaps. 4-6), while correctly pointing out the vitalistic elements of *El pensamiento de Cervantes* and hence the general unity of Castro's whole corpus of Cervantine studies as "romantic," fails to stress sufficiently the radical rift separating the early and late criticism. Castro's envisaged dichotomy in Cervantes's consciousness and writings may be a mirror of the conflicting tendencies marking Castro's own development—from the secure spiritual horizons of his early cosmopolitan scholarship and his unquestioning self-identification within Spain's minority liberal tradition (in 1928 Castro associates himself with "Erasmus's 16th-century Spanish friends" in a letter to M. Bataillon concerning the advisability of softening the tone of some of the anticlerical assertions in the latter's prologue to Dámaso Alonso's edition of the *Enchiridion* for the purpose of assuring its publication in the Spain of Primo de Rivera's dictatorship [M. Bataillon, "Erasmo, ayer y hoy," *Erasmo y el erasmismo* (Barcelona, 1977), pp. 362-63]), to a *circunstancia* painfully problematized by his historical study, a profound sense of alienation from the "illusions" of his earlier understanding, and, in his search for authentic self-knowledge, a recognition of the degree to which he and all his work were conditioned by the distinctive character of the *morada vital* of Spain. This rift is in some ways as radical as that accompanying the shift from "classic" to "romantic" in the historical reception of *Don Quixote*.

humanism that Cervantes found inspiration as he structured the fictional shapes of his exemplary works, with their "forms of a life to be desired."[22] Insofar as my study attempts to illuminate the exemplary vision of Cervantes's short stories and situate them within the spiritual climate known for its most influential spokesman as Erasmism, it can be seen as reasserting and developing the tradition in Cervantine studies initiated by Castro's *El pensamiento de Cervantes*. In a sense it is an effort to recuperate through revision the historical-critical context in which that pioneering work had fruitfully elucidated Cervantes's entire literary production, but which Castro and various disciples have subsequently attempted to dismiss as peripheral to Cervantine criticism.[23]

[22] "La ejemplaridad de las novelas cervantinas," p. 302. Castro's assertion that the reign of Philip III was a period of Christian Humanism appears to be based more on his desire to attribute the doctrinal content of the *Novelas ejemplares*, which he obviously understood as "Christian Humanist," to a thoroughly conformist impulse in Cervantes than on his accurate observation of the cultural life of the period. See J. B. Avalle-Arce's recent discussion of the deep intellectual alienation which Cervantes suffered in the Spain of the Philips, the prominence of Erasmus's ideas and attitudes in his works, and his yearning for "the world of ideas that circulated quite freely in the Spain of Charles V," "Cervantes and the Renaissance," *Cervantes and the Renaissance*, ed. M. D. McGaha (Easton, Pa., 1980), pp. 5-6. As I shall point out in my analyses of the tales, deviations from the norms, values, and expectations constituting the contemporary horizon for literary reception and from the works creating and confirming that horizon are strikingly apparent in nearly every one of them. One of the most interesting threads linking the tales under consideration and pointing to a unified consciousness informing their highly variegated structures is Cervantes's critical dialogue with and disengagement from the contemporary ascetic writings which I refer to as the literature of *desengaño*. It should be pointed out that Castro omits this revealing passage in a later, revised version of his essay. The expurgation is extremely interesting: is it simply a sign of his awareness of the inaccuracy of his earlier description of the cultural life of Philip III's Spain and his consequent recognition that acknowledgment of the *Exemplary Novels*' humanist doctrines would vitiate his central argument that they should be seen as conformist works, or is it a sign of his increasing determination to dissociate all of Cervantes's achievements in writing about man as a concrete being in this world from European humanism and, in effect, to keep his own early critical voice, that of *El pensamiento de Cervantes*, from reasserting its influence? See *Hacia Cervantes*, pp. 451-74.

[23] In his subsequent writings Castro disposes of the question of Cervantes's Erasmism more conclusively, limiting his considerations to what can be recovered from the Erasmian vision that to some extent accounted for the achievements of the "authentic" Cervantes. In *Cervantes y los casticismos españoles* (Barcelona, 1966), for example, he acknowledges that Cervantes "se interesó vivamente por la espiritualidad cristiana de inspiración erasmista," but finds its significance for the writer primarily in its general emphasis on the individual's interior spiritual life and in the way in which the type of consciousness which it nurtured might lie behind the unprecedented and entirely secular act of "structuring a new type of literary character." He argues that

In my consideration of the Erasmism of Cervantes's tales, I am not primarily concerned with the question of the specific nature of the transmission of the humanist's thought to his greatest literary disciple. Noting the inconclusiveness of the various attempts to find concrete evidence that Cervantes read Erasmus's works, Marcel Bataillon has suggested that it is more fruitful to imagine that for Cervantes, educated in the Spain of Charles V, a Spain "impregnated with Erasmus's thought," and exposed as he undoubtedly was to the humanist's essential doctrines both through the instruction of teachers such as López de Hoyos and his youthful readings, Erasmus was a powerful experience of his formative years which took root in his personality and was nourished by his subsequent experiences as a traveller, a soldier, a captive, a husband, an observer, a writer, and a disillusioned patriot and idealist. When the Erasmian vision informed his writings, Cervantes probably had no need for a specific text to borrow from or to imitate. The vision had grown with him, and it was authentically his own, transfigured by his own experience into the vision of a great spiritual heir, possessed of its own integrity, unique in its own right, and productive in its own distinctive way. As in the case of all genuine spiritual families, the disciple was drawn by natural affinities to

---

Spanish Erasmian should be defined less in terms of a body of received doctrine than in terms of the vital needs that it, as well as other spiritualist movements which preceded it historically, satisfied in the alienated sensibility of the group of Spaniards to whom its appeal was most immediate. "El interés de Erasmo por la espiritualidad de San Pablo fue aprovechado en España para finalidades no exclusivamente teológicas o doctrinales. El erasmismo—como bien se sabe—no tuvo importancia en España como 'idea,' sino como medio protector y defensivo para quienes vivían como Luis de León nos ha dicho sin ninguna reserva, y hoy sabemos por otras vías. Los conversos se aferraban a cuanto sirviera para bastarse cristianamente a sí mismos" (see pp. ix, 109). For a balanced critical exposition of Castro's final view of Cervantes's Erasmism, see M. Bataillon, "El erasmismo de Cervantes en el pensamiento de Américo Castro," *Erasmo y el erasmismo*, pp. 347-59. An intelligent attempt to reconcile Castro's early and late approaches to the question can be found in F. Márquez Villanueva's recent *Personajes y temas del Quijote* (Madrid, 1975), which maintains that Cervantes's relation to Christian Humanist thought is that of an informed and articulate antagonist. The central doctrines of Erasmus's edifying program do inform crucial scenes of the *Quixote*, but the critical scrutiny which they receive from Cervantes discloses in every case their incompatibility with the novelist's vitalism and his existentialist vision of life's manifold complexities. By attesting to the impact of Erasmian thought on Cervantes's intellectual development and creative procedures, the argument resurrects the context of *El pensamiento de Cervantes*, but in its unsympathetic interpretations of Erasmist doctrines and its failure to consider numerous scenes, particularly in *Don Quixote* II, in which the humanist vision is forcefully associated with the chivalric enterprise, it ultimately supports the late Castro's continuing disengagement of Cervantes's specific creative achievements from Erasmian inspiration.

the master, and his discovery of the predecessor was in reality the discovery of his own authentic self. Certainly the question of Cervantes's Erasmism can be ultimately answered only if one adopts a more sophisticated method of comparative study than that which has limited traditional studies of sources and influences. Bataillon concludes that what is needed are "many comparative studies which take into account not only ideas, but also their expression, and which would seize as their object typically Erasmian ideas."[24] This is the type of approach that I take at various points in my study, seeking configurations of ideas and methods of exposition linking the two writers rather than concrete verbal correspondences.[25] Cervantes's thematically richest tales in fact point quite directly to several of the central preoccupations of Erasmus's program for spiritual *renovatio*— freedom and individual fulfillment, domestic and social organization, knowledge and education, language and literature, sinfulness and moral action, and the need for a general sanctification of the secular world. A good deal of my study is devoted to the careful analysis of the way in which such preoccupations animate the fictional shapes of Cervantes's tales. It attempts to show that the *Exemplary Novels* represent

[24] See *Erasmo y España: estudios sobre la historia espiritual del siglo* XVI, trans. A. Alatorre (México, 1966), pp. 777-801; esp. p. 799. J. L. Abellán's recent *El erasmismo español* (Madrid, 1976) is content to answer the question of Cervantes's Erasmism by restating the conclusions of the studies of Castro and Bataillon (see pp. 265-81). In view of Amezúa's uncompromising rejection of the possibility of any influence of Erasmus's writings and thought on Cervantes's work (*Cervantes, creador de la novela corta española*, 2 vols. [Madrid, 1956-1958], 1:139-99) and the recent endorsement of his conclusion in C. Morón Arroyo's *Nuevas meditaciones del "Quijote"* ([Madrid, 1976], pp. 124ff.), it would appear to be all the more urgent that such studies as Bataillon calls for be made.

[25] Bataillon himself and subsequently F. Márquez Villanueva have fruitfully considered the important episode of Don Quixote's encounter with the "Caballero del Verde Gabán" in connection with Erasmus's colloquies, *The Old Men's Chat* and *The Godly Feast*, employing a method of comparison which is not encumbered by the methodological requirements of traditional influence study. Though their analyses yield very different judgments of the episode, they strongly support the conclusion that Cervantes's knew the *Colloquies* and drew on them in a most independent and creative way (see *Erasmo y España*, pp. 792-94; Márquez Villanueva, *Personajes y temas del Quijote*, pp. 159ff.). Similarly A. Vilanova has analyzed successfully the play of ideas marking Cervantes's prologue to *Don Quixote* I in connection with the *Praise of Folly*, supporting his argument for influence with some interesting correspondences of detail (see "La Moria de Erasmo y el Prólogo del Quijote," *Collected Studies in Honour of Américo Castro's 80th Year*, ed. M. P. Hornik [Oxford, 1965], pp. 423-33, and *Erasmo y Cervantes* [Barcelona, 1949]). See also Bataillon's recent reconsideration of the possible influence of the *Praise of Folly* on such ironists as Cervantes and the author of *Lazarillo de Tormes* ("Un problème d'influence d'Érasme en Espagne: L'Éloge de la Folie," *Actes du Congrès Érasme* [Rotterdam, 1969], pp. 136-47).

a complex and effective fusion of literary form and philosophical vision and that their narrative methods were so original in their time that, to recall Lope's blindness to the exemplarity which can not be isolated and extracted from its fictional container and fixed in the conveniently assimilable *sententiae* of a controlling moralist narrator, they could be understood properly only with the development of the profound insights into the symbolic nature of fiction following the breakdown in the eighteenth century of traditional rhetorical modes of criticism and the neo-classical literary theories that formulated them so persuasively.[26] Taken in its entirety, Cervantes's collection of exemplary tales, with its imaginative reach extending from the opening celebration of man's divine potential to its concluding exploration of the darkest abysses of his misery, is perhaps Spain's most imposing tribute to the breadth of vision and generosity of spirit inspiring the Christian Humanist movement and distinguishing its enduring literary products.

If we must make an effort in historical recovery in order to be able to appreciate the exemplary vision informing Cervantes's tales, we must make a similar type of effort if we are to comprehend their formal qualities, their genre, and their place in the history of narrative fiction. The European novella came into existence in Boccaccio's *Decameron* as one of the most flexible and multifarious of literary forms, assimilating a variety of traditional narrative structures and techniques, incorporating a considerable range of aesthetic effects, and, as it was widely regarded as an undignified conveyer of amusement, gossip, and novelties, escaping the confining concepts of decorum and the limitations on compositional procedures which canonization in the

[26] E. C. Riley points out that the traditional interpretation of exemplariness in literature is far too narrow to enable a full comprehension of Cervantes's tales and adds: "Over and above edifying examples and warnings there was a region where the poetically true and the exemplary were at one, and this must have been the generous sense of exemplariness that Cervantes understood" (*Cervantes's Theory of the Novel*, p. 105). A striking alteration in the reader's capacity to understand correctly the nature and workings of Cervantes's exemplary art is registered in the description of the *Novelas ejemplares* by the celebrated grammarian, G. Mayans y Siscar, in 1737—"jocosidad milesia," commendable for their style, disposition, and "la agudeza de su invención y honestidad de costumbres" (cited by W. Krauss, *Miguel de Cervantes: Leben und Werk* [Neuwied, 1966], p. 215)—and in Goethe's recognition of the affinities of his own art with that of the master: "Dagegen habe ich an den Novellen des Cervantes einen wahren Schatz gefunden, sowohl der Unterhaltung als der Belehrung. Wie sehr freut man sich, wenn man das anerkannte Gute auch anerkennen kann und wie sehr wird man auf seinem Wege gefördert, wenn man Arbeiten sieht, die nach eben den Grundsätzen gebildet sind, nach denen wir nach unserem Masse und in unserem Kreise selbst verfahren" (letter to Schiller, December 17, 1795, *Goethes Briefe*, 2:210).

official poetics of the period would no doubt have brought to it.[27] If
such variety had always been a characteristic of the early novella collections, there was, nevertheless, a uniformity visible in the general
tendency of the individual tales toward brevity, swiftly paced movement to a climactic point, and spareness in the use of any detail—
whether descriptive, rhetorical, psychological, or thematic—that might
delay the reader in his movement toward the point.[28] Based on one
of the most primitive elements in man's literary experience, the stability of the genre was to a certain extent dependent on severe limitation, and it proved increasingly precarious as writers of the sixteenth
century attempted to exploit the fictional resources of the form for
radically new purposes and effects. While courtly circles continued to
find its traditional qualities well-suited to their cultivation of wit and
conversational charm, such writers as Marguerite de Navarre and the
French adaptors of Bandello's sensational tales, Belleforest and Boais-

---

[27] From Boccaccio's concluding comment on the *Decameron*, "Conviene nella mol-
titudine delle cose, diverse qualità di cose trovarsi," to Bandello's acknowledgment
of the "disorderliness" of his collection, "E non avendo potuto servar ordine ne l'altre,
meno m'è stato lecito servarlo in queste; il che certamente nulla importa, non essendo
le mie novelle soggetto d'istoria continovata, ma una mistura d'accidenti diversi,
diversamente e in diversi luoghi e tempi a diverse persone avvenuti e senza ordine
veruno recitati," the major writers of short stories continued to recognize that the
appeal of their art rested to a great extent on its variety (see Pabst, *Novellentheorie*,
pp. 39, 74). See also R. J. Clements and J. Gibaldi, *Anatomy of the Novella: The
European Tale Collection from Boccaccio and Chaucer to Cervantes* (New York, 1977), pp.
12-16. Pabst notes that the most striking feature of the short story in its historical
development from the thirteenth to the eighteenth century is the freedom of expression which it allowed its cultivators and its resistance to the confinements of theme
or form which prescriptive literary theory generally imposes on the objects of its
attention. He emphasizes that Boccaccio "hat . . . selbst nie daran gedacht, das
Vielfältige und Unterschiedliche als Gattung oder Norm aufzufassen" and that sixteenth-century efforts, under the impact of the increasingly prestigious neo-classical
doctrines, to attribute a unified conception to the *Decameron* offer one of the most
striking examples of the incompatibility which the genre has shown through history
with the sporadic and ineffectual attempts at codification by its commentators. While
critics and defenders of short stories invoked principles of traditional rhetoric, they
never attempted to derive a theory of the novella that would accurately take into
account its fundamental constitutive features and the positive differences separating
it from the officially sanctioned genres (see pp. 22-27, 40, 73-79). For the variety of
traditional narrative forms which Boccaccio incorporated in his masterpiece, see Pabst,
Novellentheorie, pp. 28-29, and H.-J. Neuschäfer, *Boccaccio und der Beginn der Novelle:
Strukturen der Kurzerzählung auf der Schwelle zwischen Mittelalter und Neuzeit* (Munich,
1969).
[28] See E. Auerbach, *Zur Technik der Frührenaissancenovelle in Italien und Frankreich*
(Heidelberg, 1921), and W. Krömer, "Gattung und Wort *Novela* im Spanischen 17.
Jahrhundert," *Romanische Forschungen* 81 (1969):381-434.

tuau, were expanding its narrow confines by introducing elements
that were ultimately incompatible with its traditional constitutive features: the consideration of philosophical and social problems, the cultivation of sentiment, the exploration of complex psychological motivation, an increased attention to description, and the elaboration of
striking narrative units—e.g., the scene of pathos, the rhetorically
striking declamation, the generalizing excursus by character or narrator—as independent and hence discontinuous elements within the
traditional tightly ordered design. In short, the form, which had always been open in its assimilation of different socio-economic milieus,
different types of character, and different tones, settings, and historical periods, now opened up in a way which was much more radical
and which threatened its foundations and hence its very existence.[29]
The century preceding Cervantes's decision to *novelar* for the first time
in Castilian would appear to be a period of crisis in the historical
evolution of the genre, a period of breakdown and redirection in its
response to new expressive needs, themselves the result of the complex
historical pressures of this age of transition in European history. More
than any other collection of short stories of the period, Cervantes's
Novelas ejemplares would attest to the profundity of the alteration which
the genre experienced in this period. On the one hand, they represent
the full realization of the effort, initiated sporadically in Marguerite
de Navarre's *Heptaméron*, to turn the novella into a vehicle capable of
engaging with the most urgent ideological and social preoccupations
of the moment. As a novelistic monument to the humanist vision,
analogous perhaps in its "belatedness" within its spiritual tradition to
Milton's *Paradise Lost* in Renaissance epic literature, Cervantes's collection of tales is a true descendent of the *Heptaméron*, and one can
not begin to account for the evolution in narrative fiction represented
by both collections without giving some attention to the possible
impact on the novella of the most highly influential fictionalizations
of profound ideas in Europe of the sixteenth century—the *Colloquies*
of Erasmus.[30] On the other hand, Cervantes's tales represent the cul-

[29] See Krömer, "Gattung und Wort *Novela* im Spanischen 17. Jahrhundert," pp.
390-96; Clements and Gibaldi, *Anatomy of the Novella*, pp. 216-28; Auerbach, *Zur
Technik der Frührenaissancenovelle in Italien und Frankreich*, pp. 63-64.

[30] Considering L. B. Alberti's "De amicitia" in connection with the humanists'
general search for flexible, "antisystematic," forms of exposition, F. Schalk notes that
"eine persönliche erfinderische, der Novelle verwandte Kunst fliesst in seinen Büchern
zusammen mit der mächtigen Einwirkung des Humanismus" and goes on to assert
that there is a relationship of reciprocal influence between the novella and the privileged didactic genres of the humanists: "Symposion, Traktat, Dialog—und es gab
seit dem Humanismus viele Traktate und Dialoge— . . . Panegyrikus, Disputatio,

mination in the quest for new forms that marked the experimentalism occasionally visible in sixteenth-century short fiction as it turned from the brief, pointed forms that had been dominant during the first centuries of the genre's historical life. Viewed within the tradition of the early European novella, Cervantes's collection is remarkable not only for the length of the individual tales included, but also for the variety of their forms and the generic models to which they point.

While Cervantes's aspirations to be the first to *novelar* in Spanish were high, his imagination was obviously not inhibited in the slightest by an awareness of a particular model to be imitated or a set of codified rules of composition to be followed. His admirers immediately hailed his collection of novellas for its variety:

> aqueste florido abril,
> cuya variedad admira
> la fama veloz, que mira
> en él variedades mil.[31]

At the same time there are indications that his contemporary audience was somewhat bewildered by his claims to offer a collection of novellas. As we have seen, Lope, who in his willingness to consider *Amadís de Gaula* and *Orlando furioso* as distinguished examples of the genre seems not to have had a very precise awareness of what a novella was, nevertheless drew attention to the deviations in Cervantes's tales from a type of story which was familiar to him and could be invoked as representing the norms of the genre, Bandello's *Tragic Histories*. The observations of the conservative Avellaneda similarly indicate the disorienting effect which Cervantes's designation of such narratives

---

Novelle treten in einen inneren Zusammenhang miteinander" ("L. B. Albertis Buch 'De Amicitia' [Della Famiglia IV]," in *Symbola Coloniensia Iosepho Kroll sexagenario . . . oblata* [Cologne, 1949], pp. 163-71). E. Auerbach suggests that with Marguerite de Navarre's *Heptaméron* a new and rich phase in the historical development of the novella begins, as the genre situates itself more firmly within the context of the humanist philosophical vision (*Zur Technik der Frührenaissancenovelle in Italien und Frankreich*, p. 64). As I shall point out in my analyses, the *Colloquies* of Erasmus appear to have had an influence on Cervantes's composition of novellas, both in their philosophical content and in their manner of fusing ideas and fictions. W. Pabst's generally unfavorable treatment of the encounter of the European novella with humanism is severely limited by his far too exclusive association of the latter with academic theorizing, rationalistic systematization, inauthentic imitation, and logical attitudes which would inhibit creative freedom (see *Novellentheorie*, pp. 58-59, 78-79).

[31] "This flowery April,/ Whose variety is admired by/ Flying fame, who looks upon/ A thousand varieties in him" (prefatory poem by Fernando Bermúdez Carbajal, *Novelas ejemplares, Obras completas*, ed. A. Valbuena Prat, p. 771).

may have had on his contemporary readers. The works are not only improperly called exemplary, since they are "más satíricas que exemplares," but they are also inaccurately described as novellas since nearly all of them are in reality "comedias en prosa."[32] At the same time, in the enthusiastic reception which greeted Cervantes's tales in France, there are clear indications that their failure to match readers' expectations based on established conventions of the short story was so thorough that they were viewed as representing an entirely reconstituted novella, or, in fact, a new literary form. Le sieur d'Audiguier introduced his French translation of the tales as offering his public a completely new type of fiction, and Tallemant des Réaux expressed the view that the Cervantine novella must be considered as a literary form sui generis.[33]

Modern readers and literary historians have found the variety of Cervantes's tales no less challenging than his contemporary readers, but their attempts to render it intelligible in terms of familiar generic categories have been only slightly more helpful than those of his seventeenth-century readers. If one considers the various attempts at systematic classification of the *Novelas ejemplares*, one quickly discovers that critics and literary historians have been content to account for the differences in the tales by invoking some rather vaguely formulated dualistic typology—such as romantic and realistic, fantastic and *costumbrista*, idealistic and skeptical, Italianate and Spanish, imitative and original, literary and representational, normative and vitalistic, early and late, and so on—a duality that in fact turns out to be a translation into the terms of literary genre of the more basic biographical dichotomy that Cervantists continue to cling to—the "two Cervanteses." On scrutinizing it closely, one then discovers that this dichotomy, as well as the various others which it underlies, is in reality the expression of literary preferences of the modern reader, and that it carries with it a strong value judgment. There is, on the one hand, the authentic, "original," and genuinely creative Cervantes, writing the literature that significantly altered the history of prose fiction and man's literary experience, creating, through the ironic engagement with nearly all traditional forms of fiction, the great representational genre of the modern novel. On the other hand, there is a conservative, conformist, and imitative Cervantes, the man of letters who bowed to the conventional literary tastes and values of his society and its repressive institutions, such as the Inquisition, and wrote such perish-

[32] See *Don Quijote de la Mancha*, ed. M. de Riquer (Madrid, 1972), 1:7-12.

[33] See G. Hainsworth, "Quelques opinions françaises (1614-1664) sur les Nouvelles exemplaires de Cervantes (1613)," *Bulletin Hispanique* 32 (1930):63-70.

able imitations of its escapist, naively idealizing forms as *La Galatea*, *El Persiles*, and the so-called Italianate novellas. Since Menéndez y Pelayo's eloquent description of the romantic and the realistic tendencies in Cervantes's fiction, the notion of the "two Cervanteses," in several variations, has shown remarkable powers of survival, and, as I have pointed out above, we find it emerging most recently in a form which is particularly troubling for the student of the *Novelas ejemplares* in Américo Castro's arguments concerning the motivations behind their exemplarity.

The fact is that Cervantes, one of the great experimenters in the history of fiction, was receptive to a wide variety of literary forms. There was nothing exclusivistic about his reading preferences; as he himself put it, he was a man who could not resist picking up, reading, and rescuing from oblivion, as it were, the scraps of paper he found in the streets, and one need only look at the immense variety of forms and styles which he incorporates into the *Quixote* to get some idea of the catholicity of his literary tastes. Neither the single generic designation *novella*, which Cervantes himself offers us, nor the various dualities which literary historians have thus far invoked can account for the variety of the tales or, for that matter, for the form, structure, and effects of a single one. Indeed, in the failure of such attempts at classification Walter Pabst has found confirmation of his thesis concerning the nonexistence of a "classical" European novella and his general view that little is to be gained in literary study by the invocation of such insubstantial entities as types and genres. On examining the tales, Pabst goes on to remark that perhaps the most apt designation for Cervantes's collection of short fiction would be a "labyrinth" (an *Irrgarten*), a metaphor which resurrects the very *topos* by which authors and commentators, from the *Decameron* to the *Novelas ejemplares*, declared the freedom of the form in its unbounded variety.[34] Certainly one must agree with Pabst that a healthy critical nominalism which leaves the eyes open to the integrity of the individual object of study is far preferable to the facile typologies which mediate the object through a screen of modern prejudices concerning literary value. Fortunately, however, one does not have to resign oneself at this point to the choice of these two counterproductive positions. Over the past thirty years our insight into the generic possibilities of prose fiction has increased enormously, and numerous valuable studies of neglected genres, ranging from the simple minor literary forms of folktale, parable, fable, and aphorism to such inexhaustibly

[34] *Novellentheorie*, p. 117.

rich creations of man's literary imagination as romance and satire and their various subspecies—for example, chivalric, Byzantine, and hagiographic; Menippean, Lucianesque, and picaresque—have rewarded us with an increasingly sophisticated and precise knowledge of the specific forms that make up that gigantic area of non-novelistic narrative fiction, forms which can be viewed both as stable, definable literary systems and as objects with particular historical existences, involving origination, evolution, transformation, and, in some cases, death and oblivion. Anybody who reads *Don Quixote* quickly recognizes that Cervantes's consciousness of the literary conventions of traditional literary genres is highly developed, so developed in fact, that the novel itself, and particularly Part I, draws its imaginative vitality from the reiterated process of disclosing the artificiality of literary convention in its opposition to reality. The *Novelas ejemplares*, of course, assume a much less subversive attitude toward traditional generic systems, but they are no less wide-ranging in their incorporation of available forms, and they are just as subtle and, in a different way, just as original in their engagement with generic codes as is the great novel. While one part of my study looks toward the problem of their exemplarity, the other part undertakes, generally as the proper point of departure for each chapter, a careful consideration of their structure, genre, and place in literary history. Here my focus is on Cervantes's craft as a writer of short stories, as an experimenter in literary forms, and as a man who was profoundly aware of the potentialities for creative adaptation in traditional narrative. My study of the literary aspects of the works confirms in every case my arguments concerning their exemplarity and the impact of Erasmian thought on their conception. It is not simply that one finds a variety of forms which parallel the extraordinary range of thought and concern animating the tales and which indicate that it would be just as perverse to regard them as representatives of the most lifeless mechanical literature of moral instruction as to conceive their message as a bland confirmation of the most vulgar prejudices of contemporary Spain. Nor is it simply that some of their most original fictional innovations and most sophisticated accommodations of literary forms to doctrine presupposed Cervantes's intense interest in and thorough understanding of the privileged genres of the humanists—the Menippean satire and the Heliodorean romance.[35] The spiritual heritage of humanism is, in fact, visible at the most profound level of Cervantes's activity as an exper-

---

[35] M. Bataillon has noted the particular appeal which Heliodorus's *Ethiopian History*, rediscovered in the sixteenth century, had for the Erasmists (*Erasmo y España*, pp. 621-22).

imenter in narrative, and, in order to glimpse it, we must be fully
aware of the generic codes in which his short fiction is conceived and
offered to his reader. At this point the study of exemplarity and literary genre converge. Far from being inhibited by the pressures of his
culture and captive to its most reactionary literary preferences, Cervantes, in his aspiration to be the first to *novelar* in Spanish, proceeds
with absolute freedom and sovereign control of his medium. His engagement with all available literary resources is that of a writer who
understands thoroughly their potentialities and exploits them independently for his own particular needs.[36] His methods of adaptation
are always original, and they range from unprecedented hybridization,
in the combination of traditional forms of disorder in *El casamiento
engañoso y el coloquio de los perros*, and skillful accommodation, in *La
Gitanilla*'s complex fusion of ideas and romance conventions, to unraveling and reconstitution, in the critical engagement with a prestigious hagiographic form in *La fuerza de la sangre*, and violent decon-
struction, in the unexpected formal disarticulation of *El celoso extremeño*.[37]
As the latter case would indicate, Cervantes's tales can become struc-
turally most intricate and elusive precisely when they appear to be
most doctrinaire and conventional. Indeed there is hardly a tale that
fails to deviate in some radical way from the expectations that its
traditional ingredients would arouse in its audience. The disorienting
desatinos—the "swerves from the destined mark"—are clearly intended. Cervantes, whose stories so frequently strike one as childlike
in their simplicity, is at once the most indulgent and the most exacting of authors, and the numerous efforts, from Avellaneda to Una-
muno, to rewrite his fiction so as to eliminate "superfluous" or "absurd" elements, while commemorating certain readers' failures to respond
fully to the challenge in its refusal to close in the readily intelligible
way according to an insinuated "destination," are, nonetheless, continuing testimony of its power to activate its reader and enlist his
energies in its own creation. In the sense that the irregularities of
Cervantes's "Sileni" refuse to allow their reader the comforts of a stock
response and instead burden him with the obligation to cope with
unsettling violations of his vocabulary of genre, the *Novelas ejemplares*

[36] For the self-consciousness and general independence with which Cervantes manipulates traditional literary genres, see K. Reichenberger, "Cervantes und die literarischen Gattungen," *Germanisch-Romanische Monatsschrift* 13 (1963):233-46.

[37] My examination of *El casamiento engañoso y el coloquio de los perros*, which I consider
ideologically the most complex and formally the most revolutionary work of the
collection, will appear as an independent study, titled *Cervantes and the Mystery of
Lawlessness*.

stand as one of the fullest literary realizations of the characteristic nonlinear discourse of the great humanist writers of the sixteenth century, who turned to dialectical, ironic, and paradoxical modes of exposition in their efforts to explore the complexities of truth, to provoke their readers' collaboration in that exploration, and to revitalize perceptions blunted by the tyranny of familiarity and appearance.[38] The man who thoroughly understands the "familiar" beliefs which he adopts and on which he acts is in a very fundamental way a truly liberated man. To the extent that the *Novelas ejemplares* are composed in this deceptive, demanding discourse, their ultimate message may well lie in the freedom with which they dignify their reader and in the example of the creative use of freedom set by their author. In this

[38] While their liberating discourse, which engages the reader in a dialogue, separates Cervantes's stories decisively from traditional exemplary literature with its "monologic" formulations of doctrine, it links them not only with the characteristic literature of the Christian Humanists but also with *Don Quixote*, for it is the fundamental idiom of the great novel. At various points in my study I consider the central issues and narrative techniques of the short stories as they appear in the *Quixote*. Through comparative analysis I hope both to enhance our understanding of the distinctive character of each work and, by considering their mutual relationships, to contribute to our understanding of the complexity and fundamental unity of the vision informing them. Several specific points of comparison—e.g., religious attitudes; adaptations of literary conventions; the themes of nature, knowledge, and marriage—indicate the greater modernity of the *Quixote*, but they also disclose a common body of interests and preoccupations underlying both works. If it is undoubtedly naive to accept the Romantics' exaggerated conception of this unity—e.g., Friedrich Schlegel: "Wer nicht einmal sie [die Novellen] göttlich finden kann, muss den *Don Quixote* durchaus falsch verstehen" (*Seine prosaischen Jugendschriften*, 2 vols. [Vienna, 1906], 2:315)—it is perhaps no less so to conceive of an irreconcilable opposition of spirit separating the exemplary and novelistic works. A full clarification of their reciprocal relationships would, of course, require a separate study, but I hope to suggest some directions such a study might take, one of which would be to shift the focus of critical attention from the search for germs of the *Quixote* in the novellas to a careful examination and evaluation of the presence of the novellas in the *Quixote*. Given the renewed interest in the *Persiles* and the theater in recent years, such a shift would appear to be perfectly compatible with contemporary trends in Cervantine criticism, which is clearly no longer dominated by the interest in novelistic values which, because of the inexhaustible richness of *Don Quixote* as the first novel, persisted long after their decanonization by many twentieth-century writers and critics. The prominence of the humanist vision in Part II of the *Quixote* and its elevation through the ascent of Sancho Panza, the increasing conceptual complexity and ambivalence in Don Quixote's madness, and the elegiac tone surrounding his rejection by the world would suggest that the affinities of the *Novelas ejemplares* and the *Quixote* are much deeper than is commonly supposed. In general my study tends to confirm M. Bataillon's view that "La obra de Cervantes es la de un hombre que permanece, hasta lo último, fiel a ideas de su juventud, a hábitos de pensamiento que la época de Felipe II había recibido de la del Emperador" (*Erasmo y España*, p. 778).

sense they are no less progressive in the history of literature than the much more overtly revolutionary *Don Quixote*, for, while the language of its phrasing is frequently quite remote and calls for translation and mediation by the literary historian, the ultimate message to be recovered is no less valid in 1980 than it was in 1613.

CHAPTER I

El celoso extremeño
and the Classical Novella:
The Mystery of Freedom

THE "SPANISH BOCCACCIO"

WHEN CERVANTES claimed to be the first man to *"novelar"* in Spanish and Tirso de Molina paid homage to his master as the "Spanish Boccaccio," it is possible that both writers were thinking of *The Jealous Estremaduran* (*El celoso extremeño*). Of all the tales in the collection none is more directly indebted in form and content to the central tradition of the European short story, which found its classical expression in the *Decameron*, and none reveals more clearly Cervantes's mastery of the narrative techniques which Boccaccio perfected and left as the classical standard for future short story writers. While Boccaccio's collection of tales encompasses an abundance of forms and readers' attempts to isolate a quintessential classical novella therein have generally failed to do justice to its variety, Erich Auerbach is certainly right in emphasizing as distinctive formal qualities of Boccaccio's narratives the concentration on action as opposed to character or setting and the organization of the action around a single climactic point, whether in an amusing "punch line," a striking situation or occurrence, or a sudden, arresting turn of events.[1] The Boccaccian novella

---

[1] Erich Auerbach, *Zur Technik der Frührenaissancenovelle in Italien und Frankreich* (Heidelberg, 1921), chap. 4. Auerbach suggests that the sharply pointed plot of the Boccaccian tale is a formal feature deriving from its generic ancestor, the *exemplum*, with its rationalistic, "teleological" design as a demonstration of an abstract principle that resides beyond its fictional world. The feature was exaggerated by Boccaccio's imitators in Italy, who tended to strip the already economically constructed plot of

characteristically defines the motives of its action clearly and quickly at its beginning and then hastens toward the climactic point, which can be readily anticipated, as it follows logically from the premises contained in the initial situation. Unlike the *Gitanilla*, where the narrative pauses to incorporate scenes of public ritual and pageantry, strays into the discontinuous fictional world of satirical description, glances at fragmentary actions and the untold tales of peripheral characters, and points tantalizingly to suggestive, undeveloped relations between characters, the Boccaccian tale only exceptionally does anything to bring indeterminacy to its fictional world or to disorient the reader and trouble his anticipation and suspense as he moves toward the climactic point and an apprehension of the themes implicit in the action.[2] Indeed it is the impressive concentration of the Boccaccian tale that inspired Paul Heyse's influential attempt to formulate a poetics of the novella in the nineteenth century. Basing his theoretical observations on an analysis of the "falcon novella" (*Decameron*, V. 9), Heyse argues that the motif for a successful novella must have, in addition to a prominent climactic point, a sharp "silhouette," and he suggests that in the most effective novella the essentials of its arresting occurrence can be summarized in a few lines and indeed be concen-

their master's tales of any contingencies of empirical reality that could be construed as extraneous to the climactic point and pushed the novella back toward the extreme spareness of its ancestor, without, however, returning to the *exemplum's* complete subordination of design to a transcendent informing concept. While early literary theorists paid little attention to the novella and, when doing so, were far less interested in seriously analyzing its formal properties than in offering unsystematic observations concerning its "extraliterary" relations, that is, its relations to ethical, social, and educational contexts, it is interesting that one of the Renaissance neo-Aristotelian theorists who does attempt to define the genre emphasizes as an essential characteristic its teleologically constructed "Aristotelian" plot with "prologue," a "complication" or a "knotting" (*"scompiglio"*), and an "unknotting" (*"sviluppo"*) and points to Boccaccio's tales as the "Homeric" models that exemplify the perfectability of such a plot. See Francesco Bonciani, *Lezione sopra el comporre delle novelle*, summarized by Bernard Weinberg, *A History of Literary Criticism in the Italian Renaissance*, 2 vols. (Chicago, 1963), 1:538-40.

[2] The most famous exception is of course the tale of Griselda (X. 10). See also the startling disintegration of the climax of VI.1, where, in a mystification that looks forward to Cervantes's fiction, the text suddenly opens up to disclose an untold story, the "truth" of the tale suddenly appears as a problem, and the reader finds himself compelled momentarily to deal actively with puzzling, conflicting possibilities of interpretation of what he is reading (or hearing). For recent interpretations emphasizing the "troubling" elements in *The Decameron*, see Hans-Jörg Neuschäfer, *Boccaccio und der Beginn der Novelle: Strukturen der Kurzerzählung auf der Schwelle zwischen Mittelalter und Neuzeit* (Munich, 1969), and Giuseppe Mazzotta, "The *Decameron*: The Literal and the Allegorical," *Italian Quarterly* 18 (1975):53-73.

trated in a single powerful symbol. The storyteller should ask himself, as he designs his tale, "where 'the falcon' is, the specific element which distinguishes this story from a thousand others."[3] While this definition certainly fails to account for numerous stories of the *Decameron*, it nevertheless is apt in its accentuation of unity and concentration as the mark of the Boccaccian tale.[4]

[3] See the introduction to *Deutscher Novellenschatz*, ed. P. Heyse and H. Kurz (Munich, 1971), pp. xvi-xx. As Hermann Pongs points out, Heyse's remarks concerning the centrality of the symbol are undeveloped and seem to be focused primarily on problems of "external" form, e.g., unity, concentration, narrative pacing, and suspense. Pongs proceeds to explore the more profound implications of the central symbol, showing how in the greatest of the Boccaccian tales it can articulate the most fundamental themes of the story and is hence the most powerful bond in the work's "inner" unity as well. See "Über die Novelle," *Das Bild in der Dichtung*, 3 vols. (Marburg, 1927-1969), 2:97-109. It is this kind of symbolic power which we find in the central symbols of Cervantes's most concentrated tales, the house in *El celoso extremeño* and blood in *La fuerza de la sangre*. See also Pongs's analysis of Boccaccio's and Cervantes's short stories in his "Grundlagen der deutschen Novelle des 19. Jahrhunderts," *Das Bild*, pp. 110-24.

[4] I believe that the definition of a "classical novella" in terms of such basic principles, as well as a differentiation of it from other narrative genres with their distinctive processes and effects, is a valid and useful critical endeavor despite Walter Pabst's persuasive rejection of the existence of such an abstraction. Pabst's comprehensive examination of the enormous number of individuals which comprise this hypothetical species leads him to the following conclusion: "Damit ist—in Italien, Spanien, Portugal, Frankreich, vom 13. bis zum 18. Jahrhundert—nicht die Existenz einer an Formgesetze gebundenen Gattung nachgewiesen, sondern gerade das Gegenteil: die Fähigkeit und Tendenz der Novellistik, nicht nur literarischen Niederschlag zu finden, sondern eine Freiheit künstlerischen Ausdrucks zu bewahren und die Grenzen offenzuhalten zwischen Distanzierung und Vergegenwärtigung" (*Novellentheorie und Novellendichtung* [Heidelberg, 1967], pp. 26-27). Pabst's skepticism concerning the existence of the genre is primarily the result of his impressive empirical observation of the facts, the variety of which is indeed a bewildering challenge to any search for unifying structures. However, his extreme hostility to genre concepts, one suspects, is to some extent a reaction against the prestige of certain notions that have dominated modern theorizing concerning the novella, from Goethe's suggestive words on the "*unerhörte Begebenheit*" and Tieck's emphasis on the "*Wendepunkt*" to Heyse's theories on the silhouette and the central symbol, notions that are by and large unhistorical in their derivation and reductive when taken as definitive and applied uncritically. Pabst repeatedly reminds us that the great exemplars of the "classical" novella had no theories resembling those which we have adopted (e.g., "Was aber die Novellen des 'Decameron' und ihre Eigenart oder Form angeht, deren 'Gesetze' in jüngerer Zeit wieder zum Gattungsgesetz und zur 'romanischen Urform' erklärt wurden, so hat einerseits der Dichter selbst nie daran gedacht, das Vielfältige und Unterschiedliche als Gattung oder Norm aufzufassen" [p. 40]), and he points out that the greatest writers of short stories, for example, Boccaccio, Cervantes, and La Fontaine, were men who were deeply suspicious of the rigidities of systematic thinking and suggests that they undoubtedly found the form appealing in its freedom from the

In its structure, plot, and characterization the *Celoso extremeño* reveals all of these essential features of Boccaccio's "classical" novella. Its introduction characterizes the agents briefly and in general terms and defines a situation bearing in itself a potential, in fact, an *inevitable* conflict, and its central action then proceeds swiftly and directly, step by step, through the development of that conflict to the climactic scene and a concluding denouement.[5] The single central action is never

inhibiting systems of rules regulating the officially canonized literary genres, its openness to a wide variety of subjects, its fondness for burlesque and parody, and its traditional hostility to the compulsive mental habits of such figures of order as the pedant, the ascetic, and the repressive husband. In his particular way of referring to genre—"eine an Formgesetze gebundene Gattung"—and his contrast of it with "eine Freiheit künstlerischen Ausdrucks," Pabst reveals that he views genre as a codification of literary procedures that regulates and inhibits creative activity and is inevitably at odds with free expression. His critique of genres from the point of view of an expressionistic theory of literary creation and value concludes with the association of all genre theory with sterile neo-classicism, the assertion that, as the product of Occidental rationalism, it represents a perverse misapplication of scientific method to literary study, and an invocation of Goethe's observations concerning the limits of genre codifications and the lofty activities of the free genius (see pp. 258-62). When I speak of the "classical novella" in the following analysis, I am not thinking of the literary genre as a rigidly defined model (whether as an actual "classical" work or a hypostatized concept), setting norms for its imitation, exclusivist rather than inclusivist in its orientation, but rather as a recognizable system of literary elements—for example, in its plots, its agents, its narrative stances, its styles and diction, its themes, its content, its tones, and its settings—, which can be combined in a variety of ways and for a variety of effects. Such a system exists only in so far as it is immanent in the concrete works that manifest it, and, whether or not it is given theoretical formulation by writers exploiting it, it should be in fact viewed as a codification of actual practices of a type of writing in its historical evolution. A writer shares its code with his audience just as he shares with it the grammatical code of the language actualized in the sentences in which he writes. The existence of such a codification is in no way dependent on its academic formulation. Indeed the history of academic formulations of genre codes reveals a frequent misunderstanding of the codes in their actual historical manifestations, as the formulators are dominated by the rationalist impulse to control through classification and subsumption. Far from imposing itself on an author as a burden on his creative processes, the genre provides him with a system that he can freely exploit for his own expressive needs and that his own work modifies, a system that is in fact continually changing and expanding as it receives and incorporates the works manifesting it. Cervantes's *El celoso extremeño* is a powerful testimony of both the existence and the openness of generic schemes and of the way in which their actualization can in reality make possible the expression of a very original vision. At the same time it demonstrates how an audience's expectations based on its notion of genre can be skillfully manipulated for unusual effects by an author conscious of a generic code and its presence in his culture.

[5] All page references in the following analysis are to *El celoso extremeño, Novelas ejemplares*, ed. F. Rodríguez Marín, 2 vols. (Madrid, 1957-1962), vol. 2. Various critics have remarked that *El celoso extremeño* is conspicuous within Cervantes's collec-

allowed to disappear from the foreground, and all description is subordinate to its movement. While some critics have viewed the work as an example of Cervantes's realism and praised its depiction of the life and customs of Seville of the early seventeenth century,[6] the fact is that the setting of the tale is very fragmentary. The fantastic house, which certainly stands as a powerful central symbol in the tradition of some of Boccaccio's most concentrated tales, takes shape only as an agglomerate of objects and spaces related to the theme of confinement and the action of penetrating barriers. All that we see of Carrizales's bedroom is a mattress, concealing a key, a locked door, and a small hole at the base of the wall ("*la gatera*"). The interior contains a garden with orange trees, flowing water, and pictures of foliage, all presented in a description that limits itself to the generic detail and is untroubled by the retarding addition of individuated objects, because Cervantes is sketching a false paradise of confinement. We see numerous details of the street-porch ("*la casa puerta*")—the hinges on the door, the loft, the turnstile, the ground, the mule—but only because they form the principal part of the barriers that the seducer-deliverer must cross and because they form another unit of stifling confinement and dehumanization for a victim ("*un emparedado*") of the oppressor's madness. When we enter the house, we have no concrete indication of place until Cervantes needs to inform us, and he does so only in the vaguest of terms, of the presence of rooms, corners, and other more indeterminate spaces available to the servants when they

tion of tales in the tightness and linearity of its plot construction. Werner Krauss argues that Cervantes's novellas break radically with all previous novella traditions in their openness and their preference for wandering heroes, changing settings ("*Raumbewegung*"), and travel and adventure beyond the boundaries of the domestic and urban locations customary in the traditional tale. He finds *El celoso extremeño*, however, a thoroughly conventional Italianate tale in its plot, setting, and exemplary theme (see "Cervantes und der Spanische Weg der Novelle," *Studien und Aufsätze* [Berlin, 1959], pp. 93-138, esp. pp. 104, 117). Leo Spitzer emphasizes the "*geradlinnig*" and highly concentrated character of the work and points out its formal and thematic affinities with the traditional *exemplum* ("Das Gefüge einer Cervantinischen Novelle," *Romanische Stil- und Literatur Studien*, 2 vols. [Marburg, 1931], 2:141-80, esp. p. 176). See also Wolfram Krömer's discussion of the exceptional nature of *La fuerza de la sangre* and *El celoso extremeño* as tales that present a logical movement toward closure and in which not a single detail is superfluous ("Gattung und Wort *novela* im Spanischen 17. Jahrhundert," *Romanische Forschungen* 81 [1969]:381-415, esp. pp. 387-88); also, Luis Rosales, *Cervantes y la libertad*, 2 vols. (Madrid, 1960), 2:421.

[6] Amezúa insists that everything in the tale—the house, the characters, the urban setting, the songs, and the action itself—are "copied" from the reality of Seville of the time and attest to Cervantes's marvelous powers of observation. See *Cervantes, creador de la novela corta española*, 2 vols. (Madrid, 1956-1958), 2:245ff. See also F. de Icaza, *Las "Novelas ejemplares" de Cervantes* (Madrid, 1928), pp. 207-208.

vanish in flight into the darkness before the imagined approach of Carrizales. As for the urban world of Seville outside the house, Cervantes's narration is even sparer. Carrizales disappears every morning to make purchases at some unnamed location in the city, and Leonora and her attendants slip out into the darkness of early morning to attend mass in an unnamed church. The songs that, as one interpreter of Cervantes's "realism" suggests, recreate so "naturally" the atmosphere of the warm nights of Seville and "le pays de la danse et du romance,"[7] are not inserted in the text, although, as we note in the *Gitanilla*, Cervantes does not hesitate to include poetry in the tales when he wishes to do so. The allusions to the songs are made because they form the temptation for the Negro eunuch, a pathetic victim of the protagonist's obsession, and it is no accident that among the songs which Cervantes chooses to mention are the famous ballad of the "Star of Venus" and songs of Abindarráez and Abenamar, texts dealing with the passions and frustrations of youthful love, tyrannical oppression of a maiden, and the theme of confinement. When poetry is in fact included, it is limited to the highly significant fragment, appropriated from well-known texts. The lines, "A los hierros de una reja/ La turbada mano asida" ("At the bars of a grating/ The trembling hand fixed fast"), through metonym and symbol, imaginatively concentrate the situation which the narrative is describing and the themes of confinement and torment which it implies, and the fragment, "Por un verde prado" ("Through a green field"), inviting the reader to supply the following verse, "Salió mi pastora" ("my shepherdess came forth"), brings to the moment of the encounter of the custodian of the prison and the "redeemer" a glimpse of the true pastoral world, the genuine order of nature, and human freedom and vitality, all of which are opposed in the gloomy false paradise of Carrizales's house. The tale is about a man who is fanatically convinced of the value of objects and views people as objects, and the insubstantial quality of the things that form his world is one of the central ironies in its depiction of his madness. When the door springs open at the conclusion, we have the impression that the whole house, like the figment of a diseased imagination, vanishes, for we have come to view it as nothing if not a monstrous machine of confinement.[8]

---

[7] Georges Cirot, "Gloses sur les 'maris jaloux' de Cervantes," *Bulletin Hispanique* 31 (1929):1-74; see esp. p. 40.

[8] Such narrative and stylistic techniques of concentration are among the most concrete links connecting Cervantes's tale with its generic ancestor, the *exemplum*. As Hans-Robert Jauss has pointed out in his attempt to define the basic *"Stilisationsprinzip"* of the genre, "alles denkbare Beiwerk des Geschehens, das ein Verweilen in der

The narrative economy marking the description of the setting in the *Celoso extremeño* suggests that Cervantes did not want any element in his story to disturb its sharp focus on the central action. One of the major changes which he made in his text at some time between 1606, when the licentiate Porras de la Cámara presented the tale in manuscript form to the Archbishop of Seville, and 1613, when Cervantes published his collection of novellas, would appear to confirm this impression. When Cervantes first conceived the character of Loaysa, the deliverer-seducer in the tale of confinement and jealousy, he had in mind a certain class of well-to-do, idle youths in Seville, and he inserted an extensive portrayal of this class. The original passage offers a detailed description of their dress, their activities, and the organization of their societies. It employs the narrative techniques that mark Cervantes's satirical prose—a careful anatomization of objects and actions, which proliferate in long lists; grotesque exaggeration in description; and heavy value judgments by a strongly characterized satirical voice. Whether Cervantes lost interest in this class or whether he saw that his description of the multitudinous activities of this world formed a distracting element in the movement of his "Boccaccian" narrative,[9] he chose to excise the passage, referring to all the

---

Beschreibung erforderte, ist weggelassen; die Gegenstände entbehren aller Attribute." All elements serve to demonstrate the abstract principle enunciated in the title. See *Untersuchungen zur Mittelalterlichen Tierdichtung* (Tübingen, 1959), pp. 128ff. See also Hugo Friedrich's discussion of the formal attributes of the genre, its historical derivation from the literature of classical antiquity, and the theological-philosophical vision which nourished its cultivation in the middle ages (*Die Rechtsmetaphysik der Göttlichen Komödie* [Frankfurt am Main, 1942], chap. 2). Friedrich cites Humbertus de Romans' (d. 1277) precepts for the writing of *exempla*: "Solum quod facit ad rem est narrandum" (p. 28). According to traditional narrative practices and theories concerning the form and aims of the genre, Cervantes's *El celoso extremeño* is certainly the most "exemplary" of the *Exemplary Novels*.

[9] Cervantes reveals his awareness of the importance in the short story of the "point" in Sancho Panza's amusing tale of Lope Ruiz and the fickle Torralba (*Quijote*, 1:xx). Here a fast moving, suspenseful narration is needlessly delayed by the teller's interest in repeating irrelevant factual details about the identity, family, and profession of his agents and including a description of the contents of his "heroine's" traveling sack. The tale is then completely paralyzed as Sancho strays into an apparently endless description of sheep crossing a river, and it finally disintegrates as the exasperated audience refuses to tolerate its delay in getting to the point. Don Quixote's critique of Sancho's "conseja, cuento, o historia"—his denial that "saber las cabras" is "de esencia de la historia" and his request that his squire learn to compose stories like an "hombre de entendimiento"—indicate Cervantes's understanding of the extent to which the effectiveness of a tale is dependent on its concentration of what the Russian formalist critics have called "bound motifs" (see Boris Tomashevsky, "Thematics," *Russian Formalist Criticism: Four Essays*, ed. L. T. Lemon and M. J. Reis [Lincoln,

material included in it as simply things about which "much could be said; but for good considerations it is omitted."

Cervantes controls the description of setting and the definition of his agents in a way that would in fact limit our using them as a focus through which to view society. He plainly intended to maintain the central event of the story and its implicit essential themes in the foreground of his narration. His construction of that event reveals a similar type of economy, and it throws into sharp relief the central action of penetrating the forbidden areas of the confinement. The penetration proceeds in stages, but there is a similarity in the respective stages that makes them appear as variant forms of a single action rather than as its successive constituent phases. For example, we observe Loaysa lying on the ground at the crack of the door, listening, peering in, and passing tools through a tiny hole beneath it; the servants, listening at the turnstile and then peering through a hole which they make in it; and finally the *dueña* and Leonora, each prostrate on the floor whispering to each other at the "cat-hole" and passing the ointment through it.

If the act of peering surreptitiously into forbidden space and un-

Nebraska, 1965], pp. 61-95; for the more fundamental literary implications of this scene concerning artistic freedom and the distinction between literary and empirical reality, see my "Cervantes and the Freedom of the Artist," *Romanic Review* 61 [1970]:243-55). As a short story that explores the art of the short story, Sancho's tale of Torralba is comparable to the story with which Boccaccio introduces the day of the most sharply pointed tales of the *Decameron* (VI.1). Here a dreadful storyteller loses himself in endless repetitions and recapitulations and fails to find the way out of the narrative labyrinth in which he has entangled himself. Resembling the seemingly endless journey which he and his audience share, the story fails to reach a "point" and disintegrates as the exasperated listener can endure no more. Although the story is concerned with the exemplification of a social virtue—the discretion that the gracious lady reveals in extricating herself from the clutches of a bore—Boccaccio, like Cervantes, uses the occasion to dramatize the act of writing and to point to the literary values that must guide the writer. In his dull knight's mistreatment of his captive audience, he offers a grotesque contrast to his own literary technique, which is displayed in its most dazzling splendor in the following tales. That such "pointing" and elimination of the distracting details of circumstantial reality had become canonized practice and were viewed as essential features of the genre by Cervantes's time is evident if we consider the theory of the novella presented in Lucas Gracián Dantisco's *Galateo español* (1593?), a Spanish adaptation of Giovanni della Casa's *Galateo*, a work that Cervantes knew quite well. Indeed its discussion of short-story telling as an art that the courtier must practice in his efforts to cultivate good speech and social grace and its prescriptions concerning the avoidance of repetition and the importance of moving rapidly to the "remate y paradero de la novela" may be specifically echoed in Don Quixote's critique of Sancho's storytelling (see *Galateo*, ed. Colección "Cisneros" [Madrid, 1943], pp. 101-102; see also *Don Quijote de la Mancha*, 1:xx, and my "Cervantes and the Freedom of the Artist").

dermining its material defenses is repeated obsessively in these scenes, the intruder's powerful effect on the repressed forces that are waiting to be awakened within is underscored by the repeated action of lighting the candle. When Loaysa enters the Negro's loft, Luis lights a candle, and "without waiting further," the youth takes out his guitar (p. 123). Later, as the servants peep through the hole in the turnstile, "the Negro kept passing the lighted wax taper up and down his body." Following his entry into the house, the throng of females surrounds the resplendent figure, "the Negro and Guiomar, the Negress, lighting them," and Marialonso seizes a candle and inspects "the handsome musician from top to toe."[10]

As they are attracted to the demonically beautiful intruder, the group of females is repeatedly described in animal similes—the "flock" ("rebaño" [p. 127]), the "caravan" ("cáfila" [p. 127]), the "covey of doves" ("banda de palomas" [pp. 131, 151]), and the "butterfly" ("mariposa" [p. 150]). The image system brings an identity to the important series of scenes and aptly suggests the innocence, fragility, and awakening instinctuality of the female world enclosed in the house. At the same time the concluding transformation of the group into a swarm (the "caterva") and a frightened flock of predatory doves (pp. 147, 151) in the scene of the dueña's song and Guiomar's false warning, subtly intimates the movement from innocent attraction to destructive lust that follows on Carrizales's ill-fated attempt to maintain this female world in ignorance.

Another recurrent action at the different stages of the plot is the leap of jubilation, which, like the repeated fiery illumination of the intruding agent, underscores the power of the impulses that are repressed within the tyrant's order, which can break forth from such repression only in a violent way. When Loaysa succeeds in overcoming the first obstacle, he leaps in the air and gleefully turns several somersaults (p. 122); on finding the key beneath the mattress of her sleeping husband, Leonora begins to "jump for joy." And when the dueña appears with the key before the excited group of females, they toss her in the air "like students honoring a professor, exclaiming, 'Hurrah! Hurrah!' " A more complete development of this motif occurs in the orgiastic scenes of the silent dances. While Loaysa plays the "demonic zarabanda" outside the locked door, the servants cannot resist the power of the "milagroso músico" and begin to tumble about in a furious dance: "There was not an old woman who did not dance, nor

[10] "andaba el negro paseándole [a Loaysa] el cuerpo de arriba abajo con el torzal de cera encendido" (p. 133). . . . "alumbrándolos el negro y Guiomar la negra" (p. 147). . . . "de arriba abajo el bueno del músico" (p. 148).

was there a girl who did not fling herself about, all noiselessly in
strange silence." When the final barrier falls and the youth enters,
the servants almost mechanically fall back into the violent dance ("All
the girls rose and commenced to fling themselves about in a dance").[11]
The dance climaxes in a riotous scene of disorder and confusion, as
the group scatters in fear and the terrified Negro eunuch maniacally
continues to strum his untuned guitar, a conclusion that underscores
the destructive nature of the passions that the music represents.

Another recurrent action is the demonic kiss, which confirms the
possession of the menaced group by the intruding power and bonds,
so to speak, the nocturnal society. The consummate hypocrite Loaysa
twice kisses his "brother" and "disciple," the ignorant Negro, to whom
he has sworn friendship (pp. 122, 127), and in a blasphemous gesture, the diabolical intruder kisses the cross, swearing to honor the
victims who let him enter. In a grotesque scene of demonic influence
the *dueña* presses her "mouth to her lady's ear" while, lying on the
floor, she whispers to her and passes the ointment through the "cat-
hole," and she proceeds to give the maiden her blessing with "the
forced laugh of a demon" when leading her into the room of her
seducer. All the accumulated imaginative force of the repeated false
kisses converges on the one authentic kiss of the tale, the kiss of
reconciliation that the mortally wounded Carrizales plants on the brow
of his fainted wife, investing it by contrast with powerful redemptive
implications and contributing significantly to the compassionate view
of Carrizales at the conclusion.

The recurrence of such actions, motifs, and words is the mark of a
highly unified vision informing *El celoso extremeño*, and it suggests that
undoubtedly Cervantes composed the tale with a good deal of concern
for the proper selection of its details and their effective articulation in
its total design.[12] At the same time the repetitions accentuate the

---

[11] "dar brincos de contento" (p. 141). . . . "como a catedrático, diciendo, '¡Viva,
viva!' " (p. 142). . . . "No quedó vieja por bailar, ni moza que no se hiciese pedazos,
todo a la sorda y con silencio extraño" (p. 128). . . . "Levantáronse todas, y se
comenzaron a hacer pedazos bailando" (p. 150).

[12] In his penetrating analysis of the work, Leo Spitzer notes some of these recurrent
elements, and, stressing the tightness of its total structure, observes that "Cervantes
eine fest beschränkte Anzahl von 'Steinen' immer wieder und in immer anderen Sei-
tenansichten verwendet." The constituent parts are "genau abgewogen und dem Ganzen mit Intelligenz und Willen eingefügt" ("Das Gefüge einer Cervantinischen Novelle," p. 173). Moreover, the close comparative studies of the early version and the
emended published tale have demonstrated that Cervantes was clearly concerned with
coherence and precision in his choice of words and construction of sentences as he
reworked his manuscript. See Manuel Criado de Val, "De estilística cervantina; cor-

singleness of its action and endow it with the sharpened contours of dream action, in which crucial events tend to reappear obsessively in a setting of things motivated and limited by the high charge of symbolic significance which they contain. Each unit of the action, as an avatar of the central event of the destruction of barriers, in a sense contains the whole; each object acquires a heightened significance as it emerges and reemerges sharply etched against a vague background of shadows. Far from offering us a picturesque portrayal of Sevillian life or a critical commentary on its social classes, *El celoso extremeño*, with its concentrated Boccaccian plot, leads us into much darker and much more timeless areas, and it is fitting that nearly its whole action is enveloped in a nocturnal atmosphere from which there appears to be no escape. Perhaps, as he decided to excise the digression on Sevillian life, Cervantes was aware that where he really wanted to take his readers was somewhere else—into the receding dark spaces of Carrizales's tomblike house and into the psychic depths that it contains and symbolizes—to reveal to us the awful secrets that its walls conceal and then to show us the way out.

THE SITUATION OF CONFINEMENT— TRADITION AND INNOVATION

If the structure and the narrative techniques of Cervantes's *El celoso extremeño* suggest affinities with the Boccaccian narrative and its numerous descendents, the specific plot and the situation on which it is based, as well as the themes that they imply, indicate even more directly its place in the central tradition of the Italian novella. From its remote origins in the *exemplum* literature of the middle ages, the European novella was a literary genre that concerned itself primarily with the depiction of man as a social being, inescapably involved for much of his life in relationships with other members of his society.[13]

recciones, interpretaciones, interpolaciones y variantes en el *Rinconete y Cortadillo*, y en el *Zeloso extremeño*," *Anales Cervantinos* 2 (1952):231-48; also Américo Castro, " 'El celoso extremeño' de Cervantes," *Semblanzas y estudios españoles* (Princeton, 1956), pp. 271-95.

[13] See Auerbach's discussion of the object of the novella as "die Form der Diesseitigkeit, die wir Kultur nennen," the emergence of the genre at the dawn of the Renaissance as a literary means of observing, exploring, and understanding man in all his variety in the earthly life, and its attenuated interest in dealing with such essential matters as God and man's transcendental destiny (*Zur Technik der Frührenaissancenovelle in Italien und Frankreich*, chap. 1). For its increasing concentration in Cervantes's age on man as a social being, both in its themes and in its social function

One of the inexhaustible sources for its plots and moralizations was always the most fundamental of social relationships—that between the sexes. A classical novella plot is based on the conflict that inevitably follows when youth and its desires for personal and instinctual fulfillment are thwarted by repressive figures such as possessive parents, ascetic clerics, or impotent, jealous husbands. Such conflict could be exploited in a variety of ways. In its most superficial treatment it could reward the storyteller and his audience with the stimulation of pornography, arresting comedy of situation, the cruel but satisfying humor of derision at the expense of a human being victimized by his own folly, and the pleasures of witnessing the triumphant resourcefulness of youth as it demands its natural rights to experience and growth. If exploited in a more profound way, the situation of confinement and liberation could enable the writer and reader to explore the universal problems of restraint and freedom, social responsibility and individual fulfillment, the complexities that can surround moral choice, and the tensions and moral ambiguities that inevitably beset human beings united as individuals within a community.

We need only look at the *Decameron* to see the breadth of possibilities for literary treatment of this central situation of the European novella. In VII.5, Boccaccio offers a tale of an insanely jealous husband, who forbids his wife to set foot outside the walls of his house or even to look out of the window, spies on her constantly, and treats her as if she were a "prisoner sentenced to capital punishment." Like her descendents in Cervantes's tale, she discovers a crack in the walls, can not resist peering through, and discovers a beautiful young man. He widens the fissure, she ingeniously outwits the foolish husband, and the denouement celebrates her incipient career as a happy, fulfilled adulteress, even as it humiliates her tyrannical husband. In IV. 1, Boccaccio describes the sufferings of the noble young widow Ghismonda, who finds herself entrapped by her father's possessive love. An energetic, resourceful woman, she devises a plan to meet with a carefully chosen lover, employing a subterranean passage as a means of admitting the youth into her chamber. Following her father's discovery and execution of the young man, the maiden speaks eloquently for the right of a civilized human being to instinctual fulfillment, acknowledging the validity of the counterarguments based on conven-

---

(i.e., as an instrument for the cultivation of wit and *bel parlare*, and as a technique revealing the social grace necessary in Castiglione's model courtier), see Pabst, *Novellentheorie*, pp. 80-91. For Boccaccio's profound exploration of man as an individual and a social being, see Thomas Green, "Forms of Accommodation in the *Decameron*," *Italica* 45 (1968):297-313.

tional social and moral values and proposing a sophisticated compromise solution, emphasizing discretion and moral awareness, to the difficult problem raised by the conflictive demands of individual freedom and social restraint.[14]

Cervantes's interest in this situation is evident in the numerous scenes in his works developing clashes between authority figures and wives and children eager to pursue their own amorous inclinations. Perhaps his most conventional treatment of the subject is his farce, *The Jealous Old Man* (*El viejo celoso*). The play is obviously closely connected with *El celoso extremeño* in its similar subject matter, characters, sources, and even phrasing, and it provides an interesting way of approaching the much more complex and absolutely unconventional novella. I might add here that the existence of the farce and its superficial resemblance to the tale have been in part responsible for some pronounced misconceptions about the latter in Cervantine scholarship, misconceptions that have proven remarkably resistant to correction.

Whether or not we accept Grillparzer's characterization of *El viejo celoso* as the "most shameless piece in the annals of the theater," there can be no doubt that the little farce is an effective dramatic concentration of the essential conventions of the comic tale of cuckoldry which held such a privileged place in traditional collections of short stories. The characters are defined in terms of the most rudimentary of desires and fears, and in their comic repetition of their obsessions we observe the mechanical behavior that causes characters of low comedy to resemble puppets. The husband is old, impotent, and uncontrollably jealous. His obsession is reduced to the level of absurdity in his refusal to let male animals into his house, in his jealousy of the "breeze that touches" his wife, and in his mindless, automatic repetitions of his fear of neighbors, a fear based on the maxim of all suspicious husbands that the dishonor of one's wife is more frequently the result of her contact with friends than of an encounter with strangers. The wife is the traditional deprived shrew, well aware of what she is missing, cruelly disdainful of her aged spouse, and aggressively determined to use her considerable resources of wit to satisfy her physical needs. The strong emphasis on the power and violence of sexuality is supported by the presence of the adolescent Christina, who accompanies Doña Lorenza's laments concerning her frustration with a continuing tirade against the old man and an exhortation to license which echoes the temptations of Celestina in all their satanic vitality

---

[14] See Neuschäfer's analysis of the complexities of the tale and its engagement with the most profound issues raised by the theme of confinement (*Boccaccio und der Beginn der Novelle*, chap. 3).

("bring us the young man, one gallant, neat, forward, a bit daring, and most of all, young"; "[Cañizares] is a mean person, a male witch; he is old, and there's nothing worse I can say"; "I can't stop calling him old"; "if the master happens to see them, all we have to do is grab him, all together, and choke him and throw him in the well or bury him in the stable").[15] The male lover is characterized, as is frequently the case in the traditional tale of cuckoldry, as simply youthful and sexually proficient. The strident dialogue is rich in the humor of obscene allusion and well-deserved invective, and the action moves rapidly to its climax. In a scene of unforgettable comedy of situation, Doña Lorenza is overwhelmed by her violently released sexuality and hurls ingeniously obscene abuse at her husband, who, incapable of keeping up with his wife's wit as well as with all else, appears to be totally unaware of his humiliation. In the denouement we observe the merited punishment of the victim of folly, a triumph of the wit of the youthful wife, and a celebration of the restored vitality of the comic, youthful society. Despite its predominantly destructive movement toward exposure and humiliation of the fool, the little play ends on an ironically affirmative note, as all involved discover that a betrothal was simultaneous with the scene of Doña Lorenza's "liberation" and join in a song evoking the healing mysteries of the night of St. John and celebrating reconciliation, married bliss, fertility, and natural abundance. Cañizares of course excludes himself from the festive society and its song, but for all its ironies we hear it as a signal of permanent improvement in Doña Lorenza's wedded life.

The denouement of the farce is rich in ironies: a "reconciliation" has occurred; a "happy, healthy marriage" is celebrated; and a neighbor, the Celestinesque Hortigosa, has in fact proven to be a "good" neighbor, Cañizares's fears of all neighbors notwithstanding. Like so many of the Italian tales from which it descends, *El viejo celoso* concludes with the anticipation of a career of happy adultery for the oppressed woman. However, the depiction of the triumphs of an adulterous society, founded as they are on illusion and cynical deception, no matter how ingenious, rarely constitutes an untroubled happy ending to a story, and *El viejo celoso*, as well as its numerous ancestors, remains fundamentally a destructive work of literature. If we look at

---

[15] "tráyanosle galán, limpio, desenvuelto, un poco atrevido y, sobre todo, mozo"; "[Cañizares] es un malo, es un brujo, es un viejo: que no tengo más que decir"; "no me puedo hartar de decirle viejo"; "si señor los viere, no tenemos más que hacer sino cogerle entre todos y ahogarle, y echarle en el pozo o enterrarle en la caballeriza" (all citations are from *El viejo celoso, Obras completas*, ed. A. Valbuena Prat [Madrid, 1956], pp. 596-601).

the tales in Bandello's collection of short stories which Cervantes echoes in the farce and which in fact may have inspired it, we see even more clearly how pronounced the general debasement of all characters, the delight in scenes of cruel humiliation, and the preference for the primitive humor of violent sexuality and repugnant scatology marking this type of literature can be.[16] The tales focus on the folly of the repressive husband and delight in his castigation. The moral is simple, and the relation between it and the action that amusingly exemplifies it is not complicated by sophistication in character portrayal or the presentation of psychological or moral growth in the agents. As Bandello puts it in introducing the work that appears to be one of Cervantes's most immediate sources: "This Novella clearly demonstrates . . . that husbands should treat their wives well and avoid giving them the occasion for doing evil; they should not become jealous without reason, since anyone who considers the matter well will discover that the majority of those women who have sent their husbands to the land of cuckolds, have been given by them the finest occasion for doing so; for very rarely do wives who are well treated and maintained in honest freedom by their husbands fail to live as should women who are solicitous of their honor."[17] *El viejo celoso*, then, belongs to a vast family of literary works, and its ancestry can be traced at least as far back as the *Golden Ass* of Apuleius with its tale of the wife's tub, the *Disciplina Clericalis* with its *exemplum* of the foolish husband who unsuccessfully locks his wife in a tower, and the *Decameron*, which includes versions of both tales. All of these works present a climactic scene of cruelty and humiliation, which they offer as a demonstration of an elementary point concerning the relations of men and women. *El viejo celoso*, for all its technical excellences, its powerful comedy of situation, and its ironies, is a thoroughly conventional work, and it remains basically faithful to its models in its spirit, its method, and its aims.

---

[16] See Bandello, *Novelle*, I.5. The deception of the jealous victim occurs in the toilet, and the wife's activity as well as the double-entendre of her frenzied ejaculations are marked by scatological as well as sexual associations. For the debt of Cervantes's farce to Bandello's tales, as well as their resonances in the novella *El celoso extremeño*, see Stanislav Zimic, "Bandello y *El viejo celoso* de Cervantes," *Hispanófila* 31 (1967):29-41.

[17] "Essa Novella chiaramente dimostra . . . che i mariti deveno ben trattar le moglie, e non dar loro occasione di far male, non divenendo gelosi senza cagione, perciò che chi ben vi riguarderà, troverà la più parte di quelle donne che hanno mandati i loro mariti a corneto, averne da quelli avuta occasion grandissima, che rarissime son quelle da' mariti ben trattate e tenute con onesta libertà, le quali non vivano come deveno far le donne che de l'onor loro sono desiderose" (*La prima parte de le novelle del Bandello*, 9 vols. [London, 1791], 1:128-29).

In his extensive study of the sources of *El celoso extremeño* and *El viejo celoso*, Georges Cirot emphasizes the similarity of theme uniting the two works. His words are worth repeating, for they represent a continuing tendency among Cervantists to examine the tale through the convenient focus supplied by the *entremés* and to resolve any ambiguities within it by postulating its identity at some fundamental level with the far more simple farce. As Cirot puts it, both versions of the story of jealousy are "des *casos*, des problèmes de morale en action. Ce sont des leçons. Elles ont cela de commun avec l'*entremés*; et ceci encore, que le sujet traité est le même: 'la jalousie, ses inconvénients.' " All three works depict the disastrous consequences of an error and imply the simple moral: "Il faut être raisonable, d'abord en se rendant compte de ce qui est réalisable; puis en ayant confiance, sans niaiserie. . . . L'*entremés* n'est que la mise en scène féroce et forcenée du premier point, que *El celoso extremeño* expose avec plus d'agrément et d'humanité."[18] While there is certainly some truth in this interpretation, it fails to do justice to the complexity of the moral themes of Cervantes's short stories and to their originality within the tradition of the cuckoldry novella, and it completely overlooks the radical differences that separate the tales, particularly the final perfected version, from the farce, which utilizes the same sources and exploits the same fictional situation.

If we compare the novella with the farce and its conventional dramatic development of the tale of cuckoldry, we discover immediately the absence of such dominant features as the scenes of vituperation and obscene humor[19] and a strikingly anticlimactic presentation of the

---

[18] See "Gloses sur les 'maris jaloux' de Cervantes," pp. 63, 68-69; for the vast literary family which stands behind Cervantes's works and mediates our apprehension of their characters and situations, see, besides this fundamental study, Cirot's later additions to it: "*El celoso extremeño* et *l'Histoire de Floire et de Blanceflor*," *Bulletin Hispanique* 31 (1929):138-43; "Encore les 'maris jaloux' de Cervantes," *Bulletin Hispanique* 31 (1929):339-46; and "Quelques mots encore sur les 'maris jaloux' de Cervantes," *Bulletin Hispanique* 42 (1940):303-306. See also Amezúa's detailed enumeration of the literary antecedents of *El celoso extremeño*, a summary that reaches the curious conclusion that the tale's literary debts can be dismissed as insignificant because it is a masterpiece of realistic observation and a "pure" product of Cervantes's genius (see *Cervantes, creador de la novela corta española*, 2:234-48). As I hope to show in what follows, Cervantes exploitation of the complex set of literary codes surrounding the very traditional situation of his tale is a sign of his genius as a creator of literature even as it is proof of the degree to which his greatest art is nourished by and indeed dependent on literature.

[19] As Cirot has pointed out, the tale most resembles the farce in its movement and atmosphere in the scenes of disorder following the seducer's entry into the house ("Gloses sur les 'maris jaloux' de Cervantes," p. 45). It is interesting that Cervantes

forcefully anticipated climactic scene of cruelty—indeed, an abrupt abandonment of the traditional scene and a shift to an exploration of its ambiguous effects in the moral development of the husband. Such differences certainly support Cirot's conclusion that *El celoso extremeño* is informed by a more "humane" spirit than the farce, but, more importantly, they suggest that the novella may in fact be informed by a totally different spirit, that its author, in conceiving it and then modifying it carefully in the years separating its initial composition from its publication, found possibilities in the conventional situation that are very different from those he develops in his farce.

The most radical departure from the conventional situation of cuckoldry in *El celoso extremeño* lies in its treatment of the repressed wife, and the most decisive changes in Cervantes's final version of the tale indicate his growing awareness of the power and originality of her depiction and the profound implications of her actions. One of the striking aspects of *El celoso extremeño* is its demonization of the realm of instinctuality and the agents of seduction. As I pointed out above, the victims of Cañizares's repression in the farce violently demand their rights to instinctual fulfillment, and the adolescent Christina shamelessly exhorts her aunt to enjoy the pleasures of sex with a gusto that is described as satanic ("Satan is speaking through your mouth"). However, the allusion merely serves the purpose of comic invective and is balanced by the demonic imprecation of "witch" hurled at the repressor Cañizares. The action occurs in the daylight, and a concluding song celebrates a triumph of nature and vitality in the sexual act. The seducer is merely young and beautiful, and Cervantes's choice of

---

presents a scene of invective, but self-consciously mutes it, suggesting its inconsistency with the moral tone of the work and its offensiveness to the sensibilities of the reader which he invokes for his tale: "ninguna la llamó vieja que no fuese con su epíteto y adjetivo de hechicera y de barbuda, de antojadiza, y *de otros que por buen respecto se callan*" (p. 154; italics added). The narrator's expressive silence establishes the moral stance of his reader. The tendency to attenuate the invective in the revised version is heightened, as Cervantes eliminated the epithet *"puta,"* which his narrator could not manage to pass over in the first version. Similarly the role of Guiomar la negra, an *entremés* character who is surrounded by motifs of vituperation, obscenity, and grotesque humor, is slightly reduced in the published tale. F. Rodríguez Marín has published the text of the original version in his study *El Loaysa de "El celoso extremeño"* (Seville, 1901), pp. 33-93; for the reduced invective, see pp. 79-80. The reduction is an indication of the reorientation in Cervantes's thinking about the work in the years separating its initial composition from its publication. As I hope to show in what follows, one can in fact find a pattern in the numerous alterations in the text that reveals dramatically Cervantes's disengagement from the traditional literary situation of confinement and his recreation of that situation in an original, highly innovative form. In my analysis I shall refer to the original version as *"El Loaysa."*

the muffled figure of Rodomonte and three other famous knights for the tapestry that ironically comments on his "feat" of entering the house and performing sexually indicates that he has no intention of associating the young man with demonic forces. The difference in the treatment of instinctuality and seduction in the *El celoso extremeño* could hardly be greater. As in the *Coloquio de los perros*, Cervantes's most extensive exploration of the mysteries of sin, nearly the entire action of the tale unfolds in darkness, and only after what seems an interminable night does the dawn with its faint promise of redemption bring release from the demonic powers. Unlike their literary ancestors the two principal agents of the seduction are depicted in all the lurid tones in which the contemporary imagination conceived the powers of evil. If Cervantes eliminated the lengthy description of Loaysa's class in Sevillian society, the change was dictated not only by his desire for concision and concentration in his "pointed" novella, but also by his realization that its subject was far more essential than the themes of social satire. The authentic background of his character was the non-geographical realm of pure evil. Loaysa is referred to as a *"demonio"* (p. 125). There are supernatural powers of corruption in his *"milagroso"* music, which easily causes the pathetic Negro slave to betray his trust, and the *"endemoniado son"* of his saraband instantly arouses the servants' repressed passions to an orgiastic display in the grotesque, silent dance ("There was not an old woman who did not dance, nor was there a girl who did not fling herself about, all noiselessly in strange silence"). Like those of the greatest demonic figure of the period, Tirso's Don Juan Tenorio, Loaysa's activities are surrounded by motifs of blasphemy. He kisses the cross while swearing falsely that his intentions are honorable, and, when entering the house, he pronounces an oath that, for all its farcicality, reiterates his blasphemous attitude toward sacred objects. There is a touch of obscenity in his invocation of the Virgin and the Holy Spirit ("I swear by the immaculate efficacy *where it is contained most holily and most largely"*), and his vow to bind himself by the powers of the Old Testament is grotesquely disfigured by the intrusion of notarial discourse ("by the *entries and exits* of the holy Mount Lebanon").[20] Moreover, there are

---

[20] "juro por la intemerata eficacia, *donde más santa y largamente se contiene"*; "por *las entradas y salidas* del santo Líbano monte" (p. 146; italics added). See M. Bataillon, "Glanes cervantines," *Quaderni Ibero-Americani* 2 (1953):393-97; Leo Spitzer, "Y así juro por la intemerata eficacia . . . ," *Quaderni Ibero-Americani* 2 (1954):483-84. The oath rises to a climax in a resounding pronouncement in "juridical discourse," which collapses into nonsense when the vacuity of its content, initially veiled by its coherent syntax, its formidable professional terminology, and its inflated rhythm, are scruti-

occasionally traces of blasphemy in the words he inspires in his "disciples." Following his offer of the sleeping potion, one of the servants exclaims in anticipation of their orgiastic "resurrection": "may it please God that the old man sleep three days as well as nights; for we should have as many of glory."[21] Like Don Juan, Loaysa has the calculating nature of an accomplished hypocrite, and there is a striking disproportion between his power and the weakness of the people whom he exploits. The ruthlessness marking his manipulation of his victims is most evident in his treatment of the simple Negro, whom he cynically uses for his purposes while offering the temptations of music and wine and addressing him as a friend and brother. There is something very disturbing in his reception of the devotion of this childlike person, and it is not unlike Don Juan's openness to the infatuation of his most guileless victims. The brutal exploitation of the child's affection is

nized closely ("juro . . . de no salir ni pasar del juramento hecho y del mandamiento de la más mínima y desechada destas señoras, so pena que si otra cosa hiciere o quisiere hacer, desde ahora para entonces y desde entonces para ahora lo doy por nulo y no hecho ni valedero"). For the importance of this type of grotesque discourse in the depiction of devils in traditional literature, as well as its centrality in the popular culture of the carnival, see M. Bakhtin, *Rabelais and His World*, trans. H. Iswolsky (Cambridge, Mass., 1968). Loaysa's burlesque invocation of the "verdadera historia de Carlomagno con la muerte del gigante Fierabras" as he stands on the threshold of his mighty exploit activates a mock-chivalric literary code which Cervantes frequently exploits in the reductive treatment of his ambivalent redeemer (see below). For the immense popularity of the text to which he alludes—*Historia del Emperador Carlo Magno, y de los doze pares de Francia*—, its marvelous elements (e.g., the "bálsamo de Fierabras"), its naive attitude toward oaths and relics, and the ironic view that Cervantes takes toward its implausibilities in the *Quixote*, see Francisco Márquez Villanueva, "El sondable misterio de Nicolas de Piamonte: Problemas del 'Fierabrás' español," *Relecciones de literatura medieval* (Seville, 1977), pp. 95-134.

[21] "pluguiese a Dios que durmiese el viejo tres días con sus noches; que otros tantos tendríamos nosotras de gloria" (p. 130). The phrase was added in the final version (see *El Loaysa*, p. 61), and the addition is consistent with the increased demonization of the night world of instinct that marks several of Cervantes's important revisions (see below). Interestingly, whereas Cervantes is concerned to increase the demonic characterizations of his primary evildoers in the second version and does not hesitate to infect their utterances with blasphemy, he is concerned to tone down irreverences in his narrator's descriptive statements. His Quevedesque description of the *dueña*, who, consumed by lust, hastens to "collect" "el diezmo siquiera de aquel beneficio que ella había fundado" when her turn for the caresses of the youth comes, is eliminated (see p. 84). While the difficulties of logic of the first passage appear to be responsible for his excision of the reference to the "perpetua continencia" of the animals in the "monastery-house," which would prefer death to "tener generación," it is possible that an irreverent overtone was also a motive. Like many of the other changes, these point to the increased exemplarity and the higher moral tone of the final version.

one of the characteristics that link Loaysa and Carrizales, the tyrannical ruler of the infernal realm in which the story unfolds ("he embraced his good disciple, kissed his face, and immediately placed a great *bota* of wine in his hands, and a box of preserves and other sweet things").[22]

Like the devil and his various descendants in picaresque literature, Loaysa is a master of disguise, and we first behold him as a beggar lying in the street whispering his words of temptation through the crack in the door. In this serpentine posture, he persuades the gullible Negro to dig a hole through which he can pass the traditional demonic instruments of the hammer and tongs. Following his penetration of the first barrier, he leaps into the air, turns several somersaults, and proceeds to change shape, appearing as a beautiful, elegantly dressed youth.[23] The two descriptions of Loaysa are probably the most powerful expression of his demonic aspects. In each scene the youth stands in the darkness while his disciples—in one case the Negro, in the other, the uncontrollable *dueña*—pass a candle about the contours of his figure; in each case a significant part of the description is communicated through the reactions of the female society to his attractions. In an orgy of voyeuristic excitement, the servants crowd to the tiny hole in the turnstile to peer at the figure, and in the fiery glow they think they are contemplating an angel. The beauty of Loaysa, the chiaroscuro of the scenes, and the depiction of his powers to reach into the deep, forbidden areas of the psyches of those who behold him recall once again the most spectacular of the age's numerous demonic villains, Tirso's Don Juan. In the second description we see Loaysa even more exclusively through his effects on his victims. The shift is characteristic of the entire novella, as it becomes increasingly clear that the inexorable movement deeper and deeper into closed physical spaces is at the same time a movement into psychic depths. Having entered the house, Loaysa is elevated amid the throng of admirers, and Leonora and the servants form a circle about his feet as if to worship their redeemer. While the moving candle illuminates the various parts of his body, the servants gaze at the youth, and, in an

[22] "abrazó a su buen discípulo, y le besó en el rostro, y luego le puso una gran bota de vino en las manos, y una caja de conserva y otras cosas dulces" (p. 122).

[23] To be recalled is Juan-Andrés's initiation into the demonic world of the Gypsies, where he receives the emblem of the hammer and the tongs, undergoes symbolic garroting, and turns two somersaults (see below); also, Rutilio's bondage in the employ of the smith in his expiatory quest to the northern extremity of the world and his expiation in the barbarians' kingdom of death, where he must amuse his masters constantly by turning somersaults. As Sancho Panza points out, Lucifer was the first acrobat (see my *Cervantes' Christian Romance* [Princeton, 1972], pp. 113-15).

uncontrollable outburst of admiration, they utter a series of ejaculations which Cervantes describes as forming an "anatomy and a delicious fricassee" ("anatomía y pepitoria") of his physical attributes.
They hover about him all the while with the voracity of a flock of
doves feasting "in a field without fear on what other hands have sown."
"One said: 'Ah, what a beautiful forelock he has, and so well frizzled!'
Another: 'Ah, how white his teeth are!' "[24] The irrepressible outburst
of sensuality occasioned by the contemplation of Loaysa leads to the
servants' orgiastic dance and the *dueña*'s song celebrating the irresistible power of "imprisoned love" when released. Like so many of the
poems in Cervantes's fiction, the song offers a concentrated expression
of the themes of the work in which it appears. Here the song is
concretely connected with its surrounding context in that it transforms the scene in which the excited females break free of their confinement and flock to the fiery glow illuminating Loaysa into metaphor, poetic image, and symbol that universalizes its significance. The
potentially destructive power of instinct is nurtured by repression:

> Dicen que está escrito,
> Y con gran razón,
> Ser la privación
> Causa de apetito:
> Crece en infinito
> Encerrado amor.
>
> . . . .
>
> Romperá, en verdad,
> Por la misma muerte
> Hasta hallar la suerte
> Que vos no entendéis.

When released, it enslaves its victims more violently and destructively
than their repressor, unless, of course, it is met by restraints that are
rooted in the conscience of a free individual.

> Quien tiene costumbre
> De ser amorosa
> Como mariposa
> Se irá tras su lumbre,
>
> . . . .

---

[24] "en el campo sin miedo lo que ajenas manos sembraron" (p. 151). . . . . "Una
decía: '¡Ay, qué copete que tiene, tan lindo y tan rizado!' Otra: '¡Ay, qué blancura
de dientes!' " (p. 149).

> Es de tal manera
> La fuerza amorosa,
> Que a la más hermosa
> La vuelve en quimera:
> El pecho de cera,
> De fuego la gana,
> Las manos de lana,
> De fieltro los pies;
> *Que si yo no me guardo;*
> *Mal me guardaréis.*[25]

We need only compare the poem at this climactic moment of *El celoso extremeño* and its central imagery of consuming flames with the concluding song of *El viejo celoso* and its association of the improvement in Doña Lorenza's wedded life with the reestablishment of the normal rhythms and the fertility in nature to see how different the two works are in their attitudes toward the realm of instinctuality and the problem of sexual fulfillment. Cervantes is no longer concerned primarily with the vitality of the body but rather with the vitality of the ethical will, and, like so many other writers of the period, he envisions as the situation for its greatest trials and triumphs man's struggle with the destructive forces of the passions. Such is the nature of the struggle and triumph at the center of Cervantes's novella of confinement that its demonized view of instinct, a view which marks it as very close in spirit to the contemporary literature of *desengaño*,[26] is essential to its exploration of the moral nature of man.

While Loaysa is primarily a demonic figure, his function in the tale is more complex than this characterization would indicate. There is

[25] "They say that it is written,/ And with great reason,/ That privation is/ The cause of appetite:/ Imprisoned love/ increases infinitely./ . . . In truth it will break/ Through death itself/ Until it finds its destiny/ Which you do not understand./ . . . Whoever has the custom/ Of being amorous/ Like a butterfly/ Will pursue his flame,/ . . . The power of love/ Is such/ That it turns into a monster/ The most beautiful woman:/ With fire it consumes/ The breast of wax,/ The hands of wool,/ The feet of felt;/ *Unless I guard myself;/ In vain will you guard me*" (pp. 150-51).

[26] The contrast between the healing "noche de San Juan," in which imaginatively the conflict of *El viejo celoso* is resolved, and the demonic night world of the novella implies all the fundamental differences in focus that separate the two works. For the characteristic demonization of the passions in baroque literature, see Leo Spitzer, "The 'Récit de Théramène,' " *Linguistics and Literary History* (Princeton, 1967), pp. 87-134, esp. pp. 117ff. See also M. Bakhtin's discussion of the general tendency in the literature of the period to divest the traditional "grotesque image of the body" of its healthy ambivalence, to mute its powerful celebration of vitality, and to transform it into a symbol of what constituted, according to official morality, a depraved area of human experience (*Rabelais and His World*).

in fact an ambivalence in his relationship to Leonora which it is important to recognize if we are to understand the most profound implications of the work. Throughout the story Cervantes presents Loaysa's determination "to capture, by force or by stratagem, a fortress so protected" in mock-heroic terms. The "arrow" ("*virote*") is aided by officers of different ranks in his "army"; he must take into account the vigils of the sentries of the enemy posted in the fortress (i.e., Carrizales "was the watch and sentinel of his house" [p. 103]); he must carefully devise stratagems, and he must show courage in attempting such a "feat of prowess" ("tan dificultosa hazaña"). Cervantes surrounds his effort with several literary texts celebrating heroic deliverence of the imprisoned sacred object, and we need only compare the single allusion to Rodamonte for the unnamed savior of Doña Hortigosa of the farce with the numerous analogues of Loaysa as deliverer to appreciate the increased literary complexity that marks the seducer's feat in the short story. Probably the most forceful activation in the reader of a literary code of heroic deliverance lies in the extended echoes and parallels of the heroism, persistence, and ingenuity of Floire in his rescue of Blanceflor from the imprisonment in the palace of the aged emir of Babylonia. There the chaste hero employs disguises and deception, manipulates the custodian of the palace-prison by playing chess with him and intentionally losing, and smuggles himself into the maiden's tower by concealing himself in a basket of flowers.[27] A mediating text with similar implications for Loaysa's "deliverance" of the maiden from her confinement is Lope's famous ballad, the "Star of Venus," which the Negro urges the youth to sing. Here Gazul, a youthful hero, "semejante a Rodomonte," determines to deliver his lady from the clutches of an ugly Moor who is custodian of the tower of Seville. He penetrates the dark palace and in the flickering torchlight slays her sinister possessor.[28] Cervantes does not stop with the powerful evocation of the theme of heroic deliverance by allusion to medieval and contemporary chivalric romances, but, in addition, turns to classical mythology for similar effects. Loaysa, a hero-musician, is compared to Orpheus, and he enters the sepulchral

[27] For the influence of the tale of Floire and Blanceflor on Cervantes's work, an influence which could have been transmitted through the Spanish versions of the romance, published in 1512 and 1604, through Boiardo's version (in *l'Orlando innamorato*), which reveals the interesting addition that there were no male animals allowed in the oppressor's palace-tower, or through Boccaccio's *Filocolo*, see Cirot, "Gloses sur les 'maris jaloux' de Cervantes," pp. 1-74; "*El celoso extremeño* et *l'Histoire de Floire et de Blanceflor*," pp. 138-43; "Encore les 'maris jaloux' de Cervantes," pp. 339-46.

[28] See *Romancero general*, ed. B.A.E. 10:14-15.

kingdom of the fabulously wealthy Carrizales, a "Vulcan" whose wealth comes from the depths of the earth in the evil world of the Indies, to rescue his lost "Eurydice."[29] Moreover, there is even a brief association of Leonora and the guarded golden apples, an allusion suggesting, of course, the connection of Loaysa's feat and the labors of Hercules. However, Loaysa sings discordantly; his disguise as a lame beggar is more reminiscent of Guzmán de Alfarache than of the chivalric deliverer; he retreats rapidly before Guiomar's false alarm, and, in the early version of the tale, he ends his "heroic" career with the rather unheroic act of falling dead beneath his own exploding musket while participating in one of Spain's great victories. His relation to all these heroic analogues is one of travesty, and, if Cervantes chooses in his original version to exploit the power of negation springing from the systematic travesty for the purpose of social satire, in the second version he leaves it as pure negation, which aptly suits his greater interest in his character as a diabolical rather than as a social and satirical figure. However, it would be wrong to say that there is no ambivalence in the pattern of heroic references. The fact is that the maiden is imprisoned in a frightful world of repression and mutilation, that she is in desperate need of a redeemer, and that her release and birth as a human being are vitally connected with the very powers of instinct and youthfulness that Loaysa and several of his heroic analogues embody. As Frye points out in his discussion of the dungeon, deliverance, and escape archetypes in romance literature, there is something "illusory about the dungeon or whatever: however dark and thick-walled, it seems bound to turn into a womb of rebirth sooner or later."[30] As I shall point out below, the jealous Estremaduran's house does finally turn into a place of rebirth—both for Leonora and Carrizales—and for all his demonic features, and for all the destruc-

---

[29] The Vulcan myth is introduced directly in the first version as part of a highly literary description of Carrizales's awakening. In the final version Cervantes eliminated the passage, perhaps feeling that the literary inflation does not accord with the seriousness of the situation and the redeemed portrayal of Carrizales, which is about to begin. However, the myth enters obliquely in the following description: "Llegóse en esto el día, y cogió a los nuevos adúlteros enlazados en la red de sus brazos" (see *El Loaysa*, pp. 83-84). For a different interpretation of such elements, see P. Dunn's suggestive attempt to find in the tale a coherent, informing mythological pattern, based on its fragmentary allusions to classical myths ("Las 'Novelas ejemplares,' " *Suma Cervantina*, ed. J. B. Avalle-Arce and E. C. Riley [London, 1973], pp. 81-118).

[30] *The Secular Scripture: A Study of the Structure of Romance* (Cambridge, Mass., 1976), p. 134.

tion he wreaks, Loaysa is, ironically, the redeemer who delivers his own victims.

Following his entry into the house, Loaysa is replaced by the *dueña* as the dominant demonic figure in the work. Marialonso becomes the principal agent of Leonora's seduction, and Cervantes carefully associates her with the youth. Like Loaysa, she lies in a serpentine posture on the floor, whispering through the small hole to the victim of confinement, promising *"maravillas,"* and passing through it the instruments of her liberation and ruin. Just as Loaysa turns somersaults in jubilation following his entry, the *dueña* is hurled into the air several times by her companions to celebrate the acquisition of the key. The satanic powers of the figure are most strikingly presented in her treatment of Leonora in the scenes preceding her "fall," and here we observe the same ruthless manipulation of the innocent and weak by the corrupt that characterizes Loaysa's deception of the Negro. The disturbing description of her mouth at Leonora's ear and the blessing that she offers the maiden while ushering her into the room of the seducer recall the treacherous kiss of brotherhood that the hypocritical Loaysa bestows on his witless victim. Her cynical attitude toward sacred values can be nearly blasphemous, as she redefines the "king's honor" as a sanction for the indulgence of her violent instinctual drives (p. 134). Loaysa's interest in sexual pleasure is seldom mentioned, and he appears to be motivated primarily by curiosity and a perversely misdirected will to power, which finds satisfaction in the *"proezas"* of coldly manipulating reactions in other people.[31] The *dueña*, on the

---

[31] The peculiar motivation of Loaysa, his delight in the prank, his desire to perform for an admiring audience—e.g., the circle of children surrounding him, the company of his colleagues, the Negro, and the servants—, his use of numerous disguises, his ability to manipulate the witless by appealing to their secret desires, his pride in his intelligence ("todos aquellos que no fueren industriosos y tracistas, morirán de hambre" [p. 122]), and his general interest in exposing the foolishness of the self-deluded all suggest his affinities with a conventional character of the classical novella, one who was readily taken up by the picaresque fiction which emerged in the sixteenth century—the artful prankster. Disguised as a lame beggar and lying in the street, Loaysa evokes the most illustrious picaro of the age, Guzmán de Alfarache, and in his play with the Negro's illusions about his musical abilities he resembles numerous pranksters of novella literature descending from Boccaccio's masters of inventive malice, Bruno and Buffalmacco. One of the most striking things about Loaysa's characterization is the complexity of the literary codes activated by his description, his deeds, and his statements and the prominence that his literary nature assumes due to Cervantes's refusal to develop his character as an individual or as a type conceived in terms of psychological, sociological, or even physiological motivation. (The reduction of his sociological context in the revised edition makes his literary mediations all the

other hand, is driven by her instincts; and a raucous proclamation of the goodness of sensual indulgence marks her discourse throughout the story, from her mockery of her mistress in the scene of Loaysa's first appearance ("Let your worship shut herself up with her Methuselah, and let her leave us to enjoy ourselves as we can"), to her cacophonous song ("she sang the verses with more gusto than good voice") celebrating the violent power of sexuality, to the skillfully designed piece of rhetoric by which she attempts to convince Leonora of the delights she will experience in Loaysa's bed.[32] She pronounces her speech under the inspiration of the devil ("She described how much more pleasure she would find in the caresses of her young lover than of her old husband, assuring her of the secrecy and permanence of her delight, and other things similar to these, that the devil put in her mouth, full of rhetorical coloring, so convincing and effective . . ."), and, as she encloses the tearful maiden in the room of her seducer, she blesses her with "the forced laugh of a demon."[33]

---

more conspicuous.) Moreover, as I have already indicated, the various literary codes surrounding him are ambivalent both in their troubled, conflicting relations to each other and in their individual functions: for example, as artful prankster Loaysa does the unconventional thing of directing his unmasking performance not primarily at the true impostor, Carrizales, but rather at persons who strike us as more innocent than witless—Leonora and the Negro.

[32] Throughout *El celoso extremeño* music is cacophonous. The drunken Negro "en toda la noche no hizo otra cosa que tañer con la guitarra destemplada y sin las cuerdas necesarias" (p. 123); the *dueña* sings her song of lust "con más gusto que buena voz" (p. 150 [the phrase, which did not appear in the first version, is characteristic of the general tendency in Cervantes's emendations of his original tale in that it reveals his interest in undercutting any positive implications concerning the natural demands of instinct the song may have; similarly, his deletion of the introductory phrase "hacía (el cantar) mucho al caso para lo que entonces allí les pasaba" would indicate Cervantes's desire to dislodge the song from its central position as a focus of exemplarity in the tale]); and following Guiomar's false alarm, the terrified Negro scurries to his loft where he insanely strums his guitar ("tanta era [encomendado él sea a Satanás] la afición que tenía a la música" [p. 154]). The senselessly jangling music, as well as the description of the heavy snoring of Carrizales as "música a los oídos de su esposa más acordada que la del maeso de su negro" (pp. 140-41), contributes powerfully to the nightmarish atmosphere of the novella and its rush toward disintegration and madness. We might recall the festive song enjoyed by the comic society at the conclusion of *El viejo celoso* to appreciate properly the difference in tonality and the radically different treatment of instinctual forces in the novella.

[33] "Estése vuesa merced encerrada con su Matusalén, y déjenos a nosotras holgar como pudiéremos" (pp. 133-34); "cantólas con más gusto que buena voz" (p. 150); "pintóle de cuánto más gusto le serían los abrazos del amante mozo que los del marido viejo, asegurándole el secreto y la duración del deleite, con otras cosas semejantes a éstas, que el demonio le puso en la lengua, llenas de colores retóricos, tan demonstrativos, y eficaces" (p. 156); "risa falsa de demonio" (p. 157).

Several minor alterations in the second version of the tale heighten the demonic character of the world of instinct and suggest that Cervantes perceived his story and its implications in a significantly different way as he grew older. While he eliminated Loaysa's lengthy social characterization, he added the powerful passage in which the Negro illuminates him with a candle as he first appears before his dazzled audience. The description of Loaysa's somersaults following his initial entry and his discussion of the virtues of wine with the Negro are similar additions, and it is probable that Cervantes wished to exploit the traditional associations of wine as an instrument of demonic activity and celebration.[34] In the second version Cervantes places additional emphasis on the cacophony in the *dueña*'s ecstatic song, and he adds a detail suggesting violence in the orgiastic dance that it provokes ("se comenzaron a hacer pedazos bailando"—literally: "they began to tear themselves apart dancing"). As for the *dueña* herself, her role in the action is much more important in the final version, where she appears as a central character from the beginning rather than from the point toward the final phase of the tale when Loaysa passes the ointment through the hole in the turnstile (see *El Loaysa*, p. 67). More significantly, her most explicit connections with demonic forces are made in Cervantes's revisions of his manuscript. The "laugh of a demon," which accompanies her blessing of the tearful Leonora as she forces her into the seducer's bedroom, reads in the earlier version "laugh of a monkey"—"risa de mono" (see *El Loaysa*, p. 81), and the phrase "things that the devil put in her mouth," which accompanies her description of the pleasures of sexuality to the maiden, is entirely missing. In the characterization of the *dueña* in the first version of the story, the element of social satire is more pronounced than in its final version, and the narrator's analysis of her function in the action leaves us with some commonplace generalizations on the abuses of this notorious social type (pp. 156, 158).[35] As

---

[34] See *El Loaysa*, pp. 53, 55. For the vitality of the demonic banquet and the significance of wine as sacramental parody and temptation in the literature of the middle ages and the Renaissance, see Paul Lehmann, *Parodie im Mittelalter* (Munich, 1922), and M. Bakhtin, *Rabelais and His World*. Numerous masterpieces of Spanish literature, from *La Celestina* to Quevedo's *Buscón* and Calderón's *La cena del rey Baltasar*, exploit the power of this tradition. In Cervantes collection of stories banqueting motifs are most significantly developed in *El coloquio de los perros*.

[35] Ilse Nolting-Hauff points out that such denunciations of *dueñas* were ubiquitous in seventeenth-century satire and that Cervantes's satirical depiction of the type may have contributed a good deal to its standardization (see *Visión, sátira, y agudeza en los "Sueños" de Quevedo* [Madrid, 1974], pp. 148-50). The caricature can be found also in *Don Quixote* in the figure of Doña Rodríguez. However, in keeping with the

in the case of Loaysa, her evil is common to her social class, and there are few suggestions that it stems from the more essential areas which Cervantes was concerned with as he refashioned his work and aligned his villains more directly with the numinous realm of pure evil.

As I have pointed out above, the most important difference separating the tale *El celoso extremeño* from the conventional development of the cuckoldry situation as exemplified by *El viejo celoso* lies in its treatment of the heroine, and its distinguishing features are much more sharply drawn in the published form of the tale than in the early version. In the farce the world of instinctuality is represented uniformly by the wife and her companions, and their comic triumph implies a strong vindication of its value as well as a harsh condemnation of a repressive attitude toward its cultivation. In the early exemplary tale the wife is differentiated from the representatives of instinctuality, but, as Cervantes reworked his manuscript for publication, her differentiation increased from one of degree to one of essence. Although her plight resembles in certain ways that of Bandello's Bindoccia and Petrus Alfonsi's unnamed lady in the tower, figures that Cervantes had in mind as he conceived her, she has nothing in common with these strident creatures whose dauntless vitality dominates their narratives while their husbands lie in the blissful "sleep of the death of their honor." Leonora's presence remains elusive and mysterious to the end, when she slips out of her narrator's control and disappears behind the confining walls of a nunnery. We see her in fleeting glimpses—a beautiful girl of fourteen peering, perhaps curiously, perhaps timidly, out of a window, exploring a world that she will never know at first hand, hastening obediently in the half-light of dawn to return from mass to her gloomy prison before the unknown city can assume its alluring shapes, flitting silently in and out of the shadows into which her pursuer advances, the helpless quarry of a ruthless hunter, and emerging fleetingly from her swoon in her vain struggle to articulate the mystery of her guilt and innocence only to lapse back immediately into unconsciousness and vanish in the convent with a secret that appears to elude even the grasp of her creator.

In the orgiastic scene in which Loaysa displays himself in the candlelight and the servants anatomize his physical attractions in a series of breathless exclamations, the narrator tells us: "Leonora alone was silent, and she gazed at him, and he began to appear to her of better physical presence than her husband," leaving it to us to speculate on

---

dominant narrative pattern of the work, the satirical stereotype is quickly shattered by the emergence of a highly individualized and sympathetically drawn *dueña*.

the nature of the awakening and the conflicts that she is experiencing. Leonora is defined as childlike, simple, and ignorant, and the narrator frequently emphasizes the fact that her will is captive, that she belongs to others whom she obeys in ignorance. "The tender Leonora was still unaware of what had happened to her, and so, weeping with her parents, she implored their blessing, and . . . led by the hand of her husband, she proceeded to his house"; "the young bride, shrugging her shoulders, bowed her head and declared that she had no other will than that of her husband and lord, to whom she was always obedient"; "nor did her will desire anything beyond that which the will of her husband desired"; "the poor lady, convinced and persuaded by them, had to do what she had no wish to do, and would never have done voluntarily"; "Marialonso took her mistress by the hand, and almost by force, her eyes being full of tears, led her to where Loaysa was."[36]

The deprivation which the maiden suffers unawares has less to do with instinctual needs than with the far more fundamental need to be as an individual self. In *El celoso extremeño* Cervantes conceived the problem of selfhood in moral rather than psychological or existentialist terms, and in his approach and solution to it he remained true to the central traditions of Christian Humanism.[37] Unless the individual

[36] "sola Leonora callaba, y le miraba, y le iba pareciendo de mejor talle que su velado" (p. 149); "La tierna Leonora aún no sabía lo que la había acontecido, y así, llorando con sus padres, les pidió su bendición, y . . . asida de la mano de su marido, se vino a su casa" (p. 99); "encogiendo los hombros, bajó la cabeza, y dijo que ella no tenía otra voluntad que la de su esposo y señor, a quien estaba siempre obediente" (p. 100); "ni su voluntad deseaba otra cosa más de aquella que la de su marido quería" (p. 104); "la pobre señora, convencida y persuadida dellas, hubo de hacer lo que no tenía ni tuviera jamás en voluntad" (p. 132); "Tomó Marialonso por la mano a su señora, y casi por fuerza, preñados de lágrimas los ojos, la llevó donde Loaysa estaba" (pp. 156-57).

[37] As Américo Castro has demonstrated in several studies, much of Cervantes's greatest writing is informed by a more modern attitude toward selfhood, and indeed his revolutionary creation of the novel, a literary genre in which the implicit assumptions regarding its agents are radically different from the essentialist views of character dominating previous fiction, could be properly understood only with the renewed valorization of history, individuality, actuality, and particularity that marked Romantic and post-Romantic European thought (see Castro's prologue to *Don Quijote de la Mancha* [Mexico, 1960]). Cervantes certainly was capable of sensing the very real way in which a person like Don Quixote is more authentically alive than Diego de Miranda, whose routine existence bores the translator of the manuscript so much that he deletes a description of his house. As Castro suggests, Cervantes's evident sympathy for "quixotism" would imply that he saw in it a sign of vitality and individual self-creation. "La ruta del caballero manchego no es producto de su de-

is free to make a moral choice, he is incapable of engaging in activity
that distinguishes him from the beasts and that endows him with his
unique dignity as a human being.[38] While the rest of the creation is

---

mencia, sino de la necesidad de mantenerse siendo él quien ha decidido ser,—'yo sé
quien soy' dirá más tarde. La ruta de don Quijote expresa su estar siendo en él y en
Dulcinea: en ella 'tengo vida y ser' [1:307]. Ni la una ni el otro se prestan a ser
trazados geométricamente. Les basta con ser" (*Cervantes y los casticismos españoles* [Bar-
celona, 1966], p. 60). See also "La estructura del Quijote," *Hacia Cervantes* (Madrid,
1957), and "El Quijote, taller de existencialidad," *Revista de Occidente* 5 (1967):1-33.
In dealing with the problem of selfhood in the elliptically drawn figure of Leonora,
whose one significant act is the confrontation of a moral crisis, Cervantes is confining
himself to a much more traditional approach to the problem. The approach is not
necessarily inconsistent with that of the *Quixote*. Indeed one of the most interesting
links between Cervantes's works and Christian Humanist writings is his interest in
clinging to a traditional valorization of moral choice as the "essential" experience of
the self while embracing a conception of the human being that dignifies other, non-
moral forms of development and experience as well. As Vives put it, man is blessed
with Proteus's powers to transform himself into a multiplicity of forms and, in a
sense, to determine his own essence, and his transformations are so astonishing and
delightful to behold that the gods reward him with immortality (see *A Fable About
Man*, trans. N. Lenkeith, *The Renaissance Philosophy of Man*, ed. E. Cassirer, P. O.
Kristeller, J. H. Randall, Jr. [Chicago, 1948], pp. 387-93.

[38] As Pico della Mirandola put it in perhaps the most famous of the humanists'
celebrations of freedom, man alone among the creations is fashioned as a "creature of
indeterminate nature," a being who is not "limited and constrained within the bounds
of laws prescribed" by God. He is burdened with the lofty responsibility of creating
himself in whatever form he would choose. Exercising his highest faculties in proper
moral choice, he can ascend to the conditions of the superior beings in the hierarchy
of the creation and achieve the unique dignity bestowed on him as a free agent, or,
failing to do so, he can descend to the enslaved condition of the brutes, plants, and
inanimate objects (*Oration on the Dignity of Man*, trans. E. L. Forbes, *The Renaissance
Philosophy of Man*, pp. 223-54). See Fray Luis de Granada: ". . . primeramente se
dice ser el hombre imagen de Dios, porque tiene libre albedrío . . . ninguna de todas
las otras criaturas tiene esta libertad, ca todas son agentes naturales que no pueden
dejar de hacer aquello para que tienen facultad. . . . En lo cual parece que solo el
hombre es señor, y que todas la otras criaturas son como captivas y siervas, pues solo
él es libre y señor de sus obras, y ellas no" (*La introducción del símbolo de la fe* [ed.
B.A.E. 6:264]). Etienne Gilson describes the traditional Christian view of the gift of
freedom and its role in conferring identity on man: "God, therefore, not only controls
man by His providence, but also associates him with His providence; while all the
rest is simply ruled by providence, man is ruled by it and rules himself; and not only
himself but also all the rest. To say everything in one word, each human being is a
person; his acts are *personal* acts, because they arise from the free decision of a reasonable
being, and depend only on his own initiative. It is therefore precisely as such that
divine providence has to bear upon them. God, Who directs all according to His
will, has bestowed on each of us an unique privilege, a signal honour, that of association with his own divine government" (*The Spirit of Medieval Philosophy*, trans.
A.H.C. Downes [New York, 1940], p. 166). See also Hiram Haydn's study of the
persistence of this view in Renaissance Christian Humanistic thought and literature

controlled by the mechanisms of God's providence, man alone is given the responsibility to fulfill himself as a human being, and he does so by the proper exercise of his moral will. The repeated animal similes describing the imprisoned female society of Carrizales's house as its members are drawn irresistibly toward the intruder ("doves," "sheep," "flock," "swarm") do more than convey suggestions of instinctuality, appetite, timidity, and helplessness. It is a mark of Cervantes's genius as a storyteller that he has so delicately balanced the positive and negative associations of his animal imagery that it fails to coalesce in any pattern of narrow moralization. Such imagery points instead toward the deepest area of meaning connected with the house, an area in which the apparent opposition between the mechanisms of repression and the animalism that they confine collapses and both disclose unequivocally its nature as an order of subrationality and emphasize the servitude in which the entire nonhuman, "will-less" world is bound.[39] Contrary to what numerous Cervantists continue to believe, the final paragraph of the tale is more than a mere concession to conventional morality. *El celoso extremeño* is most genuinely concerned with the mystery and the powers of the human will, and its claim concerning "the little use there is in trusting to keys, turnstiles, and walls when the will remains free"[40] should not be dismissed as a commonplace exemplary appendage.

The struggle in which the passive Leonora suddenly finds herself involved is no less than a struggle to be born as a human being, and

---

(*The Counter-Renaissance* [New York, 1950], pp. 299-300). "In short, true Christian liberty is not freedom *from* anything; but freedom *to become* something—specifically, freedom to grow to the full stature of a Christian man. . . . The difference between man's position and that of the sub-rational creatures lies in the fact that although man is naturally impelled toward his goal, as are the rest, he is not *obliged* to follow it. Yet if he does not, he cannot retain his true and characteristic freedom as a man, a person, and he cannot grow to the full stature of a man—for if he deserts the end prescribed by reason, he loses his rational standing. Evil is for him, too, the privation of good, and falling short of his established and distinctive end, he drops to the level of sub-rational life." For the fortunes of these ideas in Spain, see Otis H. Green, *Spain and the Western Tradition*, 4 vols. (Madison, Wis., 1968), 2:125ff.

[39] This area of meaning is most sharply visible when the mechanisms of confinement fuse imaginatively with the world of animals, as in the settings of two crucial events of temptation—the "*gatera*," through which the *dueña* and Leonora communicate, and the loft of the stable-bastion, in which the encounter of the Negro and Loaysa occurs. To be noted is the fact that the oppressor of the instinctual society is given animal attributes: Carrizales "ronca como un animal" and prowls about his house like the dragon guarding the golden apples of the Hesperides.

[40] "lo poco que hay que fiar de llaves, tornos y paredes cuando queda la voluntad libre" (p. 171).

it is revealing that Cervantes's protagonist's most effective rewards for his deprived wife are not the traditional gifts of the repressive husbands of the Italian tales—jewels, clothing, and money—but sweets, cookies, and dolls—instruments not of compensation but rather of infantalization and dehumanization. Selfhood demands moral choice, and mature moral choice presupposes experience, which includes, of course, the experience of evil as well as of good. Carrizales will not allow his child the privilege of individual experience, and it is worth noting that Leonora's attitude toward sexuality is described not as frustration but as ignorance. The definition by negation is character- istic of the indeterminacy of her entire presentation in the tale: "he began to enjoy as well as he could the fruits of marriage, which to Leonora, who had no experience of any others, were neither sweet nor sour." Leonora's lack of identity in Carrizales's order is intimated in a variety of ways. Knowing nothing but the world of her confinement, she delights "in making dolls and in other childish diversions which showed the simplicity of her mind." A double appears, who takes her place in the presence of the tailor, for the thought of his taking her measurements drives Carrizales into an attack of jealousy. Carrizales surrounds her with slaves, and aside from his branding them, he ap- pears to view his female society with no discrimination, feeding all its members sweets, involving them in the same activities, and con- trolling their lives in such a way as to keep all of them "amused and occupied, without giving them an opportunity to reflect on their con- finement."[41]

Carrizales is drawn as a complete contrast to the elusive maiden. Throughout his life he has existed entirely for himself, exploiting human relationships for his own enjoyment and profit. From the open- ing account of his early life, in which he appears as a rootless wastrel, cultivating no ties with friends or lovers, delighting in the liberation from his family, and engaging in his most characteristic type of con- versation, the "*soliloquio*," to his return from the Indies, when he finds all friends, acquaintances, and family dead and, deciding that all other human beings are threats to his peace of mind, fortifies himself in his own isolation by building a prison in the center of civilization, we continue to see Carrizales as an active being who pursues his own inclinations with no concern for the interests of other people. When he decides to marry, he does so only after he has considered in "one

---

[41] "los frutos del matrimonio, los cuales a Leonora, como no tenía experiencia de otros, ni eran gustosos ni desabridos" (pp. 100-101); "en hacer muñecas, y en otras niñerías, que mostraban la llaneza de su condición" (p. 101); "entretenidas y ocupa- das, sin tener lugar donde ponerse a pensar en su encerramiento" (p. 101).

hundred soliloquies" the dangers of involvement with another human being and assured himself that he can fashion his spouse according to his own wishes. Carrizales's house contains fruit trees, flowing water, and domestic animals, and its walls are ornamented with tapestries depicting "females, flowers, and groves." Like a god the old man places his creation in a paradise, where everything is "redolent of virtue"—"olía a honestidad," and he keeps constant vigil over its inhabitants as if they were the mythical golden apples. It is immediately evident, however, that the innocent existence of this paradise is in reality a state of bondage and lifelessness. Its society of branded slaves, its black guardian (his castration a powerful symbol of a savage denial of instinct), the mechanical repetition marking the motionless lives of its tyrannized inhabitants, the presiding deity of Carrizales-Vulcan, the adoration of his "hair of pure gold," one of several motifs stressing its inorganic, antinatural quality, as well as occasional references to it as a tomb and to the sleep of its inhabitants as a state of death, clearly point to its moribund and demonic nature. Carrizales confines his wife in the gloomy house with the same confidence with which he hoards his countless bars of gold in a bank, and his absurd belief in the effectiveness of locks and keys as a guarantee of predictability in human behavior is symptomatic not only of his tyrannical nature but also of the failure to discriminate between things and people in his life, a failure that is one of the most frightening forms of egotism. Carrizales's fantastic house is not only a prison for the victims of his madness but also the symbol of his own prison, his own exclusion from the experience of the other and consequently from the lofty kind of moral discrimination that involves the possibility of self-transcendence. Ironically it is his disastrous failure that brings liberation, and the growth of being of Leonora that he unsuccessfully tries to prevent rewards him with his only moment of escape from his own dehumanized condition.[42]

[42] For a penetrating analysis of the "radical solipsism" in which Carrizales's life unfolds, see Américo Castro's "*El celoso extremeño* de Cervantes," pp. 271-95. For Castro the grotesque jealousy of the old man is symptomatic of an incapacity to love and to respond to "la llamada de cualquier 'logos,' o verbo animante, que el espíritu del mundo nos depare," that is, an incapacity to live authentically. ". . . la casa sepulcro estaba ya preformada en el existir trunco del mal augurado Carrizales, nacido para morir en soledad siniestra dentro de sí mismo," and his vengeance is characteristically a "hermetic" act: "quiero que así como yo fuí extremado en lo que hice, así sea la venganza que tomare, tomándola de mí mismo" (see pp. 289-90). It is characteristic of Castro's interpretation that he fails to see that Carrizales's pathetically self-focused "act of revenge," an act that radically differs from the type of vengeance sanctioned by the official values and attitudes of contemporary Spain, is also an act

The revisions which Cervantes made in his treatment of Leonora in the final text are, of course, far more significant than those which we observe in his development of the demonic society. In the early version the climactic scene of adultery is unconventional in its understatement and anticlimactic disposition, as the narrator almost immediately intrudes to impede our direct contemplation of a scene for which our anticipation has been heightened and prolonged through several stages of suspenseful plotting. It is notable that already in the first version of the tale, Cervantes refuses to reward his audience with a traditional scene of a triumphant sexual union and a humiliation of the husband of the type that was common in the Italian novella and which, as _El viejo celoso_ proves, he could compose masterfully. Instead he chooses to remove Isabel's seduction from the foreground of the narration immediately and offer in its place a commentary on the passive maiden's submission as a misfortune caused by the folly of her husband and the evils of _dueñas_. Even in its first version the seduction in _El celoso extremeño_ is far more a corruption of innocence than a celebration of instinct and a "naturalistic" morality emphasizing human fulfillment in instinctual terms. It is a profoundly ironic commentary on human weakness, of which Carrizales, as he himself announces in the madness which brings him insight, is the primary example ("an example of simplicity never seen nor heard of"). Leonora is the victim of his madness, and her "fall" is its most disastrous consequence. Carrizales's understanding of his own self-destruction accurately summarizes the implications of the tale concerning human helplessness: "as it is not possible by human effort to ward off the punishment which the divine will desires to inflict on those who do not put their desires and hopes wholly and entirely in it, it is no wonder that I have been cheated in mine, and that I myself have been the fabricator of the poison which is robbing me of life."[43] Thus the story stands as an example of pride and humility, a demonstration of the vast distance separating the divine will from the pathetic efforts of human beings to control their lives, and the dominant notes at its

---

of self-transcendence and mercy. For Castro there is nothing redemptive in the denouement of _El celoso extremeño_, nothing to compensate for the darkness that surrounds its depiction of types whom Cervantes intensely hated, aside from the vitality and circumstantiality marking his treatment of them as characters. Neither Carrizales's admission of error and pardon of his wife nor the implications of Leonora's role in the significantly revised version are of any interest to him.

[43] "como no se puede prevenir con diligencia humana el castigo que la voluntad divina quiere dar a los que en ella no ponen del todo en todo sus deseos y esperanzas, no es mucho que yo quede defraudado en las mías, y que yo mismo haya sido el fabricador del veneno que me va quitando la vida" (p. 165).

conclusion are self-prostration, guilt, madness, dissolution, and death. While Carrizales struggles through his terrible self-analysis to an act of forgiveness and the guilt-ridden Isabel thinks of expiation and shows genuine compassion for her suffering husband, the redemptive elements in the first version of *El celoso extremeño* remain in large part embryonic. The hint of spiritual growth in the characters remains no more than a hint. Cirot's summary of the tale as an example of general "faiblesse humaine" is not entirely inaccurate. Spitzer has gone on to describe the story as an "anti-novela ejemplar" in its powers of negation and its concentration on the depiction of evil, and, as I have mentioned above, Américo Castro views the tale as primarily a fictional means by which Cervantes could express his hatred of two embodiments of the "official" Spanish society at whose margins he was doomed to spend nearly his entire life.[44]

One of the most significant additions to the revised version is the phrase that Cervantes's narrator inserts in his moralizing conclusion: "I was left with the desire to arrive at the end of this incident, example, and mirror of the little use there is in trusting to keys, turnstiles, and walls *when the will remains free*."[45] On reconsidering his manuscript, Cervantes, at some point and for some reason that will probably forever elude students of his work,[46] discovered that it con-

---

[44] Cirot, "Gloses sur les 'maris jaloux' de Cervantes," p. 73; Spitzer, "Das Gefüge einer Cervantinischen Novelle," p. 176; Castro, " 'El celoso extremeño' de Cervantes" and "Cervantes se nos desliza en 'El celoso extremeño,' " *Papeles de Son Armadans* 13 (1968):205-222. See also Casalduero's observations on the tale's "desenlace negativo," its antihero, and its depiction of "la realidad antiheroica" (*Sentido y forma de "Las novelas ejemplares"* [Madrid, 1969], pp. 167-68).

[45] "yo quedé con el deseo de llegar al fin deste suceso, ejemplo y espejo de lo poco que hay que fiar de llaves, tornos, y paredes *cuando queda la voluntad libre*" (p. 171; italics added).

[46] Throughout his career as a Cervantist Américo Castro has argued that there are extraliterary reasons for the alterations in *El celoso extremeño* and that the final version is somehow less authentic than the original. Cervantes was, we are told, constrained by his fear of the censors of the Counter-Reformation (*El pensamiento de Cervantes* [Barcelona, 1972], pp. 246-48) or compelled by his desire to conform to the standards, preferences, and values of the official Spanish society from which he was excluded (" 'El celoso extremeño' de Cervantes"). When Castro finally does suggest that Cervantes was after all not concerned about "reasons of sexual morality," the flames of the Inquisition, or the need to gain social acceptance, and constructed his final text as he sincerely wanted it, his interpretation is still obsessed by his determination to find evidence everywhere of Cervantes's marginal consciousness and his embattled position in relation to his society. Thus the story focuses on the failures of an *"indiano"* and a "mocito desvergonzado," who develop within it as doubles—as members of "la clase prepotente," as prodigal youths, as emigrants to the Indies, and as unsuccessful possessors of Leonora. The key to the mystery encoded in their relationship

tained a potential theme that he had not developed in its original composition. Perhaps he may have been struck by the atmosphere of futility that enshrouds its fictional world, by the uniformly low stature of its inhabitants, and by its vindication of a pessimistic conception of human nature which had come to dominate much contemporary literature. The helplessness of all human beings in the tale, as well as its ironic commentary on the value of human effort in its treatment of the man of will, Carrizales, would certainly have appealed to such writers of *desengaño* literature as Alemán, Quevedo, and

lies in the significance of the phrase "se cansó en balde" and in a concealed, fragmentary reminiscence of a comic scene in *Orlando furioso* centering on sexual impotence. Loaysa indeed did not sleep with Leonora because he could not; such was the ultimate humiliation in Cervantes's satirical reduction of this idle, self-indulgent predecessor of the infamous Spanish *señorito* ("Cervantes prefirió que el sevillano y jacarandoso mocito no pudiera jactarse de su triunfo . . . Cervantes quiso aniquilar la virilidad de aquel mancebo" ["Cervantes se nos desliza en 'El celoso extremeño,' " pp. 205-222]). Castro's early interpretation of the changes in the published version of the tale formed part of his controversial portrait of Cervantes as one of the great "heroic hypocrites" of an age of inquisitorial tyranny and repression of free thought. The ensuing polemic among Cervantists centered frequently on *El celoso extremeño*, and a full exposition of the various arguments would add little to the clarification of the tale. A notable exception is Leo Spitzer's "Die Frage der Heuchelei des Cervantes" (*Zeitschrift für Romanische Philologie* 56 [1936]:138-78), which insists on interpreting the changes in relation to the respective formal, thematic, and tonal conventions of two very different literary genres—the novella and the farce. In its focus on the specific principles that do in fact guide writers of literary texts, this approach is far more fruitful than Castro's with its reliance on such indistinct realities as a cultural-historical period and Cervantes's individual consciousness, with all its supposed tensions and ambiguities, to account for the changes. However, the argument based on genres has various weaknesses, one being Cervantes's notorious independence of generic restrictions and his delight in transgressing them. Perhaps more to the point is the fact that from Boccaccio to Bandello and Cervantes himself, the novella has shown no reluctance to present scenes of adultery and has in fact accommodated the act of sexual love to a variety of treatments, from the farcical and debasing to the heroic, tragic, and ennobling. One need only look at Cervantes's *Coloquio de los perros*, on the one hand, and *El curioso impertinente* on the other, to see that Cervantes did not hesitate to deal with sexual love in his exemplary fiction and that he could adapt his treatment of it to various themes and standards of decorum. The best way to approach the alterations in the final version of *El celoso extremeño* is to assume that Cervantes made them *because he wanted to write a different story with different emphases and different themes* and to attempt to account for them as coherent elements in that story. As I attempt to show in the following analysis, they do in fact form integral parts of a skillfully designed story, a story that is profoundly different from its primitive version and richer in its thematic complexity. Two studies that do in fact proceed on this assumption and offer observations concerning the importance of the theme of freedom in the tale which my analysis of the alterations and consideration of intellectual backgrounds confirm are Rosales's *Cervantes y la libertad* (see 2:421-22) and Casalduero's *Sentido y forma de las "Novelas ejemplares"* (see pp. 177-80).

Calderón.[47] Throughout his major works Cervantes generally pays homage to the power of the human will and to the value of its achievements when it is allowed to exercise itself in freedom. We need only mention Preciosa's insistence that growth in being presupposes the freedom to experience temptation or the sympathetic treatment that Cervantes accords such champions of freedom as Marcela and Don Quixote to realize how anomalous Carrizales's Job-like pronouncement on humility is as an ideological position advocated by one of Cervantes's works.

As Cervantists have frequently maintained, Cervantes's failure to produce a picaresque novel is perhaps a sign of his awareness of the enormous difference in spirit separating his vision of man from that of Mateo Alemán.[48] His alteration of the early version of *El celoso extremeño* is a much more concrete, a much more dramatic testimony of his perception of that difference and of the increasing self-awareness of the writer in his old age. Leonora is suddenly a much more powerful focus of exemplarity. She is developed as an example of what the free will can in fact accomplish in the direst of straits, and, as such, she has affinities with Cervantes's most powerful female figures—Preciosa amid the license of the Gypsy world, Costanza enclosed in the dark world of the inn with its picaresque savagery, Sigismunda kidnapped by the barbarians of the north, and Transila facing the demands of the members of her husband's family, who enter her bedroom invoking the *ius primae noctis*. Her capacity to accomplish through her own will power what the tyrant could not assure through force is in its powerful irony the most effective commentary Cervantes could devise for the folly of her husband and his grotesquely exaggerated

---

[47] Spitzer emphasizes the centrality of the theme of man's helplessness in the work and its affinities with the baroque dramatic literature, which repeatedly probed this theme. "Die Novelle ist nichts als der Erweis dieser Wirkungslosigkeit der Berechnungen des Eifersüchtigen und damit menschlicher Berechnung überhaupt. Die Vorsehung Gottes ist mächtiger als alles Planen des Menschen. Um das Nutzlose menschlichen Planens zu schildern, muss Cervantes seinen Celoso ein verzwicktes System von Vorkehrungsmassregeln ersinnen lassen . . ." ("Das Gefüge einer Cervantinischen Novelle," p. 144). Spitzer fails to see any redemptive implications in the changed role of Leonora in the final version. The story offers us a glimpse into the abysses of human frailty.

[48] See, for example: Carlos Blanco Aguinaga, "Cervantes y la picaresca: notas sobre dos tipos de realismo," *Nueva Revista de Filología Hispánica* 11 (1957):313-42; Marcel Bataillon, "Relaciones literarias," *Suma cervantina*, ed. Avalle-Arce and Riley, pp. 215-32; Castro, *El pensamiento de Cervantes*, pp. 228-35; Castro, *Cervantes y los casticismos españoles* (Madrid, 1967), p. 44; Claudio Guillén, "Genre and Countergenre: The Discovery of the Picaresque," *Literature as System* (Princeton, 1971), pp. 135-58.

machinery of repression. Clearly Cervantes discovered at some point the enormous unexploited potential in his early creation of Leonora—in the emphasis on her "nonbeing" and lack of will, in the suggestive antitheses marking her relationship to both villains, in the differences separating her from the instinctual, subhuman society in which Carrizales confines her, in his own incapacity to endow her with the qualities of the Bandellian heroine, and perhaps even in the power of a literary analogue which he had allowed only an ironic function in his early version, the pure maiden of romance Blanceflor, imprisoned in the palace of the emir of Babylon and awaiting the advent of her deliverer.

Cervantes perceived that imbedded in his tale of unnatural repression and human weakness there lay another tale involving the much grander themes of human freedom, moral growth, and self-affirmation. His intentions to develop those themes are revealed by a significant number of his revisions and not merely by the spectacular change in the climactic scene, a change that Castro found intolerably implausible and ridiculed as comparable to a sudden miraculous transformation wrought by the divine intervention of the "angels of the Counter-Reformation.[49] As I have suggested above, the tendency to distinguish Leonora from her society of slaves is accentuated in the revised version. While he increases the demonization of the instinctual society and reduces its satirical referentiality, Cervantes alters some of Leonora's actions that emphasize the identity of the corrupted maiden and the evildoers. When she receives the container of ointment from the *dueña* on the night of her seduction, she can not restrain her joy: "Isabela took the vessel, and she kissed it, as if she were kissing a relic, and she told the *dueña* not to go away until she had returned with the

---

[49] ". . . cuando *El Celoso extremeño* aparece impreso en 1613, tal escena ha sufrido extraña purificación. Los ángeles de la Contrarreforma se han cernido sobre los dos amantes, y el resultado es algo mirífico: duermen en brazos uno de otro, sin que la castidad reciba menoscabo. ¡Oh maravilla! No falta sino que el portento se exorne con la advocación de algún santo, y se nos cuente en una lápida: *Siste, viator . . .*" (*El pensamiento de Cervantes*, p. 247). However "implausible" Leonora's "victory" in the bedroom might be according to the order of objective reality, and this question is far more complicated than most critics who have denounced the alteration of the climax have admitted (e.g., Amezúa, Icaza, and Rodríguez Marín), the situation is not so implausible that another storyteller of the age hesitated to use it with similarly profound implications. See Marguerite de Navarre, *Heptaméron*, XXVI. R. S. El Saffar is correct in pointing to the neglect which Leonora has suffered at the hands of the critics of the work and to the enrichment which the revised version brings to her character (see *Novel to Romance: A Study of Cervantes's "Novelas ejemplares"* [Baltimore, 1974], pp. 45-46).

news about the effectiveness of the ointment."[50] The gesture exploits the effects of desecration, a characteristic act of Loaysa, the servants, and Carrizales, the creator of human beings and false paradises, and the act strongly associates the maiden with the demonic society. In his revised version Cervantes eliminates it and removes her from a powerful pattern of negation.[51] Another slight modification in the same scene reveals Cervantes's tendency to differentiate Leonora from the representatives of uncontrolled instinct. In his first version he describes her lying on the floor, "her lips pressed to the ear of the *dueña.*" The gesture recalls the demonic kisses of Loaysa and underscores her active participation in the evil plot. In the revised version Cervantes emphasizes the victimization of the maiden by her companions, and it is not surprising that he should alter this disturbing description by having the serpentine *dueña* place "her mouth to the ear of her mistress," in the traditional pose of the demonic tempter.[52] The alteration is consistent with the earliest major change of the second version, the introduction of the *dueña* as governess—"*aya*"—and the consequent differentiation of Leonora as "pupil," a change which supports both the increased innocence and passivity of Leonora in the second version and adumbrates its most profound theme, that of spiritual growth.[53]

[50] "Tomóla Isabela el vaso, y besólo, como si besara alguna reliquia, y dijo á la dueña que no se quitase de allí hasta que volviese con las nuevas de la virtud del ungüento" (*El Loaysa*, p. 68).

[51] In his study of the alterations Castro observes the change and attributes it to "religious reasons" (" 'El celoso extremeño' de Cervantes," p. 272); he makes no mention of Cervantes's willingness to allow blasphemous elements to remain to cast their dark shadows on the world of the evildoers, and he fails to consider that, whether or not a religious scruple or fear motivated the excision, it significantly affects the reader's perception of Leonora and her role in the text. Loaysa continues to "kiss the cross" in the second version.

[52] "puestos los labios . . . en los oídos de la dueña" (*El Loaysa*, pp. 67-68).

[53] The alteration provides in the heroine's relationship to the *dueña* an analogy to the perverse relationship of Loaysa to his victim, the Negro, who is repeatedly described as his "*discípulo.*" The symmetrical relationships are in fact variants on a fundamental pattern of travestied education, which begins with Carrizales's determination to fashion his wife "a sus mañas" and informs the whole story. See also the servants' reaction when the *dueña* reveals the key: "la alzaron en peso, como a catedrático, diciendo: '¡Viva, viva!' " (p. 142). Cervantes's more sympathetic view of the heroine in the second version is visible in another change emphasizing her victimization; a minor detail differentiates her from her parents, suggesting their exploitation of her marriage: They rejoice "contentos y dichosos de haber acertado con tan buen remedio para su hija" (*El Loaysa*, p. 39); in the second version the final phrase becomes "para remedio suyo y de su hija." Similarly, although the first version devotes very little attention to her erotic demands, Cervantes may have found the

While Cervantes eliminates the blasphemous note in Leonora's elevation of the "chalice" containing the ointment, he does in fact leave untouched his depiction of her in the act of annointing her husband, as if he were a corpse. The simile, of course, belongs to a consistently developed body of imagery pointing to the moribund character of Carrizales's life and his sterile, mechanical world. At the same time the suggestion of a sacramental travesty has powerful sinister effects, and we sense here that Leonora is on the brink of her ultimate fall, which in fact follows quickly in the original version. I would emphasize that Cervantes's different conception of Leonora's character and its function in the tale does not require her transformation into an ideal of unassailable, heroic chastity such as his romance heroines, Costanza and Preciosa. Quite the contrary, she must remain an ignorant, childlike creature who endures an almost irresistible temptation to sin. She is helplessly attracted by the forces which have been savagely repressed in her and which she has not been taught to understand, and she yields to their power, to some extent even in the second version. What Cervantes added to his revised tale was the depiction of her awakening as an awakening both to her instinctual needs and to the moral implications of her will to gratify them. In the depths of this frail creature confronting the first and the only crisis of her life, we glimpse an awakening to moral consciousness, to a sense of herself as a responsible human being. As her seducer approaches in the shadows, "Isabel rejoiced greatly"; "[Leonora] rejoiced *and became distressed* at the same moment."[54] The inner world of the taciturn Leonora is much more complex in the revised tale, the result of a few strokes of the pen on the nearly total void of the original portrayal, and her paroxysm of anguish and compassion, which strikes us as unmotivated and melodramatic in the sensational first ending, is a coherent and powerful conclusion to the depiction of her simultaneous awakening to instinct and sin, to innocence and guilt. There is a terrible truth in her pathetic outburst: "although you are not

---

sensual implications of a simile describing the maiden's love of Carrizales, which he excised in his revision, inconsistent with her elevation in the second version: "el primer amor que las doncellas tienen se imprime en ellas, como el sello en la cera, y así suelen guardarle en la memoria *como el vaso nuevo el olor del licor primero con que le ocupan*" (p. 44). Of the various changes in the final version, I have found only one that would counter their dominant tendency to deemphasize the active participation of Leonora in the rebellion of the instinctual society. Describing the sleep of her husband, she says "ronca como un animal" instead of "ronca de la manera que oís" (p. 74).

[54] "Isabel se alegró en grande manera" (*El Loaysa*, p. 73); [Leonora] "se alegró *y se turbó en un punto*" (p. 147; italics added).

bound to believe anything that I may say to you, know that I have not offended you, except in thought."[55] The implications of Leonora's elliptical utterance are complex, and it is perhaps a sign of Cervantes's awareness of the complexity concealed in the understatement that a phrase introducing the climactic song describing the violence of appetite when released from repression disappeared in his published version: "and it was very much to the point in view of what happened to them then."[56] What "happened to them then" was very different from what happened to Leonora. In fact, no simple exemplary tag can adequately explain the mystery that was to unfold within the maiden.

The numerous emendations of *El celoso extremeño*, then, reveal a tendency to increase the moral complexity surrounding its polarized presentation of the worlds of life-denying repression and chaotic instinctual indulgence and to sharpen the features of Leonora as an agent who exists between the antithetical extremes of unnatural restraint and unnatural license. The simple, mutually exclusive opposites implied in the original version become linked in a complex process of reciprocal qualification, and a final resolution of their dialectical interaction is achieved in the heroine's moral action. The child no longer reacts in the mechanical way that characterizes the movements of the demonic society, which springs into motion at the sound of the forbidden music and swarms to the feast of forbidden fruits like birds flocking to a freshly sown field. Leonora undergoes her first experience and moves through conflict and crisis to a struggle in which her conscience is engaged and in which she reveals remarkable moral courage.

The major change in the manuscript is, of course, the climactic encounter, in which all the preceding action and an enormous burden of literary tradition nourishing it converge. Here, defying the expectations of reader and the narrator himself, who appears to take the traditional as the inexorable, Leonora displays courage and struggles against the force that has appeared overwhelming and that has attracted her so powerfully: "the courage of Leonora was such that, at the time when it most became her, she displayed it against the vile efforts of her astute deceiver, for they were not sufficient to vanquish her. He tired himself to no purpose, but she remained the conqueror, and they both slept."[57] The "battle" in the bed is certainly part of

[55] "puesto caso que no estáis obligado a creerme ninguna cosa de las que os dijere, sabed que no os he ofendido sino con el pensamiento" (pp. 169-70).

[56] "y hacía mucho al caso para lo que entonces allí les pasaba" (*El Loaysa*, p. 75).

[57] "el valor de Leonora fué tal, que en el tiempo que más le convenía, le mostró contra las fuerzas villanas de su astuto engañador, pues no fueron bastantes a vencerla, y él se cansó en balde, y allí quedó vencedora, y entrambos dormidos" (p. 158).

the sustained mock-heroic treatment of the seducer and his "valiant deed" ("*proeza*"), but his ignominy only throws into sharper light the true victory and the authentic heroism of the maiden.

THE MYSTERY OF FREEDOM

The most profound implications of the resistance and victory of the unaided Leonora lie not in her opposition to Loaysa and the instinctual society, but rather in her opposition to Carrizales. To appreciate them fully, we must bear in mind the central doctrines of the Christian Humanist movement concerning the perfectibility of the individual self. The whole Erasmian program for reform and its utopian vision of perfection in the family and the state, a vision that we glimpse in the background of Cervantes's *Gitanilla* (see below), were based ultimately on the creation of a new consciousness among Christians. As Erasmus and his followers tirelessly reiterated, few Christians truly understand the meaning of Christ's gift of liberty and his deliverance of his followers from the burden of the law. If a man who acts out of passion or pure self-interest is enslaved by the evil inclinations which have plagued the will since Adam's fall, the man who acts virtuously in fear of castigation is no less a slave. Erasmus found the lofty ethical vision of the classical philosophers and its ideal of the autonomous, rational individual who acts righteously because he wants to do so perfectly consistent with the gospel's call for man to pursue good spontaneously. In tracing his ideal of the perfect man, he contrasted the servile, sheeplike plodding of those who live in fear of the law, as if in a state of incarceration (those "who were confined by the commands of law as by the bars of a prison, so to speak, and who were as slaves of a guide") with the racing movements of the liberated Christian, whose pursuit of goodness is free from all external compulsion, since Christ has spiritualized the law and given it to him as an internal possession. As St. Paul had emphasized, his single law is charity, and, where the spirit of the Lord is, there is freedom and light and life. The man of law lives *under* the law, and his fear is like a tyrannical pedagogue; the spiritual man lives *in* the law and delights in actively fulfilling it. "Christians, who live spontaneously according to the law, not through the coercion of punishment, but rather through the attraction of charity, exist *in the law*. Slaves exist *under* the law; free men *in* the law."[58] To the spiritual man all is permitted, but his

[58] "qui legis praeceptis veluti cancellis quibusdam coercebantur, & ceu paedagogo serviebant"; "Christiani *in lege* versantur, qui sponte secundum legem vivunt, non

will, purified by Christ's sacrifice and revelation, will choose only what is reconcilable with the spirit of the law and with reason, which for Erasmus are close to being the same thing.[59]

The conception of freedom was fundamental to Erasmus's entire *Philosophia Christiana*. As he observed on the one hand the distasteful spectacle of the perversion of the sacred tradition of Christian liberty in the rampant ceremonialism, ritualism, and superstitious practice infesting the Catholic world and, on the other hand, the Protestants' denials of the existence of free will and their diminished conception of man as a being who, through his own efforts, could do nothing but sin,[60] he continued to affirm what he considered to be the true

cogente supplicio, sed invitante caritate. *Sub* lege sunt servi, *in* lege liberi" (*Beatus Vir, Opera Omnia*, ed. J. Le Clerc, 10 vols. [Leiden, 1703-1706], 5:182; italics added). For Erasmus's view of Christian liberty, see, in addition to the passages cited below in my text, his periphrases of Rom. 6-8 (*Opera Omnia*, ed. Le Clerc, 7:794-805). Erasmus saw in the state the guarantor of Christian liberty and an institution whose highest purpose is to allow the full moral growth of its citizens as autonomous individuals. In his *Institutio Principis Christiani* he writes: "Xenophon in Oeconomico libello scribit, divinum potius quam humanum, imperare liberis ac volentibus: sordidum enim, imperare mutis animantibus, aut coactis mancipiis: at homo divinum est animal, ac bis liberum, primum natura, deinde legibus: ideoque summae virtutis est, ac plane divinae, Regem sic temperare imperium, ut beneficium sentiat populus, servitutem non sentiat" (in *Ausgewählte Schriften* ed. Werner Welzig, 8 vols. [Darmstadt, 1967-1980], 5:188). For this aspect of Erasmus's political theory, see Eberhard von Koerber, *Die Staattheorie des Erasmus von Rotterdam* (Berlin, 1967), Chap. 2. For the centrality of the idea of freedom in Erasmus's thought and the philosophical and theological traditions behind it, see K. A. Meissinger, *Erasmus von Rotterdam* (Berlin, 1948), Chaps. 16-17, Augustin Renaudet, *Études Érasmiennes* (Paris, 1933), Chap. 4, "Le Modernisme Érasmien," and especially, Albert Alfons Auer, *Die vollkommene Frömmigkeit des Christen nach dem Enchiridion militis Christiani des Erasmus von Rotterdam* (Düsseldorf, 1954), pp. 159ff.; see p. 171: "Daran hat Erasmus immer am meisten gelegen, dass der spontane Impuls der freien Liebe nicht durch lähmende und einengende Bestimmungen abgewürgt wird und in der Trägheit des Durchschnitts oder im Mechanismus der äusserliche Gesetzerfüllung und in ethischem Minimalismus verendet."

[59] "Quod philosophi rationem, id Paulus modo spiritum, modo interiorem hominem, modo legem mentis vocat" (*Enchiridion Militis Christiani*, ed. W. Welzig, *Ausgewählte Schriften*, 1:126).

[60] See *A Diatribe or Sermon Concerning Free Will* in Erasmus-Luther, *Discourse on Free Will*, ed. and trans. E. F. Winter (New York, 1967), pp. 91, 93. In this polemical work, which takes a conciliatory stand regarding the relation between freedom and God's grace, Erasmus still asks: "What's the good of the entire man, if God treats him like the potter his clay or as he can deal with a pebble?" (p. 93). Erasmus wrote in a letter to Raffaelle Riario "if they took away my freedom, they would take away my life" (*Opus Epistolarum*, ed. P. S. Allen, 12 vols. (Oxford, 1906-1958), 2:70). As Auer points out, freedom was the "vital element" for Erasmus (see *Die vollkommene Frömmigkeit des Christen nach dem Enchiridion*, p. 26), and we find evidence of his

meaning of the gift of liberty which Christ and the first theologian St. Paul conferred on all believers. In both popular writings and theological and polemical treatises Erasmus ceaselessly stressed his ideal of the autonomous personality. In the popular dialogue *The Godly Feast* he describes the perfect man as the good king who needs no compulsion from human laws. The Holy Spirit is present in his heart directing his action, and he voluntarily does more than human laws require. Eusebius, the leader of the discussion, affirms that all Christians "should be kings of this sort," a phrase that conveys all of Erasmus's respect for the dignity of the truly liberated personality who fearlessly leads a life of moral responsibility.[61] In his *Enchiridion* Erasmus remarks on the stunted, childish character of the Christians who believe they have fulfilled their responsibility as free beings by the performance of numerous ceremonial acts. They spend their lives in "perpetual childishness and smallness of spirit," "living throughout their lives in need of tutors and under a yoke," "never growing up to the fullness of charity," and making no effort to "achieve freedom of spirit," a state of adulthood in which "there is no longer necessary a tutor who leads us through fear."[62]

---

esteem for it in all phases of his thought and program, not merely in the theological and philosophical contexts in which he deals with New Testament freedom and classical moral philosophy. We discover it in his distaste for the rigidities of scholastic systematic thought and argumentation and for the fanatical exclusivism of sectarianism, in his condemnation of physical punishment as a means of educating children, in his denunciations of parents who fail to grant their offspring the free choice of a vocation or force them into disastrous marriages, in his sympathy for the victims of dynastic marriages, in his tirades against abbots who deny monks the privilege of reading because they prefer to brutalize them and manipulate them as sheep, in his criticism of husbands who would turn their wives into ignorant slaves, in his preference for the "openness" of dialectical argumentation and its movement toward truth through the assembly of the numerous partial truths of different positions, and, of course, in his celebration through his greatest literary character, Stultitia, of the innumerable follies which human beings must be allowed to cultivate in order to perform creative and heroic acts and to bind themselves into a civilized society valuing vitality and diversity. There is perhaps nothing that marks Erasmus and Cervantes as members of the same spiritual family more clearly than the atmosphere of freedom, openness, and tolerance which one perceives throughout their works. See my *Cervantes' Christian Romance*, pp. 157-64.

[61] See *The Colloquies of Erasmus*, trans. C. R. Thompson (Chicago, 1965), p. 59.

[62] "perpetua niñería y poquedad"; "teniendo en toda la vida necessidad de ayos y biviendo siempre debaxo el yugo"; "nunca creciendo a la grandeza de la charidad"; "alcançar la libertad del espíritu"; "ya escusado es ayo que nos atraya por temor." I cite the Spanish translation of Alfonso Fernández de Madrid, El arcediano del Alcor, a text which was widely read in Spain during the first half of the sixteenth century. See *El Enquiridion o manual del caballero cristiano*, ed. Dámaso Alonso (Madrid, 1932), pp. 271-72. Erasmus's sparer Latin reads as follows: "Hinc illa perpetua in Christo

The most eloquent voice educating Spaniards in the mysteries of Christian liberty and the integrity of the "adult" moral will was that of Fray Luis de León. In his *De los nombres de Cristo* he argues that the "law of commandments" is "harsh" and "heavy," that it reaches the intellect but leaves the will unrestored. As it burdens man with an increased knowledge of sin, it commonly stimulates the will to a more active pursuit of the prohibited fruits and frequently leaves man "lost and ravaged," rent within by a "mortal war of contradictions." The "law of grace" is "most sweet"; it consists "of a healthfulness and a celestial quality which heals the damaged will," restoring its "friendship" with reason. "Engraving" on the will "an efficacious and powerful law of love, making it long for all the righteousness which the laws command," it restores man's integrity of being, uniting his warring faculties in a harmonious and loving union. "The former makes men fearful; the latter makes them loving." Recalling St. Paul, Luis de León writes: "the former makes slaves, the latter is proper for children; the former is a gloomy and punishing tutor, the latter is a

---

infantia, ut ne quid dicam gravius, quod praeposteri rerum aestimatores ea facimus plurimi, quae sola nihili sunt, iis neglectis, quae sola sufficiunt, semper sub paedagogis agentes, semper sub iugo, nec unquam ad libertatem spiritus aspirantes, nunquam ad amplitudinem caritatis crescentes. . . . At ubi venit fides, iam non sumus sub paedagogo" (*Enchiridion*, p. 220). The development of the childhood-adulthood opposition on the basis of Paul's antithesis, slavery-children of God, in the gospel passages behind Erasmus's pronouncements (Gal. 3:23-26; Rom. 8:15-24) is revealing of Erasmus's emphasis on growth, enlightenment, and maturity in his conception of the spiritual man. In the dialectical development of the ideas of repression and freedom unfolding in the revised *El celoso extremeño*, we can see a fictional and thoroughly secularized analogue of Erasmus's exhortation on freedom as it is developed by his Spanish translator: "A vosotros, hermanos, Dios os llamó para libertad. Pero mirad no uséys della para bivir desenfrenadamente y seguir las aficiones de la carne sin ningún yugo; sino que vuestra libertad toda se emplee en ayudaros y serviros unos a otros. *Y esto no tanto sea por temor no os castigue Dios, si assí no lo hazéys, ni tampoco por proprio amor porque os dé dello galardón, quanto sea principalmente por charidad y verdadero amor que os tengáys unos a otros por Dios; ca esto es amaros libre y espiritualmente como él lo manda*, pues toda su ley se encierra *bien mirado y se ensuelve* en sola esta palabra, que es 'amarás a tu próximo como a ti mesmo' " (*El Enquiridion*, pp. 273-74; the italics indicate the translator's additions to Erasmus's text; for the latter, see *Enchiridion*, p. 222). In drawing attention to such backgrounds of Cervantes's exemplary tale, I do not mean to imply that it is a religious work, but rather to suggest that its antithesis, Leonora-Carrizales, and its concern with the mentality of repression, servitude, and freedom should be understood in the context of the antitheses of law and love, ritualism and freedom, ceremonialism and authentic individual action, and Judaism and gospel liberty, which were obsessive preoccupations in the religious culture of the age and could not fail to leave their mark on all approaches to such problems as ethical choice and the nature of the individual, whether religious or secular.

spirit of regalement and consolation; the former brings servitude, the latter, honor and true liberty."[63]

Carrizales would deny Leonora the opportunity to reach the adulthood which confers authenticity on a human being and which must be won through experience and trial. Erasmus insisted that one is not born a man but rather becomes one through education in "good living" and the acquisition of the capacity to engage in mature moral action,[64] and his universally read *Enchiridion* celebrated the conception of the Christian as an enlightened, embattled warrior, living in the world of men, triumphing over the dehumanizing forces within himself through such moral acts as charity and forgiveness, and in his triumphs earning the dignity that God intended for the creature that bears his semblance. The conception accorded perfectly with the Christian Humanists' optimistic attitude toward man's capacities and toward the value of his achievements on earth and with their distaste for ascetic retreat and the authoritarian habits of mind that frequently inspired it. The individual who is truly free does good because he desires it, and he values the situation of choice; for in reality he is capable of such affirmative goodness only if he is confronted with the experience of evil. In his great treatise on man's freedom John Milton proclaimed that God does not "captivate under a perpetual childhood of prescription, but trusts him with the gift of reason to be his own chooser." He asks:

What wisdom can there be to choose, what continence to forbear without the knowledge of evil? He that can apprehend and consider vice with all her baits and seeming pleasures, and yet abstain, and yet distinguish, and yet prefer that which is truly better, he is the true wayfaring Christian. I cannot praise a fugitive and a cloistered virtue, unexercised and unbreathed, that never sallies out and sees her adversary. . . . Assuredly we bring not innocence into the world, we bring impurity much rather: that which purifies us is trial, and trial is by what is contrary. That virtue therefore which is but a youngling in the contemplation of evil, and knows not the utmost that

---

[63] "Aquélla haze temerosos, aquésta amadores." . . . "aquélla haze esclavos, ésta es propria de hijos; aquélla es ayo triste y açotador, aquésta es espíritu de regalo y consuelo; aquélla pone en servidumbre, aquésta en honra y libertad verdadera" (see *De los nombres de Cristo*, ed. F. de Onís, 3 vols. [Madrid, 1966], 2:120ff).

[64] In his treatise on education, *De Pueris Instituendis*, he asserts that, if not educated, man is worse than the animals and argues: "Quanto plus confert qui dat bene viuere quam qui dat viuere. . . . Arbores fortasse nascuntur, licet aut steriles, aut agresti foetu, equi nascuntur licet inutiles; at homines, mihi crede, non nascuntur, sed finguntur." The goal of the educator must be the creation of the liberated personality, which "sua sponte recte faciat potius quam alieno metu" (see ed. J.-C. Margolin, in *Opera Omnia*, Vol. I, pt. 2 [Amsterdam, 1971], pp. 30-32, 58).

vice promises to her followers, and rejects it, is but a blank virtue, not a pure; her whiteness is but an excremental whiteness.[65]

Leonora is an obedient child, her virtue "unpurified" by the knowledge of evil. Her "blankness" as a character, her infantilization, and her absence all point to her powerful presence as an example of the subhuman nature of the being who is denied choice. The monstrous machinery of repression, a disproportionate center of the description in the tale and an obsessive concern of its active narrator, is in reality the stifling "cloister" of law that denies existence to its inhabitants. Behind it looms the constricted mentality of authority and law which the Christian Humanists detested as inimical to dignified human fulfillment. Leonora's triumph and courage destroy the cloister, and it is a sign of Cervantes's own humanity that he allows the "birth" of his heroine to bring to life her dehumanized oppressor. Carrizales's "humiliation" in this "adultery novella" becomes in reality the moral

[65] "For God sure esteems the growth and completing of one virtuous person more than the restraint of ten vicious" (see *Areopagitica, Complete Poems and Major Prose*, ed. M. Y. Hughes [New York, 1957], pp. 727-28, 733). The traditional Christian notion of the value of the trial as it enriches virtue was infused with new life in the writings of the sixteenth-century Christian Humanists in their optimistic Christianity and emphasis on man's moral life. The trial is not only the occasion for a lesson in humility but also the opportunity to exercise freedom triumphantly. See Luis de Granada: ". . . es perfecta virtud la que tentada no cae, que provocada no es vencida, que ni en lo próspero se engríe, ni en lo adverso desfallece, y la que tan firmes raices echó en el alma, que al modo que el fuego agitado de un viento recio, léjos de apagarse se enciende más, así ella de muchos modos combatida, no solo no se rinde vencida, sino que todavía, como elegantemente dijo allá uno, cobra nuevo esfuerzo con la herida. Pues por esta doctrina puede conjeturarse qué virtud sea verdadera, cuál falsa, cuál imperfecta, cuál consumada. Así no es perfectamente honesta la mujer que guarda su honestidad sin haberla nadie provocado, sino la que tentada de muchas maneras, conserva entero y sin mancilla el pudor" (*De la retórica eclesiástica*, ed. B.A.E. 11:523). Cervantes's interest in exploring in fictional terms this conception of moral perfection is evident not only in *El celoso extremeño*, but also in *El curioso impertinente*, where the obverse side of such assumptions concerning human nature and such demands for moral perfection is held up to critical scrutiny. Here the lofty claim concerning human dignity appears as the grotesque obsession of a madman, and the fall of the tested wife would imply its unnaturalness. The denouement of the original *El celoso extremeño* accords much more with its "companion piece" in the *Quixote* than the final version. The "madman of law" and the "madman of freedom" work out their obsessions at the expense of a helpless human being, and her victimization is a lesson pointing to the helplessness of the human will and implying a pessimistic view of man's capacities. Both works are as close as Cervantes ever comes to embracing in his fiction the spirit of the contemporary literature of *desengaño*, which generally viewed the trial as a humbling rather than as a triumphant experience and "limited" the nobility man could acquire therein to the type surrounding one of the *desengañados'* favorite heroes—the "patient, innocent Job."

crisis that enables him to overcome his alienation from his true self and to reach the maturity that has eluded this "prodigal son" throughout his sixty-eight years of blighted, self-protective isolation. Swayed by his impulses to avenge himself, impulses whose propriety is endorsed by the narrator, he is stricken by dreadful pangs of self-awareness and falls into the kind of swoon which frequently in Cervantes's fiction and the meditative literary tradition behind it marks the experience of conversion or spiritual rebirth.[66] Carrizales finally meets a trial in which he is capable of triumphing, and, ironically, on the verge of death he finds his way out of his dehumanized condition and enjoys a moment of authentic being. Recognizing his own error, stifling his desire for revenge, and magnanimously forgiving Leonora for the sin that he assumes she has committed, Carrizales fleetingly emerges from the shadows of his own pseudo-existence, an existence which for nearly the whole tale is present only in the machinery of his house,[67] and he acts as Erasmus would have his *miles christianus* act in similar circumstances: "I would not call the man brave who attacks his enemy. . . . But the man who can conquer his own heart, who can love him who hates him, who can do good to him who does him ill, and who can desire good for him who wishes evil for him—that man deserves to be acclaimed as brave, and to him shall be given the reward of the magnanimous."[68]

Amid the darkness and ambiguity which trouble the denouement of this most somber of the *Exemplary Novels*, Cervantes is careful to allow each of his main characters to perform a voluntary moral act in the absence of external constraint, and the spontaneous nature of their actions contrasts sharply with the mechanical quality of nearly all the preceding movements in the narrative. Cervantes would appear to wish to connect these voluntary acts with the force that traditionally

[66] Compare the Alférez Campuzano, who, while preparing a bloody vengeance for his wife, falls asleep and awakens freed from the destructive impulse (see the discussion of the scene and its echoes of literature of conversions and miracles in my forthcoming study *Cervantes and the Mystery of Lawlessness*).

[67] In a sense the old man is an absence just as powerful as the blankness of Leonora. As Casalduero astutely observes, one can view as the true protagonist of the work the house, which embodies him during the lengthy narrative period separating his early withdrawal from the stage and his return at the conclusion. See *Sentido y forma de las "Novelas ejemplares,"* pp. 175-76. For the striking development in the characters of the husband and wife at the end, see R. El Saffar, *Novel to Romance*, pp. 45-48.

[68] "No tengo yo por fuerte al que acomete a su enemigo. . . . Mas a aquél se deve renombre de fuerte y *se le dará gualardón* de magnánimo que pudo vencer su propio coraçón, que puede querer bien a quien mal le quiere, y hazer bien a quien mal le haze, y dessear bien a quien mal le dessea" (*El Enquiridion*, p. 315; italics indicate the translator's additions). For Erasmus's Latin text, see *Enchiridion*, p. 262.

opposes the law—love; for he emphasizes in their aftermath that an awakening of each character to the reality of the other has occurred and that the awakening takes the form of an act of compassion. Both have exercised their freedom of choice to reject a powerful temptation to fulfill themselves at the expense of the other. The emphasis on physical contact and tenderness is particularly striking in that previously there has been only the slightest mention of communication between the husband and wife. The grief-stricken Leonora "came up to him, and, placing her face against his and holding him closely in her arms, she said to him: 'What is wrong, my lord, for it appears to me that you are complaining?' "; "embracing her husband, she bestowed on him greater caresses that she had ever bestowed on him before, asking him what he felt, in such tender and loving words." Whatever Carrizales may think about the motives for Leonora's tears, he pronounces words of forgiveness and kisses the unconscious maiden ("he bent down and kissed the face of Leonora in her swoon"; "the unfortunate old man kissed her as she lay in a swoon"). The most poignant expression of the intimacy, intensity, and interiority which bless their relationship at this moment of its destruction is the embrace into which they fall when overcome with grief: "When he had said this, a terrible fainting fit overtook him and made him fall so close to Leonora that their faces lay together—a strange and sad spectacle!"[69] Despite Cervantes's refusal to remove all ambiguity from Leonora's motivation and to allow Carrizales complete lucidity in his madness, the emphasis here is on maturity of feeling, genuine communication, and reconciliation. The scene of self-examination, self-exposure, and self-condemnation on the part of the dying protagonist, in which the tale lingers painfully in an abrupt deceleration of its narrative tempo, is all the more striking because the acts of physical contact that it depicts form a sharp contrast to the repeated acts of demonic physical communication that precede them. Instead of the treacherous kiss sealing the predatory bond of the self-seeking, we behold a genuine kiss of peace, sanctifying a victory over alienation from self and estrangement from the other. In a poignant scene which

[69] "se llegó a él, y poniendo su rostro con el suyo, teniéndole estrechamente abrazado le dijo:—¿Qué tenéis, señor mío, que me parece que os estáis quejando?" (p. 161); "abrazándose con su esposo le hacía las mayores caricias que jamás le había hecho, preguntándole qué era lo que sentía, con tan tiernas y amorosas palabras" (p. 162); "se inclinó y besó en el rostro de la desmayada Leonora" (p. 167); "abrazóla así desmayada el lastimado viejo" (p. 170); "Esto dicho le sobrevino un terrible desmayo, y se dejó caer tan junto de Leonora, que se juntaron los rostros: extraño y triste espectáculo" (p. 168).

recalls Milton's insights into the consequences of the mature exercise of freedom, Cervantes clearly reveals that the liberty to know and choose is intimately connected with the liberty to love. The embrace of the dying couple, the most ironic moment of this intensely ironic tale, is in fact their first act of love.

To appreciate the significance of these clear redemptive notes that sound amid the deafening cacophony of *El celoso extremeño*, we would do well to look briefly at the other masterpiece of Spanish literature that exploits the situation of repression, confinement, and liberation in order to explore the nature of man and the great theme of freedom—*La vida es sueño*. For all the obvious differences separating a drama dealing with dynastic turmoil and problems of dishonor from a tale of domestic disaster for an ill-matched married couple, the two works are strangely comparable in their most essential stratum of significance. Behind the central act of confinement in *La vida es sueño* looms the legend of Barlaam and Josaphat, where the act of repression is in reality a denial of a human being's right to progress from an infantile state of inexperience to enjoy the fullness of being that can come only through a loss of innocence and an exposure to evil. Of the numerous attempts to look for Cervantes's sources in the rich literature of confinement, none that I know has pointed to the relevance of this legend or its archetype, but in many ways it is the truest "source" for the profound mystery that unfolds in the exemplary tale.[70] In

[70] Angel González Palencia suggests the possible relationship between Cervantes's tale and a popular story which was related to him in northern Africa by a Moroccan postal employee who knew no European language ("Un cuento popular marroquí y 'El celoso extremeño' de Cervantes," *Homenaje ofrecido a Menéndez Pidal*, 3 vols. [Madrid, 1925], 1:417-23). Whatever its concrete relationship to *El celoso extremeño* might be (and as Cirot emphasizes, one can scarcely assume that a tale uncovered in the popular tradition in 1914 was current in 1580, particularly when it resembles a story published in 1613 [see "Quelques mots encore sur les 'maris jaloux' de Cervantes," pp. 305-306]), the tale is most interesting because, as is characteristic of the products of the popular imagination, it does not displace its essential psychic content through verisimilar fictionalization. Even if it originated through the inspiration of Cervantes's tale, it might tend to discard the elements localizing the action and themes and individualizing the agents and to present its universal implications in stark concentration. In the African story the confinement and denial of freedom are connected with an individual's "radical solipsism," incest, infantilization, and the denial of experience and being to the person whom the tyrant would possess. After discarding a number of wives, adults whom he evidently cannot possess, the husband buys a two-year-old girl, adopts her, and raises her "in blindness," under lock and key, because he intends to marry her. "Yo he jurado no tomar por mujer sino una niña cuyos ojos estén cerrados y que todavía mame." The child opens her eyes and asks the father: "¡Padre! ¿Hay en el mundo alguna cosa o no?" He answers: "En el mundo no hay más que yo, tú, y Dios." When an old beggar lady appears, the startled girl

Calderón's version King Basilio's effort to interfere with Divine Providence fails as disastrously as Carrizales's efforts to fashion a human being "in his own likeness" ("según mis mañas"), and both old men interpret the consequences of their acts as a lesson demonstrating the necessity of servile submission to the Supreme Will.[71] But the far more interesting point of the comparison lies in the radically different acts of the children when the towers of their confinement have fallen. Segismundo yields immediately to the most unrestrained instinctual self-indulgence imaginable, demonstrating through murder, attempted rape, attempted patricide, and uncontrollable wrath the destructive powers that man will naturally display if, liberated from the yoke of authority, he yields to the promptings of his nature. Basilio is of course wrong to deny Segismundo the right to exercise free moral choice, and that is one of the principal lessons of the play. However, Segismundo learns the proper exercise of freedom only after an abrupt vision of the corruption and mutability of all earthly life, the utter helplessness of man before the mysteries of Divine Providence, and the necessity of practicing self-restraint and virtue in order to escape damnation. The work reaches its climax in an act of double prostration, by father and son, the recognition by the chastened Segismundo, now an ideal prince, that he will rule in terror of divine retribution ("estoy temiendo en mis ansias"), and the resurrection of the tower which had confined him in his original infantile condition. Casting its disturbing shadow over the concluding restoration of order, the tower, then, stands at the beginning and the end of the play as a powerful symbol of an authoritarian view of human nature, and one of Calderón's darkest lessons is that the freedom that God has granted man alone among his creations can be exercised properly only if man can internalize the dungeon and all the fears associated with it. Man must "flee the occasion" if he is to avoid falling victim to the demonic forces within himself.

Calderón's play is a dramatic monument to the *desengañado* vision

---

asks whether there is "something in the world," and the narrative proceeds rapidly through her awakened curiosity and demand for experience to her adultery and deception of the father-husband, and to the disintegration of his world. Aware of the hopelessness of his demands, he pardons his daughter-wife and wanders in madness through the villages of the region, while she enjoys her wealth, her lover, and her youth, before becoming herself a beggar.

[71] Carrizales: "mas como no se puede prevenir con diligencia humana el castigo que la voluntad divina quiere dar a los que en ella no ponen del todo en todo sus deseos y esperanzas, no es mucho que yo quede defraudado en las mías" (p. 165). Basilio: "¡. . . son diligencias vanas/del hombre cuantas dispone/ contra mayor fuerza y causa!" (*Obras completas*, Vol. I, ed. A. Valbuena Briones [Madrid, 1969], p. 531).

of man that dominated much of Spain's cultural life of the seventeenth century. It was a vision that was nourished by traditional ascetic Christianity and was obsessed with man's natural depravity, the misery of the human condition, the destructive power of time, the probability of damnation, and the inevitability of lawlessness and conflict within man, the family, society, and the state. Nothing could be further apart in spirit from the optimistic view of man and society which animated the Christian Humanist program of reform and which found eloquent fictional expression in such romances as Cervantes's *Gitanilla* and *Los trabajos de Persiles y Sigismunda*. In several of his works Cervantes reveals his understanding of and perhaps susceptibility to the appeal of the *desengañados'* vision, but in all cases his glance in their direction is critical, and he ultimately turns away, reaffirming, if only implicitly, his allegiance to the optimistic values of his true spiritual fathers. *El celoso extremeño* is such a work, and its revised ending is perhaps the most dramatic proof we have of Cervantes's increasing sense of himself as different from such popular spokesmen for *desengaño* as Mateo Alemán, Francisco de Quevedo, and, of course, Alonso Fernández de Avellaneda, the man who contaminated his own festive masterpiece with the gloom of their somber philosophy and terminated his greatest hero's quest for universal justice by incarcerating him in the madhouse of Toledo, another of the imposing structures of confinement that loom menacingly throughout their literature.[72]

[72] One should contrast Carrizales's and Calderón's structures of confinement and the mentality that they imply with the architectural configuration that stands as a monument to the Christian Humanists' faith in the goodness of human nature, their ideal of the open personality, and their insistence on freedom as the necessary condition of human fulfillment—Rabelais's Abbaye de Thélème. Gargantua's first decree concerning its construction is that it must have no walls. The life within it is not to be structured according to clocks, schedules, or complex statutes, but rather by the promptings of its inhabitants' individual natures. The single rule for all is the guarantee of their freedom: "Fay ce que vouldras," and its adoption is based on the assumptions that human beings will naturally pursue virtue and that external constraint can only depress man, prompt him to rebel, and indeed corrupt his will by heightening the allure of the forbidden. ". . . parce que gens liberes, bien nez, bien instruictz, conversans en compaignies honnestes, ont par nature un instinct et aguillon qui tousjours les poulse à faictz vertueux et retire de vice, lequel ilz nommoient honneur. Iceulx, quand par vile subjection et contraincte sont deprimez et asserviz, detournent la noble affection, par laquelle à vertuz franchement tendoient, à deposer et enfraindre ce joug de servitude; car nous entreprenons tousjours choses defendues et convoitons ce que nous est denié" (I.57; *Oeuvres*, ed. A. Lefranc et al., 6 vols. [Paris, 1912-1955], 2:430-31). As Lucien Febvre points out, the conception of the utopia is informed by Erasmus's *Philosophia Christiana*, and Rabelais's words echo specifically his second *Hyperaspistes* (see *Le Problème de l'incroyance au xvie siècle* [Paris,

As I have pointed out above, the original version of the tale concludes with a vision of desolation. There is a mitigating element in Carrizales's pardon of his sinful wife, but its redemptive effects are severely attentuated by the overwhelming powers of negation in the action of its denouement: the protagonist's self-prostration, his acknowledgment of human helplessness and of the unfathomable mysteries of Divine Providence, and the divine retribution that brings madness, disintegration, and death to nearly all characters. The maiden escapes her confinement, and, like Segismundo, she yields to temptation immediately, and the suggestion of expiation and castigation in her ultimate confinement is pronounced.[73] There is nothing to suggest that she takes into her final prison a self of inviolable integrity or a silence that holds the secret of an inner liberation. As in Calderón's play, the prison is truly "resurrected" at the end, and it can be seen as an emblem of the entire earthly order. It is revealing that Cervantes was not content with this ending; his alterations of the maiden's conduct, his differentiation of her good nature from the demonic agents of the instinctual world, and his emphasis on her spontaneous act of will and the complexity of her interiority turn the tale into a deeply ironic, but nonetheless powerful affirmation of man's natural goodness and his capacities to exercise free will in the active pursuit of goodness and in consideration of other human beings. Calderón preserves the tower and concentrates his moral philosophy in Segismundo's injunction to himself as his instincts drive him toward

1968], pp. 288-89; also Walter Kaiser, *Praisers of Folly* [Cambridge, Mass., 1963], p. 95). Leonora's changed role in the second *El celoso extremeño* would vindicate such a conception of human nature. Her resistance dramatically reveals all that the will can accomplish "when it remains free" and points to the idleness of repressive measures as a guarantee of morality ("Que si yo no me guardo/ No me guardaréis"). The elaborate machinery of repression is in fact a stimulus to corruption, and, in its erection and destruction in the revised version of the tale, we can observe Cervantes in a critical dialogue with the attitudes of the *desengañados*, which he rejects in favor of the Erasmian vision of man that informs his most humane fiction. The changes in *El celoso extremeño* are comparable in their implications concerning Cervantes's stance vis-à-vis the literature of *desengaño* to Sancho Panza's protests that the gluttonous, loutish being who bears the name Sancho Panza in Avellaneda's *Quixote* is in reality an impostor (see *Don Quijote de la Mancha*, 2:59). See my discussion of Cervantes's critical engagement with the favored literary genres of the *desengañados*—the miracle, satire, and the picaresque novel—below in my analyses of *La fuerza de la sangre*, *El Licenciado Vidriera*, and in my forthcoming *Cervantes and the Mystery of Lawlessness.*

[73] ". . . por las malas obras que me habéis visto hacer, yo os prometo y os juro . . . que yo acabe los días que me quedaren en perpetuo encerramiento y clausura, y desde aquí prometo, sin vos, de hacer profesión en una religión de las más ásperas que hubiere" (*El Loaysa*, p. 91).

the helpless Rosaura: "let us flee the occasion" ("huyamos de la ocasión"). Cervantes destroys it entirely, and, while his work is far more tragic than the play celebrating the triumphs of its austere prince, the reaction of Cervantes's characters to adversity and the growth which he allows them in the wreckage of their world contain a far more optimistic view of human capacities and human dignity.[74]

THE CLASSICAL NOVELLA RECONSTRUCTED— EXEMPLARY UNEXEMPLARITY AND THE LIBERATION OF THE READER

Cervantes knew that his treatment of the outbreak of instinct was far from simple as he reconsidered his manuscript of *El celoso extremeño*, and it is notable that on introducing the climactic song celebrating the release of repressed appetite, he eliminated a phrase that would suggest the paradigmatic character of the simple moral contained therein: "and it was very much to the point in view of what happened to them then." There is in fact no easy moral to be inferred from the "strange and sad spectacle" that unfolds in its final scenes, and its mystery appears to elude even the creator of the work. As I mentioned above, one of the most striking departures of *El celoso extremeño* from the pattern of the tightly constructed adultery tale of the traditional novella lies in its anticlimactic presentation of the clearly anticipated scene of adultery. However, a much more puzzling dislocation of the mechanism of the Boccaccian plot occurs simultaneously, for the narrator not only interposes his moralizing commentary between reader and event, but also suddenly begins to break down as a reliable perspective through which to view the action he reports. Up to this moment Cervantes's narrator is a strong, controlling presence in the tale, conveying directly and omnisciently all information necessary to the exposition of his subjects, offering generalizing comments on the

---

[74] In its optimism, its emphasis on man's capacities to fulfill himself as a moral being in this world, and its attenuation of the ascetic implications of its denouement, Cervantes's reworking of the Barlaam and Josaphat situation is closer to Boccaccio's version (*Decameron*, IV. prologue), which characteristically emphasizes in the repressed youth's awakening and growth a discovery of the exhilarating beauty of this world, particularly the products of man's civilization, and an experience of the creative vitality of nature and instinctual life, than it is to the more traditional version presented in Calderón's drama of *desengaño*. For Boccaccio's use of the legend, as well as bibliography concerning its importance in the tradition of the European novella, see Walter Pabst, *Novellentheorie*, p. 35; for its popularity in European literature of Cervantes's age, see E. Kuhn, *Barlaam und Joasaph* (Munich, 1893).

action, frequently making moral judgements of the characters and their deeds, generally maintaining a sober, exemplary tone and, when shifting into ironic tones, making the implications of his utterances quite clear, and occasionally asserting his presence as a craftsman, who confidently shapes and manipulates his narrative.[75] Quite suddenly, at the moment when chaos is breaking out in the tightly controlled mechanistic world of the repressor, the teller appears to lose control

[75] In the opening paragraph of the story he places himself in the center of the narration with a highly rhetorical, moralizing outburst on the evils of the Indies (p. 88), and it has a powerful effect on our perception of Carrizales and his vast wealth throughout the tale. Such forceful comments continue to guide us until the "break-down." While offering a disparaging comment on his protagonist, he moralizes on the complications which the accumulation of wealth generally brings the rich man (pp. 91-92). He explains Leonora's attraction to Carrizales with a generalizing commentary on the effects of first love in young ladies (pp. 103-104); he tells us about the power of homesickness in all pilgrims and expatriates (pp. 90-91), and he generalizes about the love that Negroes have for music (p. 110). Adopting the stance of the traditional *auctor*, he gives every indication that he is absolutely omniscient concerning everything he cares to include in the tale (for the *auctorial* narrative stance, see F. K. Stanzel, *Typische Formen des Romans* [Göttingen, 1967], pp. 16-25). He concludes some harsh judgments of the idle, self-indulgent ways of Loaysa and his peers with an omission which, unlike the silences of the conclusion, is quite clear and eloquent. His abbreviation of the description with the phrase, "había mucho que decir; pero por buenos respectos se deja," in fact establishes a complicity between narrator and reader in moral understanding and in attitude toward the events, a complicity that makes the reader all the more confident in his guide and all the more passive in his response to the text. The narrator returns to this kind of statement when he tells his reader that in the interest of preserving the decorum that marks their similar view of the events he witnesses, he will be silent about the obscenities with which the servants abuse the *dueña* ("ninguna la llamó vieja que no fuese con su epitecto y adjetivo de hechicera y de barbuda, de antojadiza y de otros que por buen respecto se callan" [p. 154]). While Cervantes seemed interested in purifying the narrator's pronouncements of irreverence and cynicism (see above), he certainly allows him to be abusive in expressing his judgments of characters: "no dejaba de tentar las cuerdas de la guitarra; tanta era (encomendado él sea a Satanás) la afición que tenía a la música" (p. 154). As Marialonso summons forth the powers of rhetorical persuasion to arouse Leonora's sexual interest in Loaysa, the narrator pauses to deliver a tirade against *dueñas* (p. 156). His epithets frequently convey a judgment of his characters: he refers with sympathy to the "pobre Leonora" and the "pobre negro," and his ironic references to the "buena dueña" and the "buen extremeño" color his pronouncements with sympathy but in no way diminish the clarity of his unequivocal judgment of their behavior. Moreover, the narrator asserts his presence as a craftsman, composing a tale of which he is in total control: "éste es el nombre del que ha dado materia a nuestra novela" (p. 90); "por concluir con todo lo que no hace a nuestro propósito, digo que" (p. 90). His comments of this type suggest his thorough understanding of the case which he is reporting: "y, con todo esto, no pudo en ninguna manera prevenir ni excusar de caer en lo que recelaba; a lo menos en pensar que había caído" (p. 104); see also his foreshadowing of the outcome of the events (p. 103).

of his tale and its characters and to fail to comprehend the full significance of what is unfolding before his eyes. As Leonora enters the room of her seduction, he interprets the action with a lengthy exclamation on the uselessness of Carrizales's elaborate precautions and concludes with an analysis of the causes of the disaster.

It would have been well to ask Carrizales at this juncture, if one did not know that he was asleep, where were his prudent precautions, his jealousies, his admonitions, his persuasions, the high walls of his house, the refusal of entrance into it of even the shadow of anyone bearing the title of man, the narrow turnstile, the thick partitions, the blocked windows, the notable confinement, the large dowry that he had bestowed on Leonora, the continual gifts that he gave her, the good treatment of his serving maids and slave girls, the supply without stint of everything that he supposed to be necessary for them, or that they could desire. But, as has been said, *there was no reason for putting these questions to him, for he was slumbering more than was needful; and had he heard it, and by chance answered it, he could not have given a better reply than to shrug his shoulders, arch his eyebrows, and say:* "The whole of this to its foundations was destroyed by the cunning, as I believe, of an idle and vicious young fellow, and the wickedness of a traitorous *dueña*, combined with the inadvertence of a girl solicited and overpersuaded. *May God deliver every man from such enemies, against whom there is no shield of prudence to defend him nor any sword of modesty to cut them down.*"[76]

The most striking features of this lengthy outcry are the illusion that the character is "independent" of the narrator and the latter's failure to show a more profound understanding of the implications of what he mistakenly thinks has happened than the myopic Carrizales. Cervantes unexpectedly disjoints his narrative with a change of perspective that momentarily troubles his audience's perception of the boundaries between fiction and reality, and his narrator, suddenly stripped of his *auctorial* robes as it were, becomes, like ourselves, a

---

[76] "Bueno fuera en esta sazón preguntar a Carrizales, a no saber que dormía, que adónde estaban sus advertidos recatos, sus recelos, sus advertimientos, sus persuasiones, los altos muros de su casa, el no haber entrado en ella, ni aun en sombra, alguien que tuviese nombre de varón, el torno estrecho, las gruesas paredes, las ventanas sin luz, el encerramiento notable, la gran dote en que a Leonora había dotado, los regalos continuos que la hacía, el buen tratamiento de sus criadas y esclavas, el no faltar un punto a todo aquello que él imaginaba que habían menester, que podían desear. Pero ya queda dicho *que no había para qué preguntárselo, porque dormía más de aquello que fuera menester; y si él lo oyera, y acaso respondiera, no podía dar mejor respuesta que encoger los hombros y enarcar las cejas, y decir:* "¡Todo aqueso derribó por los fundamentos la astucia, a lo que yo creo, de un mozo holgazán y vicioso, y la malicia de una falsa dueña, con la inadvertencia de una muchacha rogada y persuadida!" *Libre Dios a cada uno de tales enemigos*, contra los cuales no hay escudo de prudencia que defienda, ni espada de recato que corte" (pp. 157-58; italics added).

puzzled observer rather than a source of truth.[77] His readiness to endorse what is obviously a superficial explanation of events which he
does not comprehend and his failure to consider the possibility of
Leonora's resistance—the traditional is the inevitable for him—mark
the beginning of a phase of the tale continuing to its very last sentence, in which the narrator is most conspicuous for his erroneous
assertions, for his failure to qualify or correct his characters' inade-
quate understanding of the events, and for the apparent misunderstanding of the characters that beclouds his attempted clarifications.
Thus he applauds Carrizales's immediate reaction to his dishonor by
emphasizing the correctness of revenge: "in spite of this, he would
have exacted the vengeance which that great wickedness demanded,
if he had been armed with weapons with which to take it. So he
determined to go back to his room, seize a dagger, and return to wipe
off the stains of his honor with the blood of his two enemies, and also
with that of all the people in his house. *With this honorable and necessary
resolution*, he returned."[78] The narrator's analysis of the causes of the

[77] The presence of an allusion to *Orlando Furioso* in the first version of this passage
(Carrizales's awakening in an empty bed echoes rather unfortunately Olympia's discovery that Bireno has abandoned her [*Furioso*, X.19-28], and the scene is described
with the conventional epic metonymy "dejó las odiosas plumas" [*El Loaysa*, p. 83])
perhaps clarifies Cervantes's startling change in the presentation of his authorial self
at this moment. For the prominence of the "helpless," self-deprecating narrative voice
in Cervantes's works, his delight in reminding the reader of his presence and the
artificiality of his creation through confusing manipulations of the "illusion of reality," and the impact of Ariosto on these narrative methods, see my *Cervantes, Aristotle,
and the "Persiles"* (Princeton, 1970).

[78] "con todo eso, tomara la venganza que aquella grande maldad requiría, si se
hallara con armas para tomarla; y así, determinó volverse a su aposento a tomar una
daga, y volver a sacar las manchas de su honra con sangre de sus dos enemigos, y aun
con toda aquella de toda la gente de su casa. *Con esta determinación honrosa y necesaria*
volvió" (pp. 159-60; italics added). The phrase is found only in the revised version,
where its apparent endorsement of the "official" solution to problems of dishonor is
all the more puzzling in view of the reality of the situation. Cervantes would appear
to want to emphasize the narrator's "desertion" of his audience and to increase the
ambiguities that it brings to the text and the difficulties it creates for the reader.
This is most obvious in the very different final sentences of the two versions, the first
neatly closing up the narrative, the second posing an unanswered question. The
change in Loaysa's fate is another element contributing to the greater "springing
open" of the novella at the moment of its anticipated closure in the second version.
Instead of dying and taking his place neatly in the economy of poetic justice controlling the original conclusion, he disappears into the Indies, replicating the career
of Carrizales and, as it were, sending the tale circling backward toward its beginning.
The change is at the same time consistent with his increased demonization in the
second work. It is in fact the culminating variant in an imaginative system based on
motifs of mechanical, futile repetition, which is visible in Cervantes's depiction of

misfortune seems no more satisfying than Carrizales's endless enumeration of his efforts to guarantee Leonora's fidelity, his claim that he treated her as an equal ("I made her my equal; I shared with her my most secret thoughts"), and his continuing refusal even to consider the possibility that she is capable of mature ethical action ("I do not blame you, you ill-advised child . . . I do not blame you, I say, because the persuasion of crafty old women and the seductive arguments of enamored youths win an easy victory and triumph over the little understanding that your youthful years possess"). At the same time his description of Carrizales's interpretation of Leonora's tears is disturbing in his silences, in his apparent adoption of the old man's point of view despite his awareness of Leonora's innocence, resistance, and genuine compassion ("he laughed the laugh of a person who was beside himself, considering the falseness of her tears"). The fact is that nobody at the end of *El celoso extremeño*, including its seemingly reliable narrator, appears to comprehend the mystery that has unfolded, and Carrizales's naive affirmation of the exemplarity of his case ("may I remain for the world an example, if not of goodness, at least

---

the world opposing freedom and in his use of repeated elements in the organization of the narrative. In the sudden "multiplication" of voices at the end of the tale and the activation of the reader among them, we can see a shift into the enlivening type of discourse which M. Bakhtin has called dialogism. In his view the Renaissance writers inherited it from the medieval popular culture of the carnival and the ancient carnivalesque literary genres, such as the Menippean satire and the Socratic dialogue, and they found it, in its flexibilities, its openness, and its powers to engage the reader, an effective means of exploring the complexity of truth and of bringing their audience, through the experience of the literary work, into vital contact with the elementary bodily life of humanity, which is frequently concealed and suppressed by the forms of official culture, its unitary modes of discourse, and the patterns of daily life. See *The Dialogic Imagination*, ed. M. Holquist, trans. C. Emerson and M. Holquist (Austin, 1981), esp. pp. 41ff. and 259ff. In terms of literary history one can see in the triumph of dialogism in Cervantes's most "classical" novella a final and complete removal of the novella from the controlling monologism of the frame, which originated in the moralizing commentaries surrounding and integrating the anecdotes of the *exempla* collections of the middle ages, survived, although in a drastically attenuated form, in the great Renaissance collections of novellas (e.g., Boccaccio's *Decameron* and Marguerite de Navarre's *Heptaméron*), and continued to sound in the highly exemplary *auctor* of the first part of *El celoso extremeño*. Cervantes's followers in Spain did not proceed in this direction, but rather, as the frame in María de Zayas's novella collection indicates, returned to the pre-Boccaccian dogmatic monologism characteristic of medieval *exempla*, an idiom which they found well suited to the proclamation of the life-denying philosophy of *desengaño*. See the discussion of the effects of dialogistic discourse in Cervantes's own Menippean satire, *El coloquio de los perros*, in my forthcoming *Cervantes and the Mystery of Lawlessness*.

of simplicity never seen nor heard of")[79] offers, in its inadequacy, an
ironic commentary on the numerous ambiguities which distinguish
the denouement of this *novella* as totally unlike the untroubled race
toward coherent closure that marks the conclusion of traditional *exempla* and their adaptations as novellas.[80] The dawn has dispelled the
shadows enveloping the night world of the moribund oppressor, but
much darkness remains as Leonora vainly struggles to relieve herself
through speech of the burden of her guilt and innocence. The tormented maiden would appear to hold the key to a resolution of all
the ambiguities, and her abbreviated outburst "sabed que no os he
ofendido sino con el pensamiento," in its tantalizing intimation of all
the complexities surrounding moral action and the immense inner
world of conscience, comes closer to a reliable disclosure of the exemplarity of the tale than any other statement in it. However, nobody
seems interested in listening to "their child," and the promise of her
utterance is never fulfilled, as she is overcome by the pain of her
admission and retreats with her secret behind the confining walls of a
nunnery, an elliptical figure whose mystery provokes the narrator to
end the tale with a confession of his own helplessness and ignorance:
"Only I do not know for what cause Leonora did not put more energy
into clearing herself and giving her jealous husband to understand
how pure and without offense she had been on that occasion; but
excitement tied her tongue."[81] While everything else in this story of
concealed spaces opens up, its most meaningful space, ironically, remains impenetrable, and the novella ends with a question mark.

To recall my point of departure, in what appears to be his most
"classical" novella, a work that selects a traditional situation and theme
and adopts the distinctive techniques of the finest Italianate novel-

[79] "hícela mi igual; comuniquéle mis más secretos pensamientos" (p. 165); "a tí
no te culpo, ¡oh niña mal aconsejada! . . . no te culpo, digo, porque persuasiones de
viejas taimadas y requiebros de mozos enamorados fácilmente vencen y triunfan del
poco ingenio que los pocos años encierran" (p. 167); "reíase él una risa de persona
que estaba fuera de sí, considerando la falsedad de sus lágrimas" (p. 163); "que quede
en el mundo por ejemplo, si no de bondad, al menos, de simplicidad jamás oída ni
vista" (p. 167).

[80] See also the narrator's unsatisfying generic designation of his tale shortly before
his concluding confession of ignorance: "ejemplo y espejo de lo poco que hay que fiar
de llaves" (p. 171). Compare, for example, the antecedent of *El celoso extremeño* in the
Disciplina Clericalis, no. XIV, or its Spanish version in Sánchez de Vercial's *Libro de
los exemplos*, no. 235 (see B.A.E. 41).

[81] "Sólo no sé que fué la causa que Leonora no puso más ahinco en desculparse y
dar a entender a su celoso marido cuán limpia y sin ofensa había quedado en aquel
suceso; pero la turbación le ató la lengua" (p. 171).

las—rapid narrative pacing, economical description, the careful pointing of a single action toward the illuminating climax, the concentrating of themes in a powerful central symbol—, the "Spanish Boccaccio" cannot resist unhinging the traditional mechanisms and infusing its conclusion with the indeterminacy that characterizes all his greatest fiction.[82] In *El celoso extremeño*, however, Cervantes's characteristic refusal to endow his works with the rigid structure of definitive pronouncement has a particular appropriateness. It has often been said that freedom is one of Cervantes's greatest themes. The tale of Leonora's confinement is, of course, directly concerned with that theme, and it is revealing that one of Carrizales's methods of increasing the stability of his anxiety-ridden world of illusion and tyranny is through the careful surveillance and censorship of its literature ("His whole house was redolent of virtue, reserve, and modesty, even in the fables which, during the long winter nights, his servants related around the hearth; owing to his presence in not a single one was the slightest sign of lasciviousness visible)."[83] As we move toward the end of *El celoso extremeño*, we note that the disintegration of Carrizales's world and the rules, rituals, and mechanisms which assure the predictability of all experience within it is simultaneous with the "generic" breakdown of the work. Just as Leonora suddenly finds herself delivered from the mechanisms controlling her existence and forced to meet the responsibility of moral choice independently, the reader unexpectedly finds himself deprived of the guidance of the conventional narrator, betrayed by the very literary codes and models which have assisted him in his efforts of comprehension, and compelled to engage actively and independently with a text that, like the house at its center, springs open and is suddenly rent by contradiction, mysterious intimations, and suggestive absences.

Cervantes's fascination with the effects of literature on behavior is evident throughout his works, and, while he can deplore the disruptive and debasing power of bad fiction, he was plainly far more interested in its victims than in those who would shy away from any experience of the alluring world of the literary imagination. There is

---

[82] See J. B. Avalle-Arce's suggestive remarks on Cervantes's rejection of the "closed" ending of his original version of the tale and the transformation of the work into "la obra que nos ofrece el mejor ejemplo de la práctica de las formas abiertas en Cervantes" (Conocimiento y vida en Cervantes," *Deslindes cervantinos* [Madrid, 1961], p. 77).

[83] "aun hasta en las consejas que en las largas noches de invierno, en la chimenea, sus criadas contaban, por estar él presente, en ninguna, ningún género de lascivia se descubría" (p. 103).

a lifelessness in his nonreaders and in his fastidiously selective readers
that clearly suggests that for him the act of reading or listening to
literature is a sign of vitality and openness to development as a human
being. As Américo Castro has shown in various illuminating studies
of the *Quixote*, the "reader" for Cervantes is, like the lover, a person
who is willing to endure the excitement and the perils of seeing beyond, and perhaps stepping beyond the world of habit, ritual, and
mechanism that accounts for so much of our daily experience.[84] Loaysa
is, of course, a sinister Orpheus who perverts the civilizing power of
poetry for his own malicious ends, but there is a sympathy in Cervantes's description of his attractiveness to the children who surround
him in the street, his appeal to the Negro eunuch, the pathetic *"emparedado"* who is driven wild by his music, and his effect on the
innocent Leonora, who yearns to be born and for whom the mysterious
sound of a voice singing a song in the night brings such relief in her
gloomy confinement.

Cervantes, then, rudely deprives his audience of the pleasures of
the passive response at the moment his heroine discovers that her role
can no longer be one of lifeless acquiescence. The reader is compelled
to undergo the enlivening experience of struggling to render intelligible the disturbing elements, of truly collaborating in the creation
of the work, and of learning that part of the elusive mystery which it
recounts lies in the discovery of the responsibility and the uncomfort-
able freedom with which the author dignifies him. *El celoso extremeño*,
which at first glance appears to be the most formulaic of Cervantes's
tales, is in reality one of his most elliptical and elusive, and the
agitation that its disorienting conclusion stimulates in its readers is
registered by the polemical quality that has characterized its interpretations. Américo Castro's various attempts to explore its tantalizing,
treacherous gaps span a half-century, and his final effort at interpretation is prefaced by the revealing admission that he has been wrong
in all his previous attempts to make sense of the climactic scene. Only
after fifty years of struggle has he finally found the key that will

---

[84] See, for example, "La palabra escrita y el 'Quijote,' " *Hacia Cervantes* (Madrid,
1967), pp. 359-408. The book is "un amante o un enemigo con el cual convivir en
enlace de amor o antipatía" (p. 375). "Los libros aparecen aquí como motivación de
la vivencia valorativa de quienes, en virtud de ella, se hacen existentes. . . . La
literatura se hace visible y el vivir individual se aureola de posibilidades poéticas—
tal es la razón de la inmarchitable belleza del *Quijote*. . . . Supuesto esencial de tan
extraño fenómeno es que la palabra escrita sea sentida como realidad de alguien,
vitalizada, y no como simple expresión de fantasías o conocimientos distanciados del
lector. Los libros intervienen aquí a causa de su *vitalidad contagiosa*, y no por ser
'depósitos de cultura' " (pp. 373-74).

unlock its secrets.[85] Perhaps in reality he is no less wrong now than before, or, to put it more accurately, perhaps he was never really wrong at all, for perhaps the quality of response to such a work as *El celoso extremeño* must be measured ultimately as much in terms of the intensity of the struggle for truth as in terms of the validity of the truth attained.

[85] "Cervantes se nos desliza en el 'El celoso extremeño,' " pp. 206, 214-15.

CHAPTER II

Cervantes's *La Gitanilla* as Erasmian Romance

THE HISTORICITY OF *LA GITANILLA*

IF WE COMPARE *La Gitanilla* with its alleged model, the *Book of Apollonius* as transmitted by Juan de Timoneda's *Patrañuelo*, or with such "purer" examples of Cervantine romance as *El amante liberal* and *La española inglesa*, we are immediately struck by the sophistication in its treatment of themes and by the difficulties they impose on its modern readers. For all their primitivism the tales of exotic lands, marvelous adventures, improbable peripeteias and recognitions, and simple conflicts between the good and evil agents are much less remote. They are told in an ethical vocabulary that is intelligible to nearly every age and culture, and insofar as they have a thematic interest, it is in the celebration of such essential and universally admired values as heroism, constant love, chastity, beauty, perseverance, courtesy, and magnanimity. In its total design the *Gitanilla* does belong to this family of stories, and it is probable that its tremendous impact on writers for the next three centuries has been due for the most part to the imaginative appeal of its compelling reworking of a thoroughly conventional situation—the restoration of an irresistibly appealing maiden from her bondage in a demonic, squalid environment to her proper identity and station within society. It is perhaps revealing that one of the first imitators of the *Gitanilla*, Antonio de Solís, extracted from the tale its basic plot and produced a more "timeless" work, a conventional drama of young lovers of different stations confronting parental opposition and triumphing in the comic recognition of the maiden's true identity.[1]

---

[1] See ed. B.A.E. 47. For Alexandre Hardy's adaptation of the tale to the stage and

Solís was a dramatist of modest abilities whose main interest undoubtedly was to please the popular audience of the Spanish *corrales* and who had no doctrinal intentions comparable to those of Cervantes's exemplary tale. It would be injudicious to jump to any conclusions concerning the contemporary understanding of Cervantes's novella on the basis of the playwright's archetypal simplification of his model. However, Solís's formulaic reduction of the work is of critical interest precisely because it leaves many elements unaccounted for, and it is these that make the work so much richer, more puzzling, and more remote for the modern reader than the naive romances. Indeed, a glance at recent criticism of Cervantes's short stories quickly reveals that *La Gitanilla* is probably the tale which has been least satisfactorily clarified. Certain fundamental problems remain to defy modern readers. The ambiguous function of the Gypsy world continues to inspire one-sided, unhistorical interpretations. For example, readers can easily discover in it Cervantes's celebration of the vitalistic nature and wild liberty characteristic of the romantic vision, or they can overlook its ambivalences and symbolic implications by viewing it as merely a representational element and one more indication of his novelist's fascination with local color and subcultures. The shadowy figure of Clemente and his tantalizing, indeterminate relationship with the heroine have provoked various contradictory interpretations, in all of which the element of speculation is pronounced.[2] The poems, which figure so prominently at the beginning and end of the tale, as well as its fragmentary scenes in Madrid, have been by and large overlooked by critics.[3] These and other obscure elements of the *Gitanilla* appear

---

his excision of all elements distracting the audience from the central action of restoring the maiden to her aristocratic class, see Esther J. Crooks, *The Influence of Cervantes in France in the Seventeenth Century* (Baltimore, 1931), pp. 146ff. For the impact of the story on literature of the following centuries, see Wolfgang von Wurzbach, "Die Preziosa des Cervantes," *Studien zur vergleichenden Literaturgeschichte* 1 (1901):391-419.

[2] See, for example, my own interpretation of Clemente's function in relation to the themes of poetry and the initiation of the poet (*Cervantes, Aristotle, and the "Persiles"* [Princeton, 1970], chap. 9). For provocative efforts to fill in the gaps that mark his characterization and action, see J. Casalduero, *Sentido y forma de las "Novelas ejemplares"* (Madrid, 1969), pp. 63-64, Harri Meier, "Personenhandlung und Geschehen in Cervantes *Gitanilla*," *Romanische Forschungen* 51 (1937):125-86, and R. El Saffar, *Novel to Romance* (Baltimore, 1974), pp. 97-98. Wolfram Krömer observes a number of tantalizing elements in the plot which are ultimately disorienting as they are not developed. Clemente, whose role appears to be that of the traditional rival, is the most striking of these "blinde Motive" ("Gattung und Wort *Novela* im Spanischen 17. Jahrhundert," *Romanische Forschungen* 81 [1969]:398-99).

[3] A failure to take the poems seriously can be observed from the remarks on their foolishness by Charles Sorel, one of Cervantes's most important seventeenth-century

to point to spiritual, social, and historical currents of sixteenth- and seventeenth-century Spanish life, and, while it is unlikely that their resistance to definitive critical interpretation will ever be completely overcome, they urgently call for clarification in the extraliterary context of Golden Age culture.

Of all Cervantes's romances, including his ambitious, carefully elaborated final work, *Los trabajos de Persiles y Sigismunda*, none is more directly and complexly involved with the historical reality of Cervantes's time than *La Gitanilla*, and none is more concerned with adapting the conventions of the genre—its ideal worlds and their demonic counterparts, its utopian narrative thrust—to an analytical engagement with problems of the real social and political worlds confronting the author. If in his ironic novella, *El celoso extremeño*, Cervantes explores the ideal of selfhood championed by Erasmus and his followers throughout Europe, in *La Gitanilla* he turns to their thought concerning human relationships, and he exploits a very different kind of traditional literary structure in order to celebrate their ideal of marriage, the family, society, and the state and to illuminate the philosophical-theological foundations upon which the great ideal rested.

La Gitanilla is a tale of courtship and rational wedded love, and its plot depicts the formation of a perfect family in the union of Juan and Preciosa. However, the imaginative reach of the work extends well beyond the ordeals of the young couple, and in the background of their triumph we look upward to the royal family ruling benignly over the larger family of Spain and to the Holy Family redeeming the entire family of mankind. Below them all we glimpse a demonic world opposing their redemptive efforts, and significantly it is presented in its aspect as a family. The conception of the family which animates *La Gitanilla* is grandiose and intensely optimistic, and its roots lie in the thought of Erasmus, for whom marriage was one of the cornerstones of his far-reaching program for the *renovatio* of Christian society. For Erasmus marriage provides the situation in which the individual can ideally realize his highest spiritual potential, through the exercise of *caritas*, amity, and brotherhood, and he envisaged orderly family life as a type of school for the good Christian, the good citizen, and the good prince. What after all is the society of mankind if not a family, whose princes, like Christ with his bride, should rule their wives and children as gentle fathers?[4]

---

disciples, to their occasional omission in twentieth-century editions and translations of the work (see G. Hainsworth, "Quelques opinions françaises [1614-1664] sur les Nouvelles exemplaires de Cervantes [1613]," *Bulletin Hispanique* 32 [1930]:63-70).

[4] The analogies of prince and father, state and family, are characteristic of all of

Many of the most remote aspects of *La Gitanilla* can be clarified if we understand the Erasmian conception of marriage and the nature of the concerns associated with it. Indeed, an important text inscribed in Cervantes's highly literary tale is one of the most influential of the various colloquies that Erasmus devoted to the subject of marriage, and its central function in the articulation of themes in *La Gitanilla* would suggest that it may have been a true "influence," an inspiration for the creation of the novella and Cervantes's most memorable female character. The colloquy provides a fruitful point of departure for the analysis of the entire Spanish text and the unraveling of some of its most difficult mysteries. However, before turning to its presence in the exemplary novella, it is necessary to consider in greater detail the Erasmian ideal of marriage and its fortunes in Spain.

THE FORMATION OF THE
ERASMIAN MARRIAGE IDEAL

The late fifteenth and early sixteenth centuries were a period of intense and disruptive controversy and radically shifting values in the history of the institution of marriage. Repelled by the spectacle of rampant concubinage among ecclesiastics, concerned about the loss of respect that the Church was suffering throughout the Christian world, and sensitive to the increasing secularization of life and to the interests of a powerful new social class and the realities of the materialistic culture which was emerging in its urban centers, clerics and humanists began to examine marriage with greater interest than in the past, exploring the possibilities that it offered the individual for self-fulfillment as a Christian and as a citizen and recognizing that the needs of a new epoch urgently demanded a revision of official doctrines and attitudes. While some of the voices calling for reform were content

---

Erasmus's writings dealing with social and political organization. See, for example, his *Institutio Christiani Matrimonii*: "Quemadmodum autem non multam laudis illi debetur, qui civitatem condere & augere potuit, gubernare non potuit: ita nihil magni faciunt, qui liberis, famulis & opibus augent rem familiarem, nisi quod partum est, recte administrent. Jam ut ex multis civitatibus constat regnum, ex multis domibus civitas, ita domus civitas quaedam est ac regnum. Quum regnum dico, gubernationem dico, alienissimam ab omni tyrannide, in qua tamen summa rerum ab uno pendeat. Is est paterfamilias. Ut vero nec regnum nec civitas constat absque concordia, ita res familiaris collabatur oportet, si adsit dissidium, praesertim inter regni Primates, maritum & uxorem" (*Opera Omnia*, ed. J. Le Clerc, 10 vols. [Leiden, 1703-1706], 5:692F). For the importance of the family in Erasmus's political thought, see Emile Telle, "Érasme et les mariages dynastiques," *Bibliothèque d'Humanisme et Renaissance* 12 (1950):7-13.

with simply challenging the traditional notion of the superiority of celibacy and recommending permission for the marriage of clerics, others, whose understanding of the crisis was not limited by an exclusive fixation on ecclesiastical decadence,[5] proceeded further, exposing the inadequacies in the traditional view of marriage and attempting to "rehabilitate" it, to dignify it with arguments that were unprecedented and directly responsive to the changing conditions of society. In the early period of European capitalism the ascending bourgeoisie was discovering in the family an institution that was well adapted to the accumulation and conservation of property and capital, and statesmen were finding in it an effective basis for national consolidation and political stability. The deficiencies of traditional pronouncements on marriage as little more than the remedy for concupiscence, as an inferior way of life to the contemplative vocation of the celibate, were obvious to many. A new ideal was called for, and it is not surprising that a flood of encomiastic writings concerning marriage, originating in the urban culture of northern Italy of the quattrocento, should spread over Europe in the early years of the sixteenth century.[6]

Deriving their doctrines primarily from the Roman family ideal, the Italians affirmed man's responsibility as a social being and a citizen, celebrated the well-ordered family as the miniature of the state, and emphasized the importance of family relationships in the moral development of the individual.[7] As Ficino puts it in his *Matrimonii Laus*, besides enjoying domestic order, companionship, and security in old age, the individual in marriage meets the lofty obligations of his humanity most easily, cultivating his social nature and exercising his God-given capacities to communicate through speech and to found laws. In domestic life he learns both to serve and to govern society, to love with an enduring love, to bear misfortune with patience, and

---

[5] For the importance of the religious reform movement in the "rehabilitation" of marriage in the sixteenth century, see Emile Telle, *L'Oeuvre de Marguerite D'Angoulême, Reine de Navarre, et La Querelle des Femmes* (Toulouse, 1937), pp. 313ff. See also Telle's other fine study of these matters, *Érasme de Rotterdam et Le Septième Sacrement: Étude d'Évangélisme Matrimonial au XVIe Siècle* (Geneva, 1954).

[6] The popularity of the topic in Florence as early as the turn of the fifteenth century is attested by the sarcastic comment of L. B. Alberti's young bachelor, Lionardo: "qui effunda grandissimi fiumi d'eloquenza in demonstrarmi e lodarmi el coniugio, la società constituta da essa primeva natura, la procreazione de' successori eredi, l'accrescimento e amplificazione della famiglia" (*I libri della famiglia, Opere volgari*, ed. C. Grayson, 3 vols. [Bari, 1960], 1:35-36).

[7] See Telle, *L'Oeuvre de Marguerite D'Angoulême, Reine de Navarre, et La Querelle des Femmes*, p. 317.

to look upon the needs and sufferings of his fellow human beings with the *pietas* that marks his relations with his parents, spouse, and children. He who would live alone, while frequently aspiring to be better than humanity, fails in fact to realize himself as a human being. Men must remember that, following the creation of man, marriage was immediately instituted by God, that it belongs to the sacred mysteries of all peoples, and that such venerable authorities as Socrates, Plato, and Hermes Trismegistus have affirmed its value. Observing that the state consists of families and that its discipline depends on domestic order, Ficino concludes his encomium by exhorting his readers as human beings bonded in friendship to marry, to procreate beings that bear God's image, and to raise and govern them for the good of the republic.[8]

The most important figure in the movement to rehabilitate marriage was Erasmus, whose voluminous writings on the subject, spanning his entire career as a reformer and educator, formed an essential part of his general program for the renovation of Christian society. Erasmus was both the spokesman for the aspirations of the new bourgeoisie and its educator, and in his religious teachings he attempted to persuade his audience that the lofty spirituality which Christians had traditionally been led to believe existed only among martyrs, ascetics, and contemplatives could be experienced outside the walls of monasteries and indeed in the activities that constitute the daily life of the layman in this world. As one historian has noted, the great aim of Erasmus was the "sanctification of lay life," and in the sixteenth century the state of marriage was synonymous with the

---

[8] See *Opera Omnia*, ed. M. Sancipriano, Vol. I, pt. 2 (Torino, 1959), pp. 778-79. See also the popular *Libellus de Dignitate Matrimonii* of Giovanni Campano, where, in addition to nearly all these arguments, we observe a more pronounced interest in the way in which the institution serves the bourgeoisie's material interests. Campano stresses the value of a spouse as an assistant in the care of one's property, adding that it is most miserable to leave one's wealth to strangers and bastards and that "matrimonium certos liberos facit non dubios instituit haeredes." It should be pointed out that Campano anticipated the principal direction that Erasmus would take in his celebration of marriage, that is, finding in Christian doctrines all the available evidence to support the dignity of the institution. Thus Campano, whose influence on Erasmus's *Declamatio Matrimonii* Telle acknowledges, points out that unlike the other sacraments, marriage was instituted before the existence of sin, that its purpose is primarily positive—to enable man's birth rather than to redeem him from sin—and that an *officium* is preferable to a *remedium*. Moreover, he mentions the significance of Christ's reality as the true Husband, of God's choice of a wedded couple for the birth of Himself, of Christ's honoring the wedding ceremony at Cana, and of the Mosaic Law's excusing the newly wedded man from military service for a year (see *Opera* [Venice, 1495], n.p.).

lay order and the active life within it. As Ficino had emphasized, marriage is the ideal state "ad res agendas."[9]

In his controversial *Encomium Matrimonii* Erasmus echoes the principal doctrines expressed in the Italian treatises. All order is based on the marriage unit, the conjugal society. In the imagery that is central in Cervantes's celebration of the same ideal, he asserts that a republic is like a garden and that it will flourish only if the gardener continually plants new shoots. No man can be a good citizen unless he enjoys the experience of producing, raising, and educating children. All civilizations have honored marriage with impressive ceremonies and rites; several have rewarded especially those citizens who produce the most children; some, like the ancient Hebrews, have exempted newlyweds from military service; and many have penalized celibates. Familiar to all Christians are the Mosaic Law's condemnation of sterile marriages and the exclusion from the temple of such men as Joachim, the father of the Virgin Mary. Society has always depended on the family for its survival, and today, more than ever before, the Turkish menace should make citizens aware of their responsibilities to produce children to defend their state. To all these arguments based on the practical considerations which are so typical of the Italian treatises, Erasmus adds traditional religious arguments in favor of marriage. Antiquity honored the institution through the myth of Orpheus's descent to hell and through the cult of Jupiter, Juno, and Lucina as gods of conjugal love and procreation, and there have been few civilizations so barbarous as to deny that marriage is a holy rite. In Christianity marriage is a particularly venerable institution. It is indeed the first of the sacraments, founded by God in paradise and, unlike the other sacraments, given to man before his fall into imperfection. Through wedded harmony man can experience and recall that blessed prelapsarian state when his will, reason, and instinct coexisted in perfect harmony and he desired naturally only what was right and rational. Christ honored matrimony by being born of a married mother

---

[9] *Matrimonii Laus*, pp. 778-79. See H. R. Trevor-Roper, "Religion, the Reformation, and Social Change," in *The European Witch-Craze of the Sixteenth and Seventeenth Centuries* (New York, 1967), pp. 1-45, esp. pp. 24-25. For Erasmus's modernity and his role in the emerging self-awareness of the bourgeoisie and the satisfaction of its demands, see Lucien Febvre, *Au Coeur religieux de xvie siècle* (Paris, 1968), pp. 76ff. "Partout où s'étendait la culture chrétienne, donc latine de langue—partout portait la voix d'Érasme. Sa voix fine, amie, insinuante. Et moderne. La plus moderne sans doute des voix de son temps. Et qu'il voulait entendre sur la bouche même des enfants—à qui il s'efforçait d' apprendre le latin correct: au départ des *Colloques*, il y a ce souci.—Ainsi, au coeur d'une société bourgeoise qui voulait s'instruire, Érasme était l'homme qui prêchait le savoir—et qui faisait tout pour le répandre" (p. 78).

and performing his first miracle at a wedding feast, and, when St.
Paul speaks of the union of Christ and the Church (Eph. 5:21-33), he
compares it to the union of man and wife joined in one flesh, an
analogy that clearly implies the exalted nature of marriage.

Such religious and political-social arguments were common in the
praises of marriage of Erasmus's predecessors. What distinguished his
writings from their treatises was the striking amount of attention that
he gives to the relationship of husband and wife and its possibilities
for perfection. Here Erasmus was truly original, and, while his optimistic views were undoubtedly a response to a widespread need of the
incipient bourgeois culture of the time for a more dignified vision of
marital relations than had been maintained traditionally—emphasizing the conservation of property and the control of concupiscence—
they did not fail to arouse the wrath of his most inveterate enemies
and to give them an opportunity to attack his "heterodoxy" throughout his life. If we look closely at the praises of marriage of such men
as Alberti, Campano, and Ficino, we discover that they confirm Werner Sombart's thesis that throughout the middle ages and the Renaissance, society tended to relegate man's most intense erotic experience—whether the sentiment and spiritual turmoil of romantic yearning
or the excitement of physical sexuality—to his extramarital existence,
and more often than not to condemn such experience from the point
of view of traditional Christian morality.[10] For example, Alberti eloquently argues for the value of the family as an institution that enables
the accumulation and preservation of wealth and contributes to the
strength and orderliness of the state. However, while he praises the
value of a wife as a custodian of her husband's possessions and admits
the value of the friendship and companionship that she provides, he
shows little interest in the possibility that deep feelings may nourish

---

[10] *Luxus und Kapitalismus* (Munich and Leipzig, 1922), chap. 3, "Die Säkularization
der Liebe." Thinkers who considered the nature of marriage tended to view love and
order as mutually exclusive states and to associate marriage with the latter. Sombart
argues that a higher valorization of sexual love is observable with the growing secularization of life which he associates with the growth of capitalism. As for the Protestant reform movement, it contributed enormously to the rehabilitation of marriage
as an institution while dethroning celibacy, but it did little to overcome its traditional disrepute as primarily a necessary concession to the bestial elements in man.
While Luther can refer to marriage as a "paradise" in his denunciations of monks,
his vision of the state is obsessed with the way in which it provides the only legitimate channel for the expression of man's concupiscent urges, and he is capable of
confessing "Scortum, facile possimus amare; conjugem, non item" and asserting that
fear of the law is the primary guarantee of marital fidelity (see Febvre, *Au Coeur
religieux du xvie siècle*, p. 80).

the conjugal bond; he continually reveals a strong contempt for woman, whom man must choose as if he were shopping for an item in the marketplace, and he regards sexual love as bestial and degrading. Indeed, when one of his interlocutors discusses it, he emphasizes that its powers and appeal are felt only in extramarital relations. While he is more optimistic concerning the value of the *benevolentia* and *mutua pietas* that must inform the conjugal relationship, Campano's emphases are basically similar to those of Alberti. A wife is the ideal custodian of property; she produces legitimate heirs to insure its maintenance; she provides companionship and care for her husband. As for sexuality, the traditional assumptions concerning the evils of appetite and marriage as a means of legitimizing concupiscence push their way to the surface repeatedly in the argument. For such thinkers, obsessed as they were with order, erotic experience—whether sentimental or physical—was fundamentally disruptive and consequently at variance with the principal aims of marriage, and it was out of the question to consider that it might indeed be an integral part of the marriage bond.[11]

It remained for Erasmus to revalue this realm of experience and to reconcile it with the more practical and religious aims of marriage. More than any other writer on the subject Erasmus strove to define the lofty spiritual possibilities of the conjugal relationship in human terms, and, while on the one hand he envisioned the friendship of man and wife as exemplifying the rationality, amity, and *caritas* celebrated by contemporary neo-Platonist theorists of love, on the other hand he did not shrink from acknowledging the important role of sexuality in marriage, transposing it from the sphere of "contaminating concupiscence" into the sphere of joyous intimacy and legitimate, healthy pleasure. Whether or not his bold revaluation is attributable primarily to his deep-seated hostility to monasticism and ascetic Christianity and his desire to dethrone the institution of celibacy from its traditional elevation as Telle suggests, Erasmus remained committed to cleansing marriage of the stigma attached to sexuality in nearly

---

[11] See Alberti, *I libri della famiglia*, II; Giovanni Campano, *De Dignitate Matrimonii*. Such attitudes are, of course, characteristic of Western civilization in general, and to discover their continuing presence in Cervantes's epoch, we need only consider Montaigne's declaration that "est ce une espece d'inceste d'aller employer à ce parentage venerable et sacré les efforts et les extravagances de la licence amoureuse. . . . Un bon mariage . . . refuse la compaignie et conditions de l'amour" (*Essais*, 3:5; see Sombart, *Luxus und Kapitalismus*, p. 58), or Torquato Tasso's assertion that the role of the lover is "inconvenientissima a coloro che come padre o madre di famiglia voglion con onestà e con amor maritale regger la casa" (*Il padre di famiglia, Opere*, ed. B. Maier, 5 vols. [Milano, 1963-1965], 4:758-59).

all his writings on the subject, from the controversial *Declamatio Matrimonii* to his defense of the prelapsarian innocence of sex in his response to Clichtove's censorship of his didactic treatise, the *Institutio Christiani Matrimonii*. His most persuasive arguments for a positive valuation of sexuality and a recognition of its central importance in marriage are based on nature, and they are presented most forcefully in the polemical *Declamatio*. According to ancient philosophers and Christian theologians, nature is rationally designed by God so that all created things have a proper purpose to fulfill in their existence. The instinct that leads man to reproduce as well as the pleasure accompanying the act of procreation belongs to the well-founded universal order, and man should properly accept it as a "magnificent gift" to be used properly and gratefully. It is absurd to maintain that the venereal instinct proceeds from sin rather than from nature. Erasmus emphasizes that marriage existed before sin entered the world, that the instinct to reproduce in animals is not regarded as sinful, and that it is in fact the human imagination alone that has tainted the sexual act: "Nor do I give heed to anyone who claims that the 'loathsome urge and prickings of desire' arise not from nature but rather from sin. What can be further from the truth? . . . In short, we, with our imagination, make loathsome what in its own nature is beautiful and holy."[12] Employing the imagery that will reappear in the central scene of his colloquy on courtship and that will emerge as a central motif in its literary descendent, Cervantes's *La Gitanilla*, Erasmus argues that nature offers man a type of rejuvenation and immortality in his offspring, which, like the "transplanted shoot of a tree," "breaks into

---

[12] "Nec audio qui mihi dicat foedam illam pruriginem et Veneris stimulos non a natura, sed peccato profectam. Quid tam dissimile veri? . . . Postremo nos imaginatione foedum reddimus, quod suapte natura pulchrum ac sanctum est" (*Declamatio in Genere Svasorio de Lavde Matrimonii Erasmi Roterodami*, ed J.-C. Margolin, *Opera Omnia*, Vol. I, pt. 5 [Amsterdam, 1975], pp. 398-400). Erasmus probably composed this "rhetorical exercise" toward the end of the fifteenth century, and he published it for the first time in 1518. It circulated widely and became one of his most inflammatory works throughout Europe (see Telle, *Érasme de Rotterdam et Le Septième Sacrement*, pp. 315-45). In 1528 a Spanish translation of the work, by Juan de Molina, appeared in Valencia. It eliminated the polemical tendencies of its Latin model to condemn the abominations of celibacy and concentrated on its principal arguments exalting the state of marriage. In concerning itself exclusively with the positive side of Erasmian thought about marriage, Molina's adaptation looks forward to Cervantes's engagement with the doctrines of the great humanist. For Molina's text and a study of its debts to Erasmus, see Francisco López Estrada, "Textos para el estudio de la espiritualidad renacentista: el opúsculo 'Sermón en loor del matrimonio' de Juan de Molina (Valencia, por Jorge Costilla, 1528)," *Revista de Archivos, Bibliotecas y Museos* 61 (1955):489-530.

leaf once again after the tree has been cut down,"[13] and he urges man to the pleasurable cultivation of his plot of land that produces the best crop—human beings.

In acknowledging the importance of sexuality in marriage and arguing for its value, Erasmus was countering the deeply entrenched hostility to man's instinctual nature which had informed most official pronouncements on marriage, from St. Augustine's response to Jovinian to those reiterated by his contemporary critics, and which indeed continued to give a puritanical flavor to such otherwise generally optimistic considerations of the subject as Alberti's *I libri della famiglia*, Campano's *Libellus de Dignitate Matrimonii*, Vives's *Institutio Feminae Christianae*, and Luis de León's *La perfecta casada*. And there can be no doubt that his arguments concerning sexuality constitute one of the strikingly "modern" aspects of his theories on marriage. However, it should be pointed out that, while acknowledging the importance of physical love and sanctioning its value, Erasmus placed much more emphasis on spiritual rather than on instinctual fulfillment. His view of the instincts is anything but that of the libertine, and his didactic writings are full of denunciations of the "epicurean" or "Turkish" license of self-indulgent Christians.[14] Moreover, all his writings on

---

[13] "planta . . . repullulat arbore excise" (*Declamatio Matrimonii*, p. 410).

[14] If it is misleading to overemphasize Erasmus's affirmative statements concerning sexual love, it is equally misleading to extract his cautionary statements and conclude that his attitudes are fundamentally puritanical. Francisco Márquez Villanueva's recent argument distinguishing Cervantes's penetrating understanding of the realities of the marital relationship from Erasmus's naive, moralizing approach to the subject proceeds on an assumption which is, in my opinion, questionable—that Erasmus' disdain for sexuality is basically similar to that of Vives (see *Personajes y temas del Quijote* [Madrid, 1975], pp. 68-70). Vives's entire view of marriage is informed by a strongly patriarchal attitude toward male dominance, a harshly misogynistic conception of the foibles of women, and an obsessive contempt for the body and instinctual needs. For example, in his *Institutio Feminae Christianae* (1523), he can observe that "quamlibet speciosum corpus feminae nihil esse aliud quam sterquilinium candido et purpureo velo opertum," that the best wives are those who take no pleasure in sex and who reduce their husbands to chastity, and that sexual enjoyment is rooted entirely in "sordida ac despicata natura" (see *Opera Omnia*, ed. G. Mayáns y Siscar, 8 vols. [Valencia, 1782-1790], 4:211-223); for Vives's "constant debasement of the body" and his view of "marital sex as a brutalizing experience justified only as a means of childbearing and as a remedy to man's concupiscence," see Carlos G. Noreña, *Juan Luis Vives* [The Hague, 1970], pp. 200-212). Márquez claims that Erasmus values marriage "sólo como instrumento, como póliza para una vida ordenada y sin sobresaltos con que granjear, además, en su día, el descanso eterno. Trátase en el fondo de una idea egoísta, prosaica y burguesa, en que la pasión no entra en juego sino como elemento disruptor. El deseo sexual seguía siendo mirado con los malos ojos connaturales con el legado teológo agustiniano" (p. 69). Certainly the vociferous

marriage, including the colloquy which determined to some extent
the thematic texture of *La Gitanilla*, are filled with cautionary statements against an immoderate reliance on sex, and much of his reasoning on the evils of clandestine marriage and the justification of divorce
is based on his awareness of the weakness of a marriage founded solely
on instinctual attraction. Indeed his fundamental ideal of marital perfection is the paradoxical notion that emerges in both his colloquy on
courtship and Cervantes's *La Gitanilla*. The ideal of chastity is truly
realized not in the confines of monastery walls but rather within a
marriage, whenever the bond uniting the two human beings is founded
in *caritas*, friendship, mutual benevolence, piety, and rationality and
is nourished by spiritual communication and the pleasures of intimacy. In words that anticipate the arguments of the hero of the colloquy on courtship and Cervantes's Preciosa, Erasmus affirms that
"chastity and purity are in fact preserved in the conjugal relationship"
and that a man "who loves conjugally is close to virginity."[15] Analyzing the conjugal bond, he asserts that nothing in nature is more firm
and happy than the union of wife and husband, in which continual
close contact is marked by faith, trust, and pleasure and is entirely
free from the dissimulation that troubles even the best of friendships.
Invoking once again the principle of natural design, Erasmus argues
that nature produces man so that he may cultivate *"benevolentia"* and
"amicitia," that no one is born for himself alone, and that a man who
rejects society is not a man. The society of marriage is the ideal society, and a man who shuns it resembles the wild animals living in
the solitudes of the wilderness. He is like Timon, the archetypal man-
hater, like the mythical giants, who in a self-destructive rebellion

---

official critics of Erasmus's doctrines of marriage did not read his various pronouncements on the subject this way. He was accused of espousing the Jovinian heresy, of
promulgating Epicurean license and naturalism, and of ignoring the damage wrought
to the natural order by Adam's fall (see his rebuttal of the critics in his *Dilutio Eorum
Quae Iodocus Clithoveus Scripsit Adversus Declamationem Des. Erasmi Roterodami Suasoriam
Matrimonii*, ed. E. Telle [Paris, 1968]). In other words, he was viewed as anything
but a puritan. In his famous colloquy, *The Epicurean*, he writes of sexual pleasure:
"Here too the godly man wins, no less than in dining. Look at it this way: the
stronger his devotion to his wife, the more pleasurable is the marriage bed" (*The
Colloquies of Erasmus*, trans. C. R. Thompson [Chicago, 1965], p. 549). As I shall
point out below, the colloquy that is echoed in Cervantes's *La Gitanilla* takes quite
an affirmative view of the joys of sexuality in a marriage, and it envisions in the
relationship of husband and wife far more than its conveniences as an instrument for
the guarantee of order and tranquility in this world.

[15] ". . . sanctissimum vitae genus est, pure casteque seruatum coniugium. . . .
minimum abest a virginitatis laude, qui ius illibatum coniugii seruat, qui vxorem
gignendae proli, non libidini habet" (*Declamatio Matrimonii*, pp. 402-404).

defied the universal order and perished, and in his insensitivity and inhumanity, his life can be fittingly compared to the existence of a stone. As for the loss of independence that accompanies marriage, Erasmus asserts that, quite the contrary, marriage is an institution enabling human beings to experience the highest kind of freedom, that is, the freedom that accompanies the decision of two human beings, acting rationally and under no compulsion, to bind themselves to each other in friendship. This is the freedom that, as we shall see, Preciosa insists on maintaining and compels her importunate lover to exercise in Cervantes's *La Gitanilla*. In a climactic moment of his oration which looks forward to Clemente's words of encouragement to Preciosa as the novella turns toward its crisis, Erasmus exhorts his audience: "If, then, you are moved in any way by honor, by filial, religious, or civic duty, or by virtue, why do you shrink away from that which God has instituted, nature has made holy, which reason advocates, and which sacred and humanist writings alike praise, which our laws enjoin, and which is approved by the agreement of all nations, and toward which the example of every great man urges us?"[16]

While the basic outlines of the Erasmian marriage ideal are clearly set forth in the polemical *Declamatio*, the humanist's emphasis on the lofty spiritual relationship that unites husband and wife is much more evident in his carefully composed didactic treatise, the *Institutio Christiani Matrimonii*, written for Catherine of Aragon nearly thirty years later. Indeed it can be argued that as a polemical document, presented behind the protective mask of the rhetorical paradox, the *Declamatio* tends to give an imbalanced view of Erasmus's attitudes toward sexuality in marriage.[17] The *Institutio* was not conceived as an antidote to the "poisons of celibacy," which Erasmus observed infecting the Christian community; one notes quickly that its sanctions of sexuality are muted, that they are not supported with the enthusiastic arguments based on nature which filled the *Declamatio*, and that they are in fact occasionally qualified by cautionary statements informed by traditional puritanical attitudes. Nevertheless, the affirmative view is clearly maintained despite the subdued tones appropriate to such a

---

[16] "Quare si quid honestum, si pietas, si religio, si officium, si virtus te mouet, cur ab eo abhorres quod Deus instituit, natura sanxit, ratio suadet, diuinae pariter et humanae literae laudant, leges iubent, omnium gentium consensus approbat, ad quod optimi cuiusque exemplum adhortatur?" (*Declamatio Matrimonii*, p. 406).

[17] One can of course argue the contrary view, that such ironic statements afford a glimpse of the true or authentic attitude of a man who was well aware of the subversive and dangerous character of such doctrines.

didactic treatise and to such a reader as Catherine of Aragon, a person who was deeply disturbed by the contemporary crisis that marriage was undergoing. Again Erasmus refuses to allow that the conjugal relationship, a part of the "well-designed nature" (*bene condita natura*) that was damaged by Adam's fall, is in itself sinful or a transmitter of the original sin that taints the newborn Christian, and again he insists that all parts of the human body were created by God as good and beautiful. He argues that physical love is a natural and effective bond in a harmonious marriage, and he proceeds to offer sensible advice on how the bride and groom should minimize the risks of alienating one another on their wedding night. Erasmus speaks of the wedding night as a solemn rite and suggests that marriage, the conjugal act, and its fruits should all be viewed positively as integral parts of the mysterious process that culminates in the rebirth of the "new man" through baptism.[18]

In the *Institutio* Erasmus develops most thoroughly his ideas on the necessity of cultivating a spiritual bond in marriage. His arguments are drawn to a great extent from neo-Platonic theories of love, and they look forward to Preciosa's education of her courtier in Cervantes's first novella.[19] Erasmus points out that lovers must learn to view each other with "philosophical eyes" and to seek the "formam animi," rather than corporeal beauty, which is subject to time and accidents of fortune. Internal beauty, internal wealth, internal nobility must "*conciliare*" Christian marriage, for only through their contemplation and the discovery therein of the ideal beauty of the creation does the couple experience the *benevolentia* that will enable their relationship to endure ("Indeed that alone is sufficient to bond enduring love and good will").[20] Erasmus acknowledges that youth in all its fervor and lack of experience must learn to achieve such a bond, and he recommends that parents exhort young couples to be patient with one another, to spend time getting acquainted, and to take a compromising approach toward the resolution of quarrels and initial difficulties, for it is through such rationally controlled efforts and not through the gratification of impulse that they can nourish an enduring love ("benevolentiam perpetuam alere"). In a comparison that eloquently pro-

---

[18] See *Institutio Christiani Matrimonii*, pp. 622C, 718D, 674F-675C, 622B; see Telle, *Érasme de Rotterdam et Le Septième Sacrement*, p. 418.

[19] For the importance of neo-Platonic doctrines in Erasmus's marriage ideal, see Telle, *Érasme de Rotterdam et Le Septième Sacrement*, pp. 418-20; for their presence in Cervantes's ideal, see below.

[20] "Ea vel sola sufficit ad conglutinandam perpetuam benevolentiam" (*Institutio Christiani Matrimonii*, p. 665B; see also pp. 665, 681-82).

claims his faith in man's capacities and responsibilities to fulfill himself by working rationally and creatively with what is given him by nature, Erasmus writes that the properly cultivated marital relationship is like the piece of pottery that the artisan carefully glues together and allows to dry slowly; he warns: "the ones nature has joined are broken more quickly than those that are held together by glue."[21] Erasmus proceeds to offer detailed advice on how the partners can approach this ideal. For example, they should offer each other companionship and continually remind themselves that a sharing of life means more than merely cohabiting: "Living together is an association of pleasures and responsibilities, play and seriousness, joyful and sad moments."[22] They should never forget the great gift of language and its communicative power to bind a society in good will. Conversation is a means of companionship, comfort, gentle guidance, and civilized dissimulation. The partners in a marriage should respect one another as equals, taking pleasure in each other's achievements and excellences and striving to realize a friendship that exemplifies Christ's teachings on the essential equality of all Christians.[23] They should delight in mutual enterprises, the most rewarding of which is perfecting themselves in virtue while embellishing a home and creating and raising children for Christ. In short, in his didactic treatise *Institutio Christiani Matrimonii* Erasmus explores at great length the ways in which man and woman are to realize the perfection that is possible in a marital relationship, the *"benevolentia"* and the *"mutua caritas"* which *"condulcabit omnia"* ("will sweeten everything"). And perhaps the most notable aspect of the work is its determination to translate the traditional theological truth that married love symbolizes the *caritas* binding Christ and the Church into such terms as can be meaningful in the concrete daily life of his fellow Christians.

[21] "citiusque franguntur ea quae natura junxerat, quam quae glutino comissa sunt" (*Institutio Christiani Matrimonii*, p. 671E; see also, p. 691).

[22] "Convictus est voluptatum & curarum, jocorum ac seriorum, laetorum ac tristium societas" (*Institutio Christiani Matrimonii*, p. 674C).

[23] Erasmus writes that they should look on one another not with the eye of the Pharisee, which maliciously probes for distinctions and hierarchies of value but rather with the simple "dovelike" eye ("columbinus elle simplex & Euangelicus oculus"), which is guided by the awareness of the fundamental bonds uniting all men and of the fact that among Christians "non oportet esse morosam aestimationem aequalitatis, quos Dominus Jesus, cuius auspiciis coeunt nuptiae, tot modis aequavit, eadem morte redemit, eodem sanguine lavit, eadem fide justificavit, eodem spiritu vegetat, iisdem roborat Sacramentis, eodem dignatur honore cognominis, fratres illos vocans ac filios Dei, ad eamdem haereditatem vitae coelestis vocavit omnes" (*Institutio Christiani Matrimonii*, p. 685C,D,E).

Nearly all the principal features of the matrimonial ideal that Erasmus traced in his didactic, exegetical, and polemical works appeared in the *Colloquies*, the collection of dialogues that rendered the *Philosophia Christiana* easily accessible in schools, houses, cities, and courts throughout Europe.[24] Perhaps the best indication of the centrality of the marriage ideal in his program of spiritual renovation is the fact that Erasmus dedicated four colloquies entirely to its exposition and dealt with it indirectly in numerous others. The matrimonial colloquies were perhaps the most popular and controversial of the dialogues, and they were among the first translated into the vernacular. Erasmus's admirers found them, in their lively dialogue and highly topical subject matter, the most suitable of the colloquies to dramatic performance; it was probably through the issues that they raised that enormous numbers of readers could understand the profound doctrines of Erasmus's "true theology" in practical terms. If, as Emile Telle observes, marriage has at all times been "le lieu 'géométrique' des préoccupations morales, sociales, économiques, physiologiques, mystiques de la société,"[25] an institution bringing the average person into an existentially meaningful encounter with such basic problems as freedom, restraint, morality, self-fulfillment, social order, and religion, in the period of the Reformation the public controversies that raged around such issues as monastic vows, celibacy, and the sacramental foundation of marriage, as well as the general demands for a new dignity in marriage raised by the new social and economic forces of a society in crisis, could only sharpen the public's sensitivity to all the vital issues associated with the institution and heighten its interest in the dialogues that attempted to confront them with such intelligence, modesty, and good humor. Certainly the strongholds of orthodoxy and tradition were aware of their appeal and their challenge. They were among the colloquies that inspired the most hostility, and like nearly all Erasmus's writings on marriage, they aroused an active response from the Sorbonne. Nearly one-quarter of the points of denunciation in its censorship of the *Colloquies* were directed against three of the matrimonial dialogues, including the one whose celebra-

---

[24] Originating as manuals and conversational guides for young students of Latin, the "*Colloques* se transformèrent pour se conformer aux tendances et aux passions du jour: ils devinrent ce que nous appellerions des cours populaires de paulinisme appliqué, à l'usage exclusif des adultes, clercs ou laïques, nobles ou roturiers, petits ou grands, hommes ou femmes, tenant à y voir clair dans l'obscurité que nous persistons à appeler du nom de Renaissance" (Telle, *Érasme de Rotterdam et Le Septième Sacrement*, p. 299).

[25] Ibid., p. 295.

tion of the marriage ideal and eloquent commentary on individual freedom and responsibility are echoed nearly a century later in Cervantes's *La Gitanilla*.[26]

As Marcel Bataillon has shown, the Erasmian *Philosophia Christi* was received in Spain with an enthusiasm unmatched in any other nation in the Catholic world. Spain was the country where the humanist's ideas seemed to be truly popularized, where, to paraphrase Juan Maldonado's letter to Erasmus, "the learned engaged in daily discussions and arguments concerning his writings, children speak only of him in their schools, and even the unlettered constantly sing his praises."[27] The immense popularity was due in large measure to the success of the *Colloquies*, translated into Spanish by such men as Alonso de Virués and Diego Morejón and made available to the public in various printed editions between 1527 and 1532. These works formed "the boldest attack launched by Spanish Erasmism in the period of its most intense propaganda."[28] As they selected specific dialogues from Erasmus's collection for publication, the Spanish editors and translators were interested not primarily in promulgating the most subversive and inflammatory criticisms in the Erasmian reform program but rather in popularizing his fundamental teachings, those intended to instruct men to exemplify in all phases of their lives, from birth to death, the piety, charity, humanity, rationality, and joy that were the cornerstones of his Christian philosophy. In the words of one of their Spanish editors, the colloquies "are necessary for living well and dying well; because, as Seneca tells us, the largest part of an individual's life should be spent in learning how to live well and the entirety of it in preparing for a good death."[29] For Erasmus the way of "good living" and preparation for the good death was not that of the ascetic or the contemplative, but rather that of the charitable Christian, the concerned citizen, the responsible family head, and the good friend. In other words, his program was a program for the active life, and his Spanish editors were true to its emphases when they included in their collection of eleven dialogues the two most important colloquies presenting his marriage ideal. An indication of the popularity of their subject and the need that society felt for their teachings is the fact that they were the first of the colloquies translated and printed in

---

[26] For the Sorbonne's censorship, see ibid., pp. 309-310.

[27] *Erasmo y España*, trans. A. Alatorre (Mexico, 1966), p. 217.

[28] Ibid., p. 309.

[29] "son necesarios para bien vivir y bien morir; porque, como dice Séneca, la mayor parte de la vida se debe gastar en aprender a bien vivir, y toda para bien morir" (see ibid., p. 289).

Spanish and circulated as single works for a few years before the collections appeared.

In the period of reaction that followed Erasmus's death and culminated in the broad censorship of his works at the Council of Trent, the *Colloquies* were frequently subjected to a censorship and condemnation, which usually lamented the powerful influence which as school textbooks they exercised in the formative years of young men and women.[30] Nevertheless, they continued to be read, and the great popularity of Pedro de Luxán's *Coloquios matrimoniales*, which reproduced Erasmus's colloquy on marriage and borrowed from his *Puerpera* and *Pietas Puerilis*, suggests both their continuing presence in Spanish cultural life and, more specifically, the continuing enthusiasm for Erasmus's doctrines concerning marriage.[31]

Perhaps the most striking testimony of the intensity and universality of the marriage controversy in the late Renaissance is the extent to which it emerged as a central theme in the literature of the age. From the narrative fiction of Marguerite de Navarre and Rabelais to the drama of Molière and the epic poetry of Milton, the various preoccupations and problems surrounding marriage continued to inspire literary exploitation and provide writers with subjects that they could count on to interest their public. Of the many great writers who addressed themselves to these issues, there was none who did so with more persistence, fascination, or profundity of thought than Cervantes.[32] It is no exaggeration to say that a fervent interest in marriage characterizes his entire literary production, from the early pastoral romance, the *Galatea*, in which the neo-Platonic spokesman, Tirsi,

[30] Ibid., pp. 501-505.

[31] Ibid., p. 649; between 1560 and 1589 eleven editions of this work appeared. As I point out below, it seems likely that Cervantes read it.

[32] For studies of various aspects of the theme of marriage in Cervantes's works, see the following: Ricardo del Arco, "Mujer, amor, celos, y matrimonio vistos por Cervantes," *Biblioteca y Boletín de Menéndez y Pelayo* 28 (1952):133-65; Marcel Bataillon, "Cervantes et la 'Mariage chrétien,' " *Bulletin Hispanique* 49 (1947):129-44; Américo Castro, *El pensamiento de Cervantes* (Barcelona, 1972), pp. 376-78; Francisco Márquez Villanueva, *Personajes y temas del Quijote*, pp. 59ff.; R. V. Piluso, *Amor, matrimonio y honra en Cervantes* (New York, 1967); C. Rodríguez-Arango Díaz, "El matrimonio clandestino en la novela cervantina," *Anuario de Historia del Derecho Español* 25 (1955):731-74; S. E. Trachmann, *Cervantes' Women of Literary Tradition* (New York, 1932). In view of the extensive literature on the subject, the slight attention that the exposition and celebration of the marriage ideal in *La Gitanilla* has received is striking. An exception is Casalduero's *Sentido y forma de las "Novelas ejemplares,"* which correctly emphasizes the centrality of the theme of marriage in all of the tales and considers the idealization of Preciosa against the background of Luis de León's *La perfecta casada* (see pp. 71-75).

envisions the culmination of love in a rational marriage, to the drama based on the experiences of his youth, *Los baños de Argel*, which includes in its rapidly shifting survey of the Islamic world of captivity a brief glimpse at the Arab marriage rite, to the final pages of the posthumous romance, the *Persiles*, in which the pilgrims discuss the problem of the validation of the "deceitful" marriage of Isabela and Andrea and the narrator caustically reminds the reader how state officials exploit the problems raised by clandestine marriages for personal profit.[33]

Probably the most striking characteristic of Cervantes's literary treatment of the theme of marriage is its complexity, a feature deriving in part from his insistence on approaching the subject in a variety of literary genres and in part from his understanding of the protean nature of the subject itself. In the farcical setting of the courtroom, he compels his audience to overhear amid the clamorous comedy of situation and character a profound analysis of the disturbing problem of psychological incompatibility and to consider, if only momentarily, the possibility that the reiterated slogan, "the worst of marriages beats the best divorce" may in fact be a principle more suited to the proper conclusion of a work of literature than to the solution of human problems.[34] In the philosophical atmosphere of the *Novelas ejemplares* he examines the marital relationship in conjunction with all the fundamental problems it raises concerning the ethical nature of man; the individual and his social relationships; freedom, self-fulfillment, and restraint; rationality and instinct; and civic responsibility. In the world of everyday reality which forms the settings for Don Quixote's wanderings, misadventures, and conversations, he can pause to let his character discourse, in the sober didactic tones that recall the human-

---

[33] *La Galatea*, ed. J. B. Avalle-Arce, 2 vols. (Madrid, 1961), 2:62; *Los baños de Argel, Obras completas*, ed. A. Valbuena Prat (Madrid, 1956), pp. 314-17. *Los trabajos de Persiles y Sigismunda*, ed. J. B. Avalle-Arce (Madrid, 1969), pp. 413, 330. Cervantes's satirical allusion to such abuses recalls Gargantua's tirade on the exploitation of clandestine marriages by clerics (Rabelais, *Le Tiers Livre*, chap. 48) and Marguerite of Navarre's tale presenting the sufferings of a victim of such practices (*Heptaméron*, 56).

[34] "más vale el peor concierto/ que no el divorcio mejor" (*El juez de los divorcios, Obras completas*, ed. A. Valbuena Prat, p. 544). One can agree with M. Bataillon and E. Telle that the little play, designed for a popular audience, makes the point quite forcefully that the "human orthodoxy" of the age was not ready to consider seriously divorce as a possible remedy for marital difficulties. The profundity of the farce, nevertheless, lies in the sensitivity with which it compels its audience to examine and reconsider the problematic character of its "orthodox" conviction. See Bataillon, "Cervantes et le 'Mariage chrétien,'" and Telle *Érasme de Rotterdam et Le Septième Sacrement*, p. 353.

ist colloquies, on the practical problems and responsibilities of a family head. And in the remote landscapes of romance he can turn from criticism and analysis to celebration, tracing an ideal of marital perfection in mythic terms. But, as we shall see, this ideal is nourished by the critical spirit which is everywhere visible in his works and in those of the man whose spirit so profoundly influenced his development.[35]

The profundity and variety in Cervantes's engagement with the problem of marriage are all the more striking if we consider the dominant view of the institution in Spain of his epoch. From Guzmán de Alfarache's discovery that one's wife is one's worst enemy, through the innumerable marital disasters depicted in the popular picaresque novels and the hopelessly destructive relations between the sexes in Maria de Zayas's feminist *novelas*, to Baltasar Gracián's codification of an ethics of solitude reflecting to some extent the darkest wisdom of the picaresque hero, Spanish literature is marked by a resurgence of the most somber of traditional ascetic attitudes concerning the married state as an obstacle to spiritual perfection and salvation, the evils of concupiscence, and the rapacity that binds and motivates people in marriages. If the innumerable pronouncements on the shortcomings of women are any indication of the prevailing attitudes of society, then it is clear that the Erasmian program for reform of this most fundamental of human relationships had failed.[36] The vision of perfection traced in the humanist's treatises and promulgated in his col-

---

[35] The question of the mode of transmission by which Erasmus's thought reached Cervantes has still not been answered satisfactorily, and it seems unlikely at this point that the traditional methods of influence study are going to lead to a definitive clarification. As Bataillon has noted, the search for "sources" has yielded very little. Indeed most of the ones which Castro discovered in support of his own "Erasmist" reading of Cervantes's works in *El pensamiento de Cervantes* will not stand up to rigorous examination. This is particularly true of those which he found in the *Colloquies*, one of the Erasmian works which circulated most widely and was most frequently subjected to censorship (see M. Bataillon, *Erasmo y España*, pp. 799-801). As I have pointed out above, Bataillon suggests that the only sensible way to pursue the subject at this point is through "estudios comparativos que tomaran en cuenta no sólo las ideas, sino también su expresión, y que tuvieran por objeto ideas típicamente erasmianas" (p. 799). In what follows I hope to reveal the presence of the *Colloquies* in Cervantes's *La Gitanilla* primarily in terms of its central ideas and their articulation in its structure, although I do believe that this is one case in which verbal correspondences between influencing and receptor texts can in fact be found.

[36] For the degeneration in the relations of the sexes, the stifling of women's freedom, and the resulting tensions within the strife-ridden Spanish society of the seventeenth century, see José Antonio Maravall, "Los españoles de 1600," *Triunfo* 532 (December 1972):15-19. For María de Zayas the prevalent codes of courtship and educational patterns are designed to impose a state of slavish submission on women.

loquies might have seemed more utopian than ever amid the fulmi-
nations that echoed from the pulpits of Spain and proliferated in the
most popular "realistic" literature of the time.[37] And yet, while Juan
de la Cerda was proclaiming that "the rod is the proper medicine for
the madness of young ladies, and parents should at no time show
tenderness to their children; rather should they maintain them in
fear," while Guzmán de Alfarache was learning through his family
misfortunes the truth that, as one contemporary moralist put it, only
through an exacerbated sense of shame can a young woman refrain
from flying "into all forms of vice like an unbridled beast and a horse
without spurs," and while Hernando de Santiago was recalling St.
Crisóstomo's words to warn his parishioners of the dangers in marriage: "What else is a woman but an enemy to friendship?"— Cervantes, perhaps recalling youthful aspirations which his own life had
sadly failed to fulfill, was quietly tracing the figure of his little Gypsy
maiden as an irresistible spokesman for the necessity of freedom in
the moral growth of an individual, whether male or female. And as
he allows her to still the wild horse raging in her infatuated courtier
and guide him to a state of perfect friendship, which, sanctified in
Christian marriage, replicates on earth the harmony of the celestial
spheres, he offers eloquent testimony to the survival of an ideal which,
although perhaps anachronistic in its time, is so modern that it continues to appeal and to elude us today.[38]

LA GITANILLA AND ERASMUS'S
COLLOQUY ON COURTSHIP

In the crucial scene that begins the courtship of Juan de Cárcamo
and Preciosa, the maiden speaks at great length on the dangers of

[37] See Thomas Hanrahan, *La mujer en la novela picaresca española*, 2 vols. (Madrid,
1967), esp. 1: chap. 5: "Ascetismo y feminismo."

[38] "la vara es medicina para la locura de las niñas; y en ningún tiempo el padre ni
la madre no deven alagar a sus hijos, sino hazerles que tengan miedo" (Juan de la
Cerda, *Vida política de todos los estados de mugeres*); "como bestia desenfrenada y como
caballo sin espuelas en todo mal" (Martín de Córdoba, *Jardín de nobles doncellas*); "Quid
aliud est mulier quam amicitiae inimica" (Hernando de Santiago, "Sermón en honor
de San José"; see Hanrahan, *La mujer en la novela picaresca española*, pp. 93-94, 135-
36, 89. In her comprehension of rational love and her insistence that time must
elapse if it is to develop, Preciosa belongs to a group of people whose understanding
of love Guzmán de Alfarache ridicules as he reflects on his marriage: "Amé con mirar
y tanta fue su fuerza contra mí, que me rindió en un punto. *No fue necesario transcurso
de tiempo, como algunos afirman y yerran*" (see Hanrahan, p. 167; italics added). For
Guzmán marriage is little more than a "remedy," and an ineffectual one at that, for
man's inherent bestiality.

infatuation, the beauty of virginity, the meaning of marriage, the necessity of proceeding circumspectly in courtship, and the importance of freedom and trust in a love relationship. She claims to be possessed by a "certain fantastic spirit" dwelling within her and stirring her to "great things" and acknowledges that her wisdom, which appears so far beyond the reach of a girl of fifteen, derives from her "natural goodness" rather than from her experience in the environment of the Gypsy world. The maturity of her speech astonishes even her guardian, who exclaims: "take heed of what you are saying, for a professor of Salamanca would not say such things! You know of love! You know of jealousy! You know of confidences! How is this? Do you take me for mad? I am listening to you as to one possessed by spirits who speaks in Latin without knowing it."[39] The laudatory exclamation is comparable to Sancho Panza's enthusiastic reaction to Don Quixote's lengthy speech to Basilio on the difficulties of married life and the obligations of a good husband in that both outbursts of admiration underscore the significance of the discourse and the prestige of its subject matter in contemporary learned and ecclesiastical circles.[40] However, in the case of Preciosa's "Latin," it is tempting to suspect Cervantes of playfully tipping his hand as a writer and inviting his reader to hear in the words of the little Gypsy the voice of one of Erasmus's most memorable heroines.

As I shall try to make clear in the following analysis, Preciosa is one of Cervantes's most literary characters, and the powerful imaginative appeal which she has held for readers and writers of the follow-

---

[39] "tengo un cierto espiritillo fantástico acá dentro, que a grandes cosas me lleva"; "¡mira que dices cosas, que no las diría un colegial de Salamanca! Tú sabes de amor, tú sabes de celos, tú de confianzas: ¿cómo es esto? que me tienes loca, y te estoy escuchando como a una persona espiritada, que habla latín sin saberlo," *Novelas ejemplares*, ed. F. Rodríguez Marín, 2 vols. (Madrid, 1957-1962), 1:38, 43; the following page references in my text are to this edition.

[40] ". . . digo dél que cuando comienza a enhilar sentencias y a dar consejos, no sólo puede tomar púlpito en las manos, sino dos en cada dedo, y andarse por esas plazas a ¿qué quieres, boca? ¡Válete el diablo por caballero andante, que tantas cosas sabes!" (*Don Quijote de la Mancha*, ed. Luis A. Murillo, 2 vols. [Madrid, 1978], 2: 204). Don Quixote's recommendations concerning the importance of "buena fama" in one's choice of a wife recall the popular treatise on marriage by the Erasmist Pedro de Luxán, *Coloquios matrimoniales* (1550); Don Quixote: "Lo primero, le aconsejaría que mirase más a la fama que a la hacienda; porque la buena mujer no alcanza la buena fama solamente con ser buena, sino con parecerlo; que mucho más dañan a las honras de las mujeres las desenvolturas y libertades públicas que las maldades secretas." Luxán: "La primera [virtud] es que sea la mujer vergonzosa, porque si una mujer no hubiese de haber más de una virtud forzosa, ésta había de ser la vergüenza. Mayor mal es para el vulgo y aun para el marido que la mujer sea públicamente desvergonzada, que no que sea secretamente mala" (Madrid, 1943), p. 21.

ing three centuries is due in part to the radiant constellation of literary, legendary, and mythic females who surround her and mysteriously
become her—St. Anne, the Virgin, Tarsiana-Truhanilla, the archetypal maiden of purity and musical harmony, Luis de León's "La perfecta casada," the ideal wife of Proverbs, Dame Poetry, Venus, Circe,
the infernal siren, the celestial siren, the folkloric "rain maiden," and
the quasi-mythical redemptive princess, Margarita of Austria. As her
numerous admirers have often recognized, there is in Preciosa an irresistibly attractive blend of spirituality and earthiness, and it is clear
that she belongs to the world of everyday reality far more than any of
these fabulous or legendary figures. However, what has not been recognized by modern readers is the degree to which the earthy side of
her characterization, which they admiringly attribute to Cervantes's
novelistic talents or his gift for the accurate observation of reality, is
in fact mediated through literary figures which, in a way similar to
that of the more familiar analogues, imaginatively expand and enhance the significance of her actions and pronouncements. If the figure
of the other dancing Gypsy maiden of Spanish literature, "La Lozana
Andaluza," looms behind Preciosa's most scathing and cynical pronouncements concerning the corruption of the society that adores her,
when she speaks in inspired tones for the value of good sense, moderation, and rationality and gently guides her lover to a state of perfect
vision and understanding, it is Erasmus's heroine who comes into view
at her side. Although the quietly sensible Maria is an unfamiliar figure
to the imagination of the modern reader and although, in her cautionary pronouncements concerning the seductive powers of the fantasy, she would oppose precisely the type of literary magic by which
Cervantes exploits her in order to transmute her descendent into myth,
her soft voice merges easily with those of the more obtrusive ideal
females who accompany Preciosa. Its tones were probably clearly audible to the sixteenth-century reader, who had to face quite seriously
the implications of the inflexible principle underlying all official marital philosophy, the principle that, as Cervantes put it in *El juez de
los divorcios*, "the worst of marriages beats the best divorce."

In his colloquy on courtship, *Proci et Puellae*, Erasmus addresses
himself to the problems attending the choice of a marital partner. He
develops his ideas in a dramatic encounter between Maria, a beautiful,
intelligent, and forceful maiden, and Pamphilus, an infatuated youth
who employs some sophisticated and some sophistical means of persuasion to win her immediate consent to a marriage. His passionate
entreaties, his lack of concern about the necessity of obtaining the
consent of her parents, and his insistence that she pronounce the three
words of consent which Erasmus elsewhere bewails as the source of so

much misery among married couples,[41] suggest, moreover, that the youth is willing to enter a clandestine marriage. Maria feels genuine affection for her suitor, but she steadfastly resists his urgings, reminding him of the gravity of any decision to marry, gently exposing the unreality of the flights of fantasy and amorous rhetoric that are spawned by passion and nourished by its obsessive cultivation, insisting that they both proceed with circumspection and parental advice, and carefully guiding him toward a position of greater moderation and rationality. Maria's wit, resourcefulness, practical intelligence, and insistence on truth undoubtedly made an unforgettable impression on Cervantes; for when he decided to trace his own embodiment of female perfection, he turned for inspiration both to her literary situation and to her very words.[42]

In the *Gitanilla* Preciosa must cope with a similar ardent youth and

---

[41] Throughout his *Institutio Christiani Matrimonii* Erasmus laments that "inter pueros ac teneras virgines tribus verbis in complexu dictis coit Matrimonium" (p. 641E). Urging that some reforms must be made in the canon law that holds that the sacramental union is sealed simply by the words of consent of the two parties, with or without an officiating priest, followed by sexual consummation, he points to the misery of "thousands of married couples" who, under the influence of passion, alcohol, panders, or other agents of momentary insanity, have hurled themselves into a "deep pit from which there is no escape" (see 641D,E; also 630E,F). Not only are countless people yoked in a union which, properly seen, is a desecration rather than a sign of Christ's loving bond with his Church; but also many find themselves torn apart from marriages in which they have realized the true *caritas* of Christ's love because of previous rash promises and acts (see 631B,C). In words which look forward to Preciosa's demand for "muchas investigaciones," Erasmus asks: "Mercaturus domum aut fundum exploras ac percontaris omnia, num jus habeat tradendi qui vendit, num quam res habeat servitutem, num gravata sit censu; conficiuntur tabulae, adhibentur testes, & stipulatio: & unde in Matrimonio contrahendo tanta temeritas, tantaque socordia?" (p. 641E).

[42] In the introduction of his translation of the colloquy, Craig Thompson points out that in her poise, intelligence, and wit, Maria is comparable to the women in Shakespeare's romantic comedies and adds that "it would be hard to point to another girl of her qualities in pre-Elizabethan literature" (*The Colloquies of Erasmus*, p. 87). It is interesting to speculate on the possible appeal of Maria both to Cervantes and to Shakespeare, who like his Spanish contemporary was, in his old age, clearly drawn to the female ideal represented by Tarsiana of the *Book of Apollonius*. As Walter Kaiser has written, "the longer one studies Erasmus, the more one realizes the extent to which his was one of the seminal minds of the modern world. It is, however, the nature of the seed, as Christ reminded his followers, that it should lose itself in the plant it forms; and Erasmus is no exception to this. Like many great teachers, he is forgotten when his pupils are not, and many who read Rabelais or Montaigne, Shakespeare or Jonson, Ariosto or Cervantes, have only heard of the scholar from Rotterdam who taught them all so much" (*Praisers of Folly* [Cambridge, Mass., 1963], p. 91). For a general study of Erasmus's views on woman, see E. Schneider, *Das Bild der Frau im Werk des Erasmus von Rotterdam* (Stuttgart, 1955).

a confession of love that is presented in some very persuasive rhetoric. Like her Erasmian model she immediately detects infatuation and is keenly aware of its dangers. Maria reminds her suitor that love blinds its victims, that time and sickness may alter the physical beauty that has enthralled him in the present, and that, when he is capable of seeing and knowing correctly, he may be miserable possessing what he had desired so ardently. She concludes: "Consider perhaps that you do not know me well enough. Nobody knows where a new shoe pinches the foot until he puts it on, no matter how well made and pretty it appears in the house of the shoemaker."[43] Preciosa replies to Juan's proposals more bluntly, but her meaning is similar: "I am aware that in those who have recently fallen in love amorous passions resemble indiscreet impulses which unhinge the will, which trampling on any inconveniences, violently hurls itself after its desire, and thinking to meet the glory of its eyes, encounters the hell of its sorrows. If it attains what it desires, the desire diminishes with the possession of the thing desired, and perhaps, the eyes of the understanding at length opening, it perceives it to be well that it should abhor what hitherto it adored for itself."[44] There is definitely a coolness in Preciosa's amatory response to her lover, and it is clear that Cervantes wishes to draw our attention to it, unaware of course that he was risking the displeasure of his future readers.[45] With a composure reminiscent of

[43] "Mira por ventura que no me ayas bien conocido. Un çapato nueuo, por bien fecho e lindo que parezca en casa del çapatero, ninguno, fasta que la calça, sabe en que parte le aprieta el pie." It is likely that Cervantes was acquainted with Erasmus's colloquies in their popular Spanish versions of the sixteenth century. I base the following study on the translation edited by M. Menéndez y Pelayo, *Colloquios de Erasmo, Origenes de la novela*, Vol. 4, N.B.A.E. 21 (Madrid, 1915). See p. 168; the following page references are to this edition. In his discussion of Cervantes's examination of ethical problems through a series of characters who are punished for moral flaws and poor judgment, Américo Castro implies that Cervantes knew Erasmus's colloquy on courtship, citing Maria's rebuke of her importunate lover (*El pensamiento de Cervantes* [Barcelona, 1972], pp. 131-32), and F. Márquez Villanueva has found in the interlocutors' jesting conversation about spirits a similarity to Don Quixote's and Sancho's discussion of enchantment (1:47) (*Fuentes literarias cervantinas* [Madrid, 1973], pp. 60-61). However, as far as I know, none of the various searches for traces of Erasmian thought in Cervantes's works has noted the relationship between the colloquy and *La Gitanilla*.

[44] "sé que las pasiones amorosas en los recién enamorados son como ímpetus indiscretos que hacen salir a la voluntad de sus quicios; la cual, atropellando inconvenientes, desatinadamente se arroja tras su deseo, y pensando dar con la gloria de sus ojos, da con el infierno de sus pesadumbres. Si alcanza lo que desea, mengua el deseo con la posesión de la cosa deseada, y quizá abriéndose entonces los ojos del entendimiento, se vee ser bien que se aborrezca lo que antes se adoraba" (pp. 38-39).

[45] For Américo Castro, Preciosa is a prime example of a series of relatively lifeless

Maria, who refuses to grant her lover a kiss and who urges him repeatedly to get to know her better and to devote more time to decisions concerning matters that affect one's whole life, Preciosa calmly tells the impassioned youth that, before making any decision, she must conduct some investigations in order to know whether he is speaking truthfully about his family and that they must spend two years in close companionship so that each of them can make a free choice in full knowledge of his and his partner's character and needs ("you will have to attend our schools for two years, during which time I shall satisfy myself of your disposition, and you of mine; at the end of this period, if you are satisfied with me and I with you, I shall submit to be your wife"). Always stressing patience, circumspection, and rationality, Preciosa suggests that in view of the gravity of the situation the youth return to Madrid and spend some time thinking

---

characters that Cervantes conceived in essentialist terms as embodiments of the ideals, values, and attitudes of the "official" society in which "deseaba vivir de manera respetable, no como paria ni 'forajido.' " Castro is far more interested in the more "authentic" products of Cervantes's imagination, that is, the characters which he created in a stance "desde fuera" and which he depicts "creating themselves" rather than exemplifying "un ideal trascendente a ellos y válido y grato para las gentes entre quienes quería vivir." He contrasts Preciosa and Dorotea, the forceful maiden of the *Quixote*: "Preciosa, la gitanilla linda, es casta *a priori* y no puede dar un beso a su amante; Dorotea (en el *Quijote*) comparte el lecho con don Fernando, y luego *se hace* su vida, derrochando energía, ingenio feminino y toda suerte de gracias y encantos" ("La ejemplaridad de las novelas cervantinas," in *Semblanzas y estudios españoles* [Princeton, 1956], p. 311). Castro's approach, which preserves the traditional dichotomy of the "two Cervanteses," a dichotomy which he conceived in different and less psychologically and sociologically oriented terms in his early *El pensamiento de Cervantes*, is very useful in illuminating Cervantes's methods of characterization, in emphasizing his revolutionary achievement in bringing to fiction an "existentialist" conception of character, in attempting in an analytical way to deal with that powerful atmosphere of actuality which, since the eighteenth century, readers have marveled at in the *Quixote*, and in probing the tensions in Cervantes's consciousness that made his achievement possible. However, in his antiexemplary and pronovelistic biases, Castro tends to overlook the fact that great fiction can indeed by created with the purpose of exploring in a mature and an authentic way important ideas, whether they happen to be "official" ideas or otherwise, and that "vitality" in the verbal reality that is literature can spring from a variety of elements—formal, ideational, or representational—and is not limited by the degree to which it reduplicates what Castro refers to as "la sensación de la vida." As for the specific case of Preciosa, one feels that Castro's biases against "exemplarity" and his continuing association of romantic and "illicit" love with authenticity and vitality in human behavior blind him to the fact that there is a good deal of "novelistic" vitality in this "*a priori*" character who, although choosing not to sleep with her suitor immediately, successfully imposes her will on the world of her novella and who has repeatedly managed to "seduce" and possess the European imagination during the last three centuries.

over his decision ("This is not a matter of so little moment that in those that time now offers us it can or ought to be decided"). While entertaining in Juan's house in Madrid, she cleverly reminds her "soldier of love" that he is "amorously inclined, impetuous, and hasty," that he might do well to calm himself and remain with his parents, and that he must proceed slowly and cautiously: "Be calm, be calm, my excited little one, and look carefully at what you do before you marry."[46] Following Juan's entry into the world of the Gypsies, Preciosa once again denounces the evils of uncontrolled passion, which transforms men into rapacious hunters and impairs their vision and their capacities to distinguish true beauty from superficial appearances (the "fine" from the "false," "gold" from "tinsel," and "sunlight" and "gold" from "shadow" and "alchemy"). In words that echo Maria's admonitions to Pamphilus at the conclusion of the colloquy (see below), she suggests that the amorous impulse will turn into enduring love only if it appeals to and is restrained by reason ("amorous instincts run wildly with loose reins until they encounter reason or disillusionment"), and she urges Juan to spend some time looking carefully at her, arguing: "the jewel once purchased, no one can get rid of it except by death, so it is well that he should have time and plenty of it to contemplate her, and again to contemplate her, and see in her the shortcomings or the virtues she possesses."[47] Preciosa characteristically views the lover's infatuation as a state of disordered vision: "during the time of this novitiate it may be that you recover your eyesight, which at present seems to have been lost, or at any rate is disordered, and then see [properly]." Both Pamphilus and Maria emphasize the necessity of correct vision, of seeing through dazzling appearances, and Pamphilus, as he takes shape toward the end of Erasmus's delicately balanced colloquy as the guide of Maria, insists that one must look for the inner essential beauty of the beloved ("your soul, whose beauty will always continue increasing with age"). While Maria with gentle irony voices her amusement at the power of his "penetrating eyes," which can perceive a soul "underneath so many

[46] "habéis de cursar dos años en nuestras escuelas, en el cual tiempo me satisfaré yo de vuestra condición, y vos de la mía; al cabo del cual, si vos os contentáredes de mí, y yo de vos, me entregaré por vuestra esposa. . . . No es éste caso de tan poco momento que en los que aquí nos ofrece el tiempo pueda ni deba resolverse. . . . Sosiega, sosiega alborotadito, y mira lo que haces primero que te cases" (pp. 40-41; 55).

[47] "los ímpetus amorosos corren a rienda suelta, hasta que encuentran con la razón o con el desengaño . . . que la prenda que una vez comprada, nadie se puede deshacer della sino con la muerte, bien es que haya tiempo, y mucho, para miralla y remiralla, y ver en ella las faltas o las virtudes que tiene" (p. 72).

folds,"[48] he proceeds to offer a summary of how he has in fact closely inspected Maria's background, family station, temperament, and interests and has assured himself of their compatibility.

Throughout the courtship of Juan and Preciosa, Cervantes stresses the fact that the maiden is not driven by the type of uncontrollable passion that motivates her suitor. "Preciosa, who was somewhat touched, rather with liking than with love, by the gallant disposition of Andrés, yet desired to inform herself if he was what he had said." As the story advances toward its conclusion, we see Cervantes continuing to point to the way in which her love emerges gradually and is nourished through constant companionship with her beloved and her recognition of his fine qualities of character: "Andrés had honorable, discreet, and loving conversations with Preciosa, and little by little she began to fall in love with the discretion and good behavior of her lover, and he, in the same manner, if his love could increase, increased it, such was the modesty, discretion, and beauty of his Preciosa."[49] Even at the conclusion of the tale, when it is clear that Preciosa has come to love Juan, she defines her feelings as affection founded on gratitude, and like Erasmus's Maria, who insists that she and her suitor confer with their parents because a marriage with parental sanction will have a greater chance of happiness than otherwise, she submits to her parents' will ("She replied . . . that her gratitude [to Juan] would not be carried further than her parents approved").[50] In Preciosa's love,

[48] "en el tiempo de este noviciado podría ser que cobrásedes la vista, que ahora debéis tener perdida, o, por lo menos, turbada, y viésedes que" (p. 40). Erasmus: "*Pam.*—Essa tu anima, cuya hermosura siempre con la edad yra cresciendo. *Mar.*— Ojos penetrables tienes, mas que de lince, si tu agora vees mi anima debaxo de tantos doblezes" (p. 168).

[49] "Preciosa, algo aficionada, más con benevolencia que con amor, de la gallarda disposición de Andrés, ya deseaba informarse si era el que había dicho" (p. 48); "Pasaba Andrés con Preciosa honestos, discretos y enamorados coloquios, y ella poco a poco se iba enamorando de la discreción y buen trato de su amante, y él, del mismo modo, si pudiera crecer su amor, fuera creciendo, tal era la honestidad, discreción y belleza de su Preciosa" (p. 80). In a good-natured, mildly coquettish exchange between Maria and Pamphilus, Erasmus makes the point that he emphasizes repeatedly in his matrimonial writings: "*Mar.*—Por ventura te parecere otra quando viniesse vna enfermedad, quando cargasse la edad, quando mudassen los años esta forma que agora te aplaze? *Pam.*—Bien veo, señora, que este xugo de juuentud, esta gentil frescura y tez, no ha de durar para siempre; por esto no tengo en tanto este tu florido e adornado tabernaculo, quanto es el huesped que dentro mora. *Mar.*—Que huesped? *Pam.*—Essa tu anima, cuya hermosura siempre con la edad yra cresciendo" (p. 168).

[50] "Respondió . . . que ya no extendería a más el agradecimiento de aquello que sus señores padres quisiesen" (p. 120). In his *Institutio Christiani Matrimonii* Erasmus repeatedly turns to the problems surrounding the role of parents in the arrangement of marriages. He acknowledges that they have forced many children into unhappy

which is marked by the determination to know its object thoroughly and which, under the guidance of reason, grows from affection and good will through friendship and companionship, Cervantes is celebrating an ideal which stands out sharply against a series of carefully drawn contrasts: the violently erupting infatuation of Juan-Andrés, who is consumed by a "flame burning in his breast" (p. 43); the uncontrollable lust of Juana Carducha, who, with no concern for the bonds of marriage or the necessity of parental consent, offers herself

marriages and vigorously objects to such coercion. However, he generally maintains that parental involvement in a child's choice of a partner is beneficial in bringing greater experience, knowledge, and moderation to the whole procedure. Lamenting the frequency of clandestine marriages and their disastrous effects on family life and consequently on the well-being of the republic (see p. 630E; also 660B ". . . si sua cuique domus negligatur, nec civitas ex his constans poterit subsistere"), he nostalgically recalls ancient customs that guaranteed, through parental participation, that nobody would marry a person whom he did not know thoroughly (see p. 642E,F), and he suggests that all marriages should be condemned unless approved by parents (see p. 649F). Typical of his conciliatory attitude toward the value of parental involvement and the rights of the contracting parties is the following statement: "Nec tutorum igitur, ne parentum tantum valeat auctoritas ut liberis aut pupillis obtrudator uxor nolentibus: nec tamen usque adeo laxandae sunt habenae licentiae, inconsultae aetati, ut furtim, ut temere, ut poti, ut incantati, ut dictis in ipso corporum complexu tribus verbis, contrahant Matrimonium, hoc est, conficiant Ecclesiae Sacramentum. Utinam vigeret illa prisca inter parentes & liberos pietas! ut nec illi secus consulerent suis quam sibi consultum vellent, nec hi dissiderent majorum suorum providentiae" (p. 650C,D). Like Erasmus, Cervantes was intensely concerned with these problems, and his sensitivity to both sides of the issue and his ultimately conciliatory stance are evident in his varying literary treatment of the subject. See, for example, the episode of Luisa in the *Persiles* and those of Dorotea, Luscinda, Leandra, and Quiteria in the *Quixote*. In the latter Don Quixote's position is at one point identical with that of Preciosa, as he emphasizes the importance of clarity of vision, notes the blinding effects of passion, and suggests that, if young people were to base their marriages solely on their feelings for one another and disregard parental advice, they would more often than not imprison themselves in a state of misery from which the only escape is death (". . . que el amor y la afición con facilidad ciegan los ojos del entendimiento, tan necesarios para escoger estado, y el del matrimonio está muy a peligro de errarse, y es menester gran tiento y particular favor del cielo para acertarle" [2:180]). Ironically, shortly thereafter, he finds himself in the position of having to defend the deceitful "love marriage" of Quiteria and Basilio as justified by "el amor" and "la disposición de los cielos." In *La Gitanilla* the importance of parental consent in the achievement of the goal of a rational marriage is voiced not only by Preciosa but also by Clemente, in his advice to the lovers as the tale approaches its climax, words that, as I shall point out below, are extremely important in the articulation of all the major themes of the work: "Agradézcote, señora, lo que en mi crédito dijiste, y yo pienso pagártelo en desear que estos enredos amorosos salgan a fines felices, y que tú goces de tu Andrés, y Andrés de su Preciosa, en conformidad y gusto de sus padres, porque de tan hermosa junta veamos en el mundo los más bellos renuevos que pueda formar la bien intencionada naturaleza" (p. 101).

to the hero in the corral of the inn; the unrestrained sexuality uniting man and wife in the precarious Gypsy marriage; the violent passion that drives Clemente's friend to murder; and the literary love that occasionally characterizes Clemente's adoration of the Gypsy maiden. The ideal represents a view of love and marriage that Erasmus's Maria espouses and that emerges in nearly all of the great humanist's writings about marriage, its possibilities, and its problems. As Maria counsels her friend: "Examine carefully and by yourself what you presently feel; look at it well before you declare it to all, and do not take counsel with emotion and carnal affection, but rather look to reason for advice, because what seems right according to emotion is temporary and momentary. But what reason determines generally pleases forever."[51] For both maidens the authentic and enduring relationship must be founded on rational love. Both suggest that such a love can grow out of the natural affection that they initially feel for their suitors, and both are keenly aware of the fragility of any marriage that is based primarily on carnal affection.

While Preciosa and Maria denounce the folly of yielding to a passion in no uncertain terms, both maidens are capable of treating the conventional rhetoric of love and courtship with humorous detachment. They are well aware that its sentimental inflation encourages self-deception, facilitates the concealment of intentions, and generally brings obscurity to an area of experience in which clarity of vision is of paramount importance, and they react to their suitors' adoption of amatory discourse with mockery and playful literal-mindedness. The first section of Erasmus's colloquy is a debate in which Pamphilus attempts to overwhelm Maria's resistance by the sophistical argumentation familiar in love debates of medieval and Renaissance literature, from Andreas Capellanus's *De Amore* to the popular contemporary *Dialoghi d'amore* of Leone Ebreo.[52] He claims that his heartless mistress, who is as hard as stone and as cruel as Mars, has slain him with

---

[51] "Este tu parecer que agora tienes, examinale bien entre ti antes que le publiques, e no tomes parecer con la aficion, mas consejate con la razon, porque lo que a la aficion le paresce, temporal es e momentaneo. Mas lo que la razon determina, perpetuamente suele agradar" (p. 170). See the words of Erasmus's spokesman Glycus in the colloquy, *The Carriage*: "Others love before they choose; I made a judicious choice before I loved" (*The Colloquies of Erasmus*, p. 192). Cervantes describes the disastrous consequences of a hasty marriage of passion in the story of Ortel Banedre (*Los trabajos de Persiles y Sigismunda*, pp. 315-26) and in *El casamiento engañoso*.

[52] In such works it is not uncommon for the lady to find herself forced to engage in debate with an importunate lover, to cut through the deception in his rhetoric, and to expose the hollowness of his arguments in favor of love (see D. W. Robertson, Jr., *A Preface to Chaucer* [Princeton, 1962], p. 418).

the poison and witchcraft of her eyes and that his life can be restored only if she relents. He finds his argument flawless in his "Achillean proofs" and capable of withstanding critical scrutiny by a "congress of logicians." Moreover, he supports his claim to be dead with the venerable doctrine, taken from "respected authors," that man's soul migrates to the object of its love, as is clearly the case in those who are divinely inspired. The learned idolatry is based on contemporary fashionable neo-Platonic theories of love,[53] and, while the doctrine of the migrations of enamored souls was echoed by numerous writers of the age, its particular formulation by Pamphilus suggests that Erasmus was addressing himself critically to Ficino's influential and seminal *Commentary on Plato's Symposium*.[54] In his discussion of simple and mutual love, Ficino offers an intricate and lengthy argument to prove that, since a lover's soul lives only in the beloved and abandons its functions in the body, the state of loving is a kind of death. If the lover is unrequited, he "lives nowhere. He is completely dead. Moreover, he never comes back to life unless indignation revives him." Ficino proceeds to ask "who will deny that a man who is loved is a homicide since he robs the loving one of his soul?" And he goes on to assert that "anyone who is loved ought in very justice to love in return, and he who does not love his lover must bear the charge of homicide." The only hope of resuscitation for the dead body lies in the possibility of mutual love. If the other lovingly receives the disembodied soul and in fact imprints the image of the lover on her own soul while sending forth that soul to the lover, the latter then rises from the dead by finding himself in the beloved's contemplation of him. In short, "though he is dead in himself, he comes to life again in the other." In an exultant apostrophe of this "happy death," Ficino speaks rapturously of the double resurrection of mutual love, for the

---

[53] ". . . tal amore è desiderio d'unione perfetta de l'amante ne la persona amata; la quale non può essere se non con la totale penetrazione de l'uno de l'altro. Questo negli animi che sono spirituali è possibile. . . . E procurando sempre la mente l'intera conversione ne la persona amata, lassa la propria, essendo sempre con maggiore affezione e pena per il mancamento de l'unione" (Leone Ebreo, *Dialoghi d'amore*, ed. S. Caramella [Bari, 1929], p. 56). See also B. Castiglione, *Il libro del Cortegiano*, ed. E. Bonora and P. Zoccola (Milano, 1972), pp. 341-42. Lope de Vega, whose writings owe a good deal to the neo-Platonic doctrines, formulates the idea succinctly in his most important work dealing critically with love, *La Dorotea*: the soul of the lover "está más donde ama que donde anima . . . assí les parece a los amantes que no la lleuan, pues que no viuen, y que ella assiste como inmortal donde la dexan" (ed. E. Morby [Madrid, 1958], p. 105).

[54] For Ficino's influence, see Jean Festugière, *La Philosophie de l'amour de Marsile Ficin et son influence sur la littérature française au xvie siècle* (Paris, 1941), chaps. 3 and 4.

favorably received lover not only regains his life but also achieves self-knowledge in his beloved, in whose soul he contemplates his own soul as reflected in a mirror.

> O, inestimable gain, when two so become one, that each of the two, instead of one alone, becomes two, and as though doubled, he who had one life before, with a death intervening, has now two. For a man who dies once and is twice resurrected has exchanged one life for two and his single self for two selves. Certainly there is a most just vengeance in reciprocal love, for a homicide must be punished by death, and who will deny that a man who is loved is a homicide since he robs the loving one of his soul?[55]

Pamphilus bases most of his argument to win Maria's consent on these doctrines. Flaunting his mastery of logic, he confronts the maiden with an intricately constructed piece of persuasion in which he maintains that he is a "lifeless corpse," that his soul is "absent from his body," and that his beloved is a cruel murderess. He explains the experience of divine possession to her, and he observes that she can bring his dead body back to life if she allows her spirit to migrate to his breast, adding that he desires "no other mirror" than the eyes of his beloved.[56]

Throughout this Platonically inspired argument, Maria responds with gentle mockery and disingenuous bewilderment, acknowledging the esoteric nature of her "philosopher's" discourse while at the same time exposing the absurdity of its doctrines when accepted literally.[57] Moreover, in a display of dialectic that matches that of her admirer,

---

[55] "O inaestimabile lucrum, quando duo ita unum fiunt, ut quisque duorum pro uno solo, duo fiat, ut tamquam geminatus qui unam habuerat vitam una interveniente morte duas iam habeat. Nam qui semel mortuus bis reviviscit, pro una vita geminam, pro se uno, se duos est consecutus. Iustissima certe est in mutuo amore vindicta. Homicida morte plectendus. Quis enim homicidam esse neget qui amatur cum animam ab amante seiungat?" (see *Marsilio Ficino's Commentary on Plato's "Symposium,"* ed. and trans. S. R. Jayne, University of Missouri Studies 19 [Columbia, 1944], pp. 51, 145). Compare Leone Ebreo's rather playful version of the "death and resurrection" of the lovers. According to the enamored Filone, the image of his Sofia has possessed his mind, drawn away all his spirits, and cut off his life (see *Dialoghi d'amore*, p. 198).

[56] Ficino claimed that the soul of the lover is "enflamed by the divine splendor glowing in the beautiful person as in a mirror, and secretly lifted up by it as by a hook in order to become God." See Paul O. Kristeller, *The Philosophy of Marsilio Ficino*, trans. V. Conant (New York, 1943), p. 267. The mirror suggests both the reflected character of divine beauty in the created world and the lover's discovery of his authentic self through the contemplation of it in the possession of the beloved.

[57] For example, when Pamphilus compares her to Mars and rebukes her for seeking glory in the shedding of human blood, Maria replies: "Dime quantos muertos vees por estas calles: quanta sangre derramada por mi causa?" (p. 164).

she proceeds to "play the sophist" with him and undermines his argument by accepting certain of its premises and drawing the contradictory conclusion that in fact the animation of his body proves the presence of an animating soul. All of this, coupled with the apparent panic of Pamphilus about his moribund state, effectively deflates the neo-Platonic rhetoric and suggests that Erasmus must have read the neo-Platonists' writings on love with a good deal of amusement.[58] At the conclusion of the dialogue he returns to the philosophical satire that dominates its beginning. Maria refuses to grant her impatient suitor even a kiss because she fears that any tiny particles of his soul that still remain in his body might slip over into her through the kiss and leave him completely lifeless. The jest is clearly aimed at the "philosophy of the kiss," which was undoubtedly very popular in the courtly circles influenced by the neo-Platonists and their vulgarizers and which received its most famous formulation in Castiglione's *Courtier*. Since the mouth "emits words, which are the interpreters of the soul," the good lover who kisses his beloved discovers that "that bond is the opening of mutual access to their souls, which, being each drawn by desire for the other, pour themselves each into the other's body by turn and mingle so together that each of them has two souls," for "a kiss has such power over the soul that it withdraws it to itself and separates it from the body."[59]

[58] As with all other major intellectual currents of the time, Erasmus's engagement with neo-Platonic philosophy is that of an eclectic. He is deeply committed and perhaps indebted to those doctrines which are congenial with his *Philosophia Christiana*—e.g., its lofty spirituality, its emphasis on rationality, its stress on the spirit as opposed to the letter (see, for example, *El Enquiridion o manual del caballero cristiano*, ed. Dámaso Alonso [Madrid, 1932], pp. 134, 291-92, 298, and *Laus Stultitiae, Ausgewählte Schriften*, ed. W. Welzig, 8 vols. [Darmstadt, 1967-1980], 2:200-211)—while he can disassociate himself easily from its tendencies toward an excessive spiritualism and a radical dualism, its heavy stress on contemplation, its esotericism and elitism, and, of course, its elaborate doctrines of love (see, for example, *The Godly Feast* and *Paráclesis*, ed. D. Alonso [Madrid, 1932], pp. 452-53). For Erasmus's hostility to occult philosophy, see F. A. Yates, *Giordano Bruno and the Hermetic Tradition* (Chicago, 1964), pp. 164-68; for his lack of interest in the neo-Platonists' metaphysical systems, see A. Renaudet, *Érasme et L'Italie* (Geneva, 1954), p. 7. The substantive links between his religious and ethical thought and Platonism are revealed in A. A. Auer, *Die vollkommene Frömmigkeit des Christen nach dem Enchiridion militis Christiani des Erasmus von Rotterdam* (Düsseldorf, 1954), *passim*. See also P. Mestwerdt, *Die Anfänge des Erasmus: Humanismus und "Devotio Moderna"* (Leipzig, 1917), chap. 1. As I shall point out below, Erasmus is indeed capable of ridiculing certain elements of the neo-Platonic doctrines of love while appropriating others to develop his own ideal of conjugal amity.

[59] "quello legame è un aprir l'adito alle anime, che tratte dal desiderio l'una dell'altra si transfundano alternamente ancor l'una nel corpo dell'altra e talmente si mescolino

To this argument, which Erasmus's readers must have found highly amusing in its allusions to contemporary fashionable writings and modes of conversation, Pamphilus adds another, equally literary but far more traditional in its resonances. He reminds his unyielding mistress of the "Court of Venus" and warns her that the vengeful god Amor will cruelly punish her if she continues to resist his persuasions. The erotic analogy of Christian love, with its conception of Amor as a divine power who demands worship, service, and suffering of his disciples and metes out punishment or reward in this life and in the afterlife, was widespread in amatory writings throughout the middle ages. Its continuing popularity in Erasmus's Europe is attested by the celebrated love penance of Amadís de Gaula, the torment of the infatuated lover in Diego de San Pedro's *Cárcel de Amor*, Cupid's violently phrased excommunication and expulsion from his temple of a heartless lady in *La Lozana Andaluza*, and the interest in such parodies as Suero de Ribera's *Missa de Amor*, where the worship of the unhappy lover carefully follows the structure of the mass, culminating in the Agnus Dei prayer to the "Lamb of God of Venus" ("Cordero de Dios de Venus"): "*Miserere nobis.*"[60]

In Pamphilus's playful threats to Maria in the name of Amor, Eras-

---

insieme, che ognun di loro abbia due anime, ed una sola di quelle due così composta regga quasi dui corpi; onde il bascio si po più presto dir congiungimento d'anima che di corpo, perché in quella ha tanta forza che la tira a sé e quasi la separa dal corpo" (*Il libro del cortegiano*, p. 342; I cite C. S. Singleton's translation, *The Book of the Courtier* [New York, 1959], pp. 349-50). It should perhaps be pointed out that the type of jocularity and philosophical parody in the exposition of the neo-Platonic doctrines which we observe in Erasmus's colloquy was not uncommon in the very treatises that popularized the doctrines in the courtly circles of the Italian Renaissance (see G. Toffanin, *Il Cinquecento* [Milano, 1929], p. 143).

[60] G. Rodríguez de Montalvo, *Amadís de Gaula*, Book II, chaps. 48-52; Diego de San Pedro, *Cárcel de Amor, Obras completas*, ed. K. Whinnom, 3 vols. (Madrid, 1971), 2: esp. pp. 84-92; Francisco Delicado, *La Lozana Andaluza*, ed. B. Damiani (Madrid, 1969), pp. 255-56; *Missa de amor*, in *Rimas inéditas de Don Iñigo López de Mendoza, Marqués de Santillana, de Fernán Pérez de Guzmán, Señor de Batres, y de otros poetas del siglo xv*, ed. Eugenio de Ochoa (Paris, 1844), pp. 389-91. For a discussion of the popularity of the order of love, the development of the imperious god of Ovid's *Ars Amatoria* under the impact of the seignorial system of service and the Christian practices of worship, and the various attitudes toward love with which writers could infuse the conception, see C. S. Lewis, *The Allegory of Love* (New York, 1958), chap. 1. For the conventional nature of this analogy in the Spanish *Cancionero* poetry of the fifteenth century, see M. R. Lida de Malkiel, "La hipérbole sagrada en la poesía castellana del siglo xv," *Revista de Filología Hispánica* 8 (1946):121-30. For its general popularity in Spanish literature of the middle ages, see C. Post's study of the "erotic hell" in his *Medieval Spanish Allegory* (Cambridge, 1915), chap. 7, and O. Green's *Spain and the Western Tradition*, 4 vols. (Madison, 1968), 1: chap. 3.

mus is addressing himself critically to the courtly attitudes toward
love service and the elaborate rules and rhetoric accompanying them,
which undoubtedly reached his young contemporaries in the popular
sentimental and chivalric romances, and which, like the neo-Platonists' mystifications, could easily become an obstacle to rational, clear-
sighted relations between the sexes. Maria's response to Pamphilus's
courtly flirtation is, in its literal-mindedness, just as devastating as
her subtle argumentation concerning the neo-Platonic premises. She
simply points out that, since Venus is goddess of the sea and she has
no interest in sailing, she is in no danger of retribution for her hard-
heartedness.

Through all the elaborate banter of the first section of the colloquy,
Erasmus emphasizes that the traditional literary language of eros,
whether neo-Platonic or courtly in its origins and in the attitudes it
formulates, is basically a language of evasion, which like lust itself is
more self-gratifying than communicative. The point is most emphatically made in Erasmus's particular formulation of the abstruse doctrine of the soul as mirror (see above), for in Pamphilus's claim to be
beholding himself in the eyes of Maria, the lofty contemplative ideal
of Platonic love is suddenly unmasked as the pose of a narcissist.

Cervantes's Preciosa is similarly resistant to the appeal of amatory
rhetoric and disdainful of the attitudes and doctrines underlying it.
This aspect of the central theme of love, courtship, and marriage is
most clearly developed in her relationship with her second suitor, the
poet-page Clemente. As I have pointed out above, various interpreters
of the work have emphasized the ambiguity surrounding this figure
in the tale, the understated quality of his bond with the heroine, the
indeterminacy marking his introduction and definition as a character,
and the peculiar way in which he vanishes as the plot turns toward
its festive conclusion and draws all its characters together. Clemente
remains to the end an elusive figure, whose appearances in the world
of the novella are fleeting and whose most important actions are literally veiled in darkness. As has often been remarked, Clemente has
an important function as a rival to Juan, as a trial which Juan must
endure in his ascent toward a pure love founded in trust and untroubled by jealousy. Moreover, it is clear that Cervantes conceived Clemente as a double of his protagonist. The parallelism of the scenes of
their introductions—the declaration of love and the offer of money to
the beloved—, the resemblances in their quests—their flights from
Madrid into a world of criminality and lawlessness, their change of
clothing, which in each case is associated with a change of identity,

and their rebaptism in the other world—,[61] their bonding and their joint triumphs as "epic" heroes in the games and competitions in the Mancha ("They were always together . . . and in all these [competitions] Andrés and Clemente were the victors"[62]), and their union in the nocturnal amoebaean song which they sing in honor of Preciosa, all suggest a single identity in the two figures. If we look at Clemente as a dark double of the protagonist, we discover that his role in the development of the theme of love is more complex than his role as rival would suggest. The doubling of characters is one of the conventional features of romance, and one of the most common effects that the romancer seeks in the procedure is the illumination of the virtues of his hero by contrast. We observe the convention in the *Persiles*, where the heroic Duke of Nemours, who hovers in the background throughout the account of the ordeals of the heroes, suddenly abandons his courtship of Auristela during her illness because, unlike the perfect lover Periandro, he is incapable of gazing on her with the ordered vision of the "eyes of the soul."[63] Clemente appears in a similar role when he surprisingly reveals his own inconstancy, confessing that he is not in love with Preciosa after all and expressing his preference for the numerous beauties of Madrid who belong to the privileged classes of society. At the same time the double of romance can have the more complex function of revealing a dark aspect that the hero must recognize in himself and overcome. The double whom the hero encounters in his descent into the lower world frequently fulfills this role, and, to recognize Cervantes's familiarity with the convention, we need only look at the wrathful Antonio's encounter with the talking wolf in the darkness of his terrible night at sea, Rutilio's confrontation of the lustful witch-wolf in his expiatory journey to the north, or Ortel Banedre's meeting with the shadowy figure in the labyrinthian streets of Lisbon whom he kills and subsequently displaces in his mother's house.[64]

The relationship of Juan and Clemente in the *Gitanilla* is much more complex than the brief confrontations of doubles in the *Persiles*,

---

[61] Preciosa's words underscore these similarities: ". . . como había don Joanes en el mundo, y que se mudaban en Andreses, así podía haber don Sanchos que se mudasen en otros nombres" (p. 99).

[62] "Andaban siempre juntos . . . de todos salían vencedores Andrés y Clemente" (pp. 98-99).

[63] See *Los trabajos de Persiles y Sigismunda*, p. 455.

[64] *Los trabajos de Persiles y Sigismunda*, pp. 76-77, 91, 316-17; see my *Cervantes' Christian Romance* (Princeton, 1972), chap. 3. For this aspect of the doppelgänger figure in romance, see Northrop Frye, *The Secular Scripture: A Study of the Structure of Romance* (Cambridge, Mass., 1976), pp. 140ff.

but, if we recognize that it is basically the same convention in a version that is thematically much more sophisticated, we can account for some of the most puzzling aspects of the page's presence in the work, particularly those emerging in his relationship to Preciosa. In his initial appearances Clemente represents a flawed experience of love which to some extent marks Juan's early courtship and which Cervantes would explore through isolation and emphasis in a shadowy double figure. Just as the Gypsy world represents in a pure form the unrestrained sexual energy that is driving Juan "as a wild horse" toward the bondage "at the feet" of Preciosa in his initial infatuation with her, so Clemente's courtship represents certain powerful illusions that Juan, like most lovers, creates about his erotic impulses and to which he then pays homage as the ultimate reality in his life. If Clemente is the "courtly" lover, he is also the "courtly" love poet, and through him Cervantes is addressing himself both to some of the destructive illusions engendered and nourished by erotic experience and to a venerable tradition of literature that man has created to confer reality and dignity on those illusions. Clemente appears to view love as an enslaving power, and his poetry would suggest the type of total absorption with one's own suffering which, if the conventions of traditional love poetry bear any connection with reality, marks a good deal of man's erotic energy and activity. Like so many lovers and poets he views his mistress as an imperious Venus, who ensnares men in her golden tresses and receives at her feet the homage of Cupid.[65] The poem that he dedicates to Preciosa, as it celebrates a sinister female principle and concentrates on love as a force of death, belongs to the numerous demonic parodies by which Cervantes sharpens our perception of the ideal love relationship and the true female principle celebrated in the romance. Preciosa's songs to St. Anne and the Queen Margarita honor the beloved female as a life-giver, associating her with the Virgin and such classical patrons of married love as Juno and Lucina and with the celestial siren and the higher Venus ("Venus casta") of the Platonic and neo-Platonic mysteries, the latter a myth

---

[65] The connection between this type of erotic experience and the hero's initial attraction to Preciosa is suggested in the narrator's description of his idolatrous pose as he listens to the recitation of Clemente's sonnet. He too is "at his mistress' feet": "tras los pies se llevaban los ojos de cuantos las miraban, especialmente los de Andrés, que así se iban entre los pies de Preciosa como si allí tuvieron el centro de su gloria" (p. 58). The narrator returns to the point in his playful lament on Juan's abasement following his deception of his parents and his conversion into the "lacayo de Preciosa": "se vino a postrarse a los pies de una muchacha, y a ser su lacayo, que, puesto que hermosísima, en fin, era gitana: privilegio de la hermosura, que trae al redopelo y por la melena a sus pies a la voluntad más exenta" (p. 78).

frequently associated with wedded love in the Renaissance.[66] Clemente's confession of love addresses his beloved as the basilisk, which metamorphoses its victim into stone, as a witch who destroys, enchants, tyrannizes, despoils, and consumes her lovers in flames, and as the traditional sinister siren, who enchants her victims with sweet song before destroying them. Invoking the conventional paradox of suffering lovers, he laments that his mistress holds him in a thrall suspended between life and death, and he reviles his beloved as arrogant and harsh.[67]

If Clemente's role as double illustrates how Cervantes imaginatively explores the themes of Erasmus's colloquy through their articulation in the conventions of romance, Preciosa's manner of dealing with the kind of love that the poet represents recalls the more direct methods of the colloquy and the specific arguments of her Erasmian ancestor. She responds to his courtly declaration with a deflationary bit of literal-mindedness and a strikingly cynical comment on the valuelessness of any spiritualizing approach to love. Seizing the phrase "suffering lover" ("pobre amador") of the final verse, she comments, "The last verse ends in 'poor' . . . That is a bad sign! Lovers should never say that they are poor, because, to my way of thinking, poverty at the beginning is a great enemy of love." In her second encounter with the poet, Preciosa again shows herself to be disdainful of the conceits of love poetry and implicitly aware of their vacuity. Perhaps alluding to the fashionable doctrine of the migration of lovers' souls, she ridicules his offer of verses: "[your verses] always come full of 'souls' and 'hearts.' But do understand, Sir Page, that I do not desire so many souls with me."[68] Her poet continues to depict his love as a thralldom, assuring her that he will worship the coin which her hand has touched "as a relic" for the rest of his life. If such language is idolatrous, it is also absurdly exaggerated; for in his next encounter with the maiden we discover that Clemente is not really in love with Preciosa. He claims that there are many women in Madrid worthier of

[66] See Erwin Panofsky, "The Neoplatonic Movement in Florence and North Italy," *Studies in Iconology* (New York, 1962), pp. 129-69.

[67] See below, my discussion of the structure of the imagery of the tale. The presence of such motifs as death, rapacity, tyranny, and destructive fire in Clemente's "literary love" associates it imaginatively with the infernal world of the Gypsies, where Cervantes creates another demonic counterweight to the perfect love of the protagonists.

[68] "En *pobre* acaba el último verso . . . ¡mala señal! Nunca los enamorados han de decir que son pobres, porque a los principios, a mi parecer, la pobreza es muy enemiga del amor" (p. 23); "siempre vienen llenos de *almas* y *corazones*. Pero sepa el señor paje que no quiero tantas almas conmigo" (p. 51).

his attention, and we must conclude that Preciosa's suspicion of the artifical language of lovers is justified. For the poet the woman appears to be little more than an occasion for the display of self-gratifying rhetoric.

If Erasmus's theme of the illusory quality of conventional amatory discourse is most strikingly developed in the figure of Clemente, it is nonetheless clearly present in the relation of Juan and Preciosa. In fact the courtly and neo-Platonic rhetoric and sentiments which enlivened Pamphilus's arguments emerge directly in Juan de Cárcamo's declaration of love, and Preciosa greets them with the same disdain that marked Maria's response. Invoking the familiar *service d'amour*, Juan insists that he wishes to serve his beloved lady, and he describes the condition of his soul in words that point to the neo-Platonic doctrines on the "marriage of minds":

Toward her my soul is wax, and on it she may imprint whatever she desires; but for preserving and retaining it, it will not be as if it were stamped on wax, but rather as if it were sculpted in marble, the hardness of which resists the lapse of time.[69]

The practical Preciosa is not at all impressed by such arguments. "Promises do not move me, gifts do not undermine my resolution, submissions do not lead me to yield; nor do I stand in awe of *the fine and subtle arguments of love*." The narrator supports her with a parenthetical comment which appears to be a gentle mockery of the abstruse doctrine of the migration of souls and a recollection of Erasmus's humorous deflation of that doctrine in Maria's refusal of the kiss re-

---

[69] "Para con ella es de cera mi alma, donde podrá imprimir lo que quisiere; y para conservarlo y guardarlo no será como impreso en cera, sino como esculpido en mármoles, cuya dureza se opone a la duración de los tiempos" (p. 37). The notion that the beloved penetrates the soul of the lover, where her image is preserved and adored regardless of her physical presence or absence and regardless of the passage of time and change, was a commonplace of neo-Platonic doctrines of love which found its way into innumerable lyric poems of the Renaissance. As Ficino puts it, "a lover imprints a likeness of the loved one upon his soul, and so the soul of the lover becomes a mirror in which is reflected the image of the loved one" (*Ficino's Commentary on Plato's "Symposium,"* p. 146). What occurs is analogous to the universal process by which the angelic mind "sees the face of God engraved within its own breast, and seeing it there, is struck with awe, and clings most avidly to it forever" (p. 170; see also p. 227). In Leone Ebreo's widely read exposition of the neo-Platonic theories of love, the enraptured Filone tells Sophia that her image is "impressed upon his mind" and adds: ". . . se la splendida bellezza tua non mi fusse intrata per gli occhi, non me ne arebbe possuto trapassar tanto, come fece, il senso e la fantasia, e penetrando sino al cuore non aría pigliata per eterna abitazione (come pigliò) la mente mia, impiendola di scultura di tua immagine" (*Dialoghi d'amore*, p. 172).

quested by her lover at the conclusion of their exchange: "Andrés (as we shall henceforth call him) had not the courage to kiss Preciosa, but rather conveyed his soul to her with his eyes. And without it, if we may say so, he left them and entered Madrid" (pp. 47-48). The Gypsy maiden adds that she has no intention of losing her virginity under the influence of "illusions and the fantasies of dreams" ("quimeras y fantasías soñadas"), and suggests that such fantasies serve only to increase the blindness afflicting the passionate lover, who is driven by his self-consuming impulses and realizes only after the gratification of his physical desires that there is no authentic bond between him and his beloved. "If he attains what he desires, desire itself diminishes with the possession of the object desired, and by chance, the eyes of the understanding at length opening, he sees that it is fitting that he should abhor what hitherto he adored for himself."[70] Following the long speech by the Gypsy elder, Preciosa returns to the theme, making it even clearer that literary language and the conventional attitudes that lie behind it are as great a threat as uncontrolled instinct to the undistorted judgment that is absolutely necessary when one

---

[70] "A mí ni me mueven promesas, ni me desmoronan dádivas, ni me inclinan sumisiones, *ni me espantan finezas enamoradas*" (p. 38; italics added); "No tuvo atrevimiento Andrés (que así le llamaremos de aquí adelante) de abrazar a Preciosilla; antes, enviándole con la vista el alma, sin ella, si así decirse puede, las dejó y se entró en Madrid" (pp. 47-48); "Si alcanza lo que desea, mengua el deseo con la posesión de la cosa deseada, y quizá abriéndose entonces los ojos del entendimiento, se vee ser bien que se aborrezca lo que antes se adoraba" (p. 39). Preciosa's exposure of the way in which the mythology and literary language of love can easily provide a mask deceptively dignifying a lover's ephemeral desire for instinctual satisfaction recalls the analysis of erotic experience in the symposium scene of Cervantes's early pastoral romance, *La Galatea*. Lenio, the critic of love, condemns "aquellas canciones," which he hears every day, "llenas de mil simples conceptos amorosos, tan mal dispuestos e intricados." He adds: "osaré jurar que hay algunas que ni las alcanza quien las oye, por discreto que sea, ni las entiende quien las hizo. Pero no menos fatigan otras que se enzarzan en dar alabanzas a Cupido, y en exagerar su poder, su valor, sus maravillas y milagros, haciéndole señor del cielo y de la tierra, dándole otros mil atributos de potencia, de mando y señorío. Y lo que más me cansa de los que las hacen, es que, cuando hablan de amor, entienden de un no sé quién que ellos llaman Cupido, que la mesma significación del nombre nos declara quién es él, que es un apetito sensual y vano, digno de todo vituperio" (ed. J. B. Avalle-Arce, 2 vols. [Madrid, 1961], 2:40). See also Cervantes's humorous treatment of the disruptive effects of the rhetoric of eros in "La Dolorida's" lament about Don Clavijo's use of "*seguidillas*" to seduce Princess Antonomasia: "si yo fuera la buena dueña que debía, no me habían de mover sus trasnochados conceptos, ni había de creer ser verdad aquel decir: 'Vivo muriendo, ardo en yelo, tiemblo en el fuego, espero sin esperanza, pártome y quédome,' con otros imposibles desta ralea, de que están sus escritos llenos. Pues ¿qué cuando prometen el fénix de Arabia, la corona de Aridiana, los caballos del Sol, del Sur las perlas, de Tíbar el oro y de Pancaya el bálsamo?" (*Don Quijote de la Mancha*, 2:334).

contemplates marriage: "of the same kind, I think, are the vows uttered by the lover, who, in order to obtain his desire, will promise the wings of Mercury and the thunderbolts of Jove, as a certain poet promised to me, and swore by the Stygian Pool." An inveterate Erasmian, the cautious Preciosa always insists that the only way to protect her love from the disastrous consequences of illusions is to rely on experience, time, and knowledge: "And you have to consider that during the time of this novitiate it may be that you recover your eyesight, which at present seems to have been lost, or which, at any rate, is disordered"; "I do not want oaths, Mr. Andrés, nor do I want promises: I only desire to leave the whole matter to the experience of this novitiate."[71]

The most striking evidence of the impact of Erasmus's colloquy on Cervantes's conception of *La Gitanilla* is to be found in the scene that is of central importance to both works—the discussion of virginity. After Maria has decisively disposed of his "literary" arguments for a quick marriage, Pamphilus reminds her that by having children a couple experiences the "glory" of renewing their youth ("renovar nuestra vejez con fruto de bendicion"). Maria counters that to do so she must "lose the gift of virginity," adding later in the argument that "virginity is universally admired" and that "chastity is a thing very pleasing to God." She asks the youth: "what do you think a more lovely thing to look upon, *a rose fresh and blooming on its bush or cut and withered in somebody's hands?*"[72] At this moment Pamphilus has fully reversed his early role as the spokesman for a foolish point of view, he now assumes the dominant position in the dialogue, and the work becomes, as is fitting in a matrimonial colloquy, a model exercise in mutual enlightenment. He gently intimates that his opponent's extremist attitudes toward virginity are unnatural and proceeds to educate her in the meaning and value of Christian marriage. Evoking the delicious abundance of the vegetable world, he suggests that the preservation of virginity in women is as unnatural as the cultivation of an orchard for its blossoms rather than for its ripe fruit. The

---

[71] "así son, según pienso, los [juramentos] del amante; que, por conseguir su deseo, prometerá las alas de Mercurio y los rayos de Júpiter, como me prometió a mí un cierto poeta, y juraba por la laguna Estigia" (p. 73); "Y habéis de considerar que en el tiempo de este noviciado podría ser que cobrásedes la vista, que ahora debéis tener perdida, o, por lo menos turbada" (p. 40); "No quiero juramento, señor Andrés, ni quiero promesas; sólo quiero remitirlo todo a la experiencia deste noviciado" (p. 73).

[72] "en opinion de todos, muy fauorable es la virginidad . . . la castidad es muy acepta a Dios . . . qual te paresce mas linda cosa de ver: *vna rosa fresca en su rosal o verla despues cortada y marchita entre las manos?*" (pp. 168-69). Italics are added here and in the following quotations from Erasmus's dialogue and Cervantes's novella.

virgin is comparable to the fallen vine, which, instead of encircling the hospitable elm tree and offering its clusters of purple grapes, lies rotting on the earth. When the clever Maria attempts to turn such argumentation by analogies back on the youth and mentions the unnaturalness of plucking a blooming rose, Pamphilus counters that, just as a good wine must be consumed rather than left to turn into vinegar, so must the rose be enjoyed before it withers on the vine. Adopting a more direct method of persuasion at this point, he allows that "a virgin maiden is *a precious gem*" but asks: "what can be a greater monstrosity than an aged virgin?" Skillfully developing the conceit of the rose, Pamphilus moves toward his most important and revolutionary argument. The blossom of virginity paradoxically blooms more beautifully when it is plucked; in its plucking more blossoms appear ("for one which *is lost many will be gained*"). Indeed, how could Maria's own flower have grown had her mother not allowed hers to be plucked? There is in fact a chaste relationship between husband and wife that is scarcely distinguishable from virginity. In it the partners, making "correct use" of the things of this world, which, as Erasmus recommends everywhere in his Pauline *Philosophia Christiana*, they should possess as if not possessing, subordinate their physical relationship to their higher spiritual unity and reproduce for Christ and their republic, learning through their relationship what in fact virginity really means. All the paradoxicality implied by the ideal of chaste marriage is emphasized in Maria's astonished reaction and Pamphilus's response: "Maria: '. . . What is this I hear? In order to learn, one must lose *the best gem which God gave me*, which is virginity?' Pamphilus: 'Why not? It is necessary *to lose in order to be able to gain.*' " Pamphilus goes on to elaborate on the paradox and enunciate an ideal of moral autonomy that is central to the ethical vision both of Erasmus and Cervantes. "Which seems more temperate to you, the person who, finding himself in the midst of delights and continually tempted to enjoy them, abstains and despises them, or the person who, confined in a monastery or removed to a desert, is virtuous by not confronting them?"[73] By this point the doctrine of virginity has come to

[73] "una donzella virgen es *vna preciosa joya.* . . . que monstruo puede ser mayor que vna virgen vieja? . . . por vna que se pierda *se ganaran muchas.* . . . *Mar.*— . . . que oygo? que para deprender se ha de perder *la mejor joya que Dios me dio*, que es la virgidad? *Pam.*—Por que no? menester es *perder para poder ganar.* . . . Qual te parece a ti que vsa mas de virtud de temperança, el que, estando en medio de los deleytes, ofreciendosele cada ora oportunidad para vsar dellos, se abstiene e los menosprecia, o el que, estando encerrado en vn monasterio o apartado en vn desierto, por no tropeçar en ello es bueno?" (pp. 168-69).

represent a life-denying force, opposed not only to nature, but also to the development of the ethically mature and liberated consciousness for which, as Erasmus repeatedly insisted, Christ called upon man to strive.[74]

In the *Gitanilla* Cervantes is unconcerned with the polemics surrounding the relative merits of celibacy and matrimony which figured so prominently in all Erasmus's writings on marriage and which made his matrimonial colloquies such relevant and controversial documents in the religious and social upheavals of the early sixteenth century. In Preciosa's speech on virginity and in her argument with her importunate suitor, there are no subtle dialectics aimed at overthrowing a repressive ascetic exaltation of virginity, just as there is no attempt to elevate virginity with traditional theological arguments. Of the various threats to the happy realization of wedded love that Erasmus considers in his colloquy, Cervantes chose for treatment in his own examination of marriage the dangers of uncontrolled passion and the illusions fostered by conventional amatory rhetoric. What undoubtedly appealed to him in the central passage of his model was its celebration, through lively debate and dramatic confrontation, of Christian marriage as an institution that sanctions the creative expression of man's natural impulses, its rich development of imagery of natural abundance and sensuous delight, and its paradoxical notion that marriage allows virginity to be maintained even as it is surrendered. Echoing the phrases of Maria, Preciosa reminds her impatient lover that her virginity is her only jewel ("A single gem do I possess . . ."), that she will not risk losing it or defiling it for gifts or the promises held by dreams and illusions, and that it is a "flower" that must not be "offended." She adds: *"Once the rose is cut from the bush, with what rapidity and facility does it wither!* This one handles it, that

---

[74] In the exchange we observe a characteristic example of Erasmus's Christian Humanism, as he appropriates a distinguished *topos* descending from classical antiquity and adapts it to his own didactic purposes. His dialogue clearly echoes the debate on the loss of virginity in Catullus's *Carmen* LXII, the so-called "Greek" epithalamium, in which youths reject the maidens' arguments against plucking the blossom. "Ut vidua in nudo vitis quae nascitur arvo/ Numquam se extollit, numquam mitem educat uvam,/ Sed tenerum prono deflectens pondere corpus/ Iam iam contingit summum radice flagellum;/ Hanc nulli agricolae, nulli coluere bubulci:/ At si forte eademst ulmo coniuncta marito,/ Multi illam agricolae, multi coluere bubulci:/ Sic virgo, dum intacta manet, dum inculta senescit;/ Cum par conubium maturo tempore adeptast,/ Cara viro magis et minus est invisa parenti." For the history of the topos which Catullus's poem bequeathed to European literature and its spectacular resurrection in epithalamic poetry of the Renaissance, see Peter Demetz, "The Elm and the Vine: Notes Toward the History of a Marriage Topos," *PMLA* 73 (1958):521-32. In the *Gitanilla* it appears in one of Preciosa's songs (see below).

one smells it, another plucks its leaves, and finally *in rough hands the flower is destroyed."* As she proceeds to speak of the blessings of marriage, she picks up the arguments and phrases of Pamphilus: "If you, sir, come for this gift alone, you cannot bear it away unless secured with the ties and bonds of marriage, for if virginity has to yield, it is only to this sacred yoke; for then its yielding would not be *its loss, but rather its employment in festivities that promise happy gains."*[75]

THE MATRIMONIAL IDEAL AND THE
POETRY OF *LA GITANILLA*

In its sharp doctrinal focus and its clear subordination of narrative and dramatic elements to the play of ideas that they serve, Erasmus's colloquy is a kind of work which is basically different from Cervantes's lengthy novella. Yet once we recognize the colloquy's impact on the fundamental conception of the exemplary tale and its actual incorporation into certain scenes that are thematically central to the novella, we can proceed to clarify several of the more ambiguous elements in the Spanish text. For example, the poems in the early part of the tale, which have been generally ignored by critics and occasionally omitted by editors and translators, can be understood as carefully integrated emblematic statements of its principal themes.

The first two songs, both in the subject that they narrate and in the circumstances surrounding Preciosa's performance of them, bring to the romance scenes of spectacular ritual celebration centering on the ideal of Christian marriage and its fruits. Depicting the heavenly family—Joachim and Anne, traditionally the models of Christian wedded love,[76] together with their offspring, the Virgin with her

---

[75] "*Cortada la rosa del rosal, ¡con qué brevedad y facilidad se marchita!* Éste la toca, aquél la huele, el otro la deshoja, y, finalmente, *entre las manos rústicas se deshace.* Si vos, señor, por sola esta prenda venís, no la habéis de llevar sino atada con las ligaduras y lazos del matrimonio; que si la virginidad se ha de inclinar, ha de ser *a este santo yugo; que entonces no sería perderla, sino emplearla en ferias que felices ganancias prometen"* (p. 39).

[76] The cult of St. Anne traditionally honored wedded love, motherhood, and family life. It developed through the late middle ages and reached its moment of greatest intensity in the early sixteenth century, a phenomenon that no doubt was related to the current widespread interest in the family in bourgeois culture. Erasmus, for example, wrote poetry to St. Anne and claimed that from his most tender childhood on he was "consumed with piety for her cult" (see Febvre, *Au Coeur religieux du xvie siècle,* p. 32). In 1584 the Pope elevated the celebration of the cult to a feast of the whole Latin Church. The cult of St. Anne was extremely popular in Cervantes's Spain, and its themes were depicted widely in the art and literature of the period (see Beda

child—and its earthly replica—King Philip III, Margarita of Austria, and the newborn infant, Philip IV—, the songs introduce the vision of perfection toward which Preciosa would aspire in her marriage ideal; associate her exile in the wilderness, her guidance of Juan toward rational love, and her redemptive powers with divine archetypes;[77] prefigure the festive celebration of her marriage and its promise of abundant fruits at the conclusion of the tale; and concentrate the central imagery of natural fertility, celestial beauty, and ascent, which penetrates the entire work and contributes significantly to its imaginative unity.[78] At the very beginning of the tale of Preciosa's ordeals,

---

Kleinschmidt, *Die Heilige Anna: Ihre Verehrung in Geschichte, Kunst und Volkstum* [Düsseldorf, 1930], pp. 334-44). Georg Schreiber has emphasized the importance of the legends of St. Anne throughout the Catholic world in the formation of humane popular attitudes toward maternity, childbearing, the value of children, and child care. "So liest sich die weitverzweigte Gesamtlegende der hl. Anna wie ein Hymnus und ein Hoheslied der ehelichen und christlichen Fruchtbarkeit" (*Mutter und Kind in der Kultur der Kirche* [Freiburg, 1918], p. 79). Schreiber's words describe the primary function of Preciosa's hymn to St. Anne in the *La Gitanilla* perfectly.

[77] Fragmentary divine myths and legends hover mysteriously about Cervantes's dancing maiden, who is kidnapped on Ascension Day and enters Madrid amid the public ceremonies of the Feast of St. Anne. One of the most prominent is the legend of St. Anne, and, in addition to adopting its central theme, the celebration of wedded love, Cervantes's tale reenacts in analogy and variation some of its specific events. Thus, like Anne's child, Mary, who dances before the altar of the temple and is adored by all who observe her, Preciosa dances to universal acclaim before the altar of the Virgin in the church of Madrid. A central scene of the legend is Anne's offering of the fruits of her marriage in the temple; in *La Gitanilla* Cervantes depicts Margarita of Austria approaching the altar of the Church of Saint Llorente and offering her newly born child to the Virgin ("las primicias de mis frutos/ Te ofrezco, Virgen hermosa" [p. 15]). The initial period of sterility in Joachim's marriage, in which he withdraws to the wilderness, leaving Anne to mourn in apparent widowhood, is comparable to the early part of *La Gitanilla*, which depicts the dissolution of a family and an exile in the wilderness, and which is marked by several motifs of sterility (see below). For the details of the legends of St. Anne, see Kleinschmidt, *Die Heilige Anna*, pp. 4-12, 252ff.

[78] This is not the place for a full treatment of the central imagery of the novella, as I am here concerned primarily with its development of the theme of marriage. However, it should be observed that one of its most powerful symbols of wedded love is the Catullian *topos* which Erasmus incorporates into his discussion of virginity. Celebrating the royal family and its offspring, the Gypsy maiden sings of Queen Margarita: "Fecunda vid,/ Crece, sube, abraza y toca/ El olmo felice tuyo,/ Que mil siglos te haga sombra,/ Para gloria de ti misma,/ Para bien de España y honra,/ Para arrimo de la Iglesia,/ Para asombro de Mahoma" (p. 14). At the same time, Margarita as the vine, St. Anne as the fruit-bearing tree, and Clemente's prophecy of the "bellos renuevos" (p. 101) which will bless Preciosa's union with Juan bring into the tale powerful traditional Christian symbols of wedded love, based on Ps. 127:3, which the Church has incorporated into the bride's mass of its liturgy: "Your wife will be

her restoration, and her perfect love, we gaze in a moment of ritual intensity on the great Christian myth celebrating the turn of history and the redemption of the entire human family.[79]

As I have pointed out above, the third poem deals with problems of love, the conventions of amatory rhetoric, and courtship. It is customary to read the fourth poem, Preciosa's prophecy to the wife of the lieutenant, for the farcical humor in its description of her character and her domestic troubles and in its mischievous allusions to her lustful proclivities. Like so many other elements in the satirical scene in the house of the struggling bureaucrat, the poem certainly contributes to the characterization of Preciosa as an intriguing combination of spirituality and worldliness. However, it should be noticed that the poem describes another marriage and another family and that, in its continuing depiction of domestic situations, the tale has taken us, so to speak, down the "Great Chain of Being," from the divine order, to the ideal social order of the court, redeemed as it is by the prince-saviour, and finally to the ordinary urban world of contemporary Spain, where most of its action unfolds. Here we discover a marriage in which both partners exhibit a good deal of violence and lust, frequently scold and beat one another, and appear to be yoked until death in a conjugal relationship plagued by tyranny, fear, mistrust, jealousy, and adultery. The brief picture of domestic chaos, which might have reminded a seventeenth-century reader of Erasmus's popular colloquy on the miseries of unhappy married life, the *Uxor Mempsigamos*,[80] presents a complete inversion of the vision of the opening poems, which it parodies effectively in its prominent imagery of animal rapacity and descent ("Protect yourself from falling down,/ Beware mainly of backward falls"[81]) and in its obscenely inverted celestial motifs—the sun and moon shining in the lady's "dark valleys"

---

like a fruitful vine/ within your house;/ your children will be like olive shoots/ around your table" (see Schreiber, *Mutter und Kind in der Kultur der Kirche*, pp. 90-91).

[79] For the symbolism of Joachim and Anne as representing the messianic promise and expectation of the Old Testament and the central moment in history when divinity entered humanity, see J. P. Asselin, "Anne and Joachim, ss.," *New Catholic Encyclopedia* (New York, 1967), 1:558-60. One can compare Cervantes's celebration in poetry of the Immaculate Conception at the moment when his wanderers have left the perilous northern world behind them, emerged from the sea, and begun the final phase of their redemptive journey to Rome (*Los trabajos de Persiles y Sigismunda*, pp. 309-11; see my *Cervantes' Christian Romance*, pp. 87-89).

[80] This colloquy was available to the Spanish public in the early translations of Erasmus's *Colloquies* (see M. Bataillon, *Erasmo y España*, pp. 386ff.), and in Pedro de Luxán's popular *Coloquios matrimoniales*, where it is adapted as the "Segundo coloquio."

[81] "Guárdate de las caídas/ principalmente de espaldas" (p. 31).

and inviting the blind to gaze at them. Thus, if we are aware of the importance of the themes of marriage, love, and courtship, we easily see that the four poems, which dominate the first quarter of the tale and indeed are recited before the action begins, form a striking emblematic prologue, announcing the principal themes and introducing the central imagery.

The most important poems in the work are those which Juan, Clemente, and Preciosa sing on the eve of the heroes' return to civilization. In the atmosphere of the pastoral symposium the heroes withdraw from the Gypsy camp to form a perfect society of friends, and, seated beneath the hospitable cork and oak trees, they discourse on such essential truths as love, beauty, and virtue. Their amoebean song is the most powerful expression of the ideal love toward which Juan moves in his purification quest. Indeed, it expands the concept of rational love, celebrated throughout the work and enunciated most frequently by Preciosa, by introducing a spiritual element that derives from neo-Platonism. Juan has not simply learned to control his impulses and to escape the blindness of his infatuation; he has in fact refined his perception of truth to such an extent that he can see through the external beauty of his beloved to her finer spiritual beauty and recognize in it the presence of divinity.[82] Lifting his thoughts to eternal truths, he likens her true beauty to the starry veil that shines above them, displaying its dazzling traces of the absolute beauty of eternity:

> Mira, Clemente, el estrellado velo
> Con que esta noche fría
> Compite con el día,
> De luces bellas adornando el cielo;
> Y en esta semejanza,
> Si tanto tu divino ingenio alcanza,
> Aquel rostro figura
> Donde asiste el extremo de hermosura.[83]

For the neo-Platonists the translunary world of the empyrean and the spheres of the fixed stars and the planets is the realm of the Cosmic

---

[82] See Ficino: "Ubi particularis amor ad particularem pulchritudinem nascitur. Sic et ad hominem aliquem ordinis mundani membrum afficimur, praesertim cum in illo perspicue divini decoris scintilla refulget" (*Ficino's Commentary on Plato's "Symposium,"* pp. 69-70).

[83] "Look upward, Clemente, and see the starry veil/ In which this chilly night/ Competes with the day,/ Adorning the heavens with lovely lights;/ And if your divine genius can reach so far,/ Figure in this image/ That face/ Where the highest degree of beauty is to be found" (p. 102).

Soul, through which the divine radiance passes before entering the darker realms of nature and matter.[84] As Juan exhorts his comrade to discover the identity of the beautiful face of Preciosa and the "starry veil,"[85] he suggests that the vision is possible only if he exercises the divine powers of his soul ("if your divine genius can reach so far"). Clemente agrees that Preciosa's beauty and the goodness visible therein are so pure that "there is no human genius sufficient to sing her praises, unless it touches on divinity."[86] Thus Juan, who begins his courtship by responding to the urgings of his "eyes of the body" ("ojos corporales"), a faculty which, according to the neo-Platonist doctrines of love echoed throughout the poem, pertains to the *anima secunda* or lower soul, has come to perceive his beloved with the highest faculty of his mind (*mens, intellectus humanus sive angelicus*), which unites him most directly with the Cosmic Mind and enables him to contemplate its supercelestial ideas.[87] In an experience recalling the neo-Platonic

---

[84] See Panofsky, "The Neoplatonic Movement in Florence and Northern Italy," p. 132, for these ideas in Ficino's writings. See also Leone Ebreo: ". . . per vedere le stelle e i cieli sempre in movimento, veniamo a conoscere i motori loro essere intellettuali e incorporei, e la sapienzia e potenzia de l'universal creatore e opifice loro" (*Dialoghi d'amore*, p. 183).

[85] Behind Juan's identification of the face of Preciosa and the "estrellado velo" is one of the most important doctrines in the neo-Platonists' celebration of the dignity of man—the theory of the microcosm. It is well to compare the poem with the more complete elaboration of the doctrine in Cervantes's early work, *La Galatea*, where it emerges in a section that borrows heavily from the writings of Mario Equicola, Pietro Bembo, Castiglione, and Leone Ebreo (see F. López Estrada, *La Galatea de Cervantes, Estudio crítico* [La Laguna de Tenerife, 1948], pp. 88-95, 110-115; also "La influencia italiana en la Galatea de Cervantes," *Comparative Literature* 4 [1952]:161-69; Geoffrey Stagg, "Plagiarism in 'La Galatea,' " *Filologia Romanza* 6 [1959]:255-76; Francisco Rico, *El pequeño mundo del hombre* [Madrid, 1970], pp. 139ff.). Lenio describes a lofty love which enables the lover to "llegar a la primera causa de las causas" by contemplating the universal beauty and design visible "en los estrellados cielos y en la máquina y redondez de la tierra," as well as in man the microcosm: "Pero lo que más los admiró y levantó la consideración, fue ver la compostura del hombre, tan ordenada, tan perfecta, y tan hermosa, que le vinieron [los antiguos filósofos] a llamar mundo abreviado, y así es verdad, que en todas las obras hechas por el mayordomo de Dios, naturaleza, ninguna es de tanto primor ni que más descubra la grandeza y sabiduría de su hacedor, porque en la figura y compostura del hombre se cifra y cierra la belleza que en todas las otras partes della se reparte, y de aquí nace que esta belleza conocida *se ama, y como toda ella más se muestre y resplandezca en el rostro, luego como se ve un hermoso rostro, llama y tira la voluntad a amarle*" (*La Galatea*, 2:60-61; italics added). For the connection between the doctrine and the praises of the physical beauty of the beloved in Renaissance lyric poetry, see Rico, *El pequiño mundo del hombre*, pp. 142-43.

[86] "Que no hay humano ingenio que le alabe,/ Si no toca en divino" (p. 102).

[87] The existence of the "divino ingenio," which Cervantes's lovers exercise at this moment of mystical vision in their quest, is a central doctrine of the neo-Platonists' view of the human being, deriving on the one hand from their belief that the divine

furor amatorius, in which the loving individual, "through the desire
for the divine beauty and the passion for Good,"[88] awakens his slumbering higher faculties, calms the affections, and reunites with the
One in the circle of love flowing from the Creator to the creation and
back, Juan and Clemente contemplate their beloved's face in the starry
skies and imagine the name of Preciosa sounding throughout the heavens, arousing wonder and awe everywhere. At this moment of mystical rapture they envision the Gypsy maiden as one of the Platonic
sirens, the celestial maidens who sit upon the turning spheres rejoicing the heavens with their song and bringing peace to the souls of
those on earth who are privileged by their virtue to hear their voices
and harmonies.

> Paz en las almas, gloria en los sentidos
> Se siente cuando canta

intellect penetrates the entire universe with its radiant effluence, animating all of its
creations to strive to reunite with it in a loving union, on the other hand from their
theory of the microcosm, which held that within man there are two superior faculties,
the higher and the lower soul, analogous to the two highest orders—the Cosmic
Mind and the Cosmic Soul—into which the Supreme Being unfolds itself in its
circular motion downward through its created hierarchies and back to itself. When
it exercises its superior faculty, the mind (designated by Ficino "intellectus humanus
sive angelicus"), the higher soul can communicate with and participate in the *intellectus divinus* of the Supreme Being. For a clear discussion of these doctrines and the
various texts by Ficino which expound and promulgate them, see Panofsky, "The
Neoplatonic Movement in Florence and Northern Italy," pp. 132-35. See also Leone
Ebreo's description of the intellect as "un piccolo razo de l'infinita chiarezza di Dio,
appropriato a l'uomo per farlo razionale, immortale e felice," the element "che ne
l'uomo corresponde al divin principio, dal qual tutte le cose hanno principio e in lui
tutte si dirizzano e riposono come in ultimo fine," and his distinction between the
pure intellect ("l'intelletto astratto") and the soul ("l'anima") (*Dialoghi d'amore*, pp.
30, 83, 176ff.). While the latter must animate the body and attend to corporeal
matters, the former is enlightened by the divine intellect ("illuminato da l'intelletto
divino" [p. 180]) and enables man to enjoy the vision of incorporeal things, eternal
forms, and universal causes. Man's pure intellect resembles the divine intellect; for
just as it "non solamente intende tutte le spezie de le cose che sono in lui, ma ancora
illumina tutti gli altri intelletti con le sue lucide ed eterne idee ovvero spezie, cosí il
nostro intelletto non solamente intende le spezie di tutte le cose, ma ancora illumina
tutte l'altre virtú conoscitive de l'uomo, accioché, se ben la lor cognizione è partic-
ulare e materiale, sia diretta da l'intelletto non bestiale, come negli altri animali" (p.
185). The climactic stanza of Cervantes's pastoral elegy (*Galatea*, pp. 177-83) envisions the dead Meliso resurrected from his "caída" into mortality and enjoying the
"hermosa clara faz serena" of the "suma gloria más perfecta." The vision is based on
the neo-Platonic conception of beauty as a ray proceeding from the divine Creator's
face, and the experience of the elegiac poet is made possible by the exercise of the
lofty faculty which enables Juan and Clemente to perceive cosmic beauties in the face
of Preciosa ("aquello que contemplo agora, y veo con el entendimiento levantado . . .").

[88] *Ficino's Commentary on Plato's "Symposium,"* pp. 115-16.

> La sirena, que encanta
> Y adormece a los más apercibidos;
> Y tal es mi Preciosa,
> Que es lo menos que tiene ser hermosa:
> Dulce regalo mío,
> Corona del donaire, honor del brío.[89]

The constellation of divine and quasi-divine maidens that has hovered about Preciosa—St. Anne, the Virgin, Margarita of Austria, Dame Poetry, the "perfecta casada" of Holy Scripture—is now complete, and, as her lovers perceive her through what the neo-Platonists referred to as the spiritual senses of sight and hearing,[90] we have reached the culminating apotheosis of the little Gypsy in Cervantes's tale.

This is not the occasion for a full analysis of the neo-Platonic content of the amoebean poem and Preciosa's response.[91] Suffice it to say

---

[89] "Peace fills the souls, the senses feel rapture/ Whenever Preciosa sings,/ The siren who enchants and calms those who are most aware;/ And such is my Preciosa,/ That the least of her qualities is her beauty:/ My sweet gift,/ The crown of grace, the honor of gallantry" (p. 103). On the sirens, whose music, as the "ultimate image of the celestial harmony," can remind the most pure and aspiring minds of the true god, see Proclus, *Platonica Theologia*, 7.36; also James Hutton, "Some English Poems in Praise of Music," *English Miscellany* 2 (1951):1-63; and E.M.W. Tillyard, *The Elizabethan World Picture* (New York, 1959), pp. 48-50. The musical powers of Preciosa to calm the affections might at the same time reflect the doctrine that music is essential to the calming of the soul before it can ascend to the transport of its encounter with beauty. See *Ficino's Commentary on Plato's "Symposium,"* pp. 115-16.

[90] See Leone Ebreo: "Ancora mi ricordo averti mostrato parte de la spirituale essenzia de la bellezza, però ch'io ti feci conoscere che, de li cinque sensi esteriori, la bellezza non entra ne l'animo umano per li tre loro materiali (cioè né per il tatto né per il gusto né per l'odorato, ché le temperate qualità né li dilettevoli tatti venerei non si chiamano belli, né manco li dolci sapori né li soavi odori si dicono belli), ma solamente per li due spirituali: cioè parte per l'audito, per li belli parlamenti orazione ragioni versi, belle musiche e belle e concordanti armonie, e la maggior parte per l'occhi, ne le belle figure e belli colori e proporzionate composizioni e bella luce e simili, li quali ti denotano quanto sia la bellezza cosa spirituale e astratta dal corpo" (*Dialoghi d'amore*, p. 316).

[91] The starry veil, with its orderly movements, the celestial harmonies of the sirens, and their power to bring order to the soul of the listener ("paz en las almas, gloria en los sentidos") are elements of Platonic and neo-Platonic philosophy that are prominent in a major tradition of Christian thought, for which Cervantes's contemporary Luis de León is one of the great spokesmen. In his *Los nombres de Cristo* the narrator directs his gaze toward heaven, "sembrado de estrellos," and discourses at great length on the peace, joy, and tranquility that the "vista hermosa del cielo" and "el concierto que tienen entre sí aquestos resplandores" bring to the beholder. Here he finds a universal design, in which the heavenly bodies never forget their true course, shine on each other in a show of love and mutual respect, and, united harmoniously as the members of a family, join their respective virtues in "una pacífica unidad de virtud." In a mysterious voice they communicate their message of harmony to the soul of the beholder and restore it to its true order, in which reason is enthroned and the trou-

that motifs of ascent are conspicuous in both poems, and that the virtue of the beloved one has elevated her to a lofty position in essential reality, which sharply contrasts with her lowly estate in the world of appearances. Her lover has moved up the Platonic "ladder of love" by recognizing and adoring her spiritual beauty ("Such is my Preciosa that the least of her qualities is her beauty"), and he has glimpsed in her the presence of the absolute beauty of the Supreme Being and reached the divine ecstasy of the perfect lover. Juan has followed Preciosa's injunction to dispel the shadows of his "disordered vision" ("turbada vista"). He has learned to lift his gaze from her bewitching feet, to look with "the eyes of the mind" ("los ojos del entendimiento"), and in the ordered vision that rewards his quest into the wilderness, he recognizes in his beloved's face the finest beauty of the microcosm and the universal splendor of the Creation that it discloses.[92]

---

blesome affections sink into repose. "La cual boz y pregón, sin ruydo, se lança en nuestras almas . . . se comiençan ellas a pacificar en sí mismas y a poner a cada una de sus partes en orden . . . este concierto y orden de las estrellas, mirándolo, pone en nuestras almas sossiego, y veremos que con sólo tener los ojos enclavados en él con attención . . . los desseos nuestros y las affecciones turbadas, que confusamente movían ruydo en nuestros pechos de día, se van quietando. . . . Y veremos que . . . lo que es señor en el alma, que es la razón, se levanta y recobra su derecho y su fuerça . . . se recuerda de su primer origen . . . queda todo el hombre ordenado y pacífico" (ed. F. de Onís, 3 vols. [Madrid, 1969], 2:150-55). In view of Casalduero's stress on the importance of *La perfecta casada* as the model of Cervantes's matrimonial ideal, it is worth pointing out that Luis de León's tract makes no attempt to associate the lofty spiritual state described by his pious interlocutors of *Los nombres de Cristo* with wedded love or, for that matter, with the contemplation of the microcosm in a beloved human being. Characteristic of the fundamental emphasis of the entire *Los nombres de Cristo* is the introduction of a secular analogue of divine realities, in this case the family, to underscore the splendor of those transcendental realities rather than to elevate the secular state. Unlike Erasmus and Cervantes, Luis de León is fundamentally a religious contemplative, and he does not share their enthusiasm for bringing into this world, to whatever extent it is possible to do so, the perfections of the transcendental order. For them it was undoubtedly the conception of the immanence of divinity in matter that was most attractive in neo-Platonic thought and not its emphasis on the transcendence of materiality through contemplation. At the same time it should be noted that, while the association of this magnificent vision of cosmic beauty and order, described by Luis de León's Marcello, with the beauty of a beloved human being, whose microcosmic perfection reflects the design of the universe, is characteristic of Renaissance neo-Platonists' theories of love (see, for example, *Ficino's Commentary on Plato's "Symposium,"* pp. 69-70), they generally made little effort to connect the matrimonial relationship with this mystical state (see below).

[92] See Leone Ebreo's discussion of the necessary worthiness of the lover who is to enjoy this supreme experience of love: "Di quella persona amata l'immagine ne la mente de l'amante avviva con la sua bellezza quella bellezza divina latente, che è la medesima anima, e gli dá attualitá al modo che gli daria essa medesima bellezza

Cervantes's effort to suffuse the joyous love of matrimony, which, as Preciosa emphasizes, looks forward to its fulfillment in procreation, with the mystical spirituality of Platonic love might strike us as odd and even paradoxical at first glance, and, to be sure, the neo-Platonic amatory treatises did not show much interest in marriage. It is characteristic that in his epistle in praise of marriage, Ficino limits his arguments to practical, civic, and ethical concerns and makes no attempt to dignify the relation of husband and wife with his contemplative doctrines of perfect love. However, we need only look at Cervantes's model; for it is precisely this combination that Erasmus developed and passed on to numerous spiritual descendants who celebrated marriage for the next two centuries.[93] Indeed, there is probably no area of his broad program for reform that demonstrates more clearly his fundamental aim of bringing the lofty piety and spirituality which had traditionally been consigned far too exclusively to contemplative and ascetic spheres of activity into the daily life of Christians in this world. Throughout his *Institutio Christiani Matrimonii* Erasmus emphasizes the possibilities for perfection in a marriage that is entered into under the guidance of reason and in which appetite and self-interest are secondary to love, friendship, companionship, and mutual understanding. In one of his discussions of Christian *caritas*, conjugal amity, and rationality, the Platonic elements in his ideal are particularly visible. After condemning inconstant lovers, who, blinded by Cupid, the son of the earthly Venus, are driven by the allurements of

---

divina esemplare. . . . l'amore di quella viene sí intenso, ardente ed efficace, che rubba li sensi la fantasia e tutta la mente, come faria essa bellezza divina quando retirasse a sé in contemplazione l'anima umana. E tanto quella immagine de la persona amata s'adora ne la mente de l'amante per divina, quanto la bellezza sua de l'anima e del corpo è piú eccellente e consimile a la bellezza divina e in lei piú reluce la sua somma sapienzia; e ancora con questo si giunta la natura de la mente de l'amante che la riceve, però che se in quella la bellezza divina è molto sommersa e latente, per essere vinta da la materia e corpo, se bene l'amato è molto bello, in lei può poco deificare, per la poca divinitá che in quella mente luce; né ancora quella può vedere nel bello amato quanta sia la bellezza sua, né può conoscere il grado della sua bellezza: onde raro è che l'anime basse e sommerse in materia amino grandi e vere bellezze, e che l'amore loro sia grandemente eccellente. Ma quando la persona amata bellissima è amata da anima chiara e levata da la materia, ne la quale la somma bellezza divina sommamente riluce, allora è grandemente deificata in lei, quale l'adora sempre per divina, e l'amore suo verso lei è grandemente intenso, efficace e ardente" (*Dialoghi d'amore*, pp. 389-90).

[93] We find, for example, a similar fusion of the ideals of Platonic love and Christian matrimony in Milton's celebration of wedded love in *Paradise Lost*: ". . . love refines/ The thoughts, and heart enlarges, hath his seat/ In Reason, and is judicious, is the scale/ By which to heav'nly Love thou may'st ascend" (8.589-92).

fleshly beauty, and whose carnal passion is in reality a form of self-love, a state in which "reason is buried" and insanity holds sway, Erasmus defines true love:

But the Philosopher says that there is also a second Cupid, born of the heavenly Venus, and that nothing is more sharp-eyed than he. He does not put out the eyes of those whom he strikes with his darts, but rather restores sight to the blind. He shows them the beauties in the souls that reflect the image of that highest beauty. This image, once glimpsed, immediately carries those who behold it away with love for it. It creates pure friendships, and once it has created them makes them firm, enabling them to grow ever better and stronger.[94]

---

[94] "Verum Philosophus ait, & alterum esse Cupidinem, e Venere coelesti prognatum, quo nihil oculatius. Is non exoculat, quos attingit suis jaculis, sed ex caecis reddit oculatos. Hic formas ostendit animorum, qui summi illius pulcri referunt imaginem, quae conspecta protinus rapit in amorem sui, jungitque puras, junctas stabilit amicitias, semper in melius majusque gliscentes" (see *Institutio Christiani Matrimonii*, pp. 681-82). The figure of a clear-sighted Cupid, representing the spiritual love inspired by the celestial Venus, was a popular figure in the neo-Platonists' discussions of love and in the works of art influenced by their doctrines. For example, Lucas Cranach the Elder depicts a "little Cupid, removing the bandage from his eyes with his own hand and thus transforming himself into a personification of 'seeing' love. To do this he bases himself most literally on Plato, for he stands on an imposing volume inscribed *Platonis opera* from which he seems to be 'taking off' for more elevated spheres" (Panofsky, "Blind Cupid," *Studies in Iconology*, p. 128). As Panofsky points out in his analysis of Titian's "Education of Cupid," Cupid's "eyes of reason" and his inspiration to contemplative love were also connected with marital affection and chaste wedded love (see pp. 165ff.). Erasmus's distinction between the heavenly and the earthly Venus is closer to Pausanius's discussion of the myth in Plato's *Symposium* and to the central medieval tradition viewing the goddesses as holding sway over virtuous and carnal love respectively (see Robertson, *A Preface to Chaucer*, pp. 125-26) than to the Florentine neo-Platonist elaborations of the myth, where the "lower" Venus signified the natural principle of generation, overseeing the creation of the innumerable forms in nature which manifest the intelligible beauty, translating "sparks of that divine glory into earthly matter," and making it apprehensible to the senses. The loves inspired by each Venus, producing on the one hand the yearning to contemplate divine beauty, on the other hand, the desire to procreate a replica of the beloved who manifests divine beauty, are both honorable (see *Ficino's Commentary on Plato's "Symposium,"* pp. 48-49). As Panofsky points out, Pico maintained Plato's earthly Venus as the goddess of carnal love and introduced a third Venus, the daughter of Saturn rather than Uranus, who occupied an intermediary position corresponding in powers and activities to that of Ficino's lower Venus (see "The Neoplatonic Movement in Florence and North Italy," pp. 144-45). Erasmus's erroneous attribution to Plato of a discussion of the opposition of a blind and a clear-sighted Cupid, an opposition that in fact did not develop until the late middle ages, as well as his adherence to a traditionalist view of the two Venuses in this particular passage, which is otherwise notable for its neo-Platonic content, is not surprising in view of his general lack of interest, as he traces his ideal of wedded love and conjugal friendship,

The fountain of all true beauty is God, "in whom whatever there is, is pure goodness," and who bountifully offers the sparks of his light to the souls of the elect, "from which there arises among the good a flame of mutual affection which is loving and chaste, as befits its source." The light of this love is untroubled by any shadows or clouds: "the love that comes into being in this way is always serene and tranquil."[95] The spiritual bond with which it unites two beings needs no witnesses or oaths. Erasmus points out that true virtue "cannot perish" ("nescit interire") and adds that "therefore inner beauty, inner riches, and inner nobility should bind Christian marriages," for the benevolence which the recognition of these invisible qualities produces will be perpetual. It is in the order of nature and Christian piety to proceed from the things of the senses to things perceived only by the "exercise of the mind" ("mentis agitatione"). Those who are smitten by the beauty of a body must recall therein true Beauty, which, as Plato declared, we are capable of recollecting, because unlike the beasts we are born with a propensity to "*honesta*." The moment of such recollection is conceived of as an "awakening from sleep,"[96] and once

---

in the contemplative and mystical heights to which the Florentines aspired in their doctrines of love and his disdain for the elaborate mythology that they developed to visualize and communicate them. For Erasmus's skeptical attitude toward the contemporary efforts of the Italian neo-Platonists to allegorize pagan mysteries and reconcile them with Christian teachings, see his *Ciceronianus*, where on at least two occasions he mocks the irresponsible exegesis of the myth of Ganymede, a myth that was commonly interpreted as an allegory of the Ascension and of the mystical ascent of the contemplative neo-Platonic lover (see *Ausgewählte Schriften*, ed. W. Welzig, 8 vols. [Darmstadt, 1967-1980], 7:176, 322).

[95] "in quo quidquid est, pura bonitas est . . . ex quibus inter bonos oritur amabilis quidam & castus ardor mutuae benevolentiae, suo fonti respondens . . . itidem sic contractus amor, semper serenus est ac tranquillus." For the doctrine of divine beauty as the purest light, glimmerings of which in beautiful people shine through the corporeal husks of materiality and arouse love in their beholders, see *Ficino's Commentary on Plato's "Symposium"*: ". . . ad hominem aliquem ordinis mundani membrum afficimur, praesertim cum in illo perspicue divini decoris scintilla refulget" (pp. 69-70; see also Ficino's discussion of the two Venuses and the translation of the sparks of divine glory into earthly matter, p. 49). Revealing his characteristic interest in reconciling the highest wisdom of the ancient philosophers with the doctrines of Christianity, Erasmus connects the notion with James's reference to divine gifts as "coming down from the Father of lights with whom there is no variation or shadow due to change" (1:17). Also to be noted is Erasmus's distinctive emphasis on the union of the "two friends" drawn together by the recognition of sparks of divinity in one another rather than on the union of the lover and divinity made manifest in the beloved. The slight difference in emphasis is a revealing indication of the limits beyond which Erasmus could not pass in his approximation to Florentine neo-Platonism, with its dominant interest in beauty and mystical experience.

[96] "Proinde, quos in amorem rapit forma corporis, veluti somnio quodam admo-

awake the lover contemplates the true beauty with the "eyes of the mind" ("mentis oculis") and can then devote himself to nourishing and bringing to perfection his union with the beloved, a union that will be marked by spirituality, rationality, clarity of vision, constancy, and trust. In Cervantes's *La Gitanilla*, at the climactic moment of the amoebaean song, which the lovers sing beneath the stars, Juan has in fact achieved the goal demanded by Preciosa at the beginning of his purification quest. He has awakened from his sleep and is looking at the maiden with the "eyes of the mind" ("ojos del entendimiento"), and, in the serenity and peace of a perfect love, he beholds the essential reality that she herself celebrates in her final song ("I consider it a greater blessing to be virtuous than to be beautiful"[97]). He knows that mortal beauty is the "least of her good qualities," and he enjoys the experience which, as Erasmus maintains, rewards all true lovers: "once the empty dreams have been shaken off, if the lover turns the eyes of his mind to the beauty of the beloved, then the illusions of insubstantial beauty immediately give way to what is truly beautiful."[98]

THE MATRIMONIAL IDEAL, THE DOUBLE, AND THE DENOUEMENT

The authentic relationship between man and wife must not be troubled by the constant threat of violence and dissolution that hangs over the fragile Gypsy marriage. For this reason Cervantes devotes considerable attention in *La Gitanilla* to the evils of jealousy. The troubling

---

nentur illius vere summique pulcri, cujus ideo Plato putat in nobis excitari reminiscentiam, quod insita si ingeniis hominum propensio quaedam ad honesta, quam in brutis nullam esse videmus" (*Institutio Christiani Matrimonii*, p. 682D).

[97] "Por mayor ventura tengo/ Ser honesta que hermosa" (p. 104).

[98] "interna igitur forma, internae opes, interna nobilitas conciliare debet Christiana conjugia . . . si discusso somnio, mentis oculos, amans intendat in latentem animi formàm, tum vere pulcris cedunt illa vanae pulcritudinis ludibria" (*Institutio Christiani Matrimonii*, p. 682D). Compare Leone Ebreo's stress on correct vision, which is repeated throughout his dialogues: "A te dunque, o Sofia, non bastino gli occhi corporei per vedere le cose belle: mirale con l'incorporei e conoscerai le vere bellezze." "Ma quelli, gli occhi de la cui mente son chiari e veggono molto piú oltre de li corporei, conoscono molto piú de l'incorporea bellezza di quello che conoscono li carnali de la corporea, e conoscono che quella bellezza che si truova ne' corpi è bassa, piccola e superficiale a rispetto di quella che si truova ne l'incorporei; anzi conoscono che la bellezza corporea è ombra e immagine de la spirituale, e participata da quella, e non è altro che il risplender che il mondo spirituale dá al mondo corporeo" (*Dialoghi d'amore*, p. 318).

connection of love and jealousy was, of course, an ubiquitous topic in
Renaissance amatory dialogues and the literary genres such as the
pastoral romance and lyric poetry which the dialogues influenced most
directly.[99] Cervantes's interest in the subject is visible throughout his
career as a writer, from Lenio's discourse in *La Galatea* on the distinction between destructive jealousy and the healthy concern of a true
lover to the demonic obsessions that torment the characters of *El celoso
extremeño* and *La casa de los celos y selvas de Ardenia* and to Sancho
Panza's complaints about his domestic distress caused by Theresa's
jealous tantrums. Cervantes's general view of jealousy and love is deeply
pessimistic. As Arnaldo points out in the *Persiles*, it is a sickness, a
"raging desperation" which "refuses to leave the soul of the lover in
peace," and which distorts his perception and brings such fear to every
moment of his life that he would gladly die.[100] Although it frequently
accompanies love, it is more a sign of "idle curiosity" than of love; it
is a self-destructive passion, a venom that consumes the very body
that produces it. Jealousy leads to the defilement of the beloved by
foolish suspicions; it brings self-debasement, it arouses an interest in
lies and gossip, it nourishes envy, and it is usually a sign of a failure
in self-confidence.[101]

While the view of jealousy as an inescapable, malign power pre-
dominates in Cervantes's writings, on occasions he expresses the aspiration to a love that is immune to its contamination. As the king
insists in *Pedro de Urdemalas*, "Jealousy is a destructive madness, and
true love/ is always free of it;/ and from a cause that is good/ no evil
effect can proceed."[102] Given his obsession with the difficulties that

---

[99] See, for example, the discussion of this "cuestión tan dificultosa" by Marcelio
and Diana in Gaspar Gil Polo's *Diana enamorada*, one of the books that the curate
saves from the bonfires in his inquisitorial examination of Don Quixote's library.
Marcelio's analysis of the illness produced by the "monstruo tan horrendo" and the
way in which it can interfere with the lovers' freedom and his ideal of a perfect love
cleansed of all debilitating suspicion anticipate Cervantes's general treatment of the
subject. See ed. Rafael Ferreres (Madrid, 1953), pp. 82-88.

[100] *Los trabajos de Persiles y Sigismunda*, pp. 429-30.

[101] *La Galatea*, 2:49-51. See also Cervantes's allegorical *romance* depicting the hor-
rid cave of jealousy and the infernal torments of the captives enslaved within it, a
work which he continued to value highly many years later when he reviewed his
writings in *Viage del Parnaso*: "Yo he compuesto romanzes infinitos,/ y el *de los zelos*
es aquel que estimo,/ entre otros, que los tengo por malditos" (ed. R. Schevill and
A. Bonilla [Madrid, 1922], p. 55). For the text of the *romance*, see *Obras completas*,
ed. A. Valbuena Prat, p. 53.

[102] "Celos son rabia, y amor/ siempre de ella está vacío; y de la causa que es buena/
mal efecto no procede" (*Pedro de Urdemalas, Obras completas*, ed. A. Valbuena Prat, p.
531).

jealousy brings to all lovers, it is only natural that in his most searching inquiry into the possibilities for perfection in a relationship between the sexes, Cervantes would directly confront this powerful threat to mutual harmony. The theme in fact emerges immediately in the encounter of Preciosa and Juan and in the latter's declaration of love. If Preciosa points out that the youth may be driven by carnal passion and blinded by an irresistible infatuation, the impetuous Juan quickly reveals that he is enslaved by the fears that jealousy produces. He requests that Preciosa avoid going to Madrid while he prepares his departure; for he fears the loss of the "good fortune that has cost him so much." The maiden reproves his lack of trust, asserting that she will never let her independence ("la libertad") be curbed by the "oppressive burden of jealousy" ("pesadumbre de los celos"), reminding him of the foolishness of the lover who "begins by being jealous" ("entra pidiendo celos"), and insisting that their relationship be founded on trust ("the first duty I desire to impose on you is that of confidence that you are to feel in me"). Her view of freedom and trust, the meaning of which her suitor must discover as she guides him toward perfection, is demonically parodied in the Gypsy world, where all live, as the elder puts it, "free from the bitter pestilence of jealousy," a freedom ensured for the most part by the terror in which the women live. [103]

If Juan's double, Clemente, initially has an important role in the development of the theme of the distortion of judgment which pro-

---

[103] "en el primero cargo en que quiero estaros es en el de la confianza que habéis de hacer de mí" (p. 42); "libres . . . de la amarga pestilencia de los celos" (p. 67). One of the disruptive forces in the troubled marriage of the lieutenant and Doña Clara, which is described in the third poem, is jealousy. In her emphatic refusal to tolerate jealousy in her relationship with Juan and in her insistence on founding their love on freedom, Preciosa is echoing fundamental principles of Erasmus's ideal of wedded love. In his *Encomium Matrimonii* the humanist denounced jealousy as a foolish sickness of lovers and proclaimed that "castus ac legitimus amor zelotypiam nescit" (p. 410). In his *Institutio Christiani Matrimonii* he discusses the illness in greater detail. After condemning archaic laws that allow a man to murder his adulterous wife, he points out that jealousy is a feature of evil love ("meretriciorum amor") rather than good conjugal love ("Christiani caritas"). However, he acknowledges that it is a terrible plague, a sickness which like the worst kind of fevers can slowly and insidiously infect its victim, and he urges man and wife to try to avoid any action, words, and gestures that might kindle suspicions in their partners (pp. 700-701). This is something Preciosa must learn, as is evident in the narrator's advice to her in the matter (see below). For the traditional view of jealousy as a morbid adjunct of carnal love in medieval writings on the subject (e.g., St. Augustine: "Whoever loves carnally must necessarily love with a pestiferous jealousy"), see Robertson, *A Preface to Chaucer*, p. 427.

duces and is reinforced by the conventional discourse of love, his primary function in the second half of the romance is that of the rival who subjects the protagonist to the trial of jealousy, and, in so doing, exposes the distortion of judgment produced by jealousy. The recitation of the page's sonnet depicting Preciosa as a courtly love goddess causes Juan to be overcome by a "thousand jealous imaginings," and, as the hapless youth turns pale and totters on the verge of a swoon, the playful narrator enters the world of his tale to scold his heroine mildly for showing so little concern about the vulnerability of lovers to such attacks.[104] In the charm by which she resuscitates the victim of jealousy, she urges him to "solicitar la bonita confiancita" ("to solicit the good little confidence" [p. 61]).

When Clemente appears as a fugitive in the camp of the Gypsies, Juan is immediately assailed by jealous impulses and tormented by irrational suspicions concerning the intentions of the page and Preciosa. His mind is "full of agitation and a thousand contrary imaginings," and he rebukes his beloved for her deceptions. He laments that "the bitter and hard presumption of jealousy" has thrown him into a state of madness and that his judgment, like that of the thief who thinks that "all men are of his occupation," is radically impaired by his uncontrollable obsession. The Gypsy maiden, who would lead her imperfect lover up the ladder toward perfect spiritual love, rebukes him for the lack of trust that he shows in allowing the "hard sword of jealousy to penetrate his soul so easily." Emphasizing once again the necessity of rationality, clarity of vision, and circumspection, she counsels him about the way in which jealousy distorts perception and admonishes him to proceed toward enlightenment with calmness and discretion:

Never does jealousy, I imagine, leave the understanding free to judge things as they really are: victims of jealousy always look through spectacles reversed, which make small things great, dwarfs giants, and suspicions truths. As you value your life and mine, Andrés, proceed in this and in all that pertains to our agreement cautiously and discreetly.[105]

---

[104] This "concern" for his character's well-being, as well as his various mischievously exaggerated condemnations of Juan as the irresponsible *miles amoris*, endears the youth to us, lightens the tone of reprobation surrounding his initial weaknesses as a lover (i.e., lust, infatuation, jealousy, possessiveness) and contributes a good deal to the festive tone that pervades the entire romance.

[105] "herido, llena de turbación el alma, y de mil contrarias imaginaciones. . . . la amarga y dura presunción de los celos . . . todos son de su condición . . . con tanta facilidad te ha penetrado el alma la dura espada de los celos. . . . Nunca los celos, a lo que imagino . . . dejan el entendimiento libre para que pueda juzgar las cosas como ellas son: siempre miran los celosos con antojos de allende, que hacen las cosas

Following her guidance, Juan survives the trial of jealousy. After becoming the inseparable friend of Clemente, he is again momentarily exposed to "the infernal sickness of jealousy," which is "so subtle and of such a nature that it works its contagion through the atoms of sunbeams" touching the beloved, but now he resists, "confident of the goodness of Preciosa."[106] At this point the purification of Juan's love is complete, his song of perfect love rises to the starry heavens, and the novella moves rapidly toward its denouement.

Cervantes's interest in setting forth an ideal of perfect love and marriage in *La Gitanilla* explains not only the peculiar function of Clemente throughout the novella but also the brief tale of intrigue which he recites in order to explain his flight from Madrid. Here we observe a clandestine courtship, the threat of parental opposition to the will of the children, deception, jealous rivals, and the probability of imperfect love, all of which leads to a violent disaster, in which "jealousy guides the sword thrusts" that take the lives of two suitors, and brings misery to the families of all the parties involved. Its parallels of situation and theme with the main plot are striking, and it is clear that just as in the cases of the Gypsy marriage and Doña Clara's family, Cervantes is working with demonic contrast as a means of sharpening our perception of his central themes.[107]

In the denouement of *La Gitanilla* we observe another interesting

---

pequeñas grandes, los enanos gigantes, y las sospechas verdades. Por vida tuya y por la mía, Andrés, que procedas en esto y en todo lo que tocare a nuestros conciertos cuerda y discretamente" (pp. 85-87).

[106] "la infernal enfermedad celosa es tan delicada y de tal manera, que en los átomos del sol se pega . . . fiado de la bondad de Preciosa" (p. 101).

[107] We observe the same structural principle at work in Cervantes's inclusion of the Gypsy grandmother's tale, which immediately follows. What at first glance appears to be a primitive anecdote based on the farcical prank contains, in its depiction of the fool's disastrous quest for hidden treasure, a parody of Juan's quest for Preciosa, who is surrounded throughout the work by imagery of the hidden treasure (see below). This is the point in *La Gitanilla* at which Preciosa, in her one moment of weakness, fears that Juan will discover the folly of his commitment to her. Emphasizing the apparent foolishness of the well-born youth, the anecdote enhances our insight into the nature of the vague fears that are troubling Preciosa and, as we resolve the ambiguities raised by its "parallels" and interpret it as ironic and its function as contrastive, it confirms our sense of Preciosa as *true treasure*. In its ambiguities and the resolution that they demand, the anecdote is similar to the narrator's ironic intrusion "condemning" Juan de Cárcamo as he contemplates his transformation into the traditional fool of love, a lackey in the train of his "triumphant" mistress, and laments his submission to the "dulce dios de la amargura," his betrayal of his family's trust, his shameful renunciation of his illustrious name, and his humiliating prostration at the feet of a "muchacha, . . . que, puesto que hermosísima, en fin era gitana" (p. 78).

adaptation of the conventions of romance narrative to the development of the central themes of courtship and marriage. It is characteristic of writers of romance to surround their final peripeteia and denouement with painful doubt and suspense, moving their action as close as possible to a catastrophic overthrow of the heroes or delaying their deliverance with a seemingly endless flow of last-minute obstacles. The logic of such narrative design is frequently at odds with plausibility, as in the case of two of Cervantes's favorite models, Heliodorus's *Aethiopika*, where Chariklea mysteriously says nothing to her parents about her identity as she and her lover move perilously toward the sacrificial stake, and the *Book of Apollonius*, where the hero's lost queen obligingly waits fifteen years in Ephesus without making any inquiries concerning the whereabouts of her husband, King Apollonius, her silence being presumably motivated by her willingness to acquiesce in the spectacular double recognition scene which her romancer feels should properly conclude a good adventure story. Such violations of plausibility have traditionally not bothered readers, and so fastidious a critic as El Pinciano acclaimed the denouement of the *Aethiopika* precisely for its insistence on postponing the deliverance until the last possible minute.[108] The conclusion of *La Gitanilla* is an excellent example of the dominance of the traditional aesthetic principle of design over the demands of plausibility, and Cervantes, one of the most self-conscious of writers, can not resist mischievously reminding us of the "logic of literary violations of logic." Following the joyous recognition scene uniting Preciosa with her parents and its disclosure of the mysterious tokens—the garments, the jewels, and the birthmark—, the benevolent Fernando de Azevedo refuses to deliver the hero from the dark dungeon where he lies in chains awaiting execution. Moreover, he allows a priest to hear the youth's confession and urge him to prepare for death, and then he has him led in chains to his wedding. The "sadism" of this scene has been noted somewhat disapprovingly by its modern editor Rodríguez Marín, but its "unnecessary cruelty" surely has less to do with Cervantes's failure to transcend the "barbarous customs" of his age, as the editor suggests, than with his clear understanding of the principles of effective storytelling, the value of infusing the final turn in his plot with as much suspense and pathos

---

[108] Heliodorus "ata siempre más y más"; "atando va siempre, y nunca jamás desata hasta el fin." One of El Pinciano's interlocutors ironically compares the effects of tension and relaxation in such plotting procedures to an execution by garroting, the confession or death of the tortured man forming the "unraveling" (see A. López Pinciano, *Philosophía antigua poética*, ed. A. Carballo Picazo, 3 vols. [Madrid, 1953], 2:85-86; also, Forcione, *Cervantes, Aristotle, and the "Persiles,"* pp. 71-76).

as possible, the advantages of a scene of public ritual for the concluding, climactic deliverance of a romance plot, and the power and conventionality of the incest archetype in romance.[109] As Cervantes describes the spectacle, in which Preciosa swoons at the sight of Juan,
"girt and fettered with so heavy a chain, his face pale and his eyes
showing traces of having wept," he pauses to note that "the bystanders" were "hanging in anxious suspense on the outcome of that incident,"[110] reminding us, as he so often does in the moments of literary
self-consciousness that punctuate his fiction, of the literary principles
determining the composition and underlying the audience's reception
of his scenes and, at the same time, of his freedom to violate those
very principles.

The troubled movement toward climax in *La Gitanilla*, with its
pronounced violations of the logic governing the order of empirical
reality and its unmistakable mark of authorial manipulation, points
primarily to such literary themes as generic conventions, authorial
freedom, and audience expectations. Indeed we discover here a typical
Cervantine assertion of the author's godlike powers over his creation,
as he quite literally compels us to watch as he displaces the Divine
Providence that conventionally controls the painfully suspended climactic denouements of romance. However, as he continues to manipulate his final peripeteia, Cervantes turns to the theme of marriage
and discovers in it a means for the continued prolongation of suspense.
A priest appears, and when he is ordered to marry the hero and the
heroine, he objects that he can not do so unless the proper procedures

---

[109] Cervantes's fragmentary introduction of the incest theme shows how playful and
arbitrary he can be in his manipulation of romance conventions. As the corregidor
torments Juan in the dungeon, the hero imagines that the older man is in love with
Preciosa, and he is stricken with jealousy. Momentarily we are compelled to view the
benevolent father in the sinister role of the possessive ogre familiar in romance,
rivaling the youthful hero for the hand of his own daughter, and suddenly the threat
of incest looms in the background as a possible obstacle to the anticipated deliverance.
At this point Cervantes's narrative glances briefly at one of its principal models, the
Book of Apollonius, where the joyous restoration at the conclusion reverses the situation
of father-daughter incest at its beginning, and the heroes escape a threat of similar
incest. In Cervantes's tale the danger is quickly averted, and the final state reverses
completely the demonic order of the Gypsy world, where, as the elder admits, incest
is a common occurrence. For the importance of the incest convention in romance, see
Frye, *The Secular Scripture*, p. 44; for the power of such archetypes and the way in
which the linkage of events in romance is based primarily on a principle of archetypal
sequence rather than logic, causality, and plausibility, see pp. 50-51.

[110] "ceñido y aherrojado con tan gran cadena, descolorido el rostro y los ojos con
muestra de haber llorado . . . y los circunstantes, colgados del fin de aquel caso" (p.
125).

have been followed. On discovering that the banns have not been published, he refuses to perform the ceremony and abruptly leaves. "And without saying another word, he walked out of the house lest any scandal should ensue and left them all in confusion."[111]

Such an obstacle is certainly at odds with traditional romance conclusions, where triumphant marriages are seldom encumbered by the complications in the official procedures that exist in reality.[112] It is

[111] "Y sin replicar más palabras, porque no sucediese algún escándalo, se salió de casa, y los dejó a todos confusos" (p. 126).

[112] In the most popular type of romance of Cervantes's age, the romance of chivalry, the "instantaneous" marriage, which, of course, was considered "clandestine" according to the laws of the time, was so common that one could call it a convention of the genre, and it is interesting that in Cervantes's tales that follow the formulas of the chivalric romance, such marriages are sometimes celebrated as part of the happy ending. See, for example, *Las dos doncellas* or the tale of Ruperta and Croriano in the *Persiles*; also, the "restoration" of Princess Micomicona-Dorotea in the *Quixote*, an episode that conforms to the patterns of chivalric literature in a highly complex and ironic way. For the frequency of the secret marriage in the romance of chivalry, see J. Ruiz de Conde, *El amor y el matrimonio secreto en los libros de caballerías* (Madrid, 1948). It is interesting that, following the consummation of the marriage of Ruperta and Croriano in the chivalric situation, Cervantes's pilgrims say nothing concerning problems that its validation might raise, while, at the conclusion of Isabela Castrucho's wedding, which belongs to the literary order of farcical comedy where the conventions of the fictional world are determined to a much greater extent by the norms of immediate actuality, the pilgrims do consider questions concerning its possible invalidation. If one attempts to arrive at Cervantes's "authentic" attitudes toward love and marriage, one must carefully consider the role of literary convention in his various engagements with the subject. Américo Castro's conclusion, on the basis of such works as *Las dos doncellas*, that Cervantes was committed to a romantic conception of love and the value of spontaneous feeling, is an oversimplification of a very complex subject (see *El pensamiento de Cervantes*, pp. 376-78). Castro briefly mentions Cervantes's introduction of the banns at the conclusion of *La Gitanilla* but hastily dismisses its significance by explaining it as a device for suspense. Here he takes advantage of the very "explanation by literary logic" which he fails to consider in the contexts that admit of such explanation according to the conventions of romance. Moreover, he ignores completely how the entire novella centers on the purification of Juan's spontaneous infatuation and depicts a movement from the blindness of irrational impulse to the lofty vision of rational love. Castro's arguments have been taken up recently by F. Márquez Villanueva, who maintains that Cervantes favors "el matrimonio de amor" and consequently makes no serious criticism of clandestine marriage and that for Cervantes "las tragedias del matrimonio no se originan de los arrojos pasionales de la juventud." If such conclusions fail to take into consideration the implications of such episodes as the tales of Leandra in the *Quixote* and Ortel Banedre in the *Persiles*, as well as such novellas as *La Gitanilla* and *La ilustre fregona*, the following conclusion presents a questionable view of the religious spirit which one can infer from Cervantes's works and of the idea of Christian liberty in the spiritual culture of the sixteenth century: "Cervantes se mantiene apegado al *consensus*

tempting to suspect that Cervantes is here looking at romance conventions with the critical spirit that led him to write the *Quixote* and to remind his readers constantly that few knights errant ever had to eat and drink and make wills as do normal human beings. However, *La Gitanilla* is anything but an "antiromance," and, while its discussion of the banns is "realistic" and collides with literary conventions, its "realism" has nothing to do with an intention of unmasking the flights from reality which one can always find concealed behind the pleasing fictions of romance. Quite the contrary, in *La Gitanilla*, as in the *Persiles*, Cervantes is resurrecting the genre which he had dealt with so mercilessly in the *Quixote*, exploiting its magical worlds and its primitive, artificial structures for a sophisticated exploration of his views of courtship, love, marriage, and human relations. When the corregidor approves of the priest's action and the young couple proceeds to a marriage that follows the laws of the time, Cervantes is aligning the lofty matrimonial ideal enunciated by Preciosa and her theories on courtship, compatibility, and the dangers of hasty marriages with the official regulations of his society and the thinking in orthodox circles that had been responsible for their institution.[113] It is well to recall that the Catholic world had responded to the universal outcry against the abuses of clandestine marriages and the pressures for desacramentalizing marriage and instituting divorce, which increased to alarming proportions in the early sixteenth century, by reaffirming the sacramental foundation of marriage and enacting leg-

---

matrimonium facit y con ello se manifiesta mucho más consecuente en su amor a la libertad cristiana que el propio Erasmo, para quien, después de tanto predicar contra las ceremonias, no había matrimonio sin la presencia solemne de sacerdote y testigos" (*Personajes y temas del Quijote*, pp. 65-70). Márquez argues that in his fictional treatment of the problems of marriage we observe the great distance separating Cervantes from Erasmus. In my view this is an area of thinking in which the affinities of the two are most pronounced, and the work in which Cervantes concerned himself most exclusively with the nature of the relationship of the sexes, *La Gitanilla*, makes this clear beyond any doubt.

[113] As the action moves out of the lower world toward its celebrative conclusion, Cervantes carefully draws attention to the ways in which the restored order is distinguished from its demonic counterpart. Just as the allusion to the banns emphasizes all that separates the civilized marriage rite from the Gypsy union of man and woman, so the description of the self-control and moderation of the local mayor following Juan's arrest draws our attention to the difference between the proper judicial procedures of civilization and the barbarous justice of the Gypsies ("no vamos a la justicia a pedir castigo: nosotros somos los jueces y los verdugos de nuestras esposas" [p. 67]; "Bien quisiera el Alcalde ahorcarle luego, si estuviera en su mano; pero hubo de remitirle a Murcia, por ser de su jurisdicción" [p. 110]).

islation to control the nuptial rite more carefully than in the past. In his *Institutio Christiani Matrimonii* Erasmus lamented that thousands of people are suffering in marriages that they had entered in the clandestine rite (see above), and, pointing out that the principle of consent as the basis for marriage is nowhere sanctioned by biblical prescription or precedent, he argued that the Church should declare marriages invalid unless they are performed before magistrates and officially recorded with witnesses to the fact that the words of consent are given in sobriety.[114] At the Council of Trent the Church proceeded to enact legislation of the type that the humanist had advocated. Embracing the traditional principle of consent and refusing to follow Protestant doctrines undermining the sacramental foundation of marriage or demanding the validation of a marriage by parental consent, the council nevertheless created compulsory legal forms for the proper enactment of the principle and declared that, if marriages did not observe these forms, they were officially regarded as "detestable." From the mid-sixteenth century onward, in all parts of the Catholic world where the council's decretals were announced and enforced, no marriage could take place if it were not registered in the priest's wedding records and preceded by the publication of the banns, so that impediments could be properly studied and people, compelled by law to be circumspect, would not hasten into the infamous marriages "por amores," which so frequently became marriages "por dolores."[115] Thus when Cervantes complicates the climax of his romance by turning the banns into an "obstacle" delaying the joyous denouement, he is in effect reflecting the sentiment that lies behind much of the most profound reformist thinking on marriage of his age, the thinking that found its most influential expression in the writings of Erasmus, that inspired the

[114] "Quod igitur controversiarum nascitur ex verbis praesentibus & futuris, ex Matrimonio rato & consummato, ex signis, nutibus, ex scriptis, magna ex parte tolletur, si dignarentur Ecclesiae Proceres statuere, nullum Matrimonium prius esse ratum, quam apud Magistratus ad hoc designatos, adhibitis testibus, clare conceptis verbis uterque sobrius ac liber alteri condicat conjugium, eaque verba scripto serventur. Quod furtim inter sese fecerant, si coitus sit, pro stupro censeatur: si consensus qualibuscumque verbis declaratus, pro simplicibus verbis habeantur: Matrimonium non sit, donec apud judices ac testes a sobriis ac liberis, solennibus verbis declaratus sit matrimonialis consensus" (pp. 651F-652A).

[115] See Herman Conrad, "Das Tridentische Konzil und die Entwicklung des Kirchlichen und Weltlichen Eherechts," in *Das Weltkonzil von Trient*, ed. G. Schreiber, 2 vols. (Freiburg, 1951), 1:297-324. See also, Hubert Jedin, *Geschichte des Konzils von Trient*, 4 vols. (Freiburg, 1951-1975), 3:141-61, and Telle, *L'Oeuvre de Marguerite D'Angoulême Reine de Navarre et La Querelle des Femmes*, p. 353.

Catholic reform at the Council of Trent, and that was to find in
Cervantes's little Gypsy its most unforgettable literary exponent.

NATURE PERFECTED

The natura bene condita

Immediately preceding the climactic vision of perfect love and universal harmony, Clemente blesses the union of the protagonists: "may
these entanglements of love turn out to have a happy ending, and
may you enjoy your Andrés, and Andrés his Preciosa, in conformity
with the wishes and pleasure of his parents, so that we may see issue
into the world from such a beautiful union the most lovely renewals
[*renuevos*—'renewals,' 'sprouts'] which the well-intentioned nature can
form."[116] His words look forward to the comic denouement of the tale
and the return of the protagonists from the wilderness. At the same
time they link the celebration of wedded love, instinctual fulfillment
within matrimony, and procreation both with the social order, which
is implied in the importance that Clemente attaches to parental sanction and the necessity of returning to the city, and with a certain
order of nature—"la bien intencionada naturaleza." The concept of
"well-intentioned nature" is in fact of fundamental importance in the
articulation of the most profound themes of the work, and there are
few other elements that point so decisively to the principal ideological
traditions that nourished its conception. Indeed the structure of the
work and particularly the puzzling function of the Gypsy world, a
natural order that dominates the middle of the narrative and imaginatively pervades its entire development, from the outburst on thieves
in the opening lines to the concluding announcement concerning the
burial of vengeance, are incomprehensible unless we understand the
implications of the concept of nature that informs its exemplarity.

As all students of the history of ideas quickly discover, the idea of
nature is one of the most elusive and multifaceted subjects in Renaissance thought. The variety of contexts in which it appears—religion,
law, ethics, statecraft, epistemology, science, and aesthetics—the contradictions one encounters in its usage, often within the works of a
single writer, and the manner in which it is invoked in self-justifica-

---

[116] "que estos enredos amorosos salgan a fines felices, y que tú goces de tu Andrés,
y Andrés de su Preciosa, en conformidad y gusto de sus padres, porque de tan hermosa
junta veamos en el mundo los más bellos renuevos que pueda formar la bien intencionada naturaleza" (p. 101).

tion by the advocates of violently opposed ideological positions make it an overwhelming challenge to anyone who would seek to sort out its meanings with clarity and continually invite the modern interpreter to fall into the trap of rendering difficult contexts in which it appears intelligible by imputing modern conceptions of nature to their authors. Indeed Etienne Gilson has remarked that the incapacity to deal with the idea of nature historically has caused contemporary readers to disfigure seriously the thought of such men as Erasmus, Rabelais, and Montaigne, and he has gone on to suggest that "ce qui manque peut-être le plus aux études poursuivies sur la littérature et la pensée du XVIe siècle, c'est une connaissance précise de ce que la philosophie médiévale enseignait touchant la Nature."[117] A good deal of misleading interpretation marks current readers' critical engagement with the view of nature in Cervantes's *La Gitanilla*, not only because of the remoteness of some of the principal ideas which inform the tale, but also because of the modernity of Cervantes's attitudes toward nature in other contexts. In what follows I would like to clarify the backgrounds in Christian Humanist thought of Clemente's allusion to the "bien intencionada naturaleza," distinguish it from the implicit vision of nature dominating the *Quixote*, and proceed to an analysis of the function of the Gypsy world in the tale, an analysis which presupposes the excursus on humanist thought.

For the Christian Humanists the realm of the "well-founded" nature was of vital importance, for its existence offered them a philosophical and religious justification for their intensely optimistic atti-

[117] "Rabelais Franciscain," *Les Idées et les lettres* (Paris, 1932), pp. 197-241, see p. 241. Noting that we are still a long way from really penetrating and comprehending the cultural climate of the sixteenth century, Lucien Febvre laments: "Nous ne sommes pas près d'avoir les cinq ou six monographies d'idées vraiment indispensables pour appuyer nos conclusions. Qui, par exemple, esquissera pour nous, avec clarté et précision, l'histoire de ce concept de 'Nature,' si riche de sens variables, et qu'on rencontre à cette époque (à d'autres aussi, du reste) sous tant de plumes ennemies?" (*Au coeur religieux du xvie siècle*, p. 66). The problem was noted by thinkers of the time. Montaigne deplored the variety, complication, and falsifying idealizations which characterized philosophers' treatment of the rules of nature (*De l'Expérience*) and John Donne lamented: "This terme the law of Nature, is so variously and unconstantly deliver'd, as I confesse I read it a hundred times before I understand it once" (*Biathanatos*; Hiram Haydn cites Donne's remark at the outset of his ambitious, impressive, and valuable compendium, "The Counter-Renaissance and the Nature of Nature," *The Counter-Renaissance* [New York, 1950], p. 461, one of the best general studies of the subject). See also A. O. Lovejoy's and G. Boas's lucid discriminations in "Some Meanings of 'Nature'," *Primitivism and Related Ideas in Antiquity* (Baltimore, 1935), pp. 447-56, an indispensable guide through the complex issues raised by the subject.

tude toward man's powers and capacities to perfect himself in this world while at the same time earning salvation in the afterlife, for their enthusiastic embrace of the great thinkers and writings of classical antiquity, and for their belief in the possibility of a general reform (*renovatio*) of Christian society. While the Lutheran reformers insisted on the total depravity of nature and its absolute separation from the realm of grace and derided the folly of the advocates of natural reason and man's ability and obligation to cooperate with God in gaining salvation, Erasmus and his followers proposed a *Philosophia Christiana* demanding that believers strive to perfect themselves, their society, and its central institutions, as well as the society of nations, through the practice of such Christian virtues as piety, charity, and brotherhood and through the exercise of the divine faculty of reason. While the Lutherans showed little interest in the prelapsarian state of man, the Erasmists maintained that the original nature gave man the models and goals for the proper exercise of his God-given powers. They argued that man's obligation on earth was the achievement of the perfection that he had known before the fall. As Erasmus put it in his *Paraclesis*, an exhortation to all Christians: "the philosophy of Jesus Christ, which he calls renascence, is nothing else than a restoration and a renovation of our nature, which in the beginning was created in purity."[118]

[118] "no es otra cosa la filosofía de Jesu Cristo, la qual él llama renacencia, sino una restauración y renovación de nuestra naturaleza, que al principio fué criada en puridad." I cite a sixteenth-century Spanish translation, edited by D. Alonso ([Madrid, 1932], p. 462). For Erasmus the relationship of grace and nature is not one of separation and tension. Grace works both within nature, since the remnants of the original nature, which was totally penetrated by the divine spirit, are still present, and from without, by restoring such remnants to their original perfection. See O. Schottenloher: "In dieser ganzen Erneuerung verband sich der Geist Christi für das Bewusstsein des Erasmus aufs engste mit den Antrieben und Kräften der Natur. . . . Für ihn, den 'alten Theologen' [Christ], gab es kein Reich der Gnade, das von der Natur geschieden werden konnte. Die Gnade wirkte in und an der Natur, die Reste der gut geschaffenen Natur aufgreifend wiederinstandsetzend und schliesslich vollendend. Christus löschte nicht aus, was er an Gutem vorfand, sondern vervollkommnete es, er zerstörte die Natur nicht, sondern vollendete sie, er besserte, was verdorben, und er erfüllte, was vermindert war. Schon das *Enchiridion* ging davon aus, dass Christus die Würde des Menschen, die ihm von der Schöpfung her eignete, wieder instandsetzte. Die wiedergeschenkte Unschuld liess Geist und Körper bereits in dieser Welt zur ursprünglichen Schönheit wieder erblühen" ("Lex Naturae und Lex Christi bei Erasmus," *Scrinium Erasmianum*, ed. J. Coppens, 2 vols. [Leiden, 1969], 2:253-99; see pp. 279-80). See also J.-C. Margolin, "L'Idée de nature dans la pensée d'Erasme," *Recherches Erasmiennes* (Geneva, 1969), pp. 9-44; esp. pp. 31-41. For the pessimistic Augustinian-Lutheran view of nature and the natural appetites in man which prevailed in the ascetic Christianity of Cervantes's contemporaries, dominated

The view of nature which the Christian Humanists developed and assimilated with the prelapsarian state of Christian theology was based to a great extent on the Aristotelian concept of nature as the proper goal or end toward which things tend and the Stoic notion of the natural order of the universe as a realm penetrated by the cosmic fire of its creator and revealing the rational design and purposiveness that characterizes the divinity. Man is a being who bears within his reason a spark of the creative logos; his authentic nature is rational, and he fulfills his nature by following his reason and pursuing virtue. Since the creator has written on man's spirit the moral law, a replica of the divine spirit, man is inclined by nature to goodness,[119] and by exer-

---

their attitudes toward marriage, and found frequent expression in their literature, see Hanrahan, *La mujer en la novela picaresca española*, 1:168. While insisting on the goodness of nature in opposition to the belief in its total ruin, characteristic of ascetic Christianity, Erasmus rejects the fully secularized view of nature as an autonomous and eternal power that was advanced by some of his Aristotelian, skeptic, and materialistic contemporaries ("sunt qui pro deo supponunt naturam; quae si aeterna est & omnipotens, profecto Deus est: si non est talis, Dei ministra est et a Deo condita. . . . Quamquam, mea sententia, religiosius est, totum hoc vel quod agit natura, vel quod secundariae causae, unius Dei energiae tribuere" [*Dilucida et Pia Explanatio Symboli*, cited by Schottenloher, "Lex Naturae," pp. 279-80]). It is perhaps well to stress this point here in view of the continuing influence of Américo Castro's *El pensamiento de Cervantes*. In one of its most fundamental and certainly most questionable arguments, it attributes to Cervantes the belief in a biological type of determinism that controls human behavior and frequently drives individuals into tragic situations. This "naturalism" forms the philosophical basis for a moral philosophy emphasizing relativism, understanding, and tolerance. Castro goes on to insist that Cervantes did not need to acquire the conception of nature as an "alta deidad" from the Italians because "Erasmus y los italianos nos las [doctrinas] habían traído a nuestra casa" (*El pensamiento de Cervantes*, p. 169).

[119] "Y en esta parte nuestra, que es en nuestro espíritu, fué donde aquel muy perfecto hazedor de todas las cosas imprimió con su dedo, que es su espíritu, una ley eterna mediante la qual siempre nos inclinamos a lo bueno y honesto, la qual fué sacada del dechado y original de su divino entendimiento" (*Enquiridion*, p. 185). One of Erasmus's most important followers in Spain, Juan de Mal Lara, observes the workings of natural reason in the "fresh" moral sensibility of children: "Aun acá los niños, guiados de la razón natural y bondad que tienen fresca en su nueva alma, cuando veen que otro iba a hacelle mal y tropieza y se lastima, dicen: 'Dios lo vido' " (*Filosofía vulgar*). The passage is cited by A. Castro, who erroneously interprets the inherent natural goodness to which it refers ("la razón natural y bondad") as meaning "vital spontaneity," a quality that man shares with the animals, and concludes that the doctrine is "anti-Christian," "ya que el niño debía poseer esas virtudes no tanto por estar cerca de su natural origen, como por la redención de la culpa primera mediante el bautismo" (*El pensamiento de Cervantes*, pp. 177, 204). Mal Lara's doctrine might well have appeared anti-Christian to Luther and his followers, with their contempt for the idolatrous belief in natural reason, but it was a fundamental tenet of the Christianity of the Erasmians, as well as of the central tradition of orthodox

cising his own reason he acts in harmony with the Right Reason which the Creator has unfolded in the universe.

This optimistic view of man's nature was easily reconcilable with the Christian conception of man's original perfection, more specifically of God's creation of him "in His own image and likeness," and with the traditional view of the fall as having damaged but not totally destroyed this original perfection. While describing the innate law of nature inscribed on man's "spirit," Erasmus observes that this part shines forth as a kind of specimen of our entire being, "revealing that we were created in the likeness of God and that we are as an image of his divine nature."[120] As for the continuing presence of the light of man's original nature following the fall, Erasmus writes: "To man whom he had created, God added an inner light [lumen ingenii], by which he clearly might see what he must reject and what he must seek out. When this light was dimmed by man's disobedience, God left nevertheless a spark, like some kind of seed for the renewal of the light. It has shone forth for us in this marvelously designed edifice of the world."[121] The presence of this light is what Paul had in mind when he suggested that it is possible that some of the gentiles could

---

Catholicism from which they emerged and to which they contributed. The common conception of the rationality of nature is exemplified perfectly throughout Luis de León's treatise on marriage, La perfecta casada, in which he repeatedly justifies his precepts by invoking the phrase: "la razón y la naturaleza pide que . . ." (see ed. E. Wallace [Chicago, 1903]).

[120] "por esta parte somos como una muestra por donde damos a entender que fuimos criados a semejança de Dios, y que somos como ymagen de su naturaleza divina" (see Enquiridion, p. 185).

[121] "Addidit homini condito lumen ingenii, quo perspiceret quid esset fugiendum, quid expetendum. Id quum esset per inobedientiam obscuratum, reliquit tamen scintillam, veluti seminarium quoddam revocandae lucis. Illuxit nobis in hac mundi fabrica mirifice condita" (In Quartum Psalmum Concio, Opera Omnia, ed. Le Clerc, 5: 255B). Compare Vives's fusion of the Stoic doctrine of the cosmic fire in nature and the Christian conception of the edenic order: "sunt in nobis igniculi quidam, seu semina virtutum a natura indita, ut Stoici Philosophi observarunt; nostri Synteresin Graeco verbo nominant, quasi conservationem et scintillam justitiae illius, qua primus auctor generis humani donatus erat a Deo; ille igniculus, adolescere modo liceret, ut illi sentiunt ad magnam nos virtutem perduceret, sed obruitur depravatis judiciis atque opinionibus . . . sancta matrona his corruptis opinionibus, integrioribus aliis et christiana dignis occurret, in suoque puero bonorum praeceptorum ac consiliorum instillatione igniculum illum, quem diximus, fovebit, semina irrigabit, ut in magnam lucem ille, haec in frugem ingentem optimamque consurgat" (Institutio Feminae Christianae, Opera Omnia, 4:260-61). The passage eloquently expresses the optimistic attitude of the humanists toward correct education as an instrument for leading man back to his original "natural" condition, for which the imagery of natural abundance is an effective correlative. For the idea of nature in Erasmus's theories of education see J.-C. Margolin, "L'Idée de nature dans la pensée d'Erasme," pp. 23-28.

glimpse the traces of God's order in nature without the benefit of revelation; it is what enabled the pagans to develop civilized forms of society in which their citizens could lead exemplary lives, and it is what inspired the ancient philosophers to discover and teach some of the most enduring social, political, and moral philosophy and values. [122] As Erasmus makes clear throughout his writings and most forcefully in those intended for his vast, nonacademic audiences, such men as Socrates, Cicero, Plato, Aristotle, Plutarch, Seneca, and even Epicurus, guided as they were by the light of nature, have left Christian civilization a legacy of wisdom to be cherished beside the teachings of the greatest "philosopher," Jesus Christ, and the greatest "theologian," St. Paul. [123]

There are two implications of Christian Humanist thought concerning the "well-founded" nature that we should bear in mind if we are to understand correctly Cervantes's celebration in *La Gitanilla* of Christian marriage, family authority, and the state-family as all belonging to the order of perfected nature. In his optimistic view of human nature, Erasmus rejected the austere dualisms characteristic of rigid stoicism and ascetic Christianity, which maintained that the affections and the instincts were a ruinous part of the human being, ever to be held in check and suppressed through discipline. To be sure, reason is the authentic nature of man, and the passions are never to be glorified as certain naturalistic philosophies had allowed, but they are not to be condemned as totally unnatural. If they are channeled according to the direction of man's true nature, that is, reason, for creative purposes, they are in fact natural and beneficial. [124] If they

---

[122] See Schottenloher, "Lex Naturae und Lex Christi bei Erasmus," pp. 256-57 and Auer's discussion of the "doctrine of the logos" and the notion of different phases of revelation in connection with Erasmus's attitudes toward pre-Christian thought (*Die vollkommene Frömmigkeit des Christen nach dem Enchiridion militis Christiani des Erasmus von Rotterdam*, pp. 126-38.

[123] See, for example, *Paráclesis*, pp. 462-63; *Enquiridion*, pp. 132-36; *The Godly Feast*. At the same time the proximity to the order of the well-founded nature of the generations which followed Adam and the clarity of its light enabled their discovery of what Erasmus's Spanish disciple, Juan de Mal Lara called *la filosofía vulgar*, the oldest and purest form of wisdom, which crystallized and was preserved and transmitted in the proverb. "Esta philosophía y manera de saber, se estendió por todo el mundo. . . . Porque, según avemos dicho, resplandeció en Adam, junto con el verdadero conocimiento de Dios, una lumbre de todas las sciencias, que sus nietos fueron rastreando, y hallaron en aquella rica mina la veta de los mejores metales que pudieron" (*Filosofía vulgar*, ed. A. Vilanova, 4 vols. [Barcelona, 1958], 1:67).

[124] See, for example, Erasmus's insistence that the sexual instinct belongs to the well-founded nature and that its expression in married love is perfectly natural: "Nu-

enslave man by overthrowing reason, overturning the proper hierarchy in the soul, and hence alienating man from his true nature, they are then, and only then, to be regarded as unnatural or antinatural. In tracing his picture of man's soul, Erasmus speaks favorably of the Peripatetic view of the possibility of restraining the passions and directing them to virtuous ends (e.g., anger can become an "awakener of virtue"). He argues that the proper relation of reason to the instincts is that of king to his subjects, controlling and ordering rather than eradicating. Recalling the division of the soul proposed by "St. Plato" in the *Timaeus*, he discusses the distinctively human *"ánima"* placed between the divine and rational spirit and the disruptive flesh, where such natural affections as filial respect, friendship, and love of one's spouse originate.[125] Arguing against the Stoics' pessimistic view of the passions and their ideal of apathy, Erasmus insists that Christ's existence offers a divine sanction of the naturalness of the affections; for Christ, in whom nature was perfect (*bene condita*) and not flawed in any way by original sin, experienced joy, sorrow, anger, and fear, as well as such corporeal appetites as hunger and thirst. The misdi-

men autem appello naturae instinctum, cuius conditor est deus. . . . Eorum membrorum rebellionem facile patiar a peccato profectam, sed ipsos stimulos arbitror esse mere naturales, eosque futuros fuisse in primis parentibus, etiam si nunquam pecassent. . . . Natura dum stimulat ad gignendum, suo fungitur officio, sollicitat ad sui propagationem, quemadmodum dum stimulat fame situe, sollicitat ad sui conseruationem" (*Dilutio Eorum Quae Iodocus Clithoveus Scripsit Adversus Declamationem Des. Erasmi Roterodami Suasoriam Matrimonii*, pp. 87-93). Erasmus makes the same point about the naturalness of marital love in his paraphrase of 1 Tim. 4:3, where, speaking of the appetites and their objects, he notes that "quicquid ab optimo Deo conditum est, id natura sua bonum esse, si quis ut oportet, & ad quod conditum est, utatur" (*Opera Omnia*, ed. Le Clerc, 7:1047C). One can compare the attitudes of Thomas More's pious Utopians: "They think, therefore, none of those pleasures are to be valued any further than as they are necessary; yet they rejoice in them, and with due gratitude acknowledge the tenderness of the great Author of Nature, who has planted in us appetites, by which those things that are necessary for our preservation are likewise made pleasant to us" (*Famous Utopias of the Renaissance*, ed. Frederic R. White [New York, 1955], p. 76).

[125] *Enquiridion*, pp. 184-92. For the importance in Renaissance psychology and anthropology of this view of the soul, which stresses the "congruent and harmonious working of the various appetites or affections (which make up the sensitive part of the soul) with the cognitive faculties" and which holds that "a healthy and virtuous soul, like a healthy and virtuous body or state or universe finds use for all of its constituent parts," see Haydn, *The Counter-Renaissance*, pp. 317-19. See also Schottenloher, "Lex Naturae und Lex Christi bei Erasmus," pp. 258-64, and Auer, *Die vollkommene Frömmigkeit des Christen nach dem Enchiridion militis Christiani des Erasmus von Rotterdam*, chap. 4.

rection of such affections and instincts toward sinful ends should not
be attributed to man's nature. Quite the contrary, it should be viewed
as a perversion of his *bene condita natura* and consequently unnatural.[126]

The other implication of the concept of the "well-founded nature"
which I would mention in connection with Cervantes's alignment of
nature and social institutions in *La Gitanilla* is the notion that the
forms of civilization that man creates by exercising his reason are in
fact natural, and that, in effect, the greater their perfection, the closer
they are to the original pure nature which Christians associate with
Eden and its perfect "gardeners." While the Christian Humanists were
intensely concerned with the corruption that mars man's activities in
society, advocated a program of critique and reform, and condemned
unsparingly the tyranny of false opinions, appearances, artifice, and
the numerous other obstacles with which society presents the individual who would pursue his authentic self as a human being and as a
Christian, their philosophy was one in which genuine primitivism had
no place, for it maintained that in ideal conditions there is absolutely
no conflict between artifice and nature. Their position is accurately
reflected by Fray Luis de Granada, an orthodox theologian of the Catholic world, in whose voluminous and influential writings several of
the fundamental attitudes and principles of the Christian Humanist
movement survived. In his translation of the *Imitatio Christi* Granada
would appear to endorse its arguments concerning reason and the
original nature of the creation. He observes that, following the fall, a
spark remained alive amid the ashes of paradise, the "buena y derecha
naturaleza," to work with divine grace for the restoration of man's
prelapsarian condition. "This is natural reason, which, although surrounded by a great darkness, still maintains the power of free judgment concerning good and evil and which recognizes the difference

---

[126] See *Disputatio de Taedio et Pavore Christi, Opera Omnia*, ed. Le Clerc, 5:1277B,
C,D. The Christian Epicureanism which Hedenius argues for in the *Epicurean*, as well
as the bewildering metamorphoses and revaluations by which Folly transforms such
traditional vices as hypocrisy, self-love, envy, vanity, and the hunger for glory into
creative forces supporting civilized life, are perhaps the most striking examples of
Erasmus's affirmative attitude toward the passions as natural and contributive to the
rational purposes of civilized man. "Grundsätzlich aber machte er weder das Wesen
der Tugend noch der Frömmigkeit aus, wider die Natur zu Sein. Erasmus glaubte
im Gegenteil zu beobachten, dass sich der Geist Christi viel eher mit den Affekten
und Kräften der Natur verband. Wie Christus nichts verlangt hat, was wider die
Natur wäre, so durften wir, die wir unter dem Gesetz der Natur lebten, das über die
Natur Gehende ruhig verehren und uns zur Nachahmung an das halten, was unserem
Mass Entsprach" (Schottenloher, "Lex Naturae et Lex Christi bei Erasmus," p. 262).

between what is true and what is false."[127] However, in his *La intro-ducción del símbolo de la fe,* he goes well beyond the influential fifteenth-century treatise in his optimism concerning the powers of reason and the value of its achievements in this world. Indeed, the luminous remnant of man's edenic nature and such natural inclinations as the love of God and filial love, inclinations that are inscribed in man's heart by "el autor de la misma naturaleza," are testimony of his dig-nity and proof of his likeness to the Creator. By using his natural reason in order to master the sciences and the arts, to invent language, and to control the elements through the arts of navigation and agri-culture, man has created in civilization a second nature and displayed powers not unlike those of his own Creator. True nature and the perfected forms of civilization, then, are in close alignment if not identical.[128]

When Cervantes in *La Gitanilla* associates the love of his protago-nists, their return from the wilderness, and Christian marriage and its fruits with the injunctions of the well-founded nature, he is giving expression to one of the central ideals of the Erasmian reform pro-gram, which saw in marriage, as an institution founded in paradise and binding human beings together in a relationship of authentic friendship, a means of elevating Christian society to a state of spiritual perfection that reflects the purity of man's primal and potential con-dition. It is well to compare Clemente's words with the most powerful moment of Erasmus's *Declamatio Matrimonii,* for the encomium em-phasizes the same elements: "If, then, you are moved in any way by honor, by filial, religious, or civic duty, or by virtue, why do you shrink away from that which God has instituted, nature has made holy, which reason advocates, and which sacred and humanist writ-ings alike praise, which our laws enjoin, and which is approved by the agreement of all nations, and toward which the example of every great man urges us?"[129]

The nature of particulars

The view of nature which is manifest in Clemente's words and which underlies the humanists' fundamental approach to man and

---

[127] "Esta es la razon natural, cercada de grande obscuridad, que tiene todavía un juicio libre del bien y del mal, y conosce la diferencia de lo verdadero y de lo falso" (*Contemptus mundi ó menosprecio del mundo y imitación de Christo, Obras,* B.A.E. 11:418).

[128] See *Obras,* B.A.E. 6:265-68.

[129] p. 406.

society assumes that the essence of any particular thing is identifiable in the genre to which the thing belongs and the end toward which, as a member of the genre, it strives, and it readily dismisses as unessential the attributes that mark the thing as individual and distinct from its generic model. As the numerous studies of Américo Castro have emphasized, the presentation of experience in the *Quixote* implies a radically different vision of nature, one that privileges the *individuality* of human beings over the laws of the genus to which they belong and one that shows remarkably little interest in a quintessential human nature and norms of conduct prescribed by that nature. There are certainly numerous traces of the humanist doctrines concerning the well-founded nature in the *Quixote*. In the various great speeches of Don Quixote of Part II we witness the chivalric madness that dominates much of his declamation in Part I metamorphose into an idealism that frequently takes the appealing shape of the humanist vision. In one of the most important of them, his discourse on the education of a prince, which he offers Sancho on the eve of his "coronation," he reminds his squire of the importance of filial love, invoking as he does so that alignment of the order of grace and the well-founded nature which is fundamental to the exemplary vision of Cervantes's novellas: "in this way you will satisfy heaven, which is not pleased when anybody despises what it has created, and you will be complying with your obligations to the well-concerted order of nature."[130] When the heathen Cide Hamete Benengeli contrasts the mutability and cyclical flux of the earthly life with the permanence of the life to follow, the narrator approvingly, if somewhat humorously, reminds us that "many without the light of faith, by the light of nature alone, have come to understand this." Don Quixote appears to accept the doctrine of the natural light of reason and the reconciliation of pagan philosophy and Christianity which it supported, for when speaking eloquently of the beauty of heroism and the good death, he does not hesitate to cite the example and the words of Julius Caesar, although the Roman spoke "as a heathen and one ignorant of the knowledge of the true God."[131] Throughout the *Quixote* Sancho Panza

---

[130] "con esto satisfarás al cielo, que gusta que nadie se desprecie de lo que él hizo y corresponderás a lo que debes a la naturaleza bien concertada" *Don Quijote de la Mancha*, 2:358. In the same speech, he reminds the future judge of the flawed condition of human nature since the fall and exhorts him to administer justice with mercy and equity.

[131] "muchos sin lumbre de fe, sino con la luz natural, lo han entendido" (2:440); "como gentil y ajeno del conocimiento del verdadero Dios" (2:228). See also Don

is linked to that primal period before writing, philosophy, and the numerous confusions of civilization, when nature's norms were clearly apprehensible to man and embodied themselves in the vast store of proverbs. Erasmus and his school collected these for the edification of civilization, an enterprise perfectly consistent with their general aim of restoring the original perfect nature.[132] In his greatest triumph, Sancho rejects the artificial and corrupt society of the duke and duchess and immediately thereafter presides over the formation of a natural community of human beings, fragmented by different religious convictions and languages but bonded by the fundamental principles of social organization according to the natural reason and philosophy which the Christian Humanists admired in the pagan thinkers— friendship and good will (*amicitia* and *benevolentia*).[133] Moreover, it

Quijote's speech on the value of the cult of fame and the pagan heroes (2:96) and the respect which he and Diego de Miranda show for "los antiguos filósofos" in their discourse on education and poetry (2:154-57).

[132] Erasmus placed the legendary Golden Age at the beginning of history following the expulsion from Eden. Although the inclination to sin was born in men, they continued for centuries to live according to the order of the original nature, which they could still glimpse with greater clarity than in the following ages. It was only after a lengthy period of gradual decline that written laws were necessary. See *Laus Stultitiae*, p. 74, and Schottenloher, "Lex Naturae und Lex Christi bei Erasmus," p. 265. This primitivist ideal appeared in the *Coloquios satíricos* of the Spanish Erasmist, Antonio de Torquemada, whose works are discussed by the censors of Don Quixote's library. The good shepherd Amintas receives two courtiers, who are lost in the forest, with hospitality, speaks to them of the beauty of nature ("Todas las cosas como las hace y produce la naturaleza desnudas y con solo el ser que su sustancia tienen son de mayor perfición que cuando los accidentes son adquiridos y postizos . . ."), and nostalgically recalls the purer order immediately following the fall, when agriculture was the universal way of life and money did not exist (N.B.E.A. 7:512-13). Proverbs, older than written philosophy and laws, embody to some extent the culture of this early period, when the recollection of Eden was still strong. Don Quixote shares the humanists' enthusiasm for the proverb and perhaps the theory of nature on which it was based: "Paréceme, Sancho, que no hay refrán que no sea verdadero, porque todos son sentencias sacadas de la mesma experiencia, madre de las ciencias todas" (1:252). As Castro has shown, the statement echoes the words of one of Erasmus's most important disciples in Spain, Juan de Mal Lara, in his collection of proverbs, *La filosofía vulgar* (see *El pensamiento de Cervantes*, pp. 182-85). While the scene of Don Quixote's speech on the Golden Age to the bewildered goatherds initially looks ironically at the utopian vision of the primal order of nature, it concludes, in one of Cervantes's characteristic reversals, by confirming its validity, celebrating the ethical values embodied in the myth—hospitality, brotherhood, kindness, and friendship— and depicting a simple society living according to them.

[133] "De cuando en cuando juntaba alguno su mano derecha con la de Sancho, y decía:—*Español y tudesqui, tuto uno: bon compaño*. Y Sancho respondía: *Bon compaño, jura Di!*" (2:450). Invoking the harmonious order of the celestial bodies, Erasmus

falls to the simple Sancho, who, inspired by his "buen natural," speaks at times like a "true theologian" about the importance of good living (2:195), to remind the frivolous duchess that beneath all the superficial distinctions of rank, wealth, and profession all human beings are united at the fundamental level of bodily life ("there's no stomach a hand's breadth bigger than any other") and that all are essentially the same in their common destiny to live, die, and occupy at the end of their respective journeys a uniformly small plot of land ("the Pope's body takes up no more feet of earth than the sexton's, though one's higher than the other; for when we go down to the pit, we all have to shrink and fit, or they make us shrink and fit, whether we like it or not—and good night!"[134]). When Sancho reacts with bewilderment to Roque Guinart's harsh castigation of his comrades and to the discovery that retributive justice is necessary even among thieves and when, aboard the galley in Barcelona, he asks: "What have these wretches done that they flog them so? And how does this single man, who goes about whistling, have the audacity to whip so many people? Surely this is hell," Cervantes is exposing the anomalous character of positive law and the disturbing "illogic" of its necessity when measured by the authentic good nature of human beings.[135]

---

writes that a society is nothing else but a "multorum amicitia iisdem legibus concorditer parentium, ac mutuis auxiliis sese tuentium." Such friendship belongs to the natural order: "[Natura] addidit genuinum affectum, inter parentes ac liberos, inter fratres ac sorores, inter cognatos & affines, inter ejusdem geniis ac civitatis homines" (*Ecclesiastes sive Concionator Euangelicus, Opera Omnia*, ed. Le Clerc, 5:1098D,E). For Erasmus's view of friendship as the fundamental bond of society and his discovery of the principle in the natural philosophy of the pagans, see Schottenloher, "Lex Naturae und Lex Christi bei Erasmus," pp. 264-69. For the central importance of friendship in Erasmus's entire Christian philosophy, see Pierre Mesnard's review of E. Telle's *Érasme de Rotterdam et Le Septième Sacrement* (*Bibliotéque d'Humanisme et Renaissance* 17 [1955]:314-19). In discussing the marital relationship, Vives speaks of the bonds of affection and good will by which God and nature unite mankind into a single family, "[illa communio ac amicitia universalis], qua cuncti homines, seu fratres ab uno rerum omnium parente Deo derivati, continentur, qua nos natura ipsa, quae prope in omnibus hominibus eadem est, inter nos caritate quadam devincit" (*Institutio Feminae Christianae, Opera Omnia*, 4:174).

[134] "no hay estómago que sea un palmo mayor que otro. . . . no ocupa más pies de tierra el cuerpo del Papa que el del sacristán, aunque sea más alto el uno que el otro; que al entrar en el hoyo todos nos ajustamos y encogemos, o nos hacen ajustar y encoger, mal que nos pese y a buenas noches" (2:299).

[135] "¿Qué han hecho estos desdichados, que ansí los azotan, y cómo este hombre solo, que anda por aquí silbando, tiene atrevimiento para azotar a tanta gente?" (2:523-24). See Erasmus's uneasy reconciliation of the philosophy of Christ, which is, of course, the reinstituted original good nature, and the necessity of positive laws. The latter are, to be sure, sparks of the pure light of Christ, but sparks that are

While such elements of the *Quixote* reveal the presence of the traditional view of nature that underlies the exemplarity of *La Gitanilla*, the work is anything but a celebration of the *bene condita natura* and the norms and institutions that it prescribes for the earthly life. Quite the contrary, insofar as one can infer a vision of nature lying behind the literary world of the *Quixote*, it is a strikingly different vision, one that values the particularity of concrete human beings and shows little concern for a universal, uniform human nature and the behavioral norms that it might imply. Everywhere in the *Quixote* Cervantes depicts human beings acting and conversing in ways which bear no relationship to an informing conceptual pattern, whether moral, philosophical, or aesthetic. Moreover, quite frequently he allows his characters' actions to conflict with expectations which he raises in his readers concerning them by initially presenting them in terms of a reductive category based on literary, professional, or class type. This pattern, which Américo Castro has studied in his later writings on *Don Quixote*, suggests a view of human nature that is far closer to that of contemporary scientific thought and skeptical philosophy than to the Christian Humanist doctrines. Indeed, to situate the vision of nature dominating the *Quixote* in its proper philosophical context we need only look at Francisco Sánchez's denunciation of the follies of those who look to nature for the dreams and fictions of universals and norms. For the skeptic nature is a vast, multifarious, confusing, and exhilarating realm of constantly changing particulars, fathomable only through the intuitive knowledge of each particular at the specific time and place of its observation.

. . . there are only individuals, only these can be perceived . . . show me in nature those things you call universals; you will give them to me in the form of particulars. Nothing do I see in them which is universal; everything is particular. . . . I am only desirous of opening the eyes and the minds of our

---

clearly visible in crystalline springs glow mysteriously, and at times faintly, in the muddy puddles that mark earthly life (*Ratio seu Compendium Verae Theologiae, Ausgewählte Schriften*, 3:200. See Schottenloher, "Lex Naturae und Lex Christi bei Erasmus," pp. 289-96; Guido Kisch, *Erasmus und die Jurisprudenz seiner Zeit* (Basel, 1960), chap. 5; and Eberhard von Koerber, *Die Staatstheorie des Erasmus von Rotterdam* (Berlin, 1967), pp. 84-89. Cervantes explores the same problem in Don Quixote's confrontation with the galley slaves, but it is not specifically the well-founded nature, embodied in Sancho Panza, which is here juxtaposed to positive law, but rather the Divine Will, the very light that illumines the order of nature, here represented by Don Quixote himself: "me parece duro caso hacer esclavos a los que Dios y naturaleza hizo libres. . . . Dios hay en el cielo, que no se descuida de castigar al malo, ni de premiar al bueno, y no es bien que los hombres honrados sean verdugos de los otros hombres" (1:273).

heedless youth and of clearing away the rubbish which obstructs the paths of the free and vast realm of nature.[136]

As for human nature, not only is it folly to speak of an essence of the species, but it is also illusory to believe in the enduring integrity of an individual: "in the case of a single man, with the passage of one hour, it cannot be said that he is the same person as before . . . so great is the indivisibility of an identity that, if you add or subtract a single point from any thing, it is no longer entirely the same thing; but the accidents are of the essence of the individual, and, as they are perpetually varying, they impress their variation upon it."[137] Such is the extreme position of the skeptic philosopher regarding human nature, and there can be no doubt that the treatment of character in the *Quixote* and, for that matter, in the entire great literary tradition which Cervantes's novel inaugurated is informed to a great extent by a similar attitude toward individual experience.[138] While the total vision of Cervantes's masterpiece would strongly imply an antiessentialist view of human nature and a conception of the law of nature in terms of the law of self-realization of the individual, it is perhaps odd that the clearest discursive formulation of a view of nature stressing singularity and unfathomable mystery appears in the exemplary *Persiles*, whose dominant view of human beings, society, and the universe is fundamentally essentialist. As I have shown elsewhere, the narrator of Cervantes's prose epic frequently exercises a subversive role in the "neo-classical" masterpiece, undermining the aesthetic principles on which it is based, reminding the reader that the "lofty" text is quite individually and subjectively determined, and suggesting that the traditional classical assumptions concerning poetic truth, decorum, and the imitation of nature as sanctions of a literary text and its fictional

---

[136] Sánchez's statement of skeptic philosophy (*Quod Nihil Scitur*), which is known to have influenced Montaigne, was written in Toulouse in 1576. I have been unable to consult the original version of this work. My citations are from the Spanish translation, *Que nada se sabe* (Buenos Aires, 1944); see pp. 104, 189.

[137] Ibid., p. 122.

[138] Sánchez's conception of man as an experiencing being, a being who eludes all definitions in terms of an enduring essence, could in fact be taken as the assumption underlying novelistic characterization in general. See Ian Watt's words on the cultural background of the rise of the novel: ". . . from the Renaissance onwards, there was a growing tendency for individual experience to replace collective tradition as the ultimate arbiter of reality . . . the unified world picture of the Middle Ages was replaced with another very different one—one which presents us, essentially, with a developing but unplanned aggregate of particular individuals having particular experiences at particular times and at particular places" (*The Rise of the Novel* [Berkeley, 1971], pp. 14, 31).

characters are questionable.[139] At one point this individualized consciousness pauses to reflect on human nature, and his digression voices a sympathy for the "nongeneric" human being in all his elusive singularity and fascinating variety:

In nature we observe many effects of which we do not know the causes; one man feels his teeth ache if he sees somebody cutting a piece of cloth with a knife; another perhaps trembles at the sight of a mouse; and I have seen another shudder over the slicing of a radish; and yet another leave the table of a formal dinner on seeing olives placed on it. If one asks of the cause of such strange things, there is no explaining it.[140]

As I shall point out below in connection with the Licenciado Vidriera's morbid compulsion to judge human beings in terms of reductive categories, the view of human nature expressed here and implicit throughout the *Quixote* is very close to that adopted in the skeptical, empirical psychology of such thinkers as Sánchez, Vives, and Huarte de San Juan. At this point I wish to emphasize the tremendous distance separating this antiessentialist way of thinking about human beings from Erasmus's emphasis on an authentic self, rational and natural, toward which the individual's quest for identity must lead.

The ambivalence marking Cervantes's concept of nature might tempt us to invoke once again that convenient catch phrase of Cervantine criticism, the two Cervanteses—the modern versus the conservative, the genius versus the craftsman—or to explain away the "exemplarity" of the *Novelas ejemplares* as Castro has done, as an effort at conformity, a silencing of the writer's authentic self as he pandered to official tastes and values. However, such an interpretation fails to take into account the fact that the complexity which Cervantes's writings reveal concerning the concept of nature is absolutely consistent with the central tradition of humanist thought that informed so much of his exemplary fiction. Indeed, if we wish to situate Cervantes's fascination with the integrity of the individual and the nonparadigmatic nature of experience in the intellectual and cultural currents of the age, it seems unnecessary to look directly to natural science and occult philosophy of such men as Telesio, Cardano, and Bruno, as Castro has done,[141]

[139] See *Cervantes, Aristotle, and the "Persiles,"* chap. 8.

[140] "Efetos vemos en la naturaleza de quien ignoramos las causas, adormécense o entorpécense a uno los dientes de ver cortar con un cuchillo un paño; tiembla tal vez un hombre de un ratón, y yo le he visto temblar de ver cortar un rábano, y a otro he visto levantarse de una mesa de respeto por ver poner unas aceitunas. Si se pregunta la causa, no hay saber decirla" (*Los trabajos de Persiles y Sigismunda*, pp. 177-78).

[141] *El pensamiento de Cervantes*, pp. 159-73. As Carlos Noreña points out, the occult sciences of such students of nature as Paracelsus, Cardanus, and Telesius failed to

although there is certainly a relationship of resemblance if not of cause-effect between Cervantes's liberation of man in literature from the shackles of "teleological" literary patterns and normative characterization and the turn toward the direct observation and empirical study of nature in contemporary science.[142] The fact is that, in his skepticism regarding the traditional approach to human nature that postulates an essential self identical in all men, in his fascination with the poetic possibilities residing in the singularity of human beings, and in his seemingly incompatible interest in writing such "essentialist" works as *La Gitanilla* and the *Persiles* and celebrating a nature of rational design and purposiveness which sets norms for the individual and the creations of his civilization, Cervantes reveals a breadth of vision which one observes in the greatest Christian Humanists, whose theories of nature are marked by the same conciliatory stance toward these very different views. One of their favorite texts was Cicero's *De Officiis*, and they were fond of invoking his accommodating definition of the law of nature:

We must realize that we are invested by nature with two characters, as it were; one of these is universal, arising from the fact of our being all alike endowed with reason and with that superiority which lifts us above the brute. From this all morality and propriety are derived, and upon it depends the rational method of ascertaining our duty. The other character is the one that is assigned to individuals in particular. . . . we must so act as not to oppose the universal laws of human nature, but, while safeguarding those, to follow the bent of our own particular nature. For it is of no avail to fight against one's nature or to aim at what is impossible of attainment. . . . Nothing is proper if it is in direct opposition to one's natural genius.[143]

If one senses here an uneasy reconciliation of the moralist and the skeptic, who acknowledges the potential for conflict in his position, it remained nevertheless a reconciliation which the Renaissance humanists found particularly appealing as they turned their attention to the immense variety in human experience in the world while attempting to establish norms which were consistent with traditional values

---

arouse much interest in Spain. Scientific activity and achievements were much more notable in the area of medicine and psychology (see "Juan Huarte's Naturalistic Humanism," *Journal of the History of Philosophy* 10 [1972]:71-76).

[142] For the development of empirical science in the sixteenth century and the enthusiastic pronouncements of its spokesmen about experience as the "mother of all wisdom," see Haydn, *The Counter-Renaissance*, chap. 4. See also Robert Lenoble, "L'Évolution de l'idée de 'Nature' du XVIe au XVIIIe siècle," *Revue de Métaphysique et de Morale* 58 (1953):108-129.

[143] *De Officiis*, I. xxx, xxxi; cited by H. Haydn, *The Counter-Renaissance*, p. 477.

and which could be universally applied. While the view of the natural order as permeated by reason and design was for the humanists easily reconcilable with the *bene condita natura* of prelapsarian man in Christian theology, an order of nature rendered perfect by the presence of grace, the allowance for the distinctive individuality of every being in the Ciceronian definition supported their intense interest in studying the manifold forms of life and civilization as objects of value and interest in themselves. Thus Erasmus can center his whole program for spiritual *renovatio* on the restoration of the well-founded nature and the application of its ethical norms in the individual, the family, the state, and all of Christendom. At the same time his fascination with nature as a realm of endless singularity is evident throughout his writings. Thus in his colloquy *Amicitia* he expresses his wonder at the marvelous deity nature, an indecipherable power whose forces are visible in the mysterious sympathies and antipathies that drive human beings as instinctual forces and to which individuals must yield if they are to achieve the fullness of being to which they are capable of growing.[144] A similar view of the realm of nature as an order of the individual with its own singular, not necessarily rational attributes, emerges in a context of aesthetic theorizing in Erasmus's *Ciceronianus*. In condemning the mechanical imitative practices and theories championed by the contemporary Ciceronians, Erasmus formulates a doctrine of authentic imitation based on a profound assimilation of the imitated model following the discovery of its suitability according to true affinities linking the individual consciousnesses of its author and his imitator. He observes that "nature created us to some extent for variety, attributing to each person his own individuality, so that you will scarcely find two human beings who have the same capacities or are interested in the same things." Every individual is unique; tastes are innumerable; and there is no style of writing that will not appeal to one temperament or another. Nature has determined that style must be the authentic mirror of the self; reading is an encounter with a real personality. Just as temperaments are infinite, readers' reactions to a piece of writing will vary according to the affinities that they feel for the self embodied in its words. After confessing his own mysterious attraction to Horace ("ingeniorum arcanam quandam affinitatem"), Erasmus observes that the "providence of nature" has created

---

[144] *The Colloquies of Erasmus*, p. 527. Erasmus characteristically qualifies his advocacy of the value of the irrational by asserting that charity and honor are natural values for all men and must never be sacrificed by an individual in his quest for self-fulfillment. The qualification echoes Cicero's advice that one should follow one's peculiar bent, but only if it is not vicious.

every human being as distinct and satisfied with himself and has given him a specific language that mirrors the unique profile of his spirit. A man of letters must follow his own nature and not spoil it by attempting to impose on it one that is alien.[145]

If Erasmus's sense of nature as individuality is clearly visible in his scientific and aesthetic treatises, it is more striking when it emerges in his ethical, religious and political writings, those works dealing most directly with his program for the restoration of the perfect nature. In the *Enchiridion* he acknowledges that every human nature is shaped in a singular way by environmental and biological forces and has distinctive needs and demands, all of which make the channeling of its impulses toward virtuous conduct and creative action a process that only its individual reason can direct. Moreover, he stresses the beauty of Christianity and the wisdom of St. Paul, its greatest saint, in their concern for every human being as a distinct individual for whom the path to salvation follows its own unique course.[146] In the

---

[145] "Ad hanc nos natura quodammodo finxit suum cuique tribuens ingenium, ut vix duos reperias, qui eadem vel possint vel ament" (*Ausgewählte Schriften*, 7:328-32). The affinities of Erasmus and Cervantes in their attitudes toward artistic creation, originality, tradition, and imitation are most evident if we compare this passage with the prologue to *Don Quixote*, I. After ridiculing the conventional conception of the writer as the *poeta doctus*, the creator of works that are sanctioned by tradition and authority and preserved in a chain of revered texts extending backwards in time to some primal, divinely revealed model, Cervantes emphatically rejects such an august lineage for his "ugly stepson." He goes on to enunciate a principle of imitation ("la imitación perfecta") which, while recognizing the importance of the proper adjustment of the literary utterance to the nature of its subject and the propriety of simplicity and clarity of style for the limited, satirical aims of the *Quixote*, at the same time places a good deal of emphasis on authenticity and self-expression. Through the "friend's" admonition to the faltering writer, Cervantes stresses that the *Quixote* is his own singular and unique creation, that his "*historia*" is "*sincera*": "este *vuestro libro* no tiene necesidad de ninguna otra cosa de aquellas que vos decís que le falta . . . esta *vuestra escritura* no mira a más que . . . salga *vuestra oración* y período sonoro y festivo, pintando, en todo lo que alcanzáredes y fuere posible, *vuestra intención*; dando a entender *vuestros conceptos* sin intricarlos y escurecerlos" (1:57-58; italics added). For the innovative character of Erasmus's theory of imitation in its stress on individuality, see H.-J. Lange, *Aemulatio Veterum sive de optimo genere dicendi: Die Entstehung des Barockstils im 16. Jahrhundert durch eine Geschmacksverschiebung in Richtung der Stile des manieristischen Typs* (Frankfurt am Main, 1974), pp. 116ff.

[146] See *Enquiridion*, pp. 164-73, esp. 168-69; 352. In all these contexts we observe Erasmus's awareness of the Aristotelian-Galenic humor psychology, which enjoyed tremendous prestige following the translation and dissemination of the works of Hippocrates and Galen in the early sixteenth century and probably had an effect in molding commonplace notions concerning human behavior comparable to Freudian theories in the twentieth century. As Haydn points out, the empirical approach to behavior which faculty psychology espoused undoubtedly contributed a great deal to the rediscovery of individuality in the sixteenth century (*The Counter-Renaissance*, chap.

Praise of Folly his ironic spokesman acknowledges the intractable variety and confusion that characterize human relations and suggests that happiness in human beings, societies, and civilization at large is built much more on a kind of balancing of flawed individual temperaments and their foibles than on the application of rational principles. And in his numerous observations on law, he argues that justice can be truly achieved only through the intense study of the distinctive and individual character of a situation, the avoidance of an inflexible reliance on the letter of the law, and the readiness to adapt or "improve" a law according to the principle of equity in its application to a particular case.[147] Indeed the empirical tendencies in Erasmus's writ-

---

7). Erasmus's qualification of his advocacy of yielding to instinctual forces by observing that individual self-fulfillment must not be pursued at the sacrifice of honor and charity is characteristic of the attitude toward the moral implications of humor psychology of even its most "scientific" proponents. While they attempted to explain behavior in materialistic terms, emphasizing the importance of hereditary, physiological, and environmental forces, they avoided a deterministic view of human action and insisted on the power of the supreme faculty, reason, and its instrument, the free will, to guide every individual to virtuous conduct (see Herschel Baker, *The Image of Man* [New York, 1961], chap. 17, esp. pp. 288ff.). For the popularity of this current of sixteenth-century naturalism in Spain, particularly among skeptic philosophers, *conversos*, and physicians and its formulation in Huarte de San Juan's *Examen de Ingenios*, one of the most influential treatises in the history of European psychological thought, see Noreña, "Juan Huarte's Naturalistic Humanism," pp. 74-75. Several studies have emphasized the coherence of Don Quixote's psychic disposition according to Huarte's theories and argued that Cervantes was familiar with his treatise (see R. Salillas, *Un gran inspirador de Cervantes: el doctor Huarte de San Juan y su Examen de ingenios* [Madrid, 1905]; Otis H. Green, "El 'ingenioso' Hidalgo," *Hispanic Review* 25 [1957]:175-93; Harald Weinrich, *Das Ingenium Don Quijotes* [Münster, 1956]). It is perhaps worth speculating that Huarte de San Juan and the entire tradition of skeptical, empirical psychology cultivated by the *converso* physicians, to which Cervantes may well have been exposed from an early age through his father, a surgeon, had a much more profound type of influence on his own psychic disposition, an influence to which his responsiveness to individuality, his sensitivity to the mysteries of self-fulfillment, his fascination with the variety in experience and human behavior, and his revolutionary introduction of the nonparadigmatic facets of experience and character into literature would attest. J.-C. Margolin has suggested that Erasmus's attachment to the particular, despite its apparent incompatibility with his belief in "une nature universelle bonne et généreuse," might be attributable in part to the influence of the medical writings of Hippocrates and Galen and the nominalist philosophical climate of contemporary medical circles ("L'Idée de nature dans la pensée d'Erasme," pp. 21-22). As Margolin notes, in his speculations concerning the particular and the universal, Aristotle had denied that medicine is a true science, because "le médecin ne soigne pas l'homme en général, mais Callias ou Socrate."

[147] For the Aristotelian concept of *epieikeia* and traditional doctrines of *aequitas* as they emerged in Erasmus's various statements on law, see Kisch, *Erasmus und die Jurisprudenz seiner Zeit*. See also, Margolin, "L'Idée de nature dans la pensée d'Erasme," pp. 30-31, and Koerber, *Die Staatstheorie des Erasmus von Rotterdam*, pp. 85-89.

ings are so relentless and so forceful that Bernhard Groethuysen has concluded that for the humanist it was difficult if not impossible to consider a human being in abstract and generalized terms, isolated from the concrete and unique experiences of a particular life.

In Erasmus's anthropology the question of life is posed, in a very special way, from within life itself, and not simply from within man as such. . . . life is a context of experienced events . . . the content of a life becomes the essential matter. The human being is not simply a subject who reacts with emotion to the events which unfold in his life and who, as subject, seeks to place himself above his life through the cultivation of an attitude which is rationalistic or voluntaristic; he is rather the human being of this life. The questions which concern him cannot be posed in dissociation from the vital context and the singular circumstances of this real life. [148]

[148] "Philosophische Anthropologie," *Mensch und Charakter* (Munich and Berlin, 1931), pp. 1-207; see pp. 186-87. In view of Américo Castro's most recent efforts to deal with the difficult problem of the psycho-social determinants of Cervantes's revolutionary achievement in conferring literary dignity on normal experience, I would emphasize that I am not concerned in this study with whatever private experience might have disposed Cervantes toward adopting such seemingly contradictory attitudes toward nature and giving expression to them in such a creative way. It is certainly plausible that his skepticism concerning the generalizing habit of mind is the mark of what social psychologists consider a "marginal" personality, one who can not avoid standing apart from the group to which he tenuously belongs and viewing the official values, attitudes, and myths which mold the consciousness of its members with some detachment. One can go on to speculate that a decisive personal experience of marginality underlies Cervantes's critique of categorical thinking, whether "official" or otherwise, and look for it in his frustrations as a soldier and a patriot, his long period of living in societies very different from his own, his "exile" as a captive and perhaps a sense of abandonment arising therefrom, his professional failures, his incapacity to achieve recognition and status within the privileged social circles of Spain, or his possible descent from a family of *conversos*. Similarly one can consider the skepticism, the empiricism, the sensitivity to the integrity of the individual, the obsessive call for tolerance, the intellectual elusiveness, the ironic detachment, and the intolerance of cant in Erasmus's writings as the marks of a marginal personality and look for its roots in his consciousness of his illegitimacy, in his sense of the hollowness of the order of life into which he was forced and for which he had no true vocation, or in his conception of himself as an outsider in his frequent relocations in different societies of Europe. In proposing that Cervantes's basic ideas on nature can be traced to a matrix of humanist thought on the subject, I do not intend to imply that such ideas transferred themselves into his consciousness by their own power, as if they had a life of their own, or that one can account for his distinctive achievement as a writer by pointing to their presence in the background of his works. Quite the contrary, Cervantes assimilated such ideas and possessed them as what Ortega would describe as authentic *"creencias,"* and he did so because of his own distinctive vital needs, which, more than likely, will forever remain a fascinating area of conjecture for Cervantists.

Er ist der Mensch dieses Lebens. It is precisely this sense of man as an "experiencing" being and life as a process—narratable but not definable—that makes Erasmus the true ancestor of Cervantes not only in his normative writings but also in his depiction of the flow of life in the first novel of European literature.

The writings of the Spanish humanists reveal the same ambivalence in the elaboration of a concept of nature. Vives upholds the existence of an authentic human nature, "identical in all men" (see above), fulfilling itself by following the moral imperatives dictated by its inner light of reason and conscience and struggling to return to its perfected prelapsarian state. "What indeed is a Christian other than a man brought back to his true nature, and, as it were, restored to his original birthright?"[149] The true order of nature is the order of the Creator, and man is capable, by following his good natural inclinations and cultivating them through proper education, of discovering its laws and ordering his own life and his society accordingly. But if Vives's championing of self-knowledge presupposes an essential self, hidden in all men, he was nevertheless fascinated with the infinite diversity in man. He discovered in one of his major projects, the exploration of man's soul, that there is in men's individual temperaments and mental dispositions [*ingenios*] not only a boundless "variety and diversity," but in fact "as much opposition as is to be found among their faces," and reached the conclusion that, while man can learn about the workings of the soul through careful observation, he can never know what its essence is.[150] Moreover, in his *De Tradendis Disciplinis* he advocates an empirical, utilitarian approach to the acquisition and use of knowledge, observing that "we cannot gain any certain knowledge" from nature, and suggesting that we should use whatever resources we have to cope with the necessities of the individual moment, provided of course that Christian piety is served.[151]

---

[149] "Quid enim est aliud christianus, quam homo naturae suae redditus, ac velut natalibus restitutus?" (*De Concordia et Discordia in Humano Genere*, I), cited by Noreña in *Juan Luis Vives*, p. 207. On the light of nature, Vives writes: "Haec mentis nostrae lux, sive censura, qua recte, qua oblique, semper tamen ad verum et bonum devergit . . ." (*De Anima et Vita*, II.4). "Deus in humanos animos de sua luce lucem derivavit, etiamque post naturae casum, tantum reliqui fecit nobis, quantum . . . in via nos profecto sistere salutis. . . . Quid ergo dici potest probabilius quam esse hominibus naturale, quo nutu suo omnes homines ferantur?" (*De Veritate Fidei Christianae*, I.4; cited by Noreña, *Vives*, p. 250).

[150] "non varietas solum ac diversitas [ingeniorum], sed adversitas quoque tanta, quanta est inter hominum facies," *De Anima et Vita, Opera Omnia*, 3:367; see also *De Disciplinis*, II.2.3. See Haydn, *The Counter-Renaissance*, p. 198.

[151] See Haydn, *The Counter-Renaissance*, p. 242.

In Juan de Mal Lara's *Filosofía vulgar*, a work which in its principal aims is an act of homage to the Erasmian view of the good original nature of man and which probably had an important general impact on Cervantes's sensibilities and his conception of the character Sancho Panza, we discover again the humanist looking at nature in the two potentially conflictive ways. In a paraphrase of the *locus classicus* in Cicero's *De Officiis*, he points out that the distinctive human nature lies in man's "participation in reason" ("in this part there is a certain element in which we all resemble one another"), but adds that there is another "special part, which each one has according to his natural inclination" and that "in order to choose a way of life, it is necessary that each individual look to his own nature."[152] Mal Lara's admonition concerning the individual's choice of profession was generally endorsed by the Christian Humanists. It appeared frequently in their writings on education, and we find it echoed by Don Quixote, in another of the "great speeches" of Part II which are informed by the humanist vision: "as to forcing them [one's children] to study this or that science, I do not think that it is right, although to persuade them will do no harm . . . you should let your son travel where his star calls him."[153]

The vision of nature which informs Cervantes's fiction and the writings of the humanists who influenced him most profoundly is marked, then, by a fundamental ambivalence emerging from the apparently contradictory tendencies to define the order of nature in essentialist and antiessentialist or particularist terms. The ambivalence can be broken down into various general antinomies in concept and attitude: rationality-irrationality and vitality; generality-singularity; design-confusion; the normative-the ethically neutral; clarity-mystery; similarity-difference; unity-variety; predictability-spontaneity; simplicity-the marvelous; confidence-awe and curiosity. Invoked constantly by the contemplative and the investigator, the rationalist and the empiricist, the theologian and the scientist, the idea of nature was complex and variable, permeated with potential contradictions, and capable of

---

[152] "en esta parte hay cierta cosa que todos nos parecemos . . . para escoger la manera de vivir, es menester que cada uno mire por su natural" (see ed. cit., 4:17-18; the passage is cited by A. Castro in *El pensamiento de Cervantes*, p. 171). For Mal Lara's debt to Erasmus, his fascination with the variety of the concrete world, and his seemingly contradictory espousal of a unifying doctrine of nature, see Castro, "Juan de Mal Lara y su 'Filosofía vulgar,' " *Hacia Cervantes* (Madrid, 1967), pp. 167-209.

[153] "en lo de forzarles [a los hijos'] que estudien esta o aquella ciencia no lo tengo por acertado, aunque el persuadirles no será dañoso . . . que vuesa merced deje caminar a su hijo por donde su estrella le llama" (2:155-56).

encompassing and dignifying an extraordinary range of human activity and attitudes. However, one of the most striking aspects of the concept and one which is perhaps most difficult for modern readers to understand is the reluctance of the majority of the thinkers of the age to invoke nature as a sanction for the indulgence of instinctual impulses. As I have pointed out above, the humanists generally looked on the passions as natural, healthy, and creative and rejected traditional habits of mind and institutions that failed to recognize that instinctual self-fulfillment is a proper and natural demand of the civilized human being. And there can be no doubt that they were receptive to traditional philosophical positions such as Epicureanism which would powerfully support their affirmative view of the whole man and his earthly existence and to theories of psychology that acknowledge the centrality of a nonrational element in the constitution of individual men.[154] However, committed to the belief that man's fundamental nature is rational and that he is a free being, despite the physiological determinants of his particular personality, they insisted that man's instinct be channeled by the direction of reason and maintained that, unless its exercise conform to the rationally discernible ideal of temperance and the Christian moral imperatives as set forth in Holy Scripture and exemplified in man's prelapsarian natural state, its expression is unnatural, and its effects are destructive. Their characteristic position was on middle ground between the opposing extremes of unnatural repression and unnatural license, extremes which in Cervantes's fiction emerge in the powerful symbolic forms of the jealous Extremaduran's grotesque monastery-house and the anarchical world of the Gypsies with its alluring "ancha libertad." The vision of man's nature in terms of biological determinism and the appeal of an ethical naturalism based on happiness, comfort, and instinctual fulfillment were

---

[154] Hiram Haydn's account of the new directions of thought leading to a revaluation of individuality, particularity, instinctuality, sentiment, and pluralism in human nature and society is brilliant and provocative, but it is somewhat misleading in its neat division of the combatants in the ideological conflict which he envisages. The fact is that the Christian Humanists form a much more varied and interesting school than Haydn would allow, precisely because they contain within their thought so many of the "counter-Renaissance" tendencies which he assigns to their adversaries. Admittedly the simplification of their position is effective for the sake of argument and clarity in a subject in which the multifarious issues and their complexity would defy almost any efforts of orderly analysis; but unfortunately the association of the Christian Humanists with Thomist philosophy (and occasionally with that of rigid Stoicism) fails to do justice to the complexities and ambivalences in their efforts of cultural synthesis, to the full extent of their modifications of traditional views in the interest of secularization, and to the remarkable breadth of their vision.

certainly familiar to them, and, when addressing themselves to the evils of repressive morality, they certainly summon forth the power of such philosophical positions. However, even in a man such as Rabelais, who fervently proclaims the value of instinctual health and finds abhorrent asceticism of any kind, we discover that the true nature of man lies in an inherent impulse to pursue virtue, which, if allowed to unfold in freedom, will lead him to a civilized life free both of unnatural restraint—whether through institutional or internal compulsion—and instinctual excess. [155] While for Rabelais the celebration of the vitality of instinctual life generally accompanies a denunciation of the tyranny of repressive and ascetic attitudes, is never presented as a sanction for license, and is in fact perfectly reconcilable with the order of the well-founded nature, in Torquato Tasso, whose tendencies are strongly ascetic and whose work anticipates in many ways the destruction of the realm of the well-founded nature and the segregation of the orders of nature and grace which characterize the spirit and literature of *desengaño* of the seventeenth century, the forceful argument for the natural order as a realm of happiness, pleasure, and

---

[155] See the ideal of human nature which Gargantua champions as he founds the utopian Abbey of Thélème, whose inhabitants will enjoy freedom and in that condition follow their "natural instinct" to be virtuous (see L. Febvre, *Le Problème de l'incroyance au xvie siècle* [Paris, 1968], pp. 289-90, and Hugo Friedrich, *Montaigne* [Bern, 1967], pp. 297-98). Febvre's words of caution concerning the ease with which modern readers allow their favored conceptions of nature to determine the perspective from which they interpret Renaissance texts are worth recalling, particularly in view of the "naturalism" which Castro's *El pensamiento de Cervantes* imputes to Cervantes (see above): "Nous sommes tellement imbus de spéculations biologiques que ce mot [Nature] suffit à nous mettre en émoi. Nous le dotons incontinent d'une majuscule. Et nous y reconnaissons, sans hésiter, la Nature des naturalistes, cette divinité, cette rivale du Dieu des théologiens, cette idole (avec la vie) des temps biologiques. . . . [Rabelais] ne dresse pas, en face du Dieu des théologiens, une idole que, usurpant les pouvoirs reconnus à ce Dieu, proposerait pour idéal aux hommes ce jeu de besoins et d'instincts qui constituent, comme nous disons, le vouloir-vivre" (p. 263). See also Douglas Bush, *Prefaces to Renaissance Literature* (New York, 1965), chap. 3, "English Poetry: God and Nature." For Rabelais's celebration of a vitalistic principle of nature, particularly when he is concerned with denouncing the antinatural forces of monstrous artifice and repressive mental habits and institutions, see Stanley G. Eskin, "Physis and Antiphysie: The Idea of Nature in Rabelais and Calcagnini," *Comparative Literature* 14 (1952):167-73. Even Montaigne, the most persuasive critic in the age of the tyranny and unnaturalness of the venerable rational law of nature and the customs which it frequently was enlisted to support and the most eloquent champion of an individualistic and instinctive law of nature, found in the gentle counsel of the beneficent mother an advocacy of temperance, moderation, and orderliness in the enjoyment of the instincts (*Essais*, 3:xiii, "De L'Expérience"; see Haydn, *The Counter-Renaissance*, pp. 477-87, and Friedrich, *Montaigne*, pp. 296-98.

instinctual gratification is unequivocally placed in the mouth of a demonic siren who enslaves the Christian knight Rinaldo:

> solo chi segue ciò che piace è saggio,
> e in sua stagion degli anni il frutto coglie.
> Questo grida natura. Or dunque voi
> indurarete l'alma a i detti suoi?[156]

The siren's arguments are effective, but Tasso counters them forcefully, when, following Rinaldo's redemption from the false paradise of the enchantress, the old man of Ascalona and Peter the Hermit instruct him in the knowledge of grace and the proper understanding of nature. As the aged seer points out, nature teaches man to follow virtue and to direct his passions to proper ends, to seek fame through honorable deeds and to express his "noble anger" in heroic battle against the enemies of the faith and the unbridled passions within the soul.

> T'alzò natura in verso il ciel la fronte,
> e ti diè spirti generosi ed alti,
> perché in su miri, e con illustri e conte
> opre te stesso al sommo pregio essalti:
> e ti diè l'ire ancor veloci e pronte,
> non perché l'usi ne' civili assalti,
> né perché sian di desidèri ingordi
> elle ministre, e da ragion discordi;
> ma perché il tuo valore, armato d'esse,
> piú fèro assalga gli aversari esterni;
> e sian con maggior forza indi ripresse
> le cupidigie, empi nemici interni.
> Dunque ne l'uso, per cui fûr concesse,
> l'impieghi il saggio duce, e le governi;
> ed a suo senno or tepide, or ardenti
> le faccia, ed or le affretti, ed or le allenti.[157]

---

[156] "He who follows pleasure and plucks the fruit in its proper season of the year, he alone is sage. Nature shouts this wisdom. Why then do you harden your soul to her counsel?" *Gerusalemme liberata*, ed. L. Bonfigli (Bari, 1930), p. 330. It should be pointed out that the same argument appears in Tasso's celebrated pastoral drama, *Aminta*, where, free of all demonic connotations, it stands as perhaps the most important of the exceptional Renaissance literary texts (other than the innumerable lyric formulations of the traditional *carpe diem* theme) celebrating the naturalness of unrestrained sensual indulgence.

[157] "Nature lifted your forehead toward heaven and gave you lofty and generous spirits, so that you might look upward and exalt youself to the highest honor with illustrious deeds; and she also gave you irascible impulses, swift and ready, not that you use them in civil conflicts, nor that they minister to your greedy desires, at

Rabelais's and Tasso's writings reveal how two very different temperaments, the one deeply sympathetic to a glorification of the instincts and their cultivation, the other deeply uneasy about their potential for destruction, could find in the humanist vision of a regenerate, perfected natural order an area for reconciliation of reason and instinct and grace and nature, as well as a sanction for a commitment to the attainment of perfection in the active life in this world. They also show how powerful arguments for an ethical naturalism postulated on a belief that the proper end of man is instinctual pleasure and that any restraint that might interfere with this end is evil can appear and bear within their means of persuasion the illustrious philosophical currents that were of great interest to the thinkers of the age.

In its manner of developing an argument concerning nature, Tasso's epic, with its episode of temptation, deliverance, and moral growth, is of course far more traditional than Rabelais's mock-epic, with its conception of a utopian "antimonastery," existing in an order of perfected nature, and the type of situation which it employs is certainly very common in the literature of the age. Committed to the traditional values of Christianity and classical moral philosophy and basically conservative in their views of the value of the institutions of civilization, writers were, in the last analysis, more concerned with the dangers of anarchy in the self and the destructive indulgence of instinct than with the dangers of repressive mental habits and institutions.[158] In their exemplary fiction, the arguments in favor of in-

---

variance with reason, but rather that your valor, armed with them, might assault the external adversaries with greater ferocity and that you might hold in check more forcefully the ungodly internal enemies of cupidity. Therefore the wise commander should govern them and put them to the use for which they were given; and according to his judgment, he should make them now tepid, now hot; at times he should quicken their pace, at times he should slow them down" (ibid., p. 386). See also the *Allegoria del poema*, where Tasso explains that the episode demonstrates that "la grazia del Signor Iddio non opera sempre negli uomini immediatamente, o per mezzi estraordinarii, ma fa molte fiate sue operazioni per mezzi naturali." He explicitly connects the realm of the sage of Ascalona with the wisdom of classical antiquity and an order of nature containing the secrets of moral philosophy. Armida's paradise and the alluring Epicurean arguments of her servants concerning the injunctions of nature are in reality deceptions employed by the devil to stir up man's potential enemies within himself. See *Le prose diverse*, ed. C. Guasti (Firenze, 1875), 1:305-307. The reduction of the sage's realm in the rewritten *Gerusalemme conquistata* is a revealing sign of the ascendence of the ascetic currents which were to dominate the baroque literature of *desengaño*.

[158] As I have suggested above, Cervantes's re-creation of *El celoso extremeño* indicates his determination to prevent the tale from becoming, in addition to a denunciation

stinctual freedom as natural are characteristically advanced by demonic agents, and they are countered by characters who, either directly or implicitly, defend the correct view of nature as a rationally designed order and an abundant source of creative energy if temperately used. The spokesmen for an incontinent nature frequently offer sophisticated and highly persuasive arguments. For example, in Sidney's *Arcadia*, a work which in its aims, sources, design, and themes is in many ways comparable with Cervantes's *Persiles*, the sorceress Cecropia attempts to overcome the resistance of the chaste Pamela to the advances of her son by invoking some distinguished philosophical doctrines concerning the unnaturalness of any restraint that is grounded in fear and the naturalness of the pursuit of pleasure. In a similar vein Milton's Comus attempts to win the chaste lady by emphasizing the innocence and naturalness of incontinence and the unnaturalness of the "lean and sallow abstinence of the Stoic," as proven by the sexual freedom of the animals. Neither lady is convinced by the "naturalist." Pamela rejects the Lucretian arguments of her adversary and reaffirms her belief in the rational design of the universe and the goodness of its Creator's laws. Milton's lady insists that the bounty of nature can be properly enjoyed only if one observes its sober law and uses its forces temperately. In these works we see that a celebration of instinctual fulfillment as natural is clearly shown to be part of a dialectical process that aims at clarifying and celebrating by contrast the good nature of reason, design, and restraint.[159]

of the mentality of the protagonist and his unnatural world, which it is in both versions, a celebration of the naturalist philosophy proclaimed in the *dueña's* song on the power of instinct and in her argument, embellished with persuasive rhetorical finery, to Leonora concerning sexual pleasure. The moral triumph of the simple, uneducated maiden becomes a vindication of the authentic good nature that Clemente invokes in the *La Gitanilla*. The structuring principle of the tale is no longer the simple opposition of unnatural repression and natural vitality (that of the *entremés*, *El viejo celoso*), but rather the dialectical movement through the antithetical extremes of unnatural, demonic restraint and unnatural, demonic license to a superior, mediating position of natural restraint and authentic freedom.

[159] *The Covntesse of Pembrokes Arcadia*, facsimile reproduction of the original 1590 edition, ed. Carl Dennis (Kent, Ohio, 1970), pp. 278-84. *Comus, a Mask, Complete Poems and Major Prose*, ed. M. Y. Hughes (New York, 1957), pp. 107-108. The Lady upbraids the tempter: "Impostor, do not charge most innocent nature,/ As if she would her children should be riotous/ With her abundance; she, good cateress,/ Means her provision only to the good/ That live according to her sober laws/ And holy dictate of spare Temperence." See N. Frye, "The Revelation to Eve," *The Stubborn Structure* (Ithaca, 1970), pp. 135-59, esp. pp. 150-51, and Eric Laguardia's detailed study of the central scene of the confrontation of the two orders of nature in important works of the English Renaissance, *Nature Redeemed: The Imitation of Order in Three Renaissance Poems* (The Hague, 1966).

The type of moral dialectic that we observe in such masterpieces of humanist literature emerges on several occasions in Cervantes's exemplary writings,[160] but nowhere is its presence more central to the work in which it appears and its articulation of themes more complex than in *La Gitanilla*. The crucial scene in its development is the lengthy depiction of the Gypsy world at the midpoint of the tale. Here we discover a realm of nature that is very different from the "bien intencionada naturaleza" that Clemente aligns with marriage, the family, the city, and the social order. Its attractions are presented in the powerful rhetoric that marks the temptations of Cecropia, Comus, and the *dueña*, and both the heroes and the reader are forced to experience its allurements, recognize its attractions and limitations, and emerge with a heightened understanding of all that distinguishes it from the authentic realm of nature, man's true home.

THE NATURAL WORLD OF THE GYPSIES

Of the various foils against which Cervantes develops his ideal of wedded love in *La Gitanilla*, the most important by far is the world of the Gypsies. As I have pointed out elsewhere, the symbolic function of the description of the Gypsy society at the center of the work is all-important in the total design of the novella.[161] Readers have plainly found in its complexities support for a wide variety of interpretations, and their disparate, frequently contradictory conclusions would suggest that Cervantes created a symbol that is fundamentally ambiguous, one that will continue to resist all efforts at one-sided interpretation. For Francisco de Icaza the long speech by the Gypsy elder at Juan-Andrés's initiation rite contains a penetrating, accurate description of the psyche of an exotic segment of the Spanish population of the time and is one more example of Cervantes's great talents as a realistic writer. The best modern Cervantine criticism is, of course, free of such exclusive concern for the value of literature as a documentary mirror of reality and has for the most part rejected as unsophisticated such readings as Icaza's. However, while considering the Gypsy world as an artistically created symbol, it has reached very different conclusions concerning its significance and function within the tale. The romantically inclined reader such as Américo Castro discovers in

---

[160] See, in addition to *El celoso extremeño*, the various scenes of temptation in the *Persiles*. In one of them Rosamunda, the lustful courtesan, defends the *ius primae noctis*, which the chaste Transila has heroically rejected, with the familiar naturalist arguments based on the animal world as a model for human behavior (see p. 117).

[161] See *Cervantes, Aristotle, and the "Persiles,"* p. 316.

its emphasis on liberty and vitality a celebration of a natural condition of man that accords with certain tendencies in Renaissance naturalistic philosophy and strikingly looks forward to the genuine primitivism of Rousseau. For the more conservative reader, such as Casalduero, the Gypsy world, in its evident barbarity, is emblematic of the theologically fallen nature and is presented in violent opposition to the order of grace; it can be properly understood only within the ideological context of Counter-Reformation theology.[162]

The fact is that Cervantes, like many other important thinkers and writers of the Renaissance who were sensitive to the multiplicity and relativity of truth and found traditional modes of discourse, in their inflexibility, unsuited to their expressive needs, was very fond of paradoxical expression. In his other-world community he created a symbol of shifting valences, one that was capable of casting illumination on a set of problems from radically different angles.[163] Thus on the

---

[162] Icaza, Las "Novelas ejemplares" de Cervantes (Madrid, 1928), pp. 151-53; Castro, El pensamiento de Cervantes, pp. 176-77; Casalduero, Sentido y forma de las "Novelas ejemplares," pp. 71-73. While the traditional interpretation emphasizing realism and costumbrismo has been generally discarded, the tendency to discern a simplistic idealization continues to interfere with the proper recognition of the complexities of the symbol, a tendency no doubt attributable in part to the influence of Castro's study, in part to the general romantic inclinations of our age. Juan Luis Alborg finds in Cervantes's presentation of Gypsy life a realistic "cuadro de género" but adds: "hasta el mismo realismo costumbrista está recubierto de una optimista y amable patina, que lo embellece y lo despoja de toda amargura y crudeza" (Historia de la literatura española, 4 vols. [Madrid, 1966-1980], 2:101). Manuel Durán stresses Cervantes's sympathy for the Gypsies' freedom and concludes that the tale is a "joyous celebration of the freedom that comes from a wandering life" (Cervantes [New York, 1974], pp. 59-60). Even Amezúa, after recognizing that Cervantes in his treatment of the Gypsies failed to exercise his abilities to portray reality as it was, finds that the stylized treatment is simply one of idealization (Cervantes, creador de la novela corta española, 2 vols. [1956-1958], 2:5-15). A more probing presentation of the romantic reading of La Gitanilla can be found in Friedrich Schürr's Cervantes: Leben und Werk des grossen Humoristen (Bern, 1963). While insisting that Cervantes's sympathy is with the happy Gypsy society as an environment that allows the natural powers of human beings to awaken and unfold and describing the Gypsy elder's speech as a "hymn to nature and the Golden Age," Schürr notes that Cervantes carefully points to a shadowy side of the community of criminals (p. 72). The more conservative view of the Gypsy world is developed by Peter N. Dunn, who correctly emphasizes the dark implications of Gypsy nature and freedom ("Las 'Novelas ejemplares,' " Suma Cervantina, ed. J. B. Avalle-Arce and E. C. Riley [London, 1973], pp. 94-96). See also Luis Rosales's remarks on the antithesis of Gypsy freedom and the Christian liberty exemplified by Preciosa (Cervantes y la libertad, 2 vols. [Madrid, 1960], 1:310-11).

[163] Compare, for example, his paradoxical method of raising and exploring profound problems in his treatment of the Canon of Toledo, "El Caballero del Verde Gabán," Zoraida—the "adherent" of the Virgin and "La Cava"—, and, of course, his

one hand it assumes the contours of an "other-world paradise," a realm providing its inhabitants with the kind of authentic self-fulfillment denied to all the "enslaved" people who accept ordinary society and its confining possibilities for professional achievement in court, commerce, or Church: "without concerning ourselves with the old proverb, 'The Church, the Sea, or the Royal Household,' we have what we want, since we content ourselves with what we have."[164] Defined in opposition to the conventional order, the Gypsy society provides a moral standard against which ceremonialism, corruption, flattery, distrust, greed, and other abuses which afflict the "civilized" society of contemporary Spain can be clarified by contrast and condemned. As such, it reinforces the satirical picture of society emerging in the early scenes of the work, particularly in Preciosa's visits to the house of the lieutenant and the gamblers' den and in the allusions to court intrigue in the poem describing Margarita of Austria's visit to the Church of San Llorente. On the other hand the Gypsy world, as a demonic order of lawlessness, terror, lust, and incest, forms the traditional lower world of romance in which an imprisoned heroine awaits the coming of a redeemer or a mysterious turn of providence that will restore her to her proper identity.

If Preciosa evokes the scandalous lust for power, honor, and wealth which dominates the palace world and historically was to be an endless source of misery to Spain's "richest and most admirable jewel," the idealistic queen (see below), the Gypsy elder reminds the novice in his initiation sermon of all that distinguishes his world from the court: "We are not troubled by the fear of losing honor, nor are we kept awake at night by the ambition to increase it; we support no political factions, and we do not get up before daybreak to present memorials or to accompany grandees or to solicit favors." The Gypsies have no interest in the luxury, artifice, and ostentatious display of pomp which mark life at the court; they cherish their huts as if they were "gilded ceilings and sumptuous palaces," they esteem the fields, forests, and mountains in their beauty above paintings and Flemish tapestries, and

---

great hero and fool, Don Quixote. As for the way in which Renaissance writers could envision another world paradoxically, see Montaigne's elusive treatment of the cannibals or Thomas More's detailed depiction of a "no-place." For the importance of the paradoxical mode in Renaissance literature, see Rosalie L. Colie, *Paradoxia Epidemica* (Princeton, 1966). On the other world, see, in addition, Harry Berger, Jr., "The Renaissance Imagination: Second World and Green World," *Centennial Review* 9 (1965):36-78.

[164] "sin entremeternos con el antiguo refrán: 'Iglesia, o mar, o casa real,' tenemos lo que queremos, pues nos contentamos con lo que tenemos" (p. 70).

they enthusiastically cultivate the virtues of "hard primitivism": endurance, hardiness, physical health, and the indifference to pain and torture: "for us the hard clods of earth are feather beds . . . we show the same face to the sun as to the frost, to sterility as to abundance."[165] Unlike the courtiers, they remain in their daily lives close to the rhythms of nature, observing the passing of day and night properly and enjoying its abundant fruits ("we are lords of the plains, of the crops, of the woods, of the forests, of the fountains, and of the rivers: the forests offer us wood free of cost; the trees fruit, the vines grapes, the gardens vegetables, the fountains water, the rivers fish, the preserves game, the rocks shade, the hills fresh air, and the caves houses"). If Preciosa's visit to the house of the *teniente* allows us to glimpse the sterility of a society in which human relationships are founded in materialism and marked by depredation, the Gypsy elder describes a more authentic community, united in friendship ("We observe inviolably the law of friendship"), opposed to the institution of private property ("Few things do we possess which are not common to all"), and committed to a life of pleasure and freedom ("our free and easy life is not subject to formalities . . . with these and other laws and statutes we maintain ourselves and live happily").[166]

All of these elements—freedom, communism, pleasure, friendship, primitivism, simplicity, and natural vitality—are, of course, traditional themes of utopian and pastoral literature, and, since *La Gitanilla* does initially expose the court society as a fallen, chaotic, and sterile order, it is tempting to see the Gypsy community as a realm of essential values, a type of "green world," which exposes by contrast the deficiencies of the real world and points toward the ideals that are

---

[165] "No nos fatiga el temor de perder la honra, ni nos desvela la ambición de acrecentarla, ni sustentamos bandos, ni madrugamos a dar memoriales, ni a acompañar magnates, ni a solicitar favores. . . . dorados techos y suntuosos palacios. . . . para nosotros son los duros terreros colchones de blandas plumas . . . un mismo rostro hacemos al sol que al yelo, a la esterilidad que a la abundancia" (pp. 68-70). For the characteristic views of nature and society and the ethical values in the philosophical tradition of "hard primitivism," as well as a survey of their literary celebrations in classical antiquity, see Lovejoy and Boas, *Primitivism and Related Ideas in Antiquity*.

[166] "somos señores de los campos, de los sembrados, de las selvas, de los montes, de las fuentes y de los ríos: los montes nos ofrecen leña de balde; los árboles, frutas; las viñas, uvas; las huertas, hortaliza; las fuentes, agua; los ríos, peces, y los vedados, caza; sombra las peñas, aire fresco las quiebras, y casas las cuevas. . . . Nosotros guardamos inviolablemente la ley de la amistad. . . . Pocas cosas tenemos que no sean comunes a todos. . . . la libre y ancha vida nuestra no está sujeta a melindres. . . . con estas y con otras leyes y estatutos nos conservamos y vivimos alegres" (pp. 66-70).

to be impressed on reality if purification is to occur.[167] Such an interpretation of the long speech of the "old and eloquent Gypsy" would
in fact resemble that of Cervantes's short-sighted hero, who enthusiastically acknowledges the "praiseworthy statutes" of the "order so
well based on reason and political foundations," embraces the "happy
life," and renounces "the profession of a gentleman and the vainglory
of his illustrious lineage."[168] However, what Juan and the majority of
modern critics who have written about *La Gitanilla* fail to see is that
Cervantes counterbalances these utopian features of his other-world
with a carefully drawn set of sinister features. Their presence brings
an ambivalence to the most powerful utopian features, namely freedom and nature. The very statement in which Juan expresses his enthusiastic acceptance of the pact, reported by the narrator in indirect
discourse, contains a most revealing "slip of the tongue," which clearly
represents a contamination of the character's discourse by the admon-
itory language of the narrator: "the novice said that . . . he only
regretted not to have come sooner to the knowledge of so pleasant a
life and that from that moment . . . he placed himself *under the yoke,
or, to put it better, under the laws* by which they lived."[169]

---

[167] For the "green world" and this literary pattern, see Northrop Frye, *Anatomy of
Criticism* (Princeton, 1957), pp. 182-83; also, *A Natural Perspective: The Development
of Shakespearean Comedy and Romance* (New York, 1965), pp. 140ff.

[168] "el novicio dijo que se holgaba mucho de haber sabido tan loables estatutos, y
que él pensaba hacer profesión en aquella orden tan puesta en razón y en políticos
fundamentos . . . renunciaba la profesión de caballero y la vanagloria de su ilustre
linaje" (p. 70).

[169] "el novicio dijo que . . . sólo le pesaba no haber venido más presto en conocimientos de tan alegre vida, y que desde aquel punto . . . lo ponía todo *debajo del
yugo, o, por mejor decir, debajo de las leyes* con que ellos vivían" (pp. 70-71, italics
added). For this type of "dialogism," with its "hybridization, mixing of accents and
erasing of boundaries between authorial speech and the speech of others," and its
importance in the history of novelistic, "multi-voiced" prose, see M. M. Bakhtin,
"Discourse in the Novel," *The Dialogic Imagination* (Austin, 1981), pp. 318-20. Cervantes's narrator's intrusions into his tale are complicated, both in their formal character (see below, note 224) and in their controlling value judgments. Another case
of a "dialogized," negative judgment of the Gypsy world appears in his moralizing
generalization following his account of Preciosa's friends' envy: "que la envidia también se aloja en los aduares de los bárbaros y en las chozas de pastores como en palacios
de príncipes" (p. 76). Here the modification of the clean antithesis of a conventional
topos through the introduction of a third member for comparison—"barbarians"—
obliquely dissociates the Gypsy world from any conventional pastoral idealization.
For value judgments that are more unstable in their ironies, see the opening denunciation of all Gypsies as thieves and the mischievously overstated reprobation of Juan
as a victim of Amor, who allows himself "a postrarse a los pies de una muchacha, y
a ser su lacayo, que, puesto que hermosísima, en fin, era gitana: privilegio de la

As Northrop Frye has made clear in numerous studies, the lower world of romance is frequently through demonic reversal and parody set over against an ideal order exemplified by the heroes and celebrated by their triumph and restoration.[170] If we look closely at Cervantes's Gypsy community, we find that, besides an enumeration of such traditional features of the lower world as violence, criminality, incest, license, and incontinence, there is a good deal of attention given to its unusual marital customs. The long discourse of the Gypsy elder, which follows the demonic ceremonies of Juan's initiation into the new society, begins with a detailed explanation of their family organization. Cervantes's description of the Gypsies' marriages is probably no more accurate than his description of their burial customs, which, as the narrator suggests and modern research has confirmed, are modeled on those of a tribe of South American Indians described in a contemporary chronicle of exploration.[171] It is in fact quite possible that Cervantes invented them and that, as he did so, he recalled his own experience of Islamic marriage rites during the years of his captivity in Algiers or his readings about the strange marital customs of ancient, Oriental, and New World societies which fascinated travelers, historians, encyclopedists, and philosophers of the sixteenth and seventeenth centuries.[172] Whatever its source may have been, Cervantes's description of the Gypsy marriage is plainly motivated neither by an anthropological-sociological interest nor by a desire to offer his audience the delights of *admiratio*. Its conception is dominated by the profound philosophical and ethical issues which the tale explores in relation to marriage and the natural order to which it belongs. Its principal function is the presentation of a demonic counterweight to

---

hermosura, que trae al redopelo y por la melena a sus pies a la voluntad más exenta" (pp. 77-78).

[170] See, for example, *A Natural Perspective*, pp. 110ff.

[171] Jorge Campos, "Presencia de América en la obra de Cervantes," *Revista de Indias* 8 (1947):371-404.

[172] See, for example, the catalogue of marital marvels presented in the typical Renaissance encyclopedia of wondrous facts, Pedro Mexía's *Silva de varia lección*, ed. J. García Soriano, 2 vols. (Madrid, 1933-1934), 1:353-58. In the "Introducción" to their edition (*Persiles y Sigismunda*; 2 vols. [Madrid, 1914], 1:ix) R. Schevill and A. Bonilla suggest that Cervantes drew on Garcilaso de la Vega's *Comentarios reales* in describing the marital customs of Transila's barbarous kingdom. Recently J. B. Avalle-Arce has argued convincingly that it is more likely that the material for the episode came from the *Repertorium . . . de Omnium Gentium Ritibus* by Johann Boehme (1520) in its Spanish adaptation by the Erasmist Francisco Thámara (1556) (see the introduction to his edition of *Los trabajos de Persiles y Sigismunda* [Madrid, 1969], pp. 14-15). For Cervantes's interest in the marital customs of the Islamic world, see his drama, *Los baños de Argel*, Act III.

the perfect marriage, which, as we have seen, the work examines in a very explicit and precise way, and its features are carefully elaborated as contrasts to the ideal.[173] As the elder immediately makes clear, in their love of freedom the Gypsies are generally opposed to ceremonies ("the free and easy life we lead is not subject to formalities or many ceremonies") and permit man and woman to live together in or outside of wedlock, as they prefer. Nothing is said of children, who figure so prominently in the ideal of wedded love affirmed by Preciosa and celebrated in her songs of St. Anne and Queen Margarita, and the only reason for marriage in the Gypsy community appears to be the enjoyment of sexual pleasure ("in this matter you can do whatever will most suit your pleasure"). If Preciosa urges caution and careful consideration by young people contemplating marriage and admonishes them to look at each other with the "eyes of reason" and avoid the blindness induced by the allurements of external beauty, the Gypsies proceed with haste and appear to make corporeal beauty the principal and sole consideration in their choices. The absence of ceremonies means, of course, that there are no laws concerning the publications of banns like those which Cervantes emphasizes in the denouement of the tale (see above), a fact that perhaps accounts for the "muchos incestos" that the Gypsy casually mentions. The elder offers Juan the pick of the maidens in the camp, asking him to inspect them and choose the one he finds most pleasing. The inspection to which he invites the youth has nothing to do with the hygienic or eugenic interests that motivated Renaissance utopian writings on marriage, and it contrasts sharply with Preciosa's Erasmian emphasis on the careful study of each other by the partners of a proposed union.[174] The women are, of course, viewed as objects to be possessed, and their consent to the will of the male in these matters is taken for

[173] In its function it is comparable to Rosamunda's speech in favor of premarital sexual instruction and the *ius primae noctis* institutionalizing it in the demonic society that the chaste, heroic maiden Transila must flee. On the affinities of Transila and Preciosa, see my *Cervantes' Christian Romance*, pp. 119-22.

[174] Preciosa's repeated emphasis on correct vision (with the "eyes of the soul") is parodied in the elder's exhortation of the youth to look at the physical endowments of the maidens and decide which one will please him most: "Mírala bien, y mira si te agrada, o si vees en ella alguna cosa que te descontente, y si la vees, escoge entre las doncellas que aquí están la que más te contentare." For the serious advocacy, for hygienic and eugenic purposes, of such inspections in utopian literature, see Thomas More's description of the marital customs in Utopia (see *Famous Utopias of the Renaissance*, pp. 82-83); also, Erasmus's colloquy "A Marriage in Name Only, or the Unequal Match" (*The Colloquies of Erasmus*, pp. 401-412). For an elegant, comprehensive survey of traditional utopian doctrines in Renaissance writings, see Harry Levin, *The Myth of the Golden Age in the Renaissance* (Bloomington, 1969).

granted. In this harshly patriarchal society the general prohibition of private property does not apply in the single case of wives and female "friends." The men assure order in the community by swearing not to covet the wives of their fellows and by tyrannically imposing a rule of terror on their own wives, who know that whenever women commit adultery, the men murder them and bury them in the "mountains and deserts as if they were wild animals." In contrast to Preciosa's ideal of moral autonomy and freely willed chastity, the chastity of the Gypsy marriage is guaranteed by fear ("by reason of this fear and dread they take care to be chaste").[175] Moreover, to ensure their pleasure and happiness, the Gypsies permit husbands to abandon wives when they grow old and choose youthful successors who are sexually more attractive and suited to their pleasure. All of this contrasts in a very precise way with Preciosa's refusal to allow a hasty union, her insistence on her own freedom of choice, her demand for an enduring marriage sanctified by the proper ceremonies, and her insistence in founding marriage not in sexual desire but rather in the friendship and understanding of two equal partners who will live together in mutual respect and rational love for a lifetime.

If these disturbing features of the Gypsy order are unnoticed by the enthralled hero, who enthusiastically enters his novitiate, Preciosa understands them perfectly, and her speech at the conclusion of the ceremony unmasks the apparent utopian characteristics as in reality the familiar temptations of the false paradise. "I do not conform to the barbarous and insolent license which these kinsmen of mine have assumed, of abandoning their wives, or of punishing them according to their humor . . . I do not wish to take for my companion one who may cast me aside for his pleasure."[176] The greater freedom enjoyed in the other-world is in reality the mask of license, self-indulgence, and patriarchal tyranny; the fuller life in harmony with nature is a surrender to incontinence and a life of barbarism.[177] The more au-

---

[175] "con la misma facilidad las matamos y las enterramos por las montañas y desiertos como si fueran animales nocivos. . . . Con este temor y miedo ellas procuran ser castas" (p. 67).

[176] "yo no me rijo por la bárbara e insolente licencia que estos mis parientes se han tomado de dejar las mujeres, o castigarlas, cuando se les antoja . . . no quiero tomar compañía que por su gusto me deseche" (p. 72).

[177] In his breathless enumeration of the gifts which a bountiful nature has bestowed on his community and his rapturous account of the heightened perception of her processes which its members enjoy, the Gypsy elder invokes a natural order of plenitude, vitality, and spontaneity. As I have suggested above, the function of this order in the total design of the tale is fundamentally ambivalent. It is clearly a positive counterweight to the spiritual sterility and stifling artifice of the corrupt court society

thentic human relationships of *amistad* can countenance the most violent kind of repression and exploitation; and the practice of communism allows the most sinister perversion of the institution of private property—slavery. To the "ancha libertad" championed by the Gypsies, Preciosa eloquently opposes the authentic freedom that a morally mature consciousness enjoys in any circumstances: "These men can quite easily hand over to you my body, but not my soul, which is free, was born free, and is to remain free, as long as I shall wish." As far as the stoical maiden is concerned, genuine freedom lies within the individual conscience, and it can never be threatened by the tyranny of external law: "the law of my own will . . . is the strongest of all laws."[178]

(see below). However, it is simultaneously a demonic counterweight to the perfected natural order of rationality and harmony invoked by Clemente, and, as such, it has clear affinities with the fallen nature of Christian theology. In its demonic aspect it is the familiar temptation of the false paradise, whose resident spirits, from Circe to Tasso's siren and Milton's Comus, have always compelled their victims and their readers to ask the question: "Wherefore did Nature pour her bounties forth/ With such a full and unwithdrawing hand,/ Covering the earth with odors, fruits, and flocks,/ Thronging the Seas with spawn innumerable,/ But all to please and sate the curious taste?" (John Milton, *Complete Poems and Major Prose* [New York, 1957], pp. 106-107). For a much less paradoxical formulation of the doctrine of an abundant nature as formidable temptation, see Calderón's *auto sacramental* based on the Circe myth (*Los encantos de la culpa*, ed. A. Valbuena Prat, *Obras completas* [Madrid, 1967], 3:414-16), where the connection between this nature and the fallen nature of Christian theology is far more direct.

[178] "Estos señores bien pueden entregarte mi cuerpo; pero no mi alma, que es libre, y nació libre, y ha de ser libre, en tanto que yo quisiere. . . . la ley de mi voluntad . . . es la más fuerte de todas" (p. 71). "Freedom" is, like "nature," an ambivalent term in Cervantes's writings, and in the paradoxical context of the description of this other-world he is carefully exploiting its ambivalence. In its positive connotations it illuminates by contrast the tyranny of custom characteristic of the artificial society of the city and court; in its negative connotations it offsets the genuine freedom of the individual to make rational moral choice regardless of the coercions in external circumstances, the freedom which Preciosa here affirms and which Leonora discovers as she copes with the persuasions of the *dueña* and the attractions of Loaysa. In its demonic aspect "la ancha libertad" of the Gypsy world resembles the "libertad" of Cruz before his conversion in *El rufián dichoso*, where it similarly is celebrated as part of man's primal paradisiacal condition ("¡Oh feliz siglo dorado,/ tiempo alegre y venturoso,/ adonde la libertad/ brindaba a la voluntad/ del gusto más exquisito!"), is connected specifically with sexual enjoyment in the masque of Venus ("¡Dulces días, dulces ratos/ los que en Sevilla se gozan, . . . do la libertad campea,/ y en sucinta y amorosa/ manera Venus camina/ y a todos se ofrece toda"), and is contrasted with the state of saintliness ("he juntado en un instante . . . una [parte], de su vida libre; otra, de su vida grave") (see *Obras completas*, ed. A. Valbuena Prat, pp. 344, 350, 343). See also Periandro's description of the ruthless Luisa, a "diosa Venus" who destroys the infatuated Ortel Banedre: "séase ella libre y desenvuelta como un cerní-

THE STRUCTURE OF THE IMAGERY
IN *LA GITANILLA*

Nearly every detail of the Gypsy marriage reveals, then, that Cervantes designed the natural world which his hero enters as a demonic inversion of the order of perfect nature with which Clemente associates wedded love. We observe the same kind of polarization in the structure of the imagery which Cervantes employs in the scene of Juan's initiation, where nearly all the central symbols and motifs connected with the true order and concentrated in the celebrative poems emerge in parody versions. Thus the poems emphasize the motif of ascent and associate the rising movement of the action of the novella with historical and mythic patterns of redemption. Preciosa's hymn to St. Anne begins with the reference to the "most precious tree" and concludes with the vision of the Holy Family in the "most lofty palace," and her song of Margarita's visit to the Church of St. Lawrence, undoubtedly drawing on the mythology of the pageants that celebrated the birth of Philip IV, describes the queen as the fertile, ascending vine and as a heavenly sphere, descending to earth to offer the fruits of her wedded love to the Virgin, who is envisioned as standing above the stars, and then reascending in all her glory to heaven.[179] In the

---

calo . . ." (*Persiles*, p. 323), and "la demasiada libertad" of Rocinante when he succumbs to the attractions of the "hacas galicianas" (*Don Quijote de la Mancha*, 1:197). In the celebration of freedom in *La ilustre fregona* Cervantes exploits the ambivalences in the concept as in *La Gitanilla*. Here freedom is the principal allurement of the picaresque order of existence, which resembles a paradise but is in reality a realm of lawlessness and violence. At the same time it is clearly opposed to the tyranny of routine in ordinary life and is celebrated as a condition in which man can enjoy a fuller existence in the pursuit of ideals and adventures. For the ambivalence in the word "*libertad*" in the age and its common association with license, animal passion, a blinding of reason, and false knowledge, see Alejandro Ramírez-Araujo, "El morisco Ricote y la libertad de conciencia," *Hispanic Review* 24 (1956):278-89. As for the other traditional utopian feature of the Gypsy "paradise," pleasure, in its emphatic confinement to the indulgence of the appetites and particularly the sexual instinct, it is clearly presented as the demonic inversion of Preciosa's "ferias que felices ganancias prometen" and the spectacle of "la alegría universal" blessing the fruits of the queen's marriage.

[179] An anonymous "relación" of the period describes a court masque honoring the newborn prince, who is hailed as the sun dispelling shadows from the entire earth, as a Hercules delivering the world from numerous monsters, and as a new Atlas receiving the terrestrial globe from his father and supporting it on his shoulders in peace and tranquility. A cloud moving through a glittering heaven above the child's temple descends and ascends continuously, bringing torch-bearing courtiers who dance in homage at the gate of the temple. With its central imagery of light, celestial bodies, jewels, and natural fertility, its powerful official symbols, its stylized move-

amoebean song Clemente and Juan would elevate the fame of the maiden to the eighth sphere, and they describe her as the siren singing amid the turning spheres and bringing peace to the pure of heart. Immediately thereafter Preciosa sings of herself aspiring to ascend to the heavens through virtue and perfect beauty ("The plant that is most humble, if it directs its growth upward, by the power of grace or nature, rises to the heavens. . . . I wish to see whether beauty has such a privilege that it will elevate me so high that I may aspire to an even loftier sphere"[180]). And in his sonnet Clemente describes the "pure, honest, healthy, and superhuman" acts of Preciosa as lifting her fame to heaven, and, employing the poetic idiom which Preciosa has come to suspect, he imagines her dazzling multitudes with the sunlight of her eyes and receiving at her feet the homage offered by Cupid. In his first encounter with Preciosa Juan announces that his

---

ments of ascent and descent, and its emphasis on music and dancing, its affinities with *La Gitanilla* go beyond those visible in Cervantes's poetry of public rituals. It is in fact interesting to speculate about the effects of this work or one similar to it on the entire conception of *La Gitanilla*. The "*relación*" also contains an account of the lavish procession in which Queen Margarita came forth from the palace to celebrate her "misa de parida" following the birth of Philip IV, the actual event narrated in Cervantes's *romance*, as well as a description of a spectacular processional masque on Low Sunday celebrating the birth of the prince and the "restoration of the time." It included floats with a painted image of the royal family receiving rays of light from the name God, written in Hebrew characters above, a symbolic heart, a terrestrial globe, and such mythological and allegorical figures as Mercury, Juno Lucina, "la pública Leticia," and "la Felicidad católica," all of which appear in Cervantes's poem. See "Relación de las fiestas de Vallodolid en 1605," ed. D. Cayetano Rosell, in *Obras completas de Cervantes*, ed. M. Rivadeneyra, 12 vols. (Madrid, 1863-1864), 2:159-250. I am not concerned here with the question as to whether Cervantes actually wrote this "*relación*," as has frequently been supposed. Whatever role such pageantry may have had in the genesis of the *La Gitanilla*, its presence in the work demonstrates the tendency of romance in every age to assimilate the marvels of public spectacles to its exploitation and celebration of official values (see Frye, *The Secular Scripture*, pp. 55ff.; for the way in which Cervantes's contemporary, Sir Philip Sidney, incorporates official pageantry in his romance, *Arcadia*, see Frances A. Yates, *Astraea: The Imperial Theme in the Sixteenth Century* [London, 1975], pp. 88-94; for the general affinities of court masque and romance, see N. Frye, "Romance as Masque," *Spiritus Mundi* [Bloomington, 1976], 148-78; for the frequency of such court spectacles in the period of Philip III, see C. Pérez Bustamante, *Felipe III* [Madrid, 1950]). As I have pointed out elsewhere, the masque which Cervantes incorporates in the *Persiles* through Periandro's dream, besides revealing the author's familiarity with this type of ritual drama, demonstrates the general principal concerning its affinities with romance (see *Cervantes' Christian Romance*, pp. 81-84).

[180] "La que es más humilde planta,/ Si la subida endereza,/ Por gracia o naturaleza/ A los cielos se levanta. . . . Quiero ver si la belleza/ Tiene tal prerrogativa,/ Que me encumbre tan arriba/ Que aspire a mayor alteza" (p. 104).

father is seeking an advantageous appointment in the court and adds that he would like "to elevate" to his "greatness the humility of Preciosa."

Juan's metamorphosis into a Gypsy begins with a reversal of this movement, as in the ceremony of his initiation ("la ceremonia de la entrada") he is compelled to turn two somersaults to the sound of two guitars. Besides representing the youth's fall into a lower world and reversing the dominant movement of ascent, the acrobatic rite parodies the orderly movements of the spheres, the divine music of the siren, their earthly analogues—the song and dances of Preciosa—and the "reales ceremonias" of Queen Margarita. The symbolic garroting of Juan, which like his somersaults recalls the expiatory quest of the dancing master, Rutilio, in the *Persiles*,[181] imaginatively associates the Gypsy world with death and inverts the motifs of renewal and fertility surrounding the perfect natural order—for example, the numerous allusions to births of children and such symbols as the life-giving tree, the vine, and the rose. It belongs to the general body of imagery of instruments of punishment which permeates the description of the Gypsy world, whose inhabitants stoically accept the pain inflicted upon them by a variety of torture machines as perfectly within the natural order of things. The hammer and tongs, emblems of the Gypsy order which the youth must hold during the ceremony, however appropriate they may be in terms of a verisimilar representation of Gypsy customs and professions, are much more important in bringing out the infernal connections of the Gypsies as fire-spirits and providing a demonic counterweight to the elaborate astral imagery surrounding Preciosa in the amoebean song and the royal family and the ministers in the poem to Margarita, which depicts the "sun of Austria," the morning star, the moon, and several of the planets as "living stars," moving through the streets of Valladolid. At the same time such emblems form a powerful imaginative inversion of one of the most conspicuous symbols of the perfect order of nature and society in the work—the cross of the great military orders. The cross is displayed by Juan as he introduces himself to Preciosa; it appears in an elevated setting on the breast of the figure of authority, Francisco de Cárcamo, as he stands on his gilded balcony and receives the admiration of the

[181] Following his imprisonment and flight Rutilio enters a dark city, where people carry torches during the day, and serves a goldsmith. From there he passes into a primitive kingdom where he must don animal skins, which he finds on a corpse hanging from a tree, and spend two years turning somersaults to amuse the barbarians. See also Sancho Panza's reference to Lucifer as the first acrobat. See my *Cervantes' Christian Romance*, pp. 113-15.

Gypsies below in one of the various hieratic scenes of adoration in the work; it is in fact contained in the little treasure chest of the foundling Preciosa in the note revealing her true identity as daughter of Fernando de Azevedo, "Knight of the Habit of Calatrava" (p. 115); and it is restored to the hero at the crucial moment of recognition, when he has achieved the goal of his quest and is ready to reenter the restored social order. An additional parody of the habit of the military order and its venerable emblem appears in the Gypsy elder's discussion of his comrades' disregard for physical suffering and his assertion that they esteem the scars on the back of a Gypsy who has been whipped as if they formed a habit: "among us to be flogged by order of the court is to have a habit on one's shoulders, which seems to the victim more precious than if he wore it on his bosom, and than if it was one of the highest orders too."[182] Another powerful symbol of the official order which is demonically transfigured in the Gypsy world is the two-headed eagle of the Hapsburgs. In her song to the queen, Preciosa hails the birth of the prince as a redeemer and unites imaginatively the Hapsburg eagle with the traditional symbol of the Virgin, the dove, and the Gospel figure of Christ as the hen sheltering her chicks under her wings (Matt. 23:37). There is perhaps no passage in the work that illustrates more clearly the way in which Cervantes creates imaginative correspondences between the proper social structure of the world in which his characters move and the religious beliefs and mythology that supported it:

> Vivas¡ oh blanca paloma!
> Que nos has de dar por crías
> Aguilas de dos coronas,
> Para ahuyentar de los aires
> Las de rapiña furiosas
> Para cubrir con sus alas
> A las virtudes medrosas.[183]

[182] "el que es azotado por justicia entre nosotros, es tener un hábito en las espaldas, que le parece mejor que si le trujese en los pechos, y de los buenos" (p. 74).

[183] "Another tongue cries, 'Whitest Dove,/ Long may you live and fill the Town/ With joy at sight of infants twain,/ The eagles of a double crown./ Ah, frighten from the realms of air/ The furies and the birds of prey,/ And shelter with your spreading wings/ The Virtues fainting from dismay.' " The poem proceeds to link the king and God ("el corazón del Rey/ en las manos de Dios mora"), and to associate Margarita with St. Anne. It describes the queen offering her fruits in the temple of the Virgin, an act that recalls Joachim's expulsion from the temple and Anne's presentation of the Virgin, events introduced into *La Gitanilla* in Preciosa's previous song. Preciosa of course enjoys the same type of idealization through imaginative association, as she enters Madrid on St. Anne's Day and dances in her church before the altar of the Virgin, just as the Virgin, St. Anne's daughter, had, according to the legend, danced

In the perverted order of the Gypsy world the elder boasts to Juan that his new comrades will transform him into an "eagle," that "there is no eagle or other bird of prey that swoops down more speedily on the victim that it spies than we on the opportunities that hold out to us any prospect of gain," and, in a specific parody of the gospel passage, he proceeds to urge his "fledgling": "Andrés, my son, for the present settle down snugly in the nest under the shelter of our wings; when the time comes we will take you out to fly, and in a place from which you are not likely to return without prey."[184]

Probably the two most important patterns of imagery in *La Gitanilla* are those based on wealth and natural regeneration. The central figure is surrounded by motifs of jewels and coins, health and fertility. Preciosa is of course the most precious of jewels, a "treasure" which her protectress must watch over constantly. Characters associate her with a variety of gems and, as is the case with many of the long line of maidens of fairy tale and romance from which she descends, her recognition and restoration are brought about by the mysterious talismanic jewels in a little treasure chest in the possession of her benevolent guardian. Francisco de Cárcamo compares her beautiful face to the images of the Catholic Monarchs on a golden doubloon (p. 58). When she sings and dances, she receives the adoration of multitudes, she wins the "prize and jewel for the best dance," and coins "rain upon her like stones on a table," for her beauty has the "power to awaken slumbering charity." When Preciosa, who unlike the rest of the Gypsies is not interested in the acquisition of money, returns the escudo that Clemente has offered her, the poet tells his "preciosa perla": "since you touch it with your hand, I shall value it as a relic so long as my life lasts."[185]

---

before the altar of the temple. At the conclusion of the tale we discover that she was kidnapped on Ascension Day. As the principal vehicle for the linkage of the characters and events of the narration with a mythological background and the religious and philosophical doctrines connected with such backgrounds, the poems of *La Gitanilla* can be compared in their function with those of Cervantes's longer romance, *Los trabajos de Persiles y Sigismunda*.

[184] "No hay águila, ni ninguna otra ave de rapiña, que más presto se abalance a la presa que se le ofrece, que nosotros nos abalanzamos a las ocasiones que algún interés nos señalen" (p. 69); "Hijo Andrés, reposad ahora en el nido debajo de nuestras alas; que a su tiempo os sacaremos a volar, y en parte donde no volváis sin presa" (p. 75). See also: "determinó el águila vieja [la abuela] a sacar a volar su aguilucha [Preciosa] y enseñarle a vivir por sus uñas" (p. 5), as well as the allusions to corrupt members of the court as harpies and birds of prey. Preciosa's homage to St. Lawrence as the "saintly Phoenix" (p. 15) unites the recurrent imagery of fire and birds in its apocalyptic aspect.

[185] "la hermosura tiene fuerza de despertar la caridad dormida" (p. 11); como le toques con la mano, le tendré por reliquia mientras la vida me durare" (p. 51).

In her visit to the gloomy house of the impoverished lieutenant and her gift of "May rain" to its world of "sterility" we feel very close to the mythic roots of romance and the archaic symbolism identifying the lost maiden, the loss of fertility, and a missing treasure. In its peculiar mingling of a magical order of fairy tale innocence and the most disabused kind of worldliness the scene epitomizes that elusive combination of innocence and experience that has made the tale and its heroine so appealing to writers during the last three centuries. The visit begins with one of the numerous scenes of adoration and spectacle which are so striking in the early part of the novella and surround the Gypsy maiden with an aura of divinity, imaginatively associating her with the venerated figures of the Virgin and the queen mother. Entering the house as a "lamb" in the "flock" of the Gypsy grandmother, who is as "rich and happy as an Easter Sunday of flowers [pascua de flores]," Preciosa shines "like the light of a torch among lesser lights" and receives the veneration of the female society awaiting her ("they all ran to her; some embraced her; others gazed at her, some blessed her, and others praised her"). In the ensuing conversation Preciosa is described as having hair of gold and eyes of emeralds and as being made of silver and sugar-paste. Doña Clara addresses the request of a prophecy to her in an incantatory series of names as if summoning forth her magical powers: "you must tell me my fortune, you child of gold, child of silver, child of pearls, child of carbuncles, child of heaven."[186] The profusion of such imagery of wealth emphasizes by contrast the impoverishment of the house, in which the female society of "maids and duennas" looks in vain to find a gold crown, a real of eight, or a real of four, and discovers that the only coin that they possess has been pawned for a pittance which has already been spent. Penuriousness, spinsterhood, spiritual poverty, and unfulfilled virginity, all presided over by a bearded old squire "de luenga barba y largos años" coalesce in the narrator's image of sterility: "one of the damsels present, seeing the sterility of the house, said . . . ." In Preciosa's conversation with the lieutenant following his arrival we observe the harshest social criticism of the work, as the maiden attributes his poverty to his refusal to follow the corrupt practices of his colleagues and thus implicates the entire society of the court in the blighted world that we discover in his house. Opposing the court society in its barrenness, poverty, corruption, and lack of

---

[186] "como la luz de una antorcha entre otras luces menores. . . . corrieron todas a ella; unas la abrazaban, otras la miraban, éstas la bendecían, aquéllas la alababan. . . . me la has de decir, niña de oro, niña de plata, y niña de perlas, y niña de carbuncos y niña del cielo" (pp. 25-27).

charity, Preciosa and her flock of Gypsies are imaginatively associated
with rebirth and fertility through the archetypal motifs of water, spring,
and treasure ("Doña Clara, with her maids and duennas, was waiting
for the Gypsies as for the rain of May"). As is generally the case in
the first half of the novella, in which Cervantes's concern with social
satire is most pronounced, the Gypsy world here is employed to provide a norm beside which the aberration represented by the society of
the city is clearly visible: "in some palaces the knaves fare better than
the wise. I am content to be a Gypsy and poor."[187]

Throughout the work we observe a coalescence of imagery of wealth
and fertility in the most important scenes idealizing Preciosa. Following her song before the adoring crowds, a "hailstorm of coins" falls
on her, and her companions must work to "harvest" them ("hacer su
agosto, y su vendimia").[188] Clemente's sonnet describes her playing

[187] "estábalas [las gitanas] esperando, como el agua de mayo ella [doña Clara] y sus
doncellas y dueñas" (p. 25); "en algunos palacios más medran los truhanes que los
discretos. Yo me hallo bien con ser gitana y pobre" (p. 34). In this scene we glimpse
Preciosa's affinities with numerous "magical" children who have a central role in the
spring and fertility rites of primitive cultures and who are perhaps the true ancestors
of the romance heroine. As the object of an incantation and a "rain-bringer" in the
barren urban world of the lieutenant, she is comparable to the chaste "rain maiden"
(*das Regenmädchen*) of northern European ritual and mythology (see *Handwörterbuch des
Deutschen Aberglaubens*, ed. E. Hoffmann-Krayer and H. Bächtold-Stäubli, 10 vols.
[Berlin and Leipzig, 1927-1942], 1:1306-1307, 4:1335).

[188] The scene of adoration is another detail suggesting the impact of public spectacle on Cervantes's conception of the tale and on its imaginative atmosphere. The
"relación" narrating the events in Valladolid following the birth of the prince describes a procession in which King Philip III went to celebrate mass at the Church
of San Llorente on the day after the birth. ". . . y al tiempo que su Majestad iba
entrando en la plaza Mayor, se comenzó á derramar mucha moneda de plata desde las
ventanas, siendo cosa de ver la grita y baraunda del pueblo por tomalla; y pudo ser
mucha, aunque la cantidad no se pudo averiguar, porque duró el esparcilla hasta que
su Majestad volvió de las completas, que su Capilla le dijo en Nuestra Señora" (p.
165). The *"relación"* provides interesting testimony of the apocalyptic numinous aspect of wealth and jewelry in official ceremony of the time, an aspect which Cervantes
exploits constantly in his romance. For example, on descending from her "riquísima
carroza toda de oro y brocado" and dazzling a multitude of onlookers ("causó gran-
dísima admiracion ver tanto número de joyas, vestidos y galas, diferentes de los otros
dias"), the queen received from the Archbishop of Burgos and a group of ecclesiastics,
who, attired in ceremonial robes, emerged from the church to welcome her, "una
vela de cera blanca, con un doblon de á diez en ella," and, "despues de haber hecho
las acostumbradas ceremonias, entraron en la iglesia" (pp. 204-205). On receiving
his audience with the Spanish monarchs, the English ambassador presented the queen
with "una rica joya, que era una águila de diamante, coronada, y el tuson por pen-
diente, con dos riquísimas perlas, que toda ella fué estimada en doce mil ducados"
(p. 215). The rich development of gem imagery around Preciosa would support Casalduero's speculation that Cervantes's creation of the *La Gitanilla* was to some extent

her tambourine and singing: "She sheds roses from her lips and pours forth pearls from her hands."[189] Preciosa describes her virginity as both "her single jewel," which she will not sell "for a price of promises and gifts," and a rose which she must guard against the "rustic hands" that would pluck it and cause it to wilt. At the same time, if surrendered in Christian marriage, it would be employed "in festivities that betoken happy profits." In the climactic nocturnal scene in which Preciosa, Juan, and Clemente retire from the Gypsy camp to form a genuine pastoral society of friendship and love and to discourse on the essential truths manifest in the true order of nature, the maiden sings of herself as a "humble plant," which, nourished by nature and grace, lifts itself toward heaven, and she immediately goes on to reveal the real meaning of all the allusions to wealth in the tale:

> En este mi bajo cobre,
> Siendo honestidad su esmalte
> No hay buen deseo que falte
> Ni riqueza que no sobre.[190]

The song recalls specifically the imagery of the hymns to St. Anne and Margarita of Austria, strengthens the imaginative identification of Preciosa with these redemptive maidens, and crowns the ascending movement of the action, elevating the humble Gypsy to the level of the divine and quasi-divine figures. In the hymns Preciosa's imagery of fertility and wealth is concentrated around each maiden. St. Anne is the "mint in which the holy die was molded that gave to God the form which he had as a man on earth." Like Preciosa a paradoxical

---

inspired by Luis de León's description of the perfect wife (*La perfecta casada*) and particularly his elaboration of Prov. 31:10: "She is far more precious than jewels" (*Sentido y forma de las "Novelas ejemplares,"* pp. 74-75). It is worth pointing out that Vives too exploited the numinous power of gems in expounding the virtues of the perfect wife. After denouncing the use of ornaments and jewelry, he speaks of "authentic," spiritual jewelry: "pyropus est, ardor conjugalis caritatis; adamas, sancti propositi firmitas . . . smaragdus, exhilaratio in domino" (*Institutio Feminae Christianae, Opera Omnia,* 4:233). One should contrast the numinous function of money in the romance, *La Gitanilla,* whether as an apocalyptic or a demonic symbol, with its novelistic treatment in the *Quixote,* where it is one of the most consistently employed "anti-magical" symbols, representing the neutral, disenchanted world of ordinary experience and the banal necessities of daily living, from which literary romance, with its characteristic vertical movements between heaven and hell, would deliver its reader.

[189] "Perlas son que derrama con las manos;/ Flores son que despide de la boca" (p. 59).

[190] "Since virtue decks with its enamel this humble copper of mine, there is no good wish which is lacking, and all riches are superfluous" (p. 103).

combination of humility and preciousness, she is described as "the most precious tree, that did so long delay to bring forth its fruit, through years which could cover it in mourning" and the "sacred sterile soil that finally gave anew all the abundance that sustains the world," allusions to the long blight in her wedded life with Joachim preceding her fertility, a part of the myth that is in a sense replicated by the action of La Gitanilla.[191] The following poem continues the development of this imagery, as Margarita, like Preciosa, is described as a "rich and admirable jewel" receiving the adoration of multitudes in her procession through the streets of Valladolid. Jewels figure prominently in the description of the pomp of the spectacle, and the newborn child is hailed as a "unique and singular pearl" and the "Mother-of-pearl of Austria" ("Nácar de Austria"), a miraculous gem that will heal all disorder in the kingdom. At the same time the queen offers her "fruits" to the Virgin, and a chorus of children addresses her as the "fecund vine that climbs," an image that associates her with the gospel symbol of Christ (John 15:1) and the symbol of the fruitful vine as the ideal wife in Psalms (see above), recalls the precious tree of St. Anne, and anticipates the ascending plant and the flowering rose of Preciosa, as well as the "most lovely shoots" ("más bellos renuevos") that Clemente associates with Christian marriage and the "bien intencionada naturaleza."

The spiritual growth of Juan is anticipated at the beginning of his quest through a similar combination of the imagery of treasure and fertility. In the house of Francisco de Cárcamo Preciosa appears once again as a healing maiden, uttering mysterious prophecies, speaking of the birth of beautiful children, and chanting magical healing words to its suffering inhabitants. The fine dramatic irony which accompanies Preciosa's skillful use of double-entendre throughout the scene

---

[191] "Casa de moneda,/ Do se forjó el cuño/ Que dió a Dios la forma/ Que como hombre tuvo"; "Arbol preciosísimo,/ Que tardó en dar fruto/ Años que pudieron/ Cubrirle de luto . . . Santa tierra estéril,/ Que al cabo produjo/ Toda la abundancia/ Que sustenta el mundo" (p. 8). The description of St. Anne as the "árbol preciosísimo," which forms part of the system of fertility imagery running through La Gitanilla and specifically associates her with Preciosa, is based on the prophetic vision in which the chaste Emerentiana glimpsed her future offspring Anne and Esmeria as trees growing from a beautiful root and bearing fresh flowers. Thus a fifteenth-century hymn addresses Anne: "Anna, die fruchtbare Wurzel, der heilbringende Baum, die du einen dreifachen Zweig hervorgebracht hast, beladen mit sieben Früchten" (see Kleinschmidt, Die Heilige Anna, pp. 253-54, 272). Moreover, the depiction of the Tree of Jesse with Anne and Joachim was common in contemporary paintings of the Holy Family. For example, a picture in a Franciscan church in Brügge shows Anne with the branch of a tree emerging from her breast with Jesse and three prophets below (see pp. 271ff.).

was undoubtedly one of the effects that led Avellaneda to describe Cervantes's novellas as excellent comedies and inspired numerous other imitators to turn them into plays. However, perhaps the most interesting of the various codes invented by Preciosa and picked up by her intended interlocutors is the one centering on the birth of a child. In the exchanges that follow the grandmother's entrance and Preciosa's query, "Is it a boy or a girl?" the speakers refer to a "delivery so secret" that it is known only to them. They express the hope that the newborn child does not die "of postnatal complications," and they speak of a birth surrounded by "marvels" and of an infant as "beautiful as gold" ("como un oro"). All of these references make it clear to Preciosa that the guardian has verified Juan's statements concerning his family's importance. However, the implications of the extended elaboration of what was undoubtedly a common cliché of popular speech are obvious, and they are supported by the references to the protagonist as "Juanico," a "boy," a "two-year-old child," and a "little gentleman."[192] Such references, as well as a profusion of diminutives throughout the scene, particularly in Preciosa's discourse ("que no sea mentirosito," "Calle, señorito," "sosiega, alborotadito," "darnos una limosnita," "sonetico tenemos," "cabecita," "confiancita"),

---

[192] Terence L. Hansen points to the phrase as one of the various folkloric motifs which appear in the tale ("Folk Narrative Motifs, Beliefs and Proverbs in Cervantes' *Exemplary Novels*," *Journal of American Folklore* 72 (1959):24-29. Whatever its origins, it was undoubtedly a common figure of speech in Cervantes's society (the expression appears in Fernando de Rojas's *La Celestina*, when Sempronio asks Celestina whether she has been successful in her visit to Melibea; see ed. D. S. Severin [Madrid, 1969], p. 103). As in the case of the hammer and tongs, the phrase should not be accounted for merely as part of a representational depiction of Gypsy life and language, but rather as part of a central pattern of imagery from which it draws its symbolic power and to which it then contributes as a symbol itself. It is worth pointing out that Cervantes does not attempt to reproduce the *ceceo* characteristic of Gypsies' discourse either for effects of verisimilitude and *costumbrismo* or, as Solís was to do in his imitation of the tale in drama, for humorous effects. The one reference to *ceceo* is very illuminating: "—¿Quiérenme dar barato, ceñores?—dijo Preciosa, que, como gitana, hablaba ceceosa, y esto es artificio en ellas; que no naturaleza" (p. 19). Cervantes's narrator uses the occasion to dissociate the Gypsy "natural" world, a world which in its perversions of nature is in reality a world of diabolical artifice, from the true nature. Its *ceceo* is such a perversion and should not be thought of as a language of natural man (see my treatment of Cervantes's engagement with current theories on natural language in his *El coloquio de los perros* in my forthcoming *Cervantes and the Mystery of Lawlessness*). In other words Cervantes inserts the realistic detail in order to introduce one of his central themes and to develop the complex *symbolic* meaning of the Gypsy world. Having accomplished this, he "abandons" realism, allowing his Gypsies throughout the remainder of the tale to speak Castillian with no concern about a violation of plausibility or a contradiction of his own statement.

associate Juan in his quest of spiritual growth with the marvelous child and cast Preciosa in the matriarchal role as guide, healer, and consoler, a role that, of course, is mythically celebrated in the poems to St. Anne, the Virgin, Margarita, and their marvelous children.[193] Preciosa's literal revival of the swooning Juan in the scene prefigures her role in his quest, and her healing chant, with its nursery-rhyme diminutives, its obtrusive incantatory rhymes creating magical resemblances in things illogically linked, and its complex function as a code between Juan and herself, forms an effective climax to the episode, poetically orchestrating the maiden's magical powers, capturing her elusive combination of worldliness and innocence, motherliness and childishness, disclosing the true nature of the relationship between her and the hero, and epitomizing the powers to control and manipulate language which she has demonstrated throughout the scene. For her chant she receives the reward of a "doubloon with two faces," a gleaming coin depicting the model couple, the Catholic Monarchs, another of the prominent emblems of the true order of nature and society whose magical shimmer is everywhere visible in the fictional world of Cervantes's first tale.

If wealth in all its associations with Preciosa has a talismanic quality and symbolizes the essential purity of the perfect nature that she embodies, it appears in the Gypsy world in its demonic aspects as the enslaving bond of a predatory society and as a source of avarice and corruption. In the first sentence the narrator stresses the fact that the Gypsies are a society of thieves: "It seems that Gypsies, both men and women, have been born into the world solely to be thieves: they are born of thieving parents, they are raised with thieves, they study to become thieves, and finally they turn into thieves, nimble and active at every turn, and the impulse to steal and the act of stealing are inseparably bound up with their existence and remain with them until they die." The striking outburst is a prelude to Preciosa's introduction, and it is motivated in part by the need to dissociate her by contrast from the lawless world of the Gypsies to which she apparently belongs.[194] Moreover, its seriousness is retroactively undercut by the

---

[193] With motherly tenderness Preciosa urges her *señorito*: "Déjate crecer un poco, para que puedas llevar los trabajos de la guerra." In the soothing intonations of the nursery rhyme, she counsels him: "Sosiega, sosiega, alborotadito, y mira lo que haces primero que te cases" (p. 55).

[194] "Parece que los gitanos y gitanas solamente nacieron en el mundo para ser ladrones: nacen de padres ladrones, críanse con ladrones, estudian para ladrones, y, finalmente, salen con ser ladrones corrientes y molientes a todo ruedo, y la gana del hurtar y el hurtar son en ellos como accidentes inseparables, que no se quitan sino con la muerte" (p. 3). One can compare the narrative technique of the opening

various ironic and playful poses that the narrator's voice assumes as the story progresses.[195] Nevertheless, it does point to a feature of the Gypsy world that is continually stressed in the tale. In the initiation sermon the elder boasts of the Gypsies' abilities to steal purses, a profession in which they are superior to all birds of prey, and advises Juan that the Gypsy education that he is to receive is an apprenticeship in thievery. If money is viewed as a source and an emblem of charity in the scene in which Preciosa's song, "awakening slumbering charity," produces a "rainstorm of coins" and in her visit to Juan's house, where Francisco de Cárcamo invites her to enter with the promise of charity and rewards her with a "golden doubloon with two faces," the "statutes and ordinances" of the Gypsies prohibit "the entry of charity in their breasts,"[196] and the Gypsy grandmother's lecture on the power of money to corrupt is a parody of all the talismanic powers of deliverance of the gems and coins associated with Preciosa and her divine analogues: "Three times, for three different offenses, have I seen myself all but placed on the ass to be flogged, and from one a silver bowl saved me, and from another a string of pearls, and from

---

paragraphs of *La ilustre fregona* and particularly the narrator's outcry concerning the evils of the picaresque world, which initiates the set of violent contrasts which the tale develops between its inhabitants and customs and the order of existence of the beautiful maiden who is, so to speak, exiled within it. In the Toledan novella the lower world has a symbolic function similar to that of the Gypsy society in the *La Gitanilla*, and it is marked by a similar ambivalence, as it unites two tendencies of traditional picaresque literature: on the one hand, the picaresque fictional world as the demonic and criminal (e.g., *Guzmán de Alfarache, El Buscón*), on the other hand, the picaresque fictional world as an order of freedom, individualism, and healthy anticeremonialism (e.g., *La vida del pícaro* [see ed. A. Bonilla, *Revue Hispanique* 9 (1902):295-330, and M. Bataillon, *Pícaros y picaresca* (Madrid, 1969), pp. 204-205]). To appreciate the full force of Cervantes's irony in these early antitheses introducing his paradoxical nocturnal worlds, one need only compare the opening of his more conventional romance, the *Persiles*, with its violent contrasts between the barbarians and the heroes.

[195] One could argue that the subversion of the moralizing generalization begins with its absurd repetition of the word *ladrones* five times. Certainly by the end of the following sentence, which describes the Gypsy grandmother as "jubilada en la ciencia de Caco" and teaching her pupil all her "gitanerías," the narrator already has assumed an individualized and playful shape whose moral judgments do not strike us as acceptable at face value.

[196] "sus estatutos y ordenanzas, que prohibían la entrada a la caridad en sus pechos" (p. 78). In one of his various intrusions to express a harsh moral judgment of the Gypsy world, the narrator reminds us of its demonic character and the absence of charity in it. After Juan receives the fugitive Clemente hospitably, explaining to him "aunque somos gitanos, no lo parecemos en la caridad," the narrator writes: "Llegóse a él Andrés y otro gitano caritativo (que aun entre los demonios hay unos peores que otros, y entre muchos malos hombres suele haber alguno bueno)" (p. 82).

the third forty reals of eight, which I had changed into coppers, giving twenty reals more for the change . . . there are no defenses which protect us and succor us more readily than the invincible arms of the great Philip. There is no passing beyond his *plus ultra*. For a doubloon of two faces the grim visage of the procurator becomes cheerful toward us, and so do those of all the ministers of death, who are harpies that prey on us poor Gypsies." Similarly, the Gypsy elder's emphasis on his fellows' capacities to resist torture in the phrase "we do not consider [the torments] worth even a cocoa bean" belongs to this general pattern of inversion.[197]

As I have pointed out above in dealing with the positive aspect of the paradoxical symbolism of the Gypsies' world, there is a good deal of imagery of natural fertility in the description of their society, and it forms part of a favorable presentation of their hard primitivism and supports a condemnation of the contrasting way of life at the court. However, it is interesting that Cervantes does not connect the abundance of their world with the theme and imagery of birth, rebirth, and rejuvenation that surround Preciosa and her divine analogues. Quite the contrary, he clearly suggests that the natural energies of the wild society are misused, directed as they are toward hedonism, the pleasures of sensuality, and anarchic self-indulgence. In the detailed description of the marriage institution nothing is said of the *"renuevos"* or *"ganancia,"* by which Preciosa and Clemente refer to the fruits of wedded love, or of the raising of children, for which St. Anne stands as a powerful symbol.[198] Indeed, the numerous motifs of renewed life

[197] "Tres veces por tres delitos diferentes me he visto casi puesta en el asno para ser azotada, y de la una me libró un jarro de plata, y de la otra una sarta de perlas, y de la otra cuarenta reales de a ocho, que había trocado por cuartos, dando veinte reales más por el cambio . . . no hay defensas que más presto nos amparen y socorran como las armas invencibles del gran Filipo: no hay pasar adelante de su *plus ultra*. Por un doblón de dos caras se nos muestra alegre la triste del procurador y de todos los ministros de la muerte, que son arpías de nosotras las pobres gitanas" (p. 45); "no lo estimamos en un cacao" (pp. 74-75). Rodríguez Marín notes that the phrase *no valer un cacao* is based on the Aztecs' use of the *cacao* as a coin of little value (see p. 75n).

[198] As Frank Pierce has recently pointed out, Juana Carducha is presented as an antithesis to Preciosa, and Cervantes's description of her as "algo más desenvuelta que hermosa" (p. 105) echoes his introduction of the Gypsy maiden as "algo desenvuelta" but "honesta" (p. 4; see "*La gitanilla*: a tale of high romance," *Bulletin of Hispanic Studies* 54 [1977]:283-95). Indeed her role as a demonic double is quite precisely developed, for she proposes an immediate, clandestine marriage of passion, "aunque a todos sus parientes les pesase" (p. 106). The destructive female is imaginatively linked with the anarchical natural order of the Gypsy world, and her proposal recalls the bestial conditions of its marriages. She offers herself in the corral of the inn,

or resurrection in the tale, which include, in addition to the pervasive imagery of vegetable fertility and the births of various children—the Virgin, Christ, Philip IV, and the child of the Gypsy code—, the rejuvenation of the somber figure of Saturn, the mythic destroyer of children, who cannot resist the contagious joy surrounding the birth of the prince and races with the procession ("Here ancient Saturn grooms and rejuvenates his beard, and, although he is sluggish, he springs lightly along, for pleasure cures his gout"[199]), the "burial of vengeance and the resuscitation of clemency" in the pardon of Juana Carducha,[200] and the resurrection of St. Lawrence, the "saintly Phoenix" of Margarita's church, who, although burned alive in Rome, "remained living in fame and in glory" ("quedó vivo/ En la fama y en la gloria"), are all countered by the profusion of instruments of execution and torture of the Gypsy world, where the garrote, the gallows, the knout, the galleys, chains, "tocas," and pulleys form part of the daily experience of its denizens and the scars left by the hangman's whip are looked upon as a sign of honor. Here we witness the ceremonial execution of a mule, and we discover that the murder of wives by husbands is apparently a common occurrence and that the official initiation ceremony is a symbolic execution of the novice by garroting.[201]

---

where Juan has gone to inspect some horses, and her temptations include, besides a life of pleasure, wealth, and property, "many newly planted vines," ("muchos majuelos"), the demonic equivalent of the flowering tree of St. Anne, the fertile vine of Margarita, and the blooming rose of Preciosa.

[199] "Aquí el anciano Saturno/ La barba pule y remoza,/ Y aunque es tardo, va ligero;/ Que el placer cura la gota" (p. 13).

[200] Whatever one may think of Cervantes's profession of carelessness and authorial freedom in appending a "misplaced" paragraph as the conclusion of his tale ("Olvidábaseme de decir como la enamorada mesonera . . ." [pp. 129-30]), his final sentence forms an ending that is imaginatively as effective in this tale of rebirth as any statement which is correct according to the logic of chronology and climactic plotting could be: ". . . a quien [la Carducha] no respondió pena alguna, porque en la alegría del hallazgo de los desposados *se enterró la venganza y resucitó la clemencia*." The antithesis imaginatively lifts the sinful adversary of the heroes out of the lower world, associates her destiny with their restoration, and implicates her in the ritualistic celebration of death and rebirth that lies behind the plot of *La Gitanilla*.

[201] As a dark kingdom of death the Gypsy world is linked imaginatively with the moribund realm of erotic experience that Clemente represents in his role as poet-lover early in the romance. For the enthralled youth, the beloved enslaves, blinds, bewitches, and kills. He describes her as the basilisk, metamorphosing her admirers into stone, and as the tyrannical love goddess, the sinister counterpart of the "chaste Venus" of Preciosa's song. Through both demonic counterweights, the one focusing on license and uncontrolled appetite, the other, on erotic sentiment and illusions, Cervantes illuminates by contrast distinct facets of his ideal of rational wedded love and the good nature in which it is founded.

In conclusion, the description of the Gypsy world and the poems that the maiden sings form imaginative focal points of the narrative, concentrating the central imagery of the work, revealing the major themes articulated in the imagery and the action, and connecting the idealized order which Cervantes celebrates in society and nature with the cosmological and religious order in which it is founded. The epiphanies of celestial order and infernal disorder in Preciosa's song of the Holy Family in the "highest palace" and the Gypsy elder's account of the statutes regulating family life in his demonic world mark the upper and lower extremes of the hierarchical world picture that dominated the Christian imagination up to the eighteenth century. Between the orders of heaven and hell we observe the two orders of nature.[202] The upper level is the original form of the Creation, the nature of Eden, infused with God's grace and rationality. Since the fall man is excluded from life in this order, and the closest he can come to a glimpse of it is in the orderly movements of the spheres and perhaps a faint recollection inspired by the sound of their celestial harmonies. Below the upper level of nature is the realm of nature as man commonly knows it, flawed by the fall, subject to decay and death, and constantly menaced by the incursions of the devil. It is here that man must experience the drama of redemption or damnation, and it is here that he must labor to perfect himself and the forms of his civilization according to the laws of the original higher order of nature, the "bien intencionada naturaleza," with its models for personal, sexual, and social fulfillment. In the *Persiles*, Cervantes's "divine comedy," we glimpse the same cosmological hierarchy in the background, and here too Cervantes employs poetry, mythological allusion, and traditional symbolism to introduce the supernatural realms of grace and damnation as a frame for the action that unfolds in the realm of nature.[203] Both works affirm man's capacities to lift himself

[202] For a succinct account of this picture, see Northrop Frye, "Romance as Masque," and "The Breaking of the Music," *Five Essays on Milton's Epics* (London, 1966), pp. 33-62. As Laguardia makes clear, Renaissance literature reveals an increased interest in the upper order of nature as furnishing models for life in the physical realm of nature and an effort to overcome the traditional segregation of the orders of spirit and nature characteristic of ascetic Christianity. (See *Nature Redeemed: The Imitation of Order in Three Renaissance Poems*, chap. 1.) This interest is perfectly consistent with what I have referred to above as the humanists' goal of the sanctification of lay life.

[203] The most important of the various epiphanies of the transcendental order behind the action of the *Persiles* is the mysterious song of Feliciana de la Voz, sweet as that of "algún ángel de los confirmados en gracia," which discloses the celestial paradise, the militant powers of hell, and the Christian vision of human history. The affinities of Preciosa and Feliciana, whose song has spellbinding powers, who sings at the altar of the Virgin, and who is a sister in that vast family of persecuted and restored maidens of romance, hardly require pointing out. See my *Cervantes' Christian Romance*,

and his civilization toward the level of redeemed nature, and both depict his movement from enslavement in a lawless natural order of barbarity and destructive energy to the state of individual freedom and enlightenment within perfected social, political, and religious institutions. Behind these works we glimpse Cervantes's optimism, his capacity to envision individual redemption on a grand scale and to view the institutions of civilization as nourishing the fulfillment of man's authentic self. Such was the vision behind the Erasmian reform movement, and its hold on Cervantes's imagination lingered on as he wrote the final pages of his life.

MARGARITA OF AUSTRIA AND THE REDEMPTION OF SPAIN: THE POLITICAL-HISTORICAL BACKGROUNDS OF *LA GITANILLA*

Preciosa's visits to the home of the lieutenant of the city and the gambling house, where "muchos caballeros" are amusing themselves, "some pacing up and down, and others playing various games,"[204] are two of the most puzzling scenes in Cervantes's loosely organized tale and point to the dimension of his work which is undoubtedly the most remote for a modern reader.[205] These scenes, together with the background action of Francisco de Cárcamo's successful petition at the court for an appointment as corregidor, the various brief satirical allusions to the corruption of court life emerging in the description of the Gypsy society and its practices, and the poetic celebration of the royal family of Margarita, Philip, and their miraculous child, form part of a pattern of political redemption which Cervantes assimilates to the various other patterns of redemption centering on the restoration of Preciosa's identity—Juan's rebirth as a being capable of spiritual love, the restoration of man's capacities to grow morally and, through such growth, to glimpse and understand the harmonious or-

---

pp. 87-90, 127-28; on the important function of poems and songs in the work, see pp. 35ff.

[204] "unos paseándose y otros jugando a diversos juegos, se entretenían" (p. 19).

[205] The judgment of a recent analyst of the work that the episode in the lieutenant's house is "nonsense" and "padding" is an accurate register of the degree to which the scene is mediated by historical events and preoccupations which have vanished from the horizons of the contemporary reader and which must be reassembled if its function and coherence within the text are to be recognized. See Jennifer Lowe, *Cervantes: Two Novelas Ejemplares, La gitanilla, La ilustre fregona* (London, 1971), p. 31. Aside from its impatience with this scene, Lowe's study makes various fine analytical observations about the structure of the two tales.

der of God's universe, the reaffirmation of Christian marriage and the traditional family structure, the redemption of man through the fruits of St. Anne's love and the gift of the Holy Family, and the restoration of the perfect nature of man's prelapsarian existence.

With their dark tonality and their fragmented events, the urban scenes bring the effects of discontinuity which characterize satirical plotting in general to the action of *La Gitanilla* and contribute a good deal to all the elements that distinguish its narrative movement from that of Cervantes's models and his own purer romances with their "teleologically" organized action. At the same time they cast Preciosa momentarily into the role of a satirical railer, and her cynical, scathing pronouncements are far more reminiscent of the worldly observations of that other illustrious Gypsy maiden of Spanish literary tradition, the Lozana Andaluza, than they are of the refined speeches and songs of her numerous ancestors in romance. When Preciosa surveys the barren world of the ingenuous lieutenant, who would be honorable and honest, and reminds him that in the perverted world of the palace the knave (*truhán*) receives more respect than the *discreto*, Cervantes is offering a brief but powerful glimpse of the notorious corruption that afflicted the court of Philip III. Her scornful admonition to her host and his family of "such distinguished ladies and gentlemen": "Bribe, Lieutenant, bribe, and your worship will have money, but do not introduce new ways, or your worship will die of hunger,"[206] contains the lesson which undoubtedly hundreds of bureaucrats learned the hard way as they beheld the scandalous depredations of the court favorites. We need only look briefly at the numerous documents— journals, correspondence, ambassadorial reports—left by observers of the court of Philip III or glance at the records of the scandalous trials of highly placed ministers which became commonplace in his reign to appreciate the evocative power of Cervantes's elliptical satirical allusions in this scene. Writing of the infamous Pedro de Franqueza's close association with the Duque de Lerma, the Venetian ambassador Bon observed that, through his insistence on bribes, the minister, "for all the inferiority and poverty of his origins, is now so esteemed and revered and has become so rich and famous to everybody that it is truly a thing of amazement." His desire for gifts is so well known to all, including the king, that "one no longer considers the bestowing of gifts upon him a vice in his conduct or an excess on the part of those who must conduct business with him, but rather a courtesy

---

[206] "Coheche vuesa merced, señor Tiniente, coheche y tendrá dineros, y no haga usos nuevos; que morirá de hambre" (pp. 32-33).

and an obligation." To deal successfully with him, "it is necessary to do what everybody does here, including the loftiest grandees of Spain and the ambassadors of all countries."[207] As Juderías concludes from his studies of the political intrigue, the scandals, and the trials of the period in which Cervantes wrote *La Gitanilla*, "the administration of the government had been turned into one gigantic auction where everything was sold to the highest bidder." At all ranks of the bureaucracy the bribe was an essential instrument for success, and the misuse of public funds by the ministers for personal profit and the plundering of the public treasury became so common that the ingenuous king, who was much more interested in the ostentatious display of public festivities celebrating royal power and in such hobbies as hunting and gambling than in overseeing the affairs of state, discovered one day that there was not enough money in his treasury for the expenses of his table and had to send his ministers through the streets of Valladolid begging for contributions from the well-to-do. When Contreras, Doña Clara, and the lieutenant all vainly search their pockets for a farthing to reward Preciosa's song and when the aged squire reveals that he had to pledge his only "real de a cuartos" in order to be able to eat, Cervantes is calling attention to the terrible situation of penury and want which afflicted many of the ministers of the Spanish state, including the king himself, whose funds, despite his favorites' assurances to the contrary, remained in a perpetual state of *empeño*.[208] At the same time the trials of such men as Franqueza and

[207] See Julián Juderías, "Los favoritos de Felipe III: Don Pedro Franqueza, Conde de Villalonga," *Revista de Archivos, Bibliotecas y Museos* 19 (1908):309-327; 20 (1909): 16-27, 223-40, esp. 19:324-25. Juderías observes that the records of Franqueza's trial offer a startling picture of the universality of the corrupt practices of the type that Preciosa advocates: "Militares y paisanos, seglares y eclesiásticos, abogados y jueces dejaron en aquellos folios amarillentos pruebas fehacientes de su ambición, de su codicia y de las malas artes que ponían en juego para lograr sus designios" (20:233). See also Stanislav Zimic's recent analysis of the sharp satire which Cervantes directs at the ruling class amid the gaiety of Pedro de Urdemalas's successful manipulation of Belica's restoration ("El gran teatro del mundo y el gran mundo del teatro en *Pedro de Urdemalas* de Cervantes," *Acta Neophilologica* 10 [1977]:55-105).

[208] See Juderías, "Un proceso político en tiempo de Felipe III: Don Rodrigo Calderón, Marqués de Siete Iglesias: su vida, su proceso y su muerte," *Revista de Archivos, Bibliotecas y Museos* 13 (1905):334-65; 14 (1906):1-31, esp. 13:347-48. For the continuing *"empeños"* which crippled the government, as well as the efforts of the ministers to delude the king by assuring him that they had the devices to effect a profitable redemption of the funds, see Pérez Bustamante, *Felipe III*, pp. 88-89. At one point the exasperated Queen Margarita upbraided the Duke of Lerma in the presence of the king and lamented that "todo estaba empeñado" (p. 89). In 1600 Luis Valle de la Cerda wrote in his *Desempeño del patrimonio de su Magestad*: "Never in seven hundred years of continuous war, nor in one hundred years of continuous peace, has

Rodrigo de Calderón, which received wide publicity and inspired the creation of numerous satirical ballads, disclosed that a few powerful ministers were accumulating truly fabulous hoards of money, jewels, and properties, and, when Preciosa reminds the lieutenant that "in some palaces knaves fare much better than the wise," her words are an accurate commentary on the Spanish court of the time. Following Preciosa's sarcastic outburst, her guardian reprimands her: "Come, come, child, speak no more; for you have already spoken much . . . speak of things suitable to a girl of your years, and do not assume airs of haughtiness, for there is none of them that does not forebode a fall," and the lieutenant exclaims: "These Gypsies are the devil incarnate!" Such reactions to Preciosa's audacity belong to the type of critical qualification that Cervantes frequently attaches to satirical pronouncement, a form of literary statement which he and many other major satirists have recognized as demonic and debasing. However, to understand their full implications, we should bear in mind that the court environment to which they were addressed was plagued by intrigue, suspicion, rivalry, fear of exposure, physical violence, anonymous libels, and, as the case of Rodrigo Calderón demonstrates, a tyrannically enforced silence on the whole population concerning probably the most infamous revelation of ministerial corruption in the period.[209]

Spain as a whole been as ruined and as poor as it is now" (cited by J. H. Elliott, "Self-Perception and Decline in Early Seventeenth-Century Spain," *Past and Present* 74 [1977]:41-61; see p. 53). To appreciate the satirical elements in *La Gitanilla* and the redemptive vision of Margarita and the prince, we should bear in mind that Spanish society of the early decades of the seventeenth century was afflicted with a pervasive sense of decline, which, as Elliott argues, was undoubtedly rooted in its experience of a series of military, economic, and demographic disasters in the final years of the sixteenth century and in its consciousness of a failure to realize the messianic national expectations which had developed from the triumphant completion of the Reconquest through the imperial reign of Charles V. While Spaniards yearned for a return to a better age and a renewal of lost energies and while *arbitristas* offered countless reform propositions—some responsible, others as fanciful as the utopian schemes depicted in contemporary satire—the feeling remained widespread that if national regeneration were to come about, it could do so only following a thorough purification of a morally diseased court society.

[209] "Ea, niña, no hables más; que has hablado mucho . . . habla de aquello que tus años permiten, y no te metas en altanerías; que no hay ninguna que no amenace caída"; "¡El diablo tienen estas gitanas en el cuerpo!" (p. 34). For the text of an edict of "perpetuo silencio" which the king issued following the public exposure of Calderón's crimes, an edict that was to take precedence over "todas y cualesquier leyes, fueros y costumbres, premáticas sanciones, provisiones ó cartas acordadas, cédulas ó consultas nuestras que haya en contrario," see Juderías, "Un proceso político en tiempo de Felipe III," 13:350-51.

The elusive scene of Preciosa's visit to the lieutenant's "sterile" house presents, then, through brief but powerful allusion, a fallen world of the court, just as the poem to Doña Clara, which Preciosa recites amid this world, depicts a deeply flawed form of marriage and family life. It is complemented by the brief scene of the gambling house, where we observe the knights of the court occupied in the idle pursuits which the leaders of Spain avidly enjoyed at the time and where the cross of Calatrava, one of the central symbols of the work, appears in a context of perversion.[210] In opposition to such blighted

---

[210] To persuade the hesitant Preciosa to enter the gambler's den, one of the knights standing behind the *"reja"* places his hand on the cross on his breast and swears that he and his associates will not harm her. The widespread addiction to gambling in the court society was observed and condemned by numerous moralists and chroniclers of the time, and it is not surprising that the great governor Sancho Panza finds himself, as he contemplates social reform, compelled to reflect on "el vicio del juego," which "se ha vuelto en ejercicio común" (*Don Quijote de la Mancha*, 2:408). The king himself lost fabulous sums at the table, and the queen learned to play cards with him in order to prevent such losses (see Pérez Bustamante, *Felipe III*, pp. 64, 88). On the actual "desecrations" of the emblems of the military orders by the ministers, who cynically bought and sold them as if they were common merchandise and frivolously bestowed them on their family members and favorites, see Juderías's accounts of the trials of the favorites. In view of the centrality of the theme of perfect marriage in *La Gitanilla* and the indeterminacy of the fragmentary scene at the gambling house, it is worth pointing out that the pernicious effects of gambling on marriage were a standard topic in didactic and satirical writings of the period, and there were few treatises on marital perfection that did not give some attention to them. See, for example, Erasmus, *Institutio Christiani Matrimonii*, p. 663A, and his colloquy "Marriage"; Luxán, *Coloquios matrimoniales*, pp. 79-80; and Luis de León, *La perfecta casada*, p. 89. Jerónimo de Mondragón writes of the insanity and self-destructiveness of gamblers: "en lo que más se muestra su locura es, que si por suerte son casados, no sólo maltratan a sus hijos, muger i demás familia, con hambre, sed i otros mil deshaires que les hazen padecer para alcançar para su maldito juego, pero aún, quando llegan con aquel insano furor de averles ido mal, los riñen, golpean i hieren malamente, sin causa ni razón alguna" (*Censura de la locura humana y excelencias della*, ed. A. Vilanova [Barcelona, 1953], p. 77). As there is some controversy among Cervantists as to whether Cervantes did in fact know this contemporary descendent of Erasmus's *Praise of Folly* (for Bataillon's recent rebuttal and rejection of Vilanova's arguments for a case of concrete influence, see "Un problème d'influence d'Érasme en Espagne: *L'Éloge de la Folie,*" *Actes du Congrès Érasme* [Amsterdam, 1971], 136-47), it is perhaps well to point out that Mondragón follows his tirade on gambling and marriage with a denunciation of the most insane form of gambling that he has witnessed: ". . . he io visto en algunos lugares de los puertos de mar, a muchos dellos que por jugar, los miserables tristemente se vendian i entregavan a las galeras, siendo el mas aspero, terrible tormento que a uno le puede dar en esta vida" (p. 78). In the *Persiles* Cervantes describes this practice. His heroes enter Perpignan and immediately encounter and save such a victim while his wife and children stand by, wailing helplessly. For all its melodramatic sensationalism, the scene includes some complexities that remove it from the context of moral simplification which frames Mondragón's unequivocal

environments we behold the house of the ideal courtier-paterfamilias, Francisco de Cárcamo, and the vision of the purified court of Preciosa's song to Queen Margarita. The venerable Francisco appears standing on his resplendent balcony displaying the red cross of Santiago emblazoned on his breast and invites the Gypsies into his house. His words, "Come up, children, for here they will give you alms," form a positive counterweight to the invitation of the gamblers that they echo, his promise of charity contrasting sharply with the offer of the *"barato,"* the tip with which the victorious gambler rewards bystanders and assistants: "Come in, come in, Gypsies, for here we shall give you a share of our winnings."[211] In Preciosa's song Cervantes combines the apocalyptic imagery which conventionally surrounded royal births in the panegyrics of the period with the imagery of fertility and sterility which is particularly characteristic of *La Gitanilla*'s imaginative atmosphere. She hails in the fruits of the royal marriage a redeemer who will deliver the court from its oppressors:

> ¡Qué de máquinas que rompe!
> ¡Qué de designios que corta!
> ¡Qué de esperanzas que infunde!
> ¡Qué de deseos mal logra!
> ¡Qué de temores aumenta!
> ¡Qué de preñados aborta![212]

As in the case of Preciosa's visit to the house of the lieutenant, the allusions take on their full range of implication only when we consider the historical background to which they clearly point. Throughout the Catholic world the opposition of Queen Margarita to the favorites who were destroying Spain was well known, and all who hoped for a purification of life at the court looked to her as a savior. Thus the Vatican advised its legate to cultivate the queen in the hope that, following her gift of an heir to the Spanish crown, Philip might abandon his life of frivolity and dedicate himself to serious matters.[213]

---

pronouncements. The husband is driven to his desperate action not by madness or vice but rather by poverty. The agents encouraging and profiting from the victims' willingness to gamble their freedom away are the ministers of the king. Even at its most "exemplary," Cervantes's fiction resists reduction according to the conventional moralizing literature with which he was familiar.

[211] "Subid, niñas; que aquí os darán limosna" (p. 52); "Entren, entren las gitanillas; que aquí les daremos barato" (p. 19).

[212] "What machinations does he crush! What schemes does he cut off! What high hopes does he implant! What desires does he frustrate! What fears does he now increase! What fertile plans does he cause to miscarry!" (p. 15).

[213] See Pérez Bustamante, *Felipe III*, p. 88.

At the same time the favorites recognized her as their enemy and attempted to isolate her from her trusted friends and advisers, to keep her under constant surveillance, and to influence the king to deprive her of the right to comment on political matters. The embattled queen was saddened by the success of her opponents and frequently remarked that she would have been happier remaining a nun in Gratz than she was occupying the throne of the most powerful kingdom in the world. However, she continued in her struggle and achieved a temporary victory with the removal from the court of her principal antagonist, Rodrigo Calderón. The news of her death in 1611 shortly after the delivery of Alfonso el Caro was greeted with an outpouring of public grief and outrage, and rumors circulated widely that Calderón had poisoned her. As Quevedo described the situation, "Public sentiment rose to a great fury at the loss of a queen of such excellence, and everybody was saying that the life of Her Majesty had been cut short, and not by a sickness, that ill-doers [*los malos*] were far more to blame for her death than illnesses [*los males*]; such was the extremity reached by public grief that it produced such extreme kinds of ranting."[214] So great was Calderón's hold on the Duke of Lerma and King Philip that, despite the rumors, he returned to power, and two months after the death of his royal enemy he triumphantly entered the Church of Santiago to receive in the presence of the grandees of Spain a habit of the illustrious military order. Whatever the truth of the rumors of Calderón's involvement may have been, the circumstances surrounding the death of Queen Margarita contributed a good deal to her apotheosis in the public imagination, and there can be no doubt that the saintliness of this young maiden, who at the age of fifteen greeted the offer of the crown of Spain with tears as she was attending to the poor in a hospital of Gratz,[215] exercised a powerful hold on the imagination of Cervantes's Spain. No wonder that on the day of her death a certain Franciscan monk, Antonio Sobrino, had a vision of the maiden's soul ascending to heaven "resplendent and beautiful, accompanied by St. John the Evangelist, of whom she was a devotee, and St. Augustine, the Great Father of the Church."[216] And no wonder that Cervantes, himself continually frustrated and disillusioned and perhaps even tainted in his own efforts to win recognition from the official powers of Spain, should choose to embody in the young queen his hopes for the regeneration of his nation and to associate her, as a

[214] *Grandes Anales*, cited by Pérez Bustamante, *Felipe III*, p. 92.

[215] Pérez Bustamante, *Felipe III*, p. 65.

[216] See Gil González Dávila, *Historia de la vida y hechos del ínclito monarca, amado y santo, D. Felipe Tercero* (Madrid, 1771), p. 161.

model of wedded love, honesty, and maternal devotion, with St. Anne, the Virgin, and his own "divine" maiden, Preciosa, who disappears on Ascension Day and returns to bestow her perfections on the world about her.[217]

PRECIOSA AND THE THEME OF POETRY

Like so many other writers of the Renaissance Cervantes looked on poetry as one of the most important of man's institutions, and he was deeply committed to it as an instrument of moral guidance. While he was aware of its powers to corrupt, to imprison people in destructive delusions, and to debase and even to destroy society, he continually reaffirmed both in theoretical statement and in practical example the lofty vision of its powers which contemporary theorists celebrated in the archetypal poets and founders of civilizations, Orpheus and Amphion. Cervantes's favorite symbol of this vision of poetry was the occasional companion of these mighty seers in the theoretical discussions with which he was familiar, Dame Poetry, a beautiful, chaste maiden who dwells close to nature in the company of nymphs representing moral and natural philosophy and who elevates all who come into contact with her. She appears in several of Cervantes's most important discussions of poetry,[218] and it is no surprise that she is one

[217] Behind the satirical modulations in *La Gitanilla* we discern the spirit of *desengaño* which animates the hermit Soldino's denunciation of the artifice of court life in the *Persiles*, Don Quixote's repeated tirades about the idleness and corruption of courtiers, and Cervantes's possibly autobiographical portrait of the frustrated young page who has fled the court while his innocence, idealism, and good cheer are still intact and has determined to seek glory as a soldier on Spain's battlefields abroad (*Don Quijote de la Mancha*, 2:226-29). However, the ideal that looms behind the criticism here is neither the autarchy and rich interiority of the Christian Stoic nor the heroic individualism of the chivalric adventurer. In comparison *La Gitanilla*'s vision of perfection is decidedly social, and it is striking that the ideal courtiers and the rulers whose successes it celebrates are presented acting in their roles as members of families. In its imaginative conception of the state as a family, the romance recalls Erasmus's program of reform, which, as I have pointed out above, found in the model of the Christian family the principles for the organization of the state and the community of states—the family of all Christians—and which maintained that in family life one receives the basic training for the good statesman and the good citizen. "Jam ut ex multis civitatibus constat regnum, ex multis domibus civitas, ita domus civitas quaedam est ac regnum" (*Institutio Christiani Matrimonii*, p. 692F). "Quid enim aliud est regnum quam magna familia?" (*Institutio Principis Christiani*, p. 178).

[218] In his most detailed description of the figure, Cervantes writes that "Moran con ella, en una misma estancia/ la diuina y moral filosofia/ el estilo mas puro y la elegancia/ . . . En fin, ella es la cifra do se apura/ lo prouechoso, honesto y deleytable,/ partes con quien se aumenta la ventura." She is opposed by "otra falsa, ansiosa, torpe

of the various divine or quasi-divine female figures who are associated with Preciosa in *La Gitanilla*.

Appearing in the scene of Clemente's pact with the Gypsy maiden, the description of Poetry parallels Preciosa's speech on virginity in the corresponding scene of the pact of the lovers immediately preceding it. Clemente addresses Preciosa as "preciosa perla," offers her a poem, and speaks to her of poetry:

> One ought to treat poetry as a most precious jewel, whose owner does not wear it every day, nor does he show it to all the world nor at every step, but only when it is suitable and when there is reason for showing it. Poetry is a most radiantly beautiful maiden, chaste, virtuous, discreet, clear-sighted, modest, a maiden who remains within the limits of the most lofty discretion. She is a friend of solitude, fountains entertain her, meadows console her, trees banish her cares, flowers delight her, and, finally, she charms and instructs all who have intercourse with her.[219]

The coalescence of Preciosa's imagery of nature and wealth around the figure of Poetry increases the suggestiveness of the association of the two maidens. For the art of poetry like chaste wedded love belongs to the order of the perfect nature, the "buen natural" which Preciosa possesses and which she preserves from corruption regardless of the barbarity in which she is immersed.

---

y vieja;/ amiga de sonaja y morteruelo,/ que ni tabanco, ni taberna dexa" (*Viage del Parnaso*, pp. 59-60). For Don Quixote, a lover of romance and the higher "truth of poetry," Poetry is a maiden who "no quiere ser manoseada, ni traída por las calles . . . es hecha de una alquimia de tal virtud, que quien la sabe tratar la volverá en oro purísimo de inestimable precio" (2:155). For the familiarity of this figure in Renaissance iconology, see Cesare Ripa, *Iconologia* (Siena, 1613), pp. 157-58. For its place in Cervantes's general view of poetry, see E. C. Riley's *Cervantes's Theory of the Novel* (Oxford, 1962), pp. 73ff.

[219] "Hase de usar de la poesía como de una joya preciosísima, cuyo dueño no la trae cada día, ni la muestra a todas gentes, ni a cada paso, sino cuando convenga y sea razón que la muestre. La Poesía es una bellísima doncella, casta, honesta, discreta, aguda, retirada, y que se contiene en los límites de la discreción más alta. Es amiga de la soledad; las fuentes la entretienen; los prados la consuelan; los árboles la desenojan; las flores la alegran; y, finalmente, deleita y enseña a cuantos con ella comunican" (p. 49). For the various details connecting Preciosa with poetry, see my *Cervantes, Aristotle, and the "Persiles,"* pp. 311-19. It is worth pointing out that in the amoebean song Clemente and Juan envision Preciosa as a "Platonic" siren, dwelling in the sphere of the fixed stars. According to an ancient tradition which enjoyed a revival in Renaissance neo-Platonism, the nine muses were associated with Plato's celestial sirens. The fixed stars are the location of Urania, the muse of cosmic knowledge and the muse traditionally invoked by the epic poet (see p. 313). For the theme of poetry in the tale, see also Karl-Ludwig Selig, "Concerning the Structure of Cervantes' *La Gitanilla*," *Romanistisches Jahrbuch* 13 (1962):273-76.

From the very beginning of the tale we notice that Cervantes is concerned not only with distinguishing chastity and rational love from lust, authentic freedom from license, and true nature from physical nature, but also with separating genuine poetry from its debased forms. Immediately we discover that Preciosa's purity is so powerful that Gypsies do not dare in her presence to "sing lewd songs or utter words that are unseemly." In her characteristic imagery of treasure Preciosa is introduced as "rich in poetry": "Preciosa grew up rich in carols, folk songs, *seguidillas*, sarabands, and other verses, especially ballads."[220] In her eagerness to exploit for personal gain the maiden's talents, her guardian solicits poems from all quarters, and the narrator speaks of the corruption of poetry caused by its commercialization, lamenting the infamous trade in false miracles which poets compose for blind men (p. 5). Preciosa, of course, remains very scrupulous about the poetry which she accepts: "she returned to Madrid, along with three other girls, . . . provided with a supply of ballads and gay carols, but all of them wholesome in tone; for Preciosa would never permit those in her company to sing immodest songs, nor did she ever sing them herself." She cautions the page-poet: "mind, sir, do not fail to bring me the ballads you speak of, but on the condition that they be seemly."[221] If the songs which the Gypsies normally cultivate with great profit appeal as pornography, the Gitanilla's chaste, beautiful songs, like those of her literary ancestor Truhanilla, who escapes the degradation of the brothel through her miraculous singing, have the power to awaken the "slumbering charity" of her listeners and reward her with vast quantities of coins. As I have pointed out above, in Preciosa's early relationship with Clemente, Cervantes explores a kind of poetry that is nourished by erotic impulses and, divorced from reality, imprisons its victims in destructive delusions. Preciosa, whose perfect nature enables her to perceive authentic poetry as well as authentic love, rejects Clemente's poetry almost as emphatically as she rejects the poetry that corrupts by its appeal to the passions.

While the effects of her singing and her repeated advocacy of the

[220] "en su presencia no osaba alguna gitana, vieja ni moza, cantar cantares lascivos ni decir palabras no buenas. . . . Salió Preciosa rica de villancicos, de coplas, seguidillas y zarabandas, y de otros versos, especialmente de romances" (pp. 4-5).

[221] "volvió a Madrid con otras tres muchachas, . . . todas apercibidas de romances y de cantarcillos alegres, pero todos honestos; que no consentía Preciosa que las que fuesen en su compañía cantasen cantares descompuestos, ni ella los cantó jamás" (pp. 10-11); "mire, señor, que no me deje de dar los romances que dice, con tal condición, que sean honestos" (p. 18).

ethical responsibility of poetry associate Preciosa with the mythical figure that Clemente describes, her relation to the luminous lady in the gentle Parnassian setting is more complicated than her relation to the other members of the constellation of ideal females that shines on the world of *La Gitanilla*. For all her purity Preciosa has come to understand very well the ways of the fallen environment in which she has lived. She remarks to her wondering audience that the experience of evil has enlivened her intellect (her *"ingenio"*) and boasts that her preceptors have been "experience" and the "devil," who teach more in a single hour than what one normally learns in a year (p. 24). In his opening outburst of admiration the narrator qualifies his praise by adding that the maiden, although pure, courteous, discreet, and intelligent, is "somewhat forward" ("algo desenvuelta"). Throughout the work Cervantes draws attention to Preciosa's shrewdness, worldliness, and mischievous boldness (*"desenvoltura"*), and he does not hesitate to show it degenerating into the caustic cynicism and acerbity which characterize some of his more disabused artistic spokesmen. Don Quixote, in one of his moments of lucid idealism, remarks that the maiden Poetry, as a lady of "the purest gold of inestimable price," should have nothing to do with "vile satires" (2:55). For all her insistence on "honestidad" in poetry, we discover that Preciosa is quite capable of declaiming satirical verse and of enjoying its characteristic obscene humor. While she reveals her control of the magical powers of healing in poetry in her revival of Juan, in Doña Clara's house she shows herself to be adept at exploiting its traditional powers to wound. The fact is that Preciosa is close to Cervantes as an artistic surrogate, far closer than the radiant figure of Lady Poetry could ever be, despite his firm convictions about the lofty aims of poetry. Perhaps it is an intuition of this affinity with his character that lies behind that mysterious, understated relationship between the maiden and the admiring Clemente, whose quest into the wilderness and whose disappearance in a world of criminality appear to have something to do with his destiny as a poet.[222]

La Gitanilla depicts the growth of a perfect love and friendship uniting Preciosa and Juan, but in a sense the real affinities of the maiden are with the narrator of the tale. Her total mastery of nearly every situation in which she finds herself and her control of the movement of the action place her in a position far superior to that of the other characters and point to her special role as agent of her creator. Moreover, the voices of both are marked by a worldliness that has

---

[222] See Forcione, *Cervantes, Aristotle, and the "Persiles,"* chap. 9.

made them masters of the language of indirection and distinguishes their discourse from that of all other voices in the narrative. Both Preciosa and Cervantes are ironists, skilled exploiters of all the possibilities for ambiguity that have lurked within language since the loss of the natural discourse of paradise. Nowhere is the privileged position of Preciosa as an alter ego of Cervantes more powerfully affirmed than in the remarkable scene when she momentarily loses control of the situation while reciting the love sonnet that sends Juan reeling into a swoon. In a shocking change of perspective the narrator enters the world of his fiction to speak privately with Preciosa, advising her to be more thoughtful in her treatment of Juan's feelings and giving her a remedy for her immediate difficulty: "Think of what you have said, Preciosa, and what you are about to say, for these are not words of praise to the page, but spears that pierce the heart of Andrés, who listens to them. Do you wish to see him, child? Then turn your eyes, and you will see him fainting on his seat in a deathlike sweat. . . . Go to him, for God's sake, and whisper a few words in his ear that may go straight to his heart and revive him from his fainting fit."[223] The maiden proceeds to follow the advice, gently whispers some reassuring words to her beloved, revives him from his swoon, and averts the danger of exposure that threatens the young couple. Of the various rifts in the text created by the narrator's remarks mingling his own world or that of his readers with the fictional world of his characters, his conference with Preciosa is certainly the most violent, and it has occasionally prompted editors and translators, i.e., its readers, to soften its impact by surrounding it with parentheses. However one may feel about its narrative logic, it forms an unforgettable moment in the tale, privileging Preciosa as having an intimate relationship with the author and depicting her, as she steps over to whisper in Juan's ear just as the narrator has whispered into hers, as having the special power to implement her author's intentions.[224]

---

[223] "Mirad lo que habéis dicho, Preciosa, y lo que vais a decir; que ésas no son alabanzas del paje, sino lanzas que traspasan el corazón de Andrés, que las escucha. ¿Queréislo ver, niña? Pues volved los ojos y veréisle desmayado encima de la silla. . . . Llegaos a él enhorabuena, y decilde algunas palabras al oído, que vayan derechas al corazón y le vuelvan de su desmayo" (pp. 59-60).

[224] The male protagonist and the narrator are united in a similar type of complicity in one of the latter's intrusions. However, the narrator's attitude toward the youth, as is generally the case in the tale, is one of playful reprobation for his surrender to love. In the important scene of Juan's declaration, the youth introduces himself as "hijo de Fulano," and the narrator adds parenthetically "que por buenos respetos aquí no se declara su nombre." The humor arising from the pretence that what we are witnessing is fact and not fiction is compounded by the protagonist's abandonment

At the conclusion of the tale Cervantes's narrator remarks that the poets of the city of Murcia took it upon themselves to "celebrate the strange case, as well as the unrivaled beauty of the little Gypsy."[225] It is certainly possible that Cervantes wished to enhance the illusion of reality in his "unerhörte Begebenheit"—the miraculous loss and recognition—by describing the process of its transformation into literature and reminding his reader of the existence of authenticating texts. However, the more important implication of the comment concerns the theme of poetry, the exemplarity of Cervantes's own art, and his view of himself as a poet. Throughout her ordeals in the lower world Preciosa has been surrounded by an aura of divinity, and now in her triumph she takes her place directly beside the hymned figures of St. Anne, the Virgin, and Queen Margarita of Austria. Cervantes's tale is itself, of course, an act of poetry, a celebration of the maiden and the good nature that she embodies and bestows upon her society. As an example of virtue to be imitated, Preciosa is indeed the highest kind of "poetic truth," the truth that Renaissance humanists envisioned when defining the imitation of nature and affirming the superiority of poetry to history. She belongs to that "golden world" which Philip Sidney saw as the true world of nature and hence the distinctive province of poetry.[226]

---

of his world of fiction to be an accomplice of the narrator in the literary hoax. The procedure continues in what follows: "Mi nombre es éste—y díjoselo—; el de mi padre ya os le he dicho; la casa donde vive es en *tal* calle, y tiene *tales y tales señas*" (p. 55; italics added). The willful absurdity of the character's shifting back and forth between the plane of his literary world and that of his narrator to confound a curious reader, whose strict moral convictions are implied by the secrecy, is retroactively even more mischievous when later on in the story the narrator reveals the names of father and son with absolutely no concern about a scandal. In such confusing manipulations of the boundary between reality and fiction, Cervantes is exploiting for his own characteristic purposes a conventional pose of the novella narrator, who, dealing commonly with recent "news" ("novelties") and scandalous events involving people known in the readers' world, frequently reveals a concern for decorum and the evils of gossip. For example, the narrator of the eighth tale in the Spanish collection of Bandello's novellas begins: "Pues este Señor (cuyo nombre quiero callar por algunos respetos) . . ." (*Historias trágicas ejemplares, sacadas de la obra del Bandello Veronés* [Salamanca, 1589], p. 206).

[225] "los poetas de la ciudad, que hay algunos, y muy buenos, tomaron a cargo celebrar el extraño caso, juntamente con la sin igual belleza de la Gitanilla" (p. 129).

[226] *An Apology for Poetry, Elizabethan Critical Essays*, ed. G. G. Smith (London, 1904), 1:156. See also Bacon's discussion of poetic imitation: "Poesy seems to bestow upon human nature those things which history denies to it. . . . For if the matter be attentively considered, a sound argument may be drawn from Poesy to show that there is agreeable to the spirit of man a more ample greatness, a more perfect order, and a more beautiful variety than it can anywhere (since the Fall) find in nature . . .

However, as I have pointed out above, in a very fundamental way Preciosa is different from her celestial analogues, and it is clear that Cervantes's exemplary prose, even when animated by his most optimistic view of poetry, is very different from the untroubled harmonies of the hymnist. Don Quixote learned the hard way that "poetic truth" has a tendency to disengage from concrete reality, and he expressed the wish that his chronicler, like those of the great epic heroes, would forget all the contingencies, all the "thrashings" that clutter the realm of true experience, and would write of him with traditional concepts of "poetic truth" as guiding principles. Cervantes, however, was seldom willing to allow his poetic truth to emerge in such pure and imaginary regions as those which his hero had encountered in the romances of chivalry, and even in *La Gitanilla*, where his characteristic determination to look at the truths of poetry ironically and critically is present but not dominant, he plants all his idealizations firmly in the world of reality. Preciosa sings that in Margarita's procession the adoring throngs intoned "hymns and chants that reveal that here on earth Glory is to be found" ("himnos y voces que muestran/ Que está en el suelo la Gloria"). Even in his most exemplary contexts and most "poetic" moments Cervantes remains a poet of the *suelo*, and in a characteristic bit of self-deprecatory mystification, he follows his statement concerning the hymns to the saintly Preciosa with the observation that a certain Licenciado Pozo's version was so accomplished that "in his verses the fame of Preciosa will endure as long as the centuries." The fact that there was a licentiate of this name in Murcia at the time, as Cervantes scholarship has assured us, is of some interest, but it does little to clarify the indeterminacy and suggestiveness that his introduction brings for a moment to the conclusion of the tale. Once again interfering with our grasp of his creation, the nar-

---

it may be fairly thought to partake somewhat of a divine nature, because it raises the mind and carries it aloft, . . . not (like reason and history) buckling and bowing down the mind to the nature of things" (*De Dignitate et Augmentis Scientiarum*, in *Essays*, ed. R. F. Jones [New York, 1937], p. 391). On the connection between the concept of the imitation of nature in aesthetics and the order of redeemed nature, which is so fundamental in humanist religious and ethical thought, see Laguardia, *Nature Redeemed*, chap. 2, which includes a discussion of the passages cited from Sidney and Bacon. For Cervantes's criticism of a tendency in Renaissance literary theorizing to interpret the Aristotelian concepts of poetic truth, imitation, and verisimilitude as enjoining an unimaginative reduplication in literature of historical fact and empirical reality, see my *Cervantes, Aristotle, and the "Persiles," passim*. An informative discussion of the variety of meanings which surrounded the concept of the imitation of nature in Renaissance poetics can be found in Harold S. Wilson's "Some Meanings of 'Nature' in Renaissance Literary Theory," *Journal of the History of Ideas* 2 (1941):430-48.

rator speaks with the double-entendre that might remind us of Preciosa's mastery of oblique statement at certain moments of the story. While there is nothing in his apparent retreat from responsibility for his text that strikes at the authenticity of its immense vision of perfection, there is, nevertheless, in his characteristic refusal to don the robes of the classical seer and in his insistence on continuing, even at the end, to speak in the flawed, infinitely suggestive idiom of fallen humanity—his own authentic idiom—a sober reminder that, if the way to the splendid truths which his heroes discover in the starry heavens is ever to be found, it is in this fallen, creaturely world that we must continue looking for it.

LA GITANILLA AS ERASMIAN ROMANCE: LITERARY FORM AND IDEAS

The presence of Erasmus's colloquy on courtship at the center of *La Gitanilla* does not clarify the total meaning and design of the later work. However, it does provide a useful key to an understanding of its intentions, its genesis, its central themes, its "exemplarity," and several of its most ambiguous structural features. To recognize its presence is not to suggest that the novella can be conveniently reduced to the tightly focused play of ideas that characterizes its Erasmian antecedent. *La Gitanilla* is a celebrative rather than an analytical work, and, in its treatment of ideas and its "informing" intellectual frame of reference, the novella is radically distinct from the colloquy, relying much more heavily on intimation and imaginative suggestion through such poetic devices as plot, imagery, symbolism, and mythological allusion than on direct assertive statement and analytical argumentation. The result is oddly enough that, while it is a much less ideological piece of writing, it undoubtedly has a much broader reach in its ideological frame of reference, and a full elucidation of the ideas that inform it would probably go well beyond the limits of the present study. I can think of nothing that more clearly illustrates the way in which literary form and complex ideas are fused in Cervantes's exemplary fiction than the way in which the central theme of marriage gives distinctive shape to the traditional conventions of romance—the two-year pact of virginal lovers, probably "borrowed" from Heliodorus's *Aethiopika*, which becomes a guarantee of knowledge, freedom, circumspection, and compatibility for a couple considering marriage; the demonic other-world, which is most notable for the details of its marital customs and statutes; the double, whose function is to illustrate the potential for deception in traditional amatory attitudes and discourse and to expose weaknesses in the protagonists as they strive for a perfect relationship; the climactic obstacles, which include the laws which the sixteenth century adopted to encourage rationality in the contraction of a marriage; the defense of embattled virginity, which is connected with a sixteenth-century ideal of chaste wedded love and Platonic amity and with the joyous perception of the order reigning throughout a harmoniously created universe; and the restoration of the lost heroine, which is imaginatively associated with the realization of the utopian aspirations of the Erasmian reform program, the spiritual renovation of the Spanish state, and the universal redemption of man and history.

CHAPTER III

El Licenciado Vidriera as a Satirical Parable: The Mystery of Knowledge

la virtud y el buen entendimiento
siempre es una y siempre es uno
—Cipión, *El coloquio de los perros*

THE PILGRIMAGE OF CURIOSITY

The heart of a fool is like a cart wheel,
and his thoughts like a turning axle.
—Ecclesiasticus

THE STRUCTURAL peculiarities of the *Licenciado Vidriera* have always been a problem with which its critical readers have had to contend. Both admirers and detractors have often pointed out that what quantitatively forms the largest part of the work is the series of discontinuous satirical observations, witty anecdotes, and philosophical aphorisms declaimed by the protagonist following his plunge into insanity. They have gone on to argue that the function of the relatively short introductory and concluding sections of the tale is to create artificially a narrative action framing the licentiate's utterances and endowing what normally would hardly have fit into a collection of novellas with an illusory shape of fiction. The key to Cervantes's meaning, then, must surely lie in the content of the protagonist's deranged discourse, and its generally abusive tenor would indicate that the author's single intention in the work is to comment satirically on the customs of his society. A large body of critical opinion has maintained that the *Li-*

cenciado Vidriera is merely a collection of satirical fragments, and Cervantists, for the most part, have agreed that its generic models are to be sought in the collections of apothegms and anecdotes which the humanists of the age were fond of compiling in imitation of such revered classical authors as Plutarch and Valerius Maximus.[1] For Marcel Bataillon, Cervantes's exemplary novella is the "supreme flower of the literature of apothegms made fashionable by Erasmism."[2] Congruent with such an interpretation is the widely held view of the glass licentiate as a spokesman for Cervantes,[3] an opinion which continued to prevail even as critics began to revise the traditional reading of the tale and pay more attention to its total design and the relation of the so-called frame to its apothegmatic center. It is undeniable that much of the licentiate's criticism of society is apt, that his rejection by a society of fools forms an ironic conclusion which supports the interpretation of his moral superiority, and that there are obvious parallels between his life and that of Cervantes—the dedication to letters and

[1] According to Francisco de Icaza, ". . . *El Licenciado Vidriera* no es sino un pretexto de Cervantes para publicar sus *Apotegmas*," and its genre as a collection of apothegms accounts for its failure as a work of art (*Las "Novelas ejemplares" de Cervantes* [Madrid, 1928], pp. 190-94). Armand Singer notes that the frame, with its account of the cause and nature of the protagonist's madness, has no bearing whatsoever on the real subject of the story, the much longer collection of the madman's pronouncements, and speaks of Cervantes's "slipshod planning" ("Cervantes' *Licenciado Vidriera*: Its Form and Substance," *West Virginia University Bulletin: Philological Papers* 8 [1951]: 13-31). William Atkinson's judgment is harsher: The work is nothing but a commentary on the Spain of the day, its presentation of its protagonist's journey is a "mistake Cervantes was not to repeat," and its "artistic value as a short story is nil" ("Cervantes, El Pinciano, and the *Novelas Ejemplares*," *Hispanic Review* 16 [1946]:189-208). An unconvincing attempt to account for the flaw in this "split" work in terms of Cervantes's lack of control of his tale can be found in R. El Saffar's *Novel to Romance* (Baltimore, 1974), pp. 51-52: "The disjunction . . . suggests on a deeper level the confusion of an author too much bound up with his character to be able either to understand him fully or to control the story of which the character is part." A succinct account of the numerous problems of interpretation surrounding the story can be found in Robert H. Russell's perceptive analysis of its disturbing depiction of "la deshumanización y la destrucción de un hombre, ya como víctima de los demás, ya como víctima de sí mismo," "*El Licenciado Vidriera*: nomenclatura y estructura," *Studia Philologica Salmanticensia* 3 (1979):242-48, a study that reached me following the completion of this chapter.

[2] *Erasmo y España* (Mexico, 1966), p. 779. As I shall try to make clear in the following pages, the Erasmism of Cervantes's tale is far more profound than Bataillon's remark would indicate.

[3] See Foulché-Delbosc: "Vidriera no es sino la máscara tras la cual se cubre el genial escritor," cited by Amezúa, *Cervantes, creador de la novela corta española*, 2 vols. (Madrid, 1956-1958), 2:193. See also Icaza, *Las "Novelas ejemplares" de Cervantes*, p. 190.

ultimately arms, the journey to Italy, the frustrations of an ambitious, unsuccessful man of letters, and the notorious susceptibility to the appeals of satire—all parallels that invite a biographical interpretation of the tale and a sympathetic response to its protagonist. Recently Otis Green has found the coherence of the novella in its artistic mimesis of Cervantes's personal experiences, its recollection of his youthful aspirations, its expression of resentment at their frustration, and its transformation of these personal elements into the basic theme of the misfortunes of an individual whose happiness is destroyed by a society that will not allow him the right to self-realization.[4] The favorable view of the glass licentiate, as a being possessed by a lofty madness, is, moreover, encouraged among critics by the fact that the author created in another work a likeable madman whose pronouncements are frequently marked by compelling insight and wisdom. While there is certainly some justification in the identification of Don Quixote and El Licenciado Vidriera,[5] the temptation to analyze the latter's obsession and behavior through the mediating focus of the former's chivalric madness has, more often than not, provided an obstacle to a proper clarification of the exemplary tale.

Whether or not the crazed man of glass is to some extent a portrait of the author, *El Licenciado Vidriera* remains an exemplary tale, and its meaning must be sought primarily in its language and design rather than in the biographical backgrounds that may have affected its genesis. For all its apparent formal discontinuities, the tale is, like all the other stories in the collection, a coherently constructed work of literature, and the connections between its narrative frame and its satirical fragments are far more intimate than is commonly supposed.

[4] "*El Licenciado Vidriera*: Its Relation to the *Viaje del Parnaso* and the *Examen de Ingenios* of Huarte," *Linguistic and Literary Studies in Honor of Helmut A. Hatzfeld*, ed. A. Crisafulli (Washington, 1964), pp. 213-20. Frank Casa stresses the unity of the tale as the "intellectual biography of a wise man who is rejected by a society he wishes to reform" ("The Structural Unity of *El Licenciado Vidriera*," *Bulletin of Hispanic Studies* 41 [1964]:242-44). As the following makes clear, I agree with Casa that the coherence of the tale must be sought in its central theme of knowledge and education, but I propose a radically different interpretation of its presentation of its protagonist. Other valuable reconsiderations of the tale which have attempted to integrate the frame and the collection of apothegms have been offered by L. Rosales, J. Casalduero, A. Oliver, and E. C. Riley (see below). For a review of recent criticism of the work and a sympathetic interpretation of its biographical implications, see Gwynn Edwards, "Cervantes' *El Licenciado Vidriera*'s Meaning and Structure," *Modern Language Review* 68 (1973):559-68.

[5] See, for example, Luis Rosales: "la locura de ambos consiste en ser únicamente verdaderos . . . El Licenciado Vidriera es un pequeño Don Quijote" (*Cervantes y la libertad*, 2 vols. [Madrid, 1960], 1:188).

In its structure *El Licenciado Vidriera* consists of three distinct parts, the first describing the protagonist's education and including his studies in Salamanca and his journey to Italy, the second recording his famous exploits as the railing philosopher, the Licenciado Vidriera, and the third narrating rapidly the restoration of his sanity, his flight from a world that values shameless impostors more than honest, sensible men, and his good death in the service of his country and his faith. Each part is introduced by a major event, which has mythic overtones and is directly allusive to the profound theme implied in the title of the work—the problem of knowledge.[6] The significance of the three events and their regulatory function in the exemplary context of the work are heightened by the unmodulated quality of the intervening action, which flows rapidly between these high points with no evident gradation to counter its centrifugal energies. The author appears to have little concern for qualitative differentiation in the numerous incidents he records or for dramatic pacing and articulation in the movement of his plot. A tendency toward the discontinuous marks the entire narrative, and a total dispersion of action is in fact prevented only by the prominence of the decisive events at the turning points of the story.

From the moment of the protagonist's awakening in the opening scene, events follow one upon another at a uniform, breathless pace. Although he dedicates himself to the contemplative life of the scholar, there is anything but tranquility in his restless pursuit of knowledge and its glories. It is perhaps surprising that in his satirical tale Cervantes shows so little interest in description. The account of Tomás Rodaja's education, travels, and declamations is in fact one of Cervantes's sparest narratives. Critics have observed, occasionally regretfully when reading the tale as a mimesis of biography or seeking within it the dynamic interaction of character and setting that distinguishes Cervantes's novelistic fiction, that the protagonist's journey to Italy offers little atmosphere or *ambiente*. Any reader who approaches the tale with the perspectives and effects of Renaissance travel literature in mind is bound to be struck immediately by the numerous verbs of action and the preponderance of the preterite tense in Cervantes's account of the journey, as well as by his preference for lists of places and things, which the narrator simply names and refuses to linger on and embody with the concrete features of circumstantial or

---

[6] The most comprehensive treatment of Cervantes's engagement with the problem of knowledge is J. B. Avalle-Arce's "Conocimiento y vida en Cervantes," *Deslindes cervantinos* (Madrid, 1961), pp. 15-80. For his fine observations on *El Licenciado Vidriera*, see pp. 61-65.

experienced realities.[7] Ironically, while the young scholar, like many other cultivators of the intellect, is an obsessive observer, a voyeur from the safe regions beyond the confines of social interaction, the narrative refuses to dwell on what he sees. It focuses instead on the action of his seeing: "All of this he looked at and noted and arranged in its proper place"; "he went by sea to Naples, where the admiration which he derived from having seen Rome was increased by that which seeing Naples aroused in him, a city in his opinion and in that of all who have beheld it the finest in Europe, and indeed in the whole world"; "he saw Palermo, and subsequently Messina; the setting and beauty of Palermo seemed splendid to him"; "he saw neither walls nor partitions, because all were covered with crutches, shrouds, chains, fetters, handcuffs, tresses of hair, waxen busts, and paintings and *retablos*"; "he saw Ghent and Brussels, and saw that the whole country was getting itself ready to take up arms and enter on a campaign in the following summer; and having satisfied the desire that compelled him to see what he had seen, he determined to return to Spain"; they told Tomás that the lady said she had been in Italy and Flanders, and to see if he knew her, he went to visit her. The result of this sight and visit was that she fell in love with Tomás, and he failed to see this . . ."[8] As for the objects of the licentiate's insatiable eye, it is not their specific features but rather their multitudinous character that the narrative emphasizes. The traveler discovers that "the life in billets is easy and varied, and every day new and pleasurable things turn

[7] See, for example, R. Schevill and A. Bonilla: ". . . no deja de ser lamentable que las impresiones recibidas por Rodaja durante su viaje por Italia sean de tan escasa sustancia." They contain "nada que nos suministre una idea, por mínima que sea, de la maravillosa cultura que por entonces poseía aquel pueblo" (*Novelas exemplares*, 3 vols. [Madrid, 1922-1925], 3:385). Atkinson criticizes the lack of any interaction between character and setting during the journey, which gives us little more than a "wine-list and a page from the guide-book" ("Cervantes, El Pinciano, and the *Novelas Ejemplares*," p. 202). The following page references to Cervantes's text are to Volume Two of F. Rodríguez Marín's edition, *Novelas ejemplares*, 2 vols. (Madrid, 1957-1962).

[8] "Todo lo miró, y notó, y puso en su punto"; "se fué por mar a Nápoles, donde a la admiración que traía de haber visto a Roma, añadió la que le causó ver a Nápoles, ciudad, a su parecer y al de todos cuantos la han visto, la mejor de Europa, y aun de todo el mundo"; "vió a Palermo, y después a Micina: de Palermo le pareció bien el asiento y belleza"; "no vió paredes ni murallas, porque todas estaban cubiertas de muletas, de mortajas, de cadenas, de grillos, de esposas, de cabelleras, de medios bultos de cera y de pinturas y retablos"; "vió a Gante, y a Bruselas, y vió que todo el país se disponía a tomar las armas para salir en campaña el verano siguiente. Y habiendo cumplido con el deseo que le movió a ver lo que había visto, determinó volverse a España"; "dijéronle a Tomás que aquella dama decía que había estado en Italia y en Flandes, y por ver si la conocía, fué a visitarla, de cuya visita y vista quedó ella enamorada de Tomás; y él sin echar de ver en ello . . ." (pp. 27-33).

up." He is overwhelmed by the abundance of wines, "so many and so different," offered by the innkeeper in Genoa: "the host named more wines and gave them more than Bacchus himself could stow away in his cellars."[9] In Rome he takes note of the "infinite number of relics of bodies of martyrs" and "the concourse and variety of races and nations." The phenomena which race past his gaze are recorded at a reckless pace in the narrative: lists of wines, relics, cities, the hills of Rome.

The Licenciado Vidriera is driven "to see Italy by curiosity," and he believes that "it would be well to see Italy and Flanders and divers other lands and countries, since long travels make men wise."[10] Unlike the pilgrimage to Rome of Cervantes's exemplary wanderers, Periandro and Auristela, the student's Italian journey is a pilgrimage of curiosity, and its object, as Casalduero\ has pointed out, is the acquisition of culture.[11] It assumes that direct\experience of the world is the way to valid knowledge, that knowledge is infinite, and that in the experience of the world's plenitude and novelties there is a delight that is worth striving for. If the principal action of Cervantes's traveler is that of seeing and taking note, his characteristic reaction is the feeling of wonder, of *admiración* and exhilaration before the multitude of novelties which he beholds in his "presente *gaudeamus*" of indulged curiosity: "Tomás also admired the fair tresses of the Genoese women, the gentility and gallant disposition of the men, and the admirable beauty of the city"; "he visited her churches, adored her relics, and admired her grandeur"; "the division of the hills within the city excited in him no less admiration"; "the European [city] the admiration of the Old World, the American the marvel of the New World"; "he arrived at Antwerp, a city no less to marvel at than those he had seen

---

[9] "la vida de los alojamientos es ancha y varia, y cada día se topan cosas nuevas y gustosas" (p. 21); "más vinos nombró el huésped, y más les dió, que pudo tener en sus bodegas el mismo Baco" (p. 25).

[10] "sería bueno ver a Italia y Flandes, y otras diversas tierras y países, pues las luengas peregrinaciones hacen a los hombres discretos" (p. 17).

[11] *Sentido y forma de las "Novelas ejemplares"* (Madrid, 1969), p. 143. Cervantists have pointed out that the licentiate's view of the benefits of travel in education accords perfectly with Renaissance precepts on education. Compare, for example, Montaigne's "le commerce des hommes y est merveilleusement propre, et la visite des pays estrangers . . . pour en rapporter principalement les humeurs de ces nations et leurs façons, et pour frotter et limer nostre cervelle contre celle d'autruy" ("De l'institution des enfans," *Essais*, ed. P. Villey, 3 vols. [Paris, 1930-1931], 1:291). Also John Milton, *Of Education, Complete Poems and Major Prose*, ed. M. Hughes (New York, 1947), p. 639.

in Italy."[12] All of this suggests that Cervantes, as he conceived the figure of his insane man of letters, glimpsed the restlessness and voracity that are characteristic of the intellect in its hunger for knowledge and that have been described, with both admiration and dismay, by philosophers and theologians throughout history. One thinks of the opening of Aristotle's *Metaphysics* and its claim that man is driven by a natural passion to know the world and delight in beholding its wonders; of Erasmus's meditation on the fruits of the tree of the knowledge of good and evil and the seductive appeal of the worldly knowledge which "comes from the earth" and causes man to swell with its possession and, as his Spanish translator puts it, "roll aimlessly until striking against death"; of Charron's description of the perpetual motion of man's inquiring mind as it flutters about the whole world in an instant, probing and meddling with insatiable curiosity, endlessly and futilely pursuing novelties, and, "like Silkworms that are intangled in Webs of their own spinning," constantly falling victim of its own reversals and contradictions; or of Hugo's paeon on the exhilarating movement of science: "La science est continuellement mouvante dans son bienfait. Tout remue en elle, tout change. . . . Cette agitation est superbe. La science est inquiète autour de l'homme; elle a ses raisons."[13] Cervantes's wanderer's restless urgings to see and to take note of what he sees are clearly manifestations of his free intellectuality, but the tale makes it clear beyond any doubt

[12] "admiráronle también al buen Tomás los rubios cabellos de las ginovesas y la gentileza y gallarda disposición de los hombres, la admirable belleza de la ciudad" (p. 25); "visitó sus templos, adoró sus reliquias y admiró su grandeza" (p. 26); "pues no le admiraba menos la división de sus montes" (p. 27); "la [ciudad] de Europa, admiración del mundo antiguo; la de América, espanto del mundo nuevo" (p. 30); "llegó a Amberes, ciudad no menos para maravillar que las que había visto en Italia" (p. 32).

[13] Aristotle, *Metaphysics*, 1.1 *The Works of Aristotle*, ed. and trans. J. A. Smith and W. D. Ross, 12 vols. (Oxford, 1908-1952), 8:980a. Erasmus, *Beatus Vir, Opera Omnia*, ed. J. Le Clerc, 10 vols. (Leiden, 1703-1706), 5:171-95; *El Enquiridion*, ed. D. Alonso (Madrid, 1932), p. 154. P. Charron, *De la Sagesse*, 1.14, trans. G. Stanhope, 2 vols. (London, 1697), 1:129-56. V. Hugo, *William Shakespeare, Oeuvres complètes*, ed. J. Massin, 18 vols. (Paris, 1967-1970), 12:197. In an ascetic inversion of the doctrine of the microcosm, Fray Alonso de Cabrera declares that man's miseries proceed from all the elements of the universe that are incorporated in his corrupted being. Deranged by original sin, man is subject in his animal nature to the violent tyranny of his emotions, passions, and appetites, while in his angelic nature he is tormented by the endlessly turning wheel of thoughts ("la rueda voluble de pensamientos, consejos, y quereres"). Cabrera's sermon is cited by F. Rico, who notes that it was appropriated nearly verbatim by the author of the apocryphal *Guzmán de Alfarache* (*El pequeño mundo del hombre* [Madrid, 1970], pp. 149-50).

that his search for knowledge is not directed toward its proper goal. In the midst of the licentiate's breathless contemplation of the relics in the shrine of Loreto, the narrator observes: "He saw the very room and apartment where the most exalted embassy, and the most important that ever occurred, was received, which all the heavens and all the angels and all the dwellers in the eternal mansions *saw and did not understand*."[14] There are indeed things which one can see clearly and fail to understand. Had he listened to the litany of Loreto with "ears of the spirit," Cervantes's scholar might have discovered the truth that was to elude him throughout his life, that the "seat of all wisdom" is with the Virgin and that its foundation is the single law of charity.

As a tale probing the mysteries of knowledge, *El Licenciado Vidriera* exploits the age-old association of wandering and curiosity and incorporates the type of pilgrimage which is familiar in wisdom literature of all ages, from the hazardous journey of the youth in the *Wisdom of Solomon*, to the famous flight of the medieval Alexander, to Petrarch's confessional account of his ascent of Mt. Ventoux, and to Rabelais's tale of Panurge's frenzied search around the world for the oracle of the Holy Bottle.[15] Indeed the misdirection of the quest outward into the world was a frequent theme of such journeys, and in Cervantes's age the traditional consciousness of the idleness of the quest of curiosity was highly developed. Thus Bartolomé Cairasco de Figueroa begins his poem *Peregrinación* by pointing to the perversion of the true pilgrimage when it is directed toward the acquisition of knowledge:

> No es Peregrinación aquel vagante,
> Inquieto y solícito camino
> Del que por ser curioso es caminante.[16]

[14] "Vió el mismo aposento y estancia donde se relató la más alta embajada y de más importancia que *vieron, y no entendieron*, todos los cielos, y todos los ángeles, y todos los moradores de las moradas sempiternas" (p. 30; italics added).

[15] Hans Blumenberg repeatedly discusses the importance of the symbol of the journey in traditional thought concerning the aims of knowledge and the value of curiosity (*Die Legitimität der Neuzeit* [Frankfurt am Main, 1966]). For the modernity of Petrarch's confession, with its dramatic presentation of a collision between the traditional Christian and a new secular attitude toward curiosity, see pp. 336-38. For the importance of curiosity and the joy of marvelous discoveries as the motives of Panurge's quest, see his exhortation of Pantagruel: "Je vous ay long temps cogneu amateur de peregrinité, et desyrant tous jours veoir et tous jours apprendre. Nous voirons choses admirables, et m'en croyez" (*Tiers Livre*, 47; *Oeuvres*, ed. A. Lefranc et al., 6 vols. [Paris, 1912-1955], 5:327).

[16] "The Pilgrimage is not that wandering, restless, and troubled way of him who for curiosity's sake is a traveler." B.A.E. 42:466; the poem is cited by Juergen Hahn in his *The Origins of the Baroque Concept of "Peregrinatio"* (Chapel Hill, 1973), pp. 15-17. The glass licentiate is one of the numerous fools that fascinated the Renaissance

And in drawing a villainous antagonist to oppose his hero Recaredo, a true pilgrim, whose journeys, which take him to Rome and the dungeons of the infidels, are aimed at the perfecting of his spiritual love and the purification of his religious faith, Cervantes presents the treacherous Arnesto as a pilgrim of curiosity: "I found my mortal enemy, Count Arnesto, who I learned was on his way to Rome, along with four servants masked, and himself disguised, motivated more by curiosity than by Catholic devotion."[17]

Probably the most famous pilgrimage of knowledge in the age was that of Odysseus, the archetypal man of curiosity, and Cervantes's association of his protagonist's wanderings with the ordeals of the Greek hero offers us a clue to his intentions in constructing the elliptical and elusive parable as a frame for the heavy, unequivocal pronouncements at its center. He describes Tomás Rodaja as a *curioso*

---

imagination, and in his obsessive curiosity, the idleness of his knowledge, and his restless movements, he resembles a certain type of figure that appeared in the rich literature of folly of the period. In his sermons based on Sebastian Brant's *Narrenschiff*, Geiler von Kaisersberg condemns the wanderer who is driven by curiosity to see other lands and peoples. Directing his attention entirely toward external and unessential things, he "begeht ein unnütze und verdamliche fürwitz," loads himself with "wissenheit und erfahrnussen," and finds himself incapable of looking inward for the kind of self-knowledge that the Christian must discover if he is to be saved. Geiler speaks of another group of madmen who are driven to still their inner despair and impatience by wandering about the world gazing at its curiosities. To emphasize their inconstancy and aimlessness, he employs the image of the spinning circle of futility: "sie lauffen herumb gleich wie ein Windtmül, die treibt der windt auff welche seiten er darzu gath." Such wandering rewards the fools with nothing but a troubled and restless spirit, and they would do well to bear in mind the proverb: "Bleib da du bist, und uberwindt, das in dir ist." He advises: "So werden dir alle Stett gleich und alle menschen recht. . . . [du] sollest dich hüten, das du nicht mit jedermann zanckest und haderest, sonder dich selbs bindest, und in allen dingen dein zungen und frefflen mundt im zaum haltest" (see *Das Kloster*, ed. J. Scheible [Stuttgart, 1845], pp. 587-90; the passage is discussed by Werner Welzig in *Beispielhafte Figuren: Tor, Abenteurer und Einsiedler bei Grimmelshausen* [Graz-Cologne, 1963], pp. 100-114). In considering the perversity in the glass licentiate's pilgrimage, one might compare the most spectacular demonization of wandering in the age, Milton's *Paradise Lost*. The devils pursue false wisdom in their underworld symposiums, "lost in wand'ring mazes" (2.561), Eve is driven to the place where she yields to the allure of forbidden knowledge by a "strange desire of knowledge by wand'ring" (9.1135-36), and she and her spouse descend into the fallen order of human history following their sin, "with wand'ring steps and slow" (12.648). The greatest pilgrim of curiosity in the epic is, of course, Satan, who, tempting "with wand'ring feet/ The dark unbottom'd infinite Abyss, embarks on his perverse voyage of discovery through the fearsome realm of Chaos (2.404-405; see ed. M. Y. Hughes [New York, 1935]).

[17] "Hallé al conde Arnesto, mi mortal enemigo, que con cuatro criados disfrazados y encubierto más por ser curioso que por ser católico, entendí que iba a Roma" (*La española inglesa, Obras completas*, ed. A. Valbuena Prat [Madrid, 1956], p. 872).

lingering among the "enjoyments and diversions (*pasatiempos*)" offered by Calypso in Venice, which "almost induced him to forget his original purpose."[18] Since Cicero's interpretation of Odysseus's temptations by the sirens as an allegorical expression of the way in which man's innate desire for knowledge, his natural curiosity, can cause him to falter in fulfilling his duty to his country, the ordeals and motives of Odysseus had frequently been assimilated to philosophical explorations of the problem of knowledge.[19] Dante had transformed him into a notorious example of a perverse lust for experience and improper knowledge, describing his defiant voyage of discovery beyond the limits set by God and finding in the destruction that rewarded his quest a somber warning for all who would place too much confidence in their merely human powers of understanding.[20] Throughout the Renaissance his adventures and ordeals continued to be invoked in connection with proper and improper knowledge. For Petrarch Odysseus is the man "who desired to see too much of the world."[21] John Colet reminded his readers that the false and fleeting things of this world lure man's eyes and desires and, with the sweet song of the sirens, easily distract him from thinking about the proper destination of his journey across the sea of life, rest in God.[22] Erasmus advises the scholar to avoid the fruitless terminological complexities of the scholastic dialecticians and likens them to the cliffs of the sirens.[23] Francisco Sánchez denounces dialectic as "another Circe who converts her lovers into asses," and, finding inspiration in Odysseus's ability to escape from the sorceress, he invites her enslaved admirers to stop braying syllogisms and to turn to "robust nature," "beautiful reality," and to become "owners and masters of the world."[24] With even more confidence in an empirical approach toward the knowledge of nature than Sánchez, who still insisted that science must seek es-

---

[18] "Por poco fueran los de Calipso los regalos y pasatiempos que halló nuestro curioso en Venecia, pues casi le hacían olvidar de su primer intento" (p. 31).

[19] *De Finibus*, 5.18; see Blumenberg, *Die Legitimität der Neuzeit*, pp. 258-59.

[20] *La divina comedia, Inferno*, 26; see Blumenberg, *Die Legitimität der Neuzeit*, pp. 333-36. For the Christian and classical attitudes toward virtue, fame, and intellectuality which converge on Dante's depiction of the disastrous consequences of Odysseus's insatiable thirst for knowledge and glory, see Hugo Friedrich, "Odysseus in der Hölle," *Romanische Literaturen*, 2 vols. (Frankfort, 1972), 2:71-118.

[21] *Trionfo della Fama*, 2.17-18; see Friedrich, "Odysseus in der Hölle," p. 116.

[22] *An Exposition of St. Paul's First Epistle to the Corinthians*, ed. and trans. J. H. Lupton (London, 1874), pp. 84-85.

[23] *De Ratione Studii*, ed. J.-C. Margolin, *Opera Omnia*, Vol. I, pt. 2 (Amsterdam, 1971), p. 118.

[24] *Que nada se sabe* (Buenos Aires, 1944), pp. 187-89.

sences of the things it observes and concluded that it can never hope to discover them, Francis Bacon reversed the lesson that Dante had celebrated in the myth, prefacing his *Instauratio Magna* with an emblem depicting Odysseus's ship sailing triumphantly through the Pillars of Hercules and bearing the inscription "Multi pertransibunt et augebitur scientia."[25] While Sánchez and Bacon could find Odysseus, the curious wanderer, a heroic example for those who would bring the benefits of new methods of science to the world, writers more exclusively concerned with man's moral responsibilities and his Christian destiny continued to present his trials as the temptations of false knowledge and his escape from them as exemplary of Christian duty and salvation. Thus in their pilgrimage to retrieve the wayward hero Rinaldo from the sorceress's false paradise, Tasso's knights, Carlo and Ubaldo, are reminded that, in its search for eternal truths, man's reason is as blind as an owl staring into the sun, and they are forced to glance back to the ill-fated voyage of Odysseus, "di veder vago e di saper," and the watery grave bearing witness to his foolish daring.[26] And in Calderón's mythological *auto*, *Los encantos de la culpa*, Odysseus, the Christian Everyman, must resist all the delights of Circe's island, which include "ciencias prohibidas" and the key to unlocking the meaning concealed in all of Nature's mysterious signatures.[27]

The allusion to Odysseus and Calypso, then, associates Cervantes's protagonist and his actions with a venerable tradition of concern with the problem of knowledge, and the myth points clearly to the illicit nature of his curiosity and to the power of knowledge as a diabolical temptation. In fact it is one of several demonic motifs that Cervantes insinuates into his account of the student's pursuit of knowledge and that anticipate the decisive moment of the parable, his fall into madness. Moreover, Cervantes's coupling of his curiosity and his "forgetfulness of his first intention" in Venice recalls specifically the Augustinian view of curiosity as a threat to man's proper use of his memory.

---

[25] See Blumenberg (*Die Legitimität der Neuzeit*, pp. 333ff.) for the implications of the reinterpretation of the myth in relation to the transvaluation of curiosity at the dawn of the modern epoch.

[26] *Gerusalemme liberata*, 14.46, 15.25-26; see ed. L. Bonfigli (Bari, 1930), pp. 326, 341.

[27] *Obras completas*, ed. A. Valbuena Prat (Madrid, 1967), 3:415. For a survey of the interpretations of the Odysseus myth in the literature of Cervantes's Spain, see Ludwig Schrader, "Odysseus im Siglo de Oro: Zur mythologischen Allegorie im Theater Calderóns und seiner Zeitgenossen," *Spanische Literatur im goldenen Zeitalter: Fritz Schalk zum 70. Geburtstag*, ed. H. Baader and E. Loos (Frankfurt am Main, 1973), pp. 401-439. The study does not, however, deal with the implications of the moralizations of the myth in relation to the problem of knowledge.

Through recollection of his origin and his transcendental destiny, the Christian turns in on himself and finds his way back to God. Curiosity, a "concupiscence of the eyes," drives him outward into the multiplicity of external things, which arrest his attention, engage his affections, and lead him to a state of forgetfulness.[28] The importance of the theme in Cervantes's tale is evident in the opening scene, when the child Tomás awakens at the foot of the tree, claims "that he had forgotten the name of the district from which he came, and that he was on his way to the city of Salamanca to seek a master whom he might serve, if only he would allow him time to study,"[29] and announces that his destiny is the pursuit of glory through learning. Thus the quest of Cervantes's fanatical scholar, whose purpose violates all Christian teaching about the proper uses of knowledge, is immediately associated with a loss of memory concerning his origin. During his journey to Italy he slips into the state of forgetfulness in Genoa as well as in Venice, for, immediately after surviving the terrors of the sea voyage, he and his companions "forgot all the past tempests in the present *gaudeamus*."[30] Such lapses are all the more striking in that he is endowed with a prodigious memory, "cosa de espanto," which wins him fame at the University of Salamanca.

As we move into the second part of the tale following the protagonist's metamorphosis into the glass licentiate, we observe what at first glance appears to be an abrupt and major change in its narrative procedures, as dialogue and indirect discourse replace reported action as the dominant narrative medium. Yet, for all the formal differences separating the two parts, the series of brief exchanges between the Licenciado Vidriera and his interlocutors should be seen as an intensification of the tendency toward the discontinuous that marks the narrative from its beginning. Here the absence of any architectonic

---

[28] *Confessions*, Book 10. See Blumenberg: ". . . die Erinnerung gibt dem Menschen den authentischen und von der Welt unabhängig machenden Bezug auf seine Herkunft, auf seine metaphysische 'Geschichte' und damit auf seine transzendente Bedingtheit. *Memoria* und *curiositas* verhalten sich wie Innerlichkeit und Äusserlichkeit, aber nicht als alternative 'Verhaltensweisen' des Menschen, sondern so, dass die Erinnerung als wesenhafte Realisierung nur durch die Gewaltsamkeit der Weltaffektion niedergehalten wird oder in dem Masse sich zur Geltung bringt, wie diese 'Reizüberflutung' abgewehrt und eingedämmt werden kann" (*Die Legitimität der Neuzeit*, p. 303).

[29] "que el nombre de su tierra se le había olvidado, y que iba a la ciudad de Salamanca a buscar un amo a que servir, por solo que le diese estudio" (p. 10).

[30] "pusieron en olvido todas las borrascas pasadas con el presente *gaudeamus*" (p. 22).

arrangement of the constituent parts and the lack of attention to pacing, subordination, development, and climax are, of course, even more striking than in the framing parable. The encounters follow upon each other rapidly, their subjects ever changing, each an autonomous unit in a list in which the sequence of individual items could evidently be rearranged in any way or expanded indefinitely. The central section of *El Licenciado Vidriera* is the most traditional part of the tale, and Cervantes undoubtedly composed it with numerous processional forms of satirical and apothegmatic literature in mind: the colloquies of Lucian; the philosophical biographies of Diogenes Laertius; such medieval forms of profession, type, and sin satire as the dance of death and the ship of fools; the popular Renaissance developments of these traditions such as Erasmus's colloquies and *The Praise of Folly*, and their contemporary Spanish descendants, Mondragón's *Censura de la locura humana y excelencias della* and Argensola's *Democrito*. However, it is important to note that the methods of exposition and disposition that Cervantes may have appropriated from such genres, all of which are marked by discontinuity and digressiveness, were ideally suited to the particular intentions that in fact distinguish his work from its satirical ancestors. The sprawling formlessness and rapid development of discrete, unsubordinated fragments, the norms of satirical writing, amplify the effects that Cervantes has already achieved in the first part of his tale. The movement and fragmentation reach full disintegration, and it is mirrored in the pathological condition of the protagonist, whose being splits apart into mind and body. The misdirection of the restless intellect in its pursuit of false knowledge turns into the disarticulated, aimless motion of madness.[31] Erasmus wrote that "multiplex est hujus mundi sapientia, divina simplicissima est," and pointed out that the fools who ceaselessly pursue this earthbound knowledge, lose themselves amid the desires of this world, where "totus flectuat atque aestuat," never find inner tranquility, and are blown about like chaff in the wind.[32]

In *Cervantes y la libertad* Luis Rosales offers an excellent analysis of

[31] Madness was linked with aimless motion and constant change in the imagination of the time. For example, Guevara, in his diatribe against seafaring, equates ship, motion, and insanity: "Es loco el navío pues siempre se mueve, es loco el marinero pues nunca está de un parecer, es loca el agua pues nunca está queda, y es loco el aire que siempre corre" (*Arte de Marear*, ed. R. O. Jones [Exeter, 1972], p. 19). In the iconography of the Renaissance a symbol of madness was the turning windmill (see C. Ripa, *Iconologia* [facsimile reproduction of the edition of Rome, 1603; Hildesheim, 1970], p. 381).

[32] See *Beatus Vir, Opera Omnia*, ed. Le Clerc, 5:183ff.

the effects of dispersion produced by the narrative of *El Licenciado Vidriera*, argues that its action fails completely to unite in a coherent configuration, contrasts its "highly insecure technique" with the "exacting and extraordinary technical control" of the author's masterpieces, and suggests that the tale belongs to an early period of Cervantes's literary activity.[33] As I have suggested above, the centrifugal nature of the action in Cervantes's tale makes the few events which do bind the proliferating fragments into a recognizable shape all the more striking. The crucial event is, of course, the licentiate's encounter with the mysterious woman, which results in his startling plunge into insanity and gives the story a sudden, unexpected change of direction. As is the case with nearly every occurrence in the framing parable, the encounter is "underwritten," so to speak, presented as a tantalizing fragment that invites the reader to fill in the empty spaces it contains with both circumstantial details and symbolic implications. In its undeveloped, allusive quality the central event has remained one of the most puzzling elements in the tale, and Cervantists are still far from agreement as to its meaning. Moreover, some have been inclined to censure it as an artistic flaw, finding that its obvious significance in its effect on the ensuing action is at odds with its brevity and its lack of motivation in terms of what preceded it in the text. Frank Casa has noted the oddity in Cervantes's inclusion of a magical fruit in what appears to be the depiction of a conventional case of scholarly melancholy, and Armand Singer has gone so far as to discount the entire episode as an unnecessary and capricious addition.[34]

Such a view is correct insofar as it emphasizes the inappropriateness

---

[33] ". . . el ritmo narrativo es más sucinto que eficaz; suprime los detalles secundarios—que nunca llegan a organizarse en un ambiente—y no destaca la importancia de ningún episodio; la narración tiene carácter de proemio y lleva al lector por la antesala de la novela y no por la novela; la acción no se concentra, se dispersa a medida que avanza, para quedar suspensa en el final; los personajes no se individualizan, y, finalmente, la fábula entrecortada y deshecha no es armónica, ni se puede reducir a unidad" (1:191). See also Julián Apraiz's judgment that the tale can hardly be considered a novella at all, since it lacks the essential feature of the genre—a coherent plot (*Estudio histórico-crítico sobre las "Novelas ejemplares" de Cervantes* [Victoria, 1901], p. 69).

[34] See Casa, "The Structural Unity of *El Licenciado Vidriera*"; Singer, "Cervantes' *Licenciado Vidriera*: Its Form and Substance." Similarly, Green is concerned to reveal the clinical accuracy in Cervantes's presentation of the madness and interprets the love philter simply as a poison that rendered the victim's disposition to melancholy more acute ("El Licenciado Vidriera: Its Relation to the *Viaje del Parnaso* and the *Examen de Ingenios* of Huarte"). El Saffar finds in the inappropriateness of the fruit and its poison a sign that Cervantes failed to understand his character and the links binding the youthful Tomás and the glass licentiate (*Novel to Romance*, p. 56).

of the licentiate's encounter with the woman as a clinically plausible cause of his mental derangement. However, it fails to see that Cervantes is far more interested in the exploitation of madness for moral and philosophical purposes than in the clinically accurate depiction of a state of psychosis. Cervantes composed this crucial scene relying on the language of myth rather than the language of science, and, in its highly concentrated and allusive nature, it was undoubtedly far less elusive for his contemporary audience than it is for the twentieth-century reader. The woman's startling appearance in the tale occurs at the climax of the licentiate's education. She is presented as a predatory temptress, "luring" the students of the university community as if they were "birds," and all that we are told of her past is that she has been in Italy and Flanders. Her attributes as a character are drastically limited; she is defined by a single action, that of temptation, and by a geographical place, the place that had attracted the curious pilgrim of knowledge. Tomás is motivated "to see" her by the same insatiable curiosity that has driven him to Flanders and Italy. The offer of the fruit to the curious student that follows may make little sense in the context of contemporary treatises describing causes and symptoms of *insania melancholicorum*, but in Cervantes's tale it is a most coherent and effective climax to a series of motifs associating education and demonic temptation that are sounded from the beginning of the tale. Indeed both parts of the protagonist's education are imaginatively linked with such temptation. He leaves his friends' home in Malaga to return to his studies in Salamanca, because, as the narrator informs us, the university city "bewitches all who have ever tasted its peaceful pleasures, compelling them to return."[35] His journey to Italy contains several motifs of temptation and impending fall— from his surrender to the persuasive arguments of the captain, who conceals from him all the burdens, the responsibilities, and the dangers of the soldier's life ("which is so near to death") and succeeds in overcoming his *discreción* by emphasizing the greater freedom and the sensuous delights that he will experience in Italy, to his forgetfulness, despite his prodigious memory, of past storms in the *gaudeamus* of life in Genoa with its beautiful women, its marvelous sights, and the innumerable wines which the innkeeper can conjure up as if by magic. Moreover, as I have pointed out above, he falls victim to the seductive allure of the sights and "regalos y pasatiempos" of Venice, which are likened by the narrator to the temptations of forgetfulness offered by

[35] "enhechiza la voluntad de volver a ella a todos los que de la apacibilidad de su vivienda han gustado" (p. 12).

the legendary temptress Calypso, who becomes an actual prefiguration of the evil woman who brings about his metamorphosis. Indeed, even as it recapitulates all these motifs in the text, the episode of the tasting of the fruit points beyond them to the archetypal Christian tale of the dangers of illicit curiosity, the temptation and fall of Adam and Eve. Once we recognize the implications of the central event of temptation and fall, the elliptical, suggestive scenes that initiate the other phases of the tale become intelligible as parts of its total design. The opening scene, which follows immediately on a title announcing the theme of knowledge and presents the child Rodaja, dressed as a *"labrador,"* sleeping at the foot of a tree beside the flowing waters of the Tormes, clearly looks forward to the scene of the tasting of the fruit, just as both scenes look forward to the brief appearance of the Hieronymite friar, who through "grace and knowledge" restores Tomás's sanity. For all its fragmentation and its disjointedness, we discern in the action of *El Licenciado Vidriera* a coherent background of archetypal symbolism that emphasizes that the protagonist's transformation must be viewed in moral terms as a fall and that his fall must be connected with his acquisition of knowledge. In the sharp outlines uniting its major events, the story assumes the shape of a parable of knowledge.[36]

---

[36] In pointing to the presence of such archetypal symbolism, I am not suggesting that the tale is a carefully designed reenactment of the myths that loom behind its major events. Cervantes is not an allegorist, and his use of such symbols is fragmentary rather than systematic, allusive and oblique rather than precise. Moreover, he is seldom interested in the sustained development of a mythic analogue characteristic of rigorous allegorical writing, and his allusions to archetypal symbols generally have a broad range of association and must be interpreted in conjunction with the other elements of the narrative—actions, themes, and characters portrayed—which condition and are in turn conditioned by their presence. Casalduero's assertion that "Cervantes recrea el pecado original" is perhaps misleading, but he is certainly right in associating Tomás's tasting of the fruit with "el pecado de la inteligencia" and in insisting that, regardless of how we choose to construe the elliptical symbolism of the scene, the one thing that we must not do is "pasar por ella como si fuera un mero recurso novelesco, porque entonces empobrecemos todo el conjunto" (*Sentido y forma de las "Novelas ejemplares,"* pp. 147-49). At the same time I would point out that there is a good deal of irony and playfulness in the evocation of the mythic background, an irony that lightens the philosophical atmosphere of the parable and that attenuates the somber tone of several of its satirical pronouncements (see below) and the bitterness implied by its conclusion. The *Licenciado Vidriera* is one of numerous "Socratic" works of the Erasmian movement which, like the Sileni Alcibiadis described by Erasmus in his influential colloquy, present their most profound truths concealed amid amusing trifles. For the general tendency of satirical literature to manipulate myths with such irony, see N. Frye, *Anatomy of Criticism* (Princeton, 1957), pp. 321-22.

THE MADNESS OF THE CYNIC

As I have suggested above, any attempt to understand the meaning of *El Licenciado Vidriera* must confront the problem of the protagonist's madness. The very title not only implies the priority of the theme of knowledge but also points to the centrality of that part of Tomás Rodaja's experience when he is insane and assumes the name of El Licenciado Vidriera. It can be argued, of course, that one of the most traditional features of the tale as a satirical narration is its presentation of a shocking metamorphosis creating an unusual perspective from which the satirical wanderer can observe a panorama of abuses.[37] However, just as the pilgrimage is most significant precisely for what distinguishes it from the traditional device of satirical exposition, so the figure of the protagonist in his transformed state and the peculiar nature of that state are far more interesting than the objects of his survey.

As in the case of *Don Quixote*, madness in Cervantes's exemplary tale is closely connected with the essential moral, philosophical, and literary themes of the work, and its presentation is fundamentally ambivalent. There is clearly something of the visionary in the insane man of letters, whose heightened intellectuality enables him to see through the illusions that fill the lives of nearly everyone else in his society and whose uncompromising morality inspires him to unmask and denounce their vices, impostures, and pretentions. In a sense there is absolutely nothing discontinuous in the abrupt change of direction in the story at the point when the protagonist is unexpectedly afflicted with insanity, for the shape that he assumes at the moment of his graduation is truly the culmination of his education. The glass of his delusion is in fact symbolic of the keen insight with which he is gifted and the freedom of a man totally dedicated to the spirit: "He told them . . . to ask him what questions they pleased, adding

---

[37] Cervantes's major satirical works—*El Licenciado Vidriera*, *El casamiento engañoso y el coloquio de los perros*, *Rinconete y Cortadillo*, and *Don Quijote de la Mancha*—exploit the device for a variety of purposes and effects. In nearly every case the particular nature of the metamorphosis is of some importance in the development of the major themes of the work, whether the metamorphosis serves the purposes of satirical castigation or the establishment of a perspective for penetrating vision. In the *Quixote* the metamorphosis can in fact become a process directly opposed to satirical depiction of character, as when a type, under the impact of concrete experience, metamorphoses into a shocking individual. The technique supports the revolutionary transformation of the work from satire into novel. The device of metamorphosis was extremely popular in the satire of Cervantes's age, which cultivated it in imitation of Lucian and Apuleius. For an analysis of its use in their writings, see Ronald Paulson, *The Fictions of Satire* (Baltimore, 1967), pp. 31-58.

that he would answer them with more understanding, because he was made of glass, and not of flesh and blood; glass, he said, is a subtle and delicate material: the soul acts through it with more promptitude and efficiency than through the body, which is heavy and earthy."[38] At the same time the metamorphosis of Tomás Rodaja is clearly satirical retribution, and as such it is quite traditional in presenting the castigation as an emblem of his folly. The scholar's fanatical devotion to the mind and the spirit is grotesquely caricatured in his removal from his body and in the terribly high price which, in his state of constant anxiety, he must pay for his knowledge. In other words, the madness of the licentiate is, in one very important sense, a precise objectified image of his foolishness.[39] The knowledge which he has pursued so avidly and recklessly has turned into poison and inflicted a dreadful torment on him. As I shall point out below, the fruits of his knowledge, which earn him the glory he seeks, are all tainted with the venom of slander and malice. While the glass of intense vision elevates, glass belongs to the order of inanimate nature, and, when Cervantes describes his protagonist crated in straw and shipped about as a breakable commodity, we witness a ridiculous satirical descent of the impostor into the world of the thing and the mechanism.[40] The descent is underscored through scatological elements, as the frenzied intellectual refuses to eat anything except bits of fruit extended to him in a chamber pot attached to a stick. Glass is also a thing of fragility, and, when the protagonist trembles beneath the thunder, fears breakage from human contact, and is domiciled in the unpopulated fields and the haylofts of inns, we observe not only a comic reduction to the subhuman orders of the thing and the animal,

[38] "Decía . . . que le preguntasen lo que quisiesen porque a todo les respondería con más entendimiento, por ser hombre de vidrio y no de carne; que el vidrio, por ser de materia sutil y delicada, obraba por ella el alma con más promptitud y eficacia que no por la del cuerpo, pesada y terrestre" (p. 37).

[39] In his satirical writings Cervantes frequently makes use of the traditional technique of *contrappasso*. See, for example, the death of Clodio, the slanderer, by an arrow through his mouth, the enchainment of Rosamunda, the lustful schemer, to Clodio (*Persiles*, 1.14), the hideous illness of the Alférez Campuzano and the physical ugliness of Cañizares in *El casamiento engañoso y el coloquio de los perros*, the repugnant physical attributes of various evildoers in the criminal world of *Rinconete y Cortadillo*, and the mistreatment of Don Quixote in the episode of the windmill, which was commonly held to be a symbol of madness (see above). See Paulson's discussion of this primordial technique of satire and its relation to the curse (*The Fictions of Satire*, pp. 9-14).

[40] See also the glass man's response to the children who bombard him with rubbish: "¿Soy yo por ventura el monte Testacho de Roma, para que me tiréis tantos tiestos y tejas?" (p. 39).

but also a grotesque *contrappasso* disclosing the isolation that he has imposed on himself from his awakening in *"soledad"* at the beginning of his pursuit of knowledge to his flight before the amorous advances of a woman. As we reflect on the validity of his angry pronouncements and the features that he shares both with the mad idealist, Don Quixote, and with Cervantes, his creator, we must not overlook the power of the traditional reductive techniques that Cervantes employs in the presentation of his madness.

The madness of the glass licentiate is fundamentally paradoxical, and Cervantes's balanced treatment of him as visionary and fool is attested by the widespread disagreement among Cervantists as to whether or not he is to be taken as a reliable spokesman for his author. As I have pointed out in commenting on the presentation of the other-world in *La Gitanilla*, Cervantes was fascinated with paradoxical pronouncement and its capacities for the expression of complex networks of ideas, and, as a general rule, any effort to arrest the movement of his paradoxes by seeking a static hierarchy in the truths that they enfold will lead to misinterpretation. Much of Cervantes's finest art involves the posing of questions that are answerable only in their formulation, and Ortega's resigned vision of Don Quijote as a question mark hovering ambiguously at the distant horizon of the Mancha while interpretors continue to grope vainly for its meaning is in reality a tribute to the depth of his insight into the work whose resistance to clarification he laments.

If the questions always remain to unsettle the minds of his readers, they can do so only when properly posed, when the problems that Cervantes allows to converge on them are recognized, understood, and evaluated within the fiction containing them. The ambivalences of Cervantes's Gypsy world, for example, are correctly understood only when one understands the issues in Renaissance thought concerning nature, freedom, ceremonialism, and social organization which are embodied imaginatively within it. While it is probable that the man of glass in isolation will continue to appeal to all ages as a powerful symbol of superhuman intelligence, uncompromising rationality, isolated hyperintellectuality, overly developed sensitivity, and life-denying spirituality, it remains undeniable that Cervantes created him deliberately and carefully as a Cynic philosopher, and it seems reasonable to suppose that he understood the issues raised by his madness in terms of that philosophy. The fact is that, in the particular shape and actions of his glass licentiate as a railing Cynic, Cervantes poses a philosophical problem with profound implications concerning ethics, epistemology, and literature, and they can be understood only if we give some attention to the issues associated with Cynic philosophy in Renaissance thought.[41]

Antonio Oliver has pointed out that numerous details link Cervantes's deranged scholar to Diogenes and other members of the Cynic school of philosophy: his beggar's dress, his staff, his manner of eating and drinking with his hands, his preference for living outdoors, his harsh criticism of society, and his six-month illness, which could represent the purifying *askesis* demanded of initiates by the Cynics and other philosophical sects. On the basis of such links and the incisiveness of the licentiate's exposure of human errors and weaknesses, Oliver concludes that Cervantes's "Diogenes" is a "reflejo ideal de la mente de Cervantes," a type of fictional superman through whom the author could express his indignation with man's inadequacies. The meaning of the tale is to be found in its untroubled resurrection of the critical

---

[41] Undoubtedly Cervantes would have understood the psychology of the glass licentiate in terms of contemporary theories concerning psychotic behavior patterns and body chemistry, that is, the disposition of the humors, which, according to traditional psycho-physiological medical doctrine, accounts for the personality features of all human beings (see Green, "El Licenciado Vidriera: Its Relation to the *Viaje del Parnaso* and the *Examen de Ingenios* of Huarte," and Casa, "The Structural Unity of *El Licenciado Vidriera*"). It has been pointed out by a twentieth-century clinical psychologist that the psychic disposition and behavior of the licentiate are perfectly coherent in terms of modern psychological theories concerning causes and patterns in neuroses and modern descriptive metaphors and terms for those patterns. Antonio Vallejo Nágera writes that Cervantes describes in the victim "con justeza de perfecto observador clínico y concienzudo alienista la evolución de una agitación catatónica aguda, que remite dejando como reliquia una idea delirante. . . . Todo es perfecto y ajustado a la realidad clínica en este caso cervantino de esquizofrenia paranoide, según nuestra opinión la mejor de las historias clínicas que debemos al ingenio complutense" (*Literatura y psiquiatría* [Barcelona, 1950], pp. 48-49). It is certainly possible, as Amezúa suggests after documenting the cases of numerous actual madmen of the sixteenth and seventeenth centuries bearing some resemblances to Cervantes's fictional character, that Cervantes was keenly interested in madness and that his character is based on his actual experience (*Cervantes, creador de la novela corta española*, 2:167ff.). While such "coherences" in the licentiate's madness may be taken to confirm Cervantes's deep interest in madness, his extraordinary powers of observation, and his concern for psychological verisimilitude and consistency in his literary characters, they in no way mean that the accurate psychological portrayal or the marvels of unusual behavior are the primary dimensions of the story. Cervantes's exemplary novella is neither a "representational" clinical history nor merely an amusing account of the antics of a real or a "possible" madman, no more so, in fact, than Erasmus's description of his mad student of good letters, Nosoponus, who in his psychosis resembles deluded people who live in fear of shattering their clay heads, is a clinical study in insanity (*Ciceronianus, Ausgewählte Schriften*, ed. W. Welzig, 8 vols. [Darmstadt, 1967-1980] Vol. 7). Among the actual madmen or types of madmen who are alleged to have provided the model for Tomás Rodaja, none dresses as Diogenes, none offers society a gratuitous, ruthless denunciation, and none is cured by "knowledge and grace."

doctrines of the ancient philosophers: All the philosophy which accounts for the origin of Cervantes's character can be traced "from Socrates to Demonax, passing through the school of Diogenes."[42]

Such readings are certainly right in attempting to illuminate the philosophical meaning of the tale on the basis of what its text says rather than how its text may confirm, through the imaginative inferences of its exegetes, modern insights anticipated by an extraordinarily prescient Cervantes into such matters as intellectuality, artistic sensitivity, love, loneliness, and communication.[43] However, I would maintain that Cervantes's tale engages with the critical philosophy which it resurrects in a far more complex and troubled way than they suppose[44] and that, to understand it, we must consider not only the

[42] "La filosofía en 'El Licenciado Vidriera,' " *Anales Cervantinos* 4 (1954):225-38. In his *Orígenes de la novela* Menéndez y Pelayo, while maintaining that the frame of the tale is merely a pretext for Cervantes's presentation of his *sententiae*, suggests that the protagonist, as spokesman for the author and as a means of dialectical philosophical exposition, resembles Demonax, the famous philosopher of Cyprus, who believed that "es de dioses corregir el error," and whose wisdom is celebrated in a Lucianic dialogue (*Orígenes de la novela*, N.B.A.E. 7 [Madrid, 1907], pp. lxxii, lxxviii).

[43] The elliptical nature of the containing parable, of course, invites such unhistorical, imaginative attempts to fill in its numerous interstices. See, for example, Luis Rosales's provocative meditation on existentialist insights into authentic being and communication and his interpretation of the constant isolation of the licentiate, intensified in his madness and fear of physical contact, as implying the lifeless state of existence of a self incapable of the enlivening recognition of the existence of the other ("el mundo del Licenciado Vidriera es el mundo de la evasión del 'tú' "). See *Cervantes y la libertad*, 1:195-213. A less successful attempt to pursue the slender implications of the text is R. El Saffar's imaginative projection of a psychological crisis accompanying the licentiate's illness, a forced confrontation with his contingency and mortality, the very realities from which he has fled in his retreat into intellectuality. While proposing such a speculative interpretation, El Saffar fails to see the various subtle ways in which the implicit narrator of the tale clearly disengages from his protagonist, and, troubled by the author's apparent identification with his flawed character, she reaches the peculiar conclusion that Cervantes misunderstood his creation and goes on to suggest a fanciful psychological drama for the author: "The work represents the nadir of Cervantes's confidence in both his possibility for success and the possibility that wisdom and intelligence have any meaning in a world governed by ignorance and prejudice" (*Novel to Romance*, pp. 50-61). Rosales is plainly right in emphasizing that, while Cervantes's glass licentiate is one of the most memorable characters of Spanish literature, it makes no sense to probe into an interiority which his elliptical portrayal simply does not offer in search of psychologically coherent or incoherent patterns. He remains a powerful symbolic figure, and, as I hope to show in the following, his creator understood quite well what he was doing in his creation.

[44] Following the completion of this chapter, I received E. C. Riley's "Cervantes and the Cynics" (*Bulletin of Hispanic Studies* 53 [1976]:189-99). As far as I know, this fine study is the first interpretation of the *Licenciado Vidriera* that deals correctly with its critical examination of Cynic philosophy.

philosophy of Diogenes and Demonax, but also the philosophy that mediated their critical spirit to the sixteenth century, the *Philosophia Christiana* of Erasmus, which embraced their doctrine while modifying it according to certain Christian principles that were in some ways profoundly antithetical to its spirit. The puzzling ambivalences which center on Cervantes's figure of Diogenes disclose certain fundamental tensions at the heart of the Erasmian Christian philosophy, and only if we bear in mind its attempted reconciliation of criticism and charity, Diogenes and Christ, can we properly understand the complexities of the Spanish tale.

In his early pastoral romance, *La Galatea*, Cervantes notes that cultivation of philosophy can easily degenerate into an exercise in exposing the defects in humanity.[45] If his words anticipate the creation of his "exemplary scholar" many years later, they also recall a traditional criticism of the school of philosophy that the scholar represents. For Cervantes's "Diogenes" embodies in a rather extreme form certain destructive tendencies in Cynic doctrine, which, when not moderated by its positive teachings concerning the pursuit of virtue, can easily produce in its philosophers the heartless inhumanity of the misanthrope. The founder of the school, Antisthenes, declared that virtue lies in self-sufficiency and complete independence of all earthly possessions and pleasures. Such complete independence, the absolute freedom from desire, is wisdom, and, if wisdom has an active side, it is to be found in the act of destruction, the rending of the illusions that enslave the majority of men. The truly independent man, of course, stands beyond the compulsions of laws and social conventions.[46] The most famous Cynic, Diogenes, claimed to belong to no country or city but rather to be a citizen of the world, but, if we are to believe the numerous stories about him, tolerance was not the product of his cosmopolitanism, as he spent most of his life living in a tub, flaunting his disregard for conventionality, railing against the illusions that victimize society, and growling at the follies of man like a dog, the animal with which he came to be associated. In Diogenes's darkly humorous advice "that one ought to hold out one's hand to a friend without closing the fingers," we perhaps hear a sardonic echo of Antisthenes's view that the "wise man was sufficient to himself." Their follower, Crates, phrased the idea more sharply when he answered the question as to what he had gained from philosophy: "A peck of lupins and to care for nobody."[47]

[45] *La Galatea*, ed. J. B. Avalle-Arce, 2 vols. (Madrid, 1961), 2:63.

[46] See Diogenes Laertius, *The Lives and Opinions of Eminent Philosophers*, trans. C. D. Yonge (London, 1895), pp. 217-23.

[47] Ibid., pp. 220, 227, 250.

The Cynics' dedication to denouncing the illusions and follies which most human beings pursue is a logical consequence of their uncompromising demands for self-sufficiency. They are obsessed with the vision of life in civilization as theatrical performance, in which the authentic being of the actor is consumed by his role, and they would constantly remind the ignorant that they are in fact possessed, indeed enslaved, by what they desire to possess, be it honor, success, wealth, material goods, or pleasure.[48] In its complexities and refinements civilization is hopelessly at odds with individual freedom and the development of the self, and in the Cynics' view it should be obliterated and replaced by a vaguely defined primitive order that allows such virtues as honesty, sincerity, simplicity, and independence of spirit to flourish. Although they profess belief in the cultivation of such positive values, their characteristic activity is negation, and their characteristic pose one of anger and violence. Regardless of whether we prefer to see its origin in an excess of black bile or in experiential trauma, whether we choose to recognize its psychological coherence as a symptom of melancholia or schizophrenia, the anger of the Licenciado Vidriera remains in Cervantes's exemplary novella, in either case, the anger of Diogenes and of the Cynics in general, and it is an anger that raises fundamental ethical and philosophical issues. Essentially moralistic in their focus and tormented by the discrepancies between appearance and reality, the Cynics are demaskers, savage renders of the veil of illusion that most people and most societies have found indispensable to viable human relations and the pursuit of happiness. Anger, of course, has many gradations, and in the noblest of Cynics we suspect that savagery is not too distant from the ecstasy of the mystic, that in reality it is an unappeased hunger for purity, an outraged idealism, and perhaps an ill-concealed sense of deprivation.[49] Cynic and mystic share a yearning for disrobing and nakedness, a *nuditas sacra*, and both are susceptible to the visionary experience as they move toward the terrible moment amid the shadows when masks drop and, divested of all disguises, truth appears, whether in the

[48] "Once he [Diogenes] was going into a theatre while everyone else was coming out of it; and when asked why he did so, 'It is,' said he, 'what I have been doing all my life' " (Ibid., p. 241).

[49] Perhaps the most powerful literary probing of the way in which the deformity of the Cynic's vision can be a measure of his frustrated ecstasy is Shakespeare's *Timon of Athens*, where an undiscriminating aspiration to universal love collapses only to be reborn in a rapture of hatred as a vision of cosmic disintegration. "That love-dream killed, his [Timon's] eyes are opened to all forms of human frailty, moral, physical, social . . . he calls down wholesale disintegration on mankind" (G. Wilson Knight, "The Pilgrimage of Hate: An Essay on *Timon of Athens*," *The Wheel of Fire: Interpretations of Shakespearean Tragedy* [London, 1974], pp. 207-239; see pp. 223-24).

dazzling brightness of eternity or in the fiery glare of infernal furnaces. Both seek a hidden truth, both seek in solitude, whether in the crowded streets of the city or in the tower in the wastelands, and there is a touch of inhumanity in both, as they reject all in their fellow human beings that fails to measure up to their absolute standards. There is a profound and disturbing irony in the proverbial wisdom that the most famous repentant Cynic of Spanish literature, Guzmán de Alfarache, invokes in one of his moments of meditation: "it is commonly said that the man who yearns for solitude has much of either God or the beast about him."[50] The "middle way," which the majority of men comfortably follow through the human community and which rewards them with the pleasures of friendship and family life and the "reduced" achievements of social success, respect, and comfort, is unknown to such solitary questers, and there is nothing coincidental in the fact that the great Cynics of literature, Timon of Athens, King Lear, Molière's Alceste, and Swift's Gulliver find that the wilderness alone is hospitable to their demanding vision.

The destructive element in Cynic philosophy was immediately recognized by the early critics of the movement,[51] and it certainly has dominated in the traditional view of its critical aspirations and methods. Indeed what Cervantes's *Licenciado Vidriera* exposes through caricature in his portrait of a Cynic had been condemned by Diogenes's contemporaries and became the object of caricaturistic treatment in Lucian's satirical colloquies. For example, Plato's encounters with his enemy, Diogenes, recorded by Diogenes Laertius, revealed clearly both the strengths and weaknesses of the Cynic position. While Diogenes convincingly defended the integrity of the particular against the excessive abstraction in Plato's idealistic approach to reality, Plato rebuked Diogenes for the spiritual pride that generally animates the Cynic program of criticism: "How much arrogance are you displaying, O Diogenes, when you think that you are not arrogant at all."[52]

---

[50] "suelen decir que el hombre que apetece soledad tiene mucho de Dios o de bestia," Mateo Alemán, *Guzmán de Alfarache*, ed. S. Gili y Gaya, 5 vols. (Madrid, 1964-1969), 4:239. Perhaps the most famous expression of this enduring fragment of "classical" wisdom is Aristotle's "man is by nature a political animal, and a man that is by nature and not merely by fortune citiless is either low in the scale of humanity or above it" (*Politics*, 1.1; see *Aristotle*, trans. H. Rackham [London, 1932], p. 9).

[51] See Donald R. Dudley, *A History of Cynicism* (London, 1937), p. 143.

[52] *The Lives and Opinions of Eminent Philosophers*, pp. 226, 236. Noting that Plato allegedly described Diogenes as "a Socrates gone mad," E. C. Riley points to an "old equation between Cynicism and madness, which Cervantes could have known, or even have arrived at independently" ("Cervantes and the Cynics," p. 193).

Lucian was very severe in exposing the pride, the isolation, the inhumanity, and the barbarism of the bad Cynic. In *Philosophies for Sale* the Cynic declares that his intention is to liberate mankind from its ills through truth and free speech. He goes on to advise those who would seek truth that they must leave the house of their parents and make their home in "a tomb or a deserted tower or even a jar," and that they should earn the admiration of society by impudence, boldness, and the proper use of abuse."[53] In its themes and reductive devices, the satirical portrait contains the formula that Cervantes was to develop centuries later in his own critical exploration of the strengths and weaknesses of the Cynic philosopher.

ERASMUS'S PARADOXICAL PORTRAIT OF THE CYNIC PHILOSOPHER: CYNICISM AND *HUMANITAS CHRISTIANA*

The tongue is an unrighteous world among our members,
staining the whole body, setting on fire the wheel of birth.
—James 3:6

I would have you wise as to what is good
and guileless as to what is evil.
—Rom. 16:19

The appeal of Cynic philosophy and its classical exemplars to the sixteenth and seventeenth centuries is far too complex a subject to be dealt with here. An adequate treatment of it would touch on many of the major spiritual and philosophical currents of the age and involve such literary figures as Erasmus, Rabelais, Des Périers, Montaigne, Cervantes, Shakespeare, Quevedo, and Molière. Suffice it to say that in its antiessentialist epistemology, its opposition to abstraction,[54] its strong emphasis on the priority of the moral category in man's life, its espousal of critique as a means of improvement for the individual and society, its suspicion of learning as an end in itself, its cosmopolitanism, as well as its belief in a transnational order of nature to which man owes his allegiance, the doctrine of the Cynics, like that

[53] *Lucian*, trans. A. M. Harmon, 8 vols. (London and Cambridge, Mass., 1913-1967), 2:467-71.

[54] "When Plato was discoursing about his 'ideas,' and using the nouns 'tableness' and 'cupness'; 'I, O Plato!' interrupted Diogenes, 'see a table and a cup, but I see no tableness or cupness' " (Diogenes Laertius, *The Lives and Opinions of Eminent Philosophers*, p. 236).

of the ancient skeptics with whom they had so much in common, offered much that was congenial to thinkers of the sixteenth century, both to the Christian Humanists dedicated to the type of spiritual reformism and ecumenical Christianity embodied in Erasmus's *Philosophia* and *Respublica Christiana* and to the philosophers of the schools and independent thinkers concerned with seeking new ways of dealing with the problem of knowledge as the old systematic philosophy crumbled away beneath the impact of nominalist thinking and the new discoveries in astronomy and geography.

At the same time the traditional weaknesses of the Cynic position were clearly visible to the humanists of the age, if for no other reason than that Lucian, one of their favorite authors, took such delight in exposing them. In their profound aversion to the dogmatic excesses and arid rigidities of scholastic philosophy, they could easily see that the Cynic's profession of anti-intellectualism frequently was in fact a mask hiding an intellectual arrogance which, although limited to the sphere of moral rather than metaphysical or scientific knowledge, was as presumptuous as the idolatrous philosophizing of the scholastics. Moreover, the fervent champions of such fundamental Christian virtues as charity and humility, they were aware that the Cynic program for a healthy critique of the illusions that enslave man could easily degenerate into pharisaic vainglory, intolerance, cruelty, and a failure to understand the nature of man's humanity.

That Erasmus saw the strengths and the weaknesses of Cynic doctrine is clear in his treatment of it in the *Enchiridion*, a work which, in its general philosophical position concerning the proper uses of knowledge and criticism, as well as in some interesting details, reveals a striking kinship with Cervantes's parable of knowledge. In Rule Six, "The Christian must reject all opinions and judgments that are vulgar and false,"[55] Erasmus emphasizes the necessity of understanding true goodness, suggests that authentic nobility derives from the individual's inner qualities rather than from his social position, and speaks of the difficulties that the Christian has in distinguishing goodness and virtue from all the false values which "los vulgares," trapped in the shadows of Plato's cave, pursue madly, "as if they were certain and true." "The truth is that the common judgment of mankind has never provided a very reasonable or certain rule for the guidance of an individual who would conduct himself in conformity with its opinions

[55] "que el christiano deve desechar todas opiniones y juyzios vulgares y falsos," (*Enquiridion*, p. 292). The following page references are to the popular sixteenth-century Spanish version of Erasmus's work.

and attitudes."[56] Asserting that the majority will always flounder about in the darkness and that the followers of Christ's truths concerning virtue, simplicity, and humility will form a small flock, Erasmus proceeds to exhort man to learn to see and distinguish amid the shadows. The world has "never been so corrupt," and Erasmus offers a list of the inversions of traditional values that reflect the pervasive disorder and disease of contemporary society. Wealth, status, and physical pleasure are its supreme values, and the lives of its members are blighted by rampant materialism, ostentation, self-indulgence, fornication, and adultery. Its leaders in both secular and spiritual affairs fail to set an example and in fact tolerate the excesses of the populace so that they can freely pursue the same type of dissolute life. Sadly there are no more governors like the ancients who, having responsibly discharged their duties, return in humility to their home with no profit other than the acquisition of a reputation for honesty. If anyone in palaces and monasteries attempts to do his duty honestly, "everybody will laugh at him, and thus he will be ridiculed as the ass among monkeys; he will go about as the target of fools and even of those who are held to be wise, and he will be unanimously dismissed as a raving madman, an idiot, an incompetent, a hypocrite, a fool, and a victim of melancholy,"[57] bitter words which might remind us of Preciosa's advice to the lieutenant concerning his failure in the palace world of Philip III, the Licenciado Vidriera's painful discovery of the court's preference for the "truhán desvergonzado" to the "discreto vergonzoso," and Sancho Panza's decision to abdicate in honorable poverty following the abuse that he receives at his court.

At this point Erasmus turns to one of his favorite modes of expression to sharpen the contrast he wishes to draw between truth and falsehood, to lengthen the gap between the appearances that enslave the world and the realities that liberate it, and to impress on his reader the necessity of learning to see with the "ojos del corazón," or, as he puts it elsewhere, with the "ojos del ánimo y del entendimiento," beyond the surfaces that the physical eye beholds. Erasmus points out in the *Sileni Alcibiadis* that Christ himself is a supremely paradoxical figure as he proclaims the power of weakness, the splendor

---

[56] "la verdad es que el juyzio común de la gente, nunca jamás fué ni es regla muy cierta, ni aun muy derecha, para regirse ombre por ella ni bivir conforme a su parecer ni conformarse con su sentir" (p. 297).

[57] "todo el mundo ha de burlar dél, y assí será escarnecido como asno entre las monas, ha de andar hecho terrero de necios y aun de los que son tenidos por cuerdos, y a una boz de todos llamado loco desvariado, bobo, inábil, ypócrita, necio, malencónico" (p. 303).

of simplicity, and the wisdom of ignorance. Here he develops a similar conception: "in Christ all things are inverted, and their names are changed and altered."[58] True nobility is the disdain for aristocrats and the affirmation of our brotherhood with Christ and of our share in the common destiny of humanity. True weapons are those that wound the bearer—Christ's crown of thorns, as well as the nails and lance of his tormentors. True riches are possessed through the disdain for the riches of Midas. True pleasure is the possession of a clear conscience, whose purification demands abhorrence of the pleasures esteemed by the world. True love is selfless and is experienced only through rejection of the selfish love that the multitude pursues. True bravery is the rejection of the impulses toward vengeance and the transcendence of the obsession with the preservation of one's honor, the honor that the world recognizes as proper in the man of valor. True knowledge is concerned with moral improvement, and by the prevailing standards of the world it is ignorance. In the eyes of society the "wise and learned man," is he who, like the Licenciado Vidriera, travels about aimlessly, determined to "know many new things," and refusing to miss "a single thing that takes place in the world," and who, proud of his ability "to speak well," can tell you of the "novelties of Rome," the activities of the king of England, events in France, customs in Scythia, and the news of the court. Erasmus condemns the presumption of such a wise man and the exclusive outward gaze of his intellect: "But I know of no greater lack of wisdom and prudence than this: to pry diligently into those affairs which are occurring far away and which are of no concern to you, yet not for a moment to consider what is going on within your breast and what concerns principally you."[59]

Erasmus points out that human affairs are "riddled throughout by error and deception" and that everywhere "good is called evil and evil is called good."[60] He exhorts his reader to resist the temptation to follow the others who stumble about in blindness, to remember that his goal is renovation and transformation in Jesus Christ, and to fix his spiritual eyes on Christ, for therein lies true vision. At the very conclusion of his argument he urges his reader to take heart in the

---

[58] "en Christo se mueven y trastruecan todas las cosas y se mudan y alteran todos los vocablos dellas" (p. 313).

[59] "Pero no sé yo que mayor falta de aviso y prudencia que ésta: escudriñar con grand diligencia lo que se haze muy lexos y que ninguna cosa te toca, y de lo que passa dentro de tu pecho y te toca principalmente, no tener ningún pensamiento" (p. 318).

[60] "todo está lleno de error y engaño, llamando bueno a lo que es malo y malo a lo que es bueno" (p. 319).

example of the "Brahmans, the Cynics, and the Stoics," who defended their views with such conviction that the contradiction and derision hurled at them constantly by the majority of the people among whom they lived could not force them to waver in their faith or to keep silent. Here we see one face of Erasmus's paradoxical engagement with Cynic philosophy. In it, as in Stoicism, he admired the boldness with which it attacked the follies which the majority of men embrace, its concern for truth, and its emphasis on such inner qualities as virtue and self-knowledge. Whenever his concern is the critique of contemporary abuses, he can invoke the rigorous Cynic or the ascetic Stoic wise man as an embodiment of healthy rationality and disciplined morality, and he apparently feels no tension surrounding the reconciliation of the ethics of such figures with his evangelical Christianity.[61] However, when his focus shifts away from the critique of the immorality of bad Christians to a presentation of an ideal of Christian conduct, both Cynic and Stoic present problems that he can not fail to recognize. Hence at the conclusion of the "veri Christianismi paradoxa" which Erasmus appends to this rule, we see a picture of the Cynic that is far different from the one with whom the Christian is urged to identify in his confrontation with the multitude of fools surrounding him.

Having concentrated on the falsehoods and evils that the Christian must reject, Erasmus turns now to the positive values that he must embrace. It is here that we can discern the development of a program of positive criticism and a firm rejection of the excesses of the Cynics' inhumanity. Invoking the Pauline conception that imbues his think-

---

[61] In the prefatory epistle to his *Institutio Principis Christiani* Erasmus invokes Diogenes as the ideal counselor of princes, alluding to the familiar anecdote in Plutarch concerning Alexander's admiration for the philosopher (" 'Ni Alexander' inquit 'essem, Diogenes esse cupiam' " [*Opus Epistolarum Des. Erasmi Roterdami*, ed. P. S. Allen, 12 vols. (Oxford, 1906-1958), 2:206]). See also the discussion of Christ, the Apostles, and Diogenes as examples of the spotless virtue that is required of anyone who would preach the word of God (*Ecclesiastes sive de Ratio Concionandi*, I, *Opera Omnia*, ed. Le Clerc, 5:777-78) and Battus's invocation of Diogenes as he prepares to defend humane letters against the hoards of philistines (*Antibarbari*, ed. K. Kumaniecki, *Opera Omnia*, Vol. I, pt. 1 [Amsterdam, 1969], p. 67). In his *Sileni Alcibiadis* Erasmus lists, beside Socrates and Christ, the most extraordinary Silenus of all, Epictetus, traditionally considered both a Stoic and a Cynic (see H. Haydn, *The Counter-Renaissance* [New York, 1950], p. 107), and the early Cynics: "Another Silenus of this kind was Antisthenes, grander with his stick, wallet, and cloak than all the riches of the greatest kings. Another Silenus was Diogenes, whom the mob considered a dog. But it was about this 'dog' that a divine observation was made by Alexander the Great" (*The "Adages" of Erasmus*, ed. and trans. M. M. Phillips [Cambridge, 1965], p. 271).

ing on nearly every subject concerning man's religious, ethical, social, and political life—the single body of Christian believers united under Christ the head—he repeatedly points to the bonds uniting all human beings over and above the divisive forces of national, geographical, professional, age, sex, and class distinctions, and he stresses the importance of charity and brotherhood. The nerves unifying the body of mankind are formed by Christian charity. The goodness of each member redounds to the benefit of all other members, the health of the whole depends on the proper functioning of the parts, and, in effect, each part is responsible to every other part. "No Christian should think that he was born for himself alone, nor should he wish to live for himself alone"; "he should consider all his goods the common property of all men"; "consider, moreover, that any man who exists, although he may appear a stranger to you, is your brother in God . . . and he is a member of the same body as you, redeemed by the same precious blood."[62] A Christian is obligated to attend to the sufferings of a brother who is spiritually ill, just as a physician approaches a sick man, with hatred for the disease and charity for its victim. The model for corrective criticism is Christ, who most frequently offered doctrine and example with humility, patience, and Christian gentleness ("mansedumbre christiana") and who abhorred anger, vituperation, and revenge.

After having proposed his Christian critical philosophy, Erasmus admits that the world is indeed full of errors worthy of ridicule and moral outrage: "Whatever type of men the truly spiritual man chooses to examine, he will see everywhere many things to laugh at, many more to weep over."[63] He then proceeds to a long denunciation of what he considers to be one of the worst evils of the time, the manner in which man uses his reason to pervert the meaning of the Bible and the saints' lives so as to justify his own sinfulness. Following the condemnation of the corruptibility of the intellect, he calls for a return to the blessed foolishness of devotion to Christ, a state that the world considers one of "desatino y locura," and that in reality is "a foolishness so wise and a madness so sane and a nonsense so discreet that, with all its little knowledge, or with all its knowledge of noth-

---

[62] "ningún christiano piense que nació para sí solo ni quiera bivir para sí solo"; "que todos sus bienes tenga por comunes a todos"; "considera, de más de esto, que cualquier ombre que sea, aunque parezca estraño, es tu hermano en el Señor . . . y es también miembro de un mesmo cuerpo donde lo eres tú, redemido por la mesma preciosa sangre que tú" (pp. 322-24).

[63] "A qualquier estado de ombres que quiera mirar el que fuere verdaderamente espiritual, verá en cada parte muchas cosas de que se ría, y muchas más de que llore" (p. 343).

ing, it knows yet how to please Christ, and it understands his words most simply and sincerely."[64]

It is curious that at this point Erasmus offers as the conclusion to this section a lengthy criticism of the Cynic philosopher, as if he represented everything that opposes the simple folly of the cross.

. . . still it is well to advise you on one thing. Although I want you to detach yourself with all your strength and determination from the judgments and opinions of the world, at the same time I do not want you to approach its matters with such uncompromising extremism and with so little circumspection that you would adopt the role of Cynic philosopher and become a scoffer or a snarler at anything you might hear or see. Nor should you be of the condition of the Cynics in condemning superciliously, as if you were perfect, whatever does not satisfy you enough. Nor should you follow them in arrogating to yourself an importunate audacity and an irksome freedom, eagerly spouting forth whatever you feel and doing so with the belief that nobody can equal you in perfection or with the intention of making all your listeners as saintly as you would like to be, all the while failing to observe proper balance and reason and failing to show patience in waiting for the proper occasion and season to make your opinions heard. At the same time you should refrain both from going about practicing slander in secret and from denouncing in public the life of anybody. Because if you do so, you will earn for yourself two evils: first, you will always be hated by everybody, and there will be nobody who will endure your sight; second, being commonly hated, or not well-liked, you will be of no benefit to anybody.[65]

The full-scale condemnation of the Cynic philosopher may strike us as strange following the admiration Erasmus expresses for the tenacity

---

[64] "la necedad tan sabia y la locura tan cuerda y el desatino tan discreto, que con todo su poco saber, o su no saber nada, sabe agradar a Christo y sabe sus palabras a la llana" (p. 351).

[65] "todavía es bien avisarte de una cosa, que assí como quiero que con todas tus fuerças te apartes muy determinadamente de las opiniones y parecer de toda estotra gente común, assí también quiero que no tomes el negocio en lo de fuera tan sin tiento ni tan por el cabo que te andes representando un filósoffo Cynico, hecho mofador o ladrador, como aquéllos, de todas quantas cosas oyeres hablar o vieres passar, ni seas de la condición de éstos en condenar luego con mucho sobrecejo y como ya muy perfeto lo que no te satisfaze tanto, ni los sigas en tener un atrevimiento importuno ni una libertad pesada, queriendo hechar luego fuera lo que sientes, y esto con pensamiento que no alcança nadie aquello que tú, o también con propósito de hazerlos luego a todos tan santos como lo querrías ser tú, sin tener en esto peso, ni razón, ni mirar oportunidad, ni aguardar sazón. Ni te cures tampoco de andar murmurando en secreto, ni menos abominando en público la vida de ninguno. Porque si assí lo hazes no puedes ganar sino dos inconvenientes: el uno, que estarás siempre en odio y desgracia de todos y no avrá nadie que no te traya sobre ojos; el otro, que estando comúnmente aborrecido, o no bien quisto, no podrás assí aprovechar a ninguno" (pp. 351-53).

of the Cynics at the conclusion of the first part of this section. However, if we consider the themes that Erasmus has developed in the following part—the essential Christian beliefs in brotherhood, the importance of charity, the obligation of all Christians to tend to their neighbors' spiritual ills, the peculiar perverseness and dangerous ingenuities of the intellect, subject as it is so often to opinion and passion, and the call for a return to the Pauline folly or ignorance in Christ—the logic of the attack on Cynic philosophy and the coherence in the paradoxical portrayal of the Cynic in the *Enchiridion* become perfectly clear. The Cynic is a man who isolates himself from the body of humanity, and his merciless manner of flaying that body is a violent perversion of Christ's healing tenderness. He is intolerant of human weaknesses and strives for a purity and a freedom that humanity cannot attain. His presumption and intellectual pride are unbounded and are equaled only by the misanthropy into which he inevitably falls because of the impossibility of his high demands.[66]

[66] In the *Praise of Folly* Erasmus offers a harsher exposure and denunciation of the inhumanity of the Cynics and the Stoics. Seneca's wise man is "devoid of all human feeling" ("ab omni prorsus humano sensu alienus"); he is "no more moved by love and pity than by hard flint." Like Cervantes's man of superior vision, he is "Arguslike," "morose and sharp-eyed," another Lynceus, who "sees everything" and "excuses nothing" ("nihil non perspiciat, nihil non ad amussim perpendat, nihil ignoscat"). He is the enemy of society, since he is incapable of tolerating the folly that binds normal human beings in their various relationships. And obsessed by the miseries of man and the tedium of life ("vitae taedium"), he will undoubtedly find the temptation of suicide as irresistible as did such illustrious sages as Diogenes and Cato. The solitude of Cervantes's proud intellectual, a condition that he does not escape until the very end of his life, should be understood in relation to the moral implications that Erasmus finds in the isolation of such a wise man, alienated as he is from everything human, "qui *solus* se ipso sit contentus, *solus* dives, *solus* sanus, *solus* rex, *solus* liber, breviter, omnia *solus*, sed suo *solius* iudicio, qui nullum moretur amicum, ipse amicus nemini, qui Diis quoque ipsis non dubitet mandare laqueum, qui quidquid in omni vita geritur, velut insanum damnet, rideatque" (see *Laus Stultitiae, Ausgewählte Schriften*, 2:64-66; also p. 44; italics added). In his satirical survey of the evils of the tongue, the *Lingua*, Erasmus pauses to remind himself that in his diatribe he might be committing one of the very sins that he is denouncing and recalls Plato's rebuke of Diogenes: "Debaccharis tu quidem in linguam maledicam, sed alia maledicentia" (ed. F. Schalk, *Opera Omnia*, Vol. IV, pt. 1 [Amsterdam, 1974], p. 332). In words that anticipate Cervantes's ambivalent engagement with Cynic philosophy and satire in the *Licenciado Vidriera* and the *Coloquio de los perros*, he observes with approval: "Cohibita est legibus veteris comoediae licentia, posteaquam lusus exierat in rabiem, et Cynici vulgo pro canibus habiti sunt, non ob aliud nisi quod recte quidem arguerent vitia mortalium, sed absque delectu personarum temporis ac loci" (p. 270). He condemns the lack of restraint of a venomous tongue "even if it utters truths" (p. 319) and calls for a humane, fraternal criticism of the type described in the *Enchiridion*: "in malis insectandis modum esse debere" (p. 332). We should heal

Erasmus proposes as an alternative to the Cynic's uncompromising condemnation of error a type of humane criticism, exemplified by St. Paul, which adopts a tolerant attitude toward human weakness, rejects the temptation of swift generalization, recognizes and attempts to meet the individuality of each person in need, and espouses courtesy, good manners, gentle dissimulation, love, persuasion, and example as the methods of reforming him. "Like St. Paul, make yourself with all men all things which you find fitting to them, adapting yourself [humanizing yourself] according to all their differences and qualities in order to win them for Christ . . . do not fail . . . in external matters to be conciliatory toward everybody and to bear their conditions with good will. . . . it is well that there be in you much courtesy and good breeding and that you receive everybody with kindness and a cheerful expression, showing anger and asperity to nobody, so that your gentle condition and politeness might be of use in attracting your neighbor, through love, to loving you and giving credit to your words."[67] The Christian critic must be firm and never shrink in cowardice from speaking freely in defense of the truth. However, he must always remember the humanity that he shares with his fellow men and the responsibilities of good will and charity that it demands.

When Erasmus exhorts his Christian critic to *humanarse* and to avoid the opposed extremes of harshness and indulgence ("humanitate emendandi sunt homines, non decipiendi"),[68] he is linking the critic's mis-

---

the weaknesses of our fellow Christians "mansueta fraternaque monitione" (p. 298) and "moderatis admonitionibus, et secretis ac blandis hortatibus" (p. 304). The act of slander is an offense against the body of Christ and all Christians, and Erasmus employs the imagery of cannibalism to emphasize its horror: "Dicam amplius, quisquis homini Christiano maledicit, Christo maledicit, vt enim ille visitur ac refocillatur in membris suis, ita laeditur et ignominia afficitur in membris suis" (p. 305). "Abstinent ab esu carnium, at interim non verentur arrodere carnes proximi sui. . . . Non comedis viscera pecudis, et comedis viscera fratris? Mordet enim omnino mordet, vulnerat, et comedit fratrem quisquis obtrectat fratri. . . . Nihil enim magis aduersatur charitati spiritus, quam inuidere frati, odisse, obtrectare, infamare" (pp. 324-25).

[67] "Hazte, pues, con todos, como sant Pablo, todo quanto vieres que les cumple, humanándote según todas las qualidades y differencias de todos por ganarlos para Christo a todos . . . no dexes con este intento acá en lo de fuera de conceder con todos y llevarles buenamente sus condiciones. . . . bien es que aya en ti toda cortesía y buena criança y que a unos y a otros hagas buen acogimiento y semblante, no mostrando pesadumbre ni azedía con nadie, de arte que tu buena condición y comedimiento aproveche para atraher assí por amor a tu próximo a que te ame y te dé crédito" (p. 352).

[68] See *Enchiridion Militis Christiani*, *Ausgewählte Schriften*, 1:302. It is characteristic of Erasmus's view of criticism that he apologetically introduces the section of his *De Conscribendis Epistolis* on *Exprobratio* with the reminder that "omnis exprobratio ab humanitate videtur recedere" (*Opera Omnia*, ed. Le Clerc, 1:462E).

sion with a principle that underlies his entire moral and educational philosophy and that a recent study has referred to as the "centre même de la pensée érasmienne"—*humanitas*.[69] For Erasmus as for so many other humanists, the notion of *humanitas* represented an ideal of man's moral and social perfectibility. It is not a state that man receives as a birthright but rather one that he must strive to attain through the proper cultivation, development, and application of the distinctly human qualities of reason, speech, and free will with which he is born. As Petrarch wrote, "a human being is an animal, dangerous, unstable, not to be trusted, wavering, savage and bloody, unless—and this is a very rare gift from God—he learns to put on humanity and to lay aside his bestial nature, in short, unless he learns to become a man instead of a mere human being."[70] In Erasmus's famous formulation the thought is put even more simply: "homines, mihi crede, non nascuntur, sed finguntur"—"men, believe me, are not born, but rather made."[71] Through education man discovers and fulfills himself as a man among other men, with whom he shares a common destiny and to whom he is united by strong fraternal bonds and responsibilities. Erasmus asserts in the *Querela Pacis* that *humanus* refers to everything that has to do with *mutua benevolentia*, and his writings continually reveal that for him the fullest state of being that an individual can attain is one that involves him directly, as a responsible member of a community, with his fellow human beings. In its emphasis on man's perfectability as a social being, Erasmus's central concept of *humanitas* has nothing to do with the free cultivation of individuality which, since Burckhardt and Michelet, we are accustomed to associate with the Renaissance view of man and very little to do with the vision of man's divine potential as celebrated in the contemplative metaphysics of contemporary Florentine neo-Platonism.

In his fine study, "Der Humanismus und das Prinzip der klassischen Geisteshaltung" Georg Weise has examined a large number of humanist writings from Petrarch up to the seventeenth century, and, through analysis of the contexts framing the appearance of the words *humanus, humanitas, studia humanitatis*, and *humaniores litterae*, he has attempted to disengage and elucidate the entire scheme of values and

---

[69] S. Dresden, "Érasme et la Notion de *Humanitas*," *Scrinium Erasmianum*, ed. J. Coppens, 2 vols. (Leiden, 1969), 2:527-45; see p. 529.

[70] "perniciosum quoque et varium et infidum et anceps et ferox et cruentum animal est homo nisi, quod rarum Dei munus est, humanitatem induere feritatemque deponere, denique nisi de homine vir esse didicerit" (ibid., p. 528).

[71] Ibid., p. 528, 530. See also, R. H. Bainton, *Erasmus of Christendom* (New York, 1969), pp. 41-42.

attitudes rooted in the fundamental concept. The terms that consistently accompany these words and phrases, whether as exact synonyms or as closely related and reconcilable concepts, are *affabilis, mitis, pietas, fides, benignitas, benevolentia, clementia, amicus, mansuetudo, moderatio, comitas, umiltà, cortesia, modestia, pazienza, riverenza, temperato, amorevole*. The most characteristic opposites and contrasts are *rudis, asper, incivilis, durezza, severo*. In words similar to Erasmus's condemnation of the Cynic, Alberti writes that "severity without humanity brings hatred rather than authority; humanity will earn all the more good will and favor the more gentle it is and the more removed from any harshness."[72] For such humanists knowledge is not esteemed as an end in itself, as an instrument of power over man or nature, and as a means of penetrating the abstruse mysteries with which theological studies had traditionally dealt, but rather, in the form of "humane letters," as a means to the attainment of *humanitas*, without which studies pursued in such areas of specialization as canon or civil law and theology might easily lead to pedantry, arrogance, and the separation of education from the achievement of man's principal goal—moral perfection. For example, Poggio refers to literary studies as those which are primarily to fashion "homines ad placabilitatem et optimos mores," the humanist Christoph Scheurl can praise Pirckheimer as one who never severed "summam humanitatem ab omnifaria eruditione," and Juan Luis Vives can lament in a letter to Erasmus that Spanish "acuta ingenia" are imbued with false opinions in their ignorance of *humanitas*.[73]

---

[72] "la severità senza umanità acquista più odio che autorità; La umanità, quanto è più facile e più sgiunta da ogni durezza, tanto più meriterà benevolenzia e grazia" (see *Zu Begriff und Problem der Renaissance*, ed. A. Buck [Darmstadt, 1969], pp. 280-325; for Alberti, see p. 305). See Rudolf Pfeiffer, *Humanitas Erasmiana* (Berlin, 1931), pp. 3-4: "Die Milderung des Allzuherben, die Lockerung des Starren und Steifen, die Beschwingung erdhafter Schwere: dies liegt ganz besonders in der Forderung der humanitas, die Anmut und Geist, Laune und Witz und die Würze der Ironie verlangt . . . ja gerade den erworbenen persönlichen Bildungsbesitz nicht eigensüchtig bei sich zu verschliessen, sondern immer freigebig von ihm den anderen mitzuteilen, Kultur zu verbreiten, erscheint als Pflicht" (see also p. 7). In his discussion of the value of knowledge and education, Vives links virtue with humanity, gentleness, courtesy, and affability, condemns arrogance and insolence, and rejects as inhumane the type of curiosity which Cervantes's failed scholar embodies: "Ne in alienas vitas inquiras, neve curiosius scruteris quid quisque agat; multae hinc suboriuntur simultates" (*Introductio ad Sapientiam, Opera Omnia*, ed. G. Mayáns y Siscar, 8 vols. [Valencia, 1782-1790], 1:34).

[73] G. Weise, "Der Humanismus und das Prinzip der klassischen Geisteshaltung," pp. 301, 311, 317. See Erasmus's interpretation of the myth of the companionship of the Graces and the Muses in his *De Pueris Instituendis* as representing the necessary

Humanitas, then, was seen as the goal of education, as a way of living at a high level of moral and social awareness, and as the fundamental wisdom orienting man in his establishment of personal goals and in his use of knowledge. Weise notes that throughout the wide range of writings gathered in his study one is struck by the unanimity with which the humanists identify *"humanitas* and *humanus* with the characteristics of friendliness, kindness, and sociability." He points out that one can, in fact, infer from their utterances a shared belief in the need for a "tempering and softening" in the development of the civilized individual's personality and manners and a firm opposition in their new educational ideal "to any individualistic cult of the self" and to any idealization of the human being as a creature who can "lift itself above the restraints of ethical and collective bonds."[74] If we bear in mind the qualities that the humanists associated with the humane personality, we can immediately see why Erasmus charged the Cynic with inhumanity and understand the extent to which Tomás Rodaja, Cervantes student of *buenas letras*, failed to grasp the essential point of his studies.

CERVANTES'S PARADOXICAL PORTRAIT OF THE CYNIC PHILOSOPHER IN *EL LICENCIADO VIDRIERA*

Both faces of the Cynic philosopher that Erasmus describes in the *Enchiridion* were visible to writers of the Renaissance, who could find in the uncompromising critic a prestigious model for healthy criticism and admonition while in the misanthrope an illustrative example for any philosophical engagement with such general problems as man's strengths and weaknesses, such social and ethical issues as courtesy, benevolence, and slander, and such practical problems as the function of criticism and satire. Clearly it is the positive side of Diogenes that appealed to Rabelais in the preface to *Le Tiers Livre*, where he likens

---

social context of education: "studiorum profectum mutua animorum benevolentia potissimum constare, unde et humanitatis literas appellavere prisci" (ed. J.-C. Margolin, *Opera Omnia*, Vol. I, pt. 2 [Amsterdam, 1971], p. 69). Cervantes's licentiate's intense study of human letters leads, of course, to the perversion of this fundamental goal of education.

[74] "Der Humanismus und das Prinzip der klassischen Geisteshaltung," p. 306. Weise stresses the "Verbindung der Geistesgaben und Kenntnisse mit der 'Sanftheit' der Sitten und der Umgangsformen als das wesentliche, immer wieder hervorgehobene Kennzeichnen des neuen Ideals der Bildung" (p. 312). See also, pp. 316-17.

his own efforts as a writer amid the chaotic conditions of the age to the Greek philosopher's insistent pounding of his tub. In Pedro de Mexía's *Silva de varia lección* Diogenes appears as an eloquent critic, and the Spanish encyclopedist insinuates through his account of a series of humorous responses by the Cynic to his questioners some of Erasmus's fundamental doctrines concerning ceremonies, education, fasting, and funerals.[75] John Lyly's *Campaspe* resurrects Diogenes as a counselor of princes, a preceptor and critic whose moral integrity, intellectual honesty, and philosophical insight win the admiration of Alexander the Great, and Thomas Middleton's satire, *Micro-cynicus, Sixe Snarling Satyres*, invokes the tradition of corrective Cynicism as a justification for fair if indeed harsh and disturbing satire.[76] Mathurin Régnier's satirist likens his critical activity to "taking up the lantern of Diogenes,"[77] and there can be no doubt that Cervantes himself associates his ideal critics, the dogs Cipión and Berganza, with the mission of Diogenes the dog, as they carry the lantern for Mahudes through the streets of Valladolid, a place where an honest man appears to be as difficult to find as in Diogenes's Athens, and remind their sinful society of the fundamentally "anticynical" principle that no man can live for himself alone. However, Cervantes's dogs are not only critics but also philosophers of criticism, and one of their various deliberations concerning the subject makes it clear that they are aware of the negative side of the Cynic position. Berganza ridicules the pretentiousness of people who ornament their conversation with Latin citations, the impostures of others who claim to be skilled Latinists while in reality they are ignorant of the most fundamental rules of grammar, and the imprudence of truly talented Latinists who are so enamored of the classical tongue that they insist on speaking it at all times, even in their dealings with uneducated shoemakers. He justifies the introduction of all his criticisms by referring to them as "philosophical matters," and his tirade culminates in the summarizing witticism: "there are some whom their being Latinists does not save from being asses." All of this provokes an outburst from his sober companion Cipión: "Do you call slander philosophy? So it goes! Canonize, Berganza, canonize the accursed plague of backbiting, and give it whatever name you please; for it will give us the name of cynics,

[75] See ed. J. García Soriano (Madrid, 1933-1934), 1:163-69.

[76] See *The Complete Works of John Lyly*, ed. R. W. Bond, 3 vols. (Oxford, 1973), 2:332-33, 355. For the conventional association of Cynic and satirist in English literature in Cervantes's age, see Robert C. Elliott, *The Power of Satire: Magic, Ritual, Art* (Princeton, 1960), pp. 164-67.

[77] See "Satyre XIV," *Oeuvres complètes* (Paris, 1853), p. 190.

which is as much as to say backbiting dogs. So for pity's sake I entreat you to be silent now and to proceed with your story."[78]

Cervantes's dogs, who stress such Christian virtues as humility and charity and who are aware of the debasing possibilities inherent in practically all criticism and its literary offshoot, satire, recall the point which Cervantes had made in his early work, *La Galatea*, about the potential danger in philosophical study, and they dissociate themselves in no uncertain terms from the excesses of Cynic denunciation. The Licenciado Vidriera, of course, does not, and it is made perfectly clear, particularly in the comical scene in which he wonders in bewilderment at the pain he feels in the wasp's sting, that he has never considered the philosophical problems underlying criticism. In fact he resembles closely the type of philosopher whom Cipión describes and condemns, and, despite the aptness of nearly all his satirical pronouncements, his fundamental position as a critic is very different from that of his author. The most interesting aspect of Cervantes's *Licenciado Vidriera* lies not in its seemingly clear-cut and at times monotonous core of processional satire, but rather in the complex system of elements that surround, infiltrate, and impinge on the satire, weakening its foundation, enveloping it in an atmosphere of ambiguity, discrediting the reliability of its pronouncer, in short, transforming what appears to be one of Cervantes's most monologic pieces of writing into his characteristic dialogic idiom, with all its radiating powers of irony. If the framing parable, with its clear intimations that the protagonist's scholarly ambitions are improperly motivated, that his striking isolation from the human community is unnatural, and that his thirst for knowledge and his startling metamorphosis are connected with demonic temptation, casts a troubling shadow on the validity of all the statements that he makes when speaking as the Licenciado Vidriera, the system of discreditation in fact penetrates the central part of the tale, although its presence is easily overlooked amid the outpouring of sensible criticism and ingenious wit. Cervantes's *Licenciado Vidriera* belongs to a body of satirical works that are most difficult to interpret precisely because they attempt to incorporate both a satirical criticism of man's follies and a puzzling self-questioning, a penetrating examination of the questionable propriety of satir-

---

[78] "es que hay algunos, que no les excusa el ser latinos de ser asnos." "¿Al murmurar llamas filosofar? ¡Así va ello! Canoniza, canoniza, Berganza, a la maldita plaga de la murmuración, y dale el nombre que quisieres, que ella dará a nosotros el de cínicos, que quiere decir perros murmuradores; y por tu vida que calles ya y sigas tu historia" (*El casamiento engañoso y coloquio de los perros, Novelas ejemplares*, ed. F. Rodríguez Marín, 2:250-51).

ical criticism in general. Like the greatest works of this type—Erasmus's *Praise of Folly*, Shakespeare's *Timon of Athens*, Molière's *Le Misanthrope*, Swift's *Gulliver's Travels*, and Cervantes's other exemplary novel, *El coloquio de los perros*—the *Licenciado Vidriera* invites simplistic interpretation because of the dominating presence within it of an unambiguous core of criticism. Its reception, like that of the other works in its tradition, has proven that the temptation to discount the self-questioning counterthrusts of its narrative is at times difficult to resist. In what follows I would like to examine the central part of the text more closely to show how Cervantes's Cynic, for all the value of his wisdom and the incisiveness of his unmasking criticism, is presented as a flawed philosopher and how Cervantes, even as he endorses much of his message, clearly detaches himself from him and exposes the limitations in his vision.

The licentiate's madness is clearly connected with superior insight. He asserts that, since he consists entirely of the "subtle and delicate materials of glass," his intellect is unencumbered by the heavy earthiness of the body and that it can respond to all questions with exceptional quickness and effectiveness. He is so successful in proving his point that the professors of Salamanca look upon him with wonder (*admiración*), evidently the emotion characteristic of the intellectual throughout the tale, and celebrate his acuity of mind (*agudeza*). His transformation into an object of curiosity and a cause of admiration is, of course, another example of the grim logic of satirical retribution, a fitting metamorphosis for a person who indulges his curiosity so relentlessly and who seeks so tirelessly the excitement of *admiratio* in experiencing the novelties of the world. However, of more importance to us here are the clear limitations in his *agudeza* which are evident in the two types of response that predominate in his exchanges with the public, the satirical observation and the witty, philosophical aphorism. As a critic the licentiate is obsessed with man's evil and hypocrisy, sees them in absolute clarity, and exposes them mercilessly. Clairvoyance in dealing with human evil, that whole realm that Cervantes probably had in mind when he wished that the *Celestina* had concealed *lo humano* a bit more than it did, is a traditional quality of the Cynic, but it can, even when it is operating most persuasively and disturbingly, present no more than a partial view of truth, and it can easily lead its possessor into the traditional intellectual and moral errors of the Cynic—undiscriminating generalization and hatred of man.

Despite his highly developed intellectual sensibility Cervantes's licentiate is guilty over and over again of pronouncing sweeping condemnations of professional, national, and racial types with no apparent concern for the distinctions among the individuals whom he thrusts into his categories. Like many other aphorists, he is captivated by a mode of discourse which, in apparently arresting and "fixing" the flow of life, offers its practitioners the illusion of intellectual control, and he is never troubled by the inconsistencies of experience that might call into question the validity of his lapidary pronouncements. He appears to believe, for example, that all *conversos* are people with a terrible secret, that all prostitutes are "pieces of baggage in Satan's army," that all printers are swindlers, and that all *dueñas* are pretentious intriguers. The procession of "todos los oficios" that he observes and denounces—notaries, scholars, muleteers, carters, sailors, apothecaries, physicians, tailors, Genovese financiers, puppeteers, bakers, fencers, judges, and friars—is certainly one of the most traditional parts of the tale, and it is undeniable that Cervantes is presenting through it his own satirical, and occasionally humorous, observations on the professions and customs of his society. However, within the larger context of the work—with its critical engagement with education, true and false wisdom, and the problem of satire—the function of the scathing observations is more complicated than in the pure processional forms of satire from which they derive. The incongruity of such ruthless stereotyping in a personality which makes claim to such fine critical powers and such subtle insight and which boasts of a superior education is obvious, and, as a striking symptom of general intellectual failure, it leads us to wonder just how reliable Cervantes's satirical *persona* is, even in those utterances that we suspect are closest to the author's views.

At this point it is perhaps worth briefly looking beyond the confines of the exemplary tale to note how consistently Cervantes draws attention to the differences between type and individual in the *Quixote*, how essential to his novelistic procedures the exposure of that difference is, and how critical he is of literary modes and theories which reduce human reality to any convenient abstractions provided by type designations. If the glass licentiate were to gaze on the world of the *Quixote* with his penetrating but narrow vision, he would undoubtedly discover in Maritornes nothing more than the features that she shares with the other members of the professional class to which she belongs, the "baggages of Satan's army"; in Doña Rodríguez he would find confirmation of his concept of the *dueña* essence, defined by a few distasteful habits that frequently afflict the members of her class—a pretentious idiom ("he told marvelous tales of their *permafoy*"), a parasitical attachment to the wealthy, and hypochondria. He would

probably confine Hadji Morato to an abstraction of nationality, Sancho
Panza to the socio-professional type of the "tosco labrador," and Don
Quixote to the social type of the idle hidalgo, and he would, of course,
limit his revelations concerning them to pointing out how they are
endowed with the foibles of all the members of the types to which
they belong. What would be of no interest to him is the observation
of such figures moving about in "nonparadigmatic" situations and
revealing elements of an individuated self which may have nothing to
do with the scheme of attributes and behavioral possibilities encompassed by the type designation and which at times may violently clash
with those attributes.

If there is any fundamental philosophical principle which we can
infer from the pervasive dialectical procedure of Cervantes's novelistic
art, that dynamic process of disengagement of individual from type
classification which compels the reader of the *Quixote* both to feel the
unmediated presence of concrete experience in what he reads and at
the same time to take note of the impoverishing abstractions of traditional idealizing and satirical modes of literature with their partial
visions of truth and their limiting theories of exemplarity and decorum, it would lie somewhere in the range of ideas which were developed traditionally in skeptic, practical philosophy and which found
eloquent expression in his age.[79] Throughout the writings of Juan Luis
Vives we observe a skeptical attitude toward the value of the gener-
alities which through rational hypothesis we bring to bear on experience, an intense consciousness of the way in which the particular
resists reduction according to a category, and a strong emphasis on
the empirical observation of the particular as the surest means of at-
taining useful knowledge. For Vives the ability to distinguish and
judge accurately is of fundamental importance, for there is such diversity in experience ("it is difficult to find two persons who are pleased
by the same thing") that the intelligent man dare not proceed with
"predetermined formulas," particularly in the realm of moral choice,
where reason and probability analysis can easily support opposite conclusions. Vives's sensitivity to individual particularity ("ingenia autem
infinita, diversissima, difformia") is well illustrated in his catalogue
of "aversions": "It would be an endless task to describe the peculiar
types of aversions of each individual. There are those who cannot
endure the noise of a handsaw, the grunting of a pig, the ripping of
a cloth, the splitting of a coal with a pair of tongs. There are those

<hr />

[79] For the importance of skepticism in Cervantes's age, see Max Horkheimer,
"Montaigne und die Funktion der Skepsis," *Anfänge der bürgerlichen Geschichtsphilosophie* (Frankfurt, 1971), pp. 96-144.

who are disturbed by certain gestures in others, their manner of walking, of sitting down, of moving their hands, of talking. And there are even those who are beside themselves on seeing a wrinkle in the dress of another person."[80]

The skeptical view of human nature informing Vives's study of the soul is presented in terms which are even more explicit by Cervantes's contemporary, the nominalist philosopher Francisco Sánchez. Again experience reveals that "there are only individuals, only these can be perceived." The empirical observation of man's psyche yields a panorama of endless variety: "How much variety does one observe? It is a marvelous thing. This individual is an accomplished thief; that one is a murderer; another is born only for grammar; another completely inept for sciences; this one is cruel and bloodthirsty from the cradle . . . one person melts away at the mere sight or smell of bile; another person never liked apples, nor can he endure the sight of someone who likes them . . . another faints at the sight or smell of a rose; this person detests women." Sánchez proceeds to push forward toward the logical conclusion of his antiessentialist view of human nature: there is indeed such variation in experience that it is wrong to think of a single individual as having an essential identity. Sánchez points out that men change from day to day and even from hour to hour ("if you add or take away a single point from anything, it is no longer entirely the same thing"), and he concludes with a striking inversion of the traditional psychological and anthropological conception of the human being: "the accidents are of the essence of the individual."[81] Such an inversion would imply a radically different conception of literary character from that which had dominated traditional fiction and literary theorizing. It would imply that the canonized techniques of characterization, whether practiced in romance, epic, or satire, based as they are on symbolization and the primacy of exemplarity in fiction, rest on fundamentally fallacious assumptions concerning the human being and the nature of human experience. Sánchez's transvaluation of accidental truth could in fact be viewed as the philosophical basis for novelistic art, and it is probable that Cervantes's exploitation of the tension between type and individual and his concern to expose the weaknesses in the traditional theories of decorum and exemplarity

---

[80] "Sunt aliae offensiones cuique peculiares, quas esset immensum persequi, ut alii serrae stridorem ferre non possunt, alii grunnitum suis, alii morderi linteum, alii frangi prunam ardentem forcipe; sunt quos offendit gestus ad certum modum compositus, sessio, incessus, motio manus, locutio; sunt quos vel ruga alienae vestis" (*De Anima et Vita*, III.xi, *Opera Omnia*, 3:471-74).

[81] See *Que nada se sabe* (*Quod Nihil Scitur*), pp. 104-105, 122.

were to some extent influenced by the currents of thought that the Spanish philosopher expressed so concisely. The passage in the *Persiles* which I have discussed above in connection with Cervantes's ideas of nature is particularly revealing concerning the affinities linking its author, in his way of thinking about individuality, with the skeptical empiricists. The garrulous narrator of the prose epic, whose reductive techniques and critical discourses on literary theory, like those of the narrators of the *Quixote*, are strongly touched by the voice of the philosophical skeptic, digresses concerning the nature of man, and in his observations the arguments of such empirical psychologists as Vives and Sánchez are clearly discernible. He speaks of the variety and strangeness in human beings' attitudes and feelings ("I have seen a man tremble on seeing a radish cut"; another's teeth ache when he "sees a cloth cut with a knife"), remarks that speculation concerning the causes of psychic phenomena is fruitless, and suggests that the most we can do in our efforts to understand individual behavior is to take note of what the particular soul under examination *does*.[82]

The Licenciado Vidriera is insensitive to whatever mysteries might reside in human particularity, and his agitated invocation of what Vives condemns as "predetermined formulas" is a symptom of his general flight from discrimination and the close engagement with other human beings that authentic discrimination requires. At this point it is well to return briefly to Vives's penetrating *De Anima et Vita*, for one of its discussions of the discriminating faculties of the mind makes

[82] *Los trabajos de Persiles y Sigismunda*, ed. J. B. Avalle-Arce (Madrid, 1969), pp. 177-78. See above, pp. 170-71. For the critical discourse of Cervantes's narrators in the *Quixote* and the *Persiles*, see my *Cervantes, Aristotle, and the "Persiles"* (Princeton, 1970), chaps. 4 and 8. The precise echoes of the writings of the empirical psychologists in the passage cited suggest that a rewarding study could be made of the links between the literary theories and practices generally represented by this narrative voice, as well as by nearly all other discursive narrators in Cervantes's works, and the philosophical skepticism supporting the developing empirical science of the age. One thinks of their general obsession with the difficulty of ascertaining truth, of such striking skeptical interludes as the editors' puzzled analysis of the changes in Sancho Panza's style of speaking and Cide Hamete Benengeli's recommendation of suspended judgment following his subjection of the narration of the descent of Don Quixote into the Cave of Montesinos to probability analysis, and of such minor details as the Moor's dramatic violation of type classification in his Christian oath and the burlesque of the syllogism in Don Quixote's narration of the cave adventure. As I have pointed out above in connection with *La Gitanilla*, the view of nature implied by Cervantes's skeptical pronouncements should be clearly separated from the "naturaleza bien concertada," a nature of rational design that can be easily deciphered by man's rational faculties and that yields inviolable ethical precepts for individual and social organization. Cervantes, like other major writers in the humanist tradition, notably Erasmus and Vives, found no difficulty in reconciling the two views of nature.

an appeal for the type of thinking that led Cervantes to turn to concrete experience and to develop literary techniques adequate to the
exploration of all the mysteries of particularity. In its description of a
flawed intellect, it leads us back to the *Licenciado Vidriera*.

Some people, through the evil custom of scorning everything, have con-
tracted the habit of being displeased by whatever they encounter, without
pausing to examine and judge. They make up for their faulty knowledge
with discontentment, refusing to approve of anything, not even what is done
with the greatest uprightness, and always probing with a systematic wickedness for whatever might be censurable. With the title of censor they greatly
flatter themselves and earn in the eyes of foolish spectators the fame of being
ingenious, as if it were not much easier and much more practicable for
anybody to condemn everything indiscriminately than to establish distinctions between good and bad, as is fitting in a man of intelligence and wisdom."[83]

By Vives's standards the "heightened" vision of Cervantes's protagonist is extremely narrow. The glass licentiate shows little interest in
pausing in order to examine carefully, to distinguish, and to judge
the individuals he confronts and condemns. He commits the traditional error of the misanthrope, and Vives's portrait of his type of
derangement might bring to mind a critical examination of misanthropy well known in the age, Lucian's *Timon, or the Misanthrope*, and
its central moment when Hermes, speaking for moderation and rationality, gently reminds the railing satirist that his victims "do not
all deserve" the sorrow that he wishes them.[84] There is a similar

---

[83] "Quidam ex prava consuetudine aspernandi omnia eum traxerunt morem ut qui-
buslibet citra judicium, citra discrimen omne, offendantur, quibus etiam hoc sapien-
tiae loco est, nihil, ne rectissimè quidem factum, approbare, in omnibus mira ini-
quitate judiciorum exquirere quod damnent; quo nomine plurimum sibi placent, et
apud stultos spectatores ingenii gloriam consequuntur; quasi vero non sit multo
promtius, et cuilibet factu facilius, promiscue damnare omnia, quàm inter bona et
mala discrimen ponere, quod ingeniosi demum est hominis et cordati" (*Opera Omnia*,
3:474).

[84] *Lucian*, 2:367; italics added. In denouncing the excesses of Cynic criticism and
proposing a method of "humane correction" and "fraternal reprehension," Erasmus
suggests that the critic must be "all things to everybody" ("Esto et tu omnibus
omnia"), which his Spanish translator interprets as an injunction that one must be
extremely sensitive to the individuality of the person whom one would correct: "Hazte,
pues, con todos, *como sant Pablo*, todo quanto vieres que les cumple, humanándote
según todas las qualidades y differencias de todos" (*Enquiridion*, p. 352). For Erasmus's insistence on considering the human being as a particular individual and, as
such, formed and bound to a significant extent by the unique circumstances of his
own life, and for his discomfort with the reductive definitions provided by traditional
anthropologies, with their abstractions and myths, see B. Groethuysen, "Philoso-

moment of complicating insight in Cervantes's tale, when, following the protagonist's satirical observations on the canonization of friars, a charitable Hieronymite appears to cure him of his torment. The dramatic technique is quite effective, and there is no need for direct commentary by character or narrator. The inadequacy in the intellect of the celebrated man of letters is suddenly illuminated sharply. His audience's acclaim of his *ingeniosidad* is but proof of Vives's assertion concerning the seductive attractiveness of dogmatic thinking to humanity, of the appeal of false wisdom to fools.

Modern readers occasionally admit with a trace of embarrassment that they have failed to respond to many of the flourishes of the licentiate's wit, assuming perhaps that the enjoyment that his moralizing pronouncements evidently bring to his audience within the tale should in fact be shared by a reader of the text. Part of the problem, of course, lies in the topical quality of satirical humor in general and specifically in the remoteness of the preoccupations and activities of seventeenth-century Spanish society from the twentieth-century reader. However, when one scrutinizes closely the spectacle of wit, that is, its pronouncement and reception, in *El Licenciado Vidriera*, one senses that a reader's exclusion from the participating audience within it has as much to do with the nature of the humor as with its content and that it may in fact be an effect that Cervantes carefully attempted to achieve. Luis Rosales has remarked that the licentiate's humorous statements lack the gaiety and generosity of understanding that characterize Cervantes's great humor, and his rather unfavorable judgment of the tale is based to some extent on its failure to offer the comic effects available in the *Quixote*.[85] I would suggest that the author knew quite well that his character was not speaking with his own authentic voice and that Cervantes was in fact presenting in his fool what he considered a diseased form of humor, a heartless humor of the mind of the type that was to flourish in Spain's literature of *desengaño*.

The characteristic witticism of the licentiate is the striking combination of disparate elements—e.g., "pimp" = "coach"—, and generally the bond uniting them and justifying their bewildering conver-

phische Anthropologie," *Mensch und Charakter* (Munich and Berlin, 1931), pp. 181-94: "Jeder Mensch hat seine Eigenart, die der Philosoph kennen muss, um ihn beraten und ihm helfen zu können . . . Der Gehalt eines Lebens wird zum Wesentlichen . . . Der Mensch des Erasmus lässt sich nicht von seiner Umwelt ablösen, in der sich sein Leben abspielt . . . Jedes menschliche Leben ist bedeutsam." Groethuysen argues that Erasmus gives expression to a fundamentally new attitude toward individuality and experience and that it was to become essential in modern definitions and evaluations of the human being.

[85] *Cervantes y la libertad*, 1:193.

gence is highly abstract and hence apprehensible by the mind rather than by the senses. Despite the formal discontinuity in the oracular segment of the tale, one quickly notes a uniformity in tone and realizes that all the startling *conceptos* that thrill the crowd of onlookers spring from a coherent, dark philosophical vision.[86] The licentiate's wit in fact feeds on analogies suggesting strife and destruction, and it is most somber when implying that the community of humanity is an aggregate of enemies. Thus he advises a husband whose wife has abandoned him to refrain from seeking her and to thank God for removing an enemy from his house. Domestic peace can be assured by a proper chain of authority, the wife commanding in the household and the husband commanding the wife. The licentiate tells a child who is considering leaving a cruel father that "the whip lashes that fathers give to their children do them honor" and suggests that by accepting them he may avoid those of the executioner.[87] He warns a crowd of spectators at a public flogging of a thief that the executioner might justifiably turn his instrument on them. The licentiate's acceptance of strife, authority, and terror as natural is implicit in his

[86] Franz H. Mautner notes the common misconception that the formal disconnectedness of the aphorism within a collection implies an essential discreteness in the pronouncement and a lack of unity in the total body of thought behind it. "Jener Schluss übersieht völlig, dass sie trotz der scheinbaren Isolierung im Werden und in der Darbietung die Gemeinsamkeit der Gewächse eines Nährbodens haben, einer einheitlichen Denk- und Erlebnismasse; so schliessen sie sich, äusserlich isoliert bleibend oder nachträglich verbunden, zum inneren System, zur einheitlichen Weltansicht zusammen." As Friedrich Schlegel put it (*Lyzeumsfragment* 103): "Viele Werke, deren schöne Verkettung man preist, haben weniger Einheit, als ein bunter Haufen von Einfällen, die nur vom Geiste eines Geistes belebt, nach Einem zielen" ("Der Aphorismus als literarische Gattung," *Der Aphorismus*, ed. G. Neumann [Darmstadt, 1976], pp. 19-74; see pp. 69-70). For the way in which a unifying system of thought can be illuminated by the brief flashes of a series of apparently disparate aphorisms, see H. Friedrich, "Pascal," *Romanische Literaturen*, 1:139-58; esp. p. 141. In her argument for the confusion of both the glass licentiate and Cervantes in this tale, El Saffar mistakes fragmentation for incoherence and maintains that there is no meaningful order in the protagonist's "bits and pieces" of knowledge ("their very fragmentation denies the totality to which they aspire") (*Novel to Romance*, pp. 59-60).

[87] "los azotes que los padres dan a los hijos honran" (p. 42). The advice recalls the biblical text which the licentiate is most fond of citing, "He who loves his son will whip him often, in order that he may rejoice at the way he turns out" (Ecclus. 30:1). The protagonist's attraction to the wisdom literature of the Old Testament, with its oracular, discontinuous style, its stern commandments, and its rather somber vision of human life, is a revealing indication of his philosophical temper. For the popularity of the biblical wisdom literature among the spokesmen for *desengaño*, and particularly the writers of picaresque fiction, with its central principle that "Militia est vita hominis super terram" (Job 7:1), see Hansgerd Schulte, *El Desengaño; Wort und Thema in der spanischen Literatur des Goldenen Zeitalters* (Munich, 1969), pp. 116ff.

most comprehensive comment on human destiny. "Being one day in a church, he saw that there were being brought in at one and the same time, an old man to bury, a child to christen, and a woman to marry, and he remarked that churches were battlefields where the old die, the young conquer, and the women triumph."[88] Unlike the characters of Cervantes's *Persiles*, who behold the same events toward the end of their pilgrimage,[89] the licentiate does not find in the spectacle an occasion for reverence before the mystery of renewal and salvation. Obsessed rather by the general destructiveness of living, he resorts to one of his favorite analogies, and the result is his most striking aphorism, undermining all conventional perspectives as it discloses the paradoxical vision of the church as a battlefield and birth as a triumphant act of war.

Whatever Cervantes may have meant by the anxiety of the protagonist, it is clear that his consciousness of death and physical decay is highly developed, and it frequently emerges to give a dark coloration to his witticisms. He amuses his host at the court by asserting that all journeys are pleasant except those that lead to the gallows. There may indeed be a profound philosophical consolation in his advice to a man who seeks a cure for envy, but, through the familiar analogy of sleep-death, it really amounts to a sardonic parody of the traditional act of the moral preceptor and a witty indulgence of the licentiate's exuberant *Schadenfreude*; "Sleep, for all the time that you are slumbering you will be the equal of the man you envy."[90] The licentiate's apparent subscription to the grim consolation is, of course, ludicrously at odds with his own hysterical fear of death, which we infer from his concern to avoid the pestilential areas between Rome and Naples and the war-torn regions of France and witness directly in the terror that he suffers in thunderstorms or at the thought of falling roof tiles. In the protagonist's response to the question as to who has been the most happy man in the world, we observe both his shallow fondness for the pun frequently characteristic of aphoristic pronouncements and an indication of his views concerning the normality of isolation, sinfulness, dissatisfaction, and damnation in the human condition: The most happy man is Nobody [Nemo] for *"Nobody knows*

[88] "Estando un día en una iglesia vió que traían a enterrar a un viejo, a bautizar a un niño y a velar a una mujer, todo a un mismo tiempo, y dijo que los templos eran campos de batalla, donde los viejos acaban, los niños vencen y las mujeres triunfan" (pp. 74-75).

[89] *Persiles*, pp. 411-12; see my *Cervantes' Christian Romance* (Princeton, 1972), pp. 138-41.

[90] "Duerme; que todo el tiempo que durmieres serás igual al que envidias" (p. 57).

his father; Nobody lives without crime; Nobody is content with his lot; Nobody goes to heaven."[91] Here the licentiate has appropriated the words of an old mock-sermon, descending from the clerical culture of the middle ages, and exploited its paradoxical pronouncements concerning the deeds of the personified negation in order to produce a trenchant aphorism, which discloses to his audience, as it attempts to resolve the unfolding paradoxes of the statements, a momentary glimpse of total desolation at the heart of human life. The *Schadenfreude* that bonds all the licentiate's aphorisms, despite their disjunct and fragmentary character, into a unified system, receives here its most concise and literal expression: "Happy is nobody, for nobody is saved."[92]

While the Licenciado Vidriera's susceptibility to categorical thinking appears to be at odds with his author's fundamental respect for the integrity of the individual and his wit, severely limited by his obsession with the destructive side of existence, it is clearly his moral conduct that contributes most to the discrediting of his vision and hence to the subversion of his authority as critic and spokesman for Cervantes. Until the restoration of his health shortly before his death, Tomás Rodaja is a man with virtually no interest in cultivating bonds with his fellow men. From the moment of the youth's appearance in the tale, asleep "en aquella soledad," Cervantes carefully draws our attention to the self-imposed isolation of his protagonist, showing him disengaging first from his birthplace and family, which he has abandoned in his determination to win fame through the acquisition of knowledge, then from his friends, whose hospitality he rejects in his eagerness to return to his studies, and finally from his country, in

---

[91] "*Nemo novit patrem; Nemo sine crimine vivit; Nemo sua sorte contentus; Nemo ascendit in coelum*" (p. 65).

[92] The metamorphosis of the text of the *sermon joyeu* demonstrates perfectly the way in which aphorists commonly revitalize literary citations, using them as the trigger for the evocation of a whole field of associated thoughts which may have nothing to do with the context from which the citation is taken. See Mautner, "Der Aphorismus als literarische Gattung," pp. 69-70. The resonances of the gospels (John 3:13; Matt. 11:27) in Rodaja's Latin aphorism form part of a larger pattern of biblical references, consisting of actual citations, symbols, and evocations of biblical style, which Cervantes coherently employs throughout the story in order to develop his principal themes. In this case we observe a travesty of the language of Christ, paralleling the licentiate's earlier denunciation of the wife of the old-clothes merchant ("*Filiae Hierusalem, plorate super vos et super filios vestros*" [p. 40]) and heightening our sense of the absurdity of the person capable of such abuse or misappropriation of sacred words. For the sources of the citation and its function in the *Licenciado Vidriera*, see my forthcoming article: "Cervantes' Praise of Nobody: The Origin and Evolution of a Renaissance Symbol."

whose army he refuses to serve.[93] We watch as various people display kindness toward Tomás, offering him both generous material assistance and the spiritual support of friendship and concern: "he arrived at Salamanca, where he was well received by his friends, and with the assistance which they provided for him he continued his studies. . . . he begged his masters to grant him permission to go back. They, being courteous and liberal gentlemen, granted him leave, and they aided him in such fashion that with what they presented him he could support himself for three years. . . . he determined to return to Spain and Salamanca to complete his studies, and as soon as he had formed this idea, he put it into execution to the very great regret of his comrade, who at the moment of saying farewell to him begged him to let him know of his health, arrival, and fortunes."[94] At no time, however, does Cervantes show Tomás revealing, through such qualities as friendship, courtesy, and concern, a moral or social sensibility commensurate with his intellectual attainments. It is not simply that there is no mention of acts or feelings of reciprocality in his dealings with others. His characteristic act in all his human relationships before his madness is withdrawal. While Cervantes's narrator initially avoids both direct negative judgment and, aside from the brief description of Tomás strutting in his bright soldierly attire ("vestido de papagayo"), caricaturistic reduction, he succeeds, through narrative techniques that are far more subtle, in activating in his reader a complex moral engagement with the protagonist whose educational triumphs he chronicles.

Once we recognize the antisocial, egocentric quality in Tomás's behavior early in the tale, we discover that the division in the work is not nearly as radical as it initially appears; for we see that the glass licentiate's madness is in reality an exacerbation of tendencies already present in his personality and behavior. The events at the beginning of his illness make this perfectly clear. A woman whom his insatiable curiosity compels him to visit falls in love with him, something that, despite all his learning, he does not understand at all: ". . . without

---

[93] ". . . dijo al capitán que era contento der irse con él a Italia; pero había de ser condición que no se había de sentar debajo de bandera, ni ponerse en lista de soldado, por no obligarse a seguir su bandera" (p. 17).

[94] "llegó a Salamanca, donde fué bien recebido de sus amigos, y con la comodidad que ellos le hicieron prosiguió sus estudios. . . . pidió a sus amos licencia para volverse. Ellos, corteses y liberales, se la dieron, acomodándole de suerte, que con lo que le dieron se pudiera sustentar tres años. . . . determinó volverse a España y a Salamanca a acabar sus estudios, y como lo pensó lo puso luego por obra, con pesar grandísimo de su camarada, que le rogó, al tiempo de despedirse, le avisase de su salud, llegada y suceso" (pp. 12, 32).

noticing what was happening, he turned a blind eye and did not care to set foot in her house unless it was under compulsion and when he was taken there by others." Her open declaration of love and offer of her possessions earn a stony refusal from the licentiate, who "attended more to his books than to other diversions."[95] With the aid of a *morisca* witch the scorned lady sends Tomás a charmed quince, a traditional love-inducing fruit, and, on tasting it, the youth falls violently ill.[96] After withering away in bed for six months, he finds his bodily health restored but suffers a strange mental aberration ("he was in good health, but he was insane with the strangest form of insanity that had ever yet been seen among the fancies of lunatics"). He believes that he is made of glass, and, terrified at the fragility of his state, he pleads with those about him to keep their distance. The scene which follows dramatically reveals his isolation:

In order to deliver him from this strange hallucination, many, without attending to his words and entreaties, took hold of him and clasped him in their arms, telling him that he should observe and see that he did not break. But what was gained by this was that the poor wretch threw himself on the ground, uttering a thousand cries, and presently fainted away, nor did he come to himself for four hours, and, when he did, he began to renew his prayers and entreaties that they should not again approach him. He begged them to speak to him from a distance.

His craving for distance and his terror at the thought of embracing another human being are symptoms of a psychic disorder which a Renaissance psychologist would probably have recognized as a form of melancholy. The fact is, however, that psychological accuracy and clinical verisimilitude, whatever they might indicate about the author's powers as an observer of human behavior, are of little consequence in the tale. Cervantes's portrait of the protagonist's illness is significant primarily in the exemplary context of the novella, and the very symptoms that point directly to both Renaissance and modern models of psychic behavior point even more directly to the essential philosophical and ethical issues that the story raises and resolves. The licentiate's hysterical fear of being approached by other human beings is in fact a humorous intensification of a concern to avoid contact with others that we observe in his normal behavior. The symptoms of his mental disorder, which is indeed caused by the tasting of a fruit, an

---

[95] "él, sin echar de ver en ello, si no era por fuerza y llevado de otros, no quería entrar en su casa . . . atendía más a sus libros que a otros pasatiempos" (p. 33).

[96] E. Panofsky points out that the quince was the "wedding fruit *par excellence*," noting that numerous texts testify "to the old custom, allegedly sanctioned by a Solonian law, of presenting couples with a dish of quinces on their wedding day" (*Studies in Iconology* [New York, 1962], p. 113).

act that neither Renaissance nor modern psychologists have attached to the syndrome of melancholy or schizophrenia, symbolize the isolation, egocentricity, and misanthropy that result from a misguided intellectualism and a pursuit of knowledge for improper reasons. As I have pointed out above, for Erasmus and his fellow humanists one of the principal goals of "good letters" is the attainment of *humanitas*. Tomás's breathless pursuit of glory through study leads to thorough dehumanization, and his terrified reaction to his friends' kind offer of an embrace, in its powerful irony, is undoubtedly the most eloquent dramatic expression of his failure in the work.[97]

Kindness, *benevolentia*, and *caritas* are among the essential characteristics of the successful scholar, and they are probably what Diego de Miranda and Don Quixote have in mind when they agree in their dialogue on the aims of education, that "learning without virtue is like pearls on a dunghill."[98] In the numerous encounters between the licentiate and the applauding mob, Cervantes carefully draws our attention to the absence of such qualities in his protagonist. If we compare Cervantes's two major efforts in satirical fiction, the *Licenciado Vidriera* and the *Coloquio de los perros*, we discover an important difference in the relationships between the satirical commentator and the procession of figures that unfolds before his gaze. Berganza's most characteristic point of view during his experience is that of the *ingénu*—naïve, unprejudiced, charitable, well-intentioned, relatively ignorant, and guided primarily by his *bien natural*. His method of discovering truth is that of the empiricist, and his denunciations are usually offered retrospectively, following his chastening experience of evil, and even then they are moderated by professions of humility and

---

[97] "quedó sano, y loco de la más extraña locura que entre las locuras hasta entonces se había visto. . . . Para sacarle desta extraña imaginación, muchos, sin atender a sus voces y rogativas, arremetieron a él y le abrazaron, diciéndole que advirtiese y mirase como no se quebrase. Pero lo que se granjeaba en esto era que el pobre se echaba en el suelo dando mil gritos, y luego le tomaba un desmayo del cual no volvía en sí en cuatro horas; y cuando volvía, era renovando las plegarias y rogativas de que otra vez no le llegasen. Decía que le hablasen desde lejos" (pp. 36-37). In his retreat into secure habitats suggestive of the animal world and its freedom from the torment of communication—the open field and the hayloft—, Cervantes's student of letters represents a violent perversion of the aim of the university, that of lifting its members out of the condition of *feritas* and bestowing *humanitas* upon them. The Spanish humanist Franceso Décio proclaimed in an inaugural address at the University of Valencia: "pecudes pene nascimur, hic autem comparamus per quod homines simus." The university is where man earns the badges of his authentic humanity ("humanitatis decora"). See F. Rico, " 'Laudes litterarum': Humanismo y dignidad del hombre en la España del Renacimiento," *Homenaje a Julio Caro Baroja* (Madrid, 1978), pp. 908-909.

[98] "letras sin virtud son perlas en el muladar" (*Don Quijote de la Mancha*, 2:154).

of concern about the evils of vituperation. Moreover, there is absolutely no ambiguity concerning his moral superiority to the figures whose foibles and vices he reveals. Unlike the dogs, who know only what nature and experience have taught them, the glass licentiate is a man of vast knowledge, and he brings to bear on his victims a point of view that is heavily burdened with dogma and opinion and that is incapable of holding judgment in abeyance as he scans his society. In other words he approaches experience as the rationalist, armed with hypotheses and categories and confident that anything he observes will confirm their validity. His perspective is that of another conventional figure of satirical literature—the misanthropic railer.

In a recent study, Robert C. Elliott has pointed out that, while the satirical railer has always offered the writer a vehicle for powerful and hyperbolic denunciation, the traditional figure has frequently invited the most profound satirists to reflect on the philosophical problems underlying their art and to engage with the question that lies at the heart of humanistic philosophy—how much can one demand of man's humanity?[99] The misanthropic satirical commentator combines high standards of excellence with a penetrating eye, and he generally finds nothing in or beneath the appearances with which human beings surround themselves in their day-to-day activities that merits a charitable judgment. Although their indignation is frequently justified by man's inadequacies, the greatest misanthropes of literature, Molière's Alceste and Swift's Gulliver, are clearly shown by their authors to be out of touch with the limits of man's humanity. There is something fundamentally unnatural in the absoluteness of their lofty expectations and demands. As Philinte, one of Molière's most persuasive spokesmen for the necessity of well-intentioned dissimulation in civilized living, points out to the outraged Alceste: "Mon Dieu des moeurs du temps mettons-nous moins en peine/ Et faisons un peu grâce á la nature humaine/ Ne l'examinons point dans la grande rigueur,/ Et voyons ses défauts avec quelque douceur."[100] As Swift's narrative makes clear to

[99] *The Power of Satire*, chap. 4.

[100] *Le Misanthrope, Oeuvres complètes*, ed. R. Jouanny, 2 vols. (Paris, 1962), 1:821. Did Molière sense that the profound meaning of *El Licenciado Vidriera* was to be sought in its critical examination of the Cynic's view of life and the consequences of his relentless demands for purity? If, as Foulché-Delbosc and Hainsworth have suggested, Molière did in fact conceive Alceste's critique of Oronte's sonnet (*Le Misanthrope*, Act I) as a dramatization of the licentiate's speech on sonneteers, the question is intriguing and might clarify the fundamental problem raised by the tale: to what extent is the protagonist identifiable with his author? See G. Hainsworth, *Les "Novelas Exemplares" de Cervantes en France au XVIIe Siècle* (Paris, 1933), p. 90.

the reader, Gulliver's puzzling blindness to the implications of the "great Humanity" and courtesy that he notes in Don Pedro, the "yahoo" sea captain who rescues him from the kingdom of the Yahoos, is a sign of a general blindness afflicting him in all his misanthropic generalizations concerning the total "yohoodom" of man.[101] In other words, certain figures whom the satirist denounces are endowed with such moral qualities that in their confrontation the satire abruptly reverses its initial direction, turns back on the railer, and dramatically reveals the narrowness and inhumanity in his vision.

As we have already noted, in the *Licenciado Vidriera* there are several characters around the central figure who, through their friendliness, courtesy, charity, and concern, draw our attention to the absence of such qualities in him—his masters, his university friends, and his traveling companion. In general the objects of his tirades appear to deserve censure and justify the indignation that seethes beneath his pronouncements. However, in two important incidents, the victims display qualities that compel us to reflect on the propriety of the protagonist's abuse and, in doing so, to question the general validity of the satirist's assertions. Following his malicious generalizations concerning the canonization of friars, a good Hieronymite, moved by *"misericordia,"* appears and heals his illness with "ciencia y gracia." If the appearance of the figure dramatically reveals the intellectual blindness of the licentiate and the discrepancies between his rationalistic categories and the realities of experience, the concentration on the friar's charitable motivation and action at this crucial moment of the narrative ironically points to the spiritual emptiness of Cervantes's protagonist, to his failure to found his program of criticism on a principle that Erasmus had emphasized in his denunciation of the Cynic philosopher and in his advocacy of a method of "humane correction" and "fraternal reprehension": love of one's fellow man.[102]

The other striking moment in which the satire turns back on the satirical railer is in his encounter with the woman at the old-clothes market. Her comment: "Upon my soul, Mr. Licentiate, your misfortune weighs heavily on me. But what can I do, for I cannot weep?" sets up the licentiate's mischievous joke and his comical misappropriation of the words of Christ: " 'Daughters of Jerusalem, weep for

---

[101] See Elliott, *The Power of Satire*, pp. 212-13.

[102] ". . . bien es que aya en ti toda cortesía . . . de arte que tu buena condición y comedimiento aproveche para atraher assí por amor a tu próximo a que te ame y te dé crédito" (*Enquiridion*, p. 352).

yourselves, and for your children.' "[103] However, at the same time her statement contains a profession of commiseration which is difficult to overlook and which forces us to consider the moral shortcomings of her calumniator's wit. She has certainly done nothing to warrant public ridicule for her Jewish ancestry, and the dialogue between her husband and the licentiate, which concludes the encounter, makes it clear that the observation is malicious and that the self-indulgent intellect of Cervantes's man of letters is fundamentally immoral in its lack of concern about its cruelty.

The woman's husband understood the malicious intention of the saying, and remarked: "Brother Glass Licentiate (for so he said that he was called), *you*

[103] "En mi ánima, señor Licenciado, que me pesa de su desgracia; pero ¿qué haré, que no puedo llorar? . . . *Filiae Hierusalem, plorate super vos et super filios vestros*" (p. 40). As in the case of the *Nemo* joke, which similarly echoes Christ's words, the licentiate's retort represents a kind of travesty which is traditional in literature presenting negative examples and their disorderly worlds. (*La Celestina, Lazarillo de Tormes*, and Quevedo's *Buscón* are spectacular cases.) In his *Parodie im Mittelalter* (Munich, 1922), P. Lehmann points out that the procedure is extremely widespread in the parodistic literature of the middle ages. The evil character is rendered all the more ridiculous or horrible as the reader contemplates his profanation of something that is sacred. In such cases the *work of literature* does not desecrate anything, although readers, even those whose sense of good and evil, the sacred and the profane, is unshakeably founded and threatened by no subversive impulses or anxieties, may find the sight of its *characters'* desecrations disturbing and even intolerable, particularly when the work offers no direct condemnation of them or no explicit moral norm by which the reader can easily maintain them in the proper perspective. As the polemical *El tribunal de la justa venganza* makes clear, Quevedo's *Buscón*, a work which is totally ironic in its vision of evil, evidently stirred up a reaction of this sort in some readers (see *Obras en verso*, ed. Astrana Marín [Madrid, 1943], pp. 1103-118). Critics who see in the Licenciado Vidriera's appropriation of the language of the New Testament a mockery of Christ miss this fundamental point (see A. Singer's discussion of the sacrilegious implications of such passages, "The Sources, Meaning, and Use of the Madness Theme in Cervantes' *Licenciado Vidriera*," *West Virginia University Bulletin: Philogical Papers* 6 [1949]:31-53; esp. p. 46). As for the possibility that such citations might elevate the licentiate to their sacred level, the context of the tale makes it quite clear that their expressive powers are not released in that direction. The licentiate would indeed speak with the powers of Christ and the Old Testament prophets, whose style he imitates, but his efforts strike the reader as presumptuous and vainglorious. Only in his concluding denunciation of the court, a powerful speech in which the perfectly constructed parallelisms and antitheses yield a cadence that echoes a style of the Old Testament, does his imitation of biblical style have an ennobling effect. But this, of course, follows the restoration of his sanity, his decision to serve his country in the wars in Flanders, and his total rejection by a society of fools. For the variety of directions in which the negative energy released by parody can flow, see Wido Hempel, "Parodie, Travestie, und Pastiche: zur Geschichte von Wort und Sache," *Germanisch-Romanische Monatsschrift* 46 (1965):150-76, esp. pp. 173ff.

have more of the knave than the madman about you." "I don't care a jot for that," he replied, *"provided that I have nothing of the stupid person about me."*[104]

Probably the most effective of the various methods which Cervantes employs to undermine the vision of his satirical commentator is a technique that comic writers of all ages have exploited to expose presumptuous impostors—dramatic self-contradiction. If we look at the procession of occupations and types that the licentiate discusses, we immediately discover that one of the faults that he consistently castigates in others is malicious speech. He laments that poets slander one another and compares them to growling curs; he condemns the abusive language of muleteers and sailors. At the same time he devotes nearly all his energies to denouncing those around him, and he evidently enjoys being approached as an expert in the art of defamation (p. 71). The licentiate is infuriated by the pretentions of others,

---

[104] "Entendió el marido de la ropera la malicia del dicho, y díjole: —Hermano Licenciado Vidriera—que así decía él que se llamaba—, *más tenéis de bellaco que de loco.* —*No se me da un ardite*—respondió él—, *como no tenga nada de necio"* (p. 40; italics added). Cervantes's railer is fond of the witticism based on the anxieties and hypocrisis of Spaniards of Jewish ancestry, and it is interesting that his other joke of this type is not surrounded by elements reflecting on its questionable propriety. Whether or not Cervantes's contemporary readers would look with such disfavor on the woman's Jewishness and her presumed unwillingness to display it that they would interpret favorably the licentiate's insistence on disclosing the truth and find the humor of the bilingual ethnic joke unqualified by moral reservations is a question that is probably impossible to answer, as it points to the most elusive and complex kinds of extraliterary considerations confronting a student of satire. Nevertheless, even if such a way of reading the scene could be demonstrated, the fact would merely prove that, in their respective moral attitudes toward the *converso* and his anxieties, there is a good deal of distance between Cervantes and both his character and his contemporary readers. For the reservations expressed by the text are concrete, and they clearly draw attention to a perverseness in the licentiate's wit and humor. An interesting contemporary discussion of satire throws some light on this problem. Like most other literary theorists of the age, Luis Alfonso de Carvallo is concerned about the dangers inherent in satirical writing, and he attempts to distinguish valuable satire from destructive vituperation. Explaining the latter, he writes: "No dexa de auer tambien Satyras perjudiciales, y maliciosas, estas tambien si van al descubierto arguye a poco ingenio del que las dize, y se tiene por necio y mal hablado, como si llamasse vn hombre a otro bujaron, y el otro llamase judio ansi avoca llena. Differente sucedio entre vn Christiano nuevo y vn labrador, que yendo cavallero le dixo el que lo era pardo, que como caualgaua tan trasero motejandole de sucio. Y el labrador con malicia de aldeano le respondio, que por no matalla en la Cruz notandole de judio." Although the licentiate's jokes clearly are of the *"ingenioso"* variety, and, as he himself insists, he is satisfied with them as long as it is admitted that *"no tenga nada de necio,"* it is important to note that for the theorist, both primitive invective and ingenious malice belong to the genre of "satyra perjudicial" (*Cisne de Apolo,* ed. A. Porqueras Mayo, 2 vols. [Madrid, 1958], 2:68-69.

but he plainly fails to observe the discrepancies between appearance and reality in his own behavior. As he moves toward the conclusion of his career as a railing Cynic, Cervantes becomes increasingly concerned to reveal dramatically his lack of self-knowledge. In his lengthy commentary on notaries Tomás proudly distinguishes his fastidious criticism from the slanderous stock responses embodied in the masses' favorite professional stereotypes. He then proceeds to abuse notaries in a peculiarly perverse manner by portraying in great detail the *vulgo*'s opinions of them, while claiming, in an unconvincing way, that he does not subscribe to them and ostentatiously citing the Latin words of Ecclesiasticus on the honor that is the proper due of the distinguished profession. The ridicule of the Cynic sinks to its most comically sublime pitch, as he pompously preaches on a correct method of defaming and dignifies it by comparing it to "other sciences" such as grammar and music: "Although I am of glass, I am not so fragile as to let myself swim with the current of the vulgar herd, which is for the most part mistaken. It appears to me that the notaries are the grammar of the slanderers, and the *la, la, la* of those who sing, for just as it is impossible to pass to other sciences except by the gate of grammar, and as the musician hums before he sings, so with those who slander; where they begin to show the malignity of their tongues is by abusing notaries!"[105] The satirical travesty, with its incongruous conception of defamation as a systematic discipline with its grammar, exercises, initiatory stages and masters, is an amusing piece of comic magnification, but the most important effect of the passage lies in its presentation of the railer criticizing others for sins of which he himself is manifestly guilty. His actions are grotesquely at odds with his principles, and he is obviously incapable of turning on his own self-deceptions the penetrating vision that his madness has given him.[106]

[105] "Aunque de vidrio, no soy tan frágil que me deje ir con la corriente del vulgo, las más veces engañado. Paréceme a mí que la gramática de los murmuradores, y el *la, la, la* de los que cantan, son los escribanos; porque así como no se puede pasar a otras ciencias si no es por la puerta de la Gramática, y como el músico primero murmura que canta, así los maldicientes, por donde comienzan a mostrar la malignidad de sus lenguas es por decir mal de los escribanos" (p. 71).

[106] It is characteristic of Cervantes's deluded man of wisdom that one of his favorite biblical texts is Ecclesiasticus and that, while he struts about citing its Latin phrases, he obviously fails to understand its emphasis on the mystery of authentic knowledge and its recurrent dark pronouncements concerning the vanity of worldly wisdom, the evils of curiosity, the madness of the learned, and the destructive powers of the tongue. See, for example: "Seek not the things that are too high for thee, and search not into things above thy ability: but the things that God hath commanded thee, think on them always and in many of his works be not curious" (3:21-22); "He who is not clever cannot be taught, but there is a cleverness which increases bitterness.

In a master stroke of caricaturistic writing, Cervantes presents an effective satirical *contrappasso* that brings to a climax the dramatic process by which his character unwittingly exposes himself as an impostor:

A wasp on one occasion stung him on the neck, and he did not dare to shake off the insect for fear of breaking himself; but despite all this he complained. Somebody asked him how he could feel the wasp's sting if his body was of glass. He replied that the wasp must be a backbiter and that the tongues and stings of backbiters were enough to destroy bodies of bronze, not to say of glass.[107]

The fool's mask momentarily drops, and we watch him as he complains about the very pain that he continually inflicts on others.

THE SATIRIST SATIRIZED

Svele la indignacion componer versos,
pero si el indignado es algun tonto, ellos tendran su
todo de peruersos.
—Cervantes, *Viage del Parnaso*

The malignant sting of the wasp has been a motif of the satirist since Callimachus's famous description of Archilochus, the legendary figure who according to tradition first turned poetry into an instrument of death. "And he drank the bitter wrath of the dog and the sharp sting of the wasp; from both of these comes the poison of his mouth."[108] If there is a bestial element in the Licenciado Vidriera's superior knowledge that points both to the inhumanity of the Cynic philosopher, the snarling dog, and to the earthly, subhuman origin of worldly wisdom (the wisdom that Erasmus, echoing James 3:15,

---

The knowledge of a wise man will increase like a flood, and his counsel like a flowing spring. The mind of a fool is like a broken jar; it will hold no knowledge" (21:12-14). "For wisdom is known through speech, and education through the words of the tongue. Never speak against the truth, but be mindful of your ignorance" (4:24-25). "Do not be called a slanderer, and do not lie in ambush with your tongue" (5:14). "But the knowledge of wickedness is not wisdom, nor is there prudence where sinners take counsel. There is a cleverness which is abominable, but there is a fool who merely lacks wisdom" (19:22-23). "To a senseless man education is fetters on his feet" (21:19).

[107] "Picábale una vez una avispa en el cuello, y no se la osaba sacudir, por no quebrarse; pero, con todo eso, se quejaba. Preguntóle uno que cómo sentía aquella avispa, si era su cuerpo de vidrio. Y respondió que aquella avispa debía de ser murmuradora, y que las lenguas y picos de los murmuradores eran bastantes a desmoronar cuerpos de bronce, no que de vidrio" (p. 75).

[108] See Elliott, *The Power of Satire*, p. 11.

had denounced as the "sabiduría animal y diabólica" leading to death),[109] there is at the same time a quality in his manner of criticizing society that illustrates how easily art can serve the beast in man. While Cervantes's parable is primarily concerned with certain ethical and epistemological aspects of the general problem of knowledge, it incorporates and develops an important literary theme that is implied by all its philosophical issues. As the glass licentiate confronts his victims, pours forth his witty venom, and earns the applause of the mob, we observe a situation that Cervantes develops frequently in his fiction in order to dramatize the act of literary creation and, in so doing, to explore theoretical problems implicit in that act. Thus, within the satirical work, the drama of the creation and reception of satire unfolds before the reader, a process analogous to the counterfeit captives' recitation of their romance-epic to a critical audience within the *Persiles*, to the composition of a prologue to *Don Quixote* I within its prologue and in the presence of an expert on prologues, and to various encounters between creating artists and critical audiences in the *Quixote*: for example, Master Pedro's recitation of the deliverance of Melisendra, Sancho Panza's narration of the tale of La Torralba, and Don Quixote's account of the underworld adventures of the Knight of the Lake.[110] In *El Licenciado Vidriera* the traditional procession of targets for the satirist's denunciation appears as an approving audience, and its behavior adds a peculiar literary dimension to the situation. Just as in the brief scene of Master Pedro's recitation, Cervantes explores in a more profound way than any literary theorist of his time the existential foundations of romance, its methods of engaging the readers' emotions, the response that it elicits, and its moral and aesthetic strengths and weaknesses, he here incorporates into a fictional situation a searching critical analysis of the literary phenomenon of satire, probing the strange fascination it has held for its audience and implicitly raising the question of its morality. In his self-reflective satirical parable, Cervantes in fact re-creates what is generally thought to be a primordial situation of satire, the extemporaneous delivery of the Cynic diatribe or *chria*, which in its loose combination of invective, anecdote, maxim, and *sententia* established certain conventions that were to retain a central place in satirical writing throughout its history.[111]

---

[109] *Enquiridion*, p. 154.

[110] See Forcione, *Cervantes, Aristotle, and the "Persiles,"* chaps. 3-5; "Cervantes and the Freedom of the Artist," *Romanic Review* 61 (1970):243-55.

[111] See Nicola Terzaghi, *Per la storia della satira* (Turin, 1932), pt. 1 ("Della Diatriba alla Satira"); Mary Claire Randolph, "The Structural Design of the Formal Verse Satire," *Philological Quarterly* 21 (1942):368-82.

Cervantes's various direct pronouncements on satire indicate that he shared the low opinion of the genre voiced by the majority of literary theorists in the age. In his poetic autobiography *Viage del Parnaso* he boasts: "Never did my humble plume soar through the region of satire, a demeaning flight which leads to vile rewards and disgraces."[112] His awareness of the traditional view of the satirist as a betrayer of the lofty purpose of poetry to "knit the bonds of social brotherhood,"[113] is powerfully expressed in the figure of Clodio in the *Persiles*, the inveterate slanderer whose art is devoted entirely to sowing discord and who refuses to be deterred from his disruptive utterances by the responsibilities of patriotism, friendship, or family loyalty. "You have offended the honor of thousands, you have destroyed illustrious reputations, you have exposed hidden secrets and defiled spotless lineages, you have not stopped short of directing your slanderous pronouncements against your king, your fellow citizens, your friends, and even your own family; and with the apparent intention of saying amusing things, you have disgraced yourself with everyone."[114] In describing this enemy of the human community, banished from England and enchained to the lascivious intriguer, Rosemond Clifford, Cervantes introduces into his prose epic the familiar exiled poet of sixteenth-century literary discussions of satire and the moral responsibility of poetry, and he considers the major issues raised by his punishment. Mauricio, here clearly speaking for Cervantes, condemns the impropriety of Clodio's defamation and points out that "*los satíricos*," "*los maldicientes*," have been justifiably "exiled and thrown

---

[112] "Nunca voló la pluma humilde mia/ por la region satirica, baxeza/ que a infames premios y desgracias guia" (p. 55). See also Don Quixote's reference to poets who take vengeance on their disdainful mistresses with "sátiras y libelos, venganza, por cierto, indigna de pechos generosos" (2:52).

[113] See Horace, *Ars Poetica*, 2.391-99. I cite Howes's translation, *The Art of Poetry*, ed. A. S. Cook (Boston, 1892), p. 29.

[114] "tú has lastimado mil ajenas honras, has aniquilado ilustres créditos, has descubierto secretos escondidos y contaminado linajes claros; haste atrevido a tu rey, a tus ciudadanos, a tus amigos y a tus mismos parientes, y en son de decir gracias te has desgraciado con todo el mundo" (*Persiles*, p. 119). The readiness to connect satirical writing with large-scale historical disasters and to view it as a menace to civilization is implied by an inquisitor's censorship of Quevedo's satires: "no sean pronóstico de los lastimosos sucesos que se vieron en Francia, . . . pues en tiempo de Francisco Primero, rey de Francia, vivió en ella un hombre de cortas obligaciones, llamado Francisco de Rabelés, el cual se picaba de ser picante y maldiciente" ("Censura" of the *Cuento de cuentos* [1630], cited by A. Castro, "La ejemplaridad de las novelas cervantinas," *Semblanzas y estudios españoles* [Princeton, 1956], p. 299). As Vélez de Guevara put the common notion, the satirist is a "bandit," a "criminal" to be hunted down in the republic (*El diablo cojuelo*, ed. F. Rodríguez Marín [Madrid, 1960], pp. 218-19).

out of their homes, without honor and with infamy, with no praise
remaining for them other than their being called ingenious villains
and villainous men of wit." In words recalling Erasmus's censure of
the Cynic philosopher for his inhumane manner of criticizing society,
he insists that "corrective criticism among human beings must be
fraternal."[115] For Clodio, as for the glass licentiate, the malicious witticism is a source of immense pleasure ("the pleasure which I receive
from saying something malicious when I say it well"), and he finds it
impossible to repress his desire to exercise his vicious tongue. Ironically it is in the grisly *contrappasso* of his death that this disruptor of
kingdoms first fulfills the only civilizing purposes of satire. The arrow
that pierces his tongue and throat points unequivocally to the enor-
mity of his sin and attests to the retribution justly merited by all
malicious satire.[116]

---

[115] "desterrados y echados de sus casas, sin honra y con vituperio, sin que les quede
otra alabanza que llamarse agudos sobre bellacos, y bellacos sobre agudos. . . . la
corrección ha de ser fraterna entre todos" (*Persiles*, pp. 119-20). Compare Don Quixote's dignified response to the vicious tirade hurled at him by the ecclesiastic who
serves the duke as moral preceptor: "Las reprehensiones santas y bien intencionadas
otras circunstancias requieren y otros puntos piden: a lo menos, el haberme reprehen-
dido en público y tan ásperamente ha pasado todos los límites de la buena reprehensión, pues las primeras mejor asientan sobre la blandura que sobre la aspereza" (2:283).
In his *"aprobación"* to the second part of the *Quixote* the licentiate Márquez Torres
distinguishes Cervantes's satire, as "blanda y suave medicina" from the "áspera reprehensión" of those who seek to be famous as "maestros de la reprehensión." The good
satirist should observe the "leyes de reprehensión cristiana," striving for cure rather
than destruction, applying to the abcesses of human behavior gentle medication rather
than the cauterizing iron, and he should imitate in Diogenes "lo filósofo y docto"
and avoid "lo cínico," which leads only to malicious slander (2:29-31). For the prominence in Renaissance theories of satire of such medical metaphors "stressing satire's
reaction on the human body for sanative purposes," see Mary Claire Randolph, "The
Medical Concept in English Renaissance Satiric Theory: Its Possible Relationships
and Implications," *Studies in Philology* 38 (1941):125-57.

[116] The peculiar linkage by chain of the familiar exiled satirist with Rosemond
Clifford, clearly a symbol of lust, recalls Erasmus's most searching inquiry into the
destructive powers in language and literature, *Lingua*, and, specifically, his discussion
of the catastrophic combination of lust and slander, the belly and the mouth, and
adulation and calumny: "Si calumniae copulem adulationem, fortasse videbor tale
iugum inducere, quale sit, si quis draconem iungat simiae." Erasmus's text similarly
refers to the arrow of slanderous utterance that punishes Clodio and contains the
admonitions that criticism of a prince should be made in private and that reproof
should be corrective and fraternal ("quae [errata proximorum] mansueta fraternaque
monitione sanare debueramus"). Mauricio's observation that "la lengua es el espejo
del alma," appears at least twice in the *Lingua* ("in nobis animi speculum est oratio").
See pp. 317-19, 304, 298, 296, 326. See my discussion of the *Lingua* and Cervantes's
treatment of the theme of language in *El Coloquio de los perros, Cervantes and the Mystery
of Lawlessness*.

While contemporary theorists tended to view all satirical utterance as unworthy of the true poet and classified satirical writing among the inferior genres of poetry, they nonetheless attempted to distinguish a valuable type of satire, one that, adhering to the practices of Horace, strikes at vices in general rather than at particular individuals, from the destructive type of witty vituperation identified with such legendary scourges as Archilochus and Hipponax and occasionally with the invectives of Juvenal.[117] Such a distinction lies behind Erasmus's defense of his satire in the dedication to the *Praise of Folly*: The liberties of the satirist should be allowed "as long as this freedom does not go to an extreme . . . he that censures the lives of men without mentioning any names—I wonder if he does not teach and warn rather than bite. . . . I also do not dip into the hidden cesspool of crimes as Juvenal did."[118] Similarly, in counseling Diego de Miranda, Don Quixote condemns "torpes sátiras," but explains:

Scold your son, sir, if he writes satires to the detriment of other men's honor; punish him and tear them up. But should he write satires after the manner of Horace for the correction of vice in general, and as elegantly as he did,

[117] In his treatise on satire the Italian neo-Aristotelian theorist, Francesco Robortello, likens satirical imitation to the pouring of black venom onto the imitated objects, and, after observing that this destructive form of poetry requires ingenuity and quickness of mind, he warns that it can easily degenerate into slander and notes that poets have been justifiably exiled from republics because of the disruptive effects of their vituperation. Robortello confronts the puzzling question of why poets take delight in defamation and suggests that its answer lies in their inherent vanity and psychological need to look down on inferiors. However, if satirical vituperation aims at thè improvement of manners by exploiting man's fear of ridicule, it is a valuable form of poetry. Robortello insists that a good satirist must be not only clever (*sagax* and *acutus*) but also moral (*bonus* and *probus*). The link between satire and Cynic philosophy which we find in Cervantes's tale is clearly stated by Robortello in his attempt to distinguish good Cynics, as satirists, from destructive critics. "Non defuerunt alii, qui diuersam ab his ineuntes rationem, non obtrectandi studio, sed potius corrigendi corruptos mores maledicentia vtebantur probitatis, ac sanctitatis plenissima. Qualis Socrates, qui improbos ea de causa in se irritauit. Quales Menippus, & Diogenes Cynici. Nam hic ideo se Canem appellari dicebat, quod hominum vitia morderet ac peruelleret" (*Explicatio Eorvm Omnivm, Qvae ad Satyram Pertinent, In Librum Aristotelis de Arte Poetica Explicationes* [facsimile reproduction of edition of Florence, 1548; Munich, 1968], pp. 26-34).

[118] "ingeniis libertas permissa fuit, vt in communem hominum vitam salibus luderent impune, modo ne licentia exiret in rabiem. . . . At enim qui vitas hominum ita taxat vt neminem omnino perstringat nominatim, queso vtrum is mordere videtur an docere potius ac monere? . . . Neque enim ad Iuuenalis exemplum occultam illam scelerum sentinam vsquam mouimus" (*Laus Stultitiae, Ausgewählte Schriften*, 2:6; the translation is from *The Essential Erasmus*, ed. and trans. J. P. Dolan [New York, 1964], p. 100).

praise him. For a poet may lawfully write against envy, and inveigh against the envious in his verses, and against other vices too, so long as he does not aim at any particular person. Though there are poets who would run the risk of banishment to the Isles of Pontus for the sake of uttering one piece of malice.[119]

While his formulation of a distinction between a legitimate and an illegitimate satire accords perfectly with prescriptions of contemporary literary theory, Cervantes is characteristically incapable of resisting the temptation to delve into everything that theory fails to take into account. His exploration of the forbidden areas of satirical writing is in some ways analogous to his penetrating engagement with all the fundamental aspects of romance literature and its reception—the appeal of the fantastic, the fluidity that characterizes the reader's capacity to believe, the manner in which imaginative projections similar to the fictions of the romancer fill the minds and affect the lives of all human beings—which were excluded from probing examination by the prestigious and easily applicable categories of classical literary theory to which he frequently paid lip service—verisimilitude, decorum, the legitimate marvelous, and exemplary truth.[120] Just as Cervantes was deeply attracted by the unrestrained fantasies of the romancer's fictional worlds, he was no less susceptible to the appeal of the freedom of expression to which the satirist traditionally laid claim, notwithstanding his protests to the contrary. However sincere Cervantes may have been in his assertion that his humble plume never soared on that ignoble flight through satirical regions, a more accurate account of his ambivalent relationship to the cankered muse of satire undoubtedly lies hidden in the peculiar testimony recorded at the notorious trial of Lope de Vega to the effect that there were only four or five people in Madrid capable of writing the libelous verses on Elena Osorio and her parents that led to the exile of the most gifted poet in

---

[119] "Riña vuesa merced a su hijo si hiciere sátiras que perjudiquen las honras ajenas, y castíguele, y rómpaselas; pero si hiciere sermones al modo de Horacio, donde reprehenda los vicios en general, como tan elegantemente él lo hizo, alábele, porque lícito es al poeta escribir contra la invidia, y decir en sus versos mal de los invidiosos, y así de los otros vicios, con que no señale persona alguna; pero hay poetas que a trueco de decir una malicia, se pondrán a peligro que los destierren a las islas de Ponto" (*Don Quijote de la Mancha*, 2:156-57) Don Quixote's discourse recalls El Pinciano's discussion of satire, which distinguishes Juvenal's acerbity from Horace's humor and offers, as the "first counsel" for satirical writing, "que reprehenda vicios generales, y no a personas particulares" (*Philosophía antigua poética*, ed. A. Carballo Picazo, 3 vols. [Madrid, 1953], 3:238).

[120] See Forcione, *Cervantes, Aristotle, and the "Persiles,"* pp. 339-48.

Spain—among them, Liñan de Riaza, Lope de Vega, and Miguel de Cervantes.[121]

Cervantes's insight into the darkness at the depths from which the satirical impulse emerges, as well as his awareness of the darkest traditions of satirical writing, is expressed most strikingly in the dialogue of Cipión and Berganza, the interlocutors of *El coloquio de los perros*. Once again Cervantes incorporates the drama of literary creation into his work and accompanies its production with a commentary on its conventions, aims, and effects. Cautioning his companion concerning the excessive liberties of the satirist, Cipión invokes the familiar distinction between proper and improper satire, but what is most interesting is his description of illicit satire:

Since I have heard say that a great poet among the ancients declared that it was difficult not to write satires, I shall consent that you may slander a little bit, but to illuminate rather than to draw blood: I mean that you should reveal but neither wound nor ridicule anybody in what you reveal; for slander is evil, although it provokes laughter in many, if it kills a single one; and if you can please without it, I shall hold you for very discreet.[122]

Satire is here associated with the uncontrollable rage of Juvenal, and, as the metaphors clearly indicate, its purpose is to kill. Cervantes's English contemporary, the Juvenalian railer John Marston, expressed the idea more bluntly through one of his spokesmen: "I'll rhyme thee dead. Look for the satire."[123] As I have pointed out above, behind all

---

[121] D. A. Tomillo and D. C. Pérez Pastor, *Proceso de Lope de Vega* (Madrid, 1901), pp. 41-42.

[122] "Por haber oído decir que dijo un gran poeta de los antiguos que era difícil cosa el no escribir sátiras, consentiré que murmures un poco de luz, y no de sangre: quiero decir que señales, y no hieras ni des mate a ninguno en cosa señalada; que no es buena la murmuración, aunque haga reír a muchos, si mata a uno; y si puedes agradar sin ella, te tendré por muy discreto" (*Novelas ejemplares*, 2:224). Cervantes's distinction between the "bloody satire" and the "illuminating satire," which would expose not primarily in order to destroy but rather to heal, recalls El Pinciano's literary dialogues, which describe licit satire, which aims at vices rather than individuals, in the imagery of light: "podrá vsar della clara y abiertamente, y, assí como el que no haze mal ama la luz, podrá el tal poeta hablar claramente delante del mundo todo, y él viuirá entre la gente más seguro" (*Philosophía antigua poética*, 3.238).

[123] *What You Will, The Works of John Marston*, ed. A. H. Bullen, 3 vols. (Boston, 1887), 2:348-49. Like Cervantes's satirical novellas Marston's play concerns itself with establishing the proper perspective for the satirist. Its solitary malcontent, Lampatho, is, like the Licenciado Vidriera, a prodigious student who is driven to black melancholy by his tireless studies and who expresses his despair and misanthropy by snarling at man's vices and follies ceaselessly. Marston exposes the shortcomings in his critical stance by juxtaposing him to another character, the hedonistic ironist

satire stands the archetypal figure of vindictive imprecation, Archilochus, who according to legend transformed the bitter wrath of the dog and the sharp sting of the wasp into the poison of his mouth, and through the verses of his invectives drove his enemies to suicide. Whatever apologies satirists may voice in defense of their art, its fundamentally destructive basis remains clear, and the boast of Archilochus "one great thing I know, how to recompense with evil reproaches him that doeth me evil," will always remain audible in it.[124] For Cervantes the excesses of satire, unlike those of the other disruptive literary genre, romance, are truly evil, and in one of the most somber passages he ever wrote, he connects the irrepressible impulse behind satire, its disturbing appeal to man, and its blighted products with original sin. Berganza is confessing that he cannot resist the impulse, and his words, appearing in Cervantes's most relentless exploration of everything in man's nature and behavior that runs counter to his desires for a true community, implicate the speaker and his artistic practices in the spectacle of evil that the work depicts. In a startling bit of Cervantine mimesis, the text points unequivocally to its own corruption and in its self-indictment implies that satire is in one sense the most apt of literary genres in the world of fallen man.

By my faith, Scipio, one must know a great deal and keep firmly in the stirrups to keep up a conversation for two hours without approaching the confines of slander; because I see in myself that, in spite of being an animal, as I am, with every few sentences that I utter, words come to my tongue like flies to wine, and every one of them is malicious and derogatory. Wherefore, I repeat what I have already said, that doing and speaking evil we inherit from our first parents and suck in with our mother's milk. This is clearly seen in the fact that hardly has a little child taken his arm out of his swaddling clothes when he raises his hand and shows signs of wanting to revenge himself upon the person by whom he supposes himself offended, and almost the first articulate word which he utters is to call his nurse or his mother a whore.[125]

Quadratus, who represents a more humane, corrective principle of satire. See Oscar James Campbell, *Comicall Satyre and Shakespeare's "Troilus and Cressida"* (San Marino, Cal., 1938), pp. 166-81.

[124] Elliott, *The Power of Satire*, p. 12. Recalling the legendary scourges, Archilochus and Hipponax, one of Carvallo's interlocutors justifies the prohibition of satire and notes that satirists "hazian tanto daño con estas perjudiciales Satiras, que muchos se ahorcaron de verse con ellas afrentados" (*Cisne de Apolo*, 2:66).

[125] "A la fe, Cipión, mucho ha de saber y muy sobre los estribos ha de andar el que quisiere sustentar dos horas de conversación sin tocar los límites de la murmuración; porque yo veo en mí, que con ser un animal, como soy, a cuatro razones que digo, me acuden palabras a la lengua como mosquitos al vino, y todas maliciosas y

In its attribution of the impulse to defame to original sin and its horrifying image of the newly born child raising its fist in indignation and abusing its mother, the passage glances directly back to the *Licenciado Vidriera*. For Cervantes's mad scholar is not only associated, through his railing and such attributes as the wasp and the Cynic dog, with the destructive satirists of legend, but he is also linked through archetypal symbolism with fallen Christian man. His curiosity and hunger for knowledge reward him with an exaggerated knowledge of evil, and, as it pours forth in his unsparing denunciations of the evils of his fellow men, its powers of contagion stimulate the evil inherent even in the most innocent.[126] In the description of the mob that follows and encircles the licentiate—its *"rueda"* forming another of the circles of futility that pervade the imaginative atmosphere of this tale of misdirected motion—and reacts gleefully to his vituperation, even when it is focused directly on its members, we notice that Cervantes curiously gives a good deal of attention to the presence of children and in fact develops as a recurrent motif of his narrative their reaction to the railer. Immediately following his emergence in public, children begin to mock and stone him. When he arrives at the court, his host instructs a guard to accompany him so that the children of the city will not harm him. At the height of his success, while the mob follows him about, applauding his derision, they continue to attack him ("yet in spite of all this he could not have defended himself from the children if his guardian had not protected him").[127]

The literary implications in the spectacle of vituperation, the howling mob, and the bestial children in Cervantes's *Licenciado Vidriera* are as powerful and as profound as those in Don Quixote's destructive assault on Master Pedro's puppets. In both cases we witness the power of art to reach our deepest emotions and satisfy our most irrational

---

murmurantes; por lo cual vuelvo a decir lo que otra vez he dicho: que el hacer y decir mal lo heredamos de nuestros primeros padres y lo mamamos en la leche. Véese claro en que apenas ha sacado el niño el brazo de las fajas, cuando levanta la mano con muestras de querer vengarse de quien, a su parecer, le ofende; y casi la primera palabra articulada que habla es llamar puta a su ama o a su madre" (*El coloquio de los perros, Novelas ejemplares*, 2:240).

[126] As a parable of knowledge, the *Licenciado Vidriera* implies that satire belongs to what, Erasmus, conflating St. Paul and St. James, denounces as the knowledge of evil, the diabolical wisdom that proceeds from the earth, inflates its possessor with vanity, plagues him with restlessness, isolates him among men, and characteristically manifests itself in mockery and persecution (*Enquiridion*, pp. 153-54).

[127] "pero, con todo esto, no se pudiera defender de los muchachos, si su guardián no le defendiera" (p. 57).

needs, and in both cases we observe Cervantes's keen interest in examining types of aesthetic experience for which contemporary literary theorists, with their insistence on the utilitarian, exemplary character of poetry and on its responsibilities to serve rationality, had little understanding or interest. In his theoretical pronouncements Cervantes may have accepted the preceptors' strictly drawn limits concerning what is and is not permitted to the writer of satire and romance. However, the problems connected with the delineation of such limits fascinated him to such an extent that he transformed them into fiction and found himself pushed by the energies of his own literary arguments into areas of artistic creation beyond the boundaries that he discursively set for himself. If in the *Quixote* he is able, through the fantasies and frustrations of his mad protagonist, to enter the forbidden realm of the illegitimate marvelous of romance, where art molds experience in accordance with man's most extravagant desires for perfection, in *El Licenciado Vidriera* he can, through his mad scholar's unsparing vision of evil, explore the forbidden world portrayed by what Scipio designates "satires of blood" as opposed to "satires of light," an imaginary world that is designed according to the logic of man's deepest fears concerning what he should not be. In Don Quixote's vision a knight errant saves a kingdom menaced by war, returns from his ordeals to wed a princess, and is welcomed by a festive society united in its love of the deliverer. In the world of the Licenciado Vidriera all men are thieves, families are held together by the bonds of terror, each member of society is isolated with his dreadful secret, and the only community that men are capable of creating is that formed by the jeering mob. While neither vision can be said to be that of Cervantes, his position is not one of complete detachment. Unlike contemporary literary theorists in his profounder understanding of the breadth of literary possibilities demanded by the imagination and vindicated by experience and tradition,[128] Cervantes never-

---

[128] "It is as difficult to account for our pleasure in vituperation as for our pleasure in tragedy. But the pleasure is there" (Elliott, *The Power of Satire*, p. 309). El Pinciano's manner of recognizing this fact of literary experience and resolving the problem that it implies is characteristic of the naïvely rationalistic spirit dominating Renaissance critical theory. In the discussion of satire in *La philosophía antigua poética*, the interlocutor El Pinciano is puzzled by Fadrique's attempt to distinguish licit and illicit satire and explains: "¡O, señor! . . . que no será escuchado el poeta que no reprehenda a personas particulares, que de ay viene el deleyte mayor a esta especie de poética" (3:239). El Pinciano frequently represents the point of view of the ingenuous Philistine, and his misunderstandings and partial truths are stages through which the dialogue moves in its dialectical formulation of truth. In this case, however, his query concerning man's "delight" in apprehending witty vituperation does not elicit a serious response from Fadrique, and it fails to raise a point that is integrated, whether

theless shares their determination to approach literary problems from what ultimately must be regarded as a perspective of morality. The ambiguities and fluidity of the moral context surrounding Don Quixote's madness and actions as well as the actions of other "victims" of romance literature in the *Quixote* can leave little doubt that Cervantes had a good deal of sympathy for his protagonist's vision and for a type of literature that, if indeed ridiculously out of touch with reality and perhaps disruptive in a well-ordered community, nevertheless can arouse some of man's loftiest hopes and inspire the noblest folly of which he is capable. In the *Licenciado Vidriera*, on the other hand, there is no such ambiguity to qualify Cervantes's dissociation from the protagonist's obsession and the primitive satire that he represents. Here madness looks downward toward man's lowest impulses—his anxieties, fears, and aggressive needs, his desires for security through categorical denunciations of others, his comfort in the presence of scapegoats, and his eagerness to avoid independent thinking by the cultivation of stock responses—and it is clear that such impulses are those that satire stirs up and plays upon.[129] Even at its best, satire, as Carvallo points out in his rather unenthusiastic defense of the genre, exploits man's fear of ridicule,[130] and, although it can be argued that in a society in need of moral purgation, such a negative corrective is a product of lofty moral intentions or even that, as Lucian puts it in his defense of his own satirical writing, a hater of evil is implicitly a lover of good,[131] it nonetheless remains true that in its destructive purpose and its

as qualification or contrast, into the theory of satire expounded in the dialogue. It remains rather an amusing and trivial case of ignorance and, as such, a revealing symptom of critical blindness.

[129] One should compare Cervantes's comical examination of vanity, derision, derogatory stereotyping, prejudice, and warfare in the episode of the braying asses in *Don Quixote* II. The devil inspires the inhabitants of the area, particularly the children, to categorize the members of the village according to their mayors' unfortunate talents and to seize every opportunity to ridicule them: "son conocidos los naturales del pueblo del rebuzno como son conocidos y diferenciados los negros de los blancos" (2:233). The passions kindled by such derision lead to constant warfare. Don Quixote's idealistic speech on the irrationality in the vituperation and in the villagers' overly sensitive reaction to trivial stereotyping, his invocation of Christ's teachings concerning love and brotherhood, and his careful definition of the just war fail to curb the folly of the army of brayers. The satirical scene reaches its climax in the pathetic flight of Don Quixote, the "victory" of the villagers in the drubbing of Sancho Panza, and the ironic reflection of the narrator that, if the victors had known of the ancient customs of the Greeks, they would have erected a monument on the location of their triumph. The Christian Humanist vision, which is prominent in Don Quixote's madness throughout Part II, seldom seems as illusory and elusive as at this comically somber moment of the novel.

[130] *El cisne de Apolo*, 2:64.

[131] *The Dead Come to Life*, Lucian, 3:33.

engagement of destructive emotions, satire, even in its most intellectual forms, bears within itself as a possibility the spectacle of the "satire of blood," the orgiastic indulgence of hatred that Cervantes depicts in the Licenciado Vidriera's confrontation with his mob. In examining this literary possibility, Cervantes allowed for no moral ambiguity, nor did he complicate his focus by introducing such exclusively aesthetic issues as those concerning narrative technique, style, and verisimilitude which we observe in Don Quixote's response to the puppet show. It may be true that the writing of the tale was to some extent a therapeutic cleansing of indignation which Cervantes felt concerning many of the objects of his protagonist's ridicule. However, Cervantes makes it clear that his satirist belongs to the society he condemns, that he is a pitiless scourge in a society where strife is the norm, and that he is a slanderer among people united in their malice. Cervantes carefully distances himself from his satirist and, in doing so, makes clear the irresponsibility and viciousness of the type of art that he represents.[132]

Perhaps Cervantes's concern to redeem the glass licentiate and his refusal to leave him in the traditional abode of the misanthrope—the cave, the desert, the stable—reveal more than the intention to end the tale by abruptly turning the satire away from the protagonist and unequivocally toward the society that rejects him. Perhaps it is an indication of Cervantes's determination to redeem satire itself, to follow his somber disclosure of all its destructive possibilities with a more positive form in which the emphasis on mending the disintegrating world it portrays is more pronounced. He could already see

---

[132] One should contrast Cervantes's critical scrutiny of the "satire of blood" with the delight in verbal abuse that marks the invectives of the most influential malcontent and railer of the age, Guzmán de Alfarache, a cynical "perro de muestra" whose irrepressible instincts for "ventear flaquezas ajenas" may well have inspired the two *Exemplary Novels* dealing with criticism. At the beginning of the second part of his "confession," the picaro compares himself to a madman throwing stones in all directions and assuming that, since everyone "has eaten the apple," all of his victims deserve the wounds that he inflicts on them. He offers a series of analogies describing the work and its reception in the imagery of punishment, suffering, and purgation— e.g., the blunderbuss that kills, the viper that poisons, the radish that nauseates, the executioner who displays a "fine tapestry" of corpses. His grotesque *captatio benevolentiae* culminates in an assault on the reader, in which he likens the reception of his work to the contemplation of bear-baiting by a bloodthirsty mob. While Guzmán adds that a "discreet reader" should avoid such a reaction, there is little in his narration that effectively counters its continual exploitation of the destructive energies in language. Alemán clearly relishes the powers of literature to arouse in readers a pleasure in the contemplation of suffering and in the orgiastic release of hatred (see *Guzmán de Alfarache*, 3:69-83, 89).

the spirit of the Licenciado Vidriera clearly emerging in the literary and cultural life of Spain—in the nightmarish fantasies of Quevedesque satire, as well as in the desolate vision of the popular picaresque narratives, with their panoramic surveys of human failings, their cultivation of railing abuse, and their antagonistic engagement with their readers.[133] He would soon watch the metamorphosis of his own heroes, Don Quixote and Sancho, into monstrous embodiments of folly when examined through the distorting lens of Avellaneda's pitiless satire, and in his reaction to the excesses of the imitation we observe his awareness of the enormous distance separating his work from the characteristic satire of his contemporaries. At the same time Cervantes could not fail to be sensitive to the resurgence in Spain's spiritual life of ascetic Christianity, which proclaimed man's depravity and the illusory quality and ultimate emptiness of the earthly existence, and to the increasing popularity among men of letters of neo-Stoicism, with its rigid morality, its dualistic conception of the division in man between mind and body, and its uncompromising view of man's enslavement to externals.[134] Whether writing as theologian or moralist,

---

[133] In his mock-epic *Viage del Parnaso* Cervantes places the author of *La pícara Justina*, López de Úbeda, beneath the banner of the crow, an emblem of debased, immoral, and slanderous poetry. In the enigmatic verses of Urganda la Desconocida at the beginning of *Don Quixote* I, he alludes critically to the destructive satire in the work. Her words in fact suggest a link in Cervantes's imagination between its abuse and his own flawed satirist: "Advierte que es desati—, / siendo de vidrio el teja—, / tomar piedras en las ma— / para tirar al veci—" (*Don Quijote de la Mancha*, 1:29). For Cervantes's distaste for *La pícara Justina* and the malicious spirit exemplified by the invectives in which its picaresque heroine delights, see Marcel Bataillon, *Pícaros y picaresca* (Madrid, 1969), pp. 53ff.; also, Bataillon, "Relaciones literarias," *Suma Cervantina*, ed. J. B. Avalle-Arce and E. C. Riley (London, 1973), pp. 219-26. For Cervantes's antipathy to the vision informing Mateo Alemán's popular *Guzmán de Alfarache*, see A. Castro, *El pensamiento de Cervantes* (Barcelona, 1972), pp. 228-35; Castro, "Perspectiva de la novela picaresca," *Hacia Cervantes* (Madrid, 1967), pp. 118-42; Castro, *Cervantes y los casticismos españoles* (Madrid, 1966), p. 44. The possibility that Cervantes's condemnation of the glass licentiate implies a general critique of picaresque fiction is all the more interesting if one takes into account the association of the Cynic and the picaresque railer in the contemporary imagination. Boileau allegedly considered writing a "vie de Diogéne le Cynique," "beaucoup plus plaisante & plus originale que celle de Lazarille de Tormes, & de Gusman d'Alfarache" (*Bolaeana ou bons mots de M. Boileau* [Amsterdam, 1742], p. 41).

[134] The logical link between the Stoic mentality and spirit of satire is perfectly obvious. It is perhaps worth pointing out that the leading proponent of European neo-Stoicism, Justus Lipsius, and his principal Spanish disciple, Francisco de Quevedo, were cultivators of Menippean satire. For the importance of neo-Stoicism and ascetic Christianity in the period, see the following: Bataillon, *Erasmo y España*, pp. 772ff. Henry Ettinghausen, *Francisco de Quevedo and the Neostoic Movement* (Oxford, 1972). K. A. Blüher, *Seneca und Spanien: Untersuchungen zur Geschichte der Seneca-*

whether invoking the authority of the patient Job or the cerebral Stoic sages who allegedly founded their philosophy on his wisdom, a large number of Cervantes's contemporaries were embracing the principle that "milicia es la vida del hombre en la tierra" and maintaining that one's survival in the struggle depends on one's adoption of a thoroughly disenchanted, harshly critical vision of man and society. The *"desengañado"* was in fact to become a dominant figure of Spanish literature of the seventeenth century. Armed with superior knowledge, gifted with a control of the devastating aphorism, frequently associated with such symbols of penetrating vision as the mirror and eyeglasses, he would undertake the mission of probing through illusions and exposing the bitter truths of human sinfulness that lie hidden behind the masks that all people wear on the stage of the world. In Rodrigo Fernández de Ribera's *Los antojos de mejor vista* (1625-1630?), a licentiate dwelling in the tower of the cathedral of Seville offers the narrator a pair of glasses through which he can observe "things as they truly are, in their very essences, without interference from the common illusions which darken the light of the most important vision." The licentiate is named El Maestro Desengaño, the glasses are made of "truth itself," and through them the narrator watches a dreadful spectacle unfold, in which judges metamorphose into vultures, doctors into hangmen, and married men into horned oxen.[135] In the greatest work in this tradition, *El Criticón*, Baltasar Gracián introduces several figures representing the principles and methods of Fernández de Ribera's licentiate—the centaur Chiron, who recommends a method of reverse vision to discover truth in a world where "todo va al revés," Argos, whose hundred eyes are connected with the superior insight necessary for survival in a world of deceit, *"el acertador,"* who specializes in relating human behavior to hidden psychological motives, *"el zahorí,"* a "veedor de todo," who can peer into human hearts as if they were made of glass, and *"el decifrador"* in Rome, who is capable of reading all the confusing ciphers of a mysterious universe. In Gracián's protagonist we witness the final phase in the ascendance of the critical hero, as the questing adventurer of this satirical transformation of the Greek romance becomes an embodiment of the penetrating, discriminating intellect that enables man to

---

Rezeption in Spanien vom 13. bis 17. Jahrhundert (Munich, 1969). Schulte, *El Desengaño: Wort und Thema in der spanischen Literatur des Goldenen Zeitalters.* Stephen Gilman, "An Introduction to the Ideology of the Baroque in Spain," *Symposium* 1 (1946):82-107.

[135] "las cosas en el mismo ser que son, sin que el engaño comun le turbe la luz de la vista mas importante" (see R. Fernández de Ribera, *Los antojos de mejor vista* [Madrid, 1871], pp. 18-19).

emerge victorious in his endless sequence of struggles with powerful illusions.[136] The Licenciado Vidriera has strong affinities with such figures, but it would be a mistake to see him as one of their progenitors. Indeed in his glass *"desengañado,"* Cervantes is addressing himself to certain principles, attitudes, methods, and characteristics of the contemporary celebrants of *"desengaño"* which could not fail to be repugnant to his sensibilities, penetrated as they were by the optimistic spirit of Erasmian Christianity—spiritual pride, inhumanity, hyperintellectuality, destructive wit, a morbid preoccupation with degeneration and decay, and the belief in the total segregation of man's emotions and instincts from his intellect.

" *'Desengaño'* and his mother Truth wander naked, but nobody wants to receive so much nakedness in his house," lamented Francisco de Miranda y Paz in his *El Desengañado* (1663).[137] The *"desengañados"* were obsessed with clothing and disguises, and they demanded nakedness, but their call was not for a return to a state of innocence and dignity but rather to a mood of total disenchantment, in which man recognizes his sinfulness and misery, broods in solitude on his physical decomposition as it runs its ineluctable course from moment to moment, and fixes his eye on the clock and his memory on dead friends. "I always live in the highest Towers, particularly where there are clocks, because in what they take away I find counsels of importance to give back. For nobody admits me to any other place, although all desire me, because *desengaño* has a very ugly face."[138] While Cervantes

---

[136] See *Obras completas,* ed. A. de Hoyo (Madrid, 1960), 1:vi; 2:i; 3:iii, v, iv. The distance separating Cervantes from the vision informing this literature is immediately evident when one compares the very different principles of bodily life implied by Sancho Panza and Andrenio respectively and recognizes the striking differences in their relationships to their masters. As has been frequently noted, the *Quixote* moves toward an "integration" of knight and squire and a breakdown of all the sharp distinctions—e.g., spirit and flesh, head and body, master and servant—separating them at the moment of their introduction in the work.

[137] "Peregrinan él [el desengaño] y su madre la verdad, desnudos. Nadie quiere tanta desnudez en su casa" (see Schulte, *El Desengaño: Wort und Thema in der spanischen Literatur des Goldenen Zeitalters,* p. 193).

[138] "Vivo siempre por las Torres más altas, particularmente donde ai relojes; porque en lo que ellos quitan, doi yo avisos de importancia. Que en otra parte, aunque todos me dessean, nadie me admite, porque tiene muy mala cara el desengaño" (R. Fernández de Ribera, *Los antojos de mejor vista,* p. 30). For the conception of time which pervades the literature of *desengaño,* see Gilman, "An Introduction to the Ideology of the Baroque in Spain"; J. Casalduero, *Sentido y forma de "Los trabajos de Persiles y Sigismunda"* (Buenos Aires, 1947), pp. 207-208; K. Vossler, *Lope de Vega und Seine Zeit* (Munich, 1947), pp. 305ff.; A. Forcione, "Lope's Broken Clock: Baroque Time in the *Dorotea,*" *Hispanic Review* 37 (1969):459-90; most recently, P. N. Skrine, *The Baroque* (London, 1978), pp. 151-64.

can comprehend and explore with some humor the vision informing El Maestro Desengaño's somber observations, it is a vision that is fundamentally alien to him, and, as his Licenciado Vidriera reminds men of their fragility and demands public exposure of all that they conceal, Cervantes reminds us of the excessiveness of his demand. But, as I have pointed out above, the fact remains that Cervantes redeems his fallen satirist, and, in so doing, he may already be looking forward to a type of satire that he can reconcile with his Christian principles. In it the protagonist will not be the misanthropic railer, but rather the helpless *ingénu*, "guileless as to what is evil"; his major source of strength will not be intellectuality, but natural wisdom, the fundamental Christian principles of charity and humility, and a dogged belief in melioration and the value of work. His concern will be truth, but he will not accompany its revelation with the ruthless candor and the undiscriminating severity of the Cynic philosopher. In the Licenciado Vidriera's withdrawal from the evil world of his diatribes and in his good death as a prudent soldier serving his community, we can discern Cervantes's aspiration to a "satire of light," his determination to unite the penetrating light of Diogenes' lamp of truth with the charity of Christ.[139]

CERVANTES AND THE MYSTERY OF KNOWLEDGE: THE RENAISSANCE BACKGROUNDS OF THE *LICENCIADO VIDRIERA* AND *DON QUIXOTE*

The seate of Trueth is in the harte, and not in the tounge.
—Henry Cornelius Agrippa, *De incertitudine et vanitate scientiarum et artium*

As I have suggested in my analysis of the parable surrounding its collection of apothegmatic pronouncements, the *Licenciado Vidriera* be-

---

[139] One can in fact see in Cervantes's mastery of his protagonist's aphoristic discourse, with its powers of "fixing" experience and releasing the destructive energies latent in language, a struggle with and a liberation from an alien language that clearly exercised a powerful hold on his imagination. The objectification of such a discourse, as M. M. Bakhtin has pointed out, can be an important process in a writer's coming to ideological consciousness and discovering his own voice (see "Discourse in the Novel," *The Dialogic Imagination* (Austin, 1981), p. 348). Cervantes's struggle is continued throughout *El coloquio de los perros*, and his liberation there is much more complete.

longs to a distinguished body of literary works that have addressed themselves directly to one of the central themes of Western thought— the nature of wisdom and the proper uses of knowledge. It is a tale of intellectual hubris written in an age that had been shaken by un- precedented upheavals in the field of knowledge, had witnessed an enormous expansion of intellectual horizons and perspectives, and had produced in the damnation of Faust the most powerful myth of intel- lectual overreaching since the story of Adam. While such optimistic thinkers as Pico della Mirandola, Carolus Bovillus, and Francis Bacon could celebrate man's Promethean powers to master his environment, whether through the discovery of hermetic texts that would illuminate all of nature's secrets or through the empirical examination of a nature freed from the teleological designs that had always hampered the best efforts of scholastic science, the majority of men continued to view knowledge as an alluring mystery, an ambivalent source of power and destruction, and a provocation to humility and idolatry. Their dis- cussions of its treacherous marvels were frequently hedged about with warnings concerning its improper uses and myths of overreaching dar- ing and destruction.[140] Curiosity continued to bear its traditional stigma, and even the most progressive thinkers recognized that, if knowledge could provide a guide to righteous living, it offered at the same time a powerful temptation to sinfulness.[141] Bacon himself, while denounc- ing an "ill-applied moderation" that might hold back man in his

[140] See Ernst Cassirer's study of Renaissance thinkers' exhilaration with man's pow- ers of understanding and creation and their characteristic reinterpretation of the myth of Prometheus (*The Individual and the Cosmos in Renaissance Philosophy*, trans. M. Do- mandi [New York, 1964], pp. 90-122); also, Eugene F. Rice Jr., *The Renaissance Idea of Wisdom* (Cambridge, Mass., 1958), chap. 4, "The Wisdom of Prometheus"; and Bernhard Groethuysen, *Philosophische Anthropologie*, chap. 8, "Der mythische Mensch." For the confidence of the magus in his hermetic philosophy and the opti- mism of the empiricists, see Haydn, *The Counter-Renaissance*, chap. 4, "The Science of the Counter-Renaissance."

[141] See Covarrubias's definition of "curiosity": "la palabra curioso u curiosidad se deriva deste adverbio *cur*, que es adverbio de preguntas, y del nombre ociosidad, porque los curiosos son muy de ordinario holgaçanes y preguntadores como su mae- stro, que su primera palabra que habló, fue cuando dixo a Eva: *Cur praecepit vobis Deus?* Plutarco escrive que en Lacedemonia davan pena y castigavan a un hombre curioso que preguntava lo que poco le iba" (*Tesoro de la lengua castellana o española* [1611], ed. M. de Riquer [Barcelona, 1943], p. 388). For the traditional negative connotations of the word and its "transvaluation" during this period, see Blumen- berg, *Die Legitimität der Neuzeit*. As in the case of many other writers of the period, "curiosity" was for Cervantes an ambivalent term. See, for example, its use in *El curioso impertinente* and in Don Quixote's instruction to governor Sancho: "la gente curiosa se ha acogido al latín, y al *regoldar* dice *erutar* . . . y esto es enriquecer la lengua" (*Don Quijote de la Mancha*, 2:361).

efforts to study "the book of God's works; divinity or philosophy," and calling for "endless progress or proficience in both," felt compelled to add a stern admonition: "only let men beware that they apply both to charity, and not to swelling; to use, and not to ostentation."[142] And in his prophetic depiction of the New Atlantis, the utopia of modern science, one occasionally glimpses in the background its literary ancestors and senses that the traditional enslavements of the island paradises of romance might still be lurking amid its abundant sensuous delights, its dazzling metamorphoses, and its houses of marvelous illusions.

In his *Introductio ad Sapientiam* Luis Vives wrote confidently of the ways in which the lifelong pursuit of learning can guide man to virtuous living and happiness. Knowledge is the "true nourishment of the soul," a "source of enjoyments and solid and perpetual delights"; "studies give seasoning and good flavor to happiness, they mitigate sadness, they curb the mad impulses of youth, they lighten the oppressive burden of old age; at home, away from home, in public, in private, in solitude, in commerce, in idleness, in business, everywhere they accompany us, they are present, or, to put it more aptly, they come to our aid and cause us to rejoice." However, the enthusiasm of the statement is tempered by a reminder that God's mysteries are impenetrable to the gaze of reason, an invocation of the warnings of St. Paul and Solomon concerning moderation in the pursuit of knowledge and the avoidance of illicit curiosity, and some harsh reminders about the dangers of intellectual pride. If the student is driven by a desire for glory and if he is presumptuous in his acquisition of learning, he will never reach the goal of knowledge, which is the liberation from the slavery of pride. In words that resonate with traditional anti-intellectualism, Vives exhorts his reader:

Banish from your studies all arrogance, for all that the most learned of mortals ever knew is no more than an infinitessimal part of what he does not know. As much knowledge as man can attain is but exiguous, obscure, and uncertain; and our minds, manacled as they are in the fetters and prisons of our bodies, stagger under the crushing weight of a massive ignorance and the deepest of shadows; and our insight is so dull that it penetrates no farther than to the most shallow surfaces of things.[143]

---

[142] *The Advancement of Learning*, cited by Don Cameron Allen, *The Legend of Noah* (Urbana, 1963), pp. 17-18.

[143] "Eruditio pastus ingenii verissimus . . . ex qua voluptates, et oblectamenta et solida, et perpetua . . . Studia res laetas condiunt, tristes leniunt, temerarios impetus juventae cohibent, senectutis molestam tarditatem levant; domi, foris, in publico, in privato, in solitudine, in frequentia, in otio, in negotio comitantur, adsunt, immo

The assault on knowledge and intellectuality is a characteristic feature of literature and thought throughout this troubled age of intellectual confidence, skepticism, and faith. From Erasmus's Stultitia, who excoriated the schoolmen and pedants, celebrated the creative vitality of the irrational forces in man, and concluded her oration by calling for a return to the simple faith of Paul's fool in Christ, to Montaigne's "countrie-clownish men," whose customs and discourses are better shaped to the "true prescription of Philosophie" than those "of our philosophers,"[144] to Shakespeare's Fool, who leads King Lear in his ordeals to his redemptive discovery of the pitiable nature of humanity, voices from all over Europe and from radically distinct areas of philosophical endeavor joined in a chorus decrying the excesses of rational speculation and reminding man that the truths that are important are simple. The intellectual currents that nourished the great procession of spokesmen for simplicity—shepherds, peasants, fools, mystics, wise animals—are numerous and often complexly fused in a single figure, and any attempt to deal systematically with them must address itself to the dominant theological, ethical, and epistemological issues of the age.[145] Moreover, while the intensity of sixteenth-century anti-intellectualism, perhaps most strikingly revealed in Luther's denunciation of reason as a whore, gives it a unique character, its roots reach back into preceding ages, and it found within tradition various congenial spokesmen with whom it could ally itself. For example, the development of fideism and skepticism, which we follow through the works of such thinkers as Vives and Sánchez to its culmination in the essays of Montaigne, can be traced to its origin in the nominalist movement in philosophy, founded by William of Ockham in the fourteenth century, with its derogation of reason, its denial of universals, and its emphasis on the individual as the only possible object of valid knowledge.[146] Similarly, the obsessive exaltation of faith and love in the spiritual life of the period, as well as the reiterated opposition to rational understanding, can be seen as a fulfillment of mystical traditions within Christianity that accompanied

---

praesunt, opitulantur, juvant. . . . Ab studiis arrogantia omnis arcenda est: nam ea quae vel doctissimus mortalium novit, non sunt minutissimum eorum quae ignorat: exiguum quiddam et obscurum et incertum est quidquid homines sciunt, mentesquae nostrae in hoc corporeo carcere devinctae, magna ignoratione et altissimis tenebris premuntur: aciemque adeo retusam habemus, ut nec summas penetremus rerum facies" (Opera Omnia, 1:16).

[144] See Haydn, The Counter-Renaissance, p. 91.

[145] The most satisfactory survey of these issues of which I am aware is Haydn's The Counter-Renaissance, chap. 2: "The Counter-Renaissance and the Vanity of Learning."

[146] Ibid., pp. 139ff.

the development of scholastic theology during the middle ages. St. Francis is reported to have said: "A single demon in hell knows more than all men on earth put together. But there is one thing of which the demon is incapable, and which is the glory of man: to be faithful to God."[147] Erasmus, a man in whom so many traditions meet, could profess immense faith in knowledge and in the power of reason to secure for man a proper understanding of the pure sources of the Christian religion and to guide him toward moral perfection as a member of his Christian family, and he could denounce repeatedly the barbarism and vanity of the ignorant. However, he never ceased to be acutely conscious of the limitations of reason and the dangers of intellectual pride. He pointed out that there is much in Holy Scripture that even the most accomplished exegete can not understand and that there are theological questions that will only confound the rational faculties. He espoused ecstatic meditation as a method of worship, and in the *Praise of Folly* he reviled, in arguments that were to be repeated throughout the age, the idolatries of scholastic theologians, as well as the follies of numerous other rationalists—astrologers, scientists, grammarians, and Stoic moralists.[148] In his meditation on the first Psalm he recalled Ezekiel's comparison of divine wisdom to waters unfathomable to man's *"ingenium,"* and, while denouncing churchmen who insist on keeping sacred letters out of the reach of laymen, he argued: "they are not understood through ingenuity, but rather through piety; the spirit teaches them, not Aristotle, grace, not reason, divine inspiration, not the syllogism."[149] And in his *Paraclesis*, which addressed the spiritual needs of his contemporaries perhaps more directly and more simply than any of his other works, he emphasized that Christianity is a "transformation rather than a reasoning." Such distinctions were voiced frequently by the Christians of the age, who, despite a variety of sectarian allegiances, found themselves united, as Eugenio Asensio has put it, in their yearning for "a shortcut to heaven" and in their striving to return to the simplicity of the primitive Church and to establish direct contact between the individual conscience and God. We hear them in St. Theresa's dis-

---

[147] Ibid., p. 94.

[148] See J. B. Payne, "Toward the Hermeneutics of Erasmus," *Scrinium Erasmianum*, 2:13-49. E. F. Rice, *The Renaissance Idea of Wisdom*, pp. 158-59. A. A. Auer, *Die vollkommene Frömmigkeit des Christen Nach dem Enchiridion militis Christiani des Erasmus von Rotterdam* (Düsseldorf, 1954), pp. 146ff.

[149] "non tam ingenio quam pietate percipiuntur. Spiritus eas docet, non Aristoteles: gratia, non ratio: afflatus non syllogismus" (*Beatus Vir, Opera Omnia*, ed. J. Le Clerc, 5:183F).

tinction between *"letrados"* and *"espirituales,"* in Gonzalo Fernández de
Oviedo's espousal of prayer: "A greater knowledge is that which one
reaches through love (*afecto*) rather than reasoning (*intelecto*)," in Ber-
nardino de Laredo's desire that the whirling "bees of thoughts which
disquiet the heart will be completely destroyed," and in Juan de Valdés's
elaboration of an authentic gnosis, emphasizing feeling, illumination,
and submissiveness and rejecting as obstacles to pure religious experience philosophy, reason, curiosity, and science.[150]

Lying behind the ambiguities that can be discerned in the attitudes
toward knowledge of such humanists as Vives, Erasmus, and Bacon
is a tradition reaching back to the most remote origins of Christianity,
holding that the Christian's impulse to know can easily degenerate
into idle curiosity and interfere with his responsibilities to pursue his
transcendental destiny through virtuous conduct in his life on earth.
Augustine had contrasted the inward illumination of the blind Tobit,
who instructed his son Tobias in the beauties of charity, with the
dazzling allurements of the external world, which arouse the "concupiscence of the eyes" and compel the Christian to indulge a certain
"vain and curious desire cloaked with the title of knowledge and science," to seek "new experiences," and to forget his origin and destiny.[151] The same spirit informs the words of St. Bernard of Clairvaux,
and in their phrasing they could almost be read as the moral of Cervantes's *Licenciado Vidriera*: "Much learning is indigestible to the stomach
of the soul, which is memory, unless it be cooked by the fire of love
[*caritas*]. Such learning will be regarded as a sin; it is a food which

[150] See Antonio Comas, "Espirituales, letrados y confesores en Santa Teresa de
Jesús," *Homenaje a Jaime Vincens Vives*, 2 vols. (Barcelona, 1965-1967), 2:85-99;
Eugenio Asensio, "El erasmismo y las corrientes espirituales afines: conversos, fran-
ciscanos, italianizantes," *Revista de Filología Española* 36 (1952):31-99; Margherita
Monreale, "Juan de Valdés as Translator and Interpreter of St. Paul: The Concept of
Gnosis," *Bulletin of Hispanic Studies* 34 (1957):89-94. Savonarola contrasted the "carnal
man" who has no intellectual interest and the "animal man" who thinks that he
knows, pointing out that the former is far closer to the spiritual life (see R. H.
Popkin, *The History of Scepticism from Erasmus to Descartes* [Assen, 1964], p. 19). For
the widespread opposition of love to knowledge in mystical thought of the sixteenth
century, see Rice, *The Renaissance Idea of Wisdom*, pp. 124ff., and Haydn, *The Counter-
Renaissance*, pp. 94-96.

[151] *Confessions*, 10; see *The Confessions of St. Augustine*, trans. John K. Ryan (Garden
City, New York, 1960), pp. 264-65. For the general emphases in Augustine's conception of wisdom and its continuing influence despite the numerous efforts by Renaissance thinkers and moralists to develop a more secularized approach to the question
of knowledge, see Rice, *The Renaissance Idea of Wisdom*, esp. chap. 1. See also Hans
Blumenberg's analysis of Augustine's critical view of curiosity in *Die Legitimität der
Neuzeit*, pp. 297-314.

turns into evil humors."[152] Amid his advocacy of the folly of the cross at the climax of his universally read *Praise of Folly* Erasmus recalls Bernard's admonition, and he reminds his audience that Christ urged man to trust not his own wisdom. God forbade eating of the tree of knowledge, as if knowledge were the "poison of happiness."[153]

The poisonous effects of knowledge continued to fascinate philosophers and thinkers throughout the Renaissance, and their writings are full of portraits of flawed men of wisdom, caricatured seekers of truth, satirical confrontations between blessed simpletons and arrogant academics, and accounts of failed education or misdirected quests for wisdom. For example, we observe Vives on his stroll through the University of Paris, an "emporium of good letters," looking for the ideal wise man, "the man who perfectly masters the circle of all the disciplines," and finding only a gallery of monsters, each of whom represents, in the concentrating and distorting focus of caricature, one of the traditional sources of wisdom.[154] We witness the titanic, dis-

---

[152] Cited by Arpad Steiner, "The Faust Legend and the Christian Tradition," *PMLA* 54 (1931):391-404; see p. 393. Steiner offers numerous statements of the pessimistic attitude toward the value of curiosity and knowledge characteristic of Christianity, from the wisdom books of the Old Testament to the writings of the Reformation period that surrounded the emergence of the Faust legend.

[153] "Eodem pertinet, quod Deus ille orbis architectus interminatur ne quid de arbore scientiae degustarent, perinde quasi scientia felicitatis sit venenum. Quamquam Paulus aperte scientiam, veluti inflantem et perniciosam improbat. Quem divus Bernardus, opinor, sequutus, montem eum in quo Lucifer sedem statuerat, scientiae montem interpretatur" (*Laus Stultitiae, Ausgewählte Schriften*, 2:196-98). The popularity in Spain of the anti-intellectualism voiced by Erasmus's *Stultitia* is evidenced by a paradoxical declamation delivered by the Spanish humanist Lope Alfonso de Herrera at the University of Alcalá in 1530. He argues that Adam's desire for knowledge rewarded him with the condition of the beast, that knowledge is closely linked to insanity, and that, in fact, "sapientia vel paululum citra insaniam sita est, vel in ipso male sani capitis jacet confinio" (see M. Menéndez y Pelayo, *Bibliografía hispano-latina clásica, Obras completas*, 66 vols. [Santander, 1940-1974], 46:267-68; F. Rico, " 'Laudes litterarum': Humanismo y dignidad del hombre en la España del Renacimiento," pp. 909-914).

[154] "Scis quantopere hic Vives desideret sapientem, quem se habiturum arbitratur, si vir extet que disciplinarum circulum quàm optimè calleat" (*In Suum Sapientem Praelectio, Opera Omnia*, 4:22-30). In such satirical characterization, plotting, and dialogue, one detects the spirit and literary techniques of Lucian, whose satires, translated and popularized by Erasmus, circulated widely and contributed significantly to the skeptical and anti-intellectual ferment of the time. For the impact on Spanish humanist writings of their recurrent critique of vain intellectuals and false philosophies, see Margherita Morreale, "Luciano y las invectivas 'antiescolásticas' en 'El scholástico' y en 'El crotalón,' " *Bulletin Hispanique* 54 (1952):370-85. Indeed one observes in both Sancho Panza and the glass licentiate affinities with Lucian's fictional characters. In his advocacy of common sense, his rejection of artifice, and the critical

astrous flights of Faust, as he indefatigably pursues all forms of knowledge in his attempts to encompass the entire universe in his mind and to master all the sources of its power. And in one of the most enduring of the numerous comic treatments of the problem of knowledge in sixteenth-century literature, we follow the restless fool Panurge on his frenzied search for an answer to the riddle that torments him, an abortive quest through which Rabelais presents an endless procession of grotesque spokesmen for the wisdom of the world.[155] While in his *Praise of Folly* Erasmus set the tone for much of the wisdom literature of the following century, in his dialogue *Ciceronianus* he created, in a tale of failed education, one of humanism's most significant embodiments of intellectual hubris. Here Erasmus addresses himself to a potential danger in the cult of good letters to which he had dedicated the work of a lifetime. In his fanatical determination to attain the ideal of Ciceronian eloquence, Nosoponus withdraws into scholarly solitude, spurning public and ecclesiastical offices, rejecting marriage and family life, and fleeing such distractions as love, jealousy, and ambition, all of which he characterizes as sicknesses. Like Cervantes's fanatical student, the Licenciado Vidriera, he is concerned to prevent the body from contaminating his intellect, nourishes himself with a few dried raisins, and, when preparing to work, fasts so that "crassa materia" does not penetrate to the "sedem liquidioris animi." He views his enterprise as a sacred calling (a *sacra res*), one that demands, like the "more secret disciplines of magic, astrology, and alchemy," a purification of all vices and emotions; he places images of Cicero above every door in his house; and he dreams constantly of his master. Working energetically for seven years and considering himself successful when the work of an entire long winter night rewards him with the completion of a single sentence, Nosoponus finally harvests

---

spirit that he displays increasingly toward the end of Part II (see below), the former is one of countless sixteenth-century descendents of Lucian's Menippus. As for the glass licentiate, we need only look at the portrait of the philosopher that Lucian presented in the popular *Icaromenippus*, a portrait that made its way into Cristóbal de Villalón's *El scholástico*: "Navegar o cultivar los campos o servir en el ejército o ejercer algún oficio me parece superfluo; yo chillo, voy sucio, me baño en agua fría, ando descalzo en el invierno y llevo una capa mugrienta, y, como Momo, voy difamando todo lo que los demás hacen" (cited by Morreale, "Luciano," p. 373).

[155] See Walter Kaiser's analysis of Rabelais's *Tiers Livre* as a work focused on the problem of knowledge (*Praisers of Folly* [Cambridge, Mass., 1963], Part II), particularly his observations on the Socratic nature of Panurge's quest, its failure, and the relation between Rabelais's satirical survey of learning and one of the most influential anti-intellectualist treatises of the age, Henry Cornelius Agrippa's *De Incertitudine et Vanitate Scientiarum et Artium* (pp. 136-50).

the fruits of his disciplined adoration of Cicero. He has compiled, in volumes too heavy to be lifted by a single man, gigantic indices of all the words and forms of expression used by his master, and he is hopelessly insane. Bulephorus, one of the interlocutors of the dialogue, describes his illness as similar to the tormenting delusion of a man who imagines that his head is made of clay and lives in fright lest any movement he makes might shatter it.

Erasmus exploits the absurd figure of Nosoponus primarily in order to develop by contrast a theory of creative imitation that allows for the importance of changing customs and tastes, the cultivation of sincerity and individuality, the pleasures of variety, and a good deal of flexibility in the play of the imagination, a type of authentic imitation that in fact accords with the practices and "spirit" of the "true" Cicero and is thoroughly incomprehensible to the contemporary deformers of his doctrines, enslaved as they are by the "letter" of his eloquently constructed prose. However, in his portrait of the pedant he continually evokes the age-old tension between Christianity and the veneration of classical antiquity in humanistic studies, and implicit throughout his arguments is his deep concern about the way in which the cultivation of good letters can interfere with the proper aims of a Christian education. Bulephorus describes a Ciceronian's oration on Christ's passion and resurrection, which in its rhetorical perfections and resplendent classical allusions won him the acclaim of his audience, but which, in its lack of "understanding and love" for the significance of Christ's redemptive sacrifice, was in reality a profanation of the spirit of Good Friday. He observes with indignation that "one who wishes to exalt in words the glory of the cross should have proposed as his model the apostle Paul rather than Cicero," and he goes on to lament the Ciceronians' pursuit of the marvelous experience of discovering relics, monuments, and ruins of classical civilization and their failure to see that Gabriel's Annunciation is a source of greater wonder than the golden rain which is said to have fallen into Danae's bedchamber. At the conclusion of the dialogue, Bulephorus points out that man must seek in knowledge primarily whatever nourishes *mutuam benevolentiam* and adds: "One studies the arts and sciences, philosophy, and rhetoric with the single purpose that we may understand Christ and celebrate his glory. This is the goal of all erudition and eloquence."[156]

---

[156] "huius [crucis] gloriam qui voluisset verbis attollere, Paulum apostolum potius sibi proponere debebat quam Ciceronem. . . . Huc discuntur disciplinae, huc philosophia, huc eloquentia, ut Christum intelligamus, ut Christi gloriam celebremus. Hic est totius eruditionis et eloquentiae scopus" (see *Ausgewählte Schriften*, 7:34, 36, 40, 144, 352, 354).

In his numerous critical examinations of the poisons of the intellect, Cervantes is one of the most important of the impressive group of Renaissance writers who concerned themselves with the problem of knowledge, and his diseased licentiate is one of the most bizarre members of a vast Renaissance literary family of misdirected scholars. A full consideration of the range and implications of Cervantes's anti-intellectualism would go well beyond the limits of this study, and it would have to deal with a complex assortment of contexts—the ridicule of bookish authority in the prologue to *Don Quixote* I, Don Quixote's oration on the respective merits of "arms" and "letters," the destructive madness of Anselmo in the *Curioso impertinente*, Diego de Miranda's discussion of the peculiarities of his son's education at Salamanca, the brief *institutio principis christiani* that Don Quixote offers Sancho on the eve of his governorship, the satirical portraits at the conclusion of *El coloquio de los perros*, the characterization of such wise men as Soldino and Mauricio in the *Persiles*, and, most importantly, the characterization of Sancho Panza and his various triumphant confrontations with men of learning.

The *Licenciado Vidriera* is Cervantes's most direct examination of the problem of knowledge. It is the tale of a failed education, and its parable of wisdom encircles its central processional satire and throws ironic light on all of the assertions of its seemingly "monologic" satirical core. For the unequivocal pronouncements of the satire are in fact the venomous fruits of the licentiate's restless pursuit of knowledge. In his early pastoral romance, *La Galatea*, we find Cervantes already conscious of the specific danger in knowledge which he was to explore in his exemplary tale. The germ of the novella is visible in Tirsi's important defense of love and his elaboration of an ethics of moderation, a passage that is deeply informed by the Peripatetic-Pauline attitude toward the proper use of the things of this world that Erasmus had championed in the *Enchiridion*. Tirsi's pairing of the perverted use of philosophy and poetry in fact looks forward to both the philosophical and literary implications of the exemplary novella:

I ask you to tell me, what praiseworthy thing there is today in the world, however good it be, which in its improper use cannot be changed into evil. Let philosophy be condemned, for often it reveals our faults, and many philosophers have been wicked; let the works of the heroic poets be burned, for with their satires and verses they vituperate and reprehend vices.

As he proceeds to advocate the golden mean in his discussion of ethics, Tirsi speaks of the kind of extremism that Cervantes will later embody and examine in his glass licentiate and his impertinently curious husband: "in everything the mean was always praised, just as the extreme was blamed, for if we embrace virtue beyond what suffices, the wise man [*el sabio*] will win the name of fool, and the just of iniquitous."[157]

Cervantes's treatment of his *sabio* and the fallen world to which he belongs is primarily destructive. His work is indeed a satire, and, despite its "dialogue" with the problem of satire, it is principally concerned with the corrosive exposure and correction of abuses that motivates all satirical writing. However, we do glimpse, if only momentarily, a counter-figure to the flawed sage, and his brief description and his function in the tale, which is as ephemeral as that of the mysterious lady who offers the student the deadly fruit and immediately disappears, tell us a good deal about the proper aims and uses of knowledge, as well as about all that the tormented intellectual is blind to as he restlessly pursues the glory of the wise:

Two years or a little more his illness lasted, when a monk of the order of Saint Jerome, who had *grace and the special knowledge* for making the dumb understand, and after a fashion speak, and for curing the insane, *moved by charity*, took upon himself to cure Vidriera; and he cured him and healed him and restored him to his original judgment, understanding, and reasoning. And when he saw him sane, he dressed him up as a scholar and had him return to the court.[158]

In his preface to Augustine's *City of God* Erasmus had written:

There are indeed some who in one way or another delight the idle with frivolous witticisms; there are others who with subtlety may teach necessary things, but who fail to bring about that what is understood is loved . . . you will understand incorrectly if you do not love what you have understood. But what benefit is there from love that is blind? Without charity, knowledge puffs up; without knowledge charity sometimes embraces the baneful

---

[157] "digo que te demando que me digas cuál loable cosa hay hoy en el mundo, por buena que sea, que el uso della no pueda en mal ser convertida. Condémnese la filosofía, porque muchas veces nuestros defectos descubre, y muchos filósofos han sido malos; abrásense las obras de los heroicos poetas, porque con sus sátiras y versos los vicios reprehenden y vituperan. . . . siempre los medios fueron alabados en todas las cosas, como vituperados los estremos; que si abrazamos la virtud más de aquello que basta, el sabio granjeara nombre de loco, y el justo de inicuo" (*La Galatea*, 2:63-64).

[158] "Dos años o poco más duró en esta enfermedad, porque un religioso de la orden de San Jerónimo, que tenía *gracia y ciencia* particular en hacer que los mudos entendiesen y en cierta manara hablasen, y en curar locos, tomó a su cargo de curar a Vidriera, *movido de caridad*, y le curó y sanó, y volvió a su primer juicio, entendimiento y discurso. Y así como le vió sano, le vistió como letrado y le hizo volver a la Corte" (p. 79; italics added).

for the beneficial. But each one calls for the assistance of the other, and joins with it in a friendly union.[159]

The Licenciado Vidriera has, of course, prided himself continually on his cleverness (*agudeza*), and his frivolous witticisms have earned him fame among the idle throng that follows him about and immediately abandons him when he can no longer satisfy its lust for the pleasure of slanderous pronouncements. He is a man who knows no charity and is driven to amass his knowledge as a means of acquiring fame. In Cervantes's exemplary tale a truly wise man does appear, a man in whom charity and knowledge, grace and science, coexist in that combination that Erasmus referred to as the "absolute perfection" toward which properly directed study strives. His role in the parable is fleeting, but his single action of using science to heal a fellow human being and his expressive silence in a world in which language has been debased in its service of ostentatious philosophy, arrogant wit, vituperation, and derision are perhaps more effective in their disclosure by contrast of the misanthropy, the idle curiosity, the vacuous babble, and the destructive philosophy of the protagonist than anything he might have done had his presence as an agent or a character been any more intrusive. The healing mystery of his true wisdom unfolds as swiftly and as imperceptibly as the workings of divine grace. Indeed there is in the very limitation of his role a type of mysterious eloquence that might remind the student of Renaissance wisdom literature of the brief, silent appearance of Gargantua before the restless babbler Panurge and the foolishly wise in the climactic symposium of Rabelais's parable of knowledge.[160]

In the *Quixote*, Cervantes juxtaposes true wisdom to mere knowledge, *sapientia* to *scientia* in the terms of the familiar Renaissance dichotomy, but the opposition is developed in a much more secularized context. The predominant concerns are epistemological rather than ethical, and it is generally the voice of empiricism and skepticism that rises to challenge the vanities of man's prideful intellect. Sancho

---

[159] "Sunt enim qui frivolis argutiis utcunque delectent ociosos. Sunt qui subtiliter doceant necessaria, sed non efficiunt, ut quod intelligitur ametur. . . . Frustra intelligas, nisi diligas quod percepisti. Ad quid autem conducit caecus amor? Scientia, si absit charitas, inflat: charitas absque scientia nonnunquam perniciosa pro salutiferis amplectitur. Sed utraque res alterius opem poscit, & conjurat amice" (*Opera Omnia*, ed. Le Clerc, 3:1248B). See also the eloquent expression of this ideal in the *Antibarbari*, the work mentioned by Cervantes's teacher, Juan López de Hoyos: Charity enables the scholar to escape from the noxious poisons of knowledge. ". . . stude non minus melior esse quam doctior, bona est scientia, charitas melior. Vtramque alteri si comitem adiunxeris, rem absolutam conficies" (pp. 95-96).

[160] *Le Tiers Livre*, chaps. 35-36; see Kaiser, *Praisers of Folly*, pp. 157-61.

Panza is the principal agent in the Quixote's anti-intellectualism, and some of his most memorable triumphs occur when he relies on his common sense to outwit the frightfully learned man of good letters, the "primo humanista," when he cheerfully mocks the nonsense of Don Quixote's pessimistic reading of the mysterious cipher of the fleeing rabbit, and when, aboard the "enchanted boat" of romance, he stands securely as an empiricist and insists on the truth of what the testimony of his senses reveals to him while his master attempts to overwhelm him with a flood of astronomical and geographical knowledge.[161]

Perhaps no single episode reveals more directly the modernity that distinguishes the anti-intellectualism of the *Quixote* from that of the *Exemplary Novels* than the adventure of the "enchanted boat." In a startling caricaturistic transformation, Don Quixote swells with intellectual pride, invokes Latin terminology and illustrious scholarly authority, babbles of "colures, lines, parallels, zodiacs, ecliptics, poles, solstices, equinoxes, planets, signs, bearings, the measures of which the celestial and terrestrial spheres are composed,"[162] and recommends the deductive application of an absurd hypothesis based on authority—that all fleas aboard a ship die when it crosses the equator—to prove to his ignorant squire that they have sailed 800 leagues and have in fact reached the Southern Hemisphere. The bewildered Sancho wonders why it is necessary "to make such an experiment" when his "very eyes" assure him that they are still in sight of the shore of the Ebro and his ears tell him that his ass is braying in dismay as he watches his master abandon him. The arrogant Don Quixote belittles Sancho's "mode of investigation," and suggests that, if he understood the concepts that he has cited, he would not think of turning to his senses to ascertain their geographical position. Manifesting the classical form of self-contradiction of the satirically drawn impostor, Don Quixote proceeds to attack the pretentiousness of ignorant people who cite Latin. The comic deflation of the pedant climaxes when the agreeable Sancho performs the recommended experiment and in a scatological discovery proves by his master's own logic that he has erred in his complex, grandiose calculations. Both victims of the blind astronomer's folly tumble into the water and nearly drown. The episode is, of course, rich in low comedy of situation and character, and it belongs to the variety of scenes burlesquing the most venerated topics

[161] *Don Quijote de la Mancha*, 2:205-207, 581-82, 261-67.

[162] "coluros, líneas, paralelos, zodíacos, clíticas, polos, solsticios, equinocios, planetas, signos, puntos, medidas, de que se compone la esfera celeste y terrestre" (*Don Quijote de la Mancha*, 2:264-65).

of the chivalric romances. However, the peculiarities in the role of Don Quixote within it, which is somewhat inconsistent with his general caricaturistic portrayal and which interferes with his development as a "novelistically" drawn character in Part II, are fully intelligible only if we recognize its allusiveness to Renaissance currents of thought concerning the problem of knowledge. Sancho Panza, for all his naïveté, is an eloquent representative of an empirical approach to the exploration of nature's secrets that was gaining force throughout the sixteenth century in opposition to the deeply entrenched scholastic mode of scientific investigation, based on authority, speculative hypothesis, and deductive reasoning. As Hiram Haydn has emphasized, an impact of the turn toward empirical observation as the proper mode of cognition is visible in nearly all fields of knowledge—in Machiavelli's determination to analyze the state and write history according to what he has learned by experience, in Vives's call for the mind to descend "to the intimate workings of nature" and his attempt to understand human psychology by observing the movements of the soul rather than by rationalistically postulating its essence, in Vesalius's insistence that the body of man is the bible for the physician and that medicine must be founded on the science of anatomy rather than on ancient textbooks, and in Tycho Brahe's insistence on painstaking astronomical observation and in his remark "that his observations of thirty-five years did not lead him to concur in Kepler's speculations, in spite of their great ingenuity." Plainly one of the principal influences on the new mentality was the experience of the voyagers to the New World and the Orient, which was dramatically revealing the errors in traditional geographical and astronomical knowledge. Jacques Cartier wrote that the "simple sailors of today have come to know the opposite of the opinions of the philosophers by true experience"; López de Gómara observed of a forbidden route that "it is already so frequented and familiar, that every day Spaniards go there very easily, and thus experience is contrary to philosophy"; and Amerigo Vespucci testified that he saw in the Antipodes "the fixed stars of the eighth sphere, of which there is no memory in our sphere, and which have never been known, up to today, by the most learned and wise of all the Ancients."[163] Indeed the emphasis on the value of experience as a source of true wisdom was so widespread in the period that we find the skeptic philosopher Francisco Sánchez suggesting that Jesus Christ was motivated by the desire to learn by experience: "Christ our Lord

---

[163] See *The Counter-Renaissance*, pp. 190-251. "The word 'experience' is almost as popular in the sixteenth century as 'reason' in the eighteenth" (p. 190).

wished to take upon Himself human miseries, so that by experiencing our calamities, he might feel more pity."[164] It is not surprising that one of the recurrent topics of skeptics and empiricists was the "theory navigator" and his companion the "theory astronomer." In the *Praise of Folly*, which was no doubt a favorite text for all skeptics of the century, Erasmus wrote that nature laughs at the scientists' pretentious conjectures as daydreams. In their ravings they "construct their countless worlds and shoot the distance to the sun, the moon, the stars and the spheres as with a thumb and a line. They postulate causes for lightning, winds, eclipses, and other inexplicable things, never hesitating for a moment, as if they had exclusive knowledge about the secrets of nature, designer of elements, or as if they visited us directly from the council of the gods." Totally immersed in their world of mental constructs, their invention of nature, and their "ideas, universals, forms without matter, primary substances, quiddities, entities," they fail to see "the ditch or stone lying across their path" and fall on their faces.[165] In Antonio de Guevara's ironic declamation, *Arte de marear*, a work that was so popular that over a half century later Cervantes drew on it in writing *El Licenciado Vidriera* and Caspar Ens literally incorporated parts of it into his *Morosophia* (1620), we observe a frequent reiteration of the antithesis "experience-learning," a contemptuous dismissal of the "theory-navigator," and a celebration of old wives' proverbial wisdom, based as it is on experience, as superior to the imposing chimerical learning of philosophers.[166] The "theory navigator" appeared again in the much more philosophical context of Sánchez's skeptical treatise: "he will be a navigator of books, and, seated very comfortably in his armchair, he will describe in great detail the most distant ports, reefs, and seas, and he will skillfully guide his ship through the kitchen or on the table; but if he ventures upon the sea and you entrust him with the helm of a ship, he will end up among those Scyllas and Charybdises which he knew how to

---

[164] *Que nada se sabe*, pp. 163-64.

[165] "Quam vero suaviter delirant, cum innumerabiles aedificant mundos, dum solem, dum lunam, stellas, orbes, tamquam pollice filove metiuntur, dum fulminum, ventorum, eclipsium ac caeterarum inexplicabilium rerum causas reddunt, nihil usquam haesitantes, perinde quasi naturae rerum architectrici fuerint a secretis, qua— sive e Deorum consilio nobis advenerint . . . ideas, universalia, formas separatas, primas materias, quidditates, ecceitates videre se praedicant . . . neque fossam aliquoties, aut saxum obvium videant" (*Laus Stultitiae, Ausgewählte Schriften*, 2:128; the English translation is taken from *The Essential Erasmus*, p. 142).

[166] Ed. R. O. Jones (Exeter, 1972), pp. 7-8. For the reminiscences of this work in Cervantes's tale, see F. Rodríguez Marín's note, *El Licenciado Vidriera*, p. 21.

describe so nicely as long as his feet were dry."[167] Similarly Antonio de Torquemada condemns physicians who rely exclusively on books, "citing mountains of texts and authorities," and insists that they should learn the healing art by experience and observation, and he compares the bookish doctor to the navigator with no experience of the sea.[168] And Montaigne, whose *Essays*, along with Cervantes's *Don Quixote*, represent probably the greatest literary expression of the Renaissance discovery of experience, compares the physician who shuns experience with the "theory-navigator": he "teaches as one who, sitting in his chaire paints seas, rockes, shelves and havens upon a board, and makes the modell of a tall ship to sail in safety; But put him to it in earnest, he knowes not what to doe nor where to begin."[169]

The tension between theory and practice, speculation and observation, and mental construct and fact runs through all these writings, and the satirical confrontation of the philosopher burdened with dogma and the unlettered advocate of practical knowledge—the simple sailors of Cartier or the old wives of Guevara—is a common feature in their critique of intellectualism. For example, in his imitation of Erasmus's *Praise of Folly*, *Morosophia*, Caspar Ens narrates an anecdote about the encounter of a heavily schooled astrologer and an ignorant peasant, who are consulted by the King of France about the weather. The former foresees fair weather, the latter, rain, and when things turn out as the peasant predicts, the king inquires about the secret of his wisdom. He replies that he bases his predictions on the activity of his ass, who always lowers his ears when anticipating rainy weather, and the admiring king rewards him and his animal handsomely and banishes his astrologer.[170] In effect Cervantes's description of the ill-fated

---

[167] *Que nada se sabe*, pp. 163-64.

[168] *Colloquios satíricos*, ed. M. Menéndez y Pelayo, N.B.A.E. 7:508.

[169] Cited by Haydn, *The Counter-Renaissance*, p. 199.

[170] *Morosophia: Id est Stulta Sapientia* (Cologne, 1620), 2:47; this compendious descendent of Erasmus's *Praise of Folly* is presented as an adaptation of Antonio Spelta's *La saggia pazzia* (1607), a work that I have been unable to consult. For the numerous critics of intellectualism in the age, whether their concerns were religious, ethical, or epistemological, the ass, the humble beast who bore Christ and conveyed God's admonition to Balaam, had a special dignity, and the paradoxical praise of its admirable qualities and superior wisdom was a characteristic theme of their writings. See, for example, Ens's argument that "asini multo potior sit, quam philosophi conditio" (1:295), and Agrippa's "Digression in praise of the Asse," which concludes his full-scale denunciation of the wisdom of the world (*Of the Vanitie and Vncertaintie of Artes and Sciences*, trans. J. Sanford [1569], ed. C. M. Dunn [Northridge, California, 1974], pp. 382-85). To appreciate the simple, wise, and pious society of Sancho and his ass in the *Quixote*, we should bear in mind the privileged position of the animal

voyage of Don Quixote, the "theory-navigator" who fails to heed the persuasive reasons of the empirical peasant, insists on imposing the intellectual constructs of his superior science on a resistant reality, and falls disastrously, is a literary reworking of a common confrontation in the wisdom literature of the age. Its implicit vindication of experience and observation as the true sources of knowledge accords perfectly with the most profound and modern themes of the *Quixote*—the unmasking of literary deception, the critical analysis of the mentality that structures itself according to myth, and the confrontation of truth.[171] For in the encounter between speculative philosopher, "anticipating" nature through hypothesis and dogma, and unlearned peasant, insisting on observing the facts, we can see an epistemological analogue of the revolutionary literary technique running through the entire novel—the depiction of the ways in which the actual activities and experiences of characters violate literary conventions, which in reality are the speculative categories concerning the trajectory of plot and the possibilities of character that constitute the expectations that a reader brings to his text and that he constantly attempts to impose on that text in his effort to render it intelligible.

While the *Quixote* poses the question concerning proper and improper knowledge primarily in a secular context and emphasizes epistemological rather than ethical issues, it would be false to overlook the common ground that it shares with the much more traditional parable of knowledge, *El Licenciado Vidriera*. Sancho Panza, for all his ignorance of books and his healthy skepticism regarding the fabrications of man's speculative reason, is not simply an inveterate empiricist. He knows that there is a *"tología"* that teaches a sacred wisdom, consisting of the simple principle of "vivir bien," and, when confronting the rational labyrinth that the legalists have constructed to ensnare him as he administers justice, he knows that one can easily solve a rationally insoluble problem by invoking the simple truth of charity, a truth that, as Erasmus put it in delineating his figure of the perfect man, the *beatus vir* of the first Psalm, is a truth more obvious but seemingly more elusive than all the complex wisdom of this world.[172]

---

not only in Holy Scripture and Christian tradition, but also in the writings of the Renaissance that addressed themselves specifically to the problem of wisdom.

[171] Cervantes was, of course, very sensitive to the ways in which an individual's sense perception is influenced by his own vital needs, and, as J. B. Avalle-Arce has pointed out, he occasionally assumes a pessimistic stance concerning the effectiveness of the empirical method of dealing with truth. See "Conocimiento y vida en Cervantes," *Deslindes cervantinos*, pp. 23ff.

[172] *Don Quijote de la Mancha*, 2:195, 425-27.

The act of charity is, as Don Quixote reminds him in the instruction that he offers the new "prince," the act in which man resembles God most closely. Erasmus emphasized that there is but one pristine law and that its profound wisdom is readily available to the simple of spirit: "Una lex Domini immaculata, sapientiam praestans parvulis." The single law of Christ is the law of charity, and the spiritual educators of men should devote less attention to the teachings of Aristotle and Plato, the subtleties of scholastic writings, and the infinite number of laws of philosophers and princes, and should instead turn their efforts to revealing the "most simple doctrine of Christ" ("Christi doctrinam, simplicissimi simplicissimam"), a "philosophy" that bears the healthiest of fruits within the believer—an innocent spirit, an impulse to act charitably, a love of one's neighbor, and the peace of a good conscience.[173]

The simple *sapientia* of charity, then, unites Cervantes's two opponents of the useless *scientia* of the world, Sancho Panza and the good friar who heals the Licenciado Vidriera. The latter is, of course, a man of knowledge, and in his combination of *ciencia* and *gracia*, he exemplifies the Erasmian principle of *humanitas*, which is so shockingly absent in the highly educated consciousness of the fanatical student of good letters who delights in flaying the society about him. *Humanitas*, of course, implies an awareness of the body of humanity to which the scholar belongs, a sense of the other, whether as individual, community, or state. As we have seen, such an awareness is notably lacking in the Licenciado Vidriera, who flees his companions, refuses service for his country, avoids the community of the city whenever it is beset with the dangers of war or plague, and, following his plunge into insanity, chooses to dwell in stables and fields and rejects even the touch of his fellow man. Erasmus wrote that the taste of the fruit of the tree of life, which is nourished by the fountain of true wisdom, rewards man with an exhilarating sense of being a vital part of something that is much greater than himself. Observing that a human being is not created to be a traitor, a defrauder, or a calumniator, he remarks: "The only profit befitting a man is to deserve well of every-

---

[173] See *Opera Omnia*, ed. Le Clerc, 5:181AB, 188E. In *El pensamiento de Cervantes* Castro draws attention to Sancho Panza's various spontaneous acts of charity and points to Erasmian doctrines that undoubtedly affected his conception as a literary character (see chap. 6). Occasionally we observe in such scenes an opposition of the type which Erasmus develops in this commentary, between the laws of the world and the higher law of charity—for example, in Sancho's resolution of the paradox of the bridge and the gallows, in his indignation as he beholds the rowers whipped in Barcelona, and in his compassion for the old galley slave who is being led in chains to his death.

body, since truly he is not born for himself, but rather for his country and his friends."[174] When he is restored to sanity, it is significant that the Licenciado Vidriera turns to the community from which he has severed himself and which he has incessantly attacked. And it is significant that, as he embraces the active life and journeys to distant lands, no longer in curiosity, but rather in devotion to his country, Cervantes defines his life and death as "prudent." Throughout most of the tale the licentiate is a hopelessly flawed man of the intellect, but in the sudden turn of events that follows on his redemption he ironically achieves the goal that has eluded him all along. He has become the true wise man, who for Cervantes can only be a true citizen, and his death on the fields of Flanders rewards him with the fame which he had sought all along. "He set off for Flanders, where the life he had begun to immortalize in letters he ended in immortalizing by arms, in the company of his good friend, Captain Valdivia, winning at his death the reputation of a wise man and a most valiant soldier."[175]

In conclusion, it is well to recall Don Quixote's discourse on letters and arms and his insistence on the fact that there is no essential distinction between the two callings as long as both serve the community. Both of the knight's ideals are realized in the life of the aged seer of the *Persiles*, Soldino, the good magician who has retreated from the court to pursue the knowledge of nature and find salvation after a full life of devotion to his country. In the background of these various contexts dealing with knowledge we glimpse Cervantes's conciliatory stance toward the traditionally conflicting claims of contemplation and action, the respective value of divine grace and human knowledge, and the relative importance of transcendental sapience and worldly knowledge, whether practical or ethical, in man's proper fulfillment of himself as a human being. In his refusal to envision the members of these various antitheses as radically opposed, in his unsparing criticism of the egotism and inhumanity of the isolated intellectual, and in his emphasis on the civic responsibilities of the man of learning, Cervantes's treatment of the problem of knowledge places him in the central stream of humanist thought, originating in the writings of certain fifteenth-century Florentine thinkers and statesmen for whom the only true wisdom is that which manifests itself in beneficial civic

[174] "Proprius hominis fructus est, bene mereri de omnibus, quippe qui non sibi natus sit, sed patriae, sed amicis" (*Opera Omnia*, ed. Le Clerc, 5:190C).

[175] "se fué a Flandes, donde la vida que había comenzado a eternizar por las letras, la acabó de eternizar por las armas, en compañía de su buen amigo el capitán Valdivia, dejando fama en su muerte de prudente y valentísimo soldado" (pp. 82-83).

action, and reaching its most influential expression in the sixteenth-century humanist reform movement led by such men as Erasmus and Budaeus.[176] As Coluccio Salutati argued, the noblest wisdom leads man to be useful to himself, his family, his friends, and his country, and the true philosopher concerns himself with moral wisdom rather than with solitary speculation on metaphysics and the order of nature. Invoking the models of Cicero and Dante, Leonardo Bruni proposed a system of education that would train citizens rather than scholars, and he claimed that a true philosopher is a "man whose family, economic, and political activity completes and perfects his intellectual work."[177] As I have pointed out above, Erasmus repeatedly insisted that no man is born for himself, that the supreme philosophy, the *Philosophia Christiana*, is centered on the law of charity, that all Christians can learn this simple philosophy and manifest it actively in their community of friends, and that the man who pursues "higher" wisdom, whether it be that of the Christian contemplative of the proud Stoic sage, is a man who cuts himself away from the body of Christians and fails to consider the principal obligation of his humanity.[178]

[176] See Rice, *The Renaissance Idea of Wisdom*, pp. 39-41.

[177] Ibid., p. 46. Compare the words of Cervantes's teacher, the Spanish Erasmist, Juan López de Hoyos: "no podemos hacer otro beneficio mayor a la república que enseñar e industriar los mancebos, de adonde salen buenos ciudadanos . . . no sólo nacimos para nosotros, sino que parte de nuestro nacimiento debemos a nuestra tierra, y parte a los amigos" (see Américo Castro, "Erasmo en tiempo de Cervantes," *Semblanzas y estudios españoles*, p. 188).

[178] As I have suggested above in connection with the lack of *humanitas* in the Cynic philosopher, in his ridicule of the absurd disembodiment of the Licenciado Vidriera's intellect, Cervantes aligns himself vigorously in another sense with the ranks of these humanists, who generally embraced an ideal of humanity that accorded to the body and the emotions a legitimate and important role in the individual's search for righteousness and happiness. Whether they turned for inspiration to Aristotle's ethics, which recognize the positive, creative function of the passions, to Cicero's moderated Stoicism, which admits, as Giannozzo Manetti put it, that, if the emotions were eliminated, there would cease to be a difference not only "tra una pecora e uno uomo, ma tra uno uomo e un tronco, o veramente un sasso, o qualunque altra cosa insensata," to Epicurean doctrines concerning pleasure and the integration of all parts of the individual, or to Christ's gentle, forgiving attitude toward human weaknesses and the comforting example of his own humanity, most evident in his fearful night in the Garden of Gesthemane, they all were in agreement that to be human meant "innanzitutto consentire con gli uomini, soffrire e godere, umanamente; amare i figli e la famiglia e la patria, nella ragione cercare non la nemica, ma la guida, la misura degli affetti" (see Eugenio Garin, *L'Umanesimo italiano: Filosofia e vita civile nel rinascimento* [Bari, 1952], pp. 75-81). However various the philosophical allies might be that distinguished the individual humanists one from another, they were nevertheless united against the common adversary—any rigorously dualistic philosophy, whether Stoic, Platonic, or Christian ascetic—that would oppose their conception of the hu-

Pursuing the same line of thought Guillaume Budaeus distinguishes wisdom from prudence, and, invoking Cicero's moral philosophy, argues that prudence is a kind of knowledge that is indispensable to one who would lead a life that is beneficial to mankind. Its contents might be less exalted than the immutable objects of "wisdom," but the "wise" man who lacks it usually suffers from an undeveloped moral sensibility and a rude lack of humanity, and he commonly yields to the temptation to display ostentatiously the empty wisdom that he has accumulated through study.[179]

It is only if we bear in mind the humanists' concern with the integration of knowledge in civic life and with the dangers in the dissociation of wisdom and prudence, that we can fully appreciate the significance of the Licenciado Vidriera's death and his paradoxical salvation in death. In the opening lines of the tale Tomás Rodaja appears sleeping at the foot of a tree in solitude ("en aquella soledad"). Cultivating his *ingenio* and his prodigious memory, he wins universal fame for his *agudeza*, but he remains in solitude. In the last line of the story he suddenly emerges from his solitude, and he appears as a good friend, a good citizen, and a "prudent and most valorous soldier," who readily confronts the dangers of history that he had continually shunned while immersed in his fragile paradise of intellectuality. Ironically he has finally achieved his initial ambition and he has truly awakened from his sleep. Purged of the venoms of all false knowledge, he has found his way back to himself, to his community, and to his body which is the body of mankind, and his prudent death for his country is, oddly enough, the first truly wise act of his life.

---

man being as a harmoniously integrated entity by postulating a rigid qualitative distinction and a continuous tension between mind and body, reason and passion. Such a dualistic vision was a common feature of the literature of Cervantes's Spain, nourished as it was by traditional ascetic religious currents and the resurgent neo-Stoicism of contemporary philosophical circles. The Licenciado Vidriera and Sancho Panza, the man of the mind and the man of the body, are the most important figures in Cervantes's fictional examination and critique of its inadequacies.

[179] Rice, *The Renaissance Idea of Wisdom*, p. 152.

CHAPTER IV

Cervantes's Secularized Miracle:
La fuerza de la sangre

THE POPULAR RELIGIOUS CULTURE OF CERVANTES'S SPAIN: PROCESSIONS, PILGRIMAGES, AND MIRACLES

ON SUNDAY, APRIL 26, 1587, the citizens of Toledo gathered to celebrate the return of their patron saint, whose remains had lain in exile in northern Europe for nearly one thousand years. Like so many other venerable Spanish relics, the bones of St. Leocadia had disappeared during the Moslem invasion, undoubtedly transported by her devotees to the safety of the Cantabrian Mountains, from which they made their way in various stages through France to the Benedictine monastery of St. Gislenus in Flanders. In 1582, fearing a menace that now came from within the divided Christian world, the Jesuit father Miguel Hernandez negotiated their release from the Flemish monastery, and after a lengthy journey across Europe they arrived five years later at their proper resting place, the Basilica of St. Leocadia in Toledo honoring the site of the saint's martyrdom.[1]

[1] See Karl Vossler, *Spanien und Europa* (Munich, 1952), p. 68. The decision to "bring home" the imperilled saint epitomizes the increasingly defensive posture of Spain of the Counter-Reformation and its determination to turn inward to its traditional sources of strength. The Spaniards' sense of the growing spiritual isolation of their country is audible in the memoirs of the prolific chronicler of the period, Esteban de Garibay y Zamalloa, who describes his efforts to persuade the Archbishop of Toledo and Philip II to save the saint by removing her from a land where she is "surrounded by heretics" and placing her in the secure kingdom of Spain, where "Catholism is flourishing" (see *Memorias de Garibay, Memorial Histórico Español* 7 (1854):312-13, 346-48).

The festivities celebrating the translation of the remains were spectacular. A solemn procession came forth from the city to receive the holy reliquary, which, elevated before an altar of the Church of the Vega, rested on a platform adorned with triumphal arches erected especially for the occasion. Eight dignitaries and canons lifted the litter to their shoulders and bore it toward the Puerta de Visagra, where magistrates of the municipal government were waiting to receive it into their city. While the astonished populace expressed its jubilation "with all kinds of music, vocal and instrumental, with dances and games, and a thousand types of merrymaking,"[2] the *regidores* carried the holy burden beneath canopies of "gold and silk" through the streets of the city, sacralizing the spaces of their daily lives by touching them with the wonder-working relics.[3] At various predetermined points on their route the celebrants halted to allow the citizens to offer their tribute to the saint in the form of "triumphal arches, and large images of saints and kings, with their elegant inscriptions written in Latin verse and in prose." When they reached "las cuatro calles," the city officials turned the holy relics over to a group of canons who in turn bore them to the Puerta del Perdón and the gate of the church, where, in a culminating epiphany, King Philip II, the royal family, and the grandees of Spain emerged from the house of the archbishop to escort the litter on the final stage of its passage. As they approached the church and the magnificent representations of the glories of "many saints of Toledo, and kings of Spain, and other princes,"[4] which the architects of the city had created for the celebra-

---

[2] "con todo genero de musicas de vozes, y otros instrumentos, con danzas y juegos, y mil maneras de regozijos" (Francisco de Pisa, *Historia de la gloriosa virgen y martyr Santa Leocadia Patrona de Toledo . . . En la qual se trata de su vida, y martyrio, y de su aparicion despues de muerta, y templos en esta ciudad a ella dedicados, y de su translacion* [facsimile of the 1605 edition of Toledo; Madrid, 1974], pp. 12ff.). The occasion is also described in Hernandez's *Vida, martirio y translacion de la virgen y martir Sancta Leocadia* (Toledo, 1591), and in Garibay's *Memorias* (pp. 441-51). The printing of such *relaciones* as Pisa's and Hernandez's indicates the importance conceded to such festivities in the epoch and existence of a market for this kind of writing.

[3] For such magical functions of relics in the maintenance of order, protection of a city, and consecration of a locale, see Heinrich Fichtenau, "Zum Reliquienwesen des früheren Mittelalters," *Beiträge zur Mediävistik* (Stuttgart, 1975), pp. 108-144, esp. 119-22. For their role in sacralizing the landscape of Europe, particularly its springs and mountaintops, see Georg Schreiber, "Strukturwandel der Wallfahrt," *Wallfahrt und Volkstum in Geschichte und Leben*, ed. G. Schreiber (Düsseldorf, 1934), pp. 45ff.

[4] "arcos triumphales, y figuras grandes de santos, y de Reyes, con sus inscripciones elegantes en versos Latinos, y en prosa . . . muchos santos de Toledo, y Reyes de España, y otros Principes." For a discussion of the "politics of relics" and the way in which such processions were traditionally designed to enable the masses to visualize

tion, the Archbishop Cardinal Gaspar de Quiroga, dressed in his pontifical robes, came forth from the church and welcomed the king, who, together with the grandees, lifted the reliquary "with great devotion," crossed the threshold of its permanent house, and laid it before the main altar. Throughout the night a specially delegated group of beneficiaries stood vigil beside the sacred coffer, holding burning candles and entoning hymns and psalms until dawn. On the following morning the cardinal conducted a pontifical mass, the coffer was opened, the authenticating documents, "instruments and testimonies" were examined, and, following their approval, King Philip locked the coffer and delivered the key to the treasurer of the church. A solemn procession bore the bones to the sacristy and their permanent abode, "a place which was appropriate for them, as it was the very palace of Our Lady the Virgin."[5] Shortly thereafter the king was to obtain from the Pope the declaration of a Plenary Jubilee for all who went in pilgrimage and prayer to the shrine during the week of the translation.

Francisco de Pisa's detailed description of the rites and the festivities of St. Leocadia's translation affords us an instructive glimpse of the pervasiveness of religious sentiment in the daily life of the period and of the theatricality with which it was cultivated and expressed. We observe how nearly all segments of the populace participated in and contributed to the colorful pageantry distinguishing the religious festivals, how religion and politics were thoroughly fused in Spanish government, and how the nation carefully designed its public spectacles to consecrate and mythologize Spanish cities and Spanish history. The organization of the procession, with its numerous divisions and its multitudes of confraternities bore witness to the hierarchical structure of Spanish society and no doubt formally incorporated nearly all of its stations. The chronicler observes that it was led by a group of "niños de la doctrina," the orphaned children whom the ecclesiastically directed schools throughout Spain adopted, educated, and restored to society. Behind them marched the bearers of 200 banners and 200 staffs, representing the confraternities of Toledo and the surrounding district, the cross of the Church of Toledo, and 110 crosses of the neighboring churches. There followed sixty virgins arrayed in

---

the continuity linking the saint, the contemporary ruler, his ancestors, and the glories of their history, see H. Fichtenau, "Zum Reliquienwesen des früheren Mittelalters," esp. pp. 131ff. At the conclusion of his account Pisa identifies Philip II and Pelayo as protectors of the saint from the barbarians, claiming that the Pelayo was responsible for the original removal of the bones.

[5] "lugar qual convenia, que fue en el proprio palacio de la Virgen nuestra Señora."

the livery of the Chapter, each of whom had received as a dower a gift of 20,000 *maravedis* for participating in the festivities, 1,000 friars of the monasteries of the area, 500 priests and clerics from eighty locations in the district, and numerous other ecclesiastics, including the inquisitors, their ministers, and their minor officials. Behind the ecclesiastics marched the 140 masters and doctors of the University of Toledo, adorned with the insignias of their respective faculties, and behind them, the members of the city government—the chief ensign, the chief mayor, and the chief constable, bearing staffs of justice and escorted by fifty-five jurats, thirty-six *regidores*, the corregidor, and their mace-bearers. The local magistrates were followed by numerous grandees of Castile, who represented the central government and who acted as harbingers of the triumphant vision of the monarchy when the king appeared at the climax of the procession.

Like so many other public rituals of the period, the spectacle in Toledo attests to the extraordinary vitality of popular religious culture in Cervantes's age and to the tremendous power it exerted on the entirety of society.[6] The banners of the 200 confraternities point to the important role throughout the Catholic world of such organizations, through which enormous numbers of citizens expressed their religious impulses in worship, ritual, and service to the community.[7]

---

[6] "Dieses Zeitalter war bemerkenswert einheitlich geformt. Es gab sich stärker und geschlossener, als es der Spätgotik vergönnt war. Der Grundgedanke des allumfassenden Reiches Gottes und der absoluten Herrschaft des Allerhöchsten glitt durch Lebensgefühl und Literatur, durch Staatsidee und Ethos, durch Musik und Schauspiel. Mehr als alle anderen Bezirke wurde aber die Volksfrömmigkeit von dieser Seelenhaltung ergriffen" (Schreiber, "Strukturwandel der Wallfahrt," pp. 27-28). Schreiber points out that triumphal translations with elaborately structured processions were frequent in the period and influenced permanently the devotional life of the inhabitants of the community receiving the relics—e.g., through holidays, festivals, and pilgrimages (see pp. 31-32). For the importance of the popular element in the cult of the saints, see Fichtenau, "Zum Reliquienwesen des früheren Mittelalters," pp. 116-17.

[7] The importance of the religious confraternities in the daily life of the time has been stressed by Schreiber. He observes a revitalization of the medieval orders, a new stress on specific doctrines and mysteries rather than a common profession as the bond uniting the members, and an emphasis on worship and religious education of their members. Their increase in number and membership (e.g., "Die Corpus Christi Bruderschaften besassen 1728 allein im bayerischen Teile des Freisinger Bistums 224910 Mitglieder") and their financial support and concrete participation in the creation of baroque art are among the most significant indications that the dominant religious and cultural movement of the time was a mass movement, the gigantic procession being one of its most characteristic manifestations. See "Der Barock und Das Tridentinum: Geistesgeschichtliche und kultische Zusammenhänge," *Das Weltkonzil von Trient*, 2 vols. (Freiburg, 1951), 1:381-425, esp. 407-416. The awarding of dowries to the

Moreover, the climax of the procession with the mightiest monarch in the world receiving the bones of a local saint is a striking example of the lively interest in relics and the reinvigorated cult of the saints, which sprang up in Catholic regions all over Europe and were sanctioned by the official political and ecclesiastical culture in response to the spread of Protestantism. And the ritual consecration of space through the contact of the saint's relics and the recommendation of devotion through pilgrimage are characteristic examples of the reaffirmation throughout the Catholic world of the value of the pilgrimage and the miraculous power of its great shrines, as well as of the increased enthusiasm for the local pilgrimage in an age when the great international pilgrimages that had been paramount in the popular devotion of the middle ages had become increasingly threatened by the religious and political upheavals that divided Europe.[8]

The impact of the popular religious culture is visible not only in such public pageants as the translation of St. Leocadia's remains but also in various forms of popular literature which flourished in the period—books of devotion, sermons, and prayers, rosary books, saints' lives, and manuals for pilgrims, consisting of devotional materials and

girls in the procession is characteristic of the active role in the age of Church organizations, which, under the inspiration of San Juan de Dios, took strong measures to support the family as a basis of social order and to prevent the spread of prostitution and illegitimate births (see G. Schreiber, *Mutter und Kind in der Kultur der Kirche* [Freiburg, 1918], pp. 82ff.). For the revitalization of traditional miracle literature by the confraternities, see G. Schreiber, *Deutsche Mirakelbücher* (Düsseldorf, 1938), p. 39.

[8] For the central place of the pilgrimage and the cult of saints, relics, and images in the daily life of Cervantes's age, see Schreiber, "Strukturwandel der Wallfahrt," pp. 21ff. "Im Zeitalter des Barock wurde die Wallfahrt von der Volksfrömmigkeit ungemein lebhaft ergriffen. Ein Hochzeitalter brach an. . . . Diese Wallfahrt verpflichtete alle, die sich zur Stadt hielten. Ganz gleich, ob sie einen Heiligen oder ein Mysterium zum Inhalt hatte. Man schmückte das Gnadenbild. Man pries es in Hymnen und Orationen. Man feierte es in Prozessionen. Man steigerte die kultische Gebärde an bestimmten Feiertagen. Auch das Kultbild kannte festa praecipua. Der städtische Künstler übernahm es in seine Vorstellungswelt und die Ausführung der schaffenden Hand. Man verteidigte es, wenn der Feind anrückte und schöpfte aus dem Heiltum den Mut zur Abwehr. Man rettete es auch zuweilen durch Flucht" (p. 23). One of the most famous literary representatives of the popular religious devotion of the period is Lope de Vega's Peribáñez, an active member of the confraternity of a local saint, an exemplary pilgrim, a zealous crusader, and a humble venerator of holy images. He remarks: ". . . sólo quiero/ que haya imágenes pintadas:/ la Anunciación,/ la Asunción,/ San Francisco con sus llagas,/ San Pedro Mártir, San Blas/ contra el mal de la garganta,/ San Sebastián y San Roque,/ y otras pinturas sagradas/ que retratos es tener/ en las paredes fantasmas" (*Peribáñez y el Comendador de Ocaña* [México, 1968], p. 98).

tourist guides and including in many cases maps, recommended stop-overs, and collections of miracles to inspire the wanderers with wonder as they approach the numinous spaces of their destinations.[9] One can get some idea of the scope of this literature by reading Bartholomé de Villalba y Estaña's forgotten work, *El Pelegrino curioso y grandezas de España* (1577), a voluminous narration of the wanderings of a youthful pilgrim among the shrines of Spain, which includes geographical descriptions, celebrations of images, catalogues of relics, edifying homilies, conversations of hermits and pilgrims, and narrations of local anecdotes, legends, and miracles.[10] The rambling compendium of popular religious lore, with its fictional plot and numerous *culto* poems, stands halfway between the pure popular forms and the numerous refined adaptations of such forms by some of the greatest writers of the period. Indeed, just as the most persuasive proof of the vitality of popular religious culture of the period can be found in such spectacular creations as Bernini's gigantic baldachin in St. Peter's, with its replication of the canopied reliquary of contemporary religious processions[11] and the countless paintings of miracles and martyrdoms by the masters of the baroque, the best indication of the vitality of the popular literary forms engendered by that culture lies in the way in which they infiltrated and nourished the most important serious literature of the day. Thus Calderón and numerous other dramatists joined the huge participating throngs in the festivals of the Holy Sacrament by writing spectacular dramas for the culminating moments of the pageants. Calderón himself described the *autos* as "sermons put into verse, questions of Sacred Theology given representable conception" ("sermones puestos en verso, en idea representable, cuestiones de la Sacra Teología").[12] Several recent studies have emphasized the decisive impact of sermons and devotional literature on the devel-

---

[9] G. Schreiber emphasizes the importance of this type of literature and its impact on baroque art ("Gerade die Kunst des Barock ist weithin geprägte Frömmigkeit und erlebte Liturgie"), and he offers a summary of its most influential forms in "Der Barock und das Tridentinum," pp. 388-91. For the pilgrim book, a medieval genre which flourished in the age, see "Strukturwandel der Wallfahrt," p. 32. Schreiber describes in detail an example of the genre in "Der heilige Berg Montserrat," *Gesammelte Aufsätze zur Kulturgeschichte Spaniens, Spanische Forschungen Der Görresgesellschaft* 10 (1955):113-60; see especially 120-28. For devotional literature of the Virgin, see Stephan Beissel, *Geschichte der Verehrung Marias im 16. und 17. Jahrhundert* (Freiburg, 1910).

[10] See ed. La Sociedad de Bibliófilos Españoles (Madrid, 1889).

[11] See Victor L. Tapié, *Baroque et Classicisme* (Paris, 1972), pp. 111-12.

[12] *La segunda esposa y triunfar muriendo, Obras completas*, ed. A. Valbuena Prat (Madrid, 1967), 3:427.

opment of the picaresque novel with its anatomy of social and moral disorder and its concern for the mysteries of sinfulness and regeneration.[13]

One of the great themes of baroque literature of all types is the pilgrimage. In some of the most memorable scenes of Tasso's celebrated epic, *La Gerusalemme liberata*, the heroic Christian army is described as a throng of pilgrims adoring the holy city and ascending to the sacred Mount of Olives to worship and reenact the mysteries of its "saint." Cervantes, Mateo Alemán, and Baltasar Gracián could make, each in different ways, the pilgrimage to Rome a central theme and a structural basis of the works they considered their masterpieces, and Lope de Vega could pour into one of his most ambitious prose narratives, *El peregrino en su patria*, sermons, accounts of pilgrimages, descriptions of shrines, poems honoring the Madonna and the wonder-working image of the Virgin of Pilar, and religious dramas.[14] At the same time the popular miracle books, which frequently formed an important part of the pilgrims' devotional readings, left an equally profound mark on the major literature of the period.[15] Cristóbal de

---

[13] The picaresque novels "son obras dedicadas a la educación ascética" (J. Casalduero, "Notas sobre La ilustre fregona," *Estudios de literatura española* [Madrid, 1962], pp. 90-102; see p. 100). See also E. Moreno Báez, *Lección y sentido del Guzmán de Alfarache* (Madrid, 1948), and Alexander Parker, *Literature and the Delinquent: The Picaresque Novel in Spain and Europe, 1599-1753* (Edinburgh, 1967). It should be recalled that Mateo Alemán, the creator of the most widely read picaresque novel in the age, was also the writer of hagiographic literature and that there are clear affinities in theme, style, tone, and structure linking his *Guzmán de Alfarache* and his *Vida de San Antonio de Padua*. See E. Cros, *Mateo Alemán: Introducción a su vida y a su obra* (Madrid, 1971), pp. 60-63.

[14] For the popularity and significance of the symbol of the pilgrimage in literature of the Counter-Reformation, see A. Vilanova, "El peregrino andante en el 'Persiles' de Cervantes," *Boletín de la Real Academia de Buenas Letras* 22 (1949):97-159; J. Hahn, *The Origins of the Baroque Concept of Peregrinatio* (Chapel Hill, 1973); Forcione, *Cervantes' Christian Romance* (Princeton, 1972), pp. 29ff.; "Lope's Broken Clock: Baroque Time in the *Dorotea*," *Hispanic Review* 37 (1969):459-90, esp. 485-90. For the history and iconography of the theme, see Samuel C. Chew, *The Pilgrimage of Life* (New Haven, 1962).

[15] For the remote origins of this traditional literary form in St. Augustine's writings, see H. Delehaye, "Les premiers *libelli miraculorum*," *Analecta Bollandiana* 29 (1910):427-34; Schreiber, *Deutsche Mirakelbücher*, p. 20. For its great popularity in Cervantes's age, see Schreiber, "Der Barock und das Tridentinum," p. 389; "Der heilige Berg Montserrat," p. 127, and, most importantly, *Deutsche Mirakelbücher*, *passim*. In his "rewritten" version of the *Quixote*, Alonso Fernández de Avellaneda appends an interesting testimony of the form's popularity at the conclusion of the lengthy *Cuento de los Felices Amantes*, a powerful but totally conventional miracle narrative which he includes as if to replace Cervantes's ambiguous miracle, *The Tale of the Captive*, with a doctrinaire celebration of the cult of the Holy Rosary. A member

Virués recast the classical epic around the deeds of Juan Garín, a fallen hero whose greatest exploit is a prodigious expiatory pilgrimage on all fours from Rome to Montserrat, where he is redeemed by the miraculous intercession of the Virgin. Cervantes, Avellaneda, and María de Zayas developed the form in prose narrative, and religious dramatists cultivated it in their plays over and over again in their efforts to

---

of the audience of the tale, in an authentically cervantine moment, is "miraculously" inspired by its telling to join the Confraternity of the Holy Rosary, and he observes: "Maravillado y suspenso en igual grado me dexa, padre, el sucesso de la historia referida y el concierto guardado en su narración, pues él la haze tan apazible quanto ella de sí prodigiosa; si bien otra igual a ella en la sustancia tengo lehída en el milagro veynte y cinco de los noventa y nueve que de la Virgen sacratíssima recogió en su tomo de *Sermones* el grave autor y maestro que por humildad quiso llamarse el Discípulo: libro bien conocido y aprovado, por cuyo testimonio a nadie parecerá apócrifo el referido milagro. Por el qual y por los infinitos que andan escritos, recogidos de diversos graves y piadosos autores, en confirmación del santo uso y devoción del rosario, protesto ser toda mi vida, de aquí adelante, muy devoto de su santa confradía" (*Don Quijote de la Mancha*, ed. Martín de Riquer [Madrid, 1972], 2:161-62). Avellaneda's reference to "infinite" numbers of miracle tales is probably no exaggeration. Throughout the Catholic world well-organized efforts were apparently made to collect, authenticate, and commit to official written record miracles confirming the holiness of the various shrines. In a pilgrim manual of 1674 a priest, Andreas Eisenhut, wrote that the Jesuit fathers who directed the religious processions in Würzburg requested all pilgrims to report to the proper religious and lay authorities any divine response that they may have received to their prayers to the Holy Blood so that its miracles could be preserved in writing, and he observed that eighteen and twenty-one miracles were accepted and permanently recorded in 1623 and 1624 respectively. A typical publication stemming from the efforts to collect miracles is entitled *Marianischer Atlass: Von Anfang vnd Vrsprung Zwölfhundert Wunderthätiger Maria-Bilder* (see G. Schreiber, *Deutsche Mirakelbücher*, pp. 73-74). Werner Weisbach points out that the miracle was the central subject in a vast body of painting and literature in the period of the Counter-Reformation and that the Catholic Church, in response to the spread of Protestantism, encouraged and exploited for propagandistic purposes the masses' receptivity to the appeal of the miraculous. "Ein Hauptmittel, mit dem die Kirche immer gearbeitet hat und das ihr auch jetzt in weitem Umfange diente, war das Wunder. Durch das Wachhalten des Wunderglaubens, durch die unausgesetzte Vorweisung und Verkündigung von Mirakeln hat sie ihre Position verankert und die breite Menge an sich gefesselt. Die Jesuiten haben ihrerseits eifrig dazu beigetragen, die Wundergläubigkeit zu befördern und die Wundersüchtigkeit des Volkes zu befriedigen. Während die protestantischen Reformatoren sich in Wesen und Wirken für Verstand und Phantasie nicht aus der allgemein menschlichen Sphäre heraushoben, war es dem Orden darum zu tun, das Leben und Handeln seines Stifters und das seines ersten grossen Missionars Franz Xaver nach und nach mit einer Fülle von übernatürlichen Geschehnissen zu umkleiden" (*Der Barock als Kunst der Gegenreformation* [Berlin, 1921], p. 37). For the importance of miracles in the religious culture of Spain of the period, see J. Caro Baroja, *La formas complejas de la vida religiosa* (Madrid, 1978), chaps. 3 and 4. "La 'voluntad del milagro' está a la orden del día" (p. 92).

astonish and edify their popular audiences. Lope de Vega's fondness
for the miracle is attested throughout his writings, and he could pause
in his prose epic to narrate the story of his own fall and deliverance
in the form of a miraculous redemption of a hermit on Montserrat,
whose desperate escape from destructive passion is imaginatively linked
with the miracle of Juan Garín, the presiding spirit of the mountain.[16]

[16] For Lope's assimilation of his biography to the literary paradigm of the miracle
narrative, see El peregrino en su patria, ed. J.-B. Avalle-Arce (Madrid, 1973), pp.
174ff. Indeed the prose epic begins with a miracle. While a group of barbarous
soldiers prepares to hang him, the pilgrim offers a long prayer to an image of the
Virgin and her child, which he carries on his breast. As the hangman places the noose
around his neck, the soldiers are touched by the beauty and nobility of the youth's
face, "God secretly moves their hearts," and they spare him (see pp. 85-92). Similarly
Cervantes's Persiles begins with the miraculous salvation of the hero, who, emerging
from the dark cave of his prison to face his executioners, lifts a glance of supplication
to heaven and is quickly delivered. In Lope's scene the parallelism of holy image and
hero as objects of adoration and instruments through which grace works its wondrous
metamorphoses should be noted, because Cervantes develops in a similar way the
miracle situation of La fuerza de la sangre, where Leocadia commends herself to the
image and then becomes a divine image on whom her antagonist gazes in the scene
of his transformation. In their fondness for symmetry and balance, striking epiphanies
of order and disorder as pivotal moments in the spectacle, the antithetical depiction
of the realms of the demonic and the divine, and the presentation of miraculous
metamorphoses and restorations, the auto and the masque, the great spectacular forms
of baroque drama, have striking affinities with the popular miracle narrative, which
indeed frequently influenced them concretely. In the masque at the center of Cervantes's El rufián dichoso, in Periandro's dream of paradise in Book II of the Persiles,
and in the duke's staging of the apparition of Dulcinea following a frightful pageant
of demons in the Quixote, we discover Cervantes employing the conventions of this
type of drama. For the structure of the masque, see Northrop Frye, "Romance as
Masque," Spiritus Mundi (Bloomington, 1976), pp. 148-78; for the court masque as
a quintessential form of "baroque" literature, see Jean Rousset, La Littérature de l'âge
baroque en France (Paris, 1954), chap. 1. One of the most powerful religious dramas
of the period, Calderón's La devoción de la cruz, presents an endless sequence of miracles through which the cross manifests its powers to save even the most hopelessly
lost of human beings. In one of its most significant doctrinal scenes its depraved
protagonist Eusebio meets a hermit who has gone into the wilderness to found a holy
order honoring the cross and who has spent over forty years composing a miracle
book, "Milagros de la Cruz." Eusebio respects the book, and his devotion to the cross
ultimately brings about the miracle that saves him from damnation. (See Comedias
religiosas, ed. A. Valbuena Prat [Madrid, 1963], 1:46; for the contemporary revitalization of the cult of the cross, visible in the founding of confraternities in its honor,
public rituals, and devotional literature, see Schreiber, "Der Barock und das Tridentinum," p. 412.) For the incorporation of situations and plots of the miracle books
in the scholastic theater of the Jesuits, the Benedictines, and other orders, see Schreiber, Deutsche Mirakelbücher, p. 74. Characteristic of the Spanish interest in the miracle
in this period is María de Zayas's adaptation of the "difunta pleiteada" theme (El
imposible vencido), in which the resurrection of the cadaver is truly miraculous, the

Indeed the burlesque miracles of the *Lazarillo de Tormes*, as well as the savage travesty of the prototype of Christian miracles, the resurrection of Lazarus, at its imaginative center, are testimony, whether through imitation or negation, of the immense popularity of the literary form in the age. And there can be no doubt that the emphasis on *"maravilla"* in the most elite literary theory and poetic practice of the time (e.g., Tasso, Marino, Góngora) had something to do with a widespread "predilection for the mysterious and the awesome" which had its roots in popular religious sentiment and the literary forms that it engendered. [17]

Cervantes may well have witnessed the triumphal festival in which the citizens of Toledo celebrated the return of their lost saint. He was living at the time in the neighboring town of Esquivias, where three

---

wonder-working agent being a crucifix. The miracle distinguishes the tale sharply from its Italian ancestor in Boccaccio's *Decameron*, where the maiden is only apparently dead, her resuscitation is associated with passionate love and sexuality, and her restoration is a triumph of human generosity (X.4). As I hope to show in the following analysis, Cervantes's *La fuerza de la sangre*, as a miracle narrative that mingles in an extremely complex way secular and religious elements, stands at some midpoint between the fully secularized miracle of Boccaccio and the pure miracles cultivated by such contemporaries as Zayas and indeed by Cervantes himself in other works. For the "difunta pleiteada" theme, see Edwin S. Morby, "The *difunta pleiteada* theme in María de Zayas," *Hispanic Review* 16 (1948):238-42.

[17] See G. Schreiber, "Der heilige Berg Montserrat," p. 127. A typical title in the hagiographic literature of the period is the following: *Flores del Yermo, pasmo de Egypto asombro del Mundo, sol del Occidente, portento de la Gracia, Vida y milagros, del grande S. Antonio Abad* (see Caro Baroja, *Las formas complejas de la vida religiosa*, p. 96). For Tasso's sensitivity to the sublime, the type of beauty that produces the stunning effect, the evolution of his literary theories away from an *imitatio*-centered poetics to one favoring *admiratio* and rhetorical effects, and the relation between such theories and his psychic and religious disposition, see Ulrich Leo, *Torquato Tasso: Studien zur Vorgeschichte des Secentismo* (Bern, 1951). Some of Tasso's most powerful poetic scenes depict supernatural events, miracles, martyrdoms, and mystical ecstasy. For the elevation of the aesthetic category of the marvelous to a prominence that it did not enjoy previously, see Hugo Friedrich's *Epochen der italienischen Lyrik* (Frankfurt, 1964), pp. 619ff. It is revealing that one of the leading spokesmen of the new poetics, the Jesuit Emanuele Tesauro, in his *Cannocchiale Aristotelico* (1655), reinterpreted Aristotle's distinctions between poetic and historical truth as meaning that poetry is a marvelous departure from the truths of daily life and went on to describe metaphor, the "mother of poetry," as "a miracle," a "bolt of lightning," a "soaring flight," a "metamorphosis on the stage," and an "intrusion of realities never before seen into the world of ordinary experience," phrases that suggest the interpenetration of the religious and the aesthetic sensibility in the period. Recalling the familiar Augustinian notion, Tesauro observes that the cosmos and nature are in fact God's book, but adds that the text is composed of intricate, mysterious ciphers and that the poet, in endowing his own fabrication with such mystery, displays powers analogous to those of divinity (see Friedrich, *Epochen der italienischen Lyrik*, pp. 654ff.).

days earlier the party escorting the remains of St. Leocadia arrived and was greeted with "festivas y devotas demonstraciones."[18] Whatever Cervantes's interest in such spectacles might have been, his writing was profoundly affected by the religious sentiment that they expressed so powerfully, from his early drama, *El trato de Argel*, which concludes with a hymn to the Virgin, intoned by a chorus of captives as they cast off their chains,[19] to the posthumous *Los trabajos de Persiles y*

[18] Cervantes was actually in Toledo on the day following the interment of the saint's remains, for he signed on April 28 a document giving his wife, Catalina, a power of attorney. See John J. Allen, *"El Cristo de la Vega* and *La fuerza de la sangre,"* *Modern Language Notes* 83 (1968):271-75.

[19] Throughout the Catholic world, the Virgin was viewed as the special protector of captives of the Turks, and the great victory of Lepanto was attributed to her intercession in response to the special prayers of the flourishing Confraternities of the Holy Rosary. "Auf Grund dieses Sieges wurde auch die Anrufung 'Hilfe der Christen' ('auxilium christianorum') in die Laurentanische Litanei eingeführt. Diese Schlacht hat die Volksfrömmigkeit stark beeindruckt. . . . Ebenfalls den Türkenkämpfen ist zugehörig das Fest Beatae Mariae Virginis de Mercede Redemptionis Captivorum (24. September)" (see Schreiber, "Strukturwandel der Wallfahrt," pp. 39-41). One of the striking features of Cervantes's religious writings, from the early drama to the posthumous prose epic, is the expression of devotion to the Virgin, and it is quite possible that the fervor marking many of them had its roots in the formative experiences of his years as soldier and captive in Italy and Africa. On the basis of the testimony of his fictional writings, his assertion in *Adjunta al Parnaso* that he frequently visited the Monasterio de Atocha, which houses one of the most venerable images of the Virgin in Spain, and his affection for the Trinitarian friars, who had arranged for his ransom in Algiers, Amezúa speculates that Cervantes was in fact a member of the Congregación del Ave María and participated regularly in its rites of worship and public processions (see *Cervantes creador de la novela corta española*, 2 vols. [Madrid, 1956-1958]; 1:123-24). Whatever truth there might be in such speculation, there can be no doubt that Cervantes, his wife Doña Catalina, and his sister, Doña Magdalena, joined the Venerable Orden Tercera de San Franciso and that, dressed in the coarse sackcloth of the Franciscans, he was borne by members of the confraternity to the Church of Discalced Trinitarians where he was buried. Moreover, in 1609 Cervantes became a member of the Confraternity of the Slaves of the Holy Sacrament of Olivar (see Amezúa, *Cervantes*, 1:122-26). For general observations concerning the importance of the Virgin in Cervantes's works, see, in addition to Amezúa, 1:106-124, A. Valbuena Prat, "Cervantes, escritor católico," *Estudios de literatura religiosa española* (Madrid, 1964), pp. 127-42, and N. Pérez, "Marie dans la Littérature Espagnole," *Maria: Études sur la Sainte Vierge*, ed. D'Hubert du Manoir, 8 vols. (Paris, 1949-1971), 2:127-40. It is clear not only that Cervantes involved himself to some extent in the religious activity that centered on the popular confraternities but also that he was very interested in the flourishing hagiographic literature of the age. According to the records of an auction in Sevilla in 1590, Cervantes acquired "quatro libritos dorados de letra francesa en 18 reales" and an "Historia de Santo Domingo en treinta," a purchase which is all the more interesting when one considers that during this period Cervantes was suffering in the most impoverished conditions of his life (see Amezúa, *Cervantes*, 1:55, who finds Cervantes's desire for such a book

Sigismunda, the prose epic depicting the triumphant pilgrimage of two heroic catechumens from the northern extremities of the world to the throne of St. Peter's in Rome. One of the most interesting registers of Cervantes's sensitivity to the intense popular religious culture of the time is his shortest novella, *La fuerza de la sangre*. The tale is set in Toledo, the heart of sacred Spain, the "ciudad santa," which Cervantes hails in the *Persiles* as "the glory of Spain and the light of her cities, who for infinite ages has sheltered in her bosom the relics of the valiant Goths, in order to resurrect their dead glory and stand once again as the illustrious mirror and preserve of Catholic ceremonies."[20] It is the story of Leocadia, a maiden who, like the patron saint of the city, whose name she bears, is a victim of savage cruelty and whose salvation is attributable to some degree to the intercession of divine powers. The tale is one of Cervantes's most melodramatic pieces of writing; its sensationalism, its inconsistencies in character, and its flagrant violations of plausibility have been frequently attacked by readers. Its "bad taste," indeed its unintelligibility, are immediately evident to all who approach it as if it were written according to the canons that appear to govern Cervantes's great representational fiction. The fact is that *La fuerza de la sangre* is controlled by a very different literary logic from that of the novel, and it demands of its modern readers a catholicity of literary taste which has seldom been manifested by its numerous critics. The literary system controlling its form is that of the miracle narrative, and only if its affiliation with the great popular genre of Cervantes's age is recognized can we appreciate its excellences and complexities. It is indeed one of the finest miracles ever written.

CERVANTES AND THE MIRACLE

Orthodox cultivation

In its formal design the Christian miracle presents an initial plunge into disorder that develops rapidly toward a point of catastrophe—for example, death, demonic possession, despair—followed by a sudden

---

incomprehensible and apparently fails to see how open Cervantes's literary works are to the influence of hagiographic texts and conventions). Cervantes undoubtedly resembled the self whom he described in *Don Quixote*: ". . . yo soy aficionado a leer, aunque sean los papeles rotos de las calles" (1:142).

[20] "gloria de España y luz de sus ciudades, en cuyo seno han estado guardados por infinitos siglos las reliquias de los valientes godos, para volver a resucitar su muerta gloria, y a ser claro espejo y depósito de católicas ceremonias" (*Persiles*, p. 327).

unexpected reversal of the downward movement and a triumphant restoration of order. In its cyclical form the plot can be viewed as a subspecies of the general narrative pattern of romance. What marks the miracle as distinctive within the vast area of romance literary forms is the fact that its emphasis does not fall primarily on the heroes' virtues as prevailing in the turn from bondage to freedom but rather on the intervention of a divine agency, which comes to the aid of heroes who are usually helpless, quite unheroic, and frequently even fallen. The protagonists of miracles are victims rather than combatants, their deliverance is a celebration of the power of grace rather than a vindication of any particular virtue that they possess, and the meaning of the situation in which they are involved is to be sought in the significance of the single central event rather than in the exemplary nature of their acts.[21] Like the *exemplum*, a literary genre with which it has close affinities, the miracle is in its structure a "teleological" literary form; it is constructed tightly around its central event, suspenseful in its rapid movement toward it, and it seldom lingers on circumstantial details that might draw its readers' attention toward the individual psychology of its characters or imply value in the particularity of their worlds.[22] There is indeed a concreteness in the fictional world of the miracle that is frequently missing in the other great hagiographic form, the saint's life, that links it with the novella, a genre whose origin it may well have influenced. However, its concreteness, visible in its attention to specific names, places, and dates and in its fondness for domestic and urban settings, is motivated primarily by its determination to authenticate the miracles to which it would bear witness and to remind the reader of the inadequacy of the everyday world in which he lives and in which the miraculous events unfold.

The traditional Christian miracle is a literary form engendered and animated by a religious mentality that is profoundly concerned with

---

[21] See Uda Ebel, *Das altromanische Mirakel: Ursprung und Geschichte einer literarischen Gattung* (Heidelberg, 1965). On the passive quality of the miracle hero and his "*Notlage*," see pp. 45-46.

[22] A sign of the generic affinities of the miracle and the *exemplum* is the fact that they are found together frequently in medieval *exempla* collections (see, for example, John Esten Keller, *Motif-Index of Mediaeval Spanish Exempla* [Knoxville, Tenn., 1949], categories "Religion" and "Rewards and Punishments"). Ebel makes an interesting attempt to distinguish the genres by isolating their respective formal and conceptual emphases and analyzing closely the transformation a miracle undergoes when incorporated into an *exempla* collection (*Das altromanische Mirakel*, see pp. 119-30). See also P. Gallais, "Remarques sur la structure des *Miracles de Notre-Dame*," *Épopées, légendes et miracles*, ed. G.-H. Allard and J. Ménard (Montreal, 1974), pp. 117-34.

the limits of man's power and the vast distance separating him from divinity, and it is not surprising that we find the form flourishing in ages of intense theological ferment and instability concerning the traditional problem of the relation between merit and grace. Ebel has suggested that it is no coincidence that the major miracle collections of the middle ages appeared at the time of St. Bernard's teachings concerning the powerlessness of man and his obligation to rely humbly on the redeeming sacrifice of Christ's blood in his quest for salvation. And it is certainly arguable that the great popularity of the miracle books in Cervantes's age and the evidence of their impact on numerous spheres of cultural life—for example, in the creation of confraternities, the increase in cultist activities and pilgrimages, and the celebration of Christian miracles in art and literature of all types—can not be separated from the controversies raging in contemporary theological circles concerning free will, the power of grace, and the mysteries of divine justice. In its emphasis on man's helplessness, its celebration of humility, and its interest in the problem of despair, the miracle is the form of romance that gives expression to one of the great themes of Spanish literature of the Counter-Reformation—the inscrutability of Divine Providence and the infinite mercy of God.[23]

---

[23] Interrupting his narration of the "miracle of the sacristan" to comment on its theological significance, Avellaneda's hermit points out that the fall of the exemplary nun was part of a divine plan revealing God's omnipotence and the power of his redeeming grace ("permitiéndolo assí su divina Magestad por su secreto juyzio y por dar muestras de su omnipotencia, la qual manifiesta, como canta la Iglesia, en perdonar a grandes pecadores gravíssimos pecados, y por mostrar también lo que vale con Él la intercesión de la Virgen gloriosíssima" [*Don Quijote de la Mancha*, 2:110]). St. Theresa's words aptly summarize the relation between man and God generally assumed by the miracle narrative: "Rogaba la Virgen al Señor que enviase a su Hijo para ser sierva de la que fuese su Madre; quería ella ser sierva, y era la Madre: quién viera qué respuesta le daba Dios. Gusanillo eres, hormiga eres que andas por la tierra, está la Virgen rogando por tí en el cielo: Señor, misericordia para aquel que me llamó, y perdón para aquel que se encomendó a mí." The passage is cited by Georg Weise, who argues that the accentuation of the distance between this world and God was characteristic of the Christian sentiment of the time, emphasizes the difference between such a religious attitude and the late medieval "familiarity" with the divine order, and suggests that there is a relationship between the prevailing ascetic vision and the fondness for heightened contrasts that marks baroque style. See "Das Element des Heroischen in der spanischen religiösen Literatur der Zeit der Gegenreformation," *Gesammelte Aufsätze zur Kulturgeschichte Spaniens, Spanische Forschungen der Görresgesellschaft* 10 (1955):161-304, esp. 223-25. For the "antithetical feeling" stemming from the awareness of God's distance (e.g., Pascal: "il y a une opposition invincible entre Dieu et nous") and the way in which it nourished so much baroque literature and manifested itself in its formal tensions, antitheses, and paradoxes, see Hugo Friedrich, "Uber die Silvae des Statius und die Frage des Literarischen Manierismus," "Pascals

Cervantes certainly did not approach these mysteries as a theologian, and it is probable that he learned more about their ambiguities while pondering the vicissitudes of his own experience in the dungeons of Algiers than while listening to the popularization of Molinist theology which undoubtedly echoed everywhere in the religious culture around him in Spain. Nevertheless, he was fascinated by them, perhaps no less so than his great contemporary Tirso de Molina, and his awareness of the major issues is evident from the early *Trato de Argel*, in which Saavedra, while acknowledging the dark ways of an all-powerful Divine Providence, exhorts his comrade to lead an active Christian life and rejects as a refuge for the weak-spirited the humble reliance on God's Providence, to the posthumous *Persiles*, in which the protagonists grapple with the problem of despair, reaffirm the "fruitfulness" of suffering, and remind themselves that human beings err in attempting to render intelligible by the standards of human reason the designs of God ("measuring and appraising his infinite mercy as if it were merchandise"—"poniendo tasa y coto a sus infinitas misericordias" [p. 97]).

With the possible exception of *El coloquio de los perros*, the *Persiles* is Cervantes's most powerful expression of the mentality implicit in the traditional miracle, and several of its episodes reveal quite clearly the design and spirit of this popular form of literature. Perhaps the most striking is the tale of Feliciana de la Voz, which culminates in a hymn to the Virgin of Guadalupe. Like most miracles the episode begins with a plunge into disorder. When her father discovers that she has secretly borne a child, the frightened maiden flees with her infant into the forest, finds refuge among a group of shepherds, and, hidden in the trunk of a tree, endures a night of terror. As she kneels enraptured before the altar of the Virgin and sings her hymn to the Immaculate Conception, "her face expressing peace, pouring forth tender tears, giving scarcely any other sign that she was a living creature," her vengeful father and her brother storm into the church, the latter brandishing a dagger.[24] The helpless maiden offers herself to her per-

---

Paradox: Das Sprachbild einer Denkform," and "Pascal," *Romanische Literaturen: Aufsätze*, 2 vols. (Frankfurt am Main, 1972), 1:34-55, 84-138, 139-58; also Stephen Gilman, "An Introduction to the Ideology of the Baroque in Spain," *Symposium* 1 (1946):82-107.

[24] "lloviendo tiernas lágrimas, con sosegado semblante, sin . . . hacer otra demostración ni movimiento que diese señal de ser viva criatura" (see *Persiles*, pp. 283-312, for the hymn, pp. 309-311). The hymn includes numerous motifs that were familiar in contemporary visualizations of the controversial doctrine: the Virgin as a temple of "limpia masa," as a resplendent figure soaring above the earth and standing with the moon beneath her feet, glowing with the light of stars, breaking the power of

secutors, but at the climactic moment the avenger forgives her and arranges for her marriage with her lover. The sudden turn of events is followed by universal rejoicing, and the deliverance is celebrated by the singer's completion of her hymn, which had been interrupted by the tumult.

Cervantes planned the *Persiles* according to the formulas for epic composition advanced by the Renaissance neo-Aristotelian literary theorists, and throughout the work he is concerned to avoid violations of verisimilitude, even in those events that are most dominated by marvelous elements. The traditional miracle, of course, exploits the wonder produced by the most flagrant kind of violations of verisimilitude and would draw its readers' attention to theological implications in the disclosure of the limitations underlying any theory of verisimilitude that reason can devise.[25] It is interesting to see how Cer-

---

the infernal serpent, and conceiving in purity the Divine Child who will redeem the world. At the conclusion of the romance Cervantes would appear to be appropriating the iconography of the Virgin of the Immaculate Conception in order to glorify his heroine. The pilgrims discover a portrait of Auristela standing crowned above the world, and in their conversation she is associated with blinding light. For the function of the hymn within the total design of the *Persiles*, see my *Cervantes' Christian Romance*, pp. 87-89. The doctrine of the Immaculate Conception was an object of intense interest in the Spanish religious culture of the time. For example, in 1593, the Jesuits declared its defense a duty for all members of the society, in 1622, at the request of the Spanish king, Pope Gregory XV officially forbade the assertion that Mary was born in sin, and in the following years the great military orders of Santiago, Alcántara, and Calatrava, showing perhaps a trace of that peculiarly Spanish obsession with *limpieza*, vowed to defend to the death the "unstained honor" of the Holy Mother. See Beissel, *Geschichte der Verehrung Marias im 16 und 17. Jahrhundert*, pp. 217-78, esp. 227-30.

[25] In its emphasis on man's incapacities the miracle narrative vindicates the Augustinian view of the miracle as "quidquid arduum aut insolitum supra spem vel facultatem mirantis apparet," rather than the scholastic view: "illa quae a Deo fiunt praeter causas nobis notas miracula dicuntur," which Ebel characterizes as more "modern" (*Das altromanische Mirakel*, see p. 34). In fact, by not explicitly and definitively removing the miracle from the possibility of comprehension by man, the latter definition can much more easily be accommodated to the more rationalistic approach to miraculous occurrences adopted by skeptics and believers alike in Cervantes's age (see below). The Augustinian view is eloquently asserted by Cervantes's contemporary Fray Luis de Granada, who emphasizes the way in which miracles in fact have causes in an order totally different from the order of natural reason and exist in fact to "humiliate reason" and cause man to fall back on faith (*Introducción del símbolo de la fe*, 2:xxix; ed. B.A.E. 6:358-59). There are no causes of miracles except God, and his deepest mysteries cannot be fathomed by reason. As I shall point out below, Cervantes would appear to endorse the Renaissance rationalists' preference for analyzing unusual phenomena as belonging to the order of nature and for accounting for their apparent incomprehensibility as attributable to man's ignorance regarding nature's occult laws. He is seldom interested in explanation by miracle, but, as some

vantes's "miracles" in the *Persiles* avoid such flagrant breaches of verisimilitude while creating an atmosphere of the miraculous through
suggestion and allusion. Thus while Feliciana's deliverance is accomplished to a great extent through the *discreción* and rationality of the
parties involved, Cervantes situates it in the temple of the Virgin and
surrounds it with allusions to the miracles of the Virgin. The pilgrims
are stricken with wonder at the sight of the "most blessed image . . .
which is the freedom of captives, the file of their manacles and the
relief of their sufferings; the most blessed image, which is health for
the sick, consolation for the afflicted, mother of orphans, and the
repair of misfortunes."[26] They behold the relics and offerings of the
innumerable devotees who were miraculously delivered from disease
and death ("crutches left behind by the crippled"; "shrouds cast aside
by the dead") by the "bountiful mercy of the Mother of mercies," and
they experience a vision of the delivered victims descending through
the air to the temple to offer the relics of their salvation to the Holy
Mother, but finding no place for them "because there was no longer
any space for them in the holy temple: so great was the number that
filled those walls."[27] Full of "astonishment," rapt in "wonder," they

of his characters agree (e.g., Cipión and Berganza and the observer of the wondrous
deliverance of the capsized ship in the *Persiles* [pp. 163-64]), there are indeed such
things as miracles, which "pasan los términos de la naturaleza." Moreover, as J. B.
Avalle-Arce has emphasized, the tension between the miraculous and the rational
which occasionally emerges in the *Persiles* does not ultimately subvert its striking set
of miracles and the religious vision that they reflect. See "Conocimiento y vida en
Cervantes," *Deslindes cervantinos* (Madrid, 1961), pp. 74-76.

[26] "santísima imagen . . . que es libertad de los cautivos, lima de sus hierros y
alivio de sus pasiones; la santísima imagen que es salud de las enfermedades, consuelo
de los afligidos, madre de los huérfanos y reparo de las desgracias" (p. 305).

[27] "muletas que dejaron los cojos . . . mortajas de que se desnudaron los muertos
. . . larga misericordia de la Madre de las misericordias . . . porque ya en el sacro
templo no cabían: tan grande es la suma que las paredes ocupan" (p. 305). In the
allusion to the vast number of relics Cervantes's work reveals what Georg Weise has
found to be a characteristic feature of the Spanish religious culture of the age, "die
kumulierende Tendenz," the fondness for the "greatest possible number" in its orchestration of the wonders of the Christian religion: "Der Zeit des Barock im Gegensatz zu dem späteren Mittelalter und seiner erdennahen mehr realistiche-vertraulicher
Auffassung, greift nicht nur jene Elemente der Betonung des Wunderbaren und über-
irdischen auf und erhebt sie zur höchsten Steigerung des Eindrucks überwältigender
Macht und Herrlichkeit. Die kumulierende Tendenz kommt in gleicher Weise in der
Hervorhebung der Erhabenheit, Würde und Einzigartigkeit zum Ausdruck" ("Das
Element des Heroischen in der spanischen religiösen Literatur," p. 213). Thus Juan
Eusebio Nieremberg wrote of the 62,200 teardrops shed by Christ on the cross and
reminded his reader that one drop of the Savior's blood could redeem "millones de
mundos." Luis de la Puente envisioned Christ's ascension as a triumphal procession
in which hosts of illustrious "*cautivos*," whom he has freed from limbo, follow him

kneel to adore the Holy Sacrament, and at this moment Feliciana lifts her "heart toward heaven" and offers her "voice to the winds" in a song that is likened to that of an "angel confirmed in grace." The listeners, their "senses suspended," are overwhelmed with mystical ecstasy. The deliverance of Feliciana immediately follows on the moment of intense devotion. A "thousand kisses" of reconciliation are quickly poured on the feet of the father-in-law by the contrite lover, freely flowing tears of despair are transformed into tears of joy, the mood of the onlookers shifts abruptly from terror to jubilation, and the pilgrims contemplate the relics, "which are numerous, most holy, and rich," confess, and receive the sacraments. And at this climactic moment the lost child, which has been absent for three days, reappears and is received by his grandfather and former persecutor, who now "tenderly bathes his face with tears and dries them with kisses and wipes them away with his grey locks."[28] While the conclusion of the episode demonstrates Cervantes's oblique, allusive technique of endowing his plausible narrative with the qualities of the orthodox Christian miracle, it provides at the same time a perfect example of the affective climate of the traditional miracle with its fondness for

---

as their captain and "millares de millares" of singing angels accompany his triumphal chariot (ibid., p. 214). In Cervantes's *Rufián dichoso* a citizen describes the miracles at the death of Doña Ana: "Oyéronse en los aires divididos coros de voces dulces de manera que quedaron suspensos los sentidos/ dijo al partir de la mortal carrera/ que once mil vírgenes estaban todas en torno de su cabecera" (*Obras completas*, ed. Valbuena Prat [Madrid, 1956], p. 355; the allusion is to the 11,000 virgin martyrs of St. Ursula, whose famous bones, on exhibit in their shrine in Cologne, dazzled pilgrims from all over Europe). At one of the most religious moments of *La fuerza de la sangre*, we witness Doña Estefanía "derramendo tantas lágrimas" on the face of the suffering protagonist that no other water was needed to revive her from her swoon. Cervantes can of course look humorously on the mentality that expresses its religious impulses with such numerical extravagance. In the *Quixote* he describes rather irreverently Don Quixote's "un millón de Avemarías," a phrase which was quickly modified in the second edition; and, as Américo Castro argues, there is no doubt some irony at the expense of popular religious attitudes in Sancho's enumeration of relics during his enthusiastic discussion of miracles with the knight (2:98-99; see *El pensamiento de Cervantes* [Barcelona, 1972], pp. 265-66).

[28] The "generic purity" of the miracle of Feliciana de la Voz and Cervantes's coherent development of the conventions of the traditional hagiographic form are all the more interesting if the tale is, as Avalle-Arce speculates, citing some interesting, if fragmentary, documentary evidence, a true story "disfrazado por leve velo de ficción" (see *Persiles*, p. 288). As in many other cases in his work, we see how the great unmasker of the violence which literature does to life is in fact a master of transfiguring life according to the patterns demanded by the idealizing fictions which he can approach so critically when he cares to. See my discussion of Cervantes's observation of hagiographic patterns in his own biography (*Cervantes' Christian Romance*, pp. 162-63).

intense, even frenzied, emotions, generally polarized according to its movement from bondage to restoration, and its exploitation of the sensational scene, generally unfolding before a crowd of awestruck witnesses. Moreover, as a miracle, it is thoroughly conventional in its subordination of characterization to the mechanics of its plot and the meaning of its central event, the incomprehensible, instantaneous metamorphoses wrought by divine grace.

There are several other episodes in Cervantes's Christian romance that have affinities with the traditional miracle narrative. Two are worth mentioning in this context because in them Cervantes does in fact allow supernatural powers to intrude into the world of normal experience and because both reveal Cervantes's interest in the darkest and perhaps greatest theme of traditional miracle literature, the mystery of sin and redemption.[29] Possessed by his uncontrollable wrath, Antonio wounds a noble who fails to address him with proper respect. In flight aboard a vessel sailing for England, he provokes and strikes a member of the crew for no apparent reason, and the captain of the ship sets him adrift in a lifeboat. In the darkness and loneliness of his nights he implores God for aid, and he is tormented by dreams in which he is devoured by wild beasts, a purgatorial vision of his own sinfulness. As he continues to pray to God and all the saints for deliverance from the "protracted death" that his life has become, he experiences remorse and sheds tears of contrition ("I increased the waters of the sea with those that poured from my eyes, not from fear of death, which revealed itself so close to me, but rather from the fear of the punishment which my sins deserved").[30] At this point the downward movement in Antonio's expiatory quest is arrested by a miraculous event, and his deliverance begins. He discovers that the darkness is less menacing than before, he perceives the stars shining dimly in the heavens and promising relief from the tempests that have continuously tossed his small boat, and he discovers that he has drifted toward an island where numerous wolves are hovering on a cliff above the boat. One of the wolves breaks the dreadful silence that has fallen on his life for several days, speaking to him "in a voice clear and

---

[29] Cervantes's most profound exploration of this mystery is his other novella that has close affinities with traditional miracle literature, El coloquio de los perros (see my forthcoming Cervantes and the Mystery of Lawlessness). The episodes that I discuss in the following pages are in the Persiles, pp. 71-98. See also my Cervantes' Christian Romance, chap. 3.

[30] "era una muerte dilatada mi vida . . . aumenté las aguas del mar con las que derramaba de mis ojos, no de temor de la muerte, que tan cercana se me mostraba, sino por el de la pena que mis malas obras merecían" (p. 76).

distinct," warning him to seek refuge elsewhere and to thank God for saving him from being torn apart by their teeth and claws. Shortly thereafter Antonio is cast ashore on another island, where the innocent, childlike maiden, Ricla, who appears to him as a "heavenly angel," sent by "the merciful heavens" to save him, rescues him from the elements. He can begin the final phase of his expiatory quest, which will eventually reach its climax in his joyous reunion with his family in Spain.

The tale of Rutilio is almost identical with that of Antonio as it traces his expiatory quest through a fall into sinfulness, bondage in the darkness of prison, a horrifying journey through the heavens to the desolate landscapes of the north, a miraculous confrontation and defeat of his sinful self, a discovery of the stars amid total darkness, his purgatorial bondage among the barbarians, his adoption of the life of the Christian hermit, and his final return to civilization. The central miracle on which his passage from bondage to deliverance pivots is Rutilio's encounter with the witch, who attempts to seduce him and metamorphoses into a ferocious wolf as he resists her advances. Rutilio succeeds in stabbing to death the monstrous embodiment of his own sin after invoking the aid of "every saint in the litany," and following his victory he is reminded to give "infinite thanks to heaven" for having delivered him from the witch's powers.

The supernatural occurrences of these two tales in the *Persiles* certainly recall the powers of hell that figure so prominently in the traditional miracle literature, but it should be pointed out that even here Cervantes avoids the introduction of demons and replaces them by agents which according to the scientific understanding of the age did exist in the world. Moreover, he is concerned to justify their plausibility and introduces a lengthy discussion of lycanthropy in the work, in which the scientist-astrologer Mauricio acknowledges the possibility of the transformations of men into beasts. Cervantes's uneasiness about the violations of plausibility in his efforts to accommodate the subject matter of Christian mysteries to the contemporary prescriptions for a classical epic surfaces on another occasion in the *Persiles* in which the action is strongly reminiscent of traditional miracle literature. As the Turks invade the coastal town of Valencia at the invitation of the treacherous Moriscos, the pilgrims seek refuge in its church and ascend to the tower, bearing the Holy Sacrament and its reliquary. While the diabolical adversary, "the common enemy of human nature," puts the village to the torch and destroys a stone cross, the heroine weeps and prays to God, "whom they had present" in the Host, to spare his temple from the flames. The prayer appears to be answered, but Cervantes would emphasize that the deliverance is attributable to natural causes: the church "did not burn, *not because of a miracle*, but rather because the doors were made of iron, and the fire which they brought to them was not very strong."[31] If such a comment would deemphasize the role of divine grace in the occurrences of the horrible night, Cervantes almost immediately turns about to insinuate once again the possibility of its involvement. The day dawns and reveals the deliverance not only of the elect in the tower, but also of the Morisca maiden Rafala, who races toward the church bearing a "cane cross in her hands" and shouting "Christian, Christian, and free, free by the grace and mercy of God!" Liberated from the oppression of her infidel father, the maiden enters the church, "her face bathed in joyful tears, and her beauty heightened by her elation" and prays to the holy images.[32] At this point, possessed by the "celestial

[31] "no ardió, *no por milagro*, sino porque las puertas eran de hierro, y porque fue poco el fuego que se les aplicó" (see *Persiles*, pp. 353-59; italics added). Cervantes's episode recreates a miracle common in hagiographic literature, and curiously the antithesis emphasizes through negation the degree to which his scene is in fact a reactualization of the paradigmatic situation. (Its effect is similar to the striking antithesis at the decisive moment in *La fuerza de la sangre* when Leocadia takes the cross "no por devoción, ni por hurto, sino llevada de un discreto designio suyo" [see below]). Compare, for example, Jean le Marchant's account of the three men who bear the image of the Virgin into the crypt of the church of Chartres and spend three days unharmed amid the flames that ravage the building (see Ebel, *Das altromanische Mirakel*, p. 79), or the tale of the monstrance, two Hosts, and a finger of St. Agatha which, suspended in the air thirty-three hours, escaped the flames that destroyed the abbey of Notre Dame de Faverney in 1608, a miracle which is said to have silenced the numerous heretics of the district (E. C. Brewer, *A Dictionary of Miracles* [Philadelphia, 1894], p. 493). The same kind of evocation and qualification of a traditional hagiographic motif appears in the episode in which Periandro witnesses the fall of a beautiful woman who is cast from the tower of a castle by her raging husband. In the background of the scene we glimpse the fall of such saints as St. Agatha Hildegardes, who is borne up by God's angels (as is Christ in the gospel miracle) when her jealous husband hurls her from his tower (see Brewer, *Dictionary of Miracles*, p. 392) and St. Ida of Toggenburg, who implores the aid of God during her fall of 400 cubits and alights gently (see Hippolyte Delehaye, *Cinq Leçons sur la Méthode Hagiographique* [Brussels, 1934], pp. 38-39). However, Cervantes's narrator points out that the lady's fall is arrested by the braking effects of her billowing skirts and appends the decisive observation: "Cosa posible sin ser milagro" (p. 373). Similarly the "resurrection" of his heroes from the "belly" of the capsized ship in which they lay "dead" and which has mysteriously drifted ashore draws the comment of an observer: ". . . no se ha de tener a milagro, sino a misterio, que los milagros suceden fuera del orden de la naturaleza y los misterios son aquellos que parecen milagros y no lo son, sino casos que acontecen raras veces" (pp. 163-64).

[32] "cruz de caña en las manos . . . '¡Cristiana, cristiana y libre, y libre por la gracia y misericordia de Dios!' . . . bañado con alegres lágrimas el rostro y acrecentando con su sobresalto su hermosura" (p. 358).

spirit," the sacristan utters his apocalyptic prophecy of the imminent overthrow of the Moriscos and the restoration of the Christian purity of the Spanish kingdom.

If all these episodes of the *Persiles* reveal Cervantes's interest in hagiographic writing, his sympathy for its themes and aims, and his mastery of the particular literary form which was collected in the numerous miracle books of his day, all of them, nonetheless, are designed with a good deal of attention to verisimilitude, and occasionally we discern a tension arising from the application of an aesthetic prescription that is fundamentally incompatible with the aims of the form. That it was literary genre and convention as well as a skeptical attitude toward the subject matter that influenced Cervantes's reserved treatment of the miraculous is proven by his most uninhibited cultivation of hagiographic material and its wonders in his religious drama. For example, in his early *Trato de Argel*, a work which celebrates the heroic Christianity of various Spanish captives who suffer daily torment in the dungeons of Algiers, withstand the constant temptation to compromise their faith, persist in their belief in the crusading mission of Spain, and are prepared to accept martyrdom with the patience and humility of Job, Cervantes presents a miracle of the Virgin, which along with the deliverance of the heroes at the conclusion confirms the presence of Divine Providence and the value of all the suffering which they endure. Attempting to escape to Oran, a captive finds himself lost in the forest, menaced by wild animals, and tormented by hunger and thirst. He calls to the Virgin of Montserrat for help ("Most blessed Mary, since it is among your most noble exploits to offer a protecting hand to the man who has fallen into misery, in this bitter moment of peril I place in your charge my body and soul"), and, awaiting his death, he falls into a deep sleep. A lion emerges from the forest and tamely lies down beside him. On awakening, he feels renewed life pulsing within himself, and "with marvelous strength" he follows the gentle beast, which, "not in reality a lion, but rather a lamb," leads him to Oran, where he offers the Virgin a prayer of thanks for her "strange charity" and vows to become her devotee.[33]

---

[33] "pues es hazaña vuestra/ al mísero caído dar la diestra . . . Santísima María,/ en este trance amargo/ el cuerpo y alma dejo a vuestro cargo" (*Obras completas*, ed. A. Valbuena Prat, pp. 137-38). The insertion of the simultaneous capture and death of the other fugitive, a double figure of the Virgin's devotee, is a puzzling, discordant element in the denouement of this miracle, and it suggests that Cervantes's religious consciousness is already troubled by the complexities evident in his later works. In this respect the scene anticipates the ironies surrounding the miraculous achievements

In Cervantes's much later *comedia de santos, El rufián dichoso*, we discover two of the traditional figures and situations of miracle literature: on the one hand, the powerful sinner who, in a moment of self-knowledge, suddenly and unexpectedly "cae en la cuenta," converts, curbs the dynamic energy that has been driving him toward self-destruction, and redirects it toward the realization of the saintly life; on the other hand, the despairing sinner who is rescued from the clutches of the devil by the intercession of the Virgin. After his conversion el Padre Cruz must contend with a swarm of demons who tempt him with the pleasures of sensuality and dance about him in a masque, singing a *romance de jacarandina* celebrating the powers of Venus. Just as Rutilio in the *Persiles* kills a diabolical antagonist who symbolizes his own flaws, Cruz puts the demons to rout, and he then turns to Doña Ana, who is sick in sin and despair and in dire need of a physician who "cura a lo divino."[34] With the intellectual pride that characterizes the great figures of despair of Spanish literature of the period, Doña Ana refuses to admit that a just God could possibly forgive her, making the mistake which Cervantes's epic hero Periandro defines as "measuring and appraising the infinite mercy of God."[35] Finding not a single good work in her life that she can weigh in the balance of God's justice, she refuses to heed Cruz's advice to hope, stubbornly claims that she would not accept God's pardon, even if offered, and screams in her agony: "My soul is being torn from me! I am dying in despair!" Cruz kneels beside her and prays to the Virgin, asking her to appeal to her "happy child" to soften the hardened heart of the sinner and win a victory over Satan in the struggle for her soul. In an act of Christlike charity ("such charity as was never imagined") he offers Ana all his own good works and burdens himself with all her sins, invoking Christ crucified and the Virgin as "bondsmen" of

---

of the Virgin in the disturbing episode of the *Cautivo* in the *Quixote*. The germ of a *Kasus* is clearly visible (see below, pp. 350, 394), and we sense that Cervantes's skepticism is barely held in check in his conception and execution of the scene. The Virgin and the sinister female figure of La Cava may already be coming together in his imagination.

[34] For the frequency in hagiographic literature of the saint's bouts with demonic temptation as acts that specially qualify him for the cure of the possessed, see Karl D. Uitti, *Old French Narrative Poetry* (Princeton, 1973), pp. 21-22.

[35] See, for example, Paulo, the tormented hermit and outlaw in Tirso de Molina's *El condenado por desconfiado*. The opposite type of spiritual disease, the excessive reliance on God's infinite mercy, was equally prominent in the literature of colossal sinners that the age produced, and Don Juan is its most famous victim. Cervantes's fascination with it is evident in his lengthy anatomy of the hideous witch, Cañizares, at the center of *El coloquio de los perros*.

his "contract" of atonement. He prays to the heavenly hosts to prevent Satan from bearing off "this sheep," which the "Great Shepherd colored red with his precious blood," and secures the repentance and confession of the dying lady. The "fortunate sinner" shouts "piously toward heaven," she sheds tears of contrition as she asks for confession, and she expires with a serenity that she has never known in life. A miracle quickly occurs, for, as her soul leaves the "prison of her body," sweet heavenly voices are heard in song, 11,000 virgins appear at her bedside, the spectators weep with wonder and joy, and el Padre Cruz's body is immediately disfigured by the horrible diseases that he must bear in his atonement for Ana's sins.[36] The final phase of the miracle occurs at the climax of the play, as the devils come forth again to subject Cruz to the temptation of despair by reminding him of his criminal past ("when he was living in freedom"). Naturally they find themselves impotent in the presence of the saint, and after some legalistic grumbling about the outrageous inequities in God's pact with them—i.e., one instant of divine grace can offset Doña Ana's forty years of vice—and voicing their irritation with the way they have always been defrauded by God in His favoritism toward the great repentant sinners of tradition, whom they list, they disappear into the abyss while the denouement celebrates the blood of the saint and his relics and the miraculous metamorphosis of his diseased body at his death (pp. 356-64).

Critical engagement: Parody, critique, and Kasus

The miraculous episodes of the *Persiles* and the religious drama indicate, then, that Cervantes understood perfectly the formal conventions and theological implications of the traditional Christian miracle narrative and that he could cultivate it in an orthodox manner when he wished to do so. However, Cervantes is anything but a doctrinaire religious writer, and his engagement with this important type of Counter-Reformation romance reveals the complexity that marks his treatment of all the traditional idealizing literary forms that nourish his fiction. Even in the orthodox *Persiles* we find beside the solemn miracles of the redemption of Antonio and Rutilio the farcical exorcism of Isabela Castrucho, a resourceful young lady whose ability to exploit people's credulity places her in a tradition of illustrious miracle-fakers extending from *Lazarillo de Tormes*'s seller of indulgences to Boccaccio's Frate Alberto, who invests his assignations with the idiotic Lisetta with the glow of the Angel Gabriel's annunciation to

---

[36] See *Obras completas*, ed. A. Valbuena Prat, pp. 352-55.

the Virgin (*Decameron*, IV, 2), and back to Lucian's grandiose charlatan Peregrinus. As the priest reads from the gospels, sprinkles the raving maiden with holy water, and holds the cross before her bed, a youth suddenly appears, as if by miracle. He immediately banishes the demons and proceeds to announce his marriage to the delivered maiden, while the wonder-stricken spectators gape in astonishment.[37] The possession and exorcism are, of course, an ingenious plan by which the girl outwits her guardian, who would marry her to someone she does not love. In the episode of Isabela's exorcism we glimpse miracles, relics, Holy Writ, and religious solemnity in a comic perspective, but Cervantes does not allow a tone of irreverence to dominate the scene, as is clearly the case in the depictions of the resourceful miracle-fakers of Lucian, Boccaccio, and the author of the *Lazarillo*. Far from being iconoclastic, the humor of this parody miracle rises precisely because the religious elements which suddenly appear as incongruous are so unshakeably founded. It is festive rather than corrosive humor, and it easily modulates into a tone of religious awe as the "resurrected" maiden and her youthful lover enter a church to be married and to contemplate the baptism of an infant and the burial of an old man. There can be no doubt, however, that we perceive here, if only briefly and in muted tones, the worldly voice of Cervantes, admiring the resourcefulness and irreverence of the energetic youths, sympathizing with their demands for freedom, while at the same time delighting in the deception of the enslaving guardian, the humorless priest, and his credulous companion. As is frequently the case in parody miracles, the audience, which in the pure miracle bears witness, expresses wonder and concentrates the tone of astonishment, and represents the edified reader, is here viewed as a throng of gulls, an easy prey for its wily manipulator.

It is in the *Quixote*, his grand antiromance, that Cervantes gives complete expression to the skeptical attitude that colors his view of all forms of romance literature and of the fondness for the reductive idealizations that marks the mentality of those who cultivate and enjoy them. The critical treatment of the miraculous in *Don Quixote* is a subject too vast to examine in great detail here, and it has been dealt with effectively in numerous important studies. From the Enlightenment to the present skeptical readers have found exhilarating the *Quixote*'s exposure of man's inclination to enslave himself in self-protecting illusions, his need for the consolation provided by superstition, and his fondness for systems of authority that thrive on ob-

---

[37] See *Persiles*, pp. 402-412.

scurantism. One need not insist that Cervantes directs the Lucianic humor of his masterpiece at such specific targets as St. Ignatius of Loyola, the cult of the Virgin, or the heightened sacramental religiosity of the Counter-Reformation, as freethinking interpreters have argued, from Diderot's suggestion that Don Quixote's adoration of Dulcinea is a burlesque of Marian devotion to L. P. May's exegesis of Don Quixote's reactions to Maese Pedro's puppets as a mockery of contemporary cults of religious images and the knight's slaying of his wineskin-giants as a burlesque of the traditional religious sensibility, capable as it is of perceiving the miraculous transformation of the sacramental wine into Christ's blood.[38] However, there can be no doubt that *Don Quixote* makes a compelling appeal for truth, which for Cervantes may well have been, as E. Chasles suggested, "more beautiful than beauty itself," and that its view of the miracle and the mentality that yearns for the comforts provided by the miracle is gently but unequivocally skeptical. As Chasles put it, the work can be viewed as "l'épitaphe du merveilleux qui est un mensonge."[39] Indeed one of the numerous elements that make Cervantes's novel a literary monument to the birth of the modern world is its relentless depiction of the inadequacies in the traditional mode of apprehending the universe as a stage for miracles, a coherently designed order replete with mystical correspondences and higher significances, as if it were, in the traditional theological parlance that continued to echo in Cervantes's age, inscribed ciphers written by the hand of God.[40] Al-

[38] See L.-P. May, *Cervantes, un fondateur de la libre-pensée* (Paris, 1947), esp. 23-30. For Diderot's interpretation, see W. Brüggemann, *Cervantes und die Figur des Don Quijote in Kunstanschauung und Dichtung der Deutschen Romantik* (Münster, 1958), p. 33. For a review of this way of reading the *Quixote* and a balanced critique of its reductive tendencies, its total failure to acknowledge Cervantes's understanding of and sympathy for the irrational needs of human beings, in short, its failure to see those elements in the text that make it for a reader such as Dostoevski "the most profound word ever uttered by humanity," see M. Robert, *Das Alte im Neuen: Von Don Quichotte zu Franz Kafka* (Munich, 1968), pp. 63-65. For Dostoevski's view of Cervantes's novel, see L. Turkevich, *Cervantes in Russia* (Princeton, 1950), pp. 115-30.

[39] ". . . quel éclat de raison! quelle sève! quelle ivresse de vérité! . . . Cervantes combat pour la vérité, qu'il croit plus belle que la beauté même" (*Michel de Cervantes: sa vie, son temps* [Paris, 1866], pp. 290-91, 297-98).

[40] See, for example, the words of instruction given by "El Descifrador" to Gracián's protagonists as they enter the final phases of their pilgrimage to Rome: "Discurrió bien quien dijo que el mejor libro del mundo era el mismo mundo, cerrado cuando más abierto: pieles extendidas, esto es, pergaminos escritos llamó el mayor de los sabios a esos cielos, iluminados de luces, en vez de rasgos, y de estrellas por letras. Fáciles son de entender esos brillantes caracteres, por más que algunos los llamen dificultosos enigmas" (*El criticón, Obras completas*, ed. Arturo del Hoyo [Madrid, 1960],

though his taste is for the exploits of the chivalric heroes rather than the wonders of the saints, Don Quixote's stance toward literature is that of a reader of miracle books, and as he wanders amid the silences of the seventeenth-century Spanish landscape, he is constantly listening for a response conforming to the wondrous patterns that fill the pages of his sacred writings. He acknowledges that his love of Dulcinea is similar to the love which all good Christians feel for the Virgin. He speaks eloquently of the value of suffering and its necessity as a forestage if the highest reward and joy are to be attained, embracing the paradox that lies at the heart both of the Christian religion and the appeal of literary romance and which in its perversity can only baffle the practical, thoroughly unascetic Sancho Panza.[41] Don Quixote knows that the resurrection of a dead man is a feat superior to the slaying of a giant, but he points out to his squire, who in a moment of endearing and healthy frivolity suggests that they change professions and become saints, that "chivalry is a religion, and there are sainted knights in glory." He describes Santiago Matamoros as "one of the most valiant saints and knights which the world ever possessed" and praises St. Paul as "a knight errant by his life and a peaceful saint in his death." And when he contemplates the spiritual disease gnawing away at the soul of the vengeful outlaw Roque Guinart, he counsels him to turn to chivalry and share with him the

---

p. 877). The full force of Cervantes's ridicule of the reliance on authority in the act of literary creation (e.g., in the prologue to *Don Quixote*, Part I) and of his self-assertive disengagements from textual models and sources (e.g., "un lugar de la Mancha de cuyo nombre no quiero acordarme") can be appreciated only if we bear in mind the traditional view that an individual writer's text is in fact inscribed within a larger and more authentic text and acquires dignity in direct proportion to its degree of approximation to that higher text. The writer is a medium transferring significances already present, and his interpositions between reader and "event-significance" should not be construed as a "creative" act. The orthodox hagiographer is, of course, vitally concerned with authenticating the events and their inherent significances, and, as a mediator, he is particularly self-effacing. See my *Cervantes, Aristotle, and the "Persiles"* (Princeton, 1970), pp. 345-48.

[41] For the ease with which Don Quixote's attitudes and actions—e.g., his penance, his ordeals, his readiness for martyrdom—can be interpreted as a sustained parody of the actions and attitudes celebrated in literary saints' lives and actually exemplified in the lives of contemporary saints—e.g., St. Theresa, who thirsted for suffering, crawled on all fours into the refectory of her cloister, weighted down by a load of stones hanging from a rope around her neck, read books of chivalry, and, as a child, planned to leave home for the Moorish kingdoms, where she could, as her hagiographer, El Padre Ribera, put it, "have her head cut off for the love of Jesus Christ and win the crown of martyrdom"—see L.-P. May, *Cervantes, un fondateur de la libre-pensée, passim* and M. Robert, *Das Alte im Neuen*, pp. 54ff.

knight's ordeals, which "taken as a penance will shorten and ease his difficult journey toward salvation."[42]

Cervantes's novel is, of course, the story of Don Quixote's failures, and throughout Part II the knight's figure appears increasingly anachronistic, as his expectations continue to be thwarted by a totally indifferent universe, in which higher powers and higher significances are conspicuous only for their absence. From the beginning of the third sally to its disastrous end in the city, here the emblem of the modern world and its new mentality, we can see a continuing series of failed miracles, and in their implications they are far more profound than the Lucianic parody miracles of the early adventures, such as the wondrous revival of Don Quixote through a draught of the "Balsam de Fierabras." The hermitage that the knight visits early in his sally is empty, the descent to the underworld with all its promise of the resurrection of the dead brings him only a disturbing insight into his own mortality,[43] the ascent of the hill at the conclusion, unlike the climactic mountaintop epiphanies of the *Persiles*, rewards him with a vision of nothing but an ordinary village of the Mancha in which he is soon to die, the "miraculous" omen of the fleeing rabbit (the *"malum signum"*), as the sober Sancho interprets it, fails to offer even the consolation that the supernatural powers of evil are interested in his torment, and the sustaining hope that Dulcinea will be resurrected vanishes as Sancho completes his self-flagellation and the knight quizzically stares at the empty fields and roads of the Mancha. While Calderón could celebrate the wondrous power of the Virgin by depicting her devotee bearing his torn-out heart across Europe to her shrine at Loreto,[44] and innumerable miracle books could celebrate over and over again the mysterious regeneration of the sinful, Don Quixote discovers in his dream discussion with Montesinos that the heart of a human being is nothing but an organ and like all organs putrifies and stinks when torn out of the breast of even the most valorous knight errant and offered to his lady, and, when he diagnoses Roque Guinart's "sickness of the soul," urges him to yield himself to treatment

---

[42] "religión es la caballería, caballeros santos hay en la gloria" (2:98-99); "uno de los más valientes santos y caballeros que tuvo el mundo . . . caballero andante por la vida, y santo a pie quedo por la muerte" (2:472-73); "y si vuestra merced quiere ahorrar camino y ponerse con facilidad en el de su salvación, véngase conmigo, que yo le enseñaré a ser caballero andante, donde se pasan tantos trabajos y desventuras, que, tomándolas por penitencia, en dos paletas le pondrán en el cielo" (2:501-502).

[43] These implications of the inexhaustible episode of Don Quixote's dream vision are skillfully presented by J. B. Avalle-Arce and E. C. Riley in "Don Quijote," *Suma Cervantina* (London, 1973), pp. 47-79, esp. 58-59, and by H. Sieber in "Literary Time in the 'Cueva de Montesinos,'" *Modern Language Notes* 86 (1971):268-73.

[44] See *A María el corazón, Obras completas*, 3:1148.

by the healing medication of God, and assures the "great sinner" that his ordeals and penitence "will carry him to Heaven in a twinkling," there is not the slightest hint that the great mystery of redemption and the instantaneous metamorphoses of grace which the "miracle-reader par excellence" awaits are about to unfold. The world that Don Quixote encounters is completely disenchanted, and the only resurrections that reward his desires—the "miraculous" resuscitation of Basilio and the deliverance of the dead Altisidora from the demons—are in fact parodies of those in which he believes, ingenious farces contrived by the craft of people about him for their own self-interest.

Behind the critical spirit of *Don Quixote*, one can discern the rationality, skepticism, and materialism of the new bourgeois culture,[45] and it is reflected most powerfully in the climactic depiction of the

---

[45] In *El pensamiento de Cervantes* Américo Castro emphasizes Cervantes's rationalistic approach to the problem of the miracle and his spiritual affinities with the Renaissance founders of modern critical thinking, for example, Pomponazzi and Vives. He notes in his works an occasionally voiced interest in interpreting apparently miraculous occurrences as natural events which, either because of their infrequency or because of their observance of occult laws of nature, elude man's easy understanding but which are nevertheless not the results of supernatural causes. Such statements as "los milagros suceden fuera del orden de la naturaleza, y los misterios son aquellos que parecen milagros y no lo son, sino casos que acontecen raras veces" (*Persiles*, pp. 163-64) and "efetos vemos en la naturaleza de quien ignoramos las causas" (ibid., p. 177) recall Cicero's skeptical doctrines concerning miracles and make a distinction that was of vital importance for Renaissance rationalists with their faith in man's capacities to understand and order his experience and their distaste for the reduced stature of the human being who is willing to resign himself to explanation by miracle (see Castro, *El pensamiento de Cervantes*, pp. 54-59). To appreciate the importance of this distinction, we need only consider the attitudes informing Luis de Granada's celebration of the great miracles that "confirm the excellence of the Christian religion." The goodness of the miracle lies in the way in which it "conquers our understanding and forces us to believe." ". . . es menester que le toque nuestro entendimiento y *lo captive y subjecte a que humilmente abrace las cosas de la fe*" (*Introducción del símbolo de la fe*, p. 359; italics added). While Cervantes's advocacy of the Ciceronian position and its implicit valorization of rationality distinguishes his view of the miracle in a fundamental way from that of the representatives of traditional orthodoxy, it is important to note that the rationalist critique of miracles had in fact been adopted by numerous religious thinkers of the sixteenth century, many of whom were quite orthodox, and that it is perhaps misleading to associate this tendency in Cervantes's complicated, ambivalent body of religious pronouncements with the precursors of modern critical thought. The fact is that the reformist Christianity of the sixteenth century had assimilated some significant aspects of the rising skeptical modes of thought that accompanied the development of the new bourgeois culture (see Lucien Febvre, *Le Problème de l'incroyance au xvie siècle* [Paris, 1968], pp. 195-218). For the integral place of skepticism in the bourgeois mentality and the historical importance of skeptic philosophy in the emancipation of the bourgeoisie in the Renaissance, see Max Horkheimer, "Montaigne und die Funktion der Skepsis," *Anfänge der bürgerlichen Geschichtsphilosophie* (Hamburg, 1971), pp. 96-144.

environment of the modern city, where Don Quixote finds himself most alienated and bewildered and of course most superfluous. Here the man for whom reading is one of the most intense and authentic of human experiences, one that binds his individual life into a pattern prescribed by his scriptures and exemplified by the models they contain, enters the printer's shop and beholds the sacred book itself transformed into commercial object, coming into existence in masses, not through the powers of the enchanter or some other agency of revelation, but rather through the monotonous movements of indifferent machines.[46] Here he listens to miraculous prophecies of an enchanted head, but the oracular utterances are unmasked as products of human ingenuity and technology, and, as the narrator discusses the machine's influence on the masses, the Inquisition's intervention in the case, and the ease with which the "maravillosa máquina" is dismantled, Cervantes allows us a glimpse of the way in which the "manufactured miracle" can become a sinister tool for the manipulation of enormous numbers of people in the modern state. Moreover, in Barcelona Don Quixote learns that the deliverance of captives from the dungeons of the infidel is achieved by money and not by the miraculous valor of crusading knights errant despite the fact that contemporary romances continue to proclaim that one heroic warrior can overcome an army of 20,000 and saints' lives continue to make assertions such as one which Cervantes perhaps noted in his own copy of St. Dominic's biography: that through the miraculous intercession of the saint and the powers of the Holy Rosary, to which he was especially devoted, the Christian

---

[46] For the "magical" powers of certain types of literature and the way in which they are aimed at affecting vitally the lives of their readers, see Northrop Frye, "Charms and Riddles," *Spiritus Mundi*, pp. 123-47, esp. 130-37. If Don Quixote in Barcelona must confront the commercialization and trivialization of literature that accompanies the development of the new materialist culture, in his visit to the orderly house of the new bourgeois world, he discovers that there is a radically different way of reading from his own which that world has adopted. Diego de Miranda informs him: "Tengo hasta seis docenas de libros, cuáles de romance y cuáles de latín, de historia algunos y de devoción otros; los de caballerías aún no han entrado por los umbrales de mis puertas. *Hojeo* más los que son profanos que los devotos, como sean de *honesto entretenimiento*, que *deleiten* con el lenguaje y admiren y suspendan con la invención, puesto que déstos hay muy pocos en España" (2:153; italics added). M. Robert describes Don Quixote as a fool who speaks and acts "als ein mit frommer Lektüre gespickter Glaubensmensch" (*Das Alte im Neuen*, p. 54). Américo Castro argues that Cervantes's fascination with the act of reading and the vital impact that the written word can have on human personality and behavior should be understood in relation to Islamic strains in Hispanic culture ("La palabra escrita y el 'Quijote,' " *Hacia Cervantes* [Madrid, 1967], pp. 359-408).

army at the Battle of Muret destroyed 20,000 of the enemy while losing but one knight and eight soldiers.[47]

Throughout the *Quixote* the traditional miracles of chivalric literature and hagiography appear frequently, and their comical distortion is consistent with the general satirical aim of the work to *desengañar*: to unmask folly, illusion, and superstition, in Chasles's words, to "dresser l'épitaphe du merveilleux qui est un mensonge," and, of course, to mock and disabuse the reader of miracle literature. And as free-thinking critics are always delighted to discover, there are moments when its searing light does not even spare the mysteries attested to by Holy Writ. When the Canon of Toledo urges the demented knight to turn to the Old Testament and historical writings for the delights that he craves from reading, Don Quixote, in one of his masterpieces of coherent nonsense, responds with the rather persuasive argument that the truths of *all* texts are primarily a matter of their individual readers' willingness to believe.[48] At another point in the novel he invokes the testimony of the Bible to support his belief in giants. However, one episode is of particular interest for the light that it sheds on the peculiar mingling of secular and religious elements in *La fuerza de la sangre*. It is the one case in the *Quixote* where we find Cervantes dealing directly with a Christian miracle and introducing the specific kind of narrative that the miracle books popularized in the religious culture of the age.

The *Historia del Cautivo* is in fact based on a miracle of the Virgin, one which was well known in the miracle literature of the sixteenth century.[49] It is a tale of the deliverance of three French knights from the dungeons of the sultan in Cairo by the miraculous intercession of the Virgin. According to one version, the three are brothers, born in the "Provincia di Piccardia, vicino alla città di Laon." The beautiful daughter of the sultan is sent to convert them to the Islamic faith by whatever means she chooses, but the Christians instead convert her

---

[47] See *Don Quijote*, 1: chap. 47; May, *Cervantes, un fondateur de la libre-pensée*, pp. 30-31.

[48] See my *Cervantes, Aristotle, and the "Persiles,"* pp. 107ff.

[49] See G. Cirot, "Le 'Cautivo' de Cervantes et Notre-Dame de Liesse," *Bulletin Hispanique* 38 (1936):378-82; H. Vaganay, "Une Source du 'Cautivo' de Cervantes," *Bulletin Hispanique* 39 (1937):153-54. For the popularity in Spanish medieval literature of accounts of Christians' miraculous escapes from the prisons of the Saracens with the aid of the Virgin and the saints, see George Camamis, *Estudios sobre el cautiverio en el Siglo de Oro* (Madrid, 1977), pp. 42-46. For the miracle's incorporation of the general folkloric motifs of the "woman who delivers the prisoner" and the "miraculous escape," see Cirot and Francisco Márquez Villanueva, *Personajes y temas del Quijote* (Madrid, 1975), pp. 104-106.

by telling her of the virtue and the uncorrupted virginity of the glorious Virgin, before, during, and after the wondrous birth of her son. Through an angel the Virgin imprints her image on the wood of the cell, and in a vision she appears to the princess, Ismeria, to announce that the knights will be delivered and that she will be baptized. The maiden takes the image, gathers her jewels and money, and flees with the Christians, who find a boat miraculously awaiting them at the Nile. While asleep the fugitives are transported to France, where they build a sanctuary honoring the image of Notre Dame de Liesse.

As G. Cirot has pointed out, there are striking similarities linking the miracle and Cervantes's tale. Zoraida, a beautiful Moorish girl who has secretly converted to Christianity and become a devotee of the Virgin, has a vision of the Holy Mother, who exhorts her to flee to Spain, the land of Christians. She frees the captive, enables him to procure a boat, and, gathering her jewels, accompanies him through a series of harrowing adventures, reversals of fortune, and unexpected recognitions, to salvation and marriage in Spain. Cervantes's tale is a far more complex and lengthy work than the miracle; it is concerned with the political, historical, and circumstantial reality of its characters' world, it individuates its agents far more than the simply motivated miracle, and it recasts many of the miraculous elements so as to maintain an air of plausibility. For example, while the miracle, in one brief stroke of the hagiographer's pen, describes the boat as being sent from heaven, Cervantes goes into great detail concerning the problems that the captives of his time faced in planning such an escape, paying particular attention to that element that he repeatedly employs to accentuate the unreality of the magical network of cause and effect visible in romance narrative—money. However, it is remarkable how close the tale is in structure and spirit to the authentic miracle narrative. Powerful religious symbols appear, visions of the Virgin motivate the characters and their acts, Divine Providence is acknowledged as guiding the action, the protagonist and the heroine are, through allusion, associated with Joseph and Mary, and, following the slowly paced introductory section describing sixteenth-century historical events and customs of the infidel world, the narrative tempo moves rapidly and suspensefully from the moment of bondage to flight, deliverance, and adoration of the image in the temple. Indeed, if we look at the total design of the *Tale of the Captive*, we find that it is one of Cervantes's most peculiar generic hybrids. At its midpoint the narrative shifts abruptly from the desultory temporal rhythms that characterize much novelistic writing, in which the intrinsic interest of subject matter and information is clearly dominant, to the dynamically structured temporality that is generally characteristic of romance narrative and that, as Ebel points out, is a distinctive feature of miracle plotting, where the reader's attention is directed toward a sequence of events and his apprehension of time is totally dominated by the suspenseful expectation of a climactic moment toward which they move.[50]

At first glance the tale appears to be in fact a recast miracle of the Virgin, accommodated to the general level of plausibility of event and density in characterization and description of setting characteristic of the novel as a whole, but a miracle nonetheless, orchestrating the traditional values of the miracle—the goodness and power of Divine Providence and the beauties of relying on the Virgin, even in the most desperate of straits. There can be no question here of a parody of the kind which we see in the more humorous treatments of the miracle in the *Quixote*. However, as various readers have pointed out, there is a deeply disturbing element within this episode, and if we look at it closely, we discover that in it Cervantes is dismantling the miracle in a much more complex and devastating way than in his numerous parody miracles. As the episode of Isabela Castrucho in the *Persiles* indicates, a parody miracle calling our attention to the absurdity in the violations of the laws of empirical reality need not undermine the religious spirit on which it is founded. In parody miracles the essential supernatural elements generally collide violently with empirical reality and generate an irreverent humor that the religious sensibility can accommodate to its vision rather easily.[51] In the tale of the captive, however, empirical reality is perfectly accommodated to the workings of the supernatural order; the disturbing element that Cervantes allows to intrude comes from a far different source. The

[50] Ebel, *Das altromanische Mirakel*, pp. 50-51. For the effects of the radically different emphases of the first and second parts of the *Historia del Cautivo*, see Kenneth Burke's discussion of the relations of form and information in literary texts ("Lexicon Rhetoricae," *Counter-Statement* [Berkeley, 1968], pp. 123-83, esp. pp. 144-45). The striking movement from history and actuality into romance and miracle visible in the tale reverses the dominant pattern of the *Quixote*, which generally shatters idealizing fictions by forcing them into an encounter with reality. However, at this moment in the novel Cervantes is complicating matters by turning about to depict life metamorphosing into art, and the direction of the *Cautivo* is perfectly consistent with the emergence of Cardenio as a real *loco enamorado*, incarnating Orlando and Amadís and, as it were, parodying the parody of Don Quixote, his double, and with the appearance of Dorotea as a real damsel in distress, incarnating the chivalric princess, Micomicona.

[51] See Lucien Febvre's discussion of the festive resurrection of Epistémon in Rabelais's *Pantagruel* and his critique of Abel Lefranc's interpretation of the episode as a cynical attack on the miracles of Christ, a scandalous parody informed by the spirit of a freethinker (*Le Problème de l'incroyance au xvie siècle*, pp. 195-218).

tyrannical sultan of the miracle, the malevolent agent who would extirpate Christianity and who creates the situation of bondage and is responsible for the dreadful pursuit, becomes in Cervantes's tale an individuated being who is endowed with such attractive characteristics as fatherly love, courtesy, kindness, and hospitality, and whose human qualities stand out in sharp contrast to the villainy of the more simply drawn agents who menace the heroes and against whom the father and the captive at one point appear to unite in defense of the maiden. Moreover, Cervantes allows us to observe him in the "non-paradigmatic" situations of ordinary life and refuses to limit our perception of him to his blocking function, which is demanded by the economy of the plot. The resulting humanization of the figure violently disrupts the rapid movement of the miracle through its conventional cycle of bondage and deliverance, and all the ambiguities of the human condition implied by the pathos of Zoraida's father as he is overwhelmed by fatherly love and begs his obsessed daughter to return, converge on the decisive, pivotal instant of this miracle and cause its expected turn toward joyous deliverance abruptly to collapse.

In the puzzling ambiguities of *The Captive's Tale*, one senses a strange and complicated blending of distinct literary conventions and genres: on the one hand a novelistic treatment of character incongruously intruding into a tale governed for the most part by the conventions of romance characterization, on the other hand an unexpected transformation of a romance miracle with its naive morality, polarizing good and evil in a simple opposition and celebrating the triumph of good, into a *Kasus*, a traditional popular form of literature that plays off against one another two compelling norms, moral claims, or systems of value, forcing the reader to ponder the ambiguities of their irresolvable conflict.[52] For our purposes, however, the important implication of the scene lies in the fact that one of the conflicting claims of the *Kasus* comes from the Christian mentality. In its subversion through the destruction of a man for whom our sympathies have been carefully enlisted, we are compelled momentarily to glimpse the achievements of Divine Providence and the miracles through which it accomplishes them as anything but a cause for unequivocal celebration.[53] In his characteristic way of using literature to explore the na-

[52] See André Jolles, *Einfache Formen* (Tübingen, 1968), pp. 171-99. I shall discuss the form at greater length below in connection with *La fuerza de la sangre*.

[53] As Spitzer has argued, the scene can be read as an indictment of the whimsicality of God's Providence (see "Linguistic Perspectivism in the *Don Quijote*," *Linguistics and Literary History* [New York, 1962], pp. 64-68). Cervantes would appear to want to heighten the ambiguity of the denouement by alluding to Cava Rumia as the geo-

ture of literature and the existential roots of the various forms of literature, Cervantes has turned his miracle of the Virgin into a critical examination of the literary genre of the miracle narrative, exposed the violent simplifications of its fictional world by confronting it with the ambiguities of real experience, and raised disturbing questions concerning the theological vision that informs it.

The examination of these various contexts in his works would indicate, then, that Cervantes was a writer whose fiction was plainly influenced in a significant way by the pervasive religious culture of his age and a writer who understood quite well the formal conventions, the spirit, and the possibilities for creative use of the various literary forms that gave expression and support to that culture. Just what Cervantes's most private attitudes and authentic beliefs in religious matters were will probably remain forever a secret, but, if the variety of positions toward religion encompassed by his fiction, some undoubtedly motivated more by the demands of literary genre than by personal conviction, is any indication, it is likely that they were extremely complex and that they may well have been troubled and unstable.[54] From the celebration of heroic, uncompromising faith of

---

graphical point where the father is abandoned. Not only is it the Virgin who seems to be presiding over the ordeals and triumphs of her devotee, but also the sinister female of legend whose treacherous lust caused the destruction of Christian Spain. See my *Cervantes' Christian Romance*, pp. 152-54. F. Márquez Villanueva has pursued this line of interpretation fruitfully in his consideration of the numerous sources that influenced Cervantes's conception of the scene. Concentrating on the "darker side" of Zoraida, he finds traces of several destructive females in her literary ancestry, imputes sinister designs to her throughout the episode, and speculates on the marital distress that surely awaits the passive *cautivo*. The fact is that the figure of Zoraida is mediated through a complicated set of literary texts and codes, and the heightened "literariness" of the tale is itself a sign of Cervantes's rejection of the traditional hagiographer's stance in constructing or bearing witness to his "miracle."

[54] The best introduction to the problems raised by Cervantes's religious thought remains Américo Castro's *El pensamiento de Cervantes*. (For a convenient collection of significant passages from many works, see Chapter 6, "Ideas religiosas.") However, in its biases toward rationalism and the view of Cervantes as a precursor of Enlightenment writing in an authoritarian and oppressive age, Castro's study divides Cervantes's numerous religious pronouncements according to the categories "orthodox" and "critical," all too hastily deals with the former as inauthentic and touched with the "dissimulation" of the Counter-Reformation ("alardes de ortodoxia"), an age of "heroic hypocrisy" (viz. Bruno), and proceeds to lavish its fine critical insight on the latter, persuasively illuminating their affiliations with Erasmian religiosity. The opportunity to explore any vitality, variety, or profundity which might exist on the orthodox side of the scheme is passed over, and Castro leaves us with a polarization that is too simple and in some ways quite misleading. Whatever one may think of the "anachronistic," "puerile," or "vulgar" mental habits that have always been prominent in popular culture, they must be scrutinized closely and objectively if one is to

El trato de Argel, a drama that looks suspiciously at the private "religion of the heart" and resonates with the militant, public Christianity preached by the followers of St. Ignatius of Loyola in their determination to spread the faith and increase the honor of a regal, all-powerful God,[55] to the pessimism of *El coloquio de los perros*, with its probings of the disturbing recesses of a distant divinity who appears to make misery and sinfulness part of his dark designs, from the *Quixote*'s criticisms of the emptiness of ceremonial religion and its intimations of the heterodox conviction that, as Sancho puts it in a moment of Erasmian eloquence that delights Don Quixote, "vivir

understand correctly a good deal of history and indeed a good deal of the elite cultural activity of any period, which they always affect in one way or another (see Fichtenau, "Zum Reliquienwesen des früheren Mittelalters," pp. 108-109). Castro's characteristic hostility to popular religious culture is evident in his continuing fascination with the "leaden books" ("libros plúmbeos"), the notorious forgeries that "sanctified" the Sacro Monte and the city of Granada by narrating the martyrdom of Saint Cecilio. In *El pensamiento de Cervantes* (pp. 317-18) and *La realidad histórica de España* ([Mexico, 1966], pp. 200-202), Castro interprets the immediate success of the "venerable texts" as an indication of a "verdadera locura supersticiosa en torno a reliquias y cuerpos de santos" and a willingness of the official ecclesiastical culture to exploit "la demencia del vulgo." In his later writings Castro tended more and more to impute his own value judgments concerning Spanish history to Cervantes and repeatedly insisted that the description at the end of the *Quixote* I of the leaden box in which an old doctor found some "pergaminos escritos con letras góticas" revealing some of the facts about Don Quixote's third sally and death is a cryptic, critical allusion to the ignorance and credulity of both the exploiters and the exploited in the scandalous affair of the "leaden books" (see *Cervantes y los casticismos españoles* [Barcelona, 1966], pp. 112-13; "El Quijote, taller de existencialidad," *Revista de Occidente* 5 [1967]:23-29; *Cómo veo ahora el Quijote* [Madrid, 1971], pp. 21-28). A more balanced view both of Cervantes's religious spirit and the Erasmian Christianity which nourished it can be found in M. Bataillon, *Erasmo y España* (Barcelona, 1977), pp. 777-806. It might be pointed out here that, despite his ironic and skeptical disposition, Cervantes may have possessed a trace of the vocation for martyrdom that was exalted everywhere in the "vulgar" religious culture of his time. Curiously, Diego de Haedo includes in his account of the tortures and martyrdoms of Christian captives in Algiers a description of the heroism of a prisoner named Miguel de Cervantes, who insisted on assuming all the guilt for the abortive escape attempt of him and fifteen other captives and who on four other occasions "estuvo a pique de perder [la vida] empalado, o enganchado, o abrasado vivo, por cosas que intentó para dar libertad a muchos." "La única explicación de la inclusión de un caso no martirial en el *Diálogo de los mártires* y de los grandes elogios que hace de Cervantes es que el 'estropeado español' representaba para el Dr. Sosa [the interlocutor of the dialogue], en una persona viva, el espíritu de todos los mártires de Argel" (G. Camamis, *Estudios sobre el cautiverio en el Siglo de Oro*, pp. 120-21).

[55] See G. Weise, "Das Element des Heroischen in der spanischen religiösen Literatur der Zeit der Gegenreformation," pp. 240ff.

bien" is the only true "tología,"[56] to the *Persiles*'s celebrative orchestration of the Christian vision of history, the mysteries of the Incarnation and Redemption, the sacraments, and the cult of the Virgin, as well as its expression of the yearning for a healing of the great schism and a restoration of a universal Christendom under the leadership of the Catholic Church—the variety and inconsistency that mark Cervantes's works dealing with Christian themes attest to an informing religious sensibility that is concerned but restless, one that is capable of experiencing the mysteries of spiritual exaltation and despair, of remorse in sinfulness and joy in righteousness, one that is vitally concerned with the great existential questions that traditionally had been answered by theological systems of thought and eager to explore fearlessly the suitability and the unsuitability of the orthodox answers. While there is very little in Cervantes's writing that can be construed in a strict sense as atheistic or heterodox, it is certainly wrong to describe his religious mentality as perfectly orthodox.[57] But it is just as wrong to classify him as a totally secular writer because a strong vein of skepticism is visible in much of his writing and because his greatest work is focused almost exclusively on the "marvelous" desires and disappointments of man living in this unmiraculous, desacralized world. Neither the view of Cervantes as orthodox spokesman for Tridentine ideology nor as freethinking, iconoclastic pioneer of the Enlightenment does justice to the vitality and incisiveness that

---

[56] *Don Quijote*, 2:195. Sancho's words echo the central theme of Erasmus's universally read *Paraclesis*, an exhortation to all Christians: "Pues quiero que sepáys que esta manera de filosofía más consiste en los afectos del ánimo que en argumentaciones, y más se muestra en bien vivir que en bien argüyr, y mejor se aprende con divinas inspiraciones que con trabajos de escuelas, y que más consiste en transformación de ánimo que no en razones naturales. Muy pocos ay que alcançan a ser letrados, pero todos pueden ser christianos, y todos pueden ser píos y santos; y aun quiérome atrever a más, y digo que todos también pueden ser theólogos" (ed. cit., pp. 461-62).

[57] Perhaps the best example of the perverse reading of the *Quixote* that invariably results when a critic attempts to argue that religious ideology has a dominant role in the novel is P. Descouzis's *Cervantes a nueva luz: El "Quijote" y el Concilio de Trento* (Frankfurt, 1966). All the rich ambiguities of the episode of the *Cautivo* are disregarded; it becomes an example of "la intención catequística-noveladora de Cervantes" because the renegade's instructions to Zoraida concerning the importance of images of the Virgin conform to the Council of Trent's decrees on the proper veneration of images (p. 81). For similarly highly selective readings that would stress orthodox elements in Cervantes's writings, see Helmut Hatzfeld, *"Don Quijote" als Wortkunstwerk* (Leipzig, 1927), "Don Quijote asceta?" *Nueva Revista de Filología Hispánica* 2 (1948):57-70, and Enrique Moreno Báez, "Perfil ideológico de Cervantes," *Suma Cervantina*, ed. J. B. Avalle-Arce and E. C. Riley (London, 1973), pp. 233-72.

characterize his engagement with religious subjects in his literary works. Cervantes's religious consciousness is profoundly undoctrinaire; it is alive with a complex ferment of spiritual and secular tendencies, and it can comfortably manifest itself at the opposite extremes of irreverent burlesque of the mental habits of the devout and hymns informed by the lofty spirituality of the most religious of his contemporaries.[58] His religious writings are most provocative when they fall between these two extremes, when they are alive with tension, and when their restlessness and their resistance to all efforts to render them easily intelligible are a register of profundity of concern. One of the most interesting and elusive of them is the shortest of his novellas, *La fuerza de la sangre*. While the little novella is not an overtly doctrinal work such as the *Persiles*, it is in some ways a more interesting testimony of the deep impact of contemporary religious culture on Cervantes's writing.

LA FUERZA DE LA SANGRE AS A MIRACLE

One of the peculiarities of the sixth novella in Cervantes's collection which is immediately apparent to the reader of the *Exemplary Tales* is the title *La fuerza de la sangre*, for it is the only title that does not point directly to the agents of the tale. The words suggest the primacy of a theme rather than an exemplary character, and as the reader discovers in the final sentence of the story, their significance is ostensibly limited to the central event of the plot. Rather surprisingly in view of the expectations aroused by the title, the nearly fatal accident is the only point inside the frame created by the last lines, the title, and the introductory allusion to Rodolfo's "illustrious blood" that the word *"sangre"* appears directly. One senses, of course, that *"sangre"* is all-pervasive in the imaginative texture of the work, and even a modern reader, whose sensibility is untouched by the distinctive resonances of the word in the religious culture of Cervantes's Spain, can respond to the associations of the symbol and admire Cervantes for his recognition of the effectiveness of understatement and insinuation in the handling of such a powerful and multivalent symbol. Readers have occasionally found Cervantes's own exegesis of the symbol at the conclusion of the tale puzzling and anticlimactic in the apparent confinement of its implications to the plausible realm of traditional ideas

---

[58] Even in the *Persiles* Cervantes can not resist turning from the solemn hymn to the Virgin to the grotesque description of the false pilgrim, who appears to confine her devotional activity to an endless series of visits to shrines (see pp. 312-15).

concerning physiology, ancestry, and social hierarchy. The fact is that, in its conceptual structure, Cervantes's final line (". . . all of which was permitted *by Heaven and the power of blood*'—"permitido todo *por el cielo y la fuerza de la sangre*")[59] hovers enigmatically between antithesis and analogy, opposition and complementarity. Its ambivalences, however, must be seen as the culmination of a tendency, running through the entire tale from its very beginning, to present and simultaneously to recoil from the miraculous. It is the final deflection from and paradoxical fulfillment of a vast promise in its title.[60]

La fuerza de la sangre is built around a central event rather than a central character, and its exemplarity emerges primarily from the themes implicit in that event rather than in the imitable virtues displayed by its heroes. Both the frame created by title and final line and the careful design of the entire work focus our attention on the crucial accident at its midpoint and confer on it the kind of dignity that marks the decisive moment of the miracle narrative.[61] In few other of his writ-

---

[59] Italics added. For the text from which my citations are drawn, see *Obras completas*, ed. A. Valbuena Prat, pp. 890-99.

[60] Esther J. Crooks's misreading or "underreading" of the title is instructive. She argues that, since Rodolfo's alteration in the tale is brought about not by the power of his ancestral "good" blood, but rather by his parents' coercion, Cervantes's title is inappropriate, and she prefers the neat, "untroubled" relationship of title and dramatic action and characterization in Alexandre Hardy's version of the story, where in fact Rodolfo's noble blood brings about remorse and reformation (see *The Influence of Cervantes in France in the Seventeenth Century* [Baltimore, 1931], pp. 140-41). The misreading registers an accurate response to the elusiveness of Cervantes's title and to his "inconsistent" handling of the symbol of blood, which are all the more apparent in their contrast to the highly rationalistic design of the French dramatist, whose readily perceptible coherence Crooks prefers. At the same time her judgment reveals a blindness to the coherently developed miracle elements in the tale, elements that are absent for the most part in the imitator's reconstruction. See also Ludwig Pfandl's misreading of the work as a simple vindication of the belief that nobility of blood necessarily accompanies honorable behavior ("edle Abstammung lässt sich nicht verleugnen") (*Geschichte der Spanischen Nationalliteratur in ihrer Blütezeit* [Freiburg im Breisgau, 1929], p. 304). Casalduero's response to the extraordinary number of associations in the title is much more satisfactory (see *Sentido y forma de las "Novelas ejemplares"* [Madrid, 1969], p. 150), although he fails to develop fully the implications of his insights and proceeds rather to a rigid theological interpretation of a tale which, in my opinion, is most interesting for the ways in which it eludes the narrow allegorizing exegesis that he offers in support of his claim.

[61] See Ebel's distinction between *Legende* and *Mirakel*: the latter "ist im Gegensatz zum Demonstrativcharakter der Legende gekennzeichnet durch seinen Wirkcharakter. Dieser Unterschied impliziert die Wiederholbarkeit des Legendenwunders, die Einmaligkeit des Mirakelgeschehens . . . [Das Mirakel] hat die unwiederholbare, einmalige Notlage zur Voraussetzung. Ihre Lösung muss endgültig sein, wenn sich Gottes Allmacht darin darstellen soll" (*Das altromanische Mirakel*, p. 51).

ings is Cervantes's eye for symmetry and balance so exacting and precise. The story divides almost perfectly into two halves, the first describing the fall of Leocadia into bondage—her abduction and rape, her secret pregnancy, her withdrawal from society in concealed dishonor, and the near-death of her child, who is laid on the very bed that was her own "sepulcher"; the second presenting her restoration— the resurrection of the child, the clarification of his lineage, her marriage, and the restoration of the scattered family.[62] The downward movement of this cyclical narrative begins with the fall of night, and darkness pervades nearly the whole of the first half of the tale. It enshrouds Leocadia's torment in the impenetrable obscurity of the chamber in which her persecutor imprisons her, her return to the church, where he abandons her, blindfolded and helpless, and her flight in terror through the shadowy streets of Toledo following her release. Rodolfo's violent act plunges the world into darkness, and its savagery is underscored by its association with loss of vision. It inflicts blindness on Leocadia's parents, "blind without the eyes of their daughter, who was the light of their eyes," it compels his victim to fall into a swoon ("for the surprise robbed her . . . even of the light of her eyes"), a darkness in which she is raped and from which she emerges only to find herself in a darkness yet more frightening ("What darkness is this? What shadows encircle me?"), and it occurs because the youth is "blind to the light of reason."[63] From the midpoint of the tale on the heroine emerges from the darkness, and the action unfolds for the most part in the daylight, rising to a climax in the processional banquet scene, in which a blinding burst of light heralds

---

[62] For commentaries on the formal symmetries of the tale, see Casalduero, *Sentido y forma de las "Novelas ejemplares,"* pp. 150-66; Robert V. Piluso, " 'La fuerza de la sangre': Un análisis estructural," *Hispania* 47 (1964):485-90; Guillermo Díaz-Plaja, "La técnica narrativa de Cervantes," *Revista de Filología Española* 32 (1948):237-68; Karl-Ludwig Selig, "Some Observations on *La fuerza de la sangre,*" *Modern Language Notes* 87 (1972):121-25.

[63] "ciegos sin los ojos de su hija, que eran la lumbre de los suyos"; "el sobresalto le quitó . . . la luz de los ojos"; "¿Qué oscuridad es ésta, qué tinieblas me rodean?"; "ciego de la luz del entendimiento" (pp. 890-92). The traditional Christian view of sin as the overthrow of the orderly control of the soul by reason and as a blinding of the "light of reason" was proclaimed everywhere in the religious culture of Cervantes's age. Georg Weise has assembled numerous typical statements of the doctrine and interpreted its obsessive reiteration as a sign of the survival in the intensely religious culture of the period of the primarily secular glorification of reason characteristic of Renaissance "neo-classical" culture. For example, Alonso Rodríguez wrote: "[las pasiones] cieguen los ojos de la razón . . . que eso es propio de la pasión, cegar la razón y disminuir la libertad de nuestro albedrío" (see "Das Element des Heroischen in der spanischen religiösen Literatur der Zeit der Gegenreformation," pp. 164-66).

the restoration of the maiden, reverses completely the fall of darkness of the opening lines, and formally punctuates the completion of the turn of the cyclical plot.

The first half of the tale is marked by the loneliness of the heroine and her alienation from a society that deprives her of her very being, looms in the background as a menacing force always quick to withhold the benefits of its esteem from the truly virtuous, makes its essential distinctions according to blood, honor, and wealth the perverse sanctions for the depredation of the weak by the strong, and appears only in the form of the derisive mob of the masked rapist and his leering cohorts. Indeed the mask of the predator and the blindfold of his victim epitomize powerfully the general state of society, in which Leocadia must retreat into solitude and her family must live a life of dissimulation, their only hope apparently being a God whose face is darkly masked and whose justice works in ways that are difficult for human beings to apprehend.[64] In the second half of the tale the demonic presentation of blood, honor, and wealth is abruptly reversed. Society appears as a friendly community united in its respect for virtue and eagerly offering its applause to the marvelous child, who, despite his poverty, is celebrated as a striking example of the good breeding that privileges virtue and wisdom above wealth. While in the opening scene the slumbering city answers the desperate screams of Leocadia with silence, here a throng of bystanders immediately presses forward to aid the trampled child, and a man of "illustrious blood" comes to his rescue in an act of marvelous charity.

Cervantes's concern for formal symmetry in his tale of fall and deliverance is evidenced by the punctuation of the decisive moments of his narrative not only by the overt reference to the suggestive symbol of blood but also by his insertion, at the beginning and end of the action, of a variation of the central miraculous event that effectively releases all the implications of that symbol—the near-death and the resurrection. At the beginning the terrified Leocadia faints and awakens in the darkness of Rodolfo's room, which is likened to the sepulcher. She momentarily feels that she is in either hell or limbo, she perceives the dim shape of her mute tormenter as a specter, and, on discovering her "wounded" condition, she asks him to kill her. At the midpoint the marvelous child, who has been trampled by a horse, just as Leocadia was "trampled" by the rapist ("desmayada me pi-

---

[64] As Ebel points out, suffering and bondage are, in the miracle narrative, frequently signs of the disturbing distance of God (*Das altromanische Mirakel*, pp. 46-66).

saste"), is carried, apparently mortally wounded, to the "bed of her sepulcher," and revives to behold joyously his mother and grandparents. When the distraught Leocadia shortly thereafter reveals her identity to Doña Estefanía, and falls into a swoon, the benevolent mother sheds healing tears on her lifeless face, and the maiden awakens to new life, "embracing the crucifix" and "converted into a sea of weeping." And at the conclusion of the tale, Leocadia falls into a faint so powerful that before her "resurrection" her pulse cannot be found and a priest is summoned to administer the last rites.

The polarization of the tale into two halves marked by violent contrasts in action, atmosphere, and tone and separated by a central event whose prominence is heightened through the contrasts that it divides, as well as the decisiveness of that event both in its instantaneous redirection of the action and in its enunciation of themes, would indicate that, in its structural features, *La fuerza de la sangre* owes a good deal to the popular narrative form that was flourishing in the numerous miracle books of the shrines throughout Catholic Europe and offering pilgrim and ordinary reader alike the consolation and entertainment of pious, suspenseful reading. If we look at the principal agents of the novella, their characterization, their situation, and their development, we discover similar affinities with the miracle narrative. As I have pointed out above, the hero of the miracle is characteristically helpless, frequently passive, and in any case an ordinary being victimized by a situation of extreme distress, whether the situation is caused by sickness, sinfulness, or persecution. Unlike the case of the other great agent of hagiographic literature, the saint, the virtues that he may have are not presented as heroic qualities to be imitated by human beings, as a vindication of the power of the human will to merit divine assistance, or as a sign of God's direct working through his human agents. The miracle hero, if virtuous, generally represents the virtue of humility. His characteristic pose is self-effacement, and his heroic act is the decision to open himself to the reception of God's grace. It is indeed the inadequacy of the human will and the vanity of traditional notions of human heroism that the miracle would emphasize. The world of the miracle, then, recognizes no human heroes, and the title of Cervantes's tale, in its uncharacteristic omission of an agent, is a reflection of the generic affiliations of the work. How tempting it might have been for Cervantes to make the tale the celebration of the constancy of Leocadia, whose name recalls the martyred patron saint of Toledo and, as the hagiographer Fer-

nando de Pisa informs us in 1602, is a name borne by many proper
girls in the Toledo of his day![65]

While the sufferings of the saint point continually to the presence
of God and are continually surrounded by the aura of the martyr's
dignity, the ordeals of the miracle hero are a source of greater tension
and perhaps authentic suspense in the narrative, as they emphasize
the hopelessness of a situation and the possible indifference of a very
distant God. The miracle hero's victimization is frequently connected
with the problem of religious doubt and despair, and an instructive
example of how the suffering of hagiographic literature can point in
such radically opposed directions can be found in Cervantes's own *El
rufián dichoso*, where the spiritual and physical agony that forces Doña
Ana to despair of God's mercy is literally transferred to the protagonist and becomes the most sublime sign of his saintliness.[66]

In Cervantes's portrayal of Leocadia and the difficulties of her plight,
which she describes as a total loss of her self ("you trampled upon me

---

[65] *Historia de la gloriosa virgen y martyr Santa Leocadia Patrona de Toledo* . . . , p. 8.
Clemencín's bewilderment at Virués's incomprehensible choice for his "epic hero" of
Garindus, the hermit of Montserrat, a man whose most memorable acts are rape and
murder and whose mightiest exploit is walking on all fours from Rome to Catalonia
in an expiatory pilgrimage (*El Monserrate*), is a dramatic indication of the peculiar
effects that arise when one attempts to accommodate miracle subject matter to literary
genres that arouse traditional expectations concerning heroism. Tasso's method of
centering the miracle of redemption on the traditional epic situation of the momentary enchantment of the hero by the sorceress is far less unsettling. One must remember, however, that such epics as Virués's and Gabriel de Mata's narration of the
"mighty deeds" of the gentle St. Francis of Assisi (*El caballero Asisio*, 1587, 1589),
and Hernández Blasco's *La universal redempción, pasión, muerte y resurreción de nuestro
Salvador Jesu Cristo y angustias de su Santísima Madre* (1584) were extremely successful
in the age (see Pfandl, *Geschichte der Spanischen Nationalliteratur in ihrer Blütezeit*, pp.
133-35). What H. R. Jauss might call a "change of the horizon of expectation" in
the reception of epic had evidently occurred, and it no doubt was directly related to
the development of a new Christocentric ideal of heroism. (See *Literaturgeschichte als
Provokation* [Frankfurt am Main, 1970].) For this ideal with its renewed emphasis on
the heroic potential in such actions and states as penance, mortification, remorse,
endurance, humility, patience, gentleness, love, and suffering, see G. Weise, "Das
Element des Heroischen in der spanischen religiösen Literatur der Zeit der Gegenreformation," pp. 175ff. To understand Cervantes's aspirations in the *Persiles*, his epic
of *"trabajos,"* as well as the initial success of the work, one must understand this
conception of the epic genre and this conception of heroism.

[66] One can compare also the martyr figure of Cloelia in the *Persiles*, who dies amid
the horrors of the kingdom of the barbarians fixing her rapturous gaze on heaven and
confessing her faith in God, with the simultaneously portrayed figure of Antonio,
whose terrible sufferings point to his enslavement in sin, his despair in the absence
of God, and the possibility of his eternal damnation.

and annihilated me"; "you dared to destroy me"; "I shall assume that I was never born in the world"),[67] and her ultimate response of resignation, we discover much that resembles the traditional situation of the miracle hero, who can do nothing but await divine assistance to relieve his suffering. When Leocadia displays the crucifix to her family following her return from Rodolfo's chamber, they "renew their tears before it," utter passionate entreaties, and pray for "miraculous punishments." Indeed the frustration of her plan to use the crucifix in order to discover the identity of her assailant and demand retribution leads to the enunciation of one of the most traditional themes of miracle literature, the limitations of human reason and the necessity of passively relying on the mercy of God. As intelligent (*discreto*) as her plan is, her father reminds her that it can easily be countered by the malicious intelligence of her adversary and bring her in fact greater misery through public dishonor. His words are very important because they decisively delimit the value of *discreción*, which, as I shall point out below, is juxtaposed throughout the tale to the supernatural and is one of the principle elements of deflection from the miracle. His methodical analysis of the various difficulties in his daughter's plan and the rationally contrived options by which they could meet them leads toward complication, breaks down in inconclusiveness, and turns into an arbitrary and contrastingly simple abandonment of reason for faith:

. . . and this being so, we shall be rather bewildered than informed, even supposing that we may be able to employ the same artifices we suspect, and hand it [the image] to the monk by the agency of a third person. What you must do, daughter, is to keep it and commend yourself to it, *so that in as much as it was the witness of your misfortune, it will permit that there be a judge who shall return to do you justice.*[68]

The maiden acknowledges the validity of the argument and, "weeping and sobbing" again, she resigns herself to her fate ("she was reduced to covering her head, as they say, and living a retired life under the protection of her parents, dressed in honorable although poor at-

[67] "me pisaste y aniquilaste"; "te atreviste a destruirme"; "yo la [cuenta] haré de que no nací en el mundo" (pp. 891-92).

[68] "y siendo esto así, antes quedaremos confusos que informados, puesto que podamos usar del mismo artificio que sospechamos, dándola [la imagen] al religioso por tercera persona; lo que has de hacer, hija, es guardarla y encomendarte a ella, que *pues ella fue testigo de tu desgracia, permitirá que haya juez que vuelva por tu justicia*" (p. 893; italics added).

tire").[69] The peculiar idiom to which the narrator draws our attention—"to cover one's head"—is another one of the motifs of concealment (e.g., masks, blindfolds, disguises, secrecy) which are so prominent in the first half of the tale. The heroine decides to wait patiently and withdraws into the nonexistence to which she claims Rodolfo's brutal act has reduced her.[70] Fearing that society will read on her brow the signs of her dishonor, she avoids all social contact, and on discovering her pregnancy, "weeping, sighing, and lamenting," she retreats even further into her isolation, cherishing the image of the crucifix as her only consolation: "I took you with the aim of reminding you always of my wrong, not in order to demand of you vengeance for it (for I do not claim that), but in order to ask you to bestow on me some consolation, with the aid of which to bear my misfortunes patiently."[71]

The characterization of Leocadia and her persecutor has troubled readers of the tale from Cervantes's age to the present. Reacting to what he no doubt considered an intolerable breach of decorum, the French dramatist Alexandre Hardy attempted to render plausible Rodolfo's altered disposition—his courtesy and rationality—and Leocadia's puzzling love for him which we witness in the final scenes of the tale by depicting him passing through intermediary stages of remorse and repentence.[72] Modern critics have continued to voice such "classical" dissatisfaction with the tale's implausibilities, both in character

---

[69] "se redujo a cubrir la cabeza, como dicen, y a vivir recogidamente debajo del amparo de sus padres, con vestido tan honesto como pobre" (p. 893).

[70] For contemporary Spanish attitudes toward honor and social esteem as more valuable than life itself, the importance of proper sexual conduct in their preservation, the ways in which an entirely innocent and virtuous person such as Leocadia could be deprived of society's "gift" (as Lope puts it, "la honra está en otro y no en él mismo"), and the way in which its loss could be felt to be a total destruction of one's identity, see Américo Castro, "Algunas observaciones acerca del concepto del honor en los siglos XVI y XVII," *Semblanzas y estudios españoles* (Princeton, 1956), pp. 319-82. The "nonexistence" of the dishonored is a state bitterly lamented by numerous heroes of the "dramas de honor" of the period; e.g., "Tello: '¡Muerto soy; mi honor es muerto! . . . ¿Qué quieres, vida, ya?' " Before resigning herself to accepting it with saintly patience, Leocadia asks her violator amid the darkness of the "sepulcher of her honor" and "the theater in which the tragedy of her misfortune was presented" to take her life: "quítamela [la vida] al momento, que no es bien que la tenga la que no tiene honra."

[71] "te llevó con propósito de acordarte siempre mi agravio, no para pedirte venganza de él, que no la pretendo, sino para rogarte me dieses algún consuelo con que llevar en paciencia mi desgracia" (p. 896).

[72] See Crooks, *The Influence of Cervantes in France in the Seventeenth Century*, p. 140.

and action, and have expressed the wish that Cervantes had given us more complexity in his agents. Hainsworth perhaps best summarizes their view:

Le dénouement est un pur effet du hasard, et ne s'explique pas par les actions ou le caractère des protagonistes. La psychologie est rudimentaire et même fausse. Leocadia, par exemple, qui a juré de haïr à jamais l'auteur de son déshonneur, ne trahit que des sentiments de joie quand, finalement, elle peut l'épouser. Le caractère de Rodolfo, conséquent, si l'on veut, dans sa bassesse, mais que le lecteur moderne trouve insupportable, ne semble pas révolter les autres personnages, ni l'auteur lui-même. En un mot, *nous ne connaissons pas dans l'oeuvre cervantesque un plus frappant exemple de mauvais goût.*[73]

Moreover, Schevill finds morally repugnant an implication in the happy ending that such an abominable act as Rodolfo's goes unpunished, apparently because he belongs to the powerful classes of society.[74] And a recent anthologizer of Spanish short stories has expurgated the allusion to Rodolfo's "indecencies" in the concluding scene when he throws himself on the fainted maiden; plainly he could not reconcile their implications with his idea of a happy ending and appropriate roles for characters in a happy ending.[75] The proper answer to all such objections, which are based on a wide assortment of aesthetic, moral, and ideological positions in these readers of different epochs and nationalities, is not to affirm with Amezúa that in the "turbulent and passionate" Spain of Cervantes's period such villains as Rodolfo were common, rapists were treated with indulgence if they married their victims, and amorous young men frequently fell into swoons and that Leocadia's sudden attraction for the man who had treated her so brutally in fact reveals the profundity of Cervantes's understanding of the psyche of a young woman in such a difficult situation.[76] This "defense" of Cervantes's art of faithfully reproducing the reality of his society, even more than the criticism of his detractors, makes it clear how inappropriate it is to judge the work according to the canons of representational fiction which are still so dominant among interpreters of Cervantes's works.

If we recognize that in *La fuerza de la sangre* Cervantes is working with the conventions of the miracle, a form in which verisimilitude is a meaningful category only through its violation, we can understand

[73] *Les "Novelas Exemplares" de Cervantes en France au XVIIe Siècle* (Paris, 1933), p. 20; italics added.

[74] R. Schevill and A. Bonilla, *Novelas ejemplares*, 3 vols. [Madrid, 1922-1925], 3:387-89.

[75] See *Spanish Stories*, ed. A. Flores (New York, 1960), pp. 86-87.

[76] See *Cervantes, creador de la novela corta española*, 2:203-233.

his simple and seemingly inconsistent characterization much more adequately. For example, as I shall point out below, Rodolfo's "indecent" gesture of hurling himself passionately on the fainted body of his bride-to-be is part of a miraculous reenactment and abrogation of the dreadful scene of the rape. Moreover, the general lack of complexity in Rodolfo's characterization is explicable if we see his connection with miracle agents. The pure miracle narrative frequently moves out of a situation of demonic possession or dominance. The links between Rodolfo and the demonic world are pronounced. The masks and grimaces of him and his cohorts as they move about their victims and taunt them; the emphasis on total confusion, violence, and darkness surrounding his actions; the reference to the chamber in which he imprisons his victim as "limbo" and "hell"; his spectral form, which Leocadia struggles to perceive in the shadows; his violation of her lifeless body, with all the implications of necrophilia and perverted sexuality; his mute, brutal response to her pathetic plea; his nearly incomprehensible mixed language, and his association with appetite and the belly in his Italian journey all are elements that associate him with the devils that inhabited the contemporary imagination and took vivid shape in its literature, painting, and didactic writing. As a literary character the relatively absent Rodolfo stands closer to the monstrous figures that swarm about Cruz in the central masque of Cervantes's *El rufián dichoso* than to the fully individuated, novelistic characters of Sancho Panza and Don Quixote. Rodolfo is a "wolf," a demonic antagonist, and his function in the economy of the narrative is to plunge the world of its "sheep" into disorder. Further characterization of him would attenuate the numinous power of evil surrounding him and might weaken the effect of the "miracle" by turning it into something that it is not—a novel, a process that does in fact unfold in the *Cautivo*'s tale. That Leocadia could love such an archetypal villain is quite implausible; it is in fact miraculous. As I shall point out below, there are complicating, antigeneric tendencies in this miracle, but they have nothing to do with the status of its agents as representational characters. Leocadia steps out of her paradigmatic role, but, unlike the characters of the *Quixote*, she does not move in the direction of real experience. To the end, she, as well as the other agents of *La fuerza de la sangre*, remain illustrative characters, and, as such, simplified, abstract, and symbolical.[77]

[77] For the distinction between illustrative and representational characterization in fiction, see R. Scholes and R. Kellogg, *The Nature of Narrative* (New York, 1971), p. 88. It is of course true that Cervantes's association of Rodolfo's villainy with his class in the first half of the story attenuates somewhat his power as an archetypal

In the nearly total darkness and constricted spaces of the first half of the tale Cervantes allows us a few brief glimpses of the presence of Divine Providence at work in the events. On awakening in the bed of the rapist, Leocadia attempts to persuade the youth to release her, promising secrecy, indicating that she understands perfectly the tremendous difference between God's judgment and the honor that the world bestows frivolously on its favorites, and shrewdly and pitifully reminding him that she can only bring herself additional suffering by revealing her dishonor. Her own words of astonishment at the wisdom of her plea suggest the presence of miraculous powers: "between me and Heaven my complaints will pass, nor shall I wish that they be heard by the world, which does not judge things according to what actually happens, but rather according to its settled opinion. I do not know how I speak to you of these truths, which normally are founded on the experience of many cases and on the passage of many years, since those of my life do not amount to seventeen."[78] Following his departure, Leocadia, "alone and imprisoned," stumbles about in the darkness of the chamber and feels her way along the wall toward a window. When she opens it, a flood of moonlight pours into the room, and she distinguishes the shapes of the furnishings, some of their colors, the frames of pictures, and, on a desk near the window, a small silver crucifix. The light that faintly glimmers in the deepest and most threatening darkness is a dim prefiguration of the burst of light that illuminates the climactic processional entry of Leocadia in the banquet scene, and in its association with the Christian mystery of Redemption and in its muted promise of deliverance, it recalls the

---

figure of evil and introduces a note of social criticism, which is subsequently dropped as the tale turns toward restoration and celebration of society. However, whether as demon or as representative of a class whose foibles Cervantes wished to condemn, Rodolfo remains an illustrative character.

[78] "entre mí y el Cielo pasarán mis quejas, sin querer que las oiga el mundo, el cual no juzga por los sucesos las cosas, sino conforme a él se le asientan en la estimación; no sé cómo te digo estas verdades, que se suelen fundar en la experiencia de muchos casos y en el discurso de muchos años, no llegando los míos a diecisiete" (p. 891). E. C. Riley has noted in Leocadia's puzzling commentary on her own wisdom a rift or disturbance in the text and interpreted it as a sign of Cervantes's awareness of his possible transgression of the principle of decorum in allowing his character to speak with such exceptional *discreción*. The comment contains an element of authorial self-justification and implies respect for the literary rule and the rational view of literature and character behind it. See *Cervantes' Theory of the Novel* (Oxford, 1962), pp. 136-37. I would add that the "no sé cómo te digo estas verdades" with its peculiar pose of helpless bewilderment before one's own wisdom is a convention of vatic discourse familiar in Christian writings from St. Paul to St. John of the Cross and that it marks the first intrusion of the miraculous into the action of the tale.

chiaroscuros of other powerful moments of bondage and despair in Cervantes's writings: Antonio's and Rutilio's lengthy vigils beneath the distant stars in their quests of expiation and Berganza's anguished contemplation of the cadaverous figure of Cañizares in the starlit patio outside her stifling chamber.

It is in the second half of *La fuerza de la sangre* that the guiding hand of Divine Providence becomes clearly visible in the ordeals of Leocadia. As I have pointed out above, the central event on which the narrative turns is the accident involving the child. The apparition of the child itself is surrounded by miraculous elements. Since readers still insist on regarding Cervantes as merely a great representational writer, it is perhaps important to stress the economy of his description of Luisico. The child is "beautiful in face, gentle in temper"; he is possessed of an "acute mind," and his actions are viewed by all as signs of noble parentage. By the age of seven he can write and read both Latin and Spanish. He arouses wonder in all who contemplate him, and, as he wanders through the streets, the multitudes spontaneously "applaud" him, "raining thousands of blessings" upon him, his parents, and his teachers. In a radical alteration of the narrative tempo of the tale, Cervantes introduces the marvelous child and offers in six sentences a concentrated account of the first seven years of his life, which are also the seven years of Leocadia's purgatorial suffering. Both the sudden disjunction of the narration and the spareness of detail are extremely effective in focusing our attention on the particular moment. By refraining from further individuation, Cervantes, at the crucial point of his narrative, brings to his text the numinous effects of the marvelous child archetype, one of the most powerful symbols of regeneration in the imagination and one which hagiographic literature of all ages has exploited repeatedly.[79] Luis is the child of Leocadia and Rodolfo and as such both the link that binds them for years after their fateful encounter and the agent of their ultimate reconciliation, the most marvelous of the various signs that

[79] C. G. Jung, "The Psychology of the Child Archetype," and "The Special Phenomenology of the Child Archetype," *Psyche & Symbol* (New York, 1958), pp. 113-47. See also Schreiber, *Mutter und Kind in der Kultur der Kirche*. A common manifestation of the archetype in hagiographic literature is the vision of the released soul of the dying saint ascending in the form of an infant to heaven (see, for example, a depiction of the death of St. Paul in the Basilica of Ottobeuren, as described by Schreiber in "Der heilige Berg Montserrat," pp. 130-31). In his startling introduction of a newborn child and a dying elder at the conclusion of the Isabela Castrucho episode in the *Persiles*, Cervantes is exploiting the latent power of the child archetype to invest its denouement with an aura of wondrous regeneration (see *Persiles*, pp. 411-12).

authenticate the maiden's identity and ensure her restoration. However, in reality, he belongs to a vast literary family of marvelous children extending in Christian culture back to the daughter of Jairus, whom Jesus raised from the dead before an astonished throng of spectators. It is not a question of looking for sources here or of arguing for precise typological connections. The child, who is struck down in the street by a horse whose rider cannot "restrain it in the fury of its career" and who lies "as if he were dead, with blood flowing profusely from his head,"[80] resembles in fact innumerable children resuscitated by divine powers following accidental death. For example, in the fifth century St. Zanobi, the bishop of Florence, prayed over the dead body of an infant child run over by a carriage in front of St. Saviour's Cathedral and immediately restored it to perfect health. If Cervantes had read the life of St. Dominic which he purchased at an auction in Seville in 1590 (see above), he might have noted that the most famous miracle performed by the founder of the great religious order was the resurrection of a youth who had fallen to his death while giving his horse free rein in a street close to the church where the saint was saying mass.[81] Moreover, in his role as the agent who miraculously reveals his parentage, Luisico has affinities with a marvelous infant common in folk tales and in hagiographic literature who, the bastard offspring of a sinful union, has the function of identifying his unknown father and saving an innocent victim from calumny.[82] As bearer of the message that ends a situation of disorder and purgatorial suffering occasioned by a dreadful act of sinfulness, his function is similar to that of the child who appears to Garín, the hermit-murderer of Montserrat, and proclaims that he can from that moment on walk upright, announcing the paradoxical metamorphosis, so central in the

---

[80] "detenerle en la furia de su carrera . . . muerto tendido en el suelo, derramando mucha sangre de la cabeza" (p. 894).

[81] See Pedro de Rivadeneira, *Les Fleurs des Vies des Saints*, ed. M. Baudovin, trans. M. Rene Gaultier (Paris, 1667), 2:107. For St. Zanobi, see Brewer, *A Dictionary of Miracles*, p. 87; for numerous examples of resurrected children, see Brewer's index, item "child." A good indication of the prominence of the theme in miracle literature can be observed in Justus Lipsius's collection of miracles of the holy image of the Virgin of Halle (1604), in which nearly a third of the wonders deal with resurrections of dead children (see *Miracles of the Virgin, or an Historical Account of the Original, and Stupendious Performances of the Image Entituled Our Blessed Lady of Halle viz. Restoring the Dead to Life, Healing the Sick, Delivering of Captives, etc. Written Originally in Latin, by Justus Lipsius; afterward translated into French, then into Dutch, and now rendered into English* [London, 1688]).

[82] See Paul Canart, "Le nouveau-né qui dénonce son père. Les avatars d'un conte populaire dans la littérature hagiographique," *Analecta Bollandiana* 85 (1966):309-333.

literature of Christian miracles, which transforms fall into fortune or, as Leocadia's parents discover on contemplating the radiant child, "*desdicha*" into "*dicha*."[83] In pointing out the various analogues of Cervantes's marvelous child in hagiographic literature, I am not suggesting that they are "sources" for his tale. I would emphasize rather that Cervantes would have the imaginative power of all these analogues converge on the *unerhörte Begebenheit* at the center of his text, and that his activation of the codes of hagiographic literature, which he and his audience knew so well, is all the more effective because of its indeterminacy. Such a technique of cumulative allusion is of course radically opposed to the traditional hagiographer's delineation of the single, precisely authenticated event of the miracle. However, I would argue that the effect of the interposition of the numerous texts that mediate the scene is not one of attenuation through literary "mirroring" or of deflection from reality into "literariness," but rather exactly the opposite, the intensification of the numinous aura surrounding the event by the evocation of the imaginative presence of a whole family of sacred writings.

While the child is surrounded by motifs of the miraculous children of hagiography, his "resurrection" is accompanied by a sudden shift in the action and atmosphere of the story which evokes imaginatively one of the most venerable of traditional miracles, the removal of blindness. Up to this moment of the tale we have seen the motif of blindness developed in a complex set of permutations, some highly abstract—for example, in the themes of sin as blindness, the inadequacy of human reason, and the inscrutability of God, and in the metaphorical usage of blindness as the state of the parents without their daughter, "the light of their eyes"—others extremely literal and concrete—for example, the references to blindfolds, masks, and dissimulating facial expressions, as well as the dark settings of the action, the nocturnal streets of Toledo, where silence and solitude "enfold" the abominable act, and Rodolfo's chamber, where the maiden tries in vain to distinguish, amid the total blackness, the outlines of her

---

[83] See *El Monserrate* (Barcelona, 1884), p. 315. For the omnipresence of the child as healer, prophet, and visionary in religious and secular folklore, see the article "Kind," *Handwörterbuch des Deutschen Aberglaubens*, ed. E. Hoffmann-Krayer and H. Bächtold-Stäubli, 10 vols. (Berlin and Leipzig, 1927-1942), 4:1333ff. The age of seven seems particularly significant in children of such magical power. One can compare the figure of Ricla in the *Persiles*. The barbarian girl, "bella como el sol, mansa como una cordera," appears before the suffering sinner as an "ángel del cielo," embraces him, offers him fruit and "pan hecho a su modo, que no era de trigo," and leads him to the spring which becomes the site of his redemption (see pp. 80-81). See also Tirso's "Pastorcillo" in *El condenado por desconfiado*.

assailant and to make out the images in the paintings that might bear clues to the identity of the child she is about to conceive. Indeed, in the society of the first half of the tale, nearly all characters are afflicted with blindness of some sort; they typically grope and stumble about in darkness; the characteristic social relationship is dissimulation. Leocadia "covers herself" and fears lest others "read dishonor written on her brow"; Rodolfo conceals his crime and perhaps his shame from his partners in evil and masks his discourse in a mixed idiom of Portuguese and Spanish; Leocadia's father laments that sincerity is a practicable virtue only in man's relations with God; the maiden exhorts her tormenter "to cover" her offense with perpetual silence, just as he has "covered" it in the darkness in which she lies, and refuses to look upon his face: "I have never beheld your face, nor do I desire to see it, because although I shall recall the outrage done to me, I do not wish to remember my offender or to preserve in my memory the image of the author of my hurt."[84]

With the appearance of the child, people begin to look at one another, and, when the grandfather asserts that, gazing on the fallen child lying in the pool of blood pouring from his head, "it appeared to him that he had beheld the face of a son of his, whom he dearly loved,"[85] it is as if all the masks, the coverings, and the shadows that have remained impenetrable to vision in the tale were suddenly lifted. The moment of healing, as is so often the case in traditional miracles, turns out to be a moment of restored vision, and the reversal that it instantaneously brings could hardly be more complete. From this central point on, the motif of seeing is stressed in all the permutations that mark the articulation of the motif of blindness in the first half of the story. The total blindness of the violent beginning becomes the blinding vision of the climatic processional scene. The clarity and the precise outlines marking the description of Leocadia's hair, her clothing, and her brilliant jewels contrast sharply with the opacity of the figures moving in the dimness of the night of the crime. Now Leocadia secretly contemplates the man whose menacing, spectral form had eluded her glance in the shadows of his chamber, and in the banquet scene she is smitten as she looks at his figure, which she now loves more than the "light of her eyes." While the images of the paintings were indistinguishable in the enveloping shadows of the

---

[84] "yo nunca he visto tu rostro, ni quiero vértele, porque ya que se me acuerde de mi ofensa, no quiero acordarme de mi ofensor ni guardar en la memoria la imagen del autor de mi daño" (p. 891).

[85] "le parecía que había visto el rostro de un hijo suyo, a quien él quería tiernamente" (p. 895).

early scenes, Rodolfo now carefully inspects the picture of the "deceptive image," by which Doña Estafanía manipulates him according to her benign purposes. While Leocadia had hidden her brow from the public's hostile gaze before the fateful accident, she now appears as a radiant cynosure uniting the society that contemplates her in adoration. Now Rodolfo's gaze on the "beautiful image of Leocadia" does not lead to the blindness of destructive passion, and at the conclusion of the tale he stares at himself proudly in "the mirror of his child's face," the link uniting him with his illustrious ancestors and descendents. And the final sentence of the tale reemphasizes the decisive moment when vision was restored miraculously to the world: "it was all made possible by the permission of Heaven and by the *power of blood*, which the valorous, illustrious, and Christian grandfather of Luisico *saw spilt on the ground.*"[86]

With the restoration of vision the shadows concealing the face of God are instantly removed, and references to the presence of Divine Providence in the action become much more frequent and more direct. The grandparents and Leocadia determine to "wait upon what God will do with the sufferer." When the child recovers and Leocadia begins her disclosure of his identity, she interprets the accident with a proverb that compactly enunciates the essential paradoxes of Christian theodicy, the paradoxes at the heart of so much of traditional miracle literature, and that reinforces the destructive-redemptive associations of the title and the central symbol of the crucifix—"when God gives the wound, He gives the medicine; the child found it in this house, and I in it the revival of some memories that I shall never be able to forget so long as my life shall last."[87] As she embraces the cross and appeals to Christ as "witness" and "judge," a scene that recalls the ubiquitous trial scene of the traditional miracle,[88] she

[86] "el espejo del rostro de su hijo . . . permitido todo por el Cielo y por la *fuerza de la sangre*, que *vió derramada en el suelo* el valeroso, ilustre y cristiano abuelo de Luisico" (p. 899; italics added).

[87] "cuando Dios da la llaga, da la medicina, la halló el niño en esta casa, y yo en ella el acuerdo de unas memorias que no las podré olvidar mientras la vida me dure" (p. 895).

[88] For the frequency of the scene in miracle literature, with the Virgin, Christ, the devil, and God cast in such roles as judge, lawyer, and witness at the trial of the helpless protagonist, see Ebel, *Das altromanische Mirakel*, pp. 30-33. Cervantes develops such a scene in *El rufián dichoso* (Act II). The astonishing testimony of an image is common in such literature, and John J. Allen has proposed the interesting possibility that a well-known local miracle of "el Cristo de la Vega," an image in the Church of St. Leocadia that bore witness by a miraculous movement of its arm to a promise of marriage given a poor maiden of Toledo by a faithless hidalgo, was in fact the source of Cervantes's tale. I would suggest that the miracle of "el Cristo de la

maintains that the near-death of her son was an event ordained by God's permissive will for her deliverance ("it was by permission of Heaven that he was trampled on"). Following her swoon the grandfather with no hesitation interprets the rape, the birth, the accident, the mysterious attraction he felt for the victim, and his vision of his son's face on the fallen child as a divine plan, and Cervantes uses the occasion to introduce the witnesses that are always so prominent in miracle narratives: "and by the divine permission of Heaven, he gave credit to the story, as if it had been proven to him by many veracious witnesses."[89]

All these references to the presence of a heavenly design in the calamities visited on Leocadia and her child release in Cervantes's text the enormous magical power that the symbol of blood enjoyed in the religious culture of the time. Blood is, of course, one of the great Christian symbols of all ages, but seldom has the fascination of the redemptive, propitiatory blood of Christ and the martyrs, the pure blood of the Virgin, and the tainted blood of sinful humanity been more intense and universal than in Cervantes's Spain. Celebrations of the goodness of sacrificial blood and the paradoxical mystery of the "rightness" of sin, the mystery that it epitomizes so powerfully, echoed from all quarters of Spanish society, from the halls of the theologians and the cells of mystics to the public square, where the populace

---

Vega," which actually accounts for very few of the miracle elements of Cervantes's story, be viewed not as a "source" with the "engendering" relationship to the receptor text traditionally attributed to sources, but rather as one of numerous "mediating texts" of miracles, all indeterminate and suggestive, that Cervantes through allusion inscribes in his tale and through which he compels his reader to engage with the "mannered" work as a miracle about miracles. I do not think that the relation of Cervantes's tale to the text evoked is one of critical contrast and ironic reduction, as Allen suggests. As I shall point out below, the miraculous is not simply embarrassed or displaced by the vital and the psychological, as indeed it is in Cervantes's more "skeptical" and more "novelistic" contexts. See *"El Cristo de la Vega* and *La fuerza de la sangre,"* pp. 271-75.

[89] "permisión fué del Cielo el haberlo atropellado . . . y él lo creyó por divina permisión del Cielo, como si con muchos y verdaderos testigos se lo hubiera probado" (p. 896). The numerous references in the tale to the process of verification, witnesses, and signs (e.g., Leocadia describes her swoon as a *"señal"*) are an indication of its affinities with hagiographic literature. (For the crucial importance of the term *signum* in the lexicon of the popular miracle literature, see Schreiber, *Deutsche Mirakelbücher,* pp. 14-16; K. H. Schäfer points out that the 465 miracle stories of the holy image of the village of Elende are designated *signa* ["Das Mirakelbuch von St. Maria im Elende am Harz," in Schreiber's *Deutsche Mirakelbücher,* pp. 135-45].) The "as if" in Cervantes's reference to witnesses to an actual intervention of divine grace is a "qualification" of the introduction of the supernatural which is consistent with a pattern of deflection from the miraculous visible throughout the work (see below).

assembled to participate in the great festivals honoring the Eucharist. "Oh Blood of the living God, Blood of infinite worth, mixed with the mud of the streets and trampled upon by vile men! Oh Angels of Heaven! How is it that you do not descend to the earth to recover this precious Blood?" A single drop of Christ's blood, even a drop of his sweat, a single one of his tears, would have sufficed to save "millions of worlds," but to show his love he poured forth "streams of blood and tears" and "cataracts of his most holy body."[90] While ascetics proclaimed such mysteries, the multitudes gazed on their public enactment in the popular *autos sacramentales* and the *comedias de santos*. For example, at the climax of Lope's *auto*, *Obras son amores*, two successive *descubrimientos* reveal a silver pelican, the symbol of Christ, seated by God with blood pouring from his breast into a chalice below and, immediately thereafter, Christ crucified, with four angels catching in chalices the blood flowing from his hands, his feet, and his side.[91] Cervantes himself, through the character Saavedra, reminded his audience that penitence is the means of acquiring "the immense treasure of his blood shed for our good," and at the climax of his *El rufián dichoso* displayed the blood-soaked garments of the martyr, the sweet-smelling "cloths of wounds" that will heal the illnesses of thousands.[92]

Everywhere in the Catholic world confraternities sprang up honoring the blood and the wounds of Christ, processions of self-flagellants attempted to actualize his passion, and pilgrims gathered to meditate on the martyrdoms and miracles of the saints toward whose shrines they made their way.[93] The painters of the period depicted the martyrdoms of the saints in the most gruesome details, and in the religious colleges of the time the novices contemplated pictures of their sufferings as part of their preparation for the martyrdom that might await them in their missionary crusades to all parts of the world.[94]

[90] "¡Oh Sangre de Dios vivo, Sangre de infinito valor, mezclada con el lodo de las calles y hollada de viles hombres! Oh Angeles del Cielo! cómo no bajáis a la tierra a recoger esta preciosa Sangre?" Juan Eusebio Nieremberg, *Prodigio del amor divino y finezas de Dios con los hombres*, cited by G. Weise, "Das Element des Heroischen in der spanischen religiösen Literatur der Zeit der Gegenreformation," pp. 248, 210-211.

[91] See N. D. Shergold, *A History of the Spanish Stage from Medieval Times until the End of the Seventeenth Century* (Oxford, 1967), p. 437.

[92] "el tesoro inmenso de su vertida sangre por bien nuestro" (*El trato de Argel*, p. 140); *El rufián dichoso*, pp. 362-64.

[93] See Schreiber, "Der Barock und das Tridentinum," pp. 385-87; "Strukturwandel der Wallfahrt," pp. 21-62.

[94] "Juan de Valdés Leal hat die abgeschlagenen Köpfe hingerichteter Märtyrer in mindestens 20 verschiedenen Bildern gemalt—ein Beweis für die Beliebtheit dieser

The yearning for suffering became a common feature of the religious sentiment of the time, and an ideal of heroism that centered on the active search for punishment was expressed frequently. The model of such heroism was of course Christ, who considered "the pains suffered for the sake of man to be delicious pleasures" and who was driven by a fervent desire "that new methods of injury and torture be invented for Himself, as He was not satisfied that the ordinary ones were sufficient to reveal His love for us." An example of the extremes to which its advocacy could drive people of the age was the Jesuit Augustin de Espinosa, who covered his body with the brandmark *S* to declare himself "from head to foot" a slave of Jesus Christ.[95] The heroism of yielding to redemptive and expiatory suffering was championed everywhere in this age that made the great sinner one of its most distinctive literary characters, from the dark galley on which the illustrious picaro Guzmán de Alfarache awakened to new life, prayed that God might

---

Darstellungen—und hat stets neue Ausdrucksformen des Schmerzes, der Agonie, des Vollbrachtseins, der erlösten Verklärung gefunden" (Ludwig Pfandl, *Geschichte der Spanischen Nationalliteratur in ihrer Blütezeit*, p. 219). For the popularity of such themes in the painting of the period and their function in the missionary training, as well as the way in which the Church exploited the power of blood in Christian mythology and legend in order to arouse the religious sentiments of the populace, see Weisbach, *Der Barock als Kunst der Gegenreformation*, pp. 34-37; for the extremes of gruesomeness that the religious taste for savagery could countenance, see Weisbach's discussion of Ribera's "Martyrdom of Saint Bartholomew" and Rubens's "Martyrdom of Saint Justus," pp. 163-70.

[95] "por delicias estar por ellos [los hombres] en penas"; "que se inventasen contra El nuevos modos de injurias y tormentos, no se contentando con los ordinarios, para descubrir el amor que nos tenía" (see Luis de la Puente, *Meditaciones espirituales*, and Juan Eusebio Nieremberg, *Prodigio del amor divino y finezas de Dios con los hombres*, cited by G. Weise, "Das Element des Heroischen in der spanischen religiösen Literatur der Zeit der Gegenreformation," pp. 273-74). For Espinosa's self-torment, see Weise, p. 239. Nieremberg wrote that the drops of blood that Christ sweated during his vigil on the Mount of Olives were a baptism that he desired "como si se bañara en agua rosada" and that "tanto ero el deseo que tenía la sangre de brotar fuera, que antes que con los azotes, espinas y clavos la abriesen puerta, se salió della sin saber por dónde" (cited by Weise, p. 281). Luis de la Puente urged man to meditate on the blood shed by Christ on the Mount of Olives and to ask himself how a God of such infinite majesty could offer such valuable blood for such a vile creature as man (see Weise, p. 235). The preciousness of the Virgin's blood was a common theme in the religious culture of the age, as were the "bloody" tears that she wept in pity for the sins of man. See, for example, Luis de León's celebration of the "destilled" blood of Mary, "la más apurada y la más delgada y más limpia, y más apta para crialla, y más agena de todo affecto bruto" (*Nombres de Cristo*, 3 vols. [Madrid, 1969], 3:232) and Sor María de Jesus de Agreda's reflections on her "bloody tears" and the blood that burst forth from under her fingernails as she watched the binding of her son's wrists (*Nueva edición de la Mística ciudad de Dios*; see Weise, pp. 288-89).

"mix" His purifying blood with his own, and rejoiced that He "banquets His friends and His chosen with poverty, ordeals, and persecutions,"[96] to the scaffold of Madrid, where the infamous Rodrigo de Calderón acted out the final scene in his miraculous transformation from murderer and swindler into saint, burning with mystical love of God, begging that his flesh be torn out, kissing his executioner, and holding in his hand the wondrous image of Christ, while multitudes wept and intoned prayers for his soul.[97] Perhaps the best indication of the fascination with the magic of bloodshed and the savagery of martyrdom and the general "cultic cruelty" (*kultische Grausamkeit*)[98] which pervaded Spanish religious sentiment of the time was Pedro de Rivadeneira's collection of saints' lives (*Flos Sanctorum*, 1599), which begins with a preface enumerating all the gruesome torments that are

[96] "banquetea a sus amigos y a sus escogidos con pobreza, trabajos, y persecuciones." In the midst of his expiatory torture he prays God to accept his blood: ". . . pidiendo al cielo que aquel tormento y sangre que con los crueles azotes vertía se juntasen con los inocentes que mi Dios por mí había derramado, y me valiesen para salvarme, y pues había de quedar allí muerto" (see *Guzmán de Alfarache*, ed. S. Gil y Gaya, 5 vols. [Madrid, 1968], 5:154, 169).

[97] Karl Vossler has suggested that in Spain of this period, perhaps more than in any other time and place in history, man "literarisierte . . . das Leben und lebte die Literatur" (*Lope de Vega und sein Zeitalter* [Munich, 1947], p. 185). It would be difficult to find a more spectacular example of the peculiar interplay of life and literature than the behavior of this strange man, who, while in prison, read every day the *Flos Sanctorum* and memorized the works of St. Theresa, lamented that he did not have 100,000 lives to give for God, described himself as the prodigal son in his final letter to his father, and, preparing for the garrote, experienced the passion of Christ and cut off the collar of his cassock to spare the executioner the possible embarrassment of fumbling in the performance of his duty before the spectators. On the day of his execution one of his enemies was found dead. In the following months numerous poets sang of his exemplary death and the paradoxical value of his criminality, sinfulness and suffering, and two years later witnesses attested to the fact that his body and the garrote wounds were still as fresh as on the day of his death. One of the greatest criminals in the history of Spanish government had successfully rewritten his life as a masterpiece of hagiographic literature. He had become the hero of a miracle. See J. Juderías, "Un proceso político en tiempo de Felipe III: Don Rodrigo Calderón, Marqués de Siete Iglesias, su vida, su proceso y su muerte," *Revista de Archivos, Bibliotecas y Museos* 14 (1906):1-31. Probably there are no facts of literary history that attest more powerfully to the reality of the *Erwartungshorizont* for the reception of Cervantes's secularized miracle that I am postulating than the immediate metamorphosis of this man from criminal to saint in the imagination of the time.

[98] Pfandl, *Geschichte der Spanischen Nationalliteratur in ihrer Blütezeit*, p. 218. For the prominence of cruelty, "die gesteigerte Klage," and "der laute Schmerzensschrei" in the art of the time, see Schreiber, "Der Barock und das Tridentinum," p. 405, Weisbach, *Der Barock als Kunst der Gegenreformation*, pp. 78ff., J. Weingartner, *Der Geist des Barock* (Augsburg, 1925), p. 17, and Caro Baroja, *Las formas complejas de la vida religiosa*, pp. 115-16.

in store for the reader in the texts that follow and proceeds to describe the scenes of cruelty in the most theatrical way imaginable.[99]

In *La fuerza de la sangre* the violence and bloodshed, the heightened emotionality, and the sharply drawn opposition in the purity of the victim and the sadism of the persecutor clearly link the story to such literature and the taste inspiring and informing it. The suggestive power of its title, the implications of its central theme, and the resonances of its understated but nonetheless savage acts of bloodshed can be understood only if we recognize the magical power of blood in the imagination of the time. Indeed, Leocadia's proverbial description of the "wound and the medicine" as belonging to God's plan, her appeal to the crucifix, the pool of blood from which the child is resurrected at the center of the tale, and the reference to the power of blood in the title coalesce in an imaginative pattern that evokes the traditional conception of Christ as doctor offering His blood as healing medicine to the victims of sinfulness and misfortune. As Luis de Gra-

---

[99] At the outset of this widely read encyclopedia of saints' lives the reader is informed about numerous methods of crucifixion, different types of whips for scourging, wheels for breaking the body, presses for crushing it as if it were a grape or an olive, steel combs and pincers for flaying, grills, branding irons, flaming masks, heated shoes and shirts, various devices for tearing bodies into pieces before they are cast into "quelque cloaque & voirie infame," ways of covering parts of the body with food delectable to hungry animals, and some methods of sexual abuse ("qui est la plus grand & ignominieux tourment qu'on leur pouvoit faire souffrir"). Suffering such torments, the saints "sonts morts avec une si étrange & admirable constance, qu'ils étonnerent & vainquisent le monde," and the lengthy description of these tortures, which cause spectators to "frissonner d'horreur," is justified, according to Ribadeneira, in order to inspire his reader to emulate the "celestial and invincible soldiers" who showed such love of Jesus, such heroic constancy, and such disdain for the earthly life. As if the endless enumeration were not enough, the prologue concludes with a recommendation that, if the reader is interested in more torments, he should consult a curious book on the instruments of torture written by an Antoine Galonius in Rome in 1590. See *Les Fleurs des Vies des Saints*, ed. M. Baudovin, trans. M. Rene Gaultier (Paris, 1667), I:n.p. While Cervantes's sensitivity to the contemporary "thirst for suffering" is evident in such works as *Los trabajos de Persiles y Sigismunda, La fuerza de la sangre*, and his religious dramas, his exposure of the perversity of such an attitude is one of the most exhilarating themes of the *Quixote*. The hero takes delight in consoling his squire after a beating by reminding him that Amadís, like Christ, was tied to a column and given 200 lashes and that the Knight of the Sun was bound in a deep pit and tortured with "enemas of snow water and sand, which nearly killed him" (1:195). He assures him that evil and suffering are necessary forestages of deliverance and happiness (the "borrascas . . . son señales de que presto ha de serenar el tiempo y han de suceder bien las cosas" [1:225]). The healthy Sancho is not easily convinced. In one of his most eloquent moments, he complains about the sadistically designed miracle in which his suffering will be rewarded with Dulcinea's resurrection: "¡Yo no sé qué tienen que ver mis posas con los encantos!" (2:314).

nada and numerous other religious writers put it, Christ is "that great Physician who came to us from Heaven."[100] A striking indication of the popularity of the conception, as well as of the general inclination of the age to "materialize" and visualize concretely the most holy of mysteries, can be found in the stage directions for José de Valdivielso's *auto, El hospital de locos*: "a curtain is drawn, and Christ appears . . . seven red ribbons come out of His breast and lead to seven vessels like those in apothecaries' shops."[101]

In the climactic moment of Leocadia's restoration to Rodolfo the miraculous elements are equally prominent. In a hieratic processional scene Leocadia herself now appears as a quasi-divine figure, resplendent with jewels and radiating light that nearly blinds the observers, as she leads her child into the banquet room guided by two damsels who "illuminate her with two wax candles mounted in silver candelabras." The appearance of the procession has all the solemnity of an intense liturgical moment, and Leocadia is described as a beautiful "image" instantaneously working wonders in those who behold her.[102]

---

[100] See Weise, "Das Element des Heroischen in der spanischen religiösen Literatur der Zeit der Gegenreformation," pp. 198, 202. A classical statement of this conception can be found in Augustine's *De Doctrina Christiana* (I. xiv. 13): "the medicine of Wisdom by taking on humanity is accommodated to our wounds. . . . Thus the Wisdom of God, setting out to cure men, applied Himself to cure them, being at once the Physician and the Medicine" (trans. D. W. Robertson, Jr. [Indianapolis, 1958], pp. 14-15). Not surprisingly, Don Quixote invokes God as "nuestro médico," who "le aplicará medicinas que le sanen" to the obstinate sinner, Roque Guinart, suffering as he is "de la enfermedad de su conciencia" (*Don Quijote de la Mancha*, 2:501).

[101] "corrose [*sic*] vna cortina, y aparece Christo . . . y del pecho le salen siete cintas encarnadas, que dan en siete caxas como de botica," cited by N. D. Shergold, *A History of the Spanish Stage from Medieval Times until the End of the Seventeenth Century*, p. 441.

[102] For the importance of mother and child in the liturgy, popular Church festivals, and religious processions, see Schreiber, *Mutter und Kind in der Kultur der Kirche*, pp. 76ff. The brilliant light surrounding mother and child is a standard feature of the iconography of Christ, the Virgin, and the saints, and it is particularly prominent in the contemporary representations of the Immaculate Conception, in which the Virgin is envisaged as "more splendid than the sun," "loftier than all constellations," "purer than light," "a reflection of eternal light," and an "unstained mirror of God" (see Beissel, *Geschichte der Verehrung Marias im 16 und 17. Jahrhundert*, pp. 247-52, 263-75). See, for example, Feliciana's hymn to the Virgin: "todo es luz . . . salió la luz del sol inacesible;/ hoy nuevo resplandor ha dado al día/ la clarísima estrella de María" (*Persiles*, p. 310). Similarly Lope de Vega: "eres del mundo esclarecido faro,/ de las naves amparo,/ porque la luz que en el extremo ardía,/ esos brazos, María/ la tienen en el Niño y Dios presente,/ lumbre de lumbre y luz indeficiente;/ lámpara del Profeta/ que por ti se interpreta,/ farol divino de tu hermosa popa,/ tres luces y un fanal de capitana . . ." (*El peregrino en su patria*, p. 90). The blinding effect of

In perhaps the most theatrical moment of a work which, in its cultivation of the element of spectacle, rhetorical declamation, and powerful states of emotional exaltation, is probably the most "baroque"[103] of Cervantes's works, the amazed spectators, "stupefied" and "astonished," rise from their seats and bow to the resplendent figure "as if it were some heavenly being that had miraculously made its appearance there." As Leocadia accepts the professed homage with humility, Rodolfo can not resist wondering: "What is this I see! Is it perchance some human angel that I am beholding?"

From this visionary moment to the conclusion we observe a se-

---

Leocadia's light on those who observe her suggests moreover the light of the glorified, which is held to be beyond the reach of human powers of perception (see Pisa, *Historia de la gloriosa virgen y martyr Santa Leocadia Patrona de Toledo . . .* , p. 8). Two of the most theatrical scenes of *La fuerza de la sangre* are surrounded by the glow of traditional religious ceremony and mythology, the climactic procession and the central moment of Leocadia's revelation of her child's identity, a scene in which Doña Estafanía appears as a *mater dolorosa*, an omnipresent figure in contemporary art, holding the fallen maiden to her breast and pouring floods of tears on her lifeless form. For the visual aspects of the processional scene, see Margarita Levisi, "La función de lo visual en *La fuerza de la sangre*," *Hispanófila* 49 (1973):59-67, and Selig, "Some Observations on *La fuerza de la sangre*," pp. 121-25.

[103] Leocadia's grandiose description of the scene of her rape as "el teatro donde se representó la tragedia de su desventura" is consistent with the theatrical design of the processional scenes of the child's passage among the throngs in the streets and Leocadia's entrance at the banquet. A conventional feature of the miracle narrative is the spectator or, more commonly, the group of spectators, whose role can be those of providing witnesses to the events and, as it were, supporting the narrator's claims of authenticity, of concentrating the proper emotional reaction of awe and astonishment before the events, and of serving as a community benefiting from the edifying effects of the wonder. In one of Lipsius's miracles, for example, a husband summons his neighbors to assist and be witnesses at the wondrous salvation of his wife from beneath a mill wheel, and the narrator writes of the astonishment of all who heard of the birth of her beautiful child shortly thereafter. At another point the narrator requests the reader to exalt Mary "with Patience and Astonishment" (*Miracles of the Virgin*, pp. 26, 32). For observations on *admiratio* as the central aesthetic category of miracle literature, as well as on the function of the spectator in the genre, see Ebel, *Das altromanische Mirakel*, pp. 33-39. One can readily see a connection between the conventions and effects of the popular genre and the masterpieces of high baroque art, for example, in Bernini's inclusion of the startled spectators in his ecstasy of St. Theresa and in the peculiar role of the pilgrim as spectator, prescribing the proper aesthetic response to the reader in Góngora's *Las soledades*. Similarly the miracle reveals the concentration on a decisive instant in a process of change which, as Heinrich Wölfflin has argued, marks baroque art, and particularly its religious art, in which the instant is frequently that of divine illumination or intervention, as fundamentally different from Renaissance art with its preference for depicting its objects and agents in their unchanging "timeless" essence (see *Kunstgeschichtliche Grundbegriffe* [Munich, 1923], pp. 178, 187).

quence of events that repeats quite specifically and reconstructs the disastrous events of the opening scene, endowing them with their true significance, metamorphosing them magically from calamity to triumph, and making of the misfortune (*"desdicha"*) the paradoxical fortune (*"dicha"*) familiar in the traditional literature of miracles. Again the image of Leocadia imprints itself on Rodolfo's soul, and the power of instinct drives him into a state of uncontrollable emotional excitement ("extremados extremos"). As in the first scene the maiden faints under the stress of the situation, and her state is likened to death; again the youth, stumbling about uncontrollably, "carried away by his amorous and inflamed passion," throws himself on the lifeless maiden, again the onlooking members of the family shriek, weep, and tear their hair in desperation as they witness the loss of "the light of their eyes" ("la luz de sus ojos").[104] Again the maiden awakens in the arms of the passionate youth, again the power of the blood drives him toward sexual union, again the house where the union is realized is "buried in silence," and again his passion will bear fruit in the conception of his children and grandchildren. However, Rodolfo's desire now corresponds to that of the maiden, marriage now sanctifies the strong urges of his physical nature, now society gathers about their union, celebrating it in banquet and song and filling their house with "jubilation," "contentment," and "joy." And now her awakening is not to the terrifying darkness of her assailant's chamber and the dishonor of her wound, but rather to the honorable embrace of her husband. Cervantes carefully underscores the "abrogation" of the early scene in the maiden's words, which like so many other elements of the tale, point to the central theme that links it to the Christian miracle literature behind it, the theme of fruitful suffering: "When I returned to consciousness and came to myself from my former swoon, I found myself, sir, in your arms without honor; but I now hold *it was for the best*, since in recovering from that which I just have experienced, I have again found myself in the arms of my foe of former days, but honored."[105] In a masterstroke of narrative illusionism[106] Cervantes

---

[104] "como si fuera alguna cosa del cielo que allí milagrosamente se había aparecido . . . '¡Qué es esto que veo! ¿Es por ventura algún ángel humano el que estoy mirando?' . . . llevado de su amoroso y encendido deseo" (p. 898).

[105] "Cuando yo recordé y volví en mí de otro desmayo, me hallé, señor, en vuestros brazos, sin honra; pero yo lo doy *por bien empleado*, pues al volver del que ahora he tenido, me hallé en los brazos del de entonces pero honrada" (p. 899; italics added).

[106] The seemingly gratuitous reference to the fact that the events of the tale occurred at a time when marriages took place "con sola la voluntad de los contrayentes, sin las diligencias y prevenciones justas y santas que ahora se usan" is probably motivated more by the aesthetic necessities of this "re-created beginning," which it

has offered at the end of his tale its true beginning, and, as we read of night and silence falling on the happy society in Toledo and glimpse a brief vision of the continuing succession of happy generations, linked by the "power of blood," it is as if seven years of misery, like a bad dream from which we awaken, in reality had never even happened. In the imaginative circling back and superimposition of a re-created beginning on its beginning, Cervantes's tale comes as close as possible to the purely miraculous without allowing itself the violations of temporal plausibility common to the fairy tale and the miracle.

THE MIRACLE SECULARIZED

Up to this point I have tried to suggest that in its structure, narrative procedures, fundamental themes, methods of characterization, imaginative atmosphere, emotional tonality, and specific events, situations, symbols, and motifs, Cervantes's *La fuerza de la sangre* can be fruitfully clarified as a work modeled on a popular narrative form which originated and flourished in the middle ages and emerged as one of the most typical literary products of the religious culture of the Counter-Reformation. This is not to say that the work is identical with its popular congeners or even that its genesis is primarily attributable to the impact of the popular genre on Cervantes, just as a clarification of some features of the *Gitanilla* by pointing to certain structural characteristics that it shares with the *Book of Apollonius* does not necessarily imply a failure to recognize the complexities of Cervantes's very original romance. As my analysis of the "conventional" elements has indicated, Cervantes's tale is a carefully designed, ingeniously narrated, and richly allusive short story, and it would be difficult to find a more exquisite version of the popular narrative form.

At this point I would turn to a complexity of the story that has nothing to do with Cervantes's distinctive adaptation of the conventional aspects of his tale. Quite the contrary, it lies in the presence of an element that is strikingly unconventional in a miracle, that indeed

renders plausible for the seventeenth-century reader, for whom the proper procedure in marriage, according to regulations established at the Council of Trent, was an issue of vital interest (see my analysis of *La Gitanilla* above), than by some compulsion that Cervantes may have felt to profess orthodox, "exemplary" values in response to the pressures of the official culture of his society or to his own peculiar psychic needs to be accepted within that culture. While the absence of the phrase might have created a troubling rift in the text for the seventeenth-century reader, its presence interrupts the rapid movement toward closure for the twentieth-century reader, and it is no surprise that A. Flores deletes it from his anthology of Spanish tales (see *Spanish Stories*, pp. 86-87).

might easily be construed as conflictive with the traditional spirit of the miracle, and that recalls some of Cervantes's critical treatments of the miracle in the *Quixote*. As I have emphasized above, the miracle is a form of romance in which the hero is in reality divine grace, and in its purest form the protagonist is a helpless suppliant who finds himself inextricably imprisoned in a hopeless situation. The miracle would deemphasize the value of human effort, advocate reliance on divine mercy, underscore the fallen nature of this world, and ever remind man of his transcendental destiny. *La fuerza del la sangre* recognizes no hero in its title; the title and the powerful central symbol of the crucifix recall the redemptive blood of Christ and the martyrs, which was widely celebrated in Cervantes's culture and indeed at some other points in his own work; and the denouement of the tale is quite explicitly connected with the unfolding of God's mysterious design. However, while all of this directs our attention to the vindication of God's Providence, there is a counterforce which Cervantes develops carefully throughout his narration that causes us to recoil from any untroubled acceptance of the miraculous implications of the action, a counterforce that operates subversively in all the major miraculous moments of the narrative, in the articulation of the three major symbols, and most strikingly in our rereading of the title itself in the final line of the story.

The first and probably the most important of these deflections of our attention from the transcendental order occurs at the moment when Leocadia in her distress discovers the silver crucifix, illuminated by the moonbeams falling through the darkness of her prison. The sharp antithesis of Cervantes's description introduces a tension that will be sustained until the end: "she saw a little crucifix, wholly of silver, which she took and slipped into the sleeve of her gown, *not from devotion*, not as a theft, *but prompted by a clever design of hers.*"[107] Almost immediately thereafter we find the cross again emerging in the two alternative perspectives as icon and clue. Following Leocadia's return, her family contemplates it as a holy image and prays before it: "she showed them the crucifix she had brought away; before the image their tears were renewed, prayers were uttered, vengeance was demanded, and miraculous chastisements were called for."[108] How-

---

[107] "vio un crucifijo pequeño, todo de plata, el cual tomó y se le puso en la manga de la ropa, *no por devoción*, ni por hurto, *sino llevada de un discreto designio suyo*" (p. 892; italics added).

[108] "les mostró el crucifijo que había traído, ante cuya imagen se renovaron las lágrimas, se hicieron deprecaciones, se pidieron venganza y desearon milagrosos castigos" (p. 893).

ever, unlike the traditional protagonist of the miracle books with their glorifications of the cults of the image, Leocadia appears to be interested in the holy image primarily as an instrument in her carefully devised plan to discover the identity of her assailant. Her father rejects her *"discreto"* plan and reasserts the traditional attitude toward the power and function of the image: "what you must do, daughter, is keep it and commend yourself to it." As the narration turns to the restoration of Leocadia's honor, Cervantes continues to present the crucifix in a double perspective, in which we are compelled to see it simultaneously as the wonder-working image of the miracles and the "neutral" instrument in Leocadia's resourceful plan. In the central recognition scene she embraces the image, invokes it as a witness of her ordeal, implores its assistance, and, continuing to clutch it, falls helplessly into a swoon, a scene which in its heightened emotionality and theatricality recalls the penitents, martyrs, and numinous moments of contemporary art. However, in the concluding recognition scene, she returns from her third swoon and responds to Rodolfo's request for proof (a *"señal"*) of her identity by producing the cross and reminding him that she alone could have stolen it on the day of its disappearance.

In Cervantes's treatment of the crucifix we discern, then, a tendency toward desacralization, visible in his concern to render ambiguous its mysterious workings within the narrative, to mute its powerful symbolic resonances, and to transform it from the talismanic "last resort" of a helpless protagonist and a bearer of divine power upon which she is totally reliant into a mere object, bereft of divine emanations and manipulated by a resourceful heroine in her efforts to triumph over her antagonist.

The same process is visible in Cervantes's articulation of the other major Christian symbols of the tale, the child and blood. Blood is the most powerful symbol in the work, and, oddly enough, its power derives in large measure from Cervantes's restrained, even evasive way of handling it. As I have pointed out above, the Christian resonances of the symbol are clearly audible, and they bring to the imaginative atmosphere of the tale all the mysteries centering on the redemptive, sacrificial blood of Jesus and the martyrs, the tainted, sinful blood of fallen humanity, and the purity of the Virgin's blood. We observe Rodolfo driven by the heated blood of his youthful instinctuality to shed the innocent blood of Leocadia and bring total confusion to her world. We sense the redemptive power in bloodshed as we witness the conception of the marvelous child in the dark night of Rodolfo's savage act. Behind the healing of the terrible wounds inflicted on the maiden and the child, who lies in a pool of blood apparently mortally wounded, we glimpse the medicine of Christ's redemptive blood exerting its restoring influence on the fallen world of the victims of the sinful act ("when God gives the wound, He gives the medicine"). In all these cases we discover the presence of the magical blood of atonement of the miracles and a powerful imaginative support for the Christian mystery of "fortunate sin" to which the traditional miracle narrative so frequently bears witness. However, as if to curtail such evocations, Cervantes, at the moment of the central miraculous event, deflects our attention from the miraculous to the scientific, and the blood that bathes the head of the trampled child becomes the cause of a purely physiological process that brings about the grandfather's glimpse of the face of his own child in the lifeless form and provokes him to his striking, charitable act of springing from his horse, thrusting his way through the crowd with no concern for his loss of dignity, and carrying the victim to his house.[109] The catastrophe is averted, and the reversal of the narrative movement has all the instantaneousness and unexpectedness of the pivotal moment of the miracle narrative, the intrusion of divine grace being displaced, however, by the old man's act of family loyalty and marvelous charity ("they were struck with surprise at such Christian behavior"). At the same time the child's resurrection, introduced with so many suggestions of the miraculous children and the resurrections of hagiographic literature, is brought about not by the treatment of "the great Physician from Heaven," but rather by the skill of the famous surgeon, who cures

---

[109] According to an ancient belief very much alive in Cervantes's age, the members of a family constitute a single body, and their blood is linked by occult affinities that can cause recognition of kinship in relatives who know nothing of their family bond. There is nothing supernatural about such mysterious powers of blood. In the *Persiles* Feliciana discusses the difficulty of identifying her infant, whom she has never seen, and hopes that "la sangre hará su oficio," a process which it works "por ocultos sentimientos" (p. 295; see also the recognition scene in *La española inglesa, Obras completas*, ed. A. Valbuena Prat, p. 863). Cervantes's words recall his rationalistic attitudes, expressed in the *Persiles*, on the difference between miracles and the mysteries of nature (see above). For the existence of this belief in the power of blood, see E. L. Rochholz, "Gold, Milch und Blut," *Germania* 7 (1862):385-428, esp. 425ff.; G. A. Kohut, "Blood Test as Proof of Kinship in Jewish Folklore," *Journal of the American Oriental Society* 24 (1903):129-44; H. Strack, *The Jew and Human Sacrifice*, trans. H. Blanchamp (New York, 1971), p. 137. Kohut suggests that the notion is closely related to the widespread belief in the accusatory power of blood, "das schreiende Blut," which Cervantes would appear to be simultaneously exploiting in the scene. The effect of the blood pouring from the child is to identify the perpetrator of the crime that has victimized his entire family. The customary call for vengeance is of course absent in Cervantes's tale of reconciliation. Cervantes's awareness of the belief in "das schreiende Blut" is evident in the Marcela episode of the Quixote: "¿Vienes a ver . . . si con tu presencia vierten sangre las heridas deste miserable a quien tu crueldad quitó la vida?" (1:185).

him with *"the greatest dexterity and expertise"* (*"grandísimo tiento y maestría"*) after discovering that his wounds were simply not as serious as they initially appeared.[110] The "reduction" of the miracle through the prominence of physiological explanations and the success of human science[111] is climaxed in the final line of the story which would appear to separate decisively the "fuerza de la sangre" from all its magical associations and indeed offer a "rewriting" of the title that "cancels out" the transcendental reverberations and all the promise of its openness. The tension that arises in the "rewritten" title of the last sentence is all the more noticeable as it concludes Cervantes's "rewriting" of the first scene in a version that emphasizes the miraculous nature of the whole tale.

All of these deflections of the reader's "tantalized" desire to construe

[110] Italics added. The doctor is a common figure in miracle literature, and his traditional role is to represent the limitations of human reason and knowledge and to stand by helplessly as he witnesses the cure that proceeds from "divine medicine" or Christ the "physician." A good contemporary example can be observed in Justus Lipsius's collection of miracles of the holy image of the Virgin of Halle (1604). Recounting the miraculous cure of a nun afflicted with convulsions, the narrator observes: "neither the ingenuity of the Physician, nor the Experience of the Chirurgion could afford her any redress; an evident sign that all human help must give place, that we ascribe the Glory to the B. Virgen only. . . . Oh wonderful but true event!" (*An Historical Account of the Original and Stupendous Performances of the Image entitled Our Blessed Lady of Halle*, p. 35). See also the numerous doctors whose failures are emphasized in the collection of miracles which Fray Luis de Granada includes in his *Introducción del símbolo de la fe*, 2:xxix. For example, he relates the case of a nun who, stricken by a crippling illness, was reduced to walking on all fours. "Ya desconfiados los médicos," she turned to the image of Jesus Christ, "comenzó á procurar con toda fe y devocion la medicina del cielo, que no podia hallar en la tierra," and was miraculously cured (see B.A.E. 6:372). In Cervantes's parody miracle of Isabela's possession in the *Persiles*, where the emphasis is on the reduction of the divine by its juxtaposition to human resourcefulness and youthful independence rather than to the effectiveness of science, a doctor is nevertheless present to express the traditional bewilderment as he examines the victim. The frequency of the theme of illness and the character of the doctor make the miracle books, despite their emphasis on the impotence of human science, an invaluable documentary source in the history of medicine and sickness (see Schreiber, *Deutsche Mirakelbücher*, pp. 56-64; E. Friess and G. Gugitz, "Die Mirakelbücher von Mariahilf in Wien [1689-1775]," Schreiber's *Deutsche Mirakelbücher*, pp. 77-134, esp. 105-112).

[111] I would emphasize the distinction between this kind of "disengagement" from the miracle of healing and its burlesque in the skeptical context of the *Quixote*, where the "bálsamo de Fierabras," the magical elixir in which Christ's body was embalmed, works a "wondrous cure" on Don Quijote, who "dijo sobre la alcuza más de ochenta paternostres y otras tantas avemarías, salves y credos, y a cada palabra acompañaba una cruz, a modo de bendición" before vomiting in disgust, and inflicts a terrible torment on the hapless Sancho, the usual "victim" of miracles in the novel (see 1:210). This passage was expurgated by the Portuguese Inquisition in 1624 (see Castro, *El pensamiento de Cervantes*, pp. 262-63).

the events of Cervantes's narrative according to the paradigms of miracle literature are consistent with an important element in the characterization of its agents and the themes that it implies. The conventional miracle would diminish the efficacy of the efforts of the agents involved and would remind its reader of the inadequacy of all human effort unless blessed by the infusion of divine grace. A good example of the antithetical association of human design and miraculous power in the orthodox Christian mentality can be observed in the *Quixote* in Basilio's jubilant exclamation following the successful staging of his false miracle: "¡No 'milagro, milagro,' sino industria, industria!"[112] Throughout *La fuerza de la sangre* the narration emphasizes the *industria* of its agents, most strikingly in its most miraculous moments. Thus Leocadia seizes the cross "not for devotion . . . but prompted by a clever design of hers." After her parents implore the image for a "miraculous punishment," she proposes with "discreet reasoning" ("discreto discurso") an intelligent plan to use the crucifix to entrap her assailant. Perfectly aware of the complexities of the secular world, she proposes to her persecutor, even as she lies on the bed of his assault, a plan of extrication that would minimize the irreparable damage done by his deed, and the narrator commends her proposal as "discreet arguments" ("discretas razones"). Before resigning herself to the passive state of the miracle protagonist, who can do no more than await divine aid in exemplary humility, Leocadia appears as a forceful figure courageously fighting off her assailant and immediately seeking an escape from her plight when Rodolfo leaves the room of her confinement. Cervantes's detailed description of the chamber is most striking for its emphasis on the maiden's acts of careful observation and intelligent interpretation:

Leocadia *felt* that she was left alone and locked in, and rising from the couch *she explored* the whole of the apartment, feeling the walls with her hands, *to see if there was* a door by which she could escape or a window out of which she could throw herself. *She found* the door, but securely locked, and *stumbled on* a window which she could open, by which the splendor of the moon entered, so clear that Leocadia *could distinguish* the colors of some damask hangings that adorned the apartment. *She perceived* that the bed was gilded and so richly furnished that it seemed to be rather the couch of a prince than of a private gentleman. *She counted* the chairs and cabinets; *she noted* the place where the door was, *and also saw* hanging on the walls some pictures, but *she could not succeed in seeing* what their subjects were. The window was large, garnished and guarded by a thick grating, and it looked into a garden which

---

[112] *Don Quijote de la Mancha*, 2:200. The customary English translation—"No miracle, no miracle; but a trick, a trick!"—fails to bring out sufficiently the force of *industria* as suggesting a "clever, intentionally contrived design."

was also shut in by high walls, obstacles which presented themselves to the project she had of throwing herself into the street. *All she saw and noted* of the size and rich ornaments of the dwelling *gave her to understand* that the owner of it must be a man of importance and wealthy, not of everyday fortune, but exceedingly rich. On a writing cabinet which was close to the window *she saw* a little crucifix, wholly of silver, which *she took*.[113]

The rapid narration of her efforts to perceive, distinguish, and analyze in the repeated verbs in the preterite tense suggests not only the astonishment that accompanies her discovery of the vast wealth of her assailant's world, but also the heightened activity of her mind, and the passage culminates in her theft of the crucifix, which the narrator informs us is part of a "discreet design" that she has already constructed. As Cervantes describes the maiden's return to her parents, he emphasizes again her resourcefulness. While Rodolfo leads her blindfolded from the house, she counts the steps leading to the street, and, aware that someone might discover her identity by following her, she enters a strange house where she pauses for a short period of time before continuing on her way. Although her "design" is rejected by her father in favor of total reliance on providential help, as the story turns toward her deliverance, Cervantes emphasizes the role that all of these actions play in the anagnorisis and restoration. She reveals the number of steps she had counted with "prudent attention" ("discreta advertencia"), and, as she prepares to inform Rodolfo's mother of the events, the latter is "filled with wonder and perplexity listening to these reflections of Leocadia, for she could not believe, although she was the witness of it, that so much prudence [*discreción*] could be possessed by someone so young."[114]

---

[113] "*Sintió* Leocadia que quedaba sola y encerrada, y levantándose del lecho anduvo todo el aposento, tentando las paredes con las manos, *por ver si había puerta* por do irse o ventana por do arrojarse; *halló puerta*, pero bien cerrada, y *topó una ventana* que pudo abrir por donde entró el resplandor de la luna, tan claro, que *pudo distinguir Leocadia* los colores de unos damascos que el aposento adornaban; *vió* que era dorada la cama, y tan ricamente compuesta, que más parecía lecho de príncipe que de algún particular caballero; *contó* las sillas y los escritorios; *notó* la parte donde la puerta estaba, y aunque *vió* pendientes de las paredes algunas tablas, *no pudo alcanzar a ver* las pinturas que contenían; la ventana era grande, guarnecida y guardada de una gruesa reja; la vista caía a un jardín, que también se cerraba con paredes altas; dificultades que se opusieron a la intención que de arrojarse a la calle tenía, *todo lo que vió y notó* de la capacidad y ricos adornos de aquella estancia *le dió a entender* que el dueño de ella debía de ser hombre principal y rico, y no comoquiera, sino aventajadamente; en un escritorio que estaba junto a la ventana *vió un crucifijo*, todo de plata, *el cual tomó*" (p. 892; italics added).

[114] "admirada y suspensa . . . escuchando las razones de Leocadia, y no podía creer, aunque lo veía, que tanta discreción pudiese encerrarse en tan pocos años" (p. 895).

The emphasis on *discreción*, reason, prudence, and human design[115] amid the apparently miraculous events that unfold in the tale is not limited to the heroine's actions. Characteristically the narrator points to the cure of the "resurrected child" as proceeding from the great "dexterity and expertise" of the famous doctor. Moreover, Leocadia's mother's *discreción* is noted as she arranges the concealment of the illegitimate birth and investigates the family of the grandchild's benefactors, and in one of the most striking moments of deflection from the miraculous, Leocadia's father appends to his admonition that his daughter fall back in humility on the power of the cross some "prudentes razones" that indicate that he is very concerned by the claims of the secular and social worlds:

Take note, my daughter, that an ounce of public dishonor wounds more painfully than five-and-twenty pounds of secret infamy; and since you can live honored with the aid of God in public, do not be pained at being dishonored in your own eyes in secret. True dishonor lies in sin, and true honor in virtue. God is offended by our speech, by our desire, and by our action, and since you have not offended Him in word or thought or deed, regard yourself as honored, for I shall hold you as such, and never look on you except as your true father.[116]

Just as in such phrases as "not for devotion, but prompted by a discreet design," the passage strikingly concentrates the fundamental tension of the story. On the one hand, it is an expression of the purest spirituality in its antithesis of true honor-true dishonor, the awareness that true honor is dependent entirely on virtue and as such is conferred on the righteous by God regardless of society's judgments. On the other hand, it includes the troubling admission, underscored in the two preceding antitheses and the central imagery of martyrdom, that an ounce of public dishonor "wounds more painfully" than a five-and-

---

[115] For the importance of *la discreción* in Cervantes's writings, see Margaret Jane Bates, *Discretion in the Works of Cervantes: A Semantic Study* (Washington, D.C., 1945); also William C. Atkinson, "Cervantes, el Pinciano, and the *Novelas ejemplares*," *Hispanic Review* 16 (1948):189-208, esp. 199ff. Atkinson correctly emphasizes both its centrality in Cervantes's system of values and its secular origins and implications: "Discretion was the science, or the art, or simply the doctrine of the relativity of all the criteria of human conduct, and is not to be learnt from the copy-book: it is to be learnt by living."

[116] "advierte, hija, que más lastima una onza de deshonra pública que una arroba de infamia secreta; y pues puedes vivir honrada con Dios en público, no te pene de estar deshonrada contigo en secreto: la verdadera deshonra está en el pecado, y la verdadera honra en la virtud; con el dicho, con el deseo y con la obra se ofende a Dios; y pues tú ni en dicho, ni en pensamiento, ni en hecho le has ofendido, tente por honrada que yo por tal te tendré, sin que jamás te mire sino como verdadero padre tuyo" (p. 893).

twenty pound measure (*una arroba*) of secret infamy, and that by maintaining public honor one can soften the dishonor which one covers with secrecy. On the one hand, the father professes a lofty religious faith, which emphasizes the clear, irreducible distinction of value between this world and the essential transcendental order and brooks no compromises of one's purest convictions; on the other hand, he engages in an elaborate casuistry informed by a conciliatory attitude toward the importance of this world and its judgments, flawed though they may be, and implicitly rejects the kind of "public suffering" that is valued so highly in the Christian tradition of martyrdom. The appended discourse on honor, with its subtle distinctions, quadruple antitheses, and syllogistic structure certainly qualifies the power of the simple admonition to rely on God's Providence and strongly reasserts the importance of the complexities of the secular world. To appreciate fully the ambiguities of the "religious spirit" here expressed, we should recall the uncompromising purity of Cervantes's early *El trato de Argel*, where Saavedra suspects any "falling back" on one's intimate, private relationship with God while conforming to the shabby practices of one's society as in reality the self-deception and mask of a weak spirit.[117] For all its evocations of miraculous elements and its structural and thematic affinities with a genre that traditionally celebrated the purest spirituality, *La fuerza de la sangre* is directly concerned with the claims of the secular world, and, at the conclusion of the father's qualification of his "heroic" counsel to rely on Providence, the narrator commends the "prudent reasons" ("prudentes razones") of his words.

In the second half of the tale the theme of *discreción* is developed primarily through Rodolfo's mother, whose ingenious manipulation of the course of the action, control over all the agents involved, and theatrical construction of the climactic "miracle" of Leocadia's dazzling entry, in which the maiden becomes "the beautiful image" that captivates the youth, make her one of the most powerful displacements of Divine Providence and its agencies[118] in Cervantes's secular-

---

[117] The combination of practicality and genuine religious conviction that we discover in Leocadia's father is observable in Clotaldo in *La española inglesa*, a man who, like the persecuted Christians to whom Saavedra refers in *El trato de Argel*, is incapable of the heroic Christianity of the martyr. He urges Isabela to conceal the family's Catholicism in her audience with Queen Elizabeth, admitting that "puesto que estaban prontos con el espíritu a recibir martirio, todavía la carne enferma rehusaba su amarga carrera" (*Obras completas*, ed. A. Valbuena Prat, p. 856).

[118] Indeed Doña Estefanía has affinities with the Virgin of the traditional miracle. She is the good mother and the embodiment of the life-giving female principles of nurture, compassion, and mercy, traditionally represented in Christian mythology by

ized miracle. Following the revelation of Leocadia's identity, Doña Estefanía immediately conceives of a plan, and from this moment to the end of the tale frequent reference is made to her *designio*, her *traza* (*plot*), her *determinación*, and her *ordenes*. She lures her son home, exploits his rather unappealing attitudes toward women, love, and marriage, delights in watching him yield to her manipulation, and prescribes roles for numerous other characters as if they were the figures of a play, a play that actually produces suspense and astonishment in its observers. As is frequently the case in Cervantes's depictions of manipulators, unpredictable elements intrude to disturb the integrity of her carefully contrived plot and perhaps remind us that even the most skillfully designed play within the infinitely complicated play of life will fail to master its intractable subject matter. Nevertheless, the resurrection of the maiden from her mortal swoon at its climax, her marriage, and the restoration of her honor are to a great extent a tribute to Doña Estefanía's resourcefulness and energy.[119]

In the climactic apotheosis of Leocadia we glimpse one of the most important of the hagiographic texts that are inscribed in Cervantes's reconstructed miracle, the legend of St. Leocadia of Toledo. The cir-

---

the Virgin: "Diciendo esto, abrazándola con el crucifijo, cayó desmayada en los brazos de Estefanía, la cual, en fin, como mujer y noble, en quien la compasión y misericordia suele ser tan natural como la crueldad en el hombre. . . ." Her revival of the fallen child on her breast suggests the miraculous healing powers of the Virgin's tears: "juntó su rostro con el suyo, derramando sobre él tantas lágrimas, que no fue menester esparcirle otra agua encima para que Leocadia en si volviese."

[119] As a character who becomes in a sense the architect of the comic action of the work in which she appears and a superb manipulator of other characters, who become role-players in her schemes and form an astonished audience of her theatrical contrivances, Doña Estefanía has affinities with several of the figures of the artist that Cervantes privileges with a special freedom within the works that contain them. It is as if she were rewriting the original script, presiding over the restoration at its climax, and carefully erasing its false beginning. It is perhaps useful to compare her with Cervantes's most powerful embodiment of the artist, Pedro de Urdemalas, another concoctor of false miracles, another transmuter of indifferent reality according to the mandates of desire, and another restorer of wronged damsels. However, if the picaresque Pedro de Urdemalas's connection with the realm of grace is not one of festive association, as in the case of Doña Estefanía, but rather one of ironic subversion and perhaps even profanation, Doña Estefanía, as artist, maintains a firm link with Divine Providence, and her contrivances bear witness to an exemplary vision that is firmly founded in a preexisting higher truth. With Pedro de Urdemalas Cervantes allows us a glimpse of a much more gigantic artist figure, one who is truly "secularized" and autonomous, one whose firm control over his texts is not overthrown by unpredictable contingencies, and who needs no sanction for his spectacularly successful machinations other than his own powerful imagination. See my *Cervantes, Aristotle, and the "Persiles,"* chap. 9.

cumstances of the life, death, and miracles of the victim of the Dacian persecution were undoubtedly familiar in the religious culture of Cervantes's Spain and particularly that of the ancient imperial capital Toledo, where three churches marked the sacred locations of her grave, her passion, and her family's home, and where an inscription in stone above the city gate honored her in a verse from an old Gothic hymn: "You are our glorious citizen, you are our native protectress"—"Tu nostra ciuis inclyta, tu es patrona vernula."[120] As I suggested at the outset of this chapter, Cervantes may well have witnessed the magnificent celebration of the translation of her bones to Toledo in 1587 and its triumphal procession, which climaxed in the apparition of King Philip II, the royal family, and the Archbishop of Toledo, who bore the coffer containing the sacred remains on the final phase of their long journey from the place of their thousand-year exile to their proper resting place in the Church of the Vega. In any event he undoubtedly had the life of the virgin martyr in mind as he composed his *La fuerza de la sangre*, and it is possible that his conception of the tale was influenced by the version of the legend that Francisco de Pisa published in 1605 in Toledo.

Pisa's account purports to be based on numerous documents which he has assembled and studied with an historian's determination to authenticate his narration. It begins with the virgin's torment and martyrdom, proceeds to her miraculous resurrection 300 years later, when she guided St. Ildefonso to her grave, and concludes with the restoration of her bones to her shrine and the celebration of their consecrating effects on her native city. Leocadia is scourged by the "ferocious wolf" Dacian, a "minister of Satan," and, while other Christians observe helplessly "with grief and pain, pouring forth tears," she is carried to a cell in the center of the city ("a deep and dark dungeon . . . where the rays of the sun were never seen"), where she is to be imprisoned in darkness, tortured, and starved. God and Jesus relieve her solitude by granting her conversation with the angels, and "spirits of light" enter to dispel the frightening shadows enveloping her. While she prays to God, asking him to protect "the sheep of his flock, whose martyred blood, in a fragrance of sweetness was rising in his esteem," she traces the sign of the cross on the rock wall of her dungeon, which miraculously softens, "as if it were butter" and offers her a permanent image. According to the chronicler, on her incarceration Leocadia was deprived of the consolation provided by her holy

[120] See Pisa, *Historia de la gloriosa virgen y martyr Santa Leocadia Patrona de Toledo*, pp. 4, 9.

books, and, since she did not even have a "cross of sticks," God gave her the miraculous image so that "she would not die without this consolation in that cavern or dungeon."[121]

If the torment of Cervantes's Leocadia in Rodolfo's dark cell and the discovery of the crucifix as a consolation resemble the events of Leocadia's martyrdom, her characterization and actions recall the perfections and divine power of the saintly figure. Neither has had any experience of society, as they have lived the pious, withdrawn life that we observe frequently in Cervantes's female ideals,[122] and in their

[121] "las ovejas de su rebaño, cuya sangre derramada subía en su acatamiento en olor de suavidad"; "no murriesse sin este consuelo en aquella sima o mazmorra" (Pisa, *Historia*, p. 3). The key moment in the saint's life becomes in Cervantes's secularized miracle a crucial but much more ambiguous moment ("no por devoción . . . sino llevada de un discreto designio suyo"). In Hardy's dramatic version the element of the miraculous disappears entirely: the crucifix becomes an image of Hercules and is reduced entirely to the function of confirming token, and the implications of the title are confined effectively to the theme of affinities of the blood uniting members of a class and a family, physiologically and characterologically. See Crooks, *The Influence of Cervantes in France in the Seventeenth Century*, pp. 140-41.

[122] See, for example, the celebrated "recogimiento" of Isabela, the heroine of *La española inglesa*, who, while awaiting the return of her beloved from his pilgrimage to Rome, never sets foot outside her house except to worship in the monastery. The most striking of Cervantes's heroines of this type is Costanza of the *Ilustre fregona*, whom we see in fleeting glimpses and whose silences are more expressive than the strident clamor of the turbulent picaresque world which seethes about her with violence and lust. It is worth pointing out how prominent the hagiographic elements are in Cervantes's other Toledan tale. Here too we find that the plot, in its total design, resembles the miracle narrative. The action begins with the rape and pregnancy of Costanza's mother and proceeds through her vow to the Virgin, her pilgrimage to the Holy Lady of Guadalupe, her entrusting herself to divine grace in her helplessness, the wondrous birth of her child, her death and the orphaning of the maiden, and the concluding miraculous restoration and its celebration by astonished throngs. The maiden's brief appearances are surrounded by mystery, and she is frequently associated with the Virgin, whom she serves with faithful and humble devotion every day of her life. We see her bowing before the holy image as she prepares for her daily chores. She is described as a "miracle worker," an "angel," a "*tragaavemarías*"; she is the "image" which Avendaño has come to adore in his "pilgrimage," an authentic pilgrimage paralleling Costanza's mother's pilgrimage to Guadalupe and contrasting with Carriazo's "*romería*" to the demonic realm of the "*almadrabas*," which is described as a sinister female. The hyperbolic descriptions of Costanza's beauty emphasize light, heavenly bodies, flowers, silver, candles, and jewels, all standard features of the contemporary iconography of the Virgin. Moreover, she is born during her mother's pilgrimage to the shrine of Our Lady of Guadalupe, and her birth takes place in a "marvelous silence" in which neither mother nor child experience pain or shed tears, an event that recalls the birth of Christ (see Alonso de Villegas Selvago, *Flos sanctorum, segunda parte y Historia general en que se escrive la Vida de la Virgen Sacratissima Madre de Dios y Señora Nuestra y las de los Santos Antiguos que fueron antes de la venida de nuestro Salvador al mundo* . . . [Zaragoza, 1586], pp. 42-45). A mys-

innocence and fragility they are woefully ill-prepared to cope with the villainy of their worldly adversaries. Before her encounter with Dacian, St. Leocadia "knew nothing more than the house of her parents and her oratory." Leocadia tells Rodolfo: "Aside from my father and my confessor, I have never spoken with a man in my life."[123] When addressing her tormentor, Cervantes's Leocadia speaks with wisdom that would belie her lack of experience, and her bewildered attribution of its origin to her suffering contains a suggestion of the presence of divine inspiration and the gifts of martyrdom. When the ruthless Dacian tempts and threatens St. Leocadia, "lifting her spirit in the contemplation of her spouse, filled with confidence and saintly fortitude, she answered with these arguments, which the Holy Spirit inspired within her." The responses of the male persecutors are similar: "On hearing these arguments, although he marveled at the discretion of the saintly virgin, Dacian became angry and furious and resolved once again to torture her, to crush her, and to break her will . . . Look how that virginal body is wounded!"; "the answer that Rodolfo gave to the discreet arguments of the wounded Leocadia was no other than to embrace her."[124] Both virgins display heroism and dignity in meeting the renewed physical abuse by their tormenters.

---

terious song heard in the night honoring her virtue and beauty is mistakenly interpreted as a hymn to Nuestra Señora del Carmen. Her refusal to acknowledge her admirers by speaking and the irresistible appeal of "su recogimiento" recall the reticence of the Virgin, who, despite her miraculous powers and knowledge, heroically refrained from speaking during the first years of her life, "excusando la admiración de ver hablar a una recién nacida," and who was commonly envisaged holding her finger to her lips above her slumbering child (see María de Jesús de Agreda, *Leyes secondas de la Esposa*, cited by Weise, "Das Element des Heroischen in der spanischen religiösen Literatur der Zeit der Gegenreformation," pp. 178-79; also Rivadeneira, *Les Fleurs des Vies des Saints*, p. 48 and Beissel, *Geschichte der Verehrung Marias im 16. und 17. Jahrhundert*, pp. 180-83). One need only compare the novella's recognition scene with its account of the fitting together of the divided parchment reading "Esta es la Señal Verdadera" with the discussion of the parchments and their Latin inscription in the authenticating process concerning St. Leocadia's remains (Pisa, *Historia*, p. 12) to see how consciously and playfully Cervantes employs hagiographic conventions in his festive celebration of his saintly heroine and the redeemed society to which she returns at the conclusion of the tale.

[123] "no sabía más de la casa de sus padres, y su oratorio" (Pisa, *Historia*, p. 2); "Fuera de mi padre y de mi confesor, no he hablado con hombre en mi vida" (*La fuerza de la sangre*, p. 892).

[124] "levantando el espiritu en contemplacion de su esposo, llena de confiança y santa fortaleza respondio estas razones, segun que el Espiritu santo se las inspirava interiormente"; "Oyendo Daciano estas razones (aunque maravillado de la discrecion de la santa virgen) vuelto en furor y saña, acordò de la afligir, domar y quebrantar. . . . Vierades lastimar aquel virginal cuerpo" (Pisa, *Historia*, p. 2); "La respuesta que dió Rodolfo a las discretas razones de la lastimada Leocadia no fue otra que abrazarla" (*La fuerza de la sangre*, p. 892).

Each maiden moves from darkness to light; each yearns for a direct vision of her husband's face; and the restoration of each is associated with the resurrection of the dead, the restoration of vision to the blind, and the redemptive power of blood. St. Leocadia vows to her persecutor that nothing can separate her from Christ: "who, bringing about our redemption with His precious blood, dressed us and adorned all Christians with blessed liberty. I certainly serve Christ, whose true light shines throughout the world; who restores vision to the blind, provides strength for the lame, fortifies the weak, and even, with His word alone, gives life to the dead and resurrects them."[125] As we have seen, Leocadia escapes from a situation of total darkness, in which she can not perceive Rodolfo, enjoys indirect, clandestine glimpses of the youth following his return from Italy, and in the final scene openly gazes on the man whom "she now loved more than the light of her eyes." St. Leocadia's reward is similar. As she is greeted by the heavenly martyrs, robed in their "immaculate vestures, washed and bleached in the blood of the lamb," "there she begins fully to enjoy the appearance and the face of the one whom she loved with living faith and unwavering hope while she was on earth."[126] In each case a marriage rewards the ordeals of the maiden: Jesus Christ places the crown of glory on the head of His bride. Leocadia, whose radiance is associated with the light of the glorified body, which blinds human sight, is wedded to Rodolfo.

By echoing the legend of St. Leocadia, Cervantes elevates his suffering heroine and associates her restoration with the triumph of the martyr. However, as the parallels that I have mentioned make clear, the relation of the exemplary novella to the legend is far more complicated than that. The reward of the saint is of course the marriage with Christ, and she welcomes death looking forward to "the delights of eternal life." Her apotheosis celebrates a liberation from this world, which is conceived as a place of exile, and from the body, which is viewed as a prison ("her blessed soul, coming out of its exile and incarceration in the body, rejoiced in great measure at its arrival at the sacred college of holy angels in Heaven").[127] Here we observe the

---

[125] "el qual obrando nuestra redempcion con su sangre preciosa, nos vistio y adornó a los Christianos de santa libertad. Yo ciertamente sirvo a Christo, cuya verdadera lumbre resplandece por todo el mundo: el qual da vista a los ciegos, es fuerça a los coxos, confirma a los flacos, y aun a los muertos con sola su palabra da vida, y resucita" (Pisa, *Historia*, p. 2).

[126] "vestiduras limpias, lavadas, y blanqueadas en la sangre del cordero"; "allí comiença a gozar perfectamente de la vista y rostro de aquel, que mientras estaba en la tierra desseava con viva fe, y firme esperança" (ibid., p. 3).

[127] "su bien aventurada anima saliendo deste destierro, y carcel del cuerpo, en gran

dualistic view of spirit and flesh, this world and the afterlife, which is characteristic of ascetic Christianity and generally of the Christian vision informing traditional saints' lives and miracles. As Hippolyte Delehaye points out, the peculiarity of the saintly hero is that his heroism begins when he dies or leaves this earth behind,[128] and the chronicler of St. Leocadia's triumphs moves toward his most rapturous moment in the concluding processional scene, in which the bones and ashes of the saint are borne through the streets amid universal jubilation. Though his style is generally the detached utterance of the professional historian and sober moralist, whose primary concerns are factual accuracy and proper ethical interpretation, the chronicler at this point cannot resist entering the ritual he is describing and sharing the jubilation of the scene. His "participation" emerges in a traditional rhetorical formula—the *topos* of diffidence and inexpressibility: "Here there was necessary another pen, one more delicate than mine, and another elegance and genius, greater than mine, to describe and place before the readers' eyes the marvelous [procession]." As Cervantes contemplates the dazzling procession centering on the divine but nonetheless very real and fleshly Leocadia at the climax of his tale, he too must abandon the stance that his narrator has generally maintained as a sober reporter of emotionally highly charged events.[129] In nearly the same words he speaks of his hand faltering: "may it be left to another pen and to another genius more delicate than mine to tell of the universal joy of all who were present."[130] But what has aroused

---

manera alegrò con su venida al sagrado colegio de los Angeles santos en el cielo" (ibid.).

[128] *Cinq Leçons sur la Méthode Hagiographique*, pp. 7-8.

[129] Such rare dislocations in the narrative voice occur primarily at the beginning of Pisa's "life," when the narrator is reporting events contained in an old text, which he may in fact be copying. The decisive moments are rendered with increased dramatic power by frequent shifts from the preterite to the present tense and in one case by an admonition of the reader to watch the torments of the martyr as if they were unfolding before his eyes: "[Daciano] *acordò* de la afligir . . . y *encarga* mucho a los soldados. . . . *Vieredes lastimar* aquel virginal cuerpo, descargando en el crueles açotes: los quales ella *sufrio* con rostro alegre" (p. 2; italics added). For the affects of such narrative techniques in hagiographic writing, see Uitti, *Old French Narrative Poetry*, pp. 42-64. In general Cervantes does not use his narrator for such effects in *La fuerza de la sangre*. For the most part the narrator is a sober, uninvolved reporter, who avoids irony and limits his self-interpositions between reader and events to occasional moralizing commentary on the reported action. See, for example, his remarks on the proper upbringing of children, on the customs of the rich, on the superior value of virtue and wisdom over the gifts of fortune, on the foolishness or prudence of the characters' actions and on the goodness of the Council of Trent's dispositions concerning marriage.

[130] "Aqui era necessaria otra pluma mas delicada, y otra mayor elegancia y ingenio que el mio, para describir y poner delante de los ojos el maravilloso . . ." (Pisa,

his uncontrollable *admiración* and stayed his hand is not a coffer of bones that bear witness to a celestial marriage and its blessings, but rather a spectacle of communal joy, friendship, piety, and family reconciliation and the Christian marriage of two human beings, drawn together by the impulses of their blood and anticipating years of "enjoyment"—"gozo"—in each other, in their children, and in their grandchildren. In the most sublime moment of her passion St. Leocadia prepares to imitate Christ in the offering of her blood and vows that nothing can deter her from serving him who "shed His precious blood to redeem mankind, who brought light to a darkened world, and who with His word alone gave life to the dead and resurrected them." With the grace that is the gift of poets of all ages Cervantes has pronounced his own word and resurrected the saint and placed her firmly on this earth. As one of the numerous sacred texts inscribed within Cervantes's exemplary novella, the legend of St. Leocadia has a highly ambivalent function, but its presence is decisive in the total design of the story. In effect, *La fuerza de la sangre* is a radical rewriting and renewal of the venerable text and its celebration of the power of blood.

In conclusion, one of the features of Cervantes's *La fuerza de la sangre* that links it most directly to the popular form of the miracle narrative is its rich orchestration of antitheses. One could say that antithesis is the dominant figure of this narration, visible in the total design of its plot, in its central body of imagery, in the abrupt shifts in its atmosphere, and in the configuration of numerous phrases and sentences, both in the narrator's account of the events and in the rhetorical declamations of the agents.[131] And it is clear that all of these concrete manifestations of antithesis are informed by the profoundly antithetical feeling behind the Christian vision of evil and redemption, of the relation between this life and the afterlife, and of the paradoxes of the Incarnation and the fortunate fall.[132] Convention-

---

Historia, p. 5); "déjese a otra pluma y a otro ingenio más delicado que el mío, el contar la alegría universal de todos" (*La fuerza de la sangre*, p. 899).

[131] See, for example, the following: "Finalmente, alegres se fueron los unos y tristes se quedaron los otros. Rodolfo llegó a su casa sin impedimento alguno, y los padres de Leocadia llegaron a la suya lastimados, afligidos, y desesperados"; "Dió voces su padre, gritó su madre, lloró su hermanico, arañóse la criada; pero ni las voces fueron oídas, ni los gritos escuchados, ni movió a compasión el llanto, ni los araños fueron de provecho alguno"; "¿Estoy en el limbo de mi inocencia o en el infierno de mis culpas?"; "Ciego de la luz del entendimiento, a oscuras robó la mejor prenda de Leocadia"; "es mejor la deshonra que se ignora que la honra que está puesta en opinión de las gentes."

[132] For St. Augustine antithesis is the most beautiful of all ornaments of discourse, since God created the world as a splendid poem and adorned it according to the

ally all such antitheses ultimately resolve themselves in the mystery of Redemption, annihilated and metamorphosed into a higher synthesis by the power of divine grace. The most interesting aspect of Cervantes's tale is not, however, its impressive articulation of such conventional antitheses, but rather its development of an area of antithesis that resists incorporation into its conventional architecture and that in fact threatens to undermine its foundations. In its consistent unsettling deflection of our attention from the miraculous, in its stress on the power of the human will, and in its recognition of the valid claims of the secular world, it allows shadows to stain the luminosity of the numinous world of the miracle which are far less easily cleansed than those cast momentarily by the powers of evil. The fact is that Cervantes, in the recoil from the miracle that he insinuates in *La fuerza de la sangre*, comes very close to giving free rein to the skeptical impulses that transformed the miracle of Zoraida's deliverance in the *Quixote* into a *Kasus*, or a type of tale that asserts the opposing claims of two distinct ways of thought or schemes of value and draws its power from the unresolved ambiguity of their restless confrontation and its resistance to closure.[133]

However, *La fuerza de la sangre* fails to become a subversion of a miracle. Tensions continue to trouble its luminous surface up to its very last line, but the opposition from which they spring should be seen as one of complementarity rather than as one of exclusivistic antagonism. The tale in fact confirms the presence of the divine within

---

fundamental antithetical principle of the opposition of good and evil (*Civitas Dei*, XI. 18; see Friedrich, *Epochen der italienischen Lyrik*, p. 551).

[133] For the openness or equipoise that characterizes the *Kasus* and its unsettling effects on a reader, who must reexamine his "hierarchy of norms," see Jolles, *Einfache Formen*, pp. 171-99. "Bestehen, Gültigkeit und Ausdehnung verschiedener Normen werden erwogen, aber diese Erwägung enthält die Frage: wo liegt das Gewicht, nach welcher Norm ist zu werten? . . . Das Eigentümliche der Form Kasus liegt nun aber darin, dass sie zwar die Frage stellt, aber die Antwort nicht geben kann, dass sie uns die Pflicht der Entscheidung auferlegt, aber die Entscheidung selbst nicht enthält— was sich in ihr verwirklicht, ist das Wägen, aber nicht das Resultat des Wägens" (pp. 190-91). The "Geistesbeschäftigung" realized and elicited by this popular form is visible throughout Cervantes's greatest writings, in his astonishing disclosures of the manner in which reality is colored by the perspective of its different percipients, in his development of profound philosophical and ethical problems through paradox, perspectivist commentary, and dialogue, and in his fondness for such anecdotes as Sancho's account of his father's argument concerning the taste of wine (a situation that Jolles mentions as one of the most typical and ubiquitous in the popular *Kasus* literature in European folklore), Sancho's confrontation of the paradox of the bridge and the gallows, or his equitable resolution of the problem of the two racers. One could say that the *Kasus* is the quintessential literary form of the ironic mentality.

the secular world, stresses the possibility of man's harmonious work-ing with God's Providence, and celebrates the value of human capac-ities and efforts. Moreover, it implies a divine sanction of social in-stitutions and all the obligations that mark man as a social as well as a religious being, from the attention to honor and the duties enjoined by the various social stations, to the responsibilities of family life, and to the supreme Christian mandate of charity. The blood of its title is the mystical blood of the Redeemer, the magically tainted blood of the primal sinner, and the desacralized blood of physiology and in-stinct, which can drive man both to brutally destructive acts at the expense of his fellows and to the procreative act which ensures the continuity of life and which binds men together in the kinships of family and class. Unlike the typical miracle narrative, Cervantes's tale does not end with an act of self-prostration, a rejection of the world, and a life of heroic devotion to a distant God, but rather with an embrace of the secular world and its perfections, in a Christian mar-riage and its fruits, all endorsed by a benign Divine Providence. Thus at the ending of what is probably his most religious exemplary no-vella, and certainly the tale that evokes most powerfully the chiaro-scuros and the tormented atmosphere of the darkest works of baroque religious literature, Cervantes takes his stand midway between the extremes marked by contemporary asceticism, with its obsessions with sinfulness and a distant all-powerful God, and skepticism, with its unsparing disclosure of the violence that superstition and fanaticism can bring about with God's puzzling apparent acquiescence.

In connection with *La Gitanilla* I have argued that the Christianity of the *Novelas ejemplares* can best be understood by recalling Erasmus's Christianity, from which it may well have derived, and his efforts to sanctify lay life by urging Christians to bring piety and faith to their activities, roles, professions, and institutions within society and to overcome the traditional mentality that would confine the religious impulse and its fulfillment to the sacralized spaces of church, pilgrim's path, and monastery. At the climax of his universally read *Paraclesis*, an "exhortation" to all the faithful, Erasmus writes disdainfully of Christians who bow in adoration before "the foot of Jesus Christ im-printed in stone" and the bejeweled images of the Savior which they proudly own, mindless of the fact that "an image, if indeed it shows us anything at all, shows us no more than the form of the body of Jesus Christ."[134] Erasmus of course has no intention of denying the

---

[134] "una señal del pie de Jesu Christo imprimida en una piedra . . . la ymagen ninguna otra cosa nos muestra, si empero algo muestra, más que la figura del cuerpo de Jesu Christo" (pp. 468-69). Erasmus put it more directly in a letter to John

miraculous powers of Christ or indeed the "mystery of the cross," which, in the *Enchiridion*, he contrasts with the wood of its image,[135] but he would ever insist that the central miracle for all Christians must remain the miracle of self-transformation, a process that is achieved in large part by the active involvement of the individual in the imitation of Christ's life and the understanding of the spirit that manifests itself through the letter of the Holy Scriptures.[136] It would be wrong to interpret Cervantes's reiterated insistence on the value of

Longlond in 1528: "Immodicam festorum multitudinem non ego solus improbo, praesertim quum hodie nullis diebus plus peccetur quam festis. . . . *Non pendet hodie religio Christianorum a miraculis*" (*Opvs Epistolarvm Des. Erasmi Roterodami*, ed. P. S. Allen and H. M. Allen [Oxford, 1928], 8:462; italics added). As Febvre has emphasized, a central feature of the religious sensibility which emerged in the great European evangelical movement of the early sixteenth century was the distaste for miracles and for those who were sensitive to their appeal. Such "skepticism" was not the exclusive privilege of rationalists and freethinkers of the age but was in fact an attitude uniting such different spokesmen for the movement as Luther, Calvin, Erasmus, and Rabelais (see *Le Problème de l'incroyance au xvie siècle*, pp. 195-218).

[135] See *Enquiridion*, p. 284. To appreciate the difference separating the humanist's attitude toward the image from that which prevailed in the Christianity of Cervantes's Spain, one can compare Erasmus's antithesis "wood-mystery" with the antithesis "wood-jewels" which emerges in Francisco de Ribera's enthusiastic account of the Virgin's gift of a miraculously transfigured crucifix to St. Theresa. According to the hagiographer, from the day of the miracle the saint "ne vit plus le bois dont la croix était formée, mais seulement ses pierres miraculeuses" (*La vida de Santa Teresa* [1590], cited by May, *Cervantes, un fondateur de la libre-pensée*, p. 27).

[136] Characteristically, in his *Virginis Matris apvd Lavretvm Cvltae Litvrgia*, Erasmus denounces those who honor the Virgin with numerous votive offerings and, when in difficulty, implore her miraculous assistance with "prolixis et ambitiosis precibus . . . de imitando quam praedicant ne cogitantes quidem." He reminds his audience that the authentic cult of the Virgin lies in the active imitation of her sobriety, her prudence, her humility, her modesty, and her chastity. Suggesting that Christians should imitate the Virgin, the ideal wife, in their own mystical marriage with Christ, Erasmus speaks of their nourishment from the holy blood of their husband as, in reality, a process of spiritual renewal brought about by the understanding and possession of his doctrine: "Nos in sponsi nostri mensa accumbentes inebriemur vino spirituali doctrinae quod nobis largiter effundit sponsus, saginemur illius sacrosancto corpore, potione sacrosancti sanguinis semper iuuenescamus secundum hominem interiorem etiam si hic exterior homo collabitur" (ed. L.-E. Halkin, *Opera Omnia*, Vol. V, pt. 1 [Amsterdam, 1977], pp. 100, 106). At the beginning of his life of St. Jerome, he stresses the hagiographer's obligation to record the truths of the daily life of the saint, ridicules traditional chroniclers' distortions of truth and exaggerations of miracles, and points out that a proper reading of a saint's life should lead the Christian to an understanding and an active imitation of the saintly model (see *Eximii Doctoris Hieronymi Stridonensis Vita, Erasmi Opuscula*, ed. W. K. Ferguson [The Hague, 1933], pp. 134-38). Thus, even when writing as hierophant and hagiographer, Erasmus is clear in expressing his sober attitude toward the miraculous elements in Christianity.

human effort and human dignity in *La fuerza de la sangre* as an ironic reflection on the presence or absence of divine grace. For Cervantes of *La fuerza de la sangre*, as for Erasmus in his influential formulations of his *Philosophia Christiana*, this world can be blessed by the restoration of the spirituality which originally informed it; there is no reason why the sacred can not go hand in hand with the secular. Perhaps the most miraculous achievement of Cervantes's "secularized miracle" lies in his own metamorphosis of the traditional genre of the monastery with its otherworldly ideal of perfection into the celebration of this antimiraculous but nonetheless deeply religious ideal.[137]

[137] The distinctively optimistic quality of the vision informing Cervantes's *Novelas ejemplares* is all the more visible when they are compared with works of a similar type by the contemporary spokesmen for *desengaño*. See, for example, the miracle narratives which Avellaneda incorporates in the place of *El curioso impertinente* and *El cautivo* in his "rewritten" *Quixote*. One describes the horrible punishment visited on a man who breaks a religious vow and marries. A guest of his house rapes his wife immediately after the birth of her child; in despair she hurls herself down a well, while her crazed husband kills the offender, batters the infant to death, and follows her to his own death (the cause of the catastrophes, the role of Divine Providence, and the presentation of the agent of revenge distinguish the tale significantly from its alleged source in Bandello's story of a Franciscan friar's lust and its consequences [*Le novelle*, 2:24]). The other narrates the case of a devotee of the Virgin and the Holy Rosary, whose plunge into the most desperate states of degradation is miraculously halted by the intercession of the Virgin, who, speaking in her image, upbraids her for her depravity, demands her self-prostration and penitence, and oversees her violent self-mortification and punishment of her tainted blood: ". . . se dió con ellas [las disciplinas] por espacio de media hora una cruelíssima diciplina sin ninguna piedad, por principio de la rigurosa penitencia que pensava hazer todos los días de su vida, de aquel sacrílego y deshonesto cuerpo, de cuya roja sangre quedó el suelo esmaltado en testimonio del verdadero dolor de sus pecados" (*Don Quijote de la Mancha*, 2:138-39). The protagonists of these miracles are viewed as the helpless playthings of a just, but very mysterious Providence, and, in the case of the more conventional of the two, *El cuento de los Felizes Amantes*, which is actually an expanded, highly theatrical version of the popular medieval *La Légende de la Sacristine*, the acts of consideration, "caer en la cuenta," conversion, expiation, and charity are all attributed to the infusion of divine grace. See also María de Zayas's account of the ordeals of Beatriz, who, after being delivered repeatedly by the Virgin from a number of absolutely frightful villains and restored to her husband, decides to abandon the treacherous world and retreats to a convent (*La perseguida triunfante*, *Desengaños amorosos*, ed. A. de Amezúa y Mayo [Madrid, 1950], pp. 333-410). To appreciate the complexities surrounding the tiny crucifix which Leocadia steals "no por devoción" in Cervantes's tale, we might compare the work to one of the great miracle dramas of the age, Calderón's *La devoción de la cruz*, with its relentless vision of helpless humanity mired in sin and anger, cleaving desperately to the cross and finding in its colossal powers the only relief in its plight.

INDEX

Alban K. Forcione is Emory L. Ford Professor of Spanish at Princeton University. He is the author of two other studies of Cervantes, *Cervantes, Aristotle, and the "Persiles"* (1970) and *Cervantes' Christian Romance: A Study of "Persiles y Sigismunda"* (1972). Professor Forcione has contributed articles and reviews to *Hispanic Review, Romanic Review, Modern Language Notes*, and *Modern Language Review*.

LIBRARY OF CONGRESS CATALOGING IN PUBLICATION DATA

Forcione, Alban K., 1938-
Cervantes and the humanist vision.
Includes index.
1. Cervantes Saavedra, Miguel de, 1547-1616. Novelas ejemplares.
2. Cervantes Saavedra, Miguel de, 1547-1616—Criticism and
interpretation. I. Title.

PQ6324.Z5F67   863'.3   82-47595
ISBN 0-691-06521-7   AACR2